The A

Fa

Monica McInerney grew up in a family of seven children in the Clare Valley wine region of South Australia. She has worked in children's television, arts marketing, the music industry, public relations and book publishing and lived all around Australia and in Ireland and England. She is the author of seven novels which were international bestsellers and have been published in translation in Europe. Her most recent novel is *Those Faraday Girls*. She now lives in Dublin with her husband.

For more information please visit
www.monicamcinerney.com

PRAISE FOR MONICA MCINERNEY

'Tender and well-observed . . . there is also plenty of McInerney's trademark wit, but have the hankies ready for this, probably her best novel yet'
Irish Independent

'An effervescent blend of romance, humour, travel and adventure'
Marie Claire

'You'll be laughing out loud one minute and crying the next'
Cosmopolitan

Also by Monica McInerney

A Taste for It

Upside Down Inside Out

Spin the Bottle

Odd One Out

Those Faraday Girls

The Alphabet Sisters

AND

Family Baggage

MONICA MCINERNEY

PAN BOOKS

The Alphabet Sisters first published 2004 by Penguin Australia
This edition published 2008 by Pan Books
Family Baggage first published 2005 by Penguin Australia
This edition published 2008 by Pan Books

This omnibus first published 2008 by Pan Books
an imprint of Pan Macmillan Ltd
Pan Macmillan, 20 New Wharf Road, London N1 9RR
Basingstoke and Oxford
Associated companies throughout the world
www.panmacmillan.com

ISBN 978-0-330-50796-7

1 3 5 7 9 8 6 4 2

A CIP catalogue record for this book is available from the British Library.

Printed in the UK by CPI Mackays, Chatham ME5 8TD

The Alphabet Sisters

To the Rum Sisters:
Ruby, Ulli and Mikaella

Acknowledgements

My thanks and love to my mum Mary, my own slightly alphabetical sisters Lea, Marie and Maura and my brothers Paul, Stephen and Rob for helping from afar with geographical details, waitressing tales, parenting tips and medical facts. My love and thanks also to my two Irish families, the Drislanes and the Dolans.

Thanks to Max and Jean Fatchen in South Australia for their recollections of General MacArthur and so much more besides; to Marea Fox and Andrew Storey in Queensland for their motel stories; and to my friends in the Clare Valley, especially Greg Cooley, Val Tilbrook, Tricia Jones and all at the Clare Library. Thanks also to Eveleen Coyle, Fiona Gillies, Nid Sangeengong, Sabine Brasseler and Michael Boyny.

Thanks to my agents, Jonathan Lloyd at Curtis Brown in London and Fiona Inglis of Curtis Brown Australia. My big thanks too, to my three publishers – everyone at Penguin Books Australia, especially Clare Forster, Ali Watts, Kirsten Abbott and Cathy Larsen; Imogen Taylor and all her team in Pan Macmillan in London; and Alison Walsh and all at Tivoli/Gill & Macmillan in Ireland.

Finally, and most of all, my love and thanks to my husband John.

Chapter One

London, England

'Your sister is married to your ex-fiancé?' Jessica's voice rose to such a pitch Bett Quinlan half expected the light bulbs to explode. 'We've worked together for nearly two years and you tell me this now?'

Bett knew right then she had made a big mistake. 'It didn't ever really come up until now.'

'Something like that doesn't need to come up. That's something you tell people within minutes of meeting. "Hi, my name's Bett, short for Elizabeth. I work as a journalist in a record company and my sister is married to my ex-husband."'

'Ex-fiancé,' Bett corrected. She tried to backtrack. 'Look, forget I mentioned it. I'm fine about it. She's fine about it. He's fine about it. It's not a big deal.' Liar, liar.

'Of course it's a big deal. It's a huge deal. And they'll both be at your grandmother's party? No wonder you're feeling sick about it.'

'I'm not feeling sick about it. I said I was a bit nervous about going home for it, not sick.'

'Tomato, tomayto. Oh, Bett, you poor thing. Which sister was it? The older one or the younger one?'

'The younger one. Carrie.' Bett felt like the words were being squeezed out of her.

'And what happened? Were they having an affair behind your back? You came home from work early one day and caught them at it in your marital – sorry, engagement – bed?'

'No, it wasn't like that.' Bett stood up. She'd definitely made a mistake. That afternoon at work she'd decided to invite her friend and colleague Jessica back for dinner to tell her the whole story. She'd hoped it would help make this trip back to Australia easier. Prepare her for people's reactions again, like a dress rehearsal. But it wasn't helping at all. It was excruciating. She ran her fingers through her dark curls, trying to take back control of the situation. 'Can I get you a coffee? Another glass of wine?'

'No thanks. Don't change the subject, either. So did you go to the wedding?'

'Would you prefer tea?'

Jessica laughed good-naturedly. 'Come on, Bett. You brought it up in the first place. Think of it as therapy. It can't have been good for you to go around with a secret like this bottled up inside you. Did you go to the wedding?'

Bett sat down again. 'I didn't, no.'

'Well, no, of course you didn't. It would have been too humiliating, I suppose.'

She blinked at Jessica's bluntness.

'Did your sister use the same wedding invitations? Just cross out your name and put hers instead?'

'That's not very funny.'

Jessica gave a sheepish smile. 'Sorry, couldn't resist. So who was the bridesmaid? Your older sister? Anna?'

'No, she wasn't there either.'

Jessica frowned. 'None of her sisters were there? What? Did it cause some huge fight between all three of you?'

In a nutshell, yes. 'It was a bit like that.'

'Really? You haven't spoken to either of your sisters since the wedding?'

'No.' Bett shifted uncomfortably in her seat. 'Or seen them.' Not since the weekend of the Big Fight. Which had followed the Friday of the Revelations. Which had followed the Weeks of the Suspicions. 'Not for three years.'

'Your grandmother's party will be the first time you've seen your sisters in *three* years?' At Bett's nod, Jessica gave a long, low whistle. 'This is more complicated than I thought. No wonder you went so weird when that fax from your grandmother arrived.'

'I didn't go weird.'

'Yes, you did. Have you got any photos of your sister and your fiancé together?'

'Why? Don't you believe me?'

'Of course I do. I just need to get the whole picture of it in my head, so I can give you all the advice you need.'

'I'd rather you didn't –'

'Please, Bett. You know how much I love looking at photos.'

That much was true. Jessica was the only person Bett had ever met who genuinely enjoyed looking at other people's holiday photos. She wouldn't just flick through a packet of snaps either, but would inspect each one, asking about the subject, the setting, the film speed used.

Jessica was being her most persuasive. 'I'm sure it will help you. This way I'll know exactly who you're talking about.'

'Thanks, anyway, but –'

'Bett, come on. You've told me half of it. I may as well see the rest.'

'Look, I –'

'Please-please-please . . .'

Bett gave in, picking up the small photo album lying on top of the bookcase in the corner of the room. At least it would take Jessica only a few minutes to get through them. She had left South Australia in such a hurry three years earlier that she hadn't taken any of her photos with her. The only ones in her album were those her parents and Lola had sent with their letters.

As Jessica gleefully started turning the pages, Bett retreated to the tiny kitchen with the dirty dishes, feeling sick and steamrolled. Thirty-two years old and she still hadn't learnt how to stand up for herself. For a fleeting moment she wondered how her sisters would have reacted in the same situation. Anna would have given Jessica a haughty stare and chilled her into silence. Carrie would have tossed her blonde head and told her laughingly and charmingly to mind her own business. But not Bett. No, she'd just felt embarrassed about having said too much and then handed the photo album over anyway. She decided to blame the wine they'd had that night for this sudden need to show and tell all. Nine parts alcohol, one part truth serum.

She came back into the living room and picked up a music magazine, trying to pretend she wasn't watching Jessica's every reaction as she pored over each photo. For a while the only sound was pages turning, interrupted by Jessica asking the occasional question.

'Is that your mum and dad?'

Bett glanced at it. A photo of her parents, arm in arm in front of the main motel building, wearing matching Santa hats, squinting into the sunshine. They'd sent it in their Christmas card the previous year. 'That's right.'

Jessica read the sign behind them. 'The Valley View Motel. Is that where you grew up?'

'We moved around a lot when we were younger, but that's where they are now.'

Jessica nodded and turned the page. 'And this is Lola? The old lady wearing too much makeup?'

Bett didn't even have to look at the photo. 'That's her.'

'Would you look at those eyebrows! They're like caterpillars on a trampoline. She was your nanny, did you tell me?'

'Sort of.' Nanny always seemed too mild a word to describe Lola. She'd certainly minded them as children. With their parents so occupied running the motels, it was Lola, their father's mother, who had practically brought up Bett and her two sisters – but she was more a combination of etiquette teacher, boot-camp mistress and musical director than nanny.

'Is she wearing fancy dress in this next photo?'

Bett glanced over. It was a picture of Lola beside her seventy-ninth birthday cake, nearly twelve months earlier. She was wearing a gaudily patterned kaftan, dangling earrings and several beaded necklaces. Nothing too out of the ordinary. 'No, that's just her.'

Jessica kept flicking the pages, and then stopped suddenly. Bett tensed, knowing she had reached Carrie and Matthew's wedding photo. Bett had wanted to throw it away the day she received it, but had stopped herself. She hadn't wanted her grandmother to be right. It was Lola who had sent the photo to her, enclosing a brief note: 'You'll probably get all dramatic and rip this up but I knew you'd want to see it.'

'This is them?' Jessica asked.

'That's them.'

Jessica studied it closely. 'Carrie's very pretty, isn't she? And he's a bit of a looker too, your Matthew. Nice perm.'

At least Jessica hadn't said what people usually said when they remarked how pretty Carrie was: 'You don't look at all alike, do you?' As for her other remark . . .

'He's not my Matthew. And it wasn't a perm. He's got naturally wavy hair.'

Jessica grinned. 'Just seeing if you defended him.' She turned the page and gave a loud hoot of laughter. 'Now we're talking. I've been dying to see proof of the Alphabet Sisters. Look at you with that mad head of curls.'

Bett tugged self-consciously at that same head of curls, now at least slightly less mad. Lola had sent her that photo, too. It had arrived with just a scrawled note, subtle as ever. 'Remember the good times with your sisters as well.' It had been taken at a country show in outback South Australia more than twenty years previously, at one of the Alphabet Sisters' earliest singing performances. Anna had been thirteen, Bett eleven, and Carrie eight. Bett could even remember the songs: 'Song Sung Blue', 'Swing Low, Sweet Chariot' and a David Cassidy pop song. Just minutes after the photo had been taken, a fly had buzzed its way straight into Anna's mouth. Her shocked expression and sudden squawk had made Bett and Carrie laugh so much both of them had fallen off the small stage, a wide plank of wood balanced on eight milk crates. The memory could still make Bett laugh.

Jessica was inspecting it very closely. 'You were a bit of a porker back then, weren't you?'

The smile disappeared. 'Well, that was nicely put, Jess, thanks.'

Jessica was unabashed. 'I always believe in calling a spade a spade. And you were a plump little thing. Look at that little belly and those rosy-red cheeks.'

Bett didn't need to look. That little belly and those rosy-red cheeks had never gone too far away. She was about to ask Jessica if she still thought she was a porker – she had gone up and down in weight so many times she hardly knew what size she was – but Jessica was too occupied with the photo. She was taking in every detail, the flicked fringes, the matching dresses, the bad make-up – all Lola's handiwork.

She glanced up at Bett. 'Not exactly the Corrs, were you?'

Bett laughed despite herself. 'I bet they didn't look that good when they were teenagers either.'

'I bet they did. Have you ever wondered if there's a fourth Corr sister, a hideously ugly one they keep locked away?' Jessica looked at the photo again. 'You're not very alike, are you? Even apart from the appalling eye makeup and the different hair colours. Unless they're wigs?'

'No, all our own work, I'm afraid.' Anna had straight black hair, Bett's was dark brown and Carrie's dark blonde. She presumed her sisters' hair colours hadn't changed in three years. She'd find out soon enough. In less than two weeks, in fact. Her stomach gave a lurch.

The fax from Lola in South Australia had arrived at Bett's work out of the blue, just the one line. If Bett didn't come home for her eightieth birthday party, she would never talk to her again.

Bett had rung her immediately. 'Lola, don't do this to me, please,' she'd said, straight to the point as soon as her grandmother answered. 'You know what it'll be like.'

'Elizabeth Quinlan, stop being such a baby. You're scared of seeing your sisters. So what? I'm nearly eighty and I've got a lot more to be scared of than you have. I could die any moment. Now, hang up, book your ticket and get here as soon as you can. I've got something I want you to do.'

Lola had obviously taken her extra-strength bossy tablets that day. 'I can't drop everything just like that, Lola. I've got a life here now.'

'And you've got a grandmother in Australia who has missed you very, very badly and wants to see you again.' Her voice had softened. 'Please, Bett. Come home. For me.'

Bett had thought about it for two days, veering between excitement and dread at the idea. One image had kept coming to her. Lola, standing in front of the motel, beaming at her, waiting to give her a hug. In the end Bett had compromised. Yes, she would come back for the party, but it would be a lightning trip. She'd arrive in South Australia the day of the party and then leave as soon as possible afterwards.

Lola hadn't been at all pleased. 'But I need you here for longer than that.'

'I can't, Lola. I've got a life here,' she'd repeated firmly. It had been a strange sensation. She wasn't used to standing up to her grandmother either.

Beside her, Jessica was going through the album again. 'It's a tricky one, that's for sure. No wonder you're so nervous. Your first meeting with your sisters and the happy couple in three years, all of you in the same motel, not to mention the added tension of a party . . .'

Bett nodded, waiting for her friend's sound advice, the helpful comments.

Jessica shut the album with a snap. 'I'd say it's going to be ferocious.'

Sydney, Australia

Anna Quinlan knew that outside the sun was shining. That less than a kilometre away the waters of Sydney Harbour were probably glinting in the sun, to a soundtrack of ferry horns, gull cries and tourist-guide commentaries.

But it could have been the Sahara Desert outside. She'd been trapped inside this coffin of a recording studio for three hours now, trying to get the voice exactly right for a new range of kitchen sponges. She'd decided the client was not just from hell, but from somewhere much deeper, hotter and even more unpleasant.

She peered through the glass of the studio window again, counting to ten as she caught sight of him. He looked like a suit-wearing spotty child who surely couldn't have driven himself to the studio today. He didn't seem old enough. She snapped back to attention as Bob, the producer/technician, pressed the button on the intercom so his voice came into her headphones.

'Anna, Henry feels you are really getting there, but he wonders whether you could combine the laugh in your voice from that first take with the kind of bubbling tone you did on the one before that last one, and add a little more lightness to the whole thing.'

Henry leaned forward, speaking into the microphone as though he was an MC at a football-club presentation night. 'Yes, loved that bubbly sound, Anna. Just perfect for our demographic. You don't mind, do you?'

Mind? Mind that she had spent three hours saying one sentence in dozens of different voices? Mind that the preschooler in the suit had tried to describe the mindset of a kitchen sponge – a kitchen sponge! – to her? 'It's determined, it's energetic, it's fun . . .'

No, it's not, Henry, she'd thought. It's a three-inch square of detergent-soaked sponge with a scouring pad on one side that you do dishes with. It isn't Russell Crowe.

She bit her tongue. Whatever you do, Anna, don't let them see you're upset. Keep cool, keep smiling, keep up the front.

She'd learned that lesson after years of unsuccessful auditions for parts. No one wanted a moody actress. It was much better to be tagged as a thorough professional, even if it was sometimes mistaken for haughtiness. And at least Henry had definitely decided that the sponge was female. Today's booking had been set up, cancelled, then set up again while Henry, his advertising agency and his market-research team argued over the best gender for their new sponge.

Anna looked at Bob for help. He was just chewing, as normal, and hitching up his trousers, unfazed, also as normal. She knew he didn't care how long the client took. He charged an hourly rate.

Some of her frustration must have shown on her face. Bob took pity on her. He spoke again, surreptitiously inclining his head towards the client. 'Anna, perhaps it would help if you visualised yourself in the sink, getting psyched up to help your housewife – sorry, homemaker – clear all those dirty dishes. And there's one particularly greasy pot that's going to need special energy, but you know it will be worth it to scrub like mad until every spot is gone.' Another barely noticeable nod at the client. 'Whenever you're ready. Tape's running.'

It worked a treat. Staring through the glass, seeing her sharp bobbed hair and immaculate makeup reflected back at her, Anna imagined Henry evolving into a dirty, grease-spattered saucepan. She imagined herself as the sponge, leaping out of nowhere and scouring his face until every spot and blackhead had disappeared, shouting all the while in a voice that was a combination of Mary Poppins and kamikaze pilot. She leaned towards the microphone. 'Let me at it! I'm the clean machine!'

Henry's pimply face broke into a huge smile. 'That's it. Perfect. Thanks, Anna.'

She had just leaned down to her bag when his voice came in again. 'But would you be able to do it one more time? I think it needs just a touch more softness, to convey the moisturiser we've included in the washing-up liquid.'

An hour later Anna was driving out of the studio carpark. The voice of the sponge was now lodged in her head and she knew from experience it would stay there for the next few days or until a new character's voice took its place. Last month her internal voice, her mind voice, had varied between a kitten stuck up a tree (for a cat food commercial), a warm-hearted nurse in an old folks' home (health insurance) and a cake waiting to be iced. That had taken three hours to get right too, before Bob stepped in once again with her motivation. 'Imagine you're the cake, Anna, okay? You're scared. You don't know which brand of icing you're about to be iced with but you sure as hell want it to be high quality. So we need a combination of fear and anticipation and . . .'

Her seven-year-old daughter, Ellen, loved it, of course. She treated Anna's repertoire of voices like a human jukebox. Lying sleepily in bed listening to a goodnight story, she'd pick and choose the voices. 'Mum, can you read this one like the Zoomer Broom?' The Zoomer Broom featured in an animated TV commercial where the ordinary household broom metamorphosed into something Harry Potter could have used for Quidditch, babbling nonsensically all the while. Ellen's other favourite was the ocean pie, a gurgly underwater voice.

Anna parked on the street across from the hospital, ten minutes late. Hurrying towards the lift, she composed her face, already hearing the disapproving tones from her neighbour, who had grudgingly agreed to collect Ellen after school and bring her here to the clinic for her latest appointment. The lift door opened and Anna spied her little daughter in the distance, standing up on a chair near the nurses' station, chatting to one of the staff. In the dozens of hospital visits since Ellen's accident, she had got to know all the nurses very well. Anna tensed, as she always did when she remembered the trauma of those first months. She decided it was time Ellen had a good spoiling: she'd give her whatever she wanted for dinner, let her watch whatever video she wanted, and then read her all the stories she wanted, as well.

By nine o'clock Anna's patience was wearing a little thin. Ellen had been alternately tearful and cranky all evening, insisting on pizza, then not eating any of it, and not settling on any one video but wanting to watch specific scenes out of five different ones. Anna had finally had enough, speaking more crossly than she intended, which set off the tears again. She then read two extra stories, purely out of guilt, hardly finding the energy for the different voices.

Ellen still wouldn't settle, hopping in and out of bed. She stood in the doorway of the living room now, tears on her face. 'Is Dad home yet?'

Anna kept her voice mild with effort. 'No, darling, he's not.'

'Where is he?'

'At work, I think.' She thought. She didn't have a clue where Glenn was. He didn't ring and tell her any more if he was going to be late, or if he was going to be home at all, in fact.

'Can you read me another story, then?'

'Sweetheart, you've had enough stories. It's time to sleep.'

'I can't sleep. I'm scared again. I keep remembering.'

The doctor's voice came into Anna's mind. 'There will be some post-traumatic stress and recurring fear, but it's important you learn to listen without making too much of it. Children are children and very skilled at knowing which buttons to press.' So what was she supposed to do? Ignore Ellen's tears? Tell her to get over it? Of course she couldn't. She pulled herself up out of the deep sofa. 'All right, Ellie. You hop back into bed and pick another story. I'll be there in a moment.'

By the time Anna got to the bedroom, Ellen had changed her mind. 'Can I have a tape instead? Can I hear Really-Great-Gran's tape?'

'Again? You sure you don't want a story tape?'

Ellen lay back and shook her head. Her dark hair fanned out on the pillow.

The tape had arrived from Lola more than two years earlier, with a note to Anna attached. 'This is for you to play to Ellen. I'm still having no part of this nonsense between you and your sisters but I'm not losing a great-granddaughter because of it. Please play her this tape so I'm not a shock each time she meets me.'

Anna put the tape in, then lay on the bed beside Ellen, stroking her hair back from her face as Lola's voice filled the room. Her still strongly Irish-accented tones were clear and precise.

'Hello, Ellen. This is your great-grandmother speaking. Now, my little dote, I've been giving a lot of thought to what you should call me and I think I've come up with the best solution. Your scoundrel of a mother started calling me Lola when she was just a child and her two sisters followed suit, but you need a different name for me, I think. And not just Great-Grandmother. I'm much better than great. So, my darling, I would like you to call me Really-Great-Gran from now on. Okay?'

There was a pause on the tape.

'Are you listening, Ellen?' Lola asked.

'Yes,' Ellen answered sleepily beside Anna.

The voice on the tape continued. 'Good girl. And are you happy with that? Happy to call me Really-Great-Gran?'

'Yes, Really-Great-Gran,' Ellen answered in the pause. She knew this ritual off by heart.

'Good girl. Now, I'm going to tell you a few stories about your mother and your grandfather, but first I'm going to sing you one or two of my favourite songs. So settle back and relax.'

Relax? Anna bit her lip as Lola started warbling 'Don't Sit Under the Apple Tree' in her falsetto voice. The last thing Lola's voice would make you do is relax. She could clear a room in seconds. Ellen didn't seem to mind. Lola could have been singing a sweetly tuned nursery rhyme, the way Ellen was reacting. Her lids were getting heavier by the second, her lips mouthing the words along with her great-grandmother's slaughtered version. Anna smiled, remembering the song. It was one of the first ones Lola had taught Anna and her sisters. There'd been a row over who got to sing the high notes. Carrie had won, hadn't she? Or was it Bett? It certainly hadn't been her, cursed with as deep a singing voice as her speaking voice. She'd always sung the bass parts.

Lola reached a shrieking crescendo, then paused on the tape, as if expecting her performance to be followed by rapturous applause. 'One of my favourites, Ellen, and one of your mum and aunts' favourites too. As is this one. Are you comfortable? Sing along with me, darling.'

As Lola embarked on 'The Good Ship Lollipop' Anna glanced down. Ellen was fast asleep.

Back in the living room, Anna poured herself a glass of wine and pressed the TV remote control. She stared at the screen, trying to pick up the plot of the thriller, fighting the desolate feeling inside her that seemed to be rising closer to the surface each day. One phrase kept occurring to her. *I'm lonely*. Lonely. Yet she had friends in Sydney, didn't she? People she could meet for coffee? And hadn't there been joint friends, other couples who came over for dinner or who they met in restaurants occasionally? Not any more. They had all slipped away the past year or so, like extras in a film, Anna thought, silently stealing away and leaving the main action to unfold. She couldn't blame them. Who would want to be around to see how she and Glenn treated each other these days?

The TV program changed to advertisements and Anna noticed without pleasure that it was her voice coming out of the mouth of the animated mobile phone on the screen. She'd done that one two years ago now and here it was back again.

She put down the glass and rubbed her face with her hands. Who was she fooling? She didn't want to talk to Glenn or any Sydney friends or colleagues. She wanted to talk to her sisters again. She wanted Carrie to sympathise with her. She wanted Bett to cheer her up with some madly melodramatic account of how bad her day had been. She wanted to tell them both how awful things had become with Glenn, especially since Ellen's accident, but how wonderful Ellen herself had been, most of the time.

She could ring her mother or father at the motel, but she'd never really confided in either of them. It had always been too hard to get the timing right. They'd be either in the kitchen cooking for house guests, or out in the bar or doing the accounts, or any of the hundred things both of them always seemed to be doing. She could ring Lola, but lately those calls hadn't been having the calming effect they used to. For the first year or two after the big fight, Lola had been understanding, trying to see each of their points of view, as she always had.

Understanding had turned to exasperation. 'This is ludicrous. I'm ashamed of the three of you, carrying on like this.' She'd tried the frosty approach for a while. 'I'm not talking to any of you while you persist in this ridiculous carry-on.' But then Lola had missed their phone calls too. 'Just because I'm talking to you doesn't mean I've forgiven any of you.' But for the past six months there had been silence on the subject. Perhaps she'd realised, as Anna herself slowly had, that that was that. It had gone on too long now for things to change.

A scream on the TV made Anna jump. A young blonde detective was being chased down a dark street by two men in suits, her face in close-up, fear-stricken. 'Oh, shush, would you,' Anna said aloud. 'You're just acting, for God's sake.' She put the remote control on the shelf under the coffee table. As she did she noticed the mail in a pile, wrapped inside the free local newspaper. How long had that been there? She picked it up and checked the date – more than two weeks old. How many times had she asked Glenn not to leave the mail there? Is this what it had come to? Each of them deliberately doing the things they knew most annoyed the other?

She flicked through the bundle. Bills. Advertising material. A fundraising letter from Ellen's school. And a thick cream envelope. She turned it over, recognising the handwriting immediately. Puzzled, she tore it open. It was an invitation. She read it again. No, not an invitation. A summons.

Clare Valley, South Australia

Lola Quinlan turned her gaze away from the vineyards visible through the window of the Valley View Motel dining room and back to the table where her youngest granddaughter was sulkily folding serviettes. 'Did I tell you what happened in the charity shop this morning, Carrie? A young woman, around about your age, perhaps a bit older, came in and said, "Could I try on that dress in the window?" And I said, "Yes, of course, but I'd much rather you used the changing room."'

Carrie didn't smile or look up. 'You've been telling that one for years, Lola.'

'Good jokes never die, you know. What did the zero say to the eight? Nice belt.' She glanced at the elegant gold watch on her thin wrist and stood up. 'Time for *Days of Our Lives*. I'm not going to offer you any help because you're doing such a marvellous job of it yourself. And you know how important I think it is for you young people to see a job through from start to finish.'

Carrie ignored her, not looking up as her grandmother came closer.

'Carrie, are you ignoring me?'

The younger woman kept her head down.

'That's fine, but don't frown like that, darling. It's very bad for the skin. If you're going to sulk, at least do it with a smile on your face. Or try doing those exercises I showed you, the ones that firm your chin. See, like this.' Lola started grimacing, stretching her lips sideways, then into a tight pout; out, then in again. 'Twenty of those a day and it's like a gym workout for your face, so I read. A little alarming for any passers-by, but that's the price we pay for endless beauty, isn't it?'

Carrie started to smile.

'That's more like it,' Lola said. 'And I know what you're thinking and, yes, I am a wizened interfering old bag of bones and quite happy to be like that.' She leaned over and kissed her granddaughter on the top of the head. At five foot nine, her posture still excellent, Lola towered over Carrie. 'But I still love you, you know.'

'If you really loved me, you wouldn't have –'

'Yes, I would have.' Lola collected her handbag. 'Will you be staying on for dinner tonight? Thursday, schnitzel night.'

'No, I'll go home, I think.'

'How are those renovations going?'

Carrie and her husband had bought an old farmhouse several kilometres south of the Valley View Motel the year before. 'Fine. Slowly.'

Lola was watching her. 'And how is Matthew, Carrie?'

Carrie turned back to the serviettes. 'He's fine. Up to his eyes in sheep manure and vet magazines as usual. You know the sort of thing.'

'You're getting on all right, are you?'

'Yes, thanks.'

'Really?'

Lola was like a human sniffer dog, Carrie thought, still not looking up. Line up a row of people and she'd sniff out each of their problems instantly. Not this time, though, Carrie decided. The days of confiding in her grandmother were well and truly over. 'Really. It's a bed of roses, in fact.'

'Rubbish. No marriage is a bed of roses. That at least was one of the positive things about Edward dying so young. We might have missed out on the good times but we missed out on some of the bad, boring times as well.' Lola was amazed, as always, at how easily the lies about her husband tripped off her tongue. 'Tell me, do you ever get bored with Matthew, Carrie?'

'Tell me, do you ever think you're overstepping the mark with your questions, Lola?'

'Oh, good Lord, yes. But people are usually so shocked, they've answered me before they've had time to think twice. Do you know what I found out this morning? That Mrs Kennedy is stepping out with her son-in-law's father at the moment. Talk about keeping it in the family. Having a grand old time, she told me.'

Carrie felt a rush of combined affection and annoyance, her usual reaction to Lola's behaviour. 'That's the only reason you're still working in that charity shop, isn't it? It's nothing to do with helping the poor or keeping yourself busy.'

Lola made an elegant gesture with her hand. 'If people choose to tell me things, there's nothing I can do about it. I see it as my gift to society: helping people unburden themselves of their problems.'

'Digging the dirt on them, you mean.'

'I noticed you changed the subject, by the way. Don't think that's the end of it.'

'I don't know what you're talking about.'

'Oh, I think you do. Now, then, I must be off. I'm going to call on your mother in the kitchen and beg some afternoon tea. I really do have the perfect set-up for an old lady, don't I? A son and daughter-in-law with their own motel and restaurant and a granddaughter who is the sweetest in the world.' Lola gave Carrie another kiss, then swept out of the room, leaving a faint trace of expensive perfume behind her.

Alone in the dining room once again, Carrie worked quietly until she had folded the last of the serviettes. With a loud sigh, she leaned back in her chair. One hundred paper swans surrounded her. This time in two days the room would be transformed for a wedding reception, the paper swans swimming elegantly up and down the rows of long tables. She'd already strung up the fairy lights the bride had requested. She'd ordered the special candles from Adelaide and they were due to arrive any moment. The bridal arch had proved tricky for a week or so. It would all come together, though. She'd done it enough times to be sure of that.

She sat back and flicked at one of the paper swans with her finger. It toppled, falling against the swan beside it, which also toppled. Within moments a whole row of them had fallen, domino-style. She could have jumped up and stopped them but instead watched idly as the last dozen or so flipped and rolled onto the unswept floor.

She didn't care. At that moment she was sick of it all. She was sick of her job. She was sick of the motel. She was sick of the fact people made such a mess while they were eating that they needed serviettes in the first place. She was feeling especially sick about her grandmother wanting to throw a birthday party for herself and insisting that Bett and Anna attend.

'But why, Lola? Why now? It'll ruin everything,' Carrie had said that morning, hoping she wasn't giving too much away. 'All that tension.'

'I've given you all three years to sort it out and you haven't even got to the starting gate. So I'm taking charge once and for all. I've written to both of them as well. Insisted they come or else. So they will, I know.'

Carrie opened her mouth to protest but one of Lola's quelling looks had blasted her way and she shut it again.

Scooping up the paper swans now and ignoring the state of some of their wings, Carrie replayed the conversation yet again. If only Lola had turned eighty a few months ago. A year ago, even. But no, it had to be now. And she had to insist on throwing a party. A huge party.

'You wouldn't be happy with a nice family dinner, you and me and Mum and Dad?' Carrie had suggested hopefully.

'Of course not. I could die any day and I want to go out with a bang. And I want Anna and Bett to see the explosion. Besides, I've got something very important I want the three of you to do for me.'

'Important? What's wrong? Lola, you're not sick, are you?'

'Don't pry, Caroline. I said I want to talk to the three of you about it. Once I have the three of you in the same room together again.'

The three of them. The three of them who hadn't spoken to each other for years, let alone been in the same room. Or the same town. Or the same country even. And whose fault was it?

Hers.

Who did everyone blame?

Her.

But now it had all changed, hadn't it? The reason none of them had spoken to each other in that time no longer existed. Which would make this reunion of Lola's even more hideous and humiliating and horrible than it would normally have been.

Carrie took her anger out on the last of the paper swans, crumpling it up in her hand and then immediately feeling guilty. 'Sorry, swannie,' she said out loud, smoothing the serviette and readjusting the little paper beak. It now looked like it had been in a washing machine. She tucked it away in her pocket. The way her luck was going this one would end up on the bride's place-mat and she'd cause a scene. Carrie had already spent enough hours calming the young woman, as she'd fretted about everything from the number of prawns to be served in the prawn cocktails to the mathematical probabilities of it raining on her wedding day.

Carrie had wanted to snap at her more than once. 'You think the wedding day is stressful? Try getting through the marriage.'

She jumped as the bell at reception rang once, twice, a third time. Right now she'd had enough of guests, too – especially guests who rang the bell more than once. She walked out, plastering a smile onto her face, knowing it was just several teeth short of a grimace. At least she was exercising her facial muscles. Lola would be pleased.

'Good afternoon,' she said to the waiting couple, her voice sickly sweet. 'I'm very sorry to have kept you.'

CHAPTER TWO

A WEEK before her flight back to Australia, Bett walked into the record company's office in the centre of London, took off her raincoat, sat down and slowly, rhythmically, banged her head against the pile of papers on her desk.

'Great new move,' Jessica said, wandering over. 'Can't see it taking off in the clubs though.'

Bett looked up, her head still on the desk. 'You should have seen this one, Jess, heard the things he was saying.'

Sprawled on the sofa in the plush Kensington hotel room, the young pop singer had fixed Bett Quinlan with a sincere blue gaze and tossed his head so a lock of blond hair shimmered across his forehead. 'I want to grow with my music but stay close to my beginnings. Most of all, I want to keep it real.'

Bett had blinked twice at him and tapped her pen against her teeth. Keep it real? That could be tricky. With all the makeup and hair gel he was wearing it was already hard to tell where his body stopped and the cosmetics industry took over. As for staying close to his beginnings – he was barely out of his teens as it was. Any closer to his beginnings and he'd be back in a pram.

There'd been a long awkward silence before he finally shifted in his seat and shot her another of his well-practised blue gazes. 'Well? Was that answer okay?'

Answer? She'd already forgotten the question. Her mind had been drifting to Lola's birthday party. Come on, Bett, concentrate. She gave herself a mental shake. 'Sorry, Grover.'

'Groover.'

'Pardon?'

'My name's Groover, not Grover.'

'Groover, sorry. Yes, that answer was great, thanks. Well-rehearsed. Well-delivered.' She ran her eye down the list of sample interview questions in the notebook in front of her, fighting an inclination to pick Groover up, tuck him under her arm and make a run for it. She could tell people he was her foster child. Her butler. Anything to get him out of the music industry before it had eaten him alive, pretty face, sweet singing voice and all.

'Where are our consciences, Jess?' Bett asked now in mock despair. 'We're sending young men to their deaths, armed with nothing but microphones.'

'Rubbish. We're sending them on their way to fame and fortune. Don't tell me you're getting all pure about music again. You child performers are all the same, pining after more innocent times, when all it took to put on a good show was a few matching outfits and a tinny backing track.'

'Yes, hilarious.' Jessica hadn't stopped teasing her about the Alphabet Sisters or the situation with her sisters since the night in Bett's flat. 'You're very cruel, you know. I thought you'd promised to leave me alone about all of that.' She should never have mentioned it to her.

'No, I promised to help toughen you up about all of that. Anyway, I can't leave you alone. I have to give you another assignment. Karl wants you to get onto it straight away.'

'He deigned to ring?' Since their boss had floated the record company on the stock market and become an instant millionaire he hadn't found it quite so necessary to come into work every day.

'Well, a quick call. Then he faxed. He's in Spain, I think. Or Portugal. He told me he wants to work you to the bone till you leave on Friday. Said he must have been off his head giving you that week off to go to your granny's party.'

'He was, actually.'

Jessica put the folder on the desk beside her. 'It's this new band from West London he's signed. He wants you to whip up a quick article for the instore mags.'

'But I can't write about them. I haven't seen them play live yet.'

'That's because they haven't played live yet. Probably never will play live. Don't even know if they can play live. Here, have a look.'

Bett took the biogs and photo. Five children in heavy eye makeup sneered at her. If they were hers she'd tell them to wash that muck off their faces and go and do their homework. 'What are they called?'

'Dogs from Hell. Except Karl calls them Puppies from Hammersmith.'

Five Go Mad in Mummy's Makeup, more like it, Bett thought. 'What on earth's Karl thinking this time?'

'He's hoping it'll revive punk. He bought the back catalogue of all these old punk bands and he wants to give them a kick-along.'

Bett looked at the photo again. 'So they're angry young musicians?'

'Oh, very angry,' Jessica laughed. 'They're furious. Cross as two sticks. Haven't stopped stamping their feet since we signed them.'

Bett turned the sample tape over, then rattled it, as if that would give her a taste of their music. The tape machine was broken and the CD player was currently propping up a bookshelf. 'What do they sound like?'

Jessica emitted a high-pitched screech, shook her head so her hair flew around, then sang in a guttural voice. '"Ravens in the night, kill the beast, anarchy rules", that kind of thing. Except on the first demo they sang an-Archie. As in the man's name. Isn't that sweet? They can't even read.'

Bett pretended to weep as she opened a new document on her computer screen. As she wrote she started speaking the words aloud in a dull monotone, silently saying goodbye to any final shred of journalistic credibility.

They're young, they're angry and they're here. London's newest music sensation, Dogs from Hell, has arrived with a bang and a wallop . . .

She stopped there, finding it hard to concentrate. More to the point, finding it hard to care about the sulky-faced brats who she knew had been chosen for their looks rather than any musical talent. She stared out the window instead, suddenly filled with gloom.

She'd been working in the press office of this small but very successful record company for two and a half years, writing media releases and puff pieces for record store magazines, as well as training their artists in interview techniques. At the start it had been a dream job, a combination of her love for music and for writing. But lately it had started to wear her down. She'd been feeling the same way about London, even though she had loved it when she first arrived. Little things seemed to be getting to her.

The night before she'd been working back late, coaching a new rap singer in radio interview techniques. It had been past nine o'clock when she left the studio, caught the tube home and started the fifteen-minute walk from the station to her basement flat, one of eight in a large three-storey Camden Town terrace house. She was tired, hungry and cold by the time her street was finally in sight. She was five steps from her door when she remembered taking her keys out of her bag that afternoon when she searched for her diary. Four steps away when she remembered seeing them on her desk and thinking 'don't forget those'. And two steps away when she realised she'd left them at work.

'In you go, then, love.' The locksmith had taken less than ten seconds to open her door. It had, however, taken him nearly two hours to arrive. Bett was frozen.

'Thanks,' she'd said, through icy-cold lips, handing over nearly fifty pounds. It was easy to see why he was so cheerful.

'Now, love, far be it from me to put myself out of a job, but have you thought about leaving a spare key with friends or family? In case this happens again?'

She'd nodded, smiled politely. She'd spent the time waiting for him thinking just that, before realising with a dull aching feeling that not only did she have no family here, but no friends close by either. Jessica lived on the other side of London. There were several other people, journalists and a band booker in one of the live music pubs, who she met occasionally for a drink, but she could hardly call them close friends. She couldn't really leave a key with them either.

She blinked now and dragged her attention back to the computer in front of her, trying to concentrate again. Cheer up, Bett, she told herself firmly. She gazed around the office, taking in all the band posters, the piles of CDs, the overflowing files of press clippings. Everything was peachy, wasn't it? She was living in the epicentre of the music industry, she had a great job, she'd never been happier.

Not only that, she was about to fly home to Australia, to see Lola and her parents for a week. And yes, all right, Anna and Glenn and Carrie and Matthew would be there, and yes, it would be awkward and uncomfortable, but she was a grown woman and she'd cope. And it would be great to see her niece, Ellen, again too, wouldn't it? Yes. Exactly. She shut her eyes tight, then opened them again, stared intently at the computer screen and started typing.

Lead singer Mutt Dagger says it's time that real music took over from the manufactured bands. 'Enough of this candy crap. People want truth and energy in their music and that's what we're giving them. This is us telling our stories with our music. And the difference is we're telling it as it is.'

Bett pressed save, then glanced down at the folder of plane tickets beside her coffee cup. She'd spent her lunch hour with her travel agent, running through all the flight details, paying the final instalment. It was only afterwards she noticed she'd conducted the entire conversation with a piece of spinach from her lunchtime salad on her front tooth, covering it so completely, in fact, it looked like she had lost a tooth, in pure witch fashion. On the way back to the office she'd had an overwhelming urge to ring her sister Anna in Sydney, to tell her about it and hear Anna's laughs. Except she didn't make those sorts of calls to her sisters any more, did she? Calls about disastrous days or wild nights, work trials or love lives or friends or recipes or hangovers or . . . anything.

The band combines a youthful energy with pure adrenalin, producing a raw, rocky sound, guitar-edged and bass-driven.

No, they don't, she thought. She typed quickly. *The band do what they're told by a middle-aged man who is living out his own musical fantasies and making a lot of money along the way out of kids reared on reality TV programs.*

She started to growl, a constant, satisfying kind of noise from the back of her throat.

Jessica peered over her own computer screen. 'Bett, are you okay?'

She stopped mid-growl to nod, then started it up again as she kept writing.

The band's drummer, Raven Deathmask, is a self-described anarchist and spotty-faced little tosshead who looks like he may still wear nappies.

Bett pressed delete and tried again.

The band's first album is a remarkable feat of hideous guitar squeals and nonsense lyrics about rebellion when the most any of the spoilt kids in this manufactured band have had to rebel against is –

Stop it, Bett. She pressed delete once more.

Dogs from Hell are a force to be reckoned with, combining youth, anger and bad haircuts –

Bett stopped writing altogether. A new, frightening thought had appeared in large letters in her head.

She didn't want to do this any more. It wasn't about music, it was about packaging. Karl had said as much to her a month ago, on one of his fleeting visits to the office. 'Just a licence to print money, Bett. Stop taking it so seriously. Pop singers, disposable music, remember?'

She looked out the window at the rain, the sky dark at four p.m. She thought of her flat. Small and cold, about as homely as a bus shelter. She thought of the Christmas just past. She had celebrated with Jessica and her family at their home in Suffolk, keeping her voice bright and cheery on the phone to her parents and Lola in South Australia. She'd felt miserable inside.

She pictured the travel agent earlier that day. 'It's such a long way to travel for seven days. You'll have only just recovered and you'll be on your way back. Are you sure you can't stay longer?'

Her words to Lola the day she'd received her fax flashed into her mind. What had she said? That she couldn't come back to Australia because she had a life here in London? What she had here wasn't a life. Not the sort of life she wanted any more, anyway.

The letters in her head were now in flashing neon. There were shadows and doubts underneath – what she would do for work and where she would live, not to mention the idea of her sisters – but she batted them away. She stared over at Jessica, amazed at what she was about to say, and even more amazed by how sure she felt about it. Do it, Bett, she thought. Quickly. Before you change your mind.

'Jessica, can you give me Karl's mobile number?'

The other woman glanced up from her computer. 'You're going to ring him? That's taking your life in your hands. Why would you want to do that?'

Do it, Bett. Be brave. Go home for good. Bett swallowed. 'I think I'm about to resign.'

In Sydney, Anna Quinlan was finishing her packing. She looked up as her daughter came into the room holding a framed photograph.

'Should I bring this, Mum?'

Anna took the photo. It was the two of them, taken twelve months previously, both smiling at the camera, Ellen's perfect six-year-old face upturned. 'Why do you want to take it, Ellie?'

'So I can show Really-Great-Gran what I used to look like. In case she's forgotten. In case she decides she doesn't like me like this either.'

'Ellie, Lola doesn't need to see that. She loves you whatever you look like.'

Ellen's voice became small. 'What if she calls me names, though? Like everyone else does?'

'Oh, Ellie, she won't. Don't think things like that.' Anna tried to keep her voice steady. How was she supposed to handle this? Ask Ellen to hold on a moment while she ran and checked the self-help books? It kept happening – just when Anna thought she had things running smoothly, out of the blue there'd be a question like this. Or a loud child's voice in the supermarket like yesterday.

'Mummy, what's wrong with that girl's face?'

'Shh, don't stare.'

Anna had at least had experience of that situation and knew the best thing to do. She had coolly answered the child. 'It's a scar. My daughter was attacked by a dog last year.' She was half tempted to carry a photo album with her. 'See,' she'd say at times like that, 'she was perfect when she was born. But then I foolishly took her to the park one afternoon and someone had a Rottweiler on the loose and the dog thought my little girl was a toy. And by the time I could drag her away from him his teeth had torn half her face.'

Anna smoothed back her daughter's hair. 'Ellie, your dad and I and your Really-Great-Gran and your gran and your grandpa love you no matter what you look like.'

'My aunties too?'

Anna's voice didn't change. 'Your aunties too. All of us, no matter what you look like, what you're wearing, how messy your hair is and how bad you smell, okay?'

That brought a glimmer of a smile. 'Even if I smell really bad and haven't brushed my hair for a year?'

'Two years even. Now, put that away and let's finish your proper packing.'

Ellen put her hands on her hips. 'I have finished. Can we run through our checklist?'

Our checklist? Anna had been hearing phrase after phrase of her own coming out of Ellen's mouth lately. She bit back another smile, not wanting Ellen to think she was laughing at her. Ellen had answered the phone ahead of the babysitter when Anna rang home several nights earlier. 'May I help you?' Ellen had said. They had spoken for a few minutes before Ellen had asked, in all seriousness, 'And were you ringing about anything in particular?' There was something about these pronouncements, and that solemn little voice and face of hers, that always went straight to Anna's core. She barely noticed Ellen's scar any more. She was aware of it – how could she not be? – but it didn't change the essence of Ellen. The body was . . . what was it? Her casing. The wrapping. Everything else was normal.

Except Glenn hadn't been able to see it that way. In his eyes, things had changed forever and it was all Anna's fault.

'I'm not the first man to feel like this, Anna. This happens to lots of marriages after a child trauma like this. I read it on the web.'

Her voice had grown icy. 'You've been researching reasons to back up why you're having an affair? Why you're walking out on us?'

'I'm not walking out on you.'

'Shall we look up the web for other ways to put it, then? Key "selfish" and "immature" into a search engine and see what websites turn up?'

'Anna, you're not making this easy.'

She had lost her temper then, hardly knowing what she was

saying. 'Glenn, I don't want to make it easy. I want to make it as excruciatingly hard for you as I can.'

Ellen had heard them fighting, Anna knew that. Ellen also knew Anna and Glenn were sleeping in separate rooms. And that her father wasn't home every night. Anna wanted to tell Ellen it wasn't her fault. He still loves you, Ellie, I know he does, she thought. It's me he doesn't love any more. It's me he blames.

Perhaps things would have been different if they'd been on steady ground before Ellen was attacked. But the foundations had been eroding for years, gaps and holes slowly appearing. Fights about his work taking up too much time. Snide remarks about her great acting career ending up in sound-recording booths. Even digs about her appearance. She'd put on a few kilos a year or two after they married, nothing too serious, so she'd thought. It had been nice to stop the endless weight watching and calorie counting that came hand in hand with a career as an actress. Until Glenn had brought home gym brochures, made pointed remarks about people letting themselves go.

'Me?' she'd said, good-humoured at first. 'Glenn, are you joking? All my clothes still fit, don't they?' Size ten at that. 'I thought you'd like to see me a bit more curvy.'

He hadn't smiled. 'I just want you to look your best.'

And that phrase had been the key, she'd discovered. He loved her, wanted her, when she looked her best. But not when her voice-over work increased and the travel between appointments lengthened and she started to get too tired to work out, wear full makeup, work constantly to keep her skin and hair in salon condition. 'Glenn, I'm a human being, not a mannequin. Would you stop going on at me all the time?'

Ellen's arrival had soothed things on one level. Glenn had shifted his attention onto her, showering his daughter with gifts and love, while he withdrew the same things from Anna. Their fights became less regular, the mood shifting from tension to indifference. They talked about Ellen, through Ellen, because of Ellen. He had been only mildly interested to hear about the fight between her and her sisters – he'd never met Matthew and had never got on with Bett or Carrie. His attention had turned to work, while she kept her days busy with Ellen and the voice-over jobs. Sometimes at night he'd be home in time to put Ellen to bed, have dinner with her, but often enough he would go out again afterwards. They were living separate lives under one roof, using guerilla tactics rather than open warfare.

Until the day in the park changed things for the worse. The long days in hospital were followed by nights of tension at home.

'How could you let this happen?'

'I was on the phone. I didn't see the dog coming.'

'You must have.'

'It's not my fault, Glenn. You think I wanted this to happen? That I wouldn't change everything, every single moment of my life, if I could make it not happen to her?'

The blame seeped into every one of their conversations.

Glenn turned further away from her, to his job – and to Julie. Anna was sure of the timing. The late nights working back with his PA had only started after Ellen had been attacked. Likewise, the weekends away at supposed conferences, business trips. She even discovered credit card bills for flowers she hadn't seen and dinners she hadn't eaten. Every corny step of it . . .

'Mum? The list?'

Anna focused back on Ellen. 'Ready when you are. Books?'

A nod from Ellen.

'Clothes? Teddies? Puzzles?'

More nods.

'Sounds good to me. You have enough for two weeks?'

Another solemn nod. 'Will I be able to help in the motel kitchen again? Even help to clean the rooms?'

She and Ellen had been back to the motel twice in the past three years, timing their two-week visits for when Carrie and Matthew were away on holiday. Ellen had enjoyed every minute, trailing behind Lola most of the time. 'Of course you can. Your grandmother would love a hand, I bet.'

'I really like it there.'

'Do you? Why?' Anna waited for her to say something about being in the country, being with her grandparents and Lola again.

'It's peaceful.'

'Peaceful?'

Ellen shuffled a little, wouldn't look at her. 'No one picks on me there.'

Anna's breath caught. A seven-year-old shouldn't be looking for peace. Shouldn't be looking forward to going to stay at her grandparents' because no one would be picking on her. But it was true, Anna knew that. Life in Sydney had been hard for Ellen since the attack. Yesterday's remark in the supermarket hadn't been the first. Her friends at school had changed towards her too, already at an age where appearance mattered. She crouched down and brushed her daughter's hair away from her face, looking straight into her eyes. 'Has it been that bad?'

There was a little pause, the smallest of nods and then Ellen started to cry, noiselessly. Anna took her into her arms and held her tight, feeling her daughter's body shuddering against hers. 'Ellie, it's all right, it's fine, it's all right,' she said over and over again. Ellen's tears didn't stop. As Anna rocked back and forth, soothing her, kissing the top of her head, another part of her mind switched into decision-making mode.

Could they stay on after Lola's birthday party? For a month or two? Longer, even? Since the attack Ellen had become fearful of everything, wetting the bed occasionally, nervous of school, of new people. But perhaps she wouldn't feel like that back in the motel, with family all around. There were good schools in the Valley these days. Could she even school Ellen herself? Of course, her work could be a problem. She doubted there'd be much demand for a voice-over artist in the Clare Valley. But perhaps she could rearrange her schedule, fly up to Sydney for a day or two a week. Or stop work altogether for a while, living off the money that Glenn, regularly, guiltily, was putting into her bank account. As for coping with seeing Carrie and Matthew every day, well, she'd face that when she had to.

Ellen's sobs had now turned into breathy gulps. Anna kissed her daughter's head again and held her tight for another moment, soothing her. 'It's all right, sweetheart. It'll be all right.'

Her voice against her mother's shoulder was muffled. 'I just get scared here sometimes.'

That was all Anna needed. She stood up, lifting Ellen onto her hip as if she was a toddler. 'I've got a good idea, then.' Holding her tight with one arm, she reached up into the wardrobe with the other and pulled out a bigger suitcase.

'Ellie, fill that one as well, will you? We might stay away a bit longer than two weeks.'

In the ladies' powder room of the Valley View Motel, Carrie Quinlan stood staring at her reflection in the full-length mirrors.

She cleared her throat. 'Bett and Anna, there's something you should know before you get here. Matthew and I have separated. And I'm not going to go into the reasons but, yes, I think it's for good.'

No, too apologetic. And maybe it would be better if she broke the news to them one by one. 'Anna, I want you to know something important. Matthew and I have decided to separate.'

Not bad. But then Anna would be the easiest to tell. Carrie took a breath. 'Bett, I don't want you to gloat but I've got some news for you.'

For a second it was as if both her sisters were standing in front of her. She pictured their reaction to her news and her temper flared. She glared at her own reflection and spoke in a fierce voice. 'Yes, I think it is for good. And no, it doesn't prove you right and it doesn't mean I shouldn't have married him in the first place. It just happened.'

She was interrupted by a knock at the door. 'Carrie?'

Carrie blushed, embarrassed. How long had her mother been outside? She didn't answer, stood stock still. She'd locked the door and put up the bright-yellow 'Sorry, I'm temporarily closed for cleaning!' sign, but it obviously hadn't been enough.

Another brisk knock. 'Carrie, did I hear you talking to yourself in there? Can you come and give me a hand moving these tables? We've got a group of Landcare people in tonight.'

Landcare-schmandcare. It was all right for them, talking to each other until the cows came home about soil levels and salinity. If only pH levels were all she had to worry about, instead of a marriage breakup, the imminent arrival of her sisters, Lola's ridiculous birthday party . . .

'Carrie?' The door handle rattled. 'Are you all right?'

Oh, perfectly all right. Couldn't be better. One final glare, a smoothing of her hair and she unlocked the door. 'Sorry, Mum. I'm coming.'

She stepped out just as her mother finished brushing specks of dust off the large banana plant by the front door. As petite as Carrie, Geraldine Quinlan was dressed in her usual trim skirt, crisp shirt and sensible shoes. Her hair was as no-nonsense as the rest of her – short, dark, neat.

She gave her daughter a speculative look. 'Is everything all right?'

'Everything's fine, Mum. Thanks.'

'Are you sure?' There was a little pause. 'You're not sick, are you? Feeling nauseous or anything . . .'

'No, it's not that.' Carrie said, colouring. Several months back, before the final big fight with Matthew, her mother had caught her reading pregnancy magazines at the reception desk. She hadn't said anything, but there had been a quick exchange of smiles.

Geraldine gave her a similar smile now. 'That's a shame.'

'Mmm,' Carrie said, trying to sound upbeat. If her mother only knew how nonexistent that possibility was these days. She gave a fake laugh. 'No, the only thing making me feel sick these days is the idea of Lola's birthday party.'

'You're not alone there.' Geraldine's lips tightened. 'It would have been nice to have been given some warning about it before she sent out all those invitations. I tried to explain to her that events like this need proper organisation, that neither you nor Jim and I can just drop everything. But of course that was like water off a duck's back.'

'I bet it was.' Carrie had actually been talking about the idea of Anna and Bett coming back making her feel sick, not the party itself. But Geraldine had never had any time for those sorts of conversations. She had been very firm about it from the start. 'You are grown women and it is up to the three of you to sort this out in your own good time.' Matthew's thoughts on her mother came to mind. 'That's just the way she is, Carrie. Anyway, you'd hate it if she was the fussy, nosy type of mother, you know that.'

She tuned back in, trying to look sympathetic as Geraldine outlined the latest episode of her silent war with Lola. It seemed she had caught Lola using the office computer to print up some sort of flyer. 'I've asked her not to do it, but she just ignores me. She goes through paper like nothing else, and never thinks to order more to replace it. I had to print out last week's menus on coloured paper, because she'd used all the white paper for a new batch of birthday invitations or some such thing.'

'She'd try the patience of a saint,' Carrie agreed, unconsciously echoing one of Lola's own Irish sayings. The difficulty was Carrie could see both sides. Lola could indeed be the most annoying, interfering, meddling old woman on the planet and Geraldine in turn was sometimes the most inflexible, single-minded, humourless woman in Australia, as Lola had once put it so succinctly. Carrie dragged out another fake laugh. 'Still, I suppose it's not every day she turns eighty.'

'No, thank God.' Geraldine glanced at her wristwatch, a functional one bought purely for timekeeping, not decorative purposes. 'So, can you come and help me move these tables? Your dad's not back from the wholesaler's yet, otherwise I'd ask him. I also want to go through the casual staff rosters with you. And I wouldn't mind your help with the new computer program, either, if you don't mind. I still can't make head nor tail of it.'

'Of course.' This was more like it. Back onto work matters, not the precarious rocky shores of emotions and feelings. Carrie felt much better as she followed her mother into the function room.

Chapter Three

In the forecourt of the Valley View Motel one week later, Len the local butcher slammed the door of his delivery van. Short, plump and with a bald pink head, he often joked that he wasn't unlike one of his tasty homemade sausages himself.

'All set for old Mrs Quinlan's hooley tonight, Jim? Sure you don't want me to DJ again?' He started speaking in a bad American accent. '"You're listening to Len's Mobile Disco, spinning the hottest new tracks for young and old."'

Jim Quinlan remembered the last time Len had DJed at a motel function. He'd had to refund half the room booking fee when the twenty-one-year-old and her parents complained. Len had been unrepentant. 'Islands in the Stream' was a classic, a beautiful song, he'd insisted. Not seven times in one night, though. 'Not this time, Len. No thanks. You just come along as our guest and enjoy yourself.'

'It's going to be some party, by all accounts. The two older girls still coming home for it?'

'That's right.' Jim wondered, not for the first time, if his family's daily activities were actually being broadcast directly to television sets around the Valley. Fifteen years they'd been here and he was still amazed at how news travelled. He made a point of looking at his watch. 'They're due any minute, actually. So if you can give me the invoice . . .'

Len gave a throaty laugh. 'The Alphabet Sisters together again. What I'd give to be a fly on the wall at that first meeting.'

Jim kept his face expressionless. It seemed the entire population of the Valley was hoping to be a fly on the wall at this reunion of his three daughters. One spray of an extra-strong pesticide and a good percentage of them would be lying on the floor, legs wriggling. It was a comforting thought. 'Good to know my family's providing so much entertainment, Len. I would have thought you'd have plenty of other things to keep you busy.'

Len was unabashed. 'Girls will be girls, won't they, Jim? I know my two can be tearing each other's eyes out one moment, giggling over a bottle of wine the next. When we first had two daughters I was a bit upset, don't mind telling you that. I wanted boys, sons, to play footy with. Now, I love it. The dramas! No need to watch soapies with them around the place.'

Jim knew Len's daughters well. As gossipy as their father, what they didn't know about people they made up. Well, let them make up what they liked about Anna, Bett and Carrie. The gossip would blow over soon enough, once something else happened in the town to grab everyone's attention. He'd actually admitted to Geraldine he was glad Lola had done what she'd done, bringing the girls back together like this. They'd both felt a twinge of guilt that they hadn't thought of it themselves. But when did they get time to sort out things like that? And neither of them had ever wanted to be the interfering kind of parent.

The phone rang, the sound echoing across the forecourt. Jim knew Geraldine was at the reception desk and would answer it, but

Len didn't. He leaned over and took the invoice out of the butcher's hand himself. 'Better run, Len. See you tonight. And thanks for the meat.'

Geraldine winked over at her husband as he came in through the front door, rolling his eyes. Len drove them both up the wall, but his meat was first rate and he delivered to their door. Holding the phone against her ear with one hand, she took the invoice from Jim with the other, mouthed a thanks and kept talking, even as she carefully filed the piece of paper in the 'Bills to be paid' folder to the left of the computer. From the bar she heard the sound of Jim picking up the plastic bin of empty bottles, ready for a trip to the recycling depot.

She concentrated on keeping the warm, friendly tone to her voice. 'That's no problem at all, Mr Lawrence. And you're still happy with that room? Very good. Thank you very much.'

This Richard Lawrence in room two was turning out to be the perfect guest, she thought as she hung up. Extending his stay week by week, keeping to himself, and so polite. Such a charming English accent too. Geraldine was mildly curious what he was up to – some sort of writing project, she'd gathered, after seeing the computer and the piles of paper spread around his room when she delivered his breakfast or cleaned his room – but she wouldn't dream of asking him for any details about it. Not like some other people in this motel . . .

She made a note in the bookings register and then, using two fingers, carefully typed the same information into the computer on the desk beside her. Carrie had been very persuasive, insisting that it really was very efficient and of course Geraldine would be able to master it. One day, perhaps. She tentatively pressed save and gave a satisfied sigh, just as a blue station wagon pulled up outside.

A casually dressed man with dark hair leapt out of the driver's seat, reached into the back for a pile of newspapers, then took the steps, two at a time and came inside. 'Mrs Quinlan? Your copies of the *Valley Times*, hot off the press. Will I leave them here?'

'Yes, thank you.' He wasn't the usual newspaper delivery man, but he did look vaguely familiar. Then again, so did half the townspeople when you'd lived in a place this long. 'Where's Pat?'

'He had a bit of an accident last night.'

'Not again. Is he all right?'

'Nothing two weeks in a drying-out clinic won't fix.'

'Oh dear. He fell off the wagon again?'

'Not so much fell as took a great, voluntary leap, I think.'

'Who are you talking about?'

They both turned. Lola had come in behind them.

'Pat from the newspaper office,' Geraldine explained. 'The man who normally does the deliveries.'

Lola nodded, giving the new arrival a good close look. His hair was a bit long but she liked those laughter lines around his eyes. 'Well, you're certainly far better looking than poor old Pat. You've taken over from him permanently, have you? Can we look forward to seeing you here every week?'

The man laughed. 'No, I'm double-jobbing. I usually do the photographs, but we've divided up his round between us today.'

She peered at him. 'I know you, don't I?'

'I know you, too, I think. From the charity shop. Lola, isn't it?'

'Cheeky monkey. It's Mrs Quinlan to you.'

A hint of a smile again and a glance at both women. 'It's just there are two Mrs Quinlans here. I didn't want to confuse myself.'

Lola clapped her hands. 'Marvellous. A man with a bit of wit about him. Are you married?'

Geraldine interrupted, exasperation in her voice. 'Lola, would you leave the poor man alone? And would you both excuse me, I need to make a few calls before the girls get here.' Not just make a few calls, but also re-organise the walk-in freezer and brief her stand-in cook about tonight's dinner preparations. Sometimes Geraldine wondered if Lola had deliberately forgotten how much work was involved in running a motel, not to mention organising birthday parties at the drop of a hat . . .

'Of course, my dear.' Lola didn't go anywhere, staring at the man for a long moment, eyes narrowed. 'I have it now. It's Daniel Hilder, isn't it?'

'You've got a very good memory.'

She batted her eyelashes in an exaggerated way. 'I never forget a good-looking face. And I remember you taking those photos when we re-opened the charity shop a few years ago. Remember, all of us old ladies dressing up? It was like a Paris fashion shoot, wasn't it?'

Daniel's lip twitched. 'A bit like that.'

'Lola, please?' Geraldine stood with the phone and a pained expression.

'We're just leaving, aren't we, Daniel?' Lola took him by the arm and steered him outside. 'Now, what are you doing back in the Valley again? I'm sure someone told me you moved away.' Who was it had told her that? Her memory was so slow these days she was surprised people didn't hear creaking sounds coming out of her skull.

'I've been in Melbourne the past few years, but I came back six months ago. My mother's still living here.'

'You were in Melbourne?' Lola remembered then exactly who he was and why she knew his name. Her smile stretched even wider. 'Well, you're a good kind boy to come and see your mother and you're very welcome home. Tell me, would you be a good kind boy to me too? I need a little hand in my room with something. Your newspaper deliveries can wait a moment, surely?'

Daniel looked amused. 'Of course they can. Lead the way.'

Geraldine watched, shaking her head, as her mother-in-law led the man across the forecourt, talking all the while. There'd be a picture needing straightening that Lola supposedly couldn't reach, or a shower rose that was pointing the wrong way or some other imaginary task that would give her the opportunity to grill her poor victim.

God help him, Geraldine thought as she reached for the phone.

'There it is, there it is,' Ellen shrieked.

Anna glanced at her daughter, who had nearly clambered out of the car seat and on to the dashboard in her excitement. 'Where, Ellie? I can't see anything.'

'There, up on the hill.'

Anna pulled the hire car onto the side of the road and looked out the opposite window. She saw vineyards and gum trees, the foundations of a house, and two vans with Clare Valley Builders written on the side in large letters parked beside it. 'I can't see anything. Are you sure?'

Ellen was laughing now. 'Mum, you're looking the wrong way.'

Anna looked down at her feet. 'No, nothing here.' Then she looked up. 'No, nothing there either. Ellie, your eyesight must be much better than mine.'

'*Muuum.*' Ellie unbuckled her seatbelt and leaned over, placed a little hand on either side of Anna's face and turned it in the right direction. 'See, there.'

'It does look a bit familiar. What does that sign say?'

'It says The Valley View Motel. Vacna . . .' Ellen struggled with the word at first. 'Vacancies. Restaurant and Bar. Function room available. What's function?'

'Another word for a party.'

'Is that where Really-Great-Gran's birthday party will be tonight?'

'I think so.' Anna gazed at the motel. Built in the 1970s, it was a perfect example of the architecture of the time: a series of building blocks, placed clunk-clunk-clunk beside one another on the hillside just north of Clare, the largest town in the Clare Valley. There were fifteen guest rooms, one row of seven facing another row of eight, with the extra room the linen store. Linking the two lines of rooms was the small bar, a tiny reception area, a medium-sized restaurant and kitchen and a large function room. Anna had always thought the motel would make the perfect setting for a retro drama series, right down to the brown carpets, white plastic bathrooms, nylon curtains and orange bedspreads.

'Mum, come on.' Ellen was tugging at her arm. 'We're not going to park here, are we?'

'You're sure you're ready? Sure you want to go there?' Anna teased.

Ellen considered the question seriously. 'I am feeling a little bit shy. I haven't seen them for a long time, have I?'

Anna knew exactly how Ellen felt. She was nervous about seeing her sisters again too, she realised. Three years on she still felt caught in the middle – trying to make peace between Carrie and Bett, she'd managed beautifully to make things worse. 'Nothing to be frightened of here, Ellie, I promise you. They're your family, remember?'

Her cheery tone convinced Ellen, but it did nothing for herself. She wished she felt fresher, more ready for this. It had only been a two-hour flight from Sydney to Adelaide, and then the same length drive from the airport to here. She'd always liked the drive from Adelaide to Clare, too. The long straight highway through flat plains and wide yellow paddocks slowly giving way to the curving roads of the Valley, vineyards and tree-covered hills on either side. But she still felt drained. It must be the tension of coming home, she thought. Or the aftermath of emotion from that morning's spat with Glenn. He'd made a point of being there to say goodbye to Ellen.

'You know I'll cry myself to sleep every night while you're away,' he'd said, as he picked the little girl up in a hug. He was so broad it took nothing out of him. Ellen could have been two, not seven.

'Me too,' Ellen had giggled, as Glenn tickled her. She had thrown back her head, laughing, completely unself-conscious with him about her scar.

'And don't forget to do me lots of drawings. And to breathe in lots of that country air.' He had done some mock deep breaths, making Ellen laugh even more. 'And you won't forget you're my favourite daughter, will you?'

Ellen shook her head.

'And not only that,' Glenn continued. 'But the best daughter in –'

'The whole wide world!' Ellen had finished it for him, as she always did.

Anna had received no such attention. She and Glenn had spoken quickly, coldly to each other. She'd been deliberately vague about how long they might be away, knowing it would annoy him. He had reminded her of the possibility he'd need to go to Singapore for business, if the office expansion ended up going ahead. She had pretended she had forgotten all about it, and enjoyed the little dart of annoyance she knew that had sent through him. How had it got so bad? she'd wondered, even as she said goodbye in her most carefree voice. Ellen hadn't noticed a thing – she hoped. She had been too busy waving until her father was long out of sight.

Anna tried to block out those thoughts and smiled across at her daughter now. 'Ready, sweetheart?'

'I'm ready, sweetheart,' Ellen replied, grinning at her own cheekiness. 'But we can't go yet.'

'Why not?'

'You have to look at yourself in the mirror first. That's what you always do.'

Anna laughed. Indeed she did. 'You don't miss a trick, do you, Miss Ellen?' She ostentatiously checked her face in the rear-vision mirror, wrinkling her nose, squinting, baring her teeth, playing up to Ellen's laughs beside her, even as she quickly took the opportunity to dab away a tiny spot of mascara and reapply her lipstick. Then she took a deep breath and started the car.

In the flower shop in the middle of Clare, Carrie glanced at her watch. The young florist noticed.

'Carrie, if you're running late, I can drop these up to the motel for you later today. The party doesn't start until seven, does it?'

Carrie didn't mind if it took all day to prepare her order. She didn't mind if she had to live in the flower shop from this moment on. Anywhere was better than being at the motel waiting for Anna and Bett to arrive.

'Carrie? Do you want me to do that?'

Carrie took a seat beside the counter. 'No, I'm in no rush at all. Honestly, take as long as you like. In fact, why don't I go and get us both a cool drink?'

'The weather hasn't helped, of course. The past week or so it's been more than thirty degrees every day. People want to head for the sea not the countryside. Still, just as well we have a few empty rooms with you girls being home again.'

'Yes, isn't it?' Anna said, trying to keep up with her mother's update on the motel occupancy rate.

Anna and Ellen had walked through the reception area into the kitchen, surprising her mother who had been wrestling with something in the walk-in freezer. Geraldine looked immaculate as ever. Not unlike a 1950s housewife, Anna had always thought. There was a brief hug, then her mother turned to Ellen, bending down, giving her a quick hug and kiss too. 'And welcome to you too, Ellen.'

Anna watched, waiting for some reaction to the scar. It wasn't the first time her mother had seen it. She had come to Sydney after the accident happened, to lend a hand, much to Anna's surprise. But it was the first time she'd seen it in months.

'Well, aren't you both looking great. Ellen, you must have grown three feet since we saw you last.' Geraldine straightened up, put her hands on her hips and stepped back.

That was the physical contact over for the visit, Anna thought. She knew it wasn't her mother's fault she wasn't a tactile person, but it had been hard at times to be her affection-craving daughter. Anna showered Ellen with hugs and cuddles and caresses, more than the child wanted sometimes. Ellen pressed close against her now, still shy, her hair forming a curtain over the right side of her face.

Geraldine busied herself in the kitchen again, passing on news over her shoulder. Anna and her sisters had always laughed at their mother's conversational style. She had to be doing something while she asked questions or relayed information, be it mopping the floor or preparing meals for guests or sometimes, in shouts, over the noise of vacuum cleaners. She'd had the same approach to mothering, in fact – fitting it in around her other, more pressing tasks.

'Carrie will be back in a moment. She's gone into town to collect the last of the flower displays for the party. Bett's flying in today too, of course. Insisted on driving herself up from Adelaide. Lola is around somewhere. I'm surprised she didn't hear the car coming in. Your father had to make a quick trip to the bottle depot this morning but he said he'd be back as soon as he could –'

'He's here now, in fact.'

They both spun around at the sound of his voice. He'd come in through the back door. 'Hello, Anna, and aren't you looking beautiful?'

'Dad! Full of charm as usual,' she said, smiling at him.

'No, just telling the truth. You took after your mother, luckily,' he said with a wink in Geraldine's direction.

Anna was amazed to see her mother get soft-eyed at the praise. Honestly, what were the two of them like? She waited, and sure enough, her father dropped a kiss on her mother's head as he went past her.

'You should be glad your parents get on so well. Mine fought all the time. That's much harder to live with,' Glenn had said in their early days, when she'd tried to explain how excluded she and her sisters had sometimes felt. 'It's unusual, though, I'll give you that. Business partnerships and marriages don't tend to last.' But her parents had always loved working together, putting across a united front, making decisions together, a true partnership. Anna had childhood memories of lying in bed at night, hearing her parents come in from locking up the motel, listening to the murmurs of conversations as they talked over their day, planned for tomorrow.

That's what she'd wanted when she met Glenn. What she'd thought she had when she met Glenn.

Anna reached up to give her father a quick kiss on the cheek, followed by a warm, close hug. He was tall, like Lola and herself, but chubby, not thin, his square, open face red from too much sunshine. She watched intently again as he got down on his haunches to be at eye level with Ellen. She'd spoken to Lola from Sydney before they left, asked her to remind her mother and father to build Ellen up as much as possible.

'And welcome to you, Miss Ellen. And aren't you looking beautiful as well? All set for the party tonight?'

Ellen nodded shyly again, struck dumb by the attention and the new surroundings.

Jim tousled Ellen's hair. 'Good girl. It's great to have you both home again.'

Ellen stared at him. 'It's not really home. My home is in Sydney.'

Jim gave a roar of laughter. 'You can't call a big city like that home, darling. Home is where the heart is. Isn't that right, Geraldine?'

'That's right, Jim.'

'But isn't my heart in my body all the time?' Ellen asked Anna, looking confused. 'Not just when I'm at home?'

'Grandpa's teasing you, Ellie. Don't mind him.'

'Best advice I've heard all day,' an Irish voice behind them said. 'Hello, my darlings. The birthday girl is here.' It was Lola, dressed in a pants-suit made of pink flowing material. She was in full makeup, with a small pink rose pinned in her white hair.

'Lola! Happy birthday!' Anna found herself rushing to meet Lola as if she was a child again herself. Now she knew for sure she was home. Lola turned from her hug with Anna, then leaned down with melodramatic groans to Ellen's height, took her face between both hands, gazed at her for a long moment and then kissed her extravagantly on both cheeks. 'That scar is fading so quickly there must be a miracle at work.'

Anna relaxed. Trust Lola to mention it, to point it out and bring it into the open. Ellen didn't seem to mind, she noticed. She was nodding. 'It is going a bit, I think, Really-Great-Gran.'

Lola gave a shout of laughter and kissed Ellen again. 'You're still calling me Really-Great-Gran, you dear little pet.'

Ellen looked delighted with herself. 'I listen to that tape a lot.'

'You're a little girl with wonderful taste. I know it in my bones.' She stood up with another groan. 'Creaking and feeble as those bones might be. Enough of dilly-dallying with this riff-raff, my dear Ellen. It's time for a tour. And may I introduce your tour leader for the day. Myself, your Really-Great-Gran.'

Ellen beamed up at her. 'But can I call you Lola, now, Really-Great-Gran? Like Mum does? Now I'm here?'

'You can call me all the names under the sun, my little darling,' Lola had said, before sweeping out of the room with her.

Anna looked out the kitchen window now and saw Lola and Ellen walking by the back fence. On one side was bushland, gum trees and scrubby earth covered in dry bark and wiry grasses. The other side of the fence marked the start of the motel grounds, with a strip of bright-green lawn, flowers and bedding plants, all their father's work. It was an island of green amid the dry South Australian landscape. As she watched, a tubby white sheep trotted up behind Lola and Ellen. Her parents had bought it the year before, to help keep the grass down around the motel. Anna saw Ellen's reaction, a shriek and then a push against her great-grandmother, looking for a shield. As her hands clenched, Anna felt her mother's eyes on her and gave an embarrassed smile. 'It's that obvious, is it? I'm trying not to run out there. The doctor says I have to be careful not to make her any more anxious than she already is.'

'Sheep have fairly blunt teeth. She'll be safe enough.'

Surely her mother wasn't making light of it? 'It was terrifying for her, Mum. For all of us.'

'I know it was. I'm not laughing at you or her. I'm saying it as it is – she'll be all right with Bumper. Besides, Bumper is so besotted with Lola she only has to whisper a word and he behaves.'

The sheep was now on one side of Lola, Ellen on the other. Lola had a hand on each of their heads and was inclining her head towards one and then another. Introducing them again, Anna realised. Probably explaining the sheep's name once more. Bumper as in Bumper Baa. Lola's idea – she'd thought it was hilarious.

Lola's voice filtered in. 'Can you feel his lovely soft wool, Ellen? Sheep have lanolin in their wool, one of nature's very best moisturisers. If you ever meet a shearer, ask to shake his hand. You'll never feel softer skin in all your life. Now, let's go and say hello to the chickens as well. They're a bad-tempered bunch. We won't worry about shaking their claws today.'

Anna turned from the window, a smile on her face. At that moment the kitchen door opened and Carrie walked in, carrying a large bundle of long brown twigs.

Anna's stomach gave a leap and the smile froze. 'Carrie. Hello.'

Carrie stopped short. 'Hello, Anna.'

Anna swallowed, kept a smile on her face. 'You look well.' She did too. Small, pretty, she looked like a dainty forest creature. Anna was unreasonably disappointed. What had she expected? Carrie to have turned into a garden troll since they'd seen each other last?

'So do you.'

Anna accepted the compliment with a brief smile. So she would want to, all the money and effort she put into it – constant dieting, fake tans, manicures, pedicures, eyebrow shaping . . .

'Have you been here long?'

'About half an hour.'

'How was the trip?'

'Fine thanks.' Anna forged ahead. She was going to be polite, she was going to handle this if it killed her. 'All set for tonight?'

'Just about, thanks.'

Geraldine looked up from the oven. 'You would have been ready days ago if Lola hadn't kept changing her mind about the way she wanted the serviettes folded. Swans one minute, bishops' hats the next. What was it you ended up with, Carrie?'

'Fans,' Carrie said shortly.

Anna gave a genuine smile. As teenagers they had spent what felt like months learning how to fold different sorts of serviettes for various functions – bishops' hats for business meetings, fans for ladies' lunches and swans for weddings. The three of them could do it in their sleep. Once upon a time Anna would have reminisced about those days, gone straight over, taken the foliage from Carrie, chatted easily and dragged her out to say hello to Ellen. Now they were standing like two store dummies, stiff and awkward, making equally stiff and awkward conversation. She tried again. 'Do you need any help?'

Carrie paused for a few moments too long. 'No thanks. Everything's under control.' She glanced around. 'Where's Ellen?'

'Lola's showing her around.'

'And Glenn?'

'He couldn't make it. Work.'

'Oh.'

Say it, Anna, say it. 'And how's Matthew?'

'Fine. Good. Busy.'

The air grew tense and the silence stretched out.

Lola had seen Carrie's car arrive. She flung open the door with a flourish, talking loudly to Ellen, deliberately interrupting. 'And here we are back in the kitchen. Oh, and look who's here, your Auntie Carrie. Carrie, you remember Ellen, our beautiful Ellen?'

Carrie turned and after a flicker of something passed over her face – shock, surprise – so quickly that only Lola noticed it, she bent down to her niece, who had gone straight over to Anna. 'Hello, Ellen. It's great to see you again. Did you have a nice trip?'

The little girl nodded, her face pressed against Anna's side.

'She's gorgeous, isn't she?' Lola said proudly. She glanced around, judging the mood. It was like Iceland in here. Time for some defrosting. 'Carrie, don't tell me that pile of twigs over there is for my party, is it? Are we having a bonfire tonight?'

'They're for the flower displays,' Carrie said sulkily. 'You told me you wanted a bush theme.'

'Did I?' Lola asked. 'Good heavens. Was I drunk?'

At Adelaide airport at that moment, Bett was walking up to the car hire desk.

A young man in a badly fitting suit smiled at her. 'Can I help you, madam?'

She smiled back. Madam? How sweet of him. A more honest query would have been 'Can I help you, you bedraggled-looking weirdo?'

'I've booked a car, thanks,' she said, handing over the paperwork. As he started pressing keys on the computer, she saw her reflection in the mirror behind him and only just stopped herself from poking her tongue out at her own rumpled, baggy-eyed reflection. She looked like the beagle she'd seen sniffing at suitcases in the arrivals hall.

Was it too late to find a gym and lose a stone? she wondered. First impressions were going to be very important. She wished that Lola had called this party two years ago, when for five glorious months, after a long bout of flu and poverty, Bett had actually been skinny, a size 12, and change rooms were welcoming places, not temples of fear and doom. Anna had always had a comforting theory about women and body fat – that there was only so much fat in the world and what it did was redistribute itself around women all over the planet. When someone on a diet lost a few kilos, another poor unsuspecting woman in a country far away would discover to her astonishment that she had gained a few. Please, God, let Anna be wrinkled and plump and Carrie scruffy and taken to wearing nylon clothes that stick to her all over. With split ends. And adult-onset pimples. Bett turned side on, sucked in her stomach as hard as she could and nearly fell over in the process.

'Is everything all right, madam?'

'Fine. Just doing some after-flight exercises.'

He looked a little suspicious.

Standing sideways again, she wondered whether it would be possible to buy a pair of those super-control tights somewhere nearby. Mind you, her only experience with a pair had been disastrous. When she finally pulled the things on, it was as if they had dragged every spare bit of flesh up with them. She'd been left with slimmish thighs, certainly, but also with the most extraordinary roll of fat over the top of them, as if she'd been stuck in a lifebuoy.

'Madam?'

The young man was now looking concerned. 'Your keys, madam. Car number fifteen.'

Pulling her case behind her, she stopped at the airport door, struck by the high temperature now she was outside the airconditioned building. It felt like someone had opened an enormous oven nearby, sending out a hot, dry rush of heat. A woman in the arrivals hall had been full of the news that it had been one of the hottest summers in years, nine days straight of temperatures in the high thirties. Bett looked around for a phone box and spied one in the carpark. She'd promised Lola she'd call and let her know she was on her way. It had been her choice to hire a car, drive up herself, arrive independently. The phone box was no cooler, the receiver hot to touch. She stared at the phone for a moment, doing the deep breathing that all the books recommended, calming herself down. Of course she could handle this. Hadn't she been out in the world for the past three years, surviving in Melbourne, Dublin and London? Making a career for herself? Be strong, Bett. Be brave, Bett. Ring and tell them you're in Adelaide and you'll be up in a few hours.

She dialled. A cross-sounding voice answered. 'Valley View Motel.'

It was Carrie. Bett hung up immediately.

'Hello? Hello?' Carrie waited a moment, then hung up. People were so rude. At least the ringing phone had got her out of the kitchen, though, before she exploded at her grandmother in front of everyone. Did Lola have any idea how hard it had been for the florist to find all those twigs?

She waited a moment to see if the caller rang back, but the phone stayed quiet. It had probably been another one of Lola's mad friends ringing up to RSVP at the last minute.

'It's not just going to be a room full of old people reminiscing, is it, Lola?' Carrie had asked her several days before. 'There seem to be a lot of croaky old voices ringing up.'

'All human life will be represented, Carrie my dear. And there'll be some reminiscing, some entertainment, a little bit of this and a little bit of that.'

'A little bit of what?'

'It's a surprise.'

'Lola, please. You're the one who is supposed to get a surprise at your party, not us. What are you planning?'

'Carrie, how many times do I have to ask you to please treat me with adoration and respect. I'm not telling. All you have to do is set up the room exactly as I've outlined, follow the running order we have discussed and then leave the rest to me.'

'You're not going to tell me why Frank from the electrical hire shop was here yesterday, are you? Or what was in that big box I saw him carrying in?'

'No, I'm not.'

'Have you finished your table settings yet, then? Are you still expecting about sixty people?'

'More like seventy now, I think. All sorts of people have told me they'd love to come. Oh, and I also invited that quiet Englishman who's staying in room two. He said he'd be delighted to attend. Actually, I think he said he'd be charmed to attend. Have you spoken to him yet? He has the most beautiful manners.'

Right then Carrie didn't care if that Englishman was the most well-mannered man in history. Honestly, her grandmother drove her *crazy* sometimes. 'Lola, you have to tell me these things. That changes everything. All the catering arrangements, everything.'

'Only slightly. Really, Carrie, you have to learn to relax or you'll give yourself high blood pressure.'

'It is you and this party and this neverending guest list that will give me high blood pressure. What are we supposed to feed these extra people?'

'Oh, they won't mind if they have to share their meals.'

'I mind, though. If I'm trying to get more business into the motel, then every occasion like this is a chance to make an impression. And I won't make a good impression if people don't get enough to eat at a birthday party for one of the owners.'

'I'm not an owner any more. I'm just the matriarch these days.'

Carrie had given in and started to laugh. 'You're just a law unto yourself, that's what you are.'

It had been funny then but it wasn't funny now. Nothing was funny now. Carrie took her pulse, felt her heart beating. Yes, it was definitely fast. And no wonder, all the pressure she was under. She heard laughing and looked out in time to see Lola, Anna and Ellen head over to Anna's favourite room, number seven. She fought off a little feeling of hurt, picked up her car keys and scribbled a quick note to her mother. She was going back into town for a long, slow cup of coffee.

Chapter Four

'At last, at last, at last.' Lola held Bett tight in another hug, then stepped back to look at her again, a wide smile on her face. She had been sitting waiting on a chair at the front of the motel for the past hour. 'You had me worried sick. I thought I'd have to start the party without you.'

Bett was surprised to find herself fighting tears. 'As if I'd let the birthday girl down.' Another hug. 'Let me look at you.' Bett took a step back, still holding Lola's hands. She'd felt bones under Lola's pink clothing. 'You've lost weight, Lola.'

Lola was looking at her just as closely. 'So have you. Not too much, thank God. I wouldn't know you without your curves.' She tucked a bit of hair behind Bett's ears. 'And your eyes are as beautiful as ever, your cheeks as rosy, and I like that colour in your hair. What's it called? Chestnut brown?'

'I don't know what it's called. It's my own colour.'

'Is there such a thing? Imagine that.'

Bett glanced around her. 'Are the –'

'Others here? No darling. I poisoned them all this morning. I decided it would make for a much more peaceful life if you and I had the place to ourselves.'

The sound of the front door opening halted any more questions. Bett looked up as her mother and father came out towards her. 'Bett! Welcome home!' She was enfolded in hugs from another two sets of arms.

An hour later, her head was spinning with news of the motel, of the Valley, of the party that night. There had been no sign of Anna or Carrie yet, and no mention of them. Her parents hadn't asked her too many questions about her life in London either. They knew some of it, of course, from her letters and phone calls, so it wasn't as if she had crawled in from the wilderness. But she had just got back from three years overseas. Shouldn't they have had more questions?

Lola was sitting on the sidelines, watching beady-eyed. Grasping a break in the conversation, she stood up with a groan loud enough to make them all look at her, then crossed to Bett and tucked her hand into her arm. 'Now, come on, Bett, I'll help you unpack. And while we do that, I want you to tell me every little thing you've been doing while you've been away.'

Lola was like a mind-reader sometimes. 'You know it all. It was in my letters.'

Lola steered her out of the kitchen. 'They were a tissue of lies. I know that and you know that. Come on, darling. You can tell me the truth now. By the way, I've organised room six for you, your favourite.'

Lola and the three girls had been sleeping in the motel rooms rather than the manager's quarters ever since the family first moved in, fifteen years before. It had been Lola's idea. She'd decided it was better to use the rooms during quiet times, rather than have them lie idle and unused, getting all musty.

As they walked out into the sunshine, Bett noticed quite a few rooms had a car parked in front of them. 'It's busy enough for this time of year.'

'Not bad, actually. Carrie has been working hard. Mostly one-nighters, though room two has been here for two weeks now. An English fellow. He's coming along tonight, actually. I called on him last week, had a very nice chat. He's researching a book or something fascinating like that. I'm dying to find out more about it.'

Bett kept her mouth shut. Many times in the past her mother had asked Lola not to call on the guests like that, but she was obviously still ignoring her. It would be a bit alarming, Bett supposed, to be booked into a motel room and have a heavily made-up old lady carrying a clinking gin and tonic appear at your door asking for your life story.

With a flourish, Lola produced the key to number six. 'Here you are, darling. All yours once again. I actually had to move a couple out that Carrie had accidentally booked in. I said there might be a problem with a nest of huntsman spiders and they seemed happy enough to move.'

'Move rooms or move motels?'

'Motels, now I think of it. Now, be sure to make yourself at home. If your luck holds and we don't get many guests, you might be able to stay put the whole time you're here. You do have neighbours, though.'

'Neighbours?'

The door to number seven beside them opened and Anna and Ellen came out. Bett's stomach flipped as she saw them for the first time in years. Anna looked as fresh and elegant as ever, immaculately made-up, wearing a white shift dress that showed off her toned, brown body. Ellen was in a pale-blue sundress, holding a straw hat. Bett stood up a little straighter, suddenly conscious of her own creased T-shirt and makeup-free face.

Lola coughed politely. 'Anna Quinlan, may I introduce your sister, Bett Quinlan. Bett Quinlan, this is Anna, your older sister.'

'Hello, Anna.'

'Hello, Bett.'

'And this is Ellen,' Lola continued. 'You remember Ellen.'

Bett looked down at the little girl, feeling Anna's eyes boring into her. Ellen was lovely, a mini version of Anna, with big eyes, straight dark hair and olive skin. Bett glanced at the scar on her cheek, keeping a big smile on her face. Lola had warned her Anna was extremely sensitive about people's reactions to Ellen's scar. She leaned down. 'Hello, Ellen.'

Ellen pressed close against Anna and wouldn't look up.

'Ellen, this is Bett, your auntie. My sister.'

Ellen still didn't look at her. Anna gave Bett a tight smile, a half shrug, as if to apologise.

Bett looked behind her, waiting for Glenn to emerge as well. Anna noticed.

'He's not here,' she said.

Bett felt the rush of colour into her face. Had Anna kept him away because of her? Because of the things she'd said about him? Oh, God. Talk about things getting off to a bad start. 'Look, he's –' Very welcome to be here, too, she'd been about to say.

'Very busy at work,' Anna said smoothly. 'He wasn't able to get away.'

Bett relaxed slightly. 'Oh. I see.'

Anna spoke again, her voice measured, in control. 'So how was your flight?'

'Fine. Long. But I had a night's stopover in Singapore, so I'm not too exhausted. And you? Did you drive down or fly?'

'We flew. Took the ten o'clock this morning.'

Lola stepped in, shaking her head. 'Well, it's a credit to the both of you. Three years' separation and look at the conversation you manage to strike up.'

'Lola, please.' Anna and Bett turned to her and spoke as one.

'Mum,' Ellen's voice was little more than a whisper, as she started pulling at her mother's hand.

Anna leaned down, stroking her daughter's hair from her face. 'You're hungry, I know. Come on, darling. We'll go and see what Grandma has for you. See you later, Bett.'

'Yes, see you, Anna. See you, Ellen.'

As they walked away towards the kitchen, Lola was half laughing, half sighing. 'You'll be the death of me. If that was the best you and Anna could do, then God knows what you'll do with Carrie. Lunge at her with a knife, probably.'

'Lola, sorry, but you have to stop all these cracks. This isn't some little tiff between us. This is big, serious stuff. Grown-up stuff.'

'Nonsense. It's been the world's most ridiculous feud. Over Matthew, of all people.'

'It wasn't just over Matthew. It was –'

'What?'

'All sorts of things,' Bett wasn't ready for this. She tried to find the words. 'Maybe we were unnaturally close all our lives, you know, with the three of us moving so much and the whole Alphabet Sisters thing.'

'So now you're blaming me?'

'Lola, of course I'm not blaming you. I loved the Alphabet Sisters, until –' She stopped short. Was that actually the truth? She grabbed her grandmother's arm. 'Can we please not talk about it right now? Just for a little while? Can you and I go inside and talk about normal things, like terrible gossip from the charity shop or the party tonight or –'

'In a moment.' Lola had heard the sound of a car coming up the driveway. 'Carrie has just arrived back and I want you to meet her. Now.'

'No.' To her own astonishment Bett leapt inside and shut the door of the room.

A second later it opened and Lola came in. 'What happened to you in London? Have you been regressing rather than aging? Don't tell me you were about to hide under the bed?' Bett had spent hours of her childhood under the bed. Looking for peace, she had insisted. Hiding from work, Lola had preferred to put it. 'I'm sure you weren't this cowardly before you went away.'

'I wasn't. And I wasn't this cowardly while I was away.'

'So you admit you're being cowardly now, wanting to hide under the bed? Did I tell you in any of my letters that your mother found some rope under one of the beds last year? Several metres of it, imagine. We had quite a discussion about what that might have been used for. I have to say I think your mother was shocked.'

Bett glared at her, trying not to laugh. 'You're the equivalent of that white noise that armies use to confound their enemies, aren't you? When they play noise at such a volume and for so long that the enemy gives in eventually.'

'Enemy? You're not my enemy. You're one of my dearest girls in the world. Now, come and meet another of my dearest girls. Her name's Carrie and she's your sister.'

At first there were fifty metres between them. Then forty. Thirty.

'Good afternoon, Carrie,' Lola called as they reached ten metres.

'Hello, Lola.'

'Carrie, may I introduce your sister?'

'Stop it, Lola,' Bett muttered. She forced herself to look directly at Carrie, taking in the blonde curls, the petite figure, dressed in jeans and T-shirt, an inch of flat brown belly showing, casual, stylish, neat. In her own mind she ballooned to Michelin Man proportions, her skirt and T-shirt turning super size, her cheeks expanding like balloons, getting redder and redder . . .

Lola interrupted her train of thought. 'But of course neither of you need any introductions. Say hello, girls.'

'Hello, Carrie.'

'Hello, Bett.'

'How was your flight?'

'Good thanks. Long.' She swallowed. 'How is –' she couldn't say Matthew's name. She tried again. 'How is work?'

A look of relief crossed Carrie's face, Bett was sure of it. Perhaps Carrie didn't want to talk about Matthew yet either. 'Fine. We're busy enough for this time of year.'

Lola was beaming between them, for all the world like a country matchmaker.

Then there seemed to be nothing else to say. 'I'd better finish getting ready for the party, then,' Carrie said briskly.

'Do you need any help?' Bett forced out the words.

'No.' Carrie answered too quickly.

'Are you sure about that, Carrie?' Lola's voice was firm.

'It's under control, thanks, Lola. See you, Bett.'

'See you, Carrie.' They stood silently as Carrie walked through the back door of the kitchen.

'Well, that went okay,' Bett said, once she was out of sight.

'Gloriously. Imagine that, all those years of rancour swept

away in one easy and honest conversation. I'm so proud of you.'

'Sarcasm is the lowest form of wit, Lola. You taught us that yourself,' Bett said, stung. She thought it had gone okay. Better than she'd expected, anyway.

'Well, it's a start, at least,' Lola said. 'Carrie probably does need help with the party, by the way, if you truly want to give her a hand.'

'Um, no. I might unpack, I think. Relax a little before the party. I've been very busy getting organised to come back.' A wave of tiredness and emotion hit her as they walked back to her motel room. 'Not that anyone in this family seems to care enough about my life to have actually asked what I've been doing in London the past few years.'

Lola surprised her with a loud burst of laughter and a kiss on her cheek. 'You definitely have regressed. You know you used to be the same at the end of some school days, especially if I dared to have something else I wanted to talk to you about. I promise we will talk about you, my dear Bettsie. We'll talk about you until we are both bored rigid or blue in the face, whichever event takes place first. But all in good time. Don't rush things, Bett. Let things happen slowly sometimes.'

Caught out, Bett grinned. 'You're a fine one to talk. The woman who's summoned us all home like this, forced it to a head.'

'I had to.' Lola decided there was no harm in dropping another hint. 'I need the three of you to do something for me.'

Bett stopped at the door to her room. This was the second time Lola had referred to something needing to be done for her. 'Lola, what is it? You're not sick or anything, are you? I mean, you look well.' As much as she could tell. Lola had gone overboard on the makeup that morning. There were smears of red blush like jam stains on each cheek.

'Right now, because you are here, I feel one hundred per cent. Patience, Bett. All will be revealed in good time. Now, come on. Let's get you unpacking and making yourself at home. Haven't I always said the devil makes work for idle hands?'

'No. Your favourite phrase was that one about too many cooks spoiling the broth. And not counting your chickens before they were hatched. And the one about water under the bridge.'

'I really am a font of wisdom. Now, you unpack while I watch.'

As she opened her case, Bett glanced at Lola. 'I thought Anna looked well. And Ellen is very sweet.'

'Anna doesn't look well. She looks exhausted. And unhappy. Something's wrong there. And Ellen is a bag of nerves as well. That scar is fading but not as quickly as it should be. The city air is no good for that child. Nor is that psychiatrist she sees every month. Have you ever heard anything more ridiculous in your life, making her go over and over the incident? The child has to move on, put it behind her, get on with life, not go back every four weeks and talk about her feelings. Now, have you had any thoughts about work yet?'

Bett laughed. 'Lola, I've just arrived.'

'It's just I had a fascinating conversation with Rebecca Carter last week. You remember Rebecca?'

'Of course.' She and Rebecca had worked side by side as reporters on the *Valley Times* for two years. Until the day Bett had left so suddenly.

'She's editor now, imagine. Filled with ideas, too. She was so interested to hear you were coming back home and looking for work locally.'

'But I'm not.'

'Of course you are. As we just said, the devil makes work for idle hands. You'll see her at the party and you can have a good talk about it with her then. So, show me what you're wearing tonight.'

Bett blinked, wondering which part of this conversation she could blame on jetlag and which part on Lola's conversational style.

'Bett? Your outfit?'

Bett took out the dress and held it against herself. She'd found it in a vintage shop in London. The style was sleeveless and simple, the fabric a rich red brocade, swirls of colour picked out with gold thread here and there.

'Beautiful. Try it on for me.'

Bett did as she was told.

Lola asked her to turn around, inspecting her from all sides. 'I think that back seam could do with taking in, to stop the skirt flaring so much. Would you like me to do it for you?'

Bett took it off and handed it over without argument. If she didn't agree, Lola was just as likely to come running after her at the party with a needle and thread.

'I'll drop it back in a little while. By the way, I don't think you're looking well either, despite what I said when you first arrived. You look like you need some fresh country air too.'

Bett glared for a moment, then a smile started on her face and a warm feeling started in her chest. 'You really are a nasty old crone, aren't you?'

'And getting worse every year.' She held her granddaughter tight against her for a moment. 'I really am very, very happy to see you.'

'I'm very, very happy to see you too. I've got something for you, by the way.'

'A present? How splendid.'

Bett reached down into her handbag, where she had been carrying the gift, not wanting to let it out of her sight. She had spent the last two weekends searching through the stalls at Camden market until she found what she wanted. She watched as Lola opened the blue velvet box. Inside was a pair of costume jewellery earrings and a matching necklace, made from extravagantly coloured glass beads of different sizes and shapes. Lola looked up, eyes wide. 'Bett, they're beautiful.'

'Do you like them?'

'I love them. Where did you get them?'

'In London. An old grey-haired woman in a rainbow cloak was hobbling along the road near the Houses of Parliament as I drove past one morning. As I got close she dissolved in a flash of silver smoke and there lying on the ground were these. So I picked them up and brought them home for you.'

Lola clapped her hands gleefully. It was one of her traditions – anything brought home from a market or charity shop had to be handed over with a story attached. 'You haven't forgotten the rules, have you? I adore them, thank you.' Bett was enveloped in another hug, and then spoken to sternly. 'Now, leave your unpacking for the time being, climb into bed there and have a quick nap. You've bags under your eyes big enough to take shopping.'

Bett did as she was told, peeping up at Lola from under the sheets, the white cotton pulled up to her nose. 'Thanks, Granny.'

'Don't you Granny me, you bold girl.' With that, Lola pulled the curtains, turned out the light and shut the door firmly behind her.

Chapter Five

Lola walked two doors down and let herself into her own room. Number four had always been her favourite, with its view over the vineyard-covered hills. She liked number fifteen, too. It was the most peaceful, when she was in that kind of mood. Number eleven was the best one in high summer, she'd discovered, nice and cool, and number eight was the best for the Christmas party season, with its excellent view over the carpark and all the shenanigans that took place there late at night.

She'd always enjoyed all the moving around, had never found it at all unsettling. Of course, it helped that the décor in each room was identical: brown carpet, pale cream walls, one double bed, one single bed, a pastel print of a vineyard scene – from France, not the Clare Valley, but the guests weren't to know that – a small table and chairs, a wardrobe which contained not just tea- and coffee-making facilities, but a bar fridge and a mini safe. There was even a full-length mirror installed on the long single door. All a person could need.

She went straight to her CD player and put on a Glenn Miller collection, a little louder than usual, then sat down and shut her eyes, all the better to review things so far. She always played Glenn Miller when she needed cheering up, and the sad truth was that's what she needed right now. Was it wrong to be feeling so disappointed? What had she expected, after all? That the girls would only have to glance at each other and all the troubles and cares of the past would melt away? That they would turn back into her little Alphabet Sisters again? It wasn't going to be as simple as that, it seemed. Not when the three of them had such stubborn, dramatic streaks. All her own fault, of course. She'd always encouraged it in them.

She still found it hard to believe this rift between the girls had lasted so long. And even harder to believe the whole row had been caused by Matthew, of all people.

'The three girls had a terrible cat fight over him, I believe,' Len the butcher, the town gossip, had said to her eagerly just after it had happened.

Lola remembered briskly suggesting he shouldn't believe everything he heard. A cat fight, indeed. But afterwards the term had quite appealed to her. Her granddaughters weren't unlike a trio of cats. Anna, the eldest, like a Siamese, all sleek and sophisticated. Carrie, the youngest, still in her kitten stage, even though she was nearly thirty. Sweet as can be one minute, hissing and spitting the next. As for Bett, her middle darling – Lola softened at the very thought of her. Bett reminded her of a lost stray sometimes, needing lots of affection and love but then repaying it in spades.

For weeks now she'd been thinking of nothing else but this reunion. She was sure the other ladies in the charity shop were sick of hearing about the three girls, and especially about their days as the Alphabet Sisters. At least Mrs Shaw, God bless her, always seemed interested.

'Was it a serious thing?' Mrs Shaw had asked. 'Like the Andrews Sisters? Proper tours and recording contracts and all of that?'

'Oh, good heavens, no,' Lola had answered. 'I started it more as a way of keeping the three of them occupied, to tell you the truth.'

It had been her idea to take on the role of minding the girls while Jim and Geraldine got on with the running of the motels. She'd been concerned how little attention the girls were getting from their parents. Too many late nights and too much roaming around unchecked hadn't been good for the three girls, she'd thought. It wasn't that they were neglected, exactly, just more in need of a firmer hand.

The new arrangement had suited everyone very well from the start. Lola's great affection for her granddaughters had turned into a love so strong it had surprised even herself. She had been so busy trying to find her feet in Australia when Jim was a child that she'd never had the luxury to enjoy being a mother. They had been very close, and still were, but being a grandmother was completely different to being a mother, she'd discovered. More carefree, more fun. Watching her granddaughters running around outside in the sunshine, or even hearing them call to each other in their Australian accents had once or twice even brought her to tears, though they were hastily wiped away. Anna, Bett and Carrie had made her feel settled here in Australia, she'd realised. Made all the hardship of the early days worthwhile.

But Lola had also discovered that three strong-minded, intelligent little girls needed more than dolls and puzzle books to keep them stimulated. 'Music has charms to sooth a savage breast', she remembered reading. She'd hoped it would have the same effect on three near savages of granddaughters. She started teaching them Irish songs she'd known since she was a child, picking out the tunes on the old piano that took up a corner of the dining room in the motel they were living in at the time.

She'd been surprised at how quickly they'd taken to it. Anna's voice had been distinctive even back then, deep and melodic. Carrie's voice had matched her looks, sweet and instantly appealing. But it was Bett who shone musically, quickly displaying not just an ear for harmonies but a real talent at the piano. Lola had silently and belatedly blessed the elderly music teacher from her own childhood, who had come to her house twice weekly and joylessly taught her scales, folk tunes and simple classical pieces. Lola had passed it all on to Bett, with much more enthusiasm, she hoped. The two of them had spent hours side by side on the wooden piano stool, graduating quickly from simple tunes to lively duets. Bett had soon started teaching herself to play more complicated songs. When they'd moved to a new motel the following year, the first thing they'd bought was a good-quality piano. It had been with them ever since.

It wasn't the piano, though, but three dresses that had marked the start of the Alphabet Sisters. Lola still couldn't think of the day she brought home that first trio of dresses without laughing. Anna had been twelve at the time, Bett ten, Carrie seven. The dresses had been made for little girls of fifteen, thirteen and eleven, but Lola folded and pinned each of them until they just about fitted. Then she lined the three girls up, eyes shut, in front of the mirror in her bedroom and then told them to take a look.

Anna was appalled. Bett was horrified. Carrie was quite pleased. The dresses were of green and red gingham, with tight bodices and flared skirts.

'We look like we should be in *Little House on the Prairie*,' Anna said in a disgusted voice.

Bett was just as alarmed. 'We look like we should be in a dustbin.'

'I think we look nice,' Carrie said.

Anna reached behind her, trying to take her dress off. 'It's all right for you, Carrie. You do look nice. Lola, can you help me get this off?'

'No, not yet. And stop pulling at it like that. You won't be able to get out of them yourselves, darling. I had to pin the backs to make them fit.'

Bett was wriggling in her dress as though it was coated in itching powder. 'Lola, please.'

Carrie had been silent, happily admiring herself in the mirror.

'Who did they belong to?'

'I asked the lady in the charity shop, and it was quite some story. They apparently belonged to a famous trio of child conjurers called the Okey Dokey Gals, who toured the world with their pet camel and a small grey-faced cat, doing magic tricks and chores around the house for anyone who took their fancy.'

'So how did their dresses end up in a charity shop?' Bett challenged.

'It was a tragic story and one for another day. So what do you think of them?'

Anna was not happy. 'They'd suit the Pokey Yokey Gals better than the Okey Dokey Gals.'

'Or the Yukky Pukky Gals,' Bett added.

Anna again. 'They'd be perfect for a country and western singing group called the Yukky Pukky Gals, in fact.'

Lola was actually pleased. 'Do you really think you look like a singing act?'

Anna nodded. 'We look like those poor kids you see forced on to talent shows on the TV.'

Carrie brightened. 'I'd like to be on one of those shows.'

'Would you, Carrie?' Lola smiled, feeling like a fisherman slowly bringing in a catch. 'That's good. Because I've entered the three of you in a competition the local TV station is running. The winners get to perform at the agricultural show next month. All proceeds to charity. Just a little effort from each of you, with my guidance, and think of all the joy you will bring to the world. Charity begins at home, remember.'

Anna groaned. 'Lola, no way. I'd die of embarrassment. Who sings in public with their sisters?'

'There is a long and honourable tradition of family singing groups.'

The three girls looked at her.

'The Von Trapps. The Partridge Family. The Osmonds. The Jackson Five. And now there's –'

'The Quinlan Sisters,' Carrie called out.

Bett wasn't impressed. 'It's not very catchy.'

'Anna, Bett and Carrie?' Lola suggested.

Carrie pouted. 'Why am I always last?'

'Because you're the thickest,' Anna said. Carrie pinched her. 'Ow! Lola, Carrie pinched me.'

'Only because she got there before me. Carrie, you are always last because your two older sisters are preparing the way for you, in the way flower girls prepare the way for a beautiful bride.'

Anna and Bett rolled their eyes. Carrie looked happier.

Lola clapped her hands. 'I have it. Anna, Bett and Carrie, the ABC Girls. No, let's make it even catchier. Not the Andrews Sisters but the Alphabet Sisters. Perfect for TV.'

Lola laughed out loud now, alone in the motel room, as she remembered their first TV appearance. Over the years the girls had got used to singing on TV, but that first time they had been overawed by the lights, the cables and the cameras, not to mention the excitable hostess. Their harmonies had disappeared, their carefully rehearsed hand movements had looked more like violent twitches and each of them had had the same panicked expressions in their eyes. The whole family – and several bemused guests – had watched it go to air on the TV in the motel bar the following week. The three girls had shrieked with embarrassment the whole way through. As Anna had said, they'd looked more like the Zombie Sisters than the Alphabet Sisters.

Lola felt a sudden welling of tears in her eyes, as the tension she'd been feeling for the past few weeks drained out of her. She'd been waiting and worrying for something to go wrong. For Anna to call and say she wasn't going to be able to make it. For Bett to say she had decided to stay in London. Lola had hardly been able to contain herself when Bett had rung to say she wasn't just coming home for the party, she was coming home for good.

Had her girls any idea at all how much she had missed them? she wondered. Not just their physical presence, but all the stories and jokes and even the rows that had shot back and forth between them all their lives, to Lola's great and constant entertainment. She wasn't fanciful enough to think that things would ever return to the glory days of the Alphabet Sisters. All the dressing up, and the attempts to get them to rehearse their songs, and those early morning drives to this show or that country TV station. And of course the fights over who got to sit in the front of the car beside her, or whose favourite song would be sung first, or which order they'd stand in. But for every fight there had been a funny moment – missed cues, out-of-tune singing, on-stage spats between them – even if Lola had to pretend to be cross with them, to try and keep some control at least. Some chance. As the past three years had shown, she had no control over them at all.

There had been a moment a year ago when she'd thought the feud was about to be over. The terrible time when Ellen was attacked by that dog. Bett and Carrie had been shocked when she'd told them and Lola knew for a fact that they had both contacted Anna in the days afterwards. Bett had written, and Carrie had rung and left a message with Glenn. But nothing more had come of it. Which was when she'd realised she was going to have to try another way . . .

Oh, if only this had all happened years ago, when her bones weren't as creaky, her mind faster, when she didn't feel so tired all the time. 'You are nearly eighty,' her doctor had said at the last visit, when Lola admitted she needed a long afternoon nap some days. 'Though you're in remarkably good nick, I'll give you that.'

'That'll be the gin,' Lola said. 'I'm preserving myself.'

'Good Irish blood, probably, and all that hard work over the years. How are those hips of yours?'

Lola had had both hips replaced five years previously. 'I feel like they've been mine forever.'

'Are you still doing those stretching exercises twice a day?'

Lola nodded. 'I'm so agile I could get a job in a Bangkok nightclub.'

The doctor had nearly choked. 'Lola, you get worse every visit and you know it. I can't give you any more advice. You already know what you have to do. Try to take things easy, don't get too stressed about anything, enjoy yourself. You deserve it.'

Of course she did. And she did try and take things easy, having her nap most afternoons, drinking eight glasses of water a day. Well, eight glasses of something every day. Surely there was plenty of water in tonic water? And on the days she didn't feel so good, there was always makeup. It helped that her skin was still in good condition. All those years of wearing inch-thick foundation, Anna had said once. Her skin probably hadn't felt a ray of sunshine in sixty years of living in Australia. She picked up her perfume bottle, an expensive French brand, one of her few luxuries, and squirted a little on her wrists. What was that joke she'd overheard two schoolboys tell last week? 'Why do girls wear makeup and perfume?' 'Because they're ugly and they stink.'

Lola put a finger on each temple and gently massaged, thinking hard. Her birthday party was just hours away and she was certainly in no mood to have the girls edging around each other the whole time, the way they had been so far today. Anna was so rigid it was amazing she'd been able to walk at all. Bett was a bag of nerves. Carrie was sulking and stomping about. None of them was being anything like their usual lovely selves.

How much further could she push them? She had been treading on thin ice today already, she knew. There had been little flashes of anger from all three of them, when she had joked and tried to ease the tension between them on their first meeting. But it was so hard to be patient. Every day she was so conscious of time ticking away from her. The idea of turning eighty had hit her with a terrible shock and propelled her into making these plans, getting them back together. There was something so *old* about being eighty. She had never had such a sense of urgency, or such a feeling that she was living on borrowed time.

She looked over at the portable bookcase and writing desk in the corner of the room. Jim had made it especially for her, so she could wheel it from room to room and feel immediately at home. The folder containing her special project was tucked well out of the way on the third shelf. Should she take it out now? Get everything out into the open? Would they be angry with her? Or would they guess the whole purpose of it was to keep them together for as long as possible? Get them working closely together again? She didn't mind if they did guess. But no, it was too soon. Besides, she wanted to reveal it in a far more dramatic fashion, and in front of as large an audience as possible.

What could they work on together in the meantime? The food was prepared and the room was arranged, so there was nothing to be done there. Then she thought of the large pile of twigs Carrie would soon be putting into vases. Or not, perhaps . . . She picked up the phone and dialled the florist shop in town.

An hour later Lola was standing in the function room with ten newly emptied vases, eight bunches of freshly delivered flowers and three stony-faced granddaughters. Carrie had been summoned from the office, Anna from the kitchen, Bett out of her bed. Ellen had been dispatched to the kitchen to find ice-cream.

Lola gave them her most winning smile. 'I know I'm the very devil for changing my mind at the last minute, but seeing the three of you together again reminded me of those wonderful room decorations you used to do for me when you were little. Do you remember that one Christmas, when you strung up mistletoe and pine cones all over the motel for me?'

Bett stared at her blankly. Perhaps it was jetlag, but she couldn't remember ever doing Christmas decorations for Lola. It had always been Geraldine in charge of the decorations. They'd be hung up neatly exactly three weeks before Christmas, then folded away just as neatly exactly twelve days after Christmas.

'And I realised it would be the icing on my birthday cake to see your flower decorations at my party tonight,' Lola continued. She patted each of them on the cheek as though they were small passing animals. 'So will you get to work? And no hard feelings about the bush theme, Carrie? I'm sure we'll find a use for all those twigs.'

Half an hour later, eavesdropping from outside, Lola was forced to admit her plan hadn't worked. It was more dysfunction than function room in there. No laughing and joking together as they merrily arranged the flowers. No cheerful 'Doesn't the room look beautiful for the party?' conversation. No lively chitchat as they took the opportunity to catch up on each other's lives. Just several frosty exchanges.

'Please don't put that vase there, Anna,' she heard Carrie say in an overly polite voice.

'Why not? I think it looks good.'

'All the flowers are to go on the side tables.'

'But you'll hardly see them once you're sitting down.'

'I've given it a lot of thought over the past few weeks and decided that is the most practical place for them.' Carrie was now speaking in a steely tone.

Outside, Lola winced. The underlying message being that Anna had no right to just march in and do what she liked . . .

There was silence for a minute or two, then she heard Bett's voice. 'Are there any more vases?'

'I'll get them for you.' Carrie, her voice still stiff.

'That's all right. I can get them.'

'They're in the cupboard under the bar.'

'Yes, I know.'

Carrie's tone was sharp again. 'It's just you've been away for so long, I thought you might have forgotten.'

After Bett came back there'd been more silence, broken only by the sound of vases being moved and stalks being snipped. Lola wasn't quite sure what to try next. Should she go in and tell some of her jokes? She'd thought of a good one. What's brown and sticky? A stick. Perhaps not. She had a feeling it would take more than a joke to fix this.

She walked into the room. The flowers were beautiful. Much nicer than the twigs had been. 'Oh, well done, girls.' There was no response. She ambled over to the piano, lifted the lid and experimentally ran her fingers up and down, playing one or two chords.

'Do you remember this one, Anna?' she said loudly. She thumped out the beginning notes of 'Don't Sit Under the Apple Tree'.

Anna shook her head.

'Poor Anna. Your memory gone and you still so young. Bett, your turn. What about this?' She played a swirly introduction to 'Danny Boy'.

Bett glanced over. 'I can't place it, Lola, sorry.'

'Too much smog in London, darling. Your brain cells obviously need a shake-up. Carrie, what about you, my dear? What's this one?' She played the introduction to 'My Favourite Things' from *The Sound of Music*.

'I'm not sure,' Carrie said, not looking up.

Lola was shocked by a surge of anger. Enough was enough. She stood up and clapped her hands, once, twice, three times. 'Right, you little buggers.'

Three startled faces turned to her. Lola rarely swore and she even more rarely used Australian swear words. 'I want to speak to the three of you. Over here, now.'

She gave them a moment to get closer and then glared at them, genuinely cross. 'I know I should be more patient with you. I know you are probably jetlagged, Bett, and you must be tired too, Anna. But I'm sorry, I've been waiting three years for this, wanting this feud to be over every single day and I can't wait any longer to get it all sorted.' She pointed a long, varnished fingertip at her middle granddaughter. 'Bett Quinlan, tell me the truth. How do you feel right now?'

Bett coloured, transported straight back to being a ten-year-old. 'I really don't want to play this, Lola.'

'Play it, Bett. How do you feel right now?'

'Lola . . .'

It was a game she had played with them when they were children. Some trick she'd picked up at a drama class or from some TV documentary. Back then she'd had a magic wand that she would point at them. The truth stick, she called it. She said it saved time. Point and talk. How are you? What's wrong? How do you feel and why? They had to answer. Back then the answers had been simple. 'I'm cross because Mum told me off.' 'I'm sad because I didn't win the race today.' 'I'm mad because the other two got more ice-cream than me.'

Lola turned away from Bett. 'All right, then. Carrie, I'll start with you instead.'

Carrie was looking at her feet.

Lola kept pointing. 'Carrie, the quicker we do this, the quicker it is over and done with.'

A long pause and then a low voice. 'I'm cross because you keep changing your mind about the decorations and it's driving me mad.'

It wasn't what Lola had hoped to hear, but it was a start. 'The customer's always right, Carrie, remember. Anna, what about you?'

Anna glared at her. 'I'm furious because I am thirty-four years old and you are treating me like a child.'

'You're all behaving like children so I'm going to treat you like children. Thank you, Anna. Bett?'

Bett hesitated. 'I'm upset because I hate this.'

'Do you really?' Lola said a silent thanks. Now she was getting somewhere. Say it, Bett, she urged. Say how much you have hated fighting with your sisters. How much you've hated being away from them. 'What do you hate exactly?'

Bett lifted her head, a picture of defiant misery. 'You telling us off. And this truth stick business. I've always hated it.'

Lola put down the imaginary stick. It had been a last-ditch effort in any case. 'Very well. I'll try some straight talking instead. You see, I've always had the idea that you might have missed each other during the past three years. That perhaps there had been times when you'd wished you could call on each other. And then I had the even more obviously ridiculous idea that all it would take for you to become friends again was to get you together to talk about it.'

No response.

'No? Then it seems in my old age I am getting not just feeble of body but feeble of mind, and I have got it all wrong. Such a shame. However, as has always been my wont, I am going to try and make the best of a bad situation.' She glared at them. 'So, my little brat-faced princesses –'

Bett suddenly had to bite back a smile. Lola hadn't called them brat-faced princesses in years.

'Do you think it would be possible for the three of you to put this ridiculous fight – all right, not ridiculous, this extremely worthwhile and valid fight – behind you for a short time? Because, girls, the way of it is I want to enjoy my party and I certainly won't if I have to see your sulky faces all night long. Or all week long. And possibly beyond that. In fact, let's say definitely beyond that.'

She ignored their looks of surprise and clapped her hands again.

The three of them jumped. 'From now on, there is to be conversation between you, do you hear me? I want some smiles too. So I hereby lay down the law. There is to be no mention whatsoever of the events of three years ago. Do you understand?'

There was a flash of temper from Anna. 'Oh, sure, Lola. As if we aren't thinking about them.'

'You can think all you like. You can think of nothing else if you like. But while you are all living and working here, I want peace and conviviality between you.' She turned to Carrie. 'I know this will be hardest on you at the moment, Carrie, Matthew being your husband and all. But I'd like you to keep him away from here for the time being. Do you think you can manage that?'

Carrie swallowed hard. If Lola only knew how easy it was going to be. She nodded, not daring to speak.

'I think it's better if he doesn't come to the party tonight, either. Tell him I'm sorry, but that's the way it has to be. There'll be enough gossiping about you all without him being there as well and everyone watching and listening to see what happens. Besides, I want all the attention to be on me, not him.' She gave a broad grin.

Carrie looked at her feet again. She'd long ago banned Matthew from coming to the party.

'So there we have it. Now, get to work please. It won't be long before my guests come marching up the carpark and there's still plenty to be organised. Carrie, ask your sisters to help you. Bett and Anna, do what she says.' She was almost at the door when she remembered something else. 'One last thing.'

They turned to her as one, like a chorus line, waiting.

She gave them a beautiful smile. 'Thank you all for being here. You've made an old lady very happy.'

Chapter Six

The function room was a mass of fairy lights. There were ten round tables, each set with white linen, sparkling glasses and gleaming cutlery. Irish music played quietly in the background, overlaid with conversations from the seventy guests, a mixture of older couples, teenagers, middle-aged women, several elderly men and even a baby in a carry-cot. There were candles and the vases of fresh flowers on the long side tables, with several bottles of wine already opened on each. Young waitresses in white shirts and black skirts were circulating with trays, collecting empty champagne glasses. Everything was in the room except the guest of honour herself.

At the door, Carrie glanced at her watch, then across the room at her oldest sister. She had stiffly asked for her help that afternoon, and just as stiffly Anna had agreed. 'Are you ready?' she mouthed.

'Ready,' Anna mouthed back.

Carrie signalled over to her other sister in the far corner by the speaker system. It had been just as hard asking Bett for help, but she'd had no choice. Lola's complicated running order for the early stages had made it impossible for Carrie to manage on her own. At Bett's nod, Carrie turned the room lights on and off and on again to get everyone's attention, then turned them off once more, leaving a spotlight over the main door. The room went quiet. Anna turned on the microphone and in her best public speaking voice – one she'd used to great effect in the children's cartoon *Hatty and the Headmistress* – made her speech: 'Please will you stand and welcome the belle of tonight's ball, the reason we're all here, the woman who is celebrating her eightieth birthday this very day – Lola Quinlan!'

Lola swept in to the sound of The Kinks' 'Lola'. She stood in the doorway for full dramatic effect, then gazed around the function room with pride and glee. The girls had done themselves and her proud. Waving majestically, she inclined her head as her friends and family started clapping, many of them laughing at her choice of music.

'You do realise it's a song about a transvestite?' Carrie had asked Lola the previous week.

'Is it?' Lola had said blithely, peering at Carrie over her glasses. 'Never mind. People will think I'm being ironic about my makeup.'

Bett watched now as Lola moved from table to table, greeting every guest in person, having a word here or a word there. She also watched people's reactions after Lola had moved on – a mixture of amazement, amusement and sometimes, outright laughter. It seemed Lola had the same effect on everyone who knew her, not just her granddaughters. It was an oddly comforting thought.

Across the room, Carrie glanced down at the running sheet in front of her. So far so good. Guests to be greeted in person at front door. Tick. Champagne to be circulated by waiting staff. Tick. In the past two days Lola had gone into a kind of white heat. 'What do you think about playing "I Do Like To Be Beside the Seaside" as the waitresses bring out the prawn cocktails?' 'Wouldn't one great big long table look better than ten round ones?' 'Do you think it's too late to ask everyone to come in costume, as pirates or gypsies or something dramatic like that?'

Carrie had finally put a stop to it. 'Lola, it's an old lady's birthday party, not a Broadway production.'

'Do you think it's like a Broadway production? Really? Which parts?'

It wasn't supposed to be a compliment, Carrie stopped herself from saying. 'I just think it might be best if you don't get too carried away. From what you've deigned to tell me, you already seem to have a lot of different activities throughout the night. People will want to talk to each other and eat their meals, remember. You need to let a bit of it happen of its own accord.'

To her surprise, Lola had agreed, taking the pen and swiping it through several items on the rundown. Probably just as well, Carrie thought – she hadn't been too sure the crowd would join in on a version of Stevie Wonder's 'Isn't She Lovely?', though Lola had been fairly confident. She had kept in two items, though – one dubbed S and the other SS.

'What do they stand for?' Carrie asked.

'Surprise and then Super Surprise.'

'I don't like surprises. Tell me.'

'You'll find out when you need to find out,' Lola had said grandly.

Which wouldn't be long now, Carrie thought with some relief. Dramatic entrance? Tick, she noted, as she watched Lola take her seat. It was all good experience, though. She'd probably be able to manage the inauguration ceremony for the President of the United States after this. It might even be simpler.

Two hours later it was ten minutes to Item Seven, the first of Lola's surprises. The starters and main courses had been served – prawn cocktails, followed by wiener schnitzels served with chips and salad. There had been three spot prizes, also Lola's idea. The lucky winners had received bottles of Lola's favourite gin. Dessert was to follow after the next set of speeches. There was a choice of fruit salad and ice-cream or homemade chocolate pudding which was in fact factory-made chocolate pudding with a slightly homemade chocolate sauce on top.

Carrie and Lola had argued about that as well. 'You can have any food you like, you know. Something special if you want.'

'I like your mother's menus. Plain, nourishing . . .'

Boring, Carrie didn't say out loud. The motel food had long been a sore point between Carrie and her mother. Geraldine had her favourites and had never seen any reason to change them. The starters were always either prawn cocktail or soup of the day – generally vegetable. The main courses were usually a choice of T-bone steak, ham steak and pineapple or wiener schnitzel, all served with chips and salad. The desserts didn't often change either: apple pie, chocolate pudding or fruit salad, all served with vanilla ice-cream. The coffee was defiantly instant, the tea made with teabags, not leaves. Geraldine billed it all on the menu as 'delicious homemade country-sized fare'. As the person who unpacked a good lot of it from the wholesaler, Carrie had argued about the term 'homemade' as well. She couldn't argue about the 'country-sized', though. The portions were always enormous.

Carrie caught Lola's eye across the function room. 'Ten minutes,' she mouthed, holding up both hands, fingers spread wide, for clarity. Lola nodded, sending her a beaming smile, before returning to her conversation with the neighbour on the table she was currently sitting at. She'd arranged the seating so there was a vacant seat at every table. 'That way I can move around all night, talk to everyone.' She'd explained her reasoning to Carrie at another one of their pre-party meetings. 'Don't you think it's silly to have me at a head table with your mother on one side and your father on the other? I can talk to them every day. I've always thought that's a ridiculous thing about weddings, actually – putting the bride and groom miles away, out of reach. They're going to spend the rest of their lives talking to each other, being beside one another, aren't they, Carrie?' She hadn't noticed Carrie's expression. 'I'm going to share myself around all night long. And I'd love it if you girls would do the same thing, take up my chairs when I'm not there. Just like those people do during the Academy Awards presentations. Have you heard about them, Carrie? Imagine doing that for a job, slipping in and taking a famous person's chair every time they nip out to the lavatory or for a cigarette. Or perhaps they go out for some drugs, would that be it?'

Carrie had stared at her for a moment, prayed for patience and then returned to the running order in front of them.

The table-swapping seemed to be working well, though. Anna and Ellen had already moved to a table on the opposite side of the room. She could see them both, Anna, with Ellen on her knee, talking to the lady from the chemist shop. Anna looked very glamorous, Carrie thought, in an elegant midnight-blue dress set off with a dramatic pair of earrings that were more art than jewellery. Ellen was all in pink, with a sweet matching hat.

On the other side of the room she could see Bett, laughing at something the local parish priest was saying. She was wearing a vintage dress for the party. Stunning material, Carrie admitted, but she knew in her heart that her own outfit was the most eye-catching. It was a deceptively simple long gold dress, with a matching gold silk wrap. She'd woven little silk flowers through her hair and taken a long time over her makeup, too.

'You look like a model,' Len from the butcher shop had said admiringly when he'd arrived with his wife. Then he'd fixed her with a beady eye. 'Matthew not here yet?'

She'd told the almost-truth. 'He's away up north on a sheep station, for the final part of his vet's training. Fantastic experience. It's just a shame it's so remote. Lola understood, of course.' She stared right at Len, daring him to ask her any more. He hadn't, but she could tell by his eagerness to get away he was dying to pass the news around to everyone in the room. Good, it would save her having to do it.

Looking at Bett again, Carrie noticed she had lost a bit of weight while she'd been in London, but she was still – well, not chubby any more, but certainly not thin. Guiltily, Carrie realised she was relieved. She'd been worried Bett would arrive back from London model-stick thin. She had a feeling Matthew preferred slender girls. She'd asked him one night as they were going to bed, in the early days, when she'd gone through a period of guilt and uncertainty. Before they had declared a blanket ban on talking about Bett.

'Matthew, did you think Bett had a better body than me?'

He'd seemed uncomfortable. 'Carrie, we promised we wouldn't talk about it.'

'But did you?'

'Carrie, I'm not answering that question.'

She'd been cross with him then, and decided to show it. 'Then you must have,' she'd said sulkily. 'Well, you should go back to her then, shouldn't you?' She had glanced up at him under her lashes. He hadn't been sure whether she was joking or not, she knew that. She had stood up, walked across the bedroom in her underwear – her extremely lacy and sexy underwear. She had discovered early on that Matthew liked sexy underwear. At the door she'd stood and relished the look on his face as he took in her body. 'I'll ring Bett, will I? See if she'll come back to you?'

Matthew was lying on the bed. 'Come here, Carrie.'

'Why?'

'You know why.'

'What will you do if I do come over?' From the look in his eye, she had a very good idea exactly what he had in mind. She'd come closer. He'd put out his hand. She'd leaned back, just out of reach.

'Don't tease me.' His voice had been husky and she'd relented, leaning forward . . . She shook the memory away. There was a time and a place for sexual fantasies and her grandmother's eightieth birthday probably wasn't it.

What would Matthew be doing now? She tried to picture him on the sheep station, two hundred kilometres away. The job offer had come out of the blue six months earlier, a perfect practical application of all he'd been learning in his latest course in veterinary farm management.

'How was today?' she'd asked in the early days, when things were still okay between them.

'Another sheep learning curve,' he'd replied.

'And the lecturer?'

'Baa-baric. He kept trying to ram all the facts home. He asked me what was wrong and then got cross when I said mutton much.'

Carrie had tried to keep a straight face. 'Have you finished?'

Matthew had just laughed at her. 'For the moment.'

'I hope that's the truth. You know I hate it when you try and pull the wool over my eyes.'

They had been good together, Carrie kept telling herself. They'd had lots of fun. They'd talked about everything. The first six months had been the most difficult, putting up with the whispers and gossip in the town, but cocooned in their belief that what had happened was bigger than both of them, had been beyond their control, they'd brazened it out. And then one of the Richards girls had a baby at the age of sixteen and the sports teacher ran off with one of the prefects at the school and there was a spate of burglaries in the Valley and everyone had plenty of things to talk about other than them.

Carrie started to feel sad and then anger took over. Had he any idea at all how hard it had been for her the past few years? And how hard it was for her tonight, facing everyone, knowing people would be talking about them? Especially knowing Bett and Anna would be watching her every move?

She was tempted for a moment to phone him, but stopped herself. She already knew what would happen. They'd just have another fight, and more likely than not she would find herself crying at the end of it. And tonight of all nights she didn't want to have blotchy skin and puffy eyes.

But she suddenly wished Matthew was there right now. That she could go across to him, whisper something funny or sexy in his ear, make it all right again that way, the way they used to do. Had done for months, until . . . She realised she was staring over at Bett when her sister caught her eye. She flushed and looked away.

Bett looked away too, embarrassed to have been caught staring at Carrie. There was no doubt about it, her younger sister looked stunning tonight. She had been proud of her own outfit, until she put it on and saw herself beside Carrie and Anna. The whole family had been summoned to Lola's room for one quick drink together before the party – a little pep talk, Lola had called it. Her father made a toast. 'We'll do this again publicly but for now, cheers to you, Lola, a wonderful mother, mother-in-law, grandmother and great-grandmother.'

'To our happy family, reunited again,' Lola had toasted in return. 'Jim, did you bring your camera? I'd love a shot of us all. And one with the three girls together again at last.'

Her father unfortunately had left his camera in the function room. 'We'll have to take that one later on,' he'd said. Bett had been relieved. She and Anna and Carrie had hardly exchanged a word with one another since the flower arranging that afternoon, let alone stood close enough to get a cheery arm-in-arm shot.

Lola had called Bett back as they were all leaving her room. 'You look marvellous, darling. Those last adjustments were just what that dress needed.'

In her room Bett had thought the now mended dress did look good, the vintage brocade such an unusual design, the colours picked up in her favourite high-heeled shoes. But one glance at Anna and Carrie and her spirits had plummeted again. 'Do you think?'

'Darling, you are my Bett, and I say you look wonderful. And you do. Some people might prefer the way Anna looks, all cool and elegant. And Carrie is a pretty young thing and she knows it and wears it well. Those are the facts. The third and final fact is that you look beautiful too. The colours are glorious and your hair is shining. I just want that glint back in your eyes that I haven't seen since you got here.'

'Sorry, Lola. Sorry to be so stupid on your birthday.'

'That's my girl.' She had pinched her cheek. 'Now, your turn to shower me with compliments. Do I look a picture? The truth now, mind.'

Bett had taken in Lola's outfit in all its glory. She was wearing a long purple taffeta skirt, a gold shimmering tunic, at least five necklaces, including her new one from Bett, and surprisingly tasteful makeup. A little too much rouge, perhaps – Bett was tempted to wipe it off then stopped herself. It would be more of a surprise to the guests if Lola arrived without her rouge, surely. 'You look sensational. Like you belong in Hollywood.'

'The very words I wanted to hear. Thank you, darling. Now go and have a good time. And by the way, you're sitting next to the Englishman from room two. Did I tell you he was a journalist too? Imagine that. You'll have lots in common to talk about.'

Bett had groaned, not in the mood for matchmaking. 'Lola, what have you done?'

'Whatever I like. It's my birthday, remember.'

Sure enough, when Bett got to her table there was a man sitting next to her. He was perhaps ten years older than her, lean, solemn-faced, wearing glasses. He was dressed in a casual suit. He smiled at her, a surprising, beautiful smile that completely lit up his face. 'Quite a party,' he said.

Bett smiled back. 'She's quite a woman.'

'Have you known her long?'

'All my life. She's my grandmother.' She held out her hand. 'I'm Elizabeth Quinlan, known as Bett.'

'Richard Lawrence.' They shook hands.

'You're English? Is that a London accent?'

'It is, yes.'

'I'm just back from there. Only this morning in fact.'

'All that way for a party? You are a social creature.'

Bett laughed. She noticed then he had very sparkly eyes behind his glasses. 'I didn't have a choice, believe me. And you're on holiday here, are you?'

'Well, a working holiday I supp –'

A slap on her back nearly sent Bett flying into the table. 'Bett Quinlan, great to see you again, love. Are you going to be back working on that newspaper?'

Her other neighbour had arrived, a man who had done the landscaping around the motel and knew the family well. He'd immediately launched into a conversation that hadn't let up through the first course. Out of the corner of her eye Bett had noticed Richard Lawrence being interrogated by his other neighbour, one of the local councillors. She heard snatches, something about doing research for a writing project. She'd been about to ask him more about it when Lola had wafted past her and whispered that it was time to move tables. 'Circulate, darling, circulate.'

Bett found the move between tables very difficult. Not quite as difficult as the walk into the function room in the first place, though. She had been intensely aware of people looking at her and talking about her. She'd kept a big smile on her face, greeting lots of old faces, friends of Lola's or people she knew from her years on the local newspaper, brightly answering their questions. Yes, she was finally back from London. No, the jetlag wasn't too bad. That stopover in Singapore had made all the difference. Yes, home for good, but she'd probably be heading off to Sydney or Melbourne fairly soon. Yes, it was great to see all the family again, not to mention a blue sky, ha ha ha.

No one had mentioned Matthew's name, or the circumstances of her leaving, not to her face anyway. No one except Len the butcher, of course. It seemed he hadn't changed his ways. She'd barely walked past after saying hello to him and his wife when she'd heard his remark, in a loud whisper that managed to carry beautifully around the room. 'That's the one I was telling you about. Her fiancé left her and ran off with the younger one. No, not the one with the child, the pretty one over there with the blonde hair.' Bett had resolutely kept moving, praying the low light hid her red cheeks.

By the time the main course had been served, she was feeling much better. The three glasses of local shiraz were helping things along beautifully too. She'd found herself sitting beside the local parish priest, who had surprised her with his rapid-fire joke delivery. She hadn't laughed so much in ages. To make things even more pleasant, one of her favourite dishes had been on offer for main course – lovely crispy wiener schnitzel, served with a pile of fat chips and salad. She knew it was deeply unfashionable to like such standard motel dining-room food, but she'd always loved her mother's cooking. Her all-time favourite was the chocolate pudding, all crunchy on the outside and molten on the inside, served with cream and ice-cream. She'd never found any reason to join in with Anna and Carrie over the years when they had tried to get Geraldine to update the menus, to offer more light and healthy options.

Bett knew full well that it was her love of her mother's kind of cooking – hearty, deep-fried, large servings – that was to blame for her constant battle with her weight. Lola had made it abundantly clear one afternoon, too, when Bett had gone to her in tears.

'It's not fair. How come Anna and Carrie got to be skinny and I didn't?'

'Anna and Carrie are skinny because they exercise a lot and they both eat like birds, Bett,' Lola had said bluntly.

'I eat like a bird too,' she'd said gloomily, knowing Lola was right. The only problem was her bird was a vulture.

She decided now to try and be disciplined and reluctantly left the last of her chips on her plate. A minute on the lips, a lifetime on the hips, she had once tried chanting. Unfortunately she'd quickly reworded it. A minute on the lips, even nicer served with chips. As she tried to ignore the chip's siren song, she felt a tap on her arm.

'Bett, have you heard the one about the horse who goes into the bar?'

'No, I haven't, Father, but I'd love to,' she said, turning to him with a smile. As she did she noticed one of the waitresses heading towards their table to pick up the plates. Oh, to hell with it. She was on holiday, wasn't she? As the priest began his joke, she picked up the last chip and popped it in her mouth.

Three tables away, Anna smiled up at the young waitress as she collected her plate. 'Thanks very much. That was delicious.'

The girl frowned. 'Why didn't you eat any of it, then? It looks like you hardly touched it.'

Anna tried not to laugh. 'I'm just not very hungry,' she said politely. She knew from experience that her mother would have called on her pool of casual waitresses for tonight – local schoolgirls, young mothers, anyone needing a bit of part-time work.

The girl looked a little uncertain. 'Will I bother bringing you a dessert then, if you're not very hungry?'

'Just a small one would be great, thanks,' she said. 'And one for my daughter. She'll be back in a moment.' Lola had come over and swept Ellen away a few minutes before. 'I want to show her off,' she'd said brightly. Ellen had happily gone off with her.

Anna tried not to react as the waitress dropped a knife onto the floor, narrowly missing her foot. She picked it up and handed it over with a smile. 'Don't worry. You're doing a great job.' Poor kid. She – and Bett and Carrie too – knew only too well what it was like to work part-time as a waitress. They'd spent their teenage years ferrying meals into the motel dining rooms. Their mother's unchanging menu items had at least meant easy serving, with no complicated sauces or cooking methods to explain. All they'd had to do was get the right meals to the right people at each table in the dining room. They'd worked out their own method of identifying each diner, scribbling one- or two-word snapshots of people in their order books. It had worked well until one evening Bett had inadvertently left her notebook on the table. When she'd come out to collect their dishes it had been to find the six people passing it around trying to work out which of them was which, from a choice of Big Nose, Ugly, Baldie, Flashy (the woman had been wearing lots of rings), Creepy Beard or Clownface. Anna remembered Bett being so mortified she'd run out of the dining room and not returned for the rest of the night.

Alone at her table for a moment, Anna looked around the room. Lola, hand in hand with Ellen, was moving regally from table to table. Her parents were standing nearby, chatting to another couple. Her father's arm was casually resting on her mother's back. Bett was still sitting two tables away, laughing at something the man beside her was saying. A possible suitor? Anna caught herself thinking. Then the man moved and Anna saw he was wearing a priest's collar. Perhaps not. Anna had wondered if Bett would arrive home with an English boyfriend. She'd casually asked Lola once whether Bett had mentioned any men in her life in any of her letters.

'Not a sinner,' Lola had said bluntly. She'd always been more than happy to keep each of them informed about the others' lives. 'I just wish she would meet someone over there. It would solve a lot of problems.'

Anna finally spotted Carrie, too, shining in her golden dress on the other side of the room. Her sister had become very skilled at running events like this, it seemed. Everything was running so smoothly, the staff checking with her constantly, looking at her with respect. Not surprising, really. Carrie had always had that confidence with people, the ability to charm them so effortlessly.

'Hello, love. Are you enjoying yourself?'

Anna turned and smiled up at her father. 'Dad, hello. Sit down.' She patted the chair beside her. 'It's a great night, isn't it? Carrie's done a very good job.'

'She has. She's doing wonders around the place, in fact. She'll have your mother and me out of a job before we know it. We'll wake up one day and she and Matthew will have taken over while we were sleeping.'

It was funny to see how naturally her father referred to Carrie and Matthew as a couple. She shouldn't have been surprised, she supposed. He'd had three years to get used to them both. 'It's all that good training you gave us as kids. Actually, I was just sitting here reminiscing about our waitressing days. That time Bett left her notebook on the table. Do you remember?'

Jim threw back his head and laughed. 'The times I've told that story. What was it again?' He reeled off the six insulting names, word perfect. 'And that time Carrie put those film people in their place. Do you remember that? When we first moved here?'

Anna laughed too, remembering it well. A film company had booked in to stay and over dinner in the public dining room openly started smoking joints. They'd become more and more obnoxious, ordering fifteen-year-old Carrie, their waitress for the night, around like a servant, complaining that there wasn't the rare brandy they wanted or the scotch they preferred. As Carrie had leaned over to change their ashtrays, one of the men had given her a pat on the bottom. 'These are just herbal cigarettes, love. Nothing to worry about.' Then he'd winked. 'Let me know if you'd like to try one.'

Without missing a beat, Carrie had removed his hand from her bottom and smiled sweetly. 'And do you see those two men over there in the bar?' She had pointed through the door at the local postmaster and the railway stationmaster, enjoying a beer together. 'They're from the drugs squad in Adelaide. Let me know if you'd like to meet them, won't you?'

Anna laughed. Not only had the film people put out their joints there and then, but they'd left Carrie a thirty dollar tip.

'Do you remember how furious Bett was?' Jim continued. 'She came marching into me in the bar. "How come Carrie always gets the tips? I'm going to start wearing a blonde wig when I'm waitressing from now on."'

Anna had forgotten that part of it. She gave a wry smile. 'So good that we've put all that fighting behind us now, isn't it, Dad?'

'I'm just glad to have you all home again,' he said simply. 'We missed you, you know. You and Bett. It's a shame it took so long.'

It was the most her father had said about it in a long time. 'It's good to be back.'

'Hi, Grandpa.' Ellen popped her head in between the two of them and then climbed onto her grandfather's lap. 'Can you do that trick where you take the coin from your ear and then put it in my ear?'

'That's not a trick, Ellie. I really do keep coins in my ear. It's much safer than the banks.'

'*Grandpa*,' Ellen said, shooting Anna a glance. 'He's joking, Mum, isn't he?'

'Oh no, Ellen. Your grandpa has a fortune in his ears.'

'Show me, Grandpa?'

He checked his watch, then touched the end of Ellen's nose. 'A little later, sweetheart. I just have to make a quick announcement about the birthday girl, but I'll be back as soon as I can.' He stood up and made a show of straightening his tie, smoothing back his hair. 'My moment of fame has come at last.'

Ellen watched him go, then turned to Anna. 'Mum, Grandpa is Lola's son, isn't he?'

'That's right.'

'They're both a little bit mad, aren't they?'

Anna burst out laughing. 'Yes, Ellie, they are.'

Bett said goodbye to the priest and moved back to her original table, carrying her fourth glass of red wine. She'd hardly have believed it possible, but she was almost enjoying herself. It seemed she just needed to keep herself mildly drunk and surrounded by a crowd at all times and she would get on just fine back here. She smiled at Richard the Englishman as she sat down beside him. 'You're enjoying yourself, I hope? All this Australian country hospitality not too much for you?'

'Good lord, no,' he said. 'In fact, I've been invited to join two local cricket teams.'

'You didn't accept, I hope. You know they only want another excuse to laugh at an English cricketer.'

'I had a funny feeling about that, actually.'

Bett laughed. 'Well, just make sure you think long and hard before you accept any offers.'

He picked up a bottle of wine and went to fill her glass. 'May I?' he asked. She accepted, impressed by his good manners.

Richard raised his voice over the sound of the Irish folk tunes. 'Lola told me all four generations of her family would be here tonight. Is that right? She seemed very happy about it.'

'That's right,' Bett said, hoping he wasn't about to ask her to introduce him to everyone. She didn't want to point out Anna and Ellen, or Carrie, she realised. She didn't want him comparing her to the other two, finding herself left on the sidelines once again. She was enjoying him too much herself. She was guiltily pleased when she noticed her father had started making his way to the microphone to introduce Lola's speech. 'Excuse me,' she said to Richard. He nodded and turned towards the front of the room too.

She wriggled around to get a better view of her father and then nearly leapt out of her seat as a sharp pain ricocheted through her right thigh. She moved and another sharp pain shot into her bottom. Bloody hell, had she sat on a spider? She lifted up her bottom an inch, lowered it and nearly shot out of her seat as the pain struck again.

Behind her, Richard noticed her jump. 'Bett, are you all right?'

'Something keeps biting me.'

'Good heavens. I promise you it's not me.'

That made her grin. 'I didn't think it was you. Don't mind me.' She couldn't get up now, make a scene, not during Lola's big moment.

Her father was now making his introduction. 'Once again, I give you my mother and the birthday girl herself, Lola Quinlan.'

The lights came on and in the front of the room was Lola, pulling back a curtain to reveal a large white screen. The guests shifted expectantly. Bett gingerly turned her seat around to make sure she had a full view, not moving her bottom, just the chair, trying to keep the insect or spider or whatever creature it was pinned underneath her bottom.

Lola waited until she had every last person's attention. 'Thank you, my darling Jim. Before I move on to the next important event of the night, I'd like to properly introduce my family to you all.

I'd invite them all up here beside me, but then you'd be looking at them not me.' There was a ripple of laughter. Lola pointed them all out, one by one. 'My son, Jim, and his wife, Geraldine, who have been so good and kind to me over the years, even when I was driving them mad.'

'Never,' Jim called across. Geraldine smiled stiffly.

'And my granddaughters. Anna, put your hand up, darling, would you? Anna's home from her successful acting life in Sydney for a little while with her daughter, my dear great-granddaughter, Ellen, who has just turned seven and is adorable.' Bett noticed Ellen was pressed against Anna, her hair hiding her scar.

'And at the table next to Anna and Ellen is my middle granddaughter, Elizabeth, known of course as Bett . . .' Bett self-conciously raised her hand as Lola continued, 'who has left behind her extremely glamorous life in London to come home and spend time with me.'

She turned and gestured towards Carrie, who was standing by the door. 'And of course my dear Carrie, there in the golden dress with the golden hair, who not only keeps me young on a daily basis, but has pulled out all the stops for tonight. Thank you, Carrie darling.'

Lola waited for the applause to come to an end before she spoke again. 'When we were first planning this evening's entertainment, I learned that a tradition these days is to have a little slideshow ready to surprise the guest of honour. Carrie suggested it and I turned her down immediately, not wanting to be embarrassed by photos of myself that I thought had long disappeared. But then I thought about it some more, and I decided, yes, perhaps it would be good, especially if I got to choose the slides, rather than have any naughty surprises.

'So I went ahead and prepared a little slide show of some of my favourite moments and I'd like to share them with you. Please, get yourselves a drink and then we'll get started.'

Uh oh, here we go, thought Bett. Anna was sitting at the table behind her, the two of them virtually back to back. She felt a tap on her shoulder and turned.

'Did you know anything about this?' Anna whispered.

Bett shook her head, surprised Anna was asking her. They both glanced over at Carrie. By the look on her face, this was a surprise to her as well.

Lola clapped her hands. 'Attention please, everyone. Anna, Bett, stop whispering over there.' She waved over at them. 'My darlings have come home especially for this, you know. So good at my age to have all the family around me again.'

In the quiet moment that followed before the slides began, two voices were clearly audible.

'Is the youngest one's husband here? The bloke that caused all the trouble?'

'No, he's been banned, I'd say.' Len the butcher's voice was easily recognisable. 'Shame, really. I was hoping to see another cat fight over him tonight.' He gave a loud laugh.

Bett stiffened. Bloody Len and his big mouth. She wished he'd go and choke on one of his own chops. From the corner of her eye she saw Anna spin around to spot the speaker. She didn't dare look in Carrie's direction. To her relief, the lights suddenly went down, the screen flickered into life and Lola's voice came over the speakers, her Irish accent strong and clear. 'Please forgive my indulgence as I reminisce a little about the past eighty years.'

A lilting Irish song started playing as slide after slide came up on the screen, with captions of the year and the place underneath. There was Lola as a child beside an enormous oak tree in front of her big family house in Ireland, standing with her parents behind her, the only child. As a young woman at a gala party, in Dublin. On her wedding day, Edward serious-faced, Lola almost a child bride. A photograph of them on the boat to Australia in the late 1930s, then several of Lola with a baby Jim on their own; by a beach; in the gateway of the Botanic Gardens in Melbourne; among a group of women, all with young children.

Bett was fascinated. She hadn't realised Lola had those photographs from Ireland, or so many from her early days in Australia. Lola had rarely spoken about those days in any detail. The memories must have been too painful for her, the three girls had decided. Bett heard whispers at the tables around her. 'She was widowed very young, wasn't she?' 'Tragic, wasn't it? Her with a young son, too.' 'Did she marry again?'

Something about the photo of Lola's house in Ireland struck a chord with Bett. She had visited it on behalf of Lola when she was living over there, taken photos of it and tried – but failed – to find anyone who remembered Lola and her family from years before. She'd like to have looked more closely at the photo but it had flashed past too quickly. She'd have to ask Lola about it another time.

The next slides were of Lola and Jim in the different guesthouses and motels they had gone on to manage all around Australia. They had moved dozens of times over the early years, from city motels to country motels, motels in farmland and motels by the sea. Geraldine and then the three girls started appearing on screen. There was a wonderful photo of Lola in her mid-fifties on holiday in Tasmania, on a beach with wind whipping through her hair, looking like a film star. Another of her in her late sixties, behind the counter of the charity shop here in the Valley, the year she had announced herself officially retired from motel work. One from her seventieth birthday party in the middle of the vineyard in front of the motel on a glorious summer day, like today. The day that she had signed over all the ownership to Jim and Geraldine. Bett remembered it clearly. Lola hadn't listened to any arguments. 'I don't want money for it. It's yours to do what you like with, as long as there's always a room and a ready supply of gin for me.'

Bett relaxed as the screen went white again. Thank God Lola hadn't included any slides of the Alphabet Sisters. She knew there were dozens of hideously embarrassing photographs from their various performances all over the country, none of which Bett ever wanted to see again. Lola usually pulled them out at any occasion. Who'd have thought she'd have respected their privacy like that tonight?

Lola's voice sounded out over the room again. 'It's been a long and eventful life, and one of the most special parts of it has been not just the joy of having three granddaughters but having three immensely talented, performing granddaughters. So I'd also like to take this opportunity to share with you some of the finest moments from their years performing as the Alphabet Sisters. Music please, maestro.'

The room filled with the sound of Perry Como singing 'The Alphabet Song'. Bett covered her face with her hands as one photo after the other of the Alphabet Sisters in an array of outfits flashed up onto the screen. There they were in the gingham dresses they'd worn for their first performance on the TV talent competition. In the matching yellow satin dresses with flared skirts. In the pink and blue skirt and shirt ensembles. The bright-green taffeta party dresses . . .

Bett made a gap in one hand and peered through, hearing the

laughter around her. It was getting worse. Why had they reached their performing peak when puff-ball skirts, fluffy hair and fluorescent colours had seemed fashionable? As Perry continued crooning in the background, working his way through the alphabet one more time, on screen the three of them moved from childhood to teenage years. It was like time-lapse photography. Bett watched herself get plumper and plumper with each passing year. There was open and loud laughter all round now. People were laughing at her or the outfits or their makeup. She covered her face, praying for the song to finish, praying for an electrical fault, an earthquake . . .

At their table Anna and Ellen were in gales of laughter. Over dinner, Ellen had been solemnly informing the lady sitting next to her that her mother and aunties had once been famous singers. Behind her, Anna had been vigorously shaking her head, smilingly denying everything. Five seconds of these slides had been the proof. There they were, squinting into the sun, standing on makeshift stages on the backs of semi-trailers, or in country halls, surrounded by balloons and crêpe-paper decorations. Another of the three of them caught mid-dance movement, looking about as elegant as scarecrows. And the dresses! They were even worse than Anna remembered.

On her lap, Ellen was in fits of giggles. 'I hope you're not laughing at me?' Anna said mock sternly.

'You all look so silly,' Ellen whispered back. 'And look at Auntie Bett's hair.'

Oh, poor Bett, Anna thought, as another slide flashed up showing Bett with her mouth caught wide open in mid-song, her mad brown curls dancing around her head. Beside her Carrie was a demure golden-haired angel. Anna judged herself critically. Her hair had been as dark and straight, her posture as excellent then as it was now. She leaned down to her daughter again and spoke in a whisper. 'We actually couldn't sing very well either. But don't tell Lola. She thought we were gorgeous.'

By the door, Carrie was enjoying every moment of the surprise slide show. She'd been taken aback at first, but was now revelling in the memories. She had loved every moment of the Alphabet Sisters. The dressing up, the singing, the applause . . . and she'd never minded any of the dresses they'd had to wear. She'd certainly never carried on about them the way Bett and Anna had, in any case.

She found herself wishing again that Matthew was there, to see this as well. He had loved hearing the stories of the Alphabet Sisters. There'd been a few awkward moments in their early days, when she had been telling him stories, wondering if he had already heard them from Bett. He had taken her hand and kissed it one night, when she'd confessed her worry. 'Carrie, Bett and I didn't talk the way you and I talk. Now, please, keep going – you were in the car with Lola on your way to a concert one day and what happened?' She bit her lip as the slides kept coming, seeing the younger, happier version of herself smiling up on the screen. Perhaps if things got better between Matthew and herself again – one day – she could show these slides to him herself . . .

The lights finally came on again, and Lola moved back in front of the screen. Was she truly wiping away a tear, Bett wondered, or was it all for show? The laughter and chat in the room quietened as all eyes turned to Lola again.

'Some wonderful memories there for me, as I'm sure you'd agree. The days working with my little Alphabet Sisters were among the happiest of my life, and ones that I had thought, sadly but inevitably, had come to an end.'

And not a moment too soon, Bett thought, the tension draining out of her. Lola's next words had her sitting upright again.

'Then something wonderful happened. My darling granddaughters agreed to the most wonderful birthday present a grandmother could ask for. I would like to share it with you all tonight.'

Oh no, Bett thought. Surely she wasn't going to talk publicly about the rift? Please don't say she was about to produce Matthew out of nowhere, stage a tearful Oprah Winfrey-style reunion between them all? She glanced at Anna, and at Carrie. Did they have any idea about this wonderful birthday present? It didn't look like it. Anna shot her a questioning glance. Bett shook her head, signalled that she had no idea either.

At the side of the room, Carrie was glancing down at the running order. She seemed just as puzzled. Bett turned around. At the back of the room Frank from the electrical shop had moved back by the slide projector and was as alert as a gun dog, waiting for Lola's signals.

The room lights went out once again, leaving a spotlight on Lola. When had she rehearsed all this? Bett wondered.

Her grandmother's voice was assured. 'For the past ten years, I have been working on what I regard as my life's project. Apart from my son and granddaughters and great-granddaughter, of course. And I have this man to thank.'

The spotlight went out. On the screen behind her was a large photo of a man in uniform.

'The American General, Douglas MacArthur,' Lola said, now pacing in front of the screen as though she was a university lecturer. 'One of the heroes of World War II, famous for a wartime speech that galvanised hearts and minds all over the free world. Yes, indeed. "I shall return," General MacArthur promised, not just to his men in the Philippines but to all the Allied forces. It became the war cry of the Pacific campaign.'

Two older people near Bett nodded and whispered to each other. They obviously remembered it, even if it was news to her.

Another slide came up. General MacArthur standing on a platform at a small railway station, his elegantly dressed wife beside him, their small son between them.

Lola's voice filled the room. 'And where did he say those momentous words? In London? No. In Washington? No. Perhaps even in Sydney? No. General MacArthur said those words on the twentieth of March 1942 on the platform of the Terowie Railway Station. Yes, the little town of Terowie, South Australia, just sixty miles from here, as he travelled by train from Alice Springs to Adelaide. What an event for that tiny place, I've always thought, with the war and worries swirling all around them. It touched me deeply. Some years ago I started imagining and thinking and putting down ideas, and before I knew what was happening my thoughts had become a short story, which became a longer story, which became a musical. Yes, I, Lola Quinlan, in the twilight of my years, found that I had written a musical.'

Lola took a big, dramatic breath and paused. 'For many months it languished in my bottom drawer. Until I shyly showed it to my three granddaughters, as we reminisced about the wonderful days of the Alphabet Sisters –'

Bett shot Anna a glance. Anna looked over at Carrie. They'd done no such thing.

'And, to my great joy, they offered there and then not just to perform it for me here at the motel, but to mount a fully staged, complete musical in the Valley for everyone to enjoy, with all proceeds going to the Valley Ambulance Fund.'

The party-goers started clapping, some of them a little uncertainly. Lola reached into a bag beside her and pulled out a bundle of leaflets. She started moving from table to table, handing out a small sheet of paper to everyone in the room. She reached Bett and handed her one with a big smile. Bett scanned it.

Many Happy Returns

A Musical for all the Family

Written by Lola Quinlan

To be performed by

The Alphabet Sisters

and the people of the Clare Valley

Clare Town Hall, March 20

Bookings Valley View Motel

All proceeds to the Buy a New Ambulance Fund

She had to grab her grandmother's arm as she started to move away. 'Lola, wait! What in God's name is all this about?'

Lola lowered her voice. 'Darling, don't blaspheme in public, especially on my birthday.'

'I'm serious.'

She patted Bett on the head. 'In a moment, darling.' She glided off.

Carrie came up to her next, looking put out. 'Is this a joke, Lola? Because it's not very funny.'

Lola was unperturbed. 'Is the musical a joke? Well, it certainly has some hilarious moments, but it has a serious side to it as well.' She sailed past her too.

Anna came up behind her and helped herself to a leaflet, a smile fixed on her face. 'You've put us in an embarrassing situation tonight, Lola.'

'Really? I thought you all looked very nice.'

'You know we can't do this. You should at least have asked us.'

'But you might have said no.'

'Of course we'd have said no. Lola, the three of us might not be here next month to take you to lunch, let alone stage your musical.'

A well-dressed woman bustled up beside them, taking a leaflet from Lola's hand. 'A tremendous idea, Lola, and aren't you girls great to do something like this for your grandmother. I love her stories about the Alphabet Sisters. It'll be a pleasure to see you all in action.'

'That's the doctor's mother,' Lola whispered as the woman moved off again.

'I don't care if she's Andrew Lloyd Webber's mother. Lola, you have to call this off.'

'But they all look so interested.'

Anna glanced around. The people in the room did appear interested, with just about everyone reading the information. On the other side of the room she saw Bett at her table, with two of the waitresses standing beside her. It looked like they were giving her their contact details. In the other corner Carrie was also surrounded by a small group of people, answering their questions as well.

A petite woman came over to Lola and Anna, clutching the leaflet. 'Will you be holding open auditions, Lola? My son is keen to get into drama school next year and the experience would be great for him.'

'Drama school!' Lola repeated. 'Isn't that marvellous. We'll be putting an ad in the *Valley Times* about the auditions, won't we, Anna?'

Anna recovered, finding a confident smile somewhere. 'We haven't talked through all the details yet, Lola, have we? Still a few grey areas to discuss.'

'Oh, nothing we can't sort out, though.'

'No, I hope not.' Anna's smile was very wide and very fake.

Across the room, as the waitresses moved away, Bett picked up the leaflet, reading the details again.

Richard Lawrence was watching her closely. He looked amused. 'Pardon me for enquiring, but are you slightly surprised about this?'

Her head shot up. Slightly? Overwhelmingly. And there was no way she was going to do it, either. But that wasn't something to admit to a complete stranger. She gave a light laugh. 'Oh, that's Lola for you. Always springing little surprises on us. She really is something else.' She moved back in her chair and yelped out loud as the worst pain yet shot into her bottom.

He looked concerned. 'Not another bite? Would you like me to look?'

'No!' She nearly shouted the word. 'I mean, no, thank you, anyway. Excuse me, will you?'

She moved through the room, dodging the waitresses carrying the trays of desserts. She practically ran into the ladies, which was blessedly empty, and started to unzip her dress. As she did so there was a tearing sound.

'Oh shit,' she said loudly. She locked herself into a cubicle and took the dress off completely. She heard another little ripping sound as the old material tore even more. What had the spiders done, eaten the skirt?

Something glistened in the seam of the material. She looked closely. They weren't spider eyes, but a whole row of silver pins. She picked one out. And not pins either. They were industrial-sized staples, their ends as sharp as needles. She groaned. Why had she trusted Lola to sew that seam? She'd thought it was strange how quickly she'd done the job that afternoon, but had been too jetlagged to comment. Now look at the mess she was in. She couldn't put the ripped dress on again, unless she wanted to treat the entire gathering to the lovely sight of her large black-undie-clad bum. And she couldn't run down to her room in her camisole, tights and shoes. Shit, shit, shit. She heard someone come in and tensed. She peered under the door. Please let it be her mother, or Anna or anyone but . . .

She recognised the gold strappy sandals. It was Carrie.

She couldn't ask her. She'd rather be here all night than ask Carrie for help.

Then the reality hit her. She could well be in here all night if she didn't ask Carrie. She had to get out there again. They'd be singing 'Happy Birthday' any minute.

'Carrie?' Her voice was small. 'Carrie?' A bit louder.

'Bett?' She sounded surprised. 'What's the matter? Are you sick?'

'I'm fine. It's just, I've, uhm, ripped my dress.'

'Just now? In there?'

'No, before I got in here. Lola mended it for me but she seems to have used a stapler rather than needle and thread.' Please don't laugh at me, she prayed.

'Come out, let me see.'

To Bett's relief, Carrie wasn't triumphant or sneering. She had a quick look. 'Oh, hell. I thought she'd stopped doing that. She just loves that stapler. It's a special upholsterer's one she got at the charity shop. I caught her stapling the curtains in her room last year. She said it was much quicker than sewing.'

'I thought a spider had bitten me, that I'd sat on a whole nest of them.'

Carrie grinned, then sobered again as the door opened and an elderly woman came in, smiled at them and went into one of the cubicles. Bett had managed to put the dress in front of her just in time. She climbed into it now, rip and all, before the woman came out.

'The staples are still in there,' Carrie whispered.

Bett whipped it off again and the two of them worked to pick them out. There were more than twenty.

Carrie shielded her as she clambered back into the dress again. As the toilet flushed, Bett turned and kept her back close to the wall.

The woman smiled at them as she washed her hands and pulled out a piece of paper towel. 'You're two of the granddaughters, aren't you?'

'That's right,' they said politely.

'You're wonderful to do that musical for your grandmother. We'll definitely be booking tickets. And all for such a good cause. The Valley could do with a whole fleet of new ambulances.'

They both smiled and nodded as the woman left the room.

'Did you know anything about this musical?' Bett asked, checking first the door was completely shut.

'Not a word. Had she said anything to you, in any of her letters?'

So Carrie had known that Lola wrote regularly to Bett. She

shook her head. 'It's ridiculous of course. There's no way we can do it.'

'Of course we can't. I don't know what she was thinking.'

There was silence for a moment and then a loud blast of music came from outside. Carrie started. 'I'd better get out there. It's the last spot prize before we sing "Happy Birthday". Look, what about this?' She took off the gold wrap from her shoulders and in a deft movement tied it around Bett's waist.

Bett sucked in her stomach, thrown by Carrie's closeness and waiting for a comment about her having put on weight. It didn't come. Instead, Carrie twisted the fabric, tucked it here and there and then tied a loose knot in the side, so the shimmering material fell in folds. 'I think it'll work. What do you think?'

Bett stepped back and looked in the full-length mirror. She wasn't sure what Carrie had done, but the effect was great. The gold wrap folded over the brocade as though it was meant to be there, adding a layer of texture to the whole outfit. 'It looks like a designer did it.'

'I saw it in *Vogue* actually. Multi-layering or something, I think it's called. Does it feel secure?'

Bett felt it. 'Yes.'

Lola's voice was clearly heard over the speakers, ordering everyone to sit down as the cake was about to arrive.

Carrie glanced at her watch. 'She's right on schedule. I'd better go.'

'Thanks a lot, Carrie.'

'You're welcome, Bett.'

It was the longest conversation they'd had in three years.

Chapter Seven

THE MAGPIES were calling into the sharp blue sky. Bumper the sheep was giving plaintive little bleats. The glass bottles were rattling as Jim Quinlan carried the first of the crates out to the bottle bank behind the kitchen. Car engines revved as guests prepared to leave the motel.

In bed in room number six, Bett groaned at all the noise. Couldn't they keep it down out there? Her poor brain was already suffering noise overload, crammed with snatches of conversation and flashes of memories from the party. What time had she gone to bed? Three or four? She peered at her bedside clock. Nine thirty. Whose bright idea had it been to have this emergency meeting about the musical at ten? And whose bright idea had it been to finish the evening with cocktails? Hers on both counts, she realised.

She leaned over, picking up the leaflet Lola had presented to her last night. She'd tried to look at it when she got back to her room, but her eyes were unable to focus, her head swirling with jetlag, too much alcohol and too many conversations. She glanced at it again now. *Many Happy Returns*. A musical for all the family. To be performed by the Alphabet Sisters and the people of the Clare Valley. Oh no it wouldn't be.

The night before, Lola had collared her on the dance floor in between the Siege of Ennis and the Walls of Limerick. 'Isn't that Carrie's wrap? What a nice touch. You're getting on so well already, then?'

Bett didn't take the bait. 'We still can't do it, Lola.'

'Can't do the musical? Of course you can. You have to have more confidence in your own abilities, Bett. I've been telling you that for years.'

'It's not about confidence, it's about . . .'

Lola smiled. 'Yes?'

Bett told the truth. 'It's about not being asked, about being presumed upon, about wondering whether any of us actually wanted to do this.'

'But I thought you would love to do it. I've been working on it for ten years.'

'Lola, you haven't. I've been gone a few years, I know, but I've never heard a squeak out of you about it.'

'I first read the article about General MacArthur ten years ago. You're just nitpicking. So will you do it or not?'

'It's not up to me. It's up to Anna and Carrie too.'

'So if they agree, you will too?'

'Lola, stop this.'

'Bett, I'm ashamed of you. Telling an old woman off on her birthday. We'll discuss it in full tomorrow when I give you the script.'

'You actually have written a script?'

'Of course. What did you think I'd done, scribbled a few notes on the back of a shopping list?'

Bett remembered an Alphabet Sisters performance that hadn't been too far from that. She'd been about to remind Lola when her grandmother glided off, cornering another man for a dance.

The party had continued for several more hours, with the DJ playing a mixture of Irish jigs, fifties dance tracks and old-style tunes. Bett had two waltzes with Richard. As they turned around the floor the second time, she noticed him laughing at something over her shoulder.

She turned in time to see Lola lift up her skirt and give a little high kick. Oh, no. Please don't let her do her *La Cage Aux Folles* impersonation here tonight. She had done it at one of the school concerts and, to Bett's eternal shame, three of her male classmates had caught sight of Lola's voluminous knickers and told the rest of the class about them. She'd been tormented by them for days: 'Does flashing your undies like that run in the family, Bett?'

'Is your grandmother always as entertaining as this?' Richard asked.

She shook her head. 'She's quite low-key tonight, actually. A little subdued. I must ask her if she's feeling okay.'

He laughed. 'I enjoyed all those photos of you and your sisters in your performing days, too. It looked like lots of fun. Certainly put my childhood days as a boy scout to shame.'

Bett just smiled. Lots of fun? In the early years, perhaps.

'You weren't tempted to do a surprise performance for Lola tonight?' he asked as they waltzed past Lola once again. 'Spring out of a birthday cake?'

'No. We broke up too many years ago for something like that.'

Another twirl. 'And why was that? You didn't want to make a career of it?'

She gave the answer she always did. Not true, but true enough. 'We were getting a bit old to be wearing matching dresses.'

Lola came up to them both. 'You're getting on. Good, good. I was sure you would. Bett's a journalist too, Richard. Did I tell you?'

'You did, Lola.'

'Richard is here researching a book, aren't you, Richard?'

'Really? What's it about?' Bett was glad to change the subject.

Lola waved her question away. 'Oh, plenty of time to hear about that tomorrow. Come on, Dicky, come and dance with me again.' And off they had gone.

Bett had also danced with her father. He had noticed her sitting at a table to the side of the dance floor and come over, bowed gallantly and asked her in extremely polite language if she would be so kind as to give him the next dance.

'If you put it so nicely,' she'd said, laughing as she took his hand. They walked out to the dance floor as the old-fashioned waltz music started up. It had taken only moments for her to match her steps to his. Jim had taught all of his daughters to waltz properly, as Lola had taught him as a boy. As children, they'd loved to crowd in on him in the motel bar after school, and, if it was quiet, take turns Foot-Dancing with him – standing on his feet and being waltzed around the room to the tune of whatever was on the radio or TV at the time.

'You're still mister twinkle-toes himself, I see,' she smiled up at him as they moved down one side of the dance floor.

'It helps when I have such a beautiful and graceful young woman to dance with,' he said.

'Charmer.'

'No, it's true, Bett. You were always the lightest on your feet.'

'Was I?'

'Yes, really. And I have to say you look a picture tonight. You've lost weight, haven't you?'

'A little,' she said, fighting a smile. Her dad had always said that to her over the years, no matter what size she was, bigger or smaller.

'Well, whatever you've done, you look great. The three of you do.'

They were silent for a few turns of the floor, then her father squeezed her hand. 'I was saying to Anna earlier, and I want to say it again to you now, we're very happy you're all home again.'

By 'we' Bett knew he meant he and Geraldine. Their father had often been the spokesman for the pair of them. 'I am too.' And she meant it, she realised.

'And you're not going to rush off again, are you? We get to have you back for a little while?'

'I don't know yet.'

'Well, there's a room here for you as long as you want it. And a job if you need it. You know that, don't you?'

She'd squeezed his hand then. 'Thanks, Dad.'

Bett turned over in bed again. The slide show came to mind, and with it a niggling thought that had occurred to her during the party. Something about one of the photos had surprised her, but between the debacle with the dress and then the rest of the party, she hadn't given it proper thought. And now her poor brain was so drenched in alcohol it wouldn't come back to her. Was it one of the Alphabet Sisters photos? Or one of Lola's? Oh, it hurt to even think . . .

She lay there hugging her pillow. Another party memory returned. Rebecca, her fellow reporter on the paper three years ago, had arrived late. Bett had noticed in a moment that she hadn't changed at all. She was tall, willowy, her hair in a stylish blonde ponytail. She'd headed straight for Bett, hugged her, poured them both a glass of wine, then made an offer, blunt as ever. 'The woman who took over from you is about to explode with a baby and I need a part-time reporter to cover for her maternity leave. The job's yours if you're interested.'

Bett had needed to shout over the noise of the music. 'I'm only home for a week or two. I'll probably be going on to Melbourne or Sydney.'

'Lola said you'd be staying here, though. Surely you've been yearning for the simple country lifestyle? Come on, Bett. Think about it.'

They'd talked about it over another glass of wine and a cocktail or two. It had started to sound so tempting. Not having to worry about moving yet. Not having to start job-hunting . . . But had she agreed to take the job or not? She really couldn't remember. Turning the pillow over to the cool side, Bett shut her eyes and gave another long, low groan.

Anna was first to arrive in the dining room. She'd left Ellen in the kitchen with Geraldine, helping to clear the guests' breakfast trays. Her mother and father had been up for hours. The function room was already back in order, the decorations tidied away, the last tray of plates and glasses going through the industrial dishwasher. Geraldine had waved away any offers of help, preferring to do it her way. Anna had been secretly relieved.

She took a seat at the window, looking out over the valley. When they first moved into the motel, the hills around them had been bare. Bit by bit the town of Clare was getting closer, houses being built on one side and across the road, a car showroom under construction to the left. The view was still beautiful, though, especially in the morning sunlight. The curving rows of grapevines across the road were a lush, glowing green against the dark soil.

'Morning.' It was Carrie.

'Morning.'

Carrie poured a coffee and took a seat at another table. 'Huge night, wasn't it?'

'A huge announcement, you mean.'

'It's ridiculous, of course.'

'Of course.'

'You did a great job organising the party, though. It all went so smoothly.'

Carrie coloured suddenly. 'Thanks.'

Anna decided to ask the question she'd been wanting to since she arrived. 'Before Lola gets here and catches me, I have to ask you something. Was Matthew okay about not coming last night?'

'He was fine. He understood,' Carrie said briskly. 'He's working up north at the moment, anyway. On a sheep station. It saved him a long trip.'

'Oh. Good.' Anna waited, but it seemed Carrie had nothing more to say about him. All right then, she wouldn't talk about him any more either. They stared out the window.

'Morning.' They turned. It was Bett, hair bedraggled, mascara around her eyes, wearing what was either a baggy pair of pyjamas or a particularly strange tracksuit. 'Has it been called off yet?'

'Any minute now,' Anna said.

The three of them sat silently, then the door opened again. Richard Lawrence stood there. 'Good morning. Am I too late for breakfast? I'm afraid I forgot to put my order out last night.'

Carrie stood up. 'It doesn't matter. I'll get something for you. Do you need our sore-head special or the puritan's delight?'

Bett translated, guessing he was probably as hungover as she was. The last time she'd seen him he was enthusiastically joining a conga line around the room. 'She means bacon and eggs for the full hangover cure or a smug continental breakfast.' She caught Carrie's surprised look. Of course she remembered the terms they gave the breakfasts. She noticed Anna was waiting to be introduced. 'Oh, sorry. I thought you two would have met last night. Richard, this is the oldest of us, Anna Quinlan, actress, and mother of one. Anna, this is Richard Lawrence from London. He's a journalist staying here at the motel while he researches a book he's writing.' Once again, she felt Carrie's eyes on her. Was she surprised Bett had learnt so much about him?

'Hello, Anna.' Richard gave her his lovely smile. 'I must say I'm thinking of throwing all that research away in exchange for another audience with your grandmother. Much more material there, I think.'

'Good. You can do the musical instead of us while you're at it,' Anna said.

He seemed surprised. 'You're not going to do it?'

'Of course they're going to do it.' Lola swept in behind him, dressed in a turquoise kaftan top over white trousers, in full makeup and jewellery. 'Dicky, dear, how are you? Marvellous dances we shared last night. You've a fine pair of hips on you. Snake hips, I'd have called you in my younger days.'

Bett was too hungover to protest at Lola's boldness for once. Her grandmother could have come in juggling puppies and wearing a sequinned bikini this morning for all she cared. She just wanted to go back to bed.

Carrie took Richard into the kitchen and handed him over to her mother, then came back and shut the door. 'So then, Lola, what's the best way to call this whole thing off?'

'Call it off? Why would we want to do that? I thought we agreed last night we'd do it?'

'No, we didn't,' Anna said.

'We can't do it, Lola,' Bett said.

'Why not?'

'Because we won't be here to do it,' Anna said patiently.

'You won't? Where will you be?'

'Well, Ellen and I are going back to Sydney, of course.' This definitely wasn't the moment to mention she'd been thinking about staying on for a month or two.

'Why?'

'Because it's where we live. Where I work. Where Ellen goes to school.'

Lola noticed Glenn wasn't mentioned. 'So? Live here for a while. It will do you both good. There are some fine schools here too.' She turned her attention to Carrie. 'What about you, Caroline? I'd have thought you'd leap at this. A chance to get back on the stage.'

'I'm very busy with the motel,' she said quickly.

'Bett, what about you? Didn't you tell me in one of your letters how much you've missed playing the piano? And you're staying here in the Valley, aren't you?'

Bett's head was throbbing now. 'I don't know for sure.'

'What about the job Rebecca offered you at the newspaper?'

'How do you know about that?'

'I told you. I had a word with her in the street last week. And I saw her talking to you last night.'

'Shall we just get a town crier to shout out everyone's secrets and be done with it?' Bett said crossly.

Lola wondered if her judgement was failing. She'd thought they'd leap at it. This called for plan B. 'Very well then. There's something else I need to tell you. The other reason I brought you all back here.'

Three heads shot up. They'd been waiting for this.

Lola paused dramatically. 'I was at the doctor's last week. She's worried about me.' She was too. Worried that Lola was drinking too much. She'd promised her she'd cut back after the party. And perhaps she would.

'Worried about what?' Bett asked the question for all of them.

She had their attention. Good. Now, use it. 'The fact that I am a very elderly lady and that my time on this earth is fast running out.'

'Your doctor actually said that to you?' Carrie exclaimed.

'She didn't put it exactly like that. But all I'm saying is who knows how long I might be here?' That was true enough, she thought – who knew how long any of them would be around? 'And it would mean so much to me if the three of you staged the musical,' Lola continued in her most cajoling voice. 'Anna, the local schools are very good, you know. There's even a choice of denominations, though I don't know what you believe these days. And, Bett, Rebecca tells me the job she's offering is part-time and for six months, which would suit you well, too. Plenty of time for rehearsals. And you, Carrie, well, of course we'll all lend a hand with the motel. But surely you'll be able to make time to learn your lines for the lead role.'

'The lead?'

Lola gave a light laugh. 'I keep forgetting you haven't actually read the script. Yes, I'd thought of you for the lead, Carrie. You as musical director, Bett, unless you would like to get up on stage again? No, I thought not. And, Anna, I actually saw you as the director of the entire production. We'd change the billing, to read "Written by Lola Quinlan, Directed by Anna Quinlan, Music by Bett Quinlan, Starring Carrie Quinlan". Oh, I can see the programs now.' A calculated pause followed, before she lowered her voice. 'Of course, once you've all read it you might have your own ideas.'

Bett knew at that moment how sheep felt when they were being nosed into a pen by a collie.

'So you have actually finished it?' Anna was still suspicious.

'Indeed I have,' Lola said proudly. 'I have had to resist some extra special finishing touches, but I do believe it is nearly there. About two hours with an interval. Seven main characters, a chorus, lots of minor characters. You'd be able to involve half the Valley if you wanted. There are even one or two parts for children. I was thinking of Ellen if you think she is up to it. And I've even written in a cameo for the Alphabet Sisters. Imagine. That was sheer indulgence on my part. You might decide to take that out.'

'We haven't decided anything.' Anna spoke for them all.

'Of course you haven't. You have to read it first.' Lola reached into the bag beside her. 'So here you are, your reading copies, hot off the press. Mind you, by the looks of the three of you, you might want to wait until those hangovers have passed. Why you insist on mixing the grape and the grain I don't know. Wine one minute, spirits the next. Yes, Bett, I saw you with those cocktails at the end of the night. I stuck to gin and tonics all evening so my system knew exactly what to expect and here I am right as rain.' She finished handing out the folders. 'So, now I'm off back to my room to write some thankyou cards.' She was off back for a sleep, actually. She was extremely hungover. 'So will we meet here tonight to see what you think?'

The scripts were nearly an inch thick. 'Tonight?' Anna squeaked, in nothing like her usual modulated tone. 'It'll take longer than that to read it, let alone to make decisions about it.'

'It's not as if we can drop everything, Lola. I've got a motel to run, remember,' Carrie added.

Bett said nothing. She just wanted someone to carry her to her bed.

'Very well, then,' Lola said. 'Shall we say tomorrow afternoon? Excellent. You can prepare all your questions and then we'll meet again. Splendid.'

Richard walked in from the kitchen at that moment, carrying a plate of bacon and eggs and a large mug of coffee.

Lola smiled at him. 'Ah, Dicky, all sorted then? Good. Enjoy your breakfast, won't you?'

'I will. And did you enjoy your meeting?'

Lola gave a happy sigh. 'It was marvellous.'

Later that day, after a long refreshing sleep, Lola made her way to the kitchen. Lunch had been served some hours before and the preparations for dinner were still to be done. It was Lola's favourite time in the motel. The large silver table in the middle of the kitchen was cleared and shining. The air was still filled with cooking smells. Geraldine was in the office sorting accounts. Carrie had gone home for the afternoon to make a start on reading the script. Anna and Ellen had gone for a picnic. Bett was in her room. Lola helped herself to a cup of tea and the remains of last night's chocolate pudding dessert. She had just opened the newspaper to the crossword when her son walked in.

'You look well set up. Geraldine not here?'

Lola made a show of looking under her cup and saucer. 'I can't see her, no.'

Jim grinned. 'I never learn, do I? Ask an obvious question –'

'Get a clever answer. How are you, Jimmy? Sit down here and talk to your old mother.'

They rarely had the opportunity, but Lola loved these moments, looking at her fine strong son, enjoying the energy that buzzed off him. So hard to think this nearly sixty-year-old man was the same little fellow who had traipsed from motel to motel with her in those early days. It had never been a bother to him. Sunny-natured he was, through some stroke of luck. God knows his father had been anything but sunny-natured.

Jim made himself a cup of tea. 'Can I get you anything else, Lola? More tea? More pudding?'

'I've had exactly as much as I want, down to the last crumb, darling, thank you. I want to hear you talk, that's what I want.'

They took a sip of tea. 'The girls seem to be getting on fine,' Jim said.

'Do you think?' Lola smiled.

'Well, I thought there might have been a bit of unpleasantness, on account of the situation with Matthew and all, but so far so good.'

'So far so splendid,' Lola agreed.

'If we could just get the three of them back cleaning and waitressing, it'd be like old times, wouldn't it? Do you remember those nights, when you were first training the girls? You had them all balancing books on their heads and carrying trays of glasses. We must have gone through a dozen that first night.'

'Their postures are excellent, though, Jim. You have to admit that.'

'It was great novelty value, too, having the three of them waitressing. Especially when you'd get them to sing at the end of the shift. I never saw anything like those tips in all my years in motels.'

'It is years now, isn't it? But you've never regretted going into the motel business with me, have you? Resented all that moving around?'

'Of course I have. Bringing me up like a gypsy. My entire childhood spent in kitchens and bars, never knowing how long I'd call one place home.'

Lola leaned back and smiled. She always enjoyed it when Jim teased her like this. 'That's right. And don't forget you were chained to the sink since you were barely able to walk.'

'Exactly. Rinsing glasses, washing pots and pans. Do you know I was the only boy in any of my schools who had dishpan hands?'

'And don't forget I always used to drag you out of those schools, just as you started to make friends.'

'Not to mention ruining any chance I had of being a professional footy player. Remember that time we moved motels three weeks before the grand final?'

'I'd forgotten that. Probably the best thing for you. You'd be a mass of broken bones and bruises if you'd gone on with the sport.'

'The move after that was the best one we ever made, of course.'

'Was it? Why?'

Jim laughed. 'It was where I met Geraldine.'

'Of course.' Geraldine had been working in the kitchen of that next motel, training as a cook. When Lola and Jim had moved on again, two years later, Geraldine had come with them, as his wife, and already pregnant with Anna.

Lola often wondered if Jim had ever noticed that she and Geraldine couldn't bear one another. Oh, they were both polite on the surface – with all of them living in such close proximity, there had to be good manners. But it had still been difficult. In the early days, Lola had seriously considered moving to another motel, leaving Geraldine and Jim to their own devices. But then the girls had come along and Lola had quite simply fallen in love with them. Since then she'd made a pact with herself to keep things fine between her and Geraldine. Jim was devoted to her, but Lola still couldn't see why. She was too much of a cold fish, in Lola's opinion. Buttoned-up. More interested in Jim and the motel than her daughters. It always hurt Lola to see the three girls trying to get Geraldine's attention and usually failing. It had been another reason for her to shower them with attention. If she had needed any more reasons.

Lola reached into her bag, took out a folder and passed it to her son.

'For me?'

'For you. For you and Geraldine, in fact.'

'What is it?'

'Have a look and tell me what you see.'

'Tickets.' He opened them. 'First-class train tickets.' There were two sets, one for a two-night trip on the legendary *Ghan* from Adelaide through the desert centre of Australia to Darwin. The other for the *Indian Pacific*, a four-day journey from Sydney across the Nullarbor Plain to Perth. In another folder were plane tickets for their connecting flights. He glanced through them too. 'All in the name of Jim and Geraldine Quinlan.'

Lola loved these sorts of moments. 'And now look at the dates.'

'Departing from Adelaide next week? And not coming back for a month? Lola, we can't take these.'

'Of course you can. I insist.' She held up her hand to quell his protest. 'I'll run the place while you're away. And don't tell me I can't because I was doing it long before you even had a notion. And I've got the girls to help me now, as you so rightly pointed out. I've been in touch with Geraldine's stand-by cook and she said she'd love the work. Carrie already knows this place backwards. Bett is a terrific cleaner once she sets her mind to it. And so is Anna, as long as you give her ten pairs of gloves. Ellen could help, too. And all three of them are very good waitresses. I'll take care of all the rosters myself.'

'Have you asked the girls about this? No, don't answer that one. And presumably you're going to tell me these tickets are non-refundable and that if we don't take them now and do as you say you'll never talk to me again?'

Lola nodded happily.

'And you've got the rest of your argument all worked out too, I suppose. That we haven't had a holiday in years and this is the best chance to do it.'

'That's right.'

Jim was grinning. 'So I'd better go straight to Geraldine and tell her to start packing, is that it?'

'In a nutshell. Come here, darling.' She reached up and gave him a big kiss on the forehead. 'Thank you, Jimmy. You always were such an obedient boy.'

CHAPTER EIGHT

IN HER room the next day, Bett stopped midway through unpacking the last items from her suitcase. She'd checked the bookings register and it looked like she'd have this room for the next few nights at least. That had always been the drawback of sleeping in the motel rooms, having to pack up quickly and do a hasty but thorough cleaning job when real guests turned up. As teenagers, the three of them had got it down to a fine art. Carrie held the record, having once moved all her belongings, remade the bed and cleaned, polished and vacuumed a room in the time it had taken the guests to walk from the reception desk to their car and drive around to the parking space in front of the room.

When they were in their mid-teens, their father had presented each of them with a large box on wheels. The boxes were perfect for storing or transporting their clothes, pictures, vases, posters – all the things they liked to bring into the rooms to make them their own. Even better, they looked official enough when they were being wheeled in and out of rooms. Their boxes of tricks, he called them. Lola had called them their personality boxes, after seeing them lined up side by side one afternoon, when they'd hurriedly needed to move out of their rooms. Anna's had been full of makeup samples, a small gold-framed mirror, a theatre magazine, a book of tips on stagecraft and a length of fake fur that she had taken to wearing dramatically wrapped around her shoulders. Bett's box of tricks had held a smaller box crammed with music cassettes, a portable tape player, a bundle of imported pop magazines, sheet music for the piano, empty chip packets and books. Carrie, animal-mad at the time, had stored her two cloth mice toys, a book of horse tales and three packets of plastic farmyard animals.

Bett had to force the wardrobe door shut. There was only just enough room for the shirts, skirts and dresses she had brought on the plane with her. The rest of her things were coming by ship. She'd slowly put together a whole new wardrobe over the past three years, having taken hardly any of her belongings when she'd left the Valley in such a hurry. She remembered ringing Lola from Melbourne a few weeks after the big fight and apologising for leaving so much behind. 'Mum told me you'd packed up all my things. Thanks, Lola. You've gone to so much trouble for me.'

'No I haven't.'

'But she said you'd packed up all my things and stored them.'

'I did. But I didn't go to any trouble. I just flung everything into lots of boxes and taped them shut. You'll have your work cut out whenever you decide to come back.'

It had turned out to be a good thing, in a way. Being forced to start from scratch, on a very small budget, most of her clothes had been picked up at vintage shops and second-hand clothing stores around Dublin and London. The high-street shops had never been any good for her, stocked with clothes made for women with far smaller and more willowy bodies than she possessed. And vintage clothes had their own appeal, or so she'd convinced herself. She'd smiled at the irony. After years of protesting about being forced to wear vintage clothes as the Alphabet Sisters costumes, she'd voluntarily started going out and buying them for herself.

A noise at the open door interrupted her thoughts. It hadn't quite been a knock, more of a soft shuffle against the wood. She turned in time to see Ellen duck out of sight.

'Hi, Ellie,' she called, in a bright cheery voice.

There was no reaction from Ellen. 'Hi, Ellie. You can come in if you like,' Bett said again, in a more normal voice.

The little girl came in, sidling against the cupboard.

Bett smiled at her. 'How are you?'

'Good.' The voice was very soft.

'Have you been helping Grandpa with the bottles?' She'd seen the two of them pushing the trolley that morning, her father giving Ellen little rides back and forth.

A nod.

'And did you have a good time at Lola's party?'

Another nod.

Bett wasn't sure what to talk to Ellen about. It had been years since she'd had anything to do with a child. And she didn't really know Ellen any more, did she? There was a big difference between a four-year-old and a seven-year-old girl. Especially one who had been through what Ellen had been through. Bett had a flash of how Lola used to talk to them – as if they were her co-conspirators, her equals. Could she talk to Ellen about her weight-loss and lack-of-boyfriend troubles? No, not much common ground there. They could talk about children's TV programs, perhaps, except Bett hadn't seen any in years.

Ellen was fiddling with the bottle of sunscreen Bett had left on the cupboard. She was feeling just as shy, Bett realised. Oh, the sweet thing. 'Come and sit here beside me, Ellie, and let's have a chat.' She left her unpacking and sat down on the floor, patting the carpet beside her.

Ellen hesitated. 'On the floor?

Isn't that what children did? Sit on floors? 'That's right. Would you rather a cushion? I didn't realise you were from a royal family.' She bit her lip. Keep your sarcasm to yourself, Bett. She is a child.

To her surprise, Ellen smiled. 'If I was royal, it would have to be a velvet cushion, wouldn't it?'

'With tassels,' Bett agreed solemnly.

'What's a tassel?'

'A sort of – um, a sort of ponytail of thread attached to the edge, like a decoration.'

'Yes, I'd have tassels. And a waiter standing there with a silver tray and some drinks.'

This was more like it. 'And what sort of drinks would we have? You mean we, don't you? You are planning on sharing?'

'Perhaps.' The little smile again. 'It would be chocolate milk for me and for you . . .'

Bett waited.

'Beer.'

'Not champagne?'

A shake of the head. 'Beer.'

Bett pulled a face. 'And after we've had our drinks, what will we do?'

'Play in the castle.'

'On our own? Or have we got pets?' Oh, bloody hell. Now what had she done by bringing up animals?

'No dogs. I'm scared of big dogs now.'

I bet you are, Bett thought, glancing quickly at the scar again. She was surprised Ellen had even mentioned dogs. She couldn't help herself blurting out a question. 'Do you remember much about it, Ellen?'

A little nod.

Should she be asking this? 'You must have been very brave, afterwards. It must have been very scary.'

The little girl wasn't looking at her now. She was concentrating on her feet. She shrugged.

'And you're so much better now, aren't you?' Bett said, feeling like a car hurriedly reversing out of a one-way street. Back to the game, quick. 'So we won't have a dog. Will we have a cat, then?'

'No, a sheep. Like Bumper.'

Good. They were back on track. 'What a great idea.'

A voice from outside interrupted them. 'Bett? Are you there? Is Ellen with you? I need some help.'

Bett had never been so glad to hear her mother's voice calling. 'Come on, sweetheart. It sounds like you've got potatoes to peel.'

Geraldine appeared at the door. 'There you are, Ellen. Come in and help taste some of tonight's desserts, would you? I can't tell if they're ready.'

Ellen skipped off cheerfully. Bett put away her empty suitcase and checked the time. Nearly three o'clock. She'd better hurry. Time for their first production meeting, as Lola was calling it. A get-out-of-this-if-we-can meeting, Bett was calling it. She peered into the kitchen as she went past. Geraldine was back at the stove, Jim at the table with Ellen on his knee, bowls of chocolate pudding in front of them. They were poring over a map of Australia and a pile of travel brochures.

Bett had been taken aback at the news of her parents' holiday. 'Don't take it personally now, Bett,' Lola had said to her that morning. 'They're not in a hurry to get away from you. It's a practical decision. Your poor parents haven't been away properly in years, and casual staff are so expensive. With the three of you home to lend a hand this is the perfect opportunity for them to get away.'

'But we've all just got here.'

'And you'll see plenty of them when they get back.' She had pulled Bett close, planted a big kiss on her forehead, then lowered her voice. 'I've actually done it deliberately, so I can have you all to myself. You know I never liked sharing you girls with your parents.'

Anna, Carrie and Lola were already in the function room when she arrived. Anna was explaining to Lola that it might be better if she left them alone for a little while. 'We want to talk about it on our own first, Lola. You know, in case –'

'You hurt my feelings?' At Anna's guilty nod, Lola laughed. 'I'm eighty, darling. I've no feelings left to hurt. No, talk away amongst yourselves and I'll look forward to hearing what you've got to say.' She gave them a cheery wave, then moved through the front door, around the side of the motel to the back of the function room. She'd been in earlier and opened all the windows, knowing their voices would float out. She'd even taken a chair out there. Silly things, as if she was going to let them talk about her musical without her hearing.

The sisters pulled their chairs around a table in the centre of the room, the scripts and a plunger of coffee in front of them. Bett shot both of them a look. Anna was as sleekly turned out as ever – designer clothes, dramatic silver jewellery, all thin lines and sharp hair. Carrie looked like she was on her way to film a shampoo ad, bouncy blonde hair and trim body, in hipster jeans and tight-fitting T-shirt. Bett tucked her unruly hair behind her ears, tugged at her waisted jeans and fortunately not tight-fitting T-shirt.

'So,' Anna said, taking charge. The mood was tense. 'Have you both read it?'

Carrie and Bett nodded.

'And what did you think?'

Neither Bett nor Carrie spoke, both looking down at their scripts. Anna waited a moment. Still nothing. Then she leaned forward and spoke, her voice very low and very firm. 'When I was at acting school, there were sometimes things I had to do that I didn't like. Pretend to be a dog. Stand in a chorus line when I'd rather have been the lead. It happens at work still. I have to take on some jobs I'd rather not because that's just the way it is. Sometimes you have to do things you would rather not, either to please other people or because they need to be done.'

Bett tried not to react. She'd always hated it when Anna lectured them like this.

Carrie felt like rolling her eyes. Who did Anna think she was? Their mother?

'Now, I don't know whether Lola spent ten years or ten minutes on this, but I think we owe it to her at least to talk properly about it. You both know as well as I do how good she was to us. Right now putting on a musical is the last thing I want to do, to be perfectly honest. But the way I see it is, the sooner we at least talk about it, and decide whether we do it or not, the sooner it's over.'

Bett stared at her script some more. The worst thing about Anna was that apart from being so bossy she was also so often completely and maddeningly right.

'I'm not asking you to do it for me,' Anna continued. 'I'm asking you to do it for Lola. It would make her very happy.'

Carrie looked up then. 'It's easy for you to say. She's been driving me and Mum bananas the past few months.'

'She's been driving Mum bananas for more than thirty years, Carrie, and you know it. And as for you – just think of it as good practice for when you and Matthew have children. If you can handle Lola, you'll be able to handle any naughty child.' She ignored Carrie's intake of breath and poured herself some more coffee.

Outside, Lola was weighing up whether to be hurt by anything she'd heard. After a moment's reflection, she decided not to be. Nothing there she hadn't known, anyway.

Anna took a sip of coffee before tapping the script in a business-like manner. 'So then, shall we start again? What did you both think of it?'

Recalling several of the scenes, Bett suddenly found herself trying not to laugh. 'It was certainly different,' she offered. She noticed quick answering grins from Carrie and Anna, before their shutters came down again. Different – the word used in the Valley for anything a bit challenging or out of the ordinary, a polite way of saying appalling. 'I like your dress, Anna. It's different.' 'You've had a new hair cut, Bett. Gee, it's different.'

'Let me rephrase that,' Bett said. 'I think it's the maddest piece of musical theatre I have ever read in my life.'

Anna's lip twitched. 'I'd agree with that. Carrie?'

Carrie still looked a little sulky. 'If you ask me it's like she took all her favourite pieces from all her favourite musicals, flung them into a blender with a few lines of dialogue and this is what came out.'

By the window, Lola smiled serenely. Good girl, Carrie. That was exactly what she had done.

Bett turned to Anna. 'Could you actually work out what was going on?'

'I think so. It's set in Terowie, at wartime, where the townspeople –'

'Or the villagers, as she calls them,' Carrie interrupted.

'The villagers get wind that General Douglas MacArthur is coming through on a train –'

Cue three verses of 'Chattanooga Choo Choo', Bett recalled.

'And a big row breaks out between two rivals in the local Country Women's Association over who will organise the welcoming party at the railway station. Which develops into a full-scale row – amazingly like the fight scene from *West Side Story*. And of course the son of one rival and the daughter of the other are secretly in love.'

'And just happen to be called Romeo and Juliet, those two common names in 1940s Australia,' Carrie said.

Lola bristled. They might well have been common names in Terowie. How were the girls to know? She listened closely as Anna, Bett and Carrie took it in turns relating the story. They might have been laughing at her musical, but at least it meant they were talking about something.

'But then Juliet starts falling for the young American GI who is organising MacArthur's visit. And Romeo gets jealous and they split up.'

'So the GI starts feeling guilty for wreaking all this havoc on a small town and confesses as much to the lad-about-town who's been watching all the antics from afar.'

'Who happens to be the nephew of a train driver and has the bright idea to get the GI himself to dress up as General MacArthur and arrive at the platform one day early. So the CWA women scurry around and prepare his welcoming party.'

'And then they pretend that for security reasons he'll have to do it all over again, so they bring the train through again the next day, except this time of course it's the real MacArthur.'

'And the other group gets to serve their morning tea and do the welcoming party, too, and that's when General MacArthur delivers his big "I shall return" speech.'

'And the GI and the cheeky lad-about-town laugh to themselves about the fact he has already returned.'

Ingenious, Lola thought proudly.

Anna leaned back elegantly in her chair. 'And they all live happily ever after, including the couple. Cue "Happy Talk" from *South Pacific*.'

'Has Lola actually made up all the General MacArthur business?' Bett asked.

'No, it's true,' Carrie said. 'I checked on the Internet this morning. He did stop in Terowie and that is where he made that famous speech. But I don't think any of that other stuff happened, especially the war scenes in the beginning.'

'No, I'd hardly imagine Mrs MacArthur singing "My Favourite Things" to her scared little son in that first scene, when they're flying in from the Philippines,' Anna said.

'And I don't reckon the Terowie villagers came out every day, gazed at their cornfields and sang "Oh What a Beautiful Morning",' Bett added, fighting another smile.

'At least she didn't have the CWA catering women singing that "MacArthur Park" song.' Anna was actually laughing now. 'I was sure I could see it coming. A chorus row of women upset because their cakes had been left out in the rain.'

Outside, Lola wasn't laughing. She had written a scene just like that. She'd only taken it out because she wasn't sure if they would be able to manage rain special effects at the Clare Town Hall.

'There were some good bits, though, didn't you think?' Carrie said. 'I loved the scene where the couple are dancing around the local football oval, singing "I Am Sixteen Going on Seventeen".'

Anna raised an eyebrow. 'You mean the scene that is a direct lift from *The Sound of Music*?'

'Well, that was always my favourite scene in the film, too,' Carrie said defensively. 'And I also liked that scene the night of the first MacArthur's visit, when the lead actress sings "I Could Have Danced All Night" from *My Fair Lady*.'

Bett knew that song well. It had been Carrie's most popular solo moment in the Alphabet Sisters days.

'But I don't think it works when the next day she sings "I Like To Be in America",' Anna said. 'Not when she's been going on about how much she loves the Australian countryside and that man, Romeo, or whatever his name is.'

'But that's the whole thing,' Carrie said passionately. 'She thinks she loves Romeo, but now her head has been turned by MacArthur and his GI and all the drama and talk of America. She's torn between her simple life in the country and the pursuit of her dreams.'

Anna stared at her. 'You've really lived this, Carrie, haven't you?'

'Well, I can see what Lola's trying to say,' Carrie said blushing. 'And I think that song is perfect there.'

That song which just happened to be Carrie's second-favourite song from the Alphabet Sisters days, Bett thought. She'd just realised what Lola had done.

Anna's tone was now extremely businesslike. 'And what did you both think of the Alphabet Sisters cameo in the second act?'

Bett's smile disappeared. 'I crossed it out.' She didn't look at Carrie.

'I did too,' Carrie said, not looking at Bett either.

Anna felt the tension in the room increase. She glanced between the two of them. 'Fine. I'll cross it out too.' She patted her script.

'Here's what I think. It's completely mad, of course, and it needs a bit of work, but it could be done. That's if Lola is actually serious about it.'

Lola popped her head up over the window ledge. 'I'm quite serious.'

They all jumped. Anna frowned. 'Lola, this is supposed to be a private meeting.'

'Don't be ridiculous. You must have known I'd be eavesdropping outside. But you spoke too low for my poor old ears at the end there. What did you all think of it?'

'It's actually very good,' Anna said.

'Don't sound so surprised,' Lola said.

'I really enjoyed it,' Bett said.

'I knew you would.'

'There's definitely something in there for everybody,' Carrie said.

'That was my whole intention. So it could work?'

'Well, yes,' Anna said. 'But it's not like the Alphabet Sisters performances, Lola. It isn't just the three of us standing up singing a few tunes wearing matching dresses. It would need a hall for a start.'

'I've booked it.' She waved the flyer at them. 'For March twentieth. It's the anniversary of General MacArthur's visit. Perfect, don't you think?'

'That's so soon. What about sets? Costumes?'

'Len the butcher said he'd be happy to help. He's not a bad carpenter. I've been tucking bits and pieces away for costumes from the charity shop for the past few months. If you don't like them, we could hire some in Adelaide.'

'And what about a band?'

Lola gestured grandly at Bett. 'Who needs a band when we've

got Bett? You could use the piano here for rehearsals and we could move it to the town hall for the show. Though there are lots of talented musicians in the Valley if you wanted more than piano.'

Bett was going through the song list. Lola had looked after her too. She had chosen many of her favourites, ones with lots of bright piano music.

Anna was leafing through the script again. When she first left drama school in Sydney, she'd joined a musical theatre group that put on mini musicals for corporate functions. That was how she had met Glenn. He'd been organising the Real Estate Association Christmas party. She'd picked up all sorts of tricks and tips for staging a show on a budget – how to use one backdrop for lots of different scenes, and how to make rapid scene changes to keep the action moving. Lola's script was surprisingly good, but she could see where a little cutting here and there would help it . . .

Lola was now all eagerness and excitement. 'I thought you could put an ad in the paper calling for auditions. I've got some wording for it here, look.' She waved another bit of paper at them.

Bett wasn't convinced. 'It's still very tight time-wise.'

Anna took a diary out of her bag. 'Not if we got moving with the auditions, then started rehearsals twice a week. Carrie, would this room be available?'

'I'd have to check the bookings, but it's usually free on weeknights. And we haven't got any weddings for a couple of months. But hold on a moment. Are you all going to stay in the Valley? Here in the motel?' Carrie looked from Anna to Bett. This was moving too quickly for her. 'What about your work, Anna? And Glenn?'

Anna's face was expressionless. 'If we did decide to do the musical, I could juggle work. Go up to Sydney for two days a week. Ellen could come with me.' She didn't mention Glenn.

'No, Ellen couldn't, actually.' Lola gave a guilty smile. 'She'll be in school here. I spoke to the principal today. She's a friend of mine. She said they can certainly find a place for her.'

Carrie turned to her other sister, fighting a feeling of panic. It was one thing hiding Matthew's absence from her sisters for days, but for weeks? 'And you, Bett? What about your work?'

Lola stepped in again. 'She's accepted a part-time job at the *Valley Times*. Haven't you, Bett?'

Bett stared at Lola in amazement. She'd only phoned Rebecca that afternoon. She'd decided to accept the job first and worry later about living so close to Carrie and Matthew.

The mobile beside Anna started vibrating. She checked the number. 'Excuse me,' she said, walking outside to answer the call. 'Glenn?'

'Anna, hello. How are things? How's Ellen?'

'Fine. How are you?' So stiff, so awkward with each other.

'Fine, fine. Big news up here. The Singapore trip is on. I leave in two days.'

'I see. How long will you be away for?'

'Three weeks to begin with. But it's only eight hours' flight from Sydney. I'll be back and forth. I'll still ring Ellen every night, of course. In fact, I'm thinking about getting her a mobile.'

'A mobile? She's only seven years old, Glenn.'

'I like the idea of her having one anyway. To keep her safe.'

One more dig at her failure as a parent. Anna felt very tired, even as she realised he'd just helped her make the final decision. 'As it turns out, Glenn, that works out well. We're going to stay here in the Valley for a month or so.' She didn't tell him about the musical. He wouldn't have been interested.

His anger came down the phone line like a sonic wave. 'Just like that? Without discussing it with me? At least I told you the

Singapore trip was on the cards. What if I hadn't been going there? When was I going to get to see Ellen?'

She walked further away from the motel building, her voice low, the anger only just controlled. 'When would you want to see Ellen? In between nights at Julie's house? In between conferences? Work trips?'

'Anna, I love her. She's my daughter. You know I see her as much as I can. And just because I'm not with her every hour of the day doesn't mean I'm not thinking about her. What are you going to do about her schooling? Your work?'

Anna had to sit down on a bench, her chest tight with anger. 'I don't know yet. We're still sorting it out.' There was a long pause and then she had to ask. 'Is Julie going to Singapore?'

He tried to bluster through it. 'Well, she's my senior assistant and it's a big deal to set up a brand-new office. I couldn't be expected to do it on my own.'

'Is Julie going as your lover as well as your assistant, Glenn?' Anna's voice was smooth. He wouldn't have guessed for a moment that her stomach was churning, her hands were sweating. She wanted the truth.

'Julie's coming with me, yes.'

So it was still happening. 'Look, Glenn, I can't talk now. I'll ring you tomorrow.'

There was a pause, then he spoke again. 'Okay, then. Fine. So will you give Ellen my love?'

'I will. Goodbye.' She hung up and sat for a moment trying to quell the desire to throw up. She felt her heart. It was racing. Her skin was clammy. She shut her eyes for a moment, waited for her breathing to calm, and then stood up. She used all the years of drama school training to put a smile on her face as she walked back into the function room. 'That's all sorted. Glenn's got to go to Singapore for work for a while, so the timing couldn't have been better. We can definitely stay.'

Still outside, leaning in through the window, Lola noticed Bett was humming one of the songs under her breath. Carrie was mouthing some lines. Anna was the only one who seemed a little distracted. Perhaps she'd had to fight with Glenn to be able to stay on. He'd always been possessive. Still, they'd talk about it later. She gazed at her three granddaughters. 'So have you definitely made a decision? Will you do it?'

Anna looked at Bett, who looked at Carrie, who looked back at Anna. Then they all turned to Lola. 'We'll do it.'

Chapter Nine

In the function room a week later, Bett was practising songs on the piano for the following night's auditions.

Their parents had left for their holiday that morning. Lola, Anna, Bett, Carrie and Ellen had stood waving on the forecourt as the two of them had driven off, smiling and waving back. They'd all been thinking it, but it was Lola who said it out loud. Jim and Geraldine were like newlyweds off on their honeymoon.

'What's a honeymoon?' Ellen asked.

'A holiday for people who have just got married,' Anna answered.

'Did you and Dad have a honeymoon?'

'Yes, for two weeks.' They'd gone to an exclusive resort in Fiji. Glenn had confessed on the plane on the way over that he'd heard it was an excellent place for networking business contacts.

'Why didn't you take me?'

Anna ruffled her hair. 'You weren't born yet.'

Ellen turned to Carrie. 'Have you ever had a honeymoon, Auntie Carrie?'

Bett and Carrie both stiffened. 'I have, Ellen, yes.'

'And you, Auntie Bett?'

Before Bett had a chance to answer, Lola gave a very loud moan. They all spun towards her, alarmed. 'Lola, what's the matter? Are you all right?'

She moaned again. 'It's just my arthritis, I think. It comes and goes in this damp weather.'

It hadn't rained in weeks and Bett knew for a fact that Lola didn't suffer from arthritis. Short of screaming 'Quick! Change the subject!' at the top of her voice, her grandmother couldn't have been any more obvious. But it had worked. The five of them had walked back into the motel and even managed to have a peaceful enough meeting about the work rosters.

Bett was on reception duty that night. She'd already interrupted her piano playing twice to welcome guests and give out room keys. Carrie had been in the bar earlier, serving rounds of drinks to a small group of people. It was now dark in there. Bett assumed Carrie had closed it all up and gone home for the night. Anna had been in the kitchen when Bett had passed through earlier. She'd been preparing the guests' breakfast trays, reading through the ticked forms, distributing little boxes of cereal, portions of jam and sachets of sugar. Ellen had been beside her, standing on a chair. With her tongue visible between her lips, she'd been folding the red paper serviettes into passable fans.

Bett finished playing 'Oh What a Beautiful Morning' and picked up the sheet music for 'Chattanooga Choo Choo'. She loved the smoothness of the piano keys under her fingers, the familiar tunes filling the room around her, the feeling of being in charge of the music, adding elaborate notes here and there. She worked her way through each of the songs, memories of different Alphabet Sisters performances coming back to her – singing 'My Favourite Things' to an audience of five, two of them dogs, at an agricultural show in New South Wales. She remembered one hot, dry day in country Queensland, midway through their version of 'Boogie Woogie Bugle Boy', when the three of them had inexplicably got the giggles so badly that Bett and then Carrie had fallen off the stage. It had almost become their party trick.

She stopped playing, walked to the window and stared out into the carpark. Being back in the Valley again was sparking all sorts of memories. Not just about Matthew, and the terrible fight with Anna and Carrie, but everything that had happened afterwards as well. Her mind had been filled with thoughts of it all week.

The morning after the fight, she'd got up at dawn, packed one small bag, filled her car with petrol and started driving. From a roadside motel en route to Melbourne she'd phoned the *Valley Times* office and taken leave without pay until further notice. She'd called a friend from journalism college now based in Melbourne and explained what had happened. By nightfall, she was set up in her friend's spare room.

The next three months had passed in a kind of frenzy. With too much time on her hands, she'd started drinking too much, talking too much to cover the hurt and confusion. She had found some freelance work with city newspapers, started falling in and out of bars with a fluid, rowdy gang of reporters, sub-editors, photographers. She hadn't told anyone the real reason she was in Melbourne. She'd done her best to block it out of her mind and nearly succeeded.

Until the night in Carlton, seeing a band in a new club, she had bumped into an old work colleague from home. She'd been surprised to see him. 'I didn't realise you were in Melbourne.'

'I didn't know you were here either.'

She didn't know if he knew the circumstances of her leaving the

Valley, but she was strangely glad to see a familiar face. He bought her a drink, then another one. She hadn't eaten all day and ignored the light-headed feeling. The vodka fuelled her confidence, helped her pretend to be carefree, as they swapped stories of newspaper life, keeping it light, fun.

It got later, and the band finished playing. They went for another drink, on to a late-night bar together for more vodka and then she found herself back in his flat, alone with him. She had been talking all night and remembered getting upset, even crying a little about something. Had it been about Carrie and Matthew? The fight with Anna? All of that and more. He had taken her in his arms and given her a sympathetic hug and that's when the evening had changed. She was the one who'd changed it into a closer hug, a different sort of hug. She'd made it happen. Insisted on it. She wanted to kiss him, touch him in a way she'd never done with Matthew. She wanted to rid herself of memories of Matthew, to feel different, to behave in a way she'd never behaved. She wanted to cancel out any tears and vulnerability she'd shown him that evening, wanted to cover it over with sex, sweat, kissing, stroking, thrusts, arched backs and marking nails and biting mouths . . .

When she awoke the next morning, wild and reckless Bett was long gone, leaving ashamed and hungover Bett lying there naked beside him. She lifted his arm from her waist, moved away, trying not to make any noise. 'Don't wake up. Please don't wake up,' she prayed, edging out of the room, into the living room, gathering her clothes, bag and jacket, dressing, then slipping out quickly. She didn't leave a note. It was a big city. They never had to see each other again.

Back home she'd taken to her bed for the rest of the day. By nightfall she'd been desperate to talk to someone about it. Too shy to tell her flatmate, unable to ring her sisters, she'd called Lola and told her everything. As she sketched the story, moments kept coming back to her, making her nearly yelp aloud in embarrassment. Oh, God. Had she really cried in his arms? Another shudder as she remembered insisting on kissing him. Insisting on having sex with him. She'd felt it in her body all day, a warm kind of ache, between her legs, on her skin. Memories that would have been sensual, pleasant, if they hadn't made her want to howl in shame.

Lola had been non-judgemental. 'Perhaps it was better that it was someone you knew, not a complete stranger. Did you use contraception?'

'Yes. Yes, we did.'

'Do you want to see him again?'

'Of course I don't. How could I face him?' Then she'd started crying. 'I'm unhappy, Lola. That's not me. I don't do things like that. I don't know what's happening to me.'

'Bett, it was a one-night stand, not a mass murder. Keep it in perspective. Do you want to come back home?'

'I can't.'

'You can. You'd get used to seeing Carrie and Matthew together.'

'Lola, I don't want to see Carrie and Matthew together. I don't want everyone watching me to see how I react, people talking about me behind my back.'

'This is such a scandal people would be talking about it in front of your back, believe me. Darling, have you lost your sense of humour somewhere? Come on, it's a broken romance. Millions of people have those every day.'

'But I never wanted to be like millions of other people. And I'm sick of making a mess of things.' The words started tumbling out of her. 'I wanted to be fearless and do something wonderful and splendid and remarkable and I haven't and I don't think I ever will. I'm scared all the time, Lola.'

'Scared of what?'

'Of being embarrassed. Of making a fool of myself.'

'You'll have to be more specific. Everyone is scared of those things. You need to be clearer with me, darling.'

Bett only had to think for a moment. 'I'm scared of loads of things. Of being on my own.' Of sex, whether she did it properly or not. But she didn't want to tell Lola that. She thought of other things instead. 'I'm scared of seeing my body in mirrors in changing rooms in clothes shops, and snooty shop assistants making fun of me.' She managed to laugh. 'I'm scared of stupid things, too. Like eating oysters. Reverse parking. Aeroplanes. Mobile phones . . .'

'Is that all? I thought you were scared about serious things.'

'They're serious to me.'

'But you can overcome all of them. You know the saying, Bett. You have to face your fears.'

'Where do I start? Make a list? Tick them off?'

'Leave it with me. For now, get into your pyjamas, go to bed and have an early night. Don't have a drink. Be patient. And calm down.'

The first decree had arrived exactly three days later. Just a postcard, addressed to Bett, with one line in the centre.

Eat an oyster.

That's all it said. For a moment she thought it was a new marketing ploy, targeting people one by one. Then she recognised the handwriting. Lola's. She phoned her. 'What do you mean, eat an oyster?'

'You're scared of them. So face them. Go and eat one. Then write to me – don't phone me – and tell me how you got on.'

She did it. She hated it but she did it nevertheless. Her report to Lola was also sent on a postcard. *I went to a seafood restaurant last night with my flatmate Yvonne. She ordered oysters and I ate one. It was the most disgusting thing I have ever eaten, like swallowing a salty slug that has been lying in water in the sun and gone bad. It took three glasses of wine to get the taste out of my mouth.*

The reply came by return post. *Good, brave girl.*

For the next four weeks the one-line postcards arrived like clockwork. *Go to the theatre on your own. Go out to dinner on your own.* Each time, Bett took on the task, and wrote home to tell Lola exactly what had happened. A week later, another card would arrive. *Good, brave girl*, with another task set beside it.

Then a surprising one arrived.

Go and live overseas.

She phoned Lola immediately. 'That's a bit of a jump, isn't it? From oysters to overseas?'

'I've been leading up to it. I've been pushing you to go for years. The money is burning a hole in my pocket.'

Lola had given each of the girls a return airfare to the place of their choice for their twenty-fifth birthday. Anna had gone to America for an acting course. Glenn had followed her out and proposed to her as they took a horse and carriage ride around Central Park. 'Blech, so tacky,' Carrie had said. 'Bet he had the carriage-driver playing violin as well.' Carrie had headed off on a round-Asia trip, which then turned into a year away. But between study and work, Bett had never found time to leave Australia. 'I can't take it from you, Lola.'

'Don't give me that nonsense. Your sisters took it gladly and so should you. And I'll throw in some spending money as well. Let's call it the interest I've earned on the capital because you've taken so long to decide to take it.'

'You can't afford it either, Lola.'

'Darling, you haven't the faintest idea whether I am poorhouse material or a very rich old lady, and I'm not going to tell you. Just take it and run. I was going to leave you this money in my will. I might as well give it to you now, so I can see how you spend it.'

'I can't.'

'Why not? Are you scared?'

Bett laughed. 'Yes, I am actually.'

'Of what? The flight? Moving to a new country?'

'All of that.'

'You know the best way to deal with that.'

And so it had happened. Bett finally agreed to accept the fare, and two weeks after that conversation found herself in Dublin.

It had been hard at first. She'd brought herself to Ireland, not a new improved fearless model. The first month she stayed in a youth hostel in the centre of Dublin. She'd been worried she would be the oldest person there and was surprised when no one cared what age she was. With an Irish passport courtesy of Lola, she set off looking for work in newspapers, before realising that was the old her. She had imaginary conversations with Lola. 'What do you like?' 'Music. Writing.' 'Can you combine the two?' She discovered she could, by getting a job behind the bar in one of Dublin's many music venues and writing the occasional review of the gigs for music newspapers, websites and magazines.

She found a flatshare on the North Circular Road, near the Phoenix Park, sharing a four-storey red-brick terraced house with young Irish students, Nigerians, Asians, Romanians, their friendship confined to nods and hellos on the steep steps leading up to the red-painted front door. She walked to work through the fruit markets, dodging delivery trucks, stepping over cabbages, kiwi fruit, sometimes even mangoes squashed onto cobblestones.

She started living a strange upside-down life, working in the night time, sleeping in the daytime, seeing as many as ten live bands a week in the venues she worked in. She made friends with other bar staff, the sound engineers, the woman who took the money at the door. Just as the late nights started to lose their appeal, a chance conversation with Karl over the bar while one of his early signings played to an empty room led to a move to London and the job in his record company. It had been exciting, leaving one new city for another. She'd felt brave, adventurous, free . . .

But then she had started to miss things, too. Being free meant being unconnected, untethered. Which was fine when she was happy. But not when things were uncertain, when out of the blue she would find herself longing for conversations with Anna – and even with Carrie. She discovered a horoscope website, and read their signs each day, trying to guess what might be happening in their lives. Walking through a department store one afternoon she smelt a familiar perfume and was overwhelmed by a feeling of missing Anna. She asked for a sample. For the rest of the day Bett felt oddly comforted that Anna was nearby.

There'd been only one communication between them in the three years, when Lola told her about Ellen being attacked. Bett had been shocked by the news. That same night she sent Anna a card, brief, to the point, telling her how sad she was to hear about Ellen. She heard nothing back. After that, there hadn't been another opportunity. Not until the excuse of the eightieth birthday party had arrived.

Images of Anna and Carrie came to mind now. Things weren't as she'd expected with them. Anna wasn't as snooty or as aloof as the imaginary Anna she had been carrying in her mind these years. And Carrie wasn't as smug or self-satisfied as she'd expected either. In fact, they both seemed . . . what? Bett wondered. Normal? Familiar? Even a little troubled?

The phone rang, making her jump. She ran out to the reception desk. 'Valley View Motel. Can I help you?'

'What are you doing, darling?' It was Lola.

'Looking over the songs,' Bett improvised. 'Where are you?'

'In my room. I could see you staring out the function-room window and I wondered if you needed any help.'

'No, I'm fine. I'm finished for today, I think. I know enough for the auditions tomorrow anyway.'

'Good girl. Come and talk to me, would you? And would you bring the outfit you're going to wear to work tomorrow and let me have a look at it?'

Bett laughed. 'Lola, that's very sweet of you but it's a part-time job, not my first day at school.'

'I know. But first impressions can count. You want to be feeling good when you go in there, meeting people you haven't seen for a few years.'

'I saw Rebecca last week.'

'Indulge me, darling.'

Ten minutes later she was in Lola's room, carrying the clothes she'd chosen to wear to the newspaper office in the morning. It was a vintage skirt, dark-red silk, which she planned to wear with a simple white shirt. Her shoes were good. Italian leather, stylish but still very comfortable.

Lola put her head to one side and looked for a moment like a bright-eyed bird. 'Just about exactly right, I think. You have learned something while you've been away. Earrings?'

Bett held up the pair she planned to wear. They were also dark red, made from old glass beads. She'd found them at a Dublin market stall.

'Very nice. More to the point, how do you feel in the whole outfit?'

'Good, I think.'

'That's more important. And remember you are Bett who is thirty-two, who has been living in Dublin and London, who has eaten an oyster and gone to the theatre on her own, among many other brave things. Remember all that tomorrow.'

Bett smiled. 'Why? Is someone planning on springing *This Is Your Life* on me?'

'I just want you to feel good about yourself, no matter what happens, no matter who you meet.'

Bett softened. Lola knew there would be people at the office from three years ago when the whole business with Carrie and Matthew had blown up. 'Why do you do it, Lola?'

'Do what?'

'Put up with us. All of us. How can you be bothered?'

'Because I love you. And because I love making you do as I tell you. So you'll keep the chin up tomorrow, no matter what? Promise me?'

'I promise you.'

Lola gave a contented sigh and lay back on her bed. 'I never thought I'd say it but one of the bonuses of being an elderly decrepit old bag of bones like I am is that no one pays any attention to the way you look. You're just some old woman, not some thin woman or fat woman or ugly woman or beautiful woman. You're just old.'

'And does that bother you?' Bett asked as she returned her skirt to the hanger. 'Do you miss things about being young?'

'Of course, but I can't change it. I am old. On my last legs, probably, the clock ticking away as we speak.'

'Stop that, you old ghoul.' Bett sat down beside Lola on the bed. It was always a treat to have her to herself. 'Do you ever think about it, though, Lola? Are you scared of dying?'

'Why? Are you about to try and kill me?'

'No, not tonight. I like you tonight. But do you think about it?'

'Of course I do. Most people do. That's why you have to try and fill up each day as much as you can, in case it's your last day.'

'But if you truly lived life like that, you'd never go to work, would you? Or wash dishes. Or sweep floors. Because you wouldn't want to spend your last day on earth doing boring things like that.'

'Exactly. Which is why I don't let a day go past without having a gin and tonic. No point rationing it out, in case the day I choose not to have one is the day I die. And think how much work I'll save the embalmer, from all the gin I've consumed over the years. I'm sure I'm half embalmed as it is.'

'You are getting more appalling every year.'

Lola gave a happy smile. 'Yes, I know.'

Bett picked up Lola's left hand and started moving her wedding ring around, the way she had done since she was a little girl and she and Lola were talking like this. She knew every twist of gold. 'Do you still miss Edward, Lola?'

'He's been gone sixty years, Bett. You get used to anything after that length of time.'

'What was he like? What were the two of you like together?'

'Why are you interested so suddenly?'

Bett put down Lola's hand and smoothed the bedcover, idly noting a tiny cigarette burn on one corner. Guests always did ignore the sign about no smoking in bed. 'I was thinking about it last night. That we have been coming to you for years with every detail about every little aspect of our lives, moaning and groaning, and maybe it's your turn to talk, and ours to listen. I was thinking about your slide show, those photos you had of Ireland and the early days. I want you to know that if you feel like reminiscing about those days, about Edward, what it was like when you and Dad started running the guesthouses and all of that, or if there is anything else you want to talk about, I'm here, okay?'

Lola burst out laughing. She reached up to touch the curly head beside her. 'Darling, thank you very much. If anything comes up I'll be sure to call you.'

'I mean it, Lola.'

'And I do too.'

In the kitchen of her house, Carrie glanced up at the clock. Nearly ten o'clock. He should be here any moment. She checked her appearance again, smoothed down her dress, straightened the knives and forks on the table. She was nervous, she realised. Of her own husband.

Of her estranged husband, to be accurate.

She went out onto the verandah. The paddocks all around the house were dark for as far as she could see. In the daytime she liked the peace and quiet. In the night time, without Matthew, it gave her the creeps. She jumped at the sound of a bird in the gum trees behind the house, then jumped again at a rustle in the agapanthus lining the driveway. It was a hot evening, but she still shivered.

She longed for a return of the days when the very sight of the house would give her a lift. She and Matthew had spent months searching for their ideal home. They had agreed on everything – they wanted an old-style, stone house, with a full return verandah, preferably with open fireplaces for those cold Clare winter nights. They wanted just a small block of land, perhaps an acre or two. Ideally, they would find a house that already had the major renovations done – all the plumbing and rewiring. And they wanted at least three bedrooms.

'Four,' she'd said.

'You want three children?' he'd laughed.

'At least,' she'd said airily. 'And as soon as possible.'

'Not too soon.'

She should have picked up the hints then, shouldn't she? But no, she'd chosen to ignore him, to go on making plans, picking out nursery colours, before they even had a nursery, let alone a baby . . .

They'd found this house by accident. One weekend Matthew had collected her from the motel after work and for a change they'd gone for a drive rather than head back to the small unit they were renting. They'd taken one of the dirt roads just to the south of the town, winding up between the vineyards. And there it had been. A hand-painted For Sale sign at the end of a track leading up to an old stone house. They'd driven straight up and found the owners inside – a pair of middle-aged hippies, there was no other way to describe them. They'd been living in the Valley for the past two years but had decided to head north to the tropical heat and rainforests of Queensland. They hadn't listed the house with any real estate agents, preferring to let the buyer find them, they'd earnestly explained. Matthew and Carrie had been squeezing each other's hands underneath the table. The house had almost everything they had been looking for – the original stone work, the verandah, the slate floors. It had been rewired and the plumbing was in reasonable condition. The main problem had been the colours the walls had been painted, tangerine and purple, swirls of this and that. 'I think they studied at the Marijuana School of Interior Decoration', Matthew had whispered as they toured around. But it hadn't put them off. They'd made an offer the next day. Two months later they'd moved in.

Carrie forced herself to stay outside now, leaning against the verandah post she'd painted herself, waiting for the sound of his car. He'd been surprised at her call that afternoon, she knew that. No wonder, considering what she had shouted at him last time they had spoken, several weeks ago now. 'It's over, Matthew. We're finished. Can't you see that?'

He'd sounded wary on the phone. Exhausted. But he'd agreed to make the long drive from the station he was working at, to hear what it was she had to say. That counted for something, surely.

The problem was she didn't really know what she wanted to say to him. She jumped as a flicker of light was reflected against the pale bark of the gum trees. Car headlights. Matthew? Her heart started beating faster as the car came closer . . .

Three hours later the peace of the farmhouse was broken by the sound of a long, shuddering snore from the other side of the double bed.

'Shut up, Matthew,' Carrie said crossly into the darkness. She gave him a sharp pinch, which caused a moment's break in his loud snoring, before he settled back into it again. She sat up looking at him. Well, that had gone really well. It had been after midnight by the time he'd finally arrived. She'd worn a track in the verandah from her pacing, had nearly leapt out of her skin each time car headlights appeared down the road. By the time he had rung to say he'd had serious engine trouble and been stuck on the side of the road trying to fix it for the past two hours, she'd been beside herself with worry. She'd also been a little drunk from the red wine she'd been sipping out of nervousness. When he'd finally arrived she'd wanted to fly at him in anger and frustration, but the thought of Anna and Bett laughing at her and her broken marriage had kept her voice low and sweet. She greeted him, offered him a beer.

She had led the way into their living room, smiling as he took a chair – not his usual chair, she noticed – offering him a sandwich, some cheese. It was too late for the dinner she'd prepared. He'd shaken his head, watching her closely, as nervous of her as she was of him, she realised.

'So how was work today?' she asked cheerily, even though the sight of him – dirty, exhausted, his clothes covered in dust – supplied her with the answer.

He ran his fingers through his hair. She knew the gesture well. It meant he was tired and it also meant he was feeling impatient. 'Can we cut to the chase here, Carrie? What did you want to talk about?'

He was angry, too. And she supposed he had every right to be. She'd kicked him out of the house after all. Hung up on him each time he'd called. Returned his letters unopened and unanswered. She felt a dart of shame that, yes, perhaps he had some right to be cross with her. So what did she want to talk to him about? She didn't know any more. 'Us, I suppose.'

'What else have you got to say? I thought you'd made yourself pretty clear.'

She took some heart from the fact he had at least come tonight, long drive, long day and all. She decided to tell him the truth. 'It's about Bett.'

He ran his fingers through his hair again.

'She's staying on in the Valley. She's taken a job at the local paper again.' She debated whether to tell him about Lola's musical, then decided against it. This was about Bett, not Lola.

'Has she? Good on her.'

'So how does it make you feel?'

'About her job? Carrie, it's got nothing to do with me. It's up to Bett where she wants to work.'

'I don't mean about her job. I mean how do you feel about Bett being close by again.'

She saw a flash of something – temper? – cancelling out the exhaustion in his eyes. 'Carrie, I feel what I felt when you asked me about Bett three weeks ago. Six months ago. A year ago. I can't keep telling you.'

'I don't believe you.'

He raised his voice at her then. 'Because you don't want to believe me. And I can't do anything about that. Jesus, Carrie, it's like banging my head against a brick wall, and I'm sick of it –' He stopped there. 'Listen, can I have a shower, have a coffee maybe? Can we talk about it after that?'

She turned her back, shrugged. She saw in the reflection in the window that he stood and looked at her for a few moments, before he went to the bathroom. She took her drink out onto the verandah, waited for him to join her, calming herself, preparing the words again, hoping to make herself understood this time. Twenty minutes later she was still waiting.

She had walked into their bedroom and found him asleep on top of the bed, half undressed. He'd been so exhausted it seemed he hadn't even got to the shower, simply lain down on their bed and fallen asleep. And he was still asleep. No amount of clanging saucepans or poking had stirred him. She had felt a ripple of guilt looking down at him, at the boyish face asleep on the pillow, the light-brown hair tousled, dirty.

Staring at him in the bed beside her now, she was reminded of earlier days, in the first year of their marriage, when he'd arrive home from similar busy, dirty days working out on farms and stations. She'd greet him at the door with a kiss, putting her finger on his mouth to stop him talking, leading him into the bathroom where she'd slowly undress him, and then herself, moving him into the shower, still silent, now kissing him on the lips, on the shoulder, on the brown skin of his arms, on his flat brown belly, lower down until he would be groaning against the side of the shower. And after that it would be into the bedroom, where he would return the favour, no longer tired, stroking and caressing her, until she could hardly bear it and would pull him down into her. The memory stirred her now, and she moved in closer to him.

'Matthew?'

She touched his back through his T-shirt. No response. She ran her hand down his side and he flinched. She waited, tried again, moving lower towards his crotch. He muttered something, moved away, lying on his front, out of reach.

'Forget it, then,' she said loudly, crossly. When had this happened? The two of them who had barely been able to keep their hands off each other since the first night they met. She thumped the pillow in frustration. How had she made such a mess of things?

She fought back tears, fanning angry feelings instead. If it hadn't been for Lola, the way she had started talking incessantly about how much she missed the three of them, how she had dreamt about the Alphabet Sisters again, she'd never have been in this position. Lola had never said it, but Carrie knew what was beneath it all – it was all Carrie's fault, for stealing Matthew from

Bett. If she had never done that, they would all be living happily ever after, wouldn't they? She hadn't been able to get the guilty feelings out of her mind, at the same time that Matthew's work started taking him away for stretches at a time. When he was home, they seemed to fight. And not just about having a baby any more, either. They'd found plenty of other subject matter instead. Finally, in a fit of temper two months earlier, she had said they needed a trial separation.

He'd been shocked. 'Why?'

'Because it's not right. We shouldn't have got together. You should have stayed with Bett.'

'Carrie, we've been through this. I fell in love with you. It would have been wrong for me to stay with her.'

'Maybe it wouldn't have. Maybe that's what you should have done. It was a test of your love for Bett.'

'What?'

'You know, like a temptation. And you failed. And now we're both being punished.'

'What are you talking about? Have you had religious cranks staying at the motel?'

She couldn't explain it any better. And then he'd got angry, and they had rowed about all sorts of other things, until they had both been glad when he had stormed out and she had told him not to come back.

At the back of her mind were Bett and Anna's voices. 'We told you so.' She couldn't bear it. What a horrible, awful, unfair mess, she thought, curling tighter into a ball on the very edge of the bed.

Beside her Matthew gave another loud snore. It was all she could do not to smother him with her pillow.

In her room at the motel, Anna was lying on her bed, with Ellen tucked in beside her fast asleep. Anna's eyes were wide open as she stared into space. Her skin felt clammy, her stomach was churning, she felt exhausted but unable to sleep. She was in the country, the fresh air – wasn't she supposed to feel better? Truth was, she'd never felt so tired or so awful in her life.

She'd had another fight with Glenn on the phone that evening. More guilt, more blaming, more heated words, all in hushed tones so that Ellen, in the bath, couldn't hear. She'd come out wrapped in a towel, and asked, 'Is that Daddy?' At Anna's nod, she'd reached for the phone and settled herself on the bed, chattering away to him, all the solemn little phrases tumbling out of her. 'Is work busy?' 'Is Singapore hot like here?' 'Will you bring me a present when you come home?' As if things were perfectly normal with them all. And then the worst of it. 'Will you say hello to Julie for me too?' Anna had nearly been sick. Ellen was friendly enough with her father's lover to send her messages.

When Ellen had handed back the phone, Anna had barely been able to speak to him, only keeping her voice civil because she knew Ellen was listening to every word. Afterwards, she'd wanted to throw the mobile across the room, hoping to see it smash, the parts fly into all corners. On the verge of doing that, in sight of Ellen or not, it had started ringing again. Not Glenn this time, but her booking agent, Roz. She apologised for ringing so late, but explained that a big job had come up from one of her past clients. Was Anna available?

'They've specifically asked for you. It's a good gig, Anna. You could do it in your sleep.' It was the voice-over for three separate teenage sex-education videos, as well as a series of radio ads directed at parents and teachers. If the response was good, there could even be follow-up commercials. 'Top rates, too. For a few days' work, maximum. Can you do it?'

Anna had massaged her temple with her spare hand. She'd promised Ellen they would have a long break together. God knows they both needed it. But this job would pay well. Which would mean she wouldn't need to take Glenn's money, for a little while at least. The thought made her feel good. 'Of course I can,' she'd said.

Ellen murmured in her sleep. Anna pressed a kiss on her head. Lola's ban on any talk of Matthew came to mind. Was that the key to life? Simply ignoring any difficult subject? Should she have ignored the fact that Glenn had become bored with her? Just kept on smiling, attending social functions with him, perhaps taken a lover or two of her own? Ignored the calls from Julie, the intimacy in her phone conversations with Glenn proof that their relationship had changed from colleagues to lovers? Just kept smiling, smiling, smiling? Until her face hurt and her body ached with the tension?

She'd managed to avoid the subject here beautifully so far. She had skilfully answered her parents' few questions about him, deftly explaining his absences from these home visits, murmuring something about work pressures and promotions and overseas trips. There was no risk of Carrie and Bett asking after him – they'd made their feelings about Glenn clear three years ago. She'd felt Lola's eyes on her, as ever, waiting for the questions, but so far, nothing.

Not that she would answer them anyway. 'Yes, Lola, Bett and Carrie were right that night. I did make a very bad decision years ago and I've lived with it ever since. I did ignore all my own instincts, went ahead with a marriage to someone who I knew only cared about my face and my body, not my heart, definitely not my mind or soul.'

But how did she fix the unfixable? Did she go to Bett and Carrie and admit that they had been right? That the terrible things they had shouted at her, the night of their big fight, had actually turned out to be true? That her marriage was over, that she was exactly what they accused her of becoming – cold, fake, self-obsessed? Would they say it had served her right, that she had made her bed when she married Glenn for his money, his social standing, his contacts?

In her arms, Ellen gave a little wriggle. Anna held her tighter and shut her eyes, tired of thinking, willing sleep to come to her, too.

Matthew was gone by the time Carrie woke up the next morning. She looked for a note, an apology. Nothing.

'That's why!' she shouted out the door, to no one but the birds in the paddocks opposite. 'You don't talk to me, you don't tell me anything any more. It's no wonder it's ruined.' She burst into tears and ran back into their bedroom, grabbing the pillow he had slept on and sobbing until it was wet under her cheek.

Chapter Ten

Bett tried out her new swivel chair again, giving it a little spin and ending up facing Rebecca's office across the corridor. A stack of newspapers lay on the desk beside her. She'd already skimmed through them, enjoying every article, getting up to date with the ins and outs of Clare Valley life. There were stories about water shortages next to photos of largest-ever pumpkins, schoolchildren's charity efforts alongside politicians handshaking.

She'd had a long meeting with Rebecca that morning. Apart from writing general news and feature stories, Rebecca wanted her to write the editorial for a new project, a twelve-page supplement on the Valley's tourist attractions, sponsored by the tourism commission. 'They've asked for lots of colour, all the sights and smells and tastes, so I want you and the photographer to actually try everything out, so you can write it from the visitor's perspective.'

'You want me to do it? The new girl?' It was a dream assignment.

Rebecca laughed. 'Yes, I know. I'd rather be doing it myself. Let me tell you, being editor's not all it's cracked up to be.'

Bett had returned to her desk, feeling buoyed and enthusiastic about a writing project for the first time in months. She started drawing up a list of subjects: the wine-tasting tours, the gourmet cooking course in one of the Clare Valley's grand country homes, the overnight sleeping under the stars experience at the Valley's oldest sheep station, the guided historical walk along the path of the old railway line . . . This was more like it, she thought. She wrote the lead sentence of an article in her head, as she often did for practice. *Bett Quinlan, 32, announced today that she was very happy to be back working for a real newspaper.*

She had picked up the phone to dial one of the tour operators when a voice behind her made her jump. 'Bett Quinlan, as I live and breathe.' It was Neil, the grey-haired sports reporter who'd been with the paper since it started. 'It's great to see you. Welcome back on board.'

She stood and hugged him. 'Great to see you too, Neil.' It had been good to see lots of her old colleagues. They'd asked after London, after her family, normal things. No one had mentioned Matthew yet.

'I've been hearing all about your grandmother's musical. Don't suppose you've got a part for an old fellow like me?' He burst into the first line of 'The Sound of Music'.

'Auditions are on tomorrow night. Why don't you come along?'

'You know, I just might. I wouldn't mind treading the boards one more time.' He gave a quick little soft-shoe shuffle before he walked away.

Rebecca came out of her office. 'I'm thinking about coming along myself.'

'You're kidding? Do you want to be in it?'

'Of course not. But I wouldn't want to miss the chance of seeing some of the locals auditioning. Much better than watching those reality shows on telly. Now then, Hildie's just come in, the photographer you'll be doing the tourism supplement with.' She poked her head into one of the side rooms and called out. 'Hildie, are you around? Come and meet our new reporter.' Then she lowered her voice. 'You might remember him, actually. It was before my time in the Valley, but he used to work here before he went to Melbourne for a few years. I snapped him up when he came back last year.' She smiled over Bett's head at the new arrival.

'Bett Quinlan, all the way from London, I'd like you to meet Daniel Hilder.'

Bett turned and felt the colour run from her face. Her one-night stand had just walked into the room.

In the gym at the country club, Anna looked up at the clock. She'd only been on the treadmill for ten minutes and she was already breathless, feeling out of shape after just a few days away from exercise. She could almost hear her personal trainer's voice. 'A little every day keeps age and fat away.' Too bad. She could do nothing about her age and it wasn't as if she needed to lose weight at the moment. If anything, she needed to put some on. Irony of ironies – now the pressure was off, now Glenn was gone and she could put on some weight if she wanted, she wasn't hungry. She could let herself go completely if she wanted. It wasn't as if there was another man on the sidelines dying to see her naked body.

'Hello, Anna.'

She turned. It was Richard Lawrence, dressed in shorts and a T-shirt, a towel over his shoulder. It was the first time she'd seen him since the morning after Lola's party. He certainly looked much fresher today. Taller than she remembered. Still wearing his glasses. His hair was cropped very short. He looked quite like an athlete, she thought. Like a marathon runner, in fact. Lean and spare.

'Richard, how are you?' She coolly reached forward and turned off the treadmill, gradually adjusting her steps as the belt slowed. She'd always taken care stepping off this kind of equipment, especially since Bett had rung her in Sydney some years before and recounted her humiliating first and last visit to this gym. She had mistimed stepping off the treadmill and been catapulted backwards onto the rowing machine, landing on another woman and pushing her onto the floor as well. It was one of Anna's favourite Bett stories. She had nearly cried laughing while Bett was telling her.

Richard smiled. 'I'm well, thank you. I didn't realise you liked to work out here too.'

'Occasionally. But I'm not in the mood this morning. I think I'll try the natural air approach and walk back to the motel instead.'

'Do you mind if I join you? I've been hoping to have the chance to talk to you again.'

She stood in front of him, a towel in her hands. Years ago she had decided to get it out into the open when men made approaches to her like this. 'Really, Richard, you're being very forward. Are you trying to pick me up?'

'I don't know yet,' he said calmly. 'You're certainly very beautiful, and I like that spark in your eye, but I like to be able to have a conversation with my lovers, not just look at them. So it's probably too early to tell.'

To both their surprise, she burst out laughing. 'That is the best answer I have ever heard. What about your workout?'

He grinned. 'We could walk the long way back, couldn't we?'

Out at her house, Carrie was feeling sick. A book lay on the wooden boards beside her. She'd come home from the motel for a quick break after lunch, hoping for a message from Matthew, an email, perhaps even a letter. She'd found nothing. Pacing the house, feeling restless, she'd tried the TV, then the radio, before crouching in front of the bookshelf in the hall. It was filled mostly with magazines and textbooks. Neither of them was a great reader. She'd come across one of Matthew's few books, a collection of English vet stories. As she flicked through it, his bookmark had fallen out.

It was an old photograph of Matthew and Bett together, arm in arm.

At six o'clock, Bett came running up the path to the motel and practically burst into Lola's room. 'You knew he was working there, didn't you? That's why you said all those things about me looking as good as I could. I thought you meant the other stuff but you meant Daniel Hilder, didn't you?'

'Hello, darling. Did you have a good day at work?'

'Lola, I mean it. Why didn't you warn me?'

'What was I going to say? "Best of luck at work tomorrow, and by the way that man you had the one-night stand with in Melbourne three years ago is working there now so you might want to make sure you've got your lipstick on straight." Really, Bett, wasn't it better to be surprised? Think of how much you would have been worrying last night if you'd known he'd be there this morning.'

'But have you any idea how embarrassing it was? If it's not bad enough knowing people are talking about me and Carrie and Matthew. Why don't we just put me on the back of a truck and drive up and down the main street, letting people laugh at me for all the mistakes I've made in my life?'

'That's a great idea. I wish I'd thought of it. We could get sponsors, perhaps?'

'It's not funny, Lola.'

'Did Daniel laugh at you?'

'No.'

'Did he call all your colleagues over and tell them what happened between the two of you?'

'No.'

'Perhaps he didn't remember it himself.'

'Of course he remembered it. You don't forget a night like that, do you? Or perhaps he has forgotten it? Oh God, that's even worse.'

'The poor man can't win,' Lola said, laughing. 'You'd be furious with him if he did say something about it and furious with him if he'd forgotten it. He's very nice, you know. And you told me the sex was quite something, once you stopped all the crying and talking and got on with it.'

'Did I really tell you that?' She realised that, yes, she probably had. The state she had been in at that stage she was practically stopping complete strangers and telling them intimate details about her life.

'I just can't bear it,' she wailed, as she relived the brief and stilted conversation she'd had with Daniel that morning, with Rebecca standing between them chatting away unawares. 'I knew I shouldn't have come back here, Lola. Anna and Carrie and I are on eggshells with each other. Mum and Dad are still in their own little world. I'd have been better off staying in London.' She was shocked at the feel of a hand across her cheek. 'Did you just slap me?'

'It wasn't a slap, it was a flick of my fingers. Quite a different thing. I was scared you were about to become hysterical and I didn't have a bucket of water handy.'

Bett stood open-mouthed.

Lola took Bett's face between both hands and looked her right in the eyes. 'Bett, face him. Face every single thing life throws at you.

Daniel was kind to you that night, wasn't he? And everything you told him was the truth? Perhaps it was a good thing for him, too, a crash course in understanding women. Perhaps he's been kinder to his own wife or girlfriend because of some of the things you said to him.'

'Wife? Is he married now?'

'No, although there was a serious girlfriend in Melbourne, from what I could drag out of him the other day when I remembered who he was. A live-in girlfriend, that's the phrase, I believe. Horrible term, makes me think of velvet-covered sofas for some reason.'

'Was he living with her when I slept with him? Oh no, that's even worse.'

'I don't think so. He'd only been with her for a year or two, I think.' Lola laughed. 'Bett, don't look so horrified. You didn't get pregnant, did you? Catch anything from him? He didn't have lice? Scabies? AIDS? Don't look so surprised. I watch TV soaps, remember. I know every disease going.' She looked at her watch. 'Darling, the auditions will be starting soon. Do you want to stand in front of a gathering of people in a state like this? And no, you can't get under the bed, so stop looking over there. Go for a walk. Think about things and remember how lucky you are.'

'Lucky? That my most embarrassing moment has come back to haunt me?'

'That's not your most embarrassing moment. You told me your most embarrassing moment was last year when you walked around the centre of London for an afternoon without realising you had your dress tucked in your knickers.'

Bett howled. 'Apart from that.'

'See, you've had more embarrassing moments than you realise. There's no need to carry on as if this is the one that will tip you over the edge.'

'Can't you be kind to me?'

'I am being kind. Cruel to be kind. Bett, go for a walk. Be glad of your good strong legs and stop worrying about tiny things that don't matter. Do you know, I've just remembered another one. That time you made the speech at school and called the guest of honour by the wrong name the whole way through –'

'No more, Lola, or I swear I'll –'

'You'll do what? Elizabeth Quinlan, are you threatening your feeble eighty-year-old grandmother? Get out now or I'll call the police.'

An hour later, Lola was in a new outfit and full makeup, sitting behind a small table at the function room door, greeting people effusively as they came in. Ellen was sitting beside her, politely handing out registration forms to each person.

'Sandra, marvellous to see you,' Lola beamed. 'And which of your daughters is this? And what will you be singing, dear? Celine Dion? Oh, one of my favourites. Here, fill out this form, would you? We'll get started as soon as we can.'

Anna, Bett and Carrie stood at the other end of the room, watching the people stream in and sit down on the chairs lining the walls.

'I can't believe the turn-out,' Anna said. 'I thought we'd be searching for people to audition.'

Bett had a flicker of nerves. 'Do you actually know how to run one of these things?'

'Of course I do. I've been to a million of them. We'll do the warm-up songs, then get everyone to sing a verse and chorus of their chosen song, ask them to stop midway through if we think they're terrible, or hear them to the end if they're okay. Then if we want them, we call their agents and make an offer.'

Bett's lip twitched. She noticed Carrie was trying not to smile too. 'I don't think Len the butcher or Mrs Gill from the primary school are going to have agents.'

'You know what I mean. We need to run it professionally, set the standard from the start. It's going to be hard enough to pull this off in a few weeks as it is, starting from scratch, without any professional actors or musicians or performers, apart from me.' There was a tiny pause. 'And you two, of course.'

'A lot of the people here have got experience,' Carrie said briskly. 'I think you'll be surprised, Anna.'

'I hope I am.'

'Hello, Carrie.'

Carrie turned. It was Kaylene, one of Len's daughters. She worked in one of the Valley hairdressers, although Carrie didn't go to her any more, since she'd learned what a gossip she was. Carrie smiled a welcome nevertheless. The more the merrier tonight. 'Hi, Kaylene. You know Anna? And Bett?'

Kaylene nodded at the other two. 'God, I didn't ever think I'd see you Quinlans standing in the same room. I heard you had a ferocious row over Matthew.'

'Did you?' Anna said coolly. The three of them were standing close to one another and without realising it inched even closer.

'Mmm. Someone said you hadn't spoken in three years.'

Anna, in the middle, put one arm around Bett and the other around Carrie. 'Then it seems that someone was wrong, Kylie.'

'Kaylene.'

'Sorry, Kaylene. We wouldn't let a silly thing like a row about a man upset us, would we, Bett, Carrie?' Behind their backs, she was pinching them both hard.

'Of course not.'

'No.'

'If anything, it's brought us even closer together,' Anna added.

There was no need to lay it on too thick, Bett thought. She didn't dare look at Carrie.

Kaylene seemed disappointed.

'And you've come to audition, Kaylene, have you?' Anna asked nicely.

Kaylene coloured. 'I thought I'd give it a try. I like dancing and my mother says I'm a good singer.'

Bett took pity on her. 'Thanks for coming, Kaylene. Take a seat, won't you, and we'll get started as soon as we can.'

As she moved away Anna grinned. 'Good thing she left when she did. I was about to tell her I'd slept with Matthew too.'

'Anna!' Carrie and Bett were genuinely shocked.

Anna's eyes were full of mischief. 'Only joking.'

Turning back to the piano, fighting a smile, Bett didn't see Daniel Hilder come into the room behind her. Or see Lola greet him with a kiss on the cheek. Or see him take a seat at the back out of her line of vision.

Twenty minutes later the room was filled to capacity. The plan was for Lola to welcome everyone, briefly sketch the musical, then pass it over to Anna who would run the auditions. 'It's your baby, now,' Lola had told them that afternoon. 'I've done my bit. I want to enjoy it all at the end, when all the hard work has been done.'

'You're not going to sit in on every rehearsal, making comments?' Anna asked.

'Me, make comments? What do you take me for? No, I'm leaving it all to you and spending the time with Ellen instead.'

Lola hadn't been surprised when Ellen had said she didn't want to be in the musical. She'd already noticed how self-conscious the little girl was. 'Excellent news, Ellen,' she'd said cheerfully. 'That means you and I can keep each other company while the others get on with the hard work.'

Lola made her way to the front of the room now. Bett enjoyed some of the group's reactions as they took in her outfit – the blue silk shirt, so shiny it could have been a Barry White cast-off, the flared trousers, the crocheted vest in enough colours to rival Joseph's technicoloured coat. Lola waited dramatically for the chatter to stop, then gave a little bow. 'Thank you all for coming. It's the most wonderful turn-out. You may have heard this is my life's work, something I have been planning for nearly ten years –'

Two months, Bett corrected.

'And I am thrilled that so many of you are here tonight to audition, or to at least be entertained by the others' auditions while planning on sneaking off yourselves before we call you up. Hello there, Rebecca. Yes, I can see you edging out the back there.' There was a ripple of laughter. 'Let me set the scene – *Many Happy Returns* is based on the true story of the American war hero General Douglas MacArthur, and his historic visit to the tiny town of Terowie in 1942, in the middle of World War II. My story begins . . .'

Bett gazed around the room as Lola gave a precis of the storyline. There were several people she remembered from her newspaper days, but many she didn't know. A late arrival coming in the door caught her eye. Richard Lawrence. She wasn't surprised to see him. He'd been curious about the whole musical since Lola's party. She brought her attention back to Lola's speech.

'So you'll see it's the age-old story of family against family, young love thwarted, a town pulling together against the odds, the tyranny and ferociousness of war, all to a soundtrack of lots of marvellous old songs from my favourite – sorry, everyone's favourite – musicals.' There was a burst of applause, then Lola held up her hand again. 'So now, over to my granddaughter Anna.'

Anna moved forward, all glamour and poise. 'Good evening, everyone, and thanks for coming. We'll have a warm-up or two, and then we'll hear you do your individual pieces.'

At the piano, Bett watched as Lola made a poor attempt to slip unnoticed out of the room with Ellen. At Anna's nod, she played the intro, then moved smoothly into the first song, 'Do-Re-Mi' from *The Sound of Music*. There were only a few voices to begin with but as she kept playing, more people joined in. By the end of the third verse everyone was singing, even if not all of them were in tune. Bett ignored what looked like Anna wincing, and moved into the second warm-up song, 'Boogie Woogie Bugle Boy'. Things got a little livelier.

Anna stood up hurriedly at the end of the second verse, stopping them there. 'Terrific, we're off to a good start. Now, then, time for the solo spots.'

'There's not hidden cameras here or anything, is there?' Bett overheard one man ask another. 'This is getting a bit too much like that *Popstars* program for my liking.'

'Just sing any old way. Think of the free beer afterwards.'

Bett grinned. It had been Carrie's idea to add the offer of free drinks to the advertisements. 'Otherwise we won't get any men at all, and we need them for the villagers, and the soldiers, not to mention General MacArthur.'

At the desk, Anna picked out a registration form at random. 'Right, then. We'll start with Louise singing "Bohemian Rhapsody". When you're ready, Louise.'

In room seven, Lola was sitting on the side of Ellen's bed, telling stories about the girls' childhood. 'I called it my Collection of Cries, Ellen. I had a whole row of jars and as soon as I'd hear your mother cry, or Bett, or Carrie, I'd sneak up behind them and capture their cries in the jar, then quickly put the lid on. It was marvellous. They'd stop crying immediately.'

Ellen was giggling. 'And have you still got all the jars?'

Lola sadly shook her head. 'No. Unfortunately three bold little girls opened all the lids one afternoon. You've never heard such a racket. Five years' worth of tears and tantrums released in a moment. It took me some quick talking to convince the police nothing terrible had happened. As for the poor motel guests – they didn't know what had hit them.'

Ellen moved further down in her bed. 'Can you tell me another story?'

'I will, of course. But not tonight. It's past all good great-granddaughters' bedtimes.'

'But wait, Lola. I've got another question.'

Lola waited. She was well used to these delaying tactics. Anna had been exactly the same as a child. 'One more question, then.'

'Why have you got a funny voice?'

'What do you mean a funny voice?'

'You talk differently to other people. You talk like this: "It's past all good great-granddaughters' bedtimes".'

Lola laughed out loud. Ellen had just perfectly mimicked her Irish accent. She was definitely Anna's daughter. 'That, my love, is called an Irish accent, not a funny voice.'

'I like it.'

'Good. I'll keep it, then.' She kissed Ellen's forehead. 'Night night, sweetheart. Sleep well. And I'm three doors down if there's anything you need, okay? And Mummy will be here soon, too, just as soon as she's finished the auditions.'

'Night night, Lola.' Ellen's voice was barely audible. Lola waited at the door for a few minutes until she was sure the little girl was content. After a minute she heard the sound of regular breathing and let herself out. Dear little thing.

Letting herself back into her own room, Lola suddenly felt exhausted. She'd have liked to sit and watch every moment of the auditions. She'd have liked to sit in on every production meeting, too. Painted the sets, helped Bett work out the music, sew the costumes, even. But she didn't have the energy for it any more. The spirit was more than willing, but the flesh was getting weaker all the time. Oh, yes, she was in better nick than most eighty-year-olds, there was no doubt about it, but it was all downhill from here and she didn't like it one bit.

She opened the bar fridge and mixed herself a gin and tonic. She'd have a little read, a little think, a little drink and then a good night's sleep. She was longing for her bed, in fact. They didn't warn you of that in the growing old books, did they? That some days all you would ever want to do is sleep, just like a baby. It was true, the older you became, the more your life went backwards, your hair thinning, your teeth falling out, your bladder getting a life of its own. What would be next to go? Her marbles?

She sat upright in her chair. No, she was damned if that was how she was going to go. She'd made it this far, she was going to keep at it. As soon as she started lolling about, getting lazy, giving in, it would all collapse around her. She hadn't let it happen when she was young and she wouldn't now.

She deliberately moved to the hard chair, and sat there, more awake, remembering Bett asking her if she missed being young.

She'd thought about it since and decided she missed one very simple thing. Running. She missed being able to run, wished, just one more time, that she could run like she used to run as a child in Ireland, across the fields behind the house, through the soft rain or on the mild summer days, with the grass and the chestnut trees lush with new growth all around her, feeling the ground beneath her feet, muddy at times, and the long grass against her bare legs. Her favourite route had been from the front door of the big house, down the drive to the oak tree outside the main gate. She'd touch it once, twice, three times for luck, then run back as fast as she could.

She took a sip of gin and moved to turn on the TV, then changed her mind, preferring her own thoughts. She'd been remembering a lot from her childhood recently, ever since she had gone through the few photos she had, picking them out so Frank from the electrical shop could turn them into slides for her. He'd dropped the originals back that afternoon, and come in for a chat, full of questions. He was off to Ireland himself for a holiday in a few months and was keen to hear tips, asking did she want anything brought back or did she want him to call at her old house and take photos?

She'd patted him on the hand. 'Kind Frank, thank you but no. Bett did that for me when she was there a few years ago.' Not that Lola had ever looked closely at the photos Bett sent back that time. Well, there'd been no need to, had there? It wasn't as if they had meant anything to her. All the same, she'd sent Bett a note, thanking her for going to all the trouble of travelling there, talking to locals, taking the photos. And then she had never raised the subject again. She'd had more than the occasional twinge of guilt. Wanting to tell someone the truth. But too much time had gone past by now for it to matter any more, surely.

She took another sip of her drink and turned to her crossword.

She'd finish the last few clues, then go to bed. As she reached for her pen and reading glasses, there was a crackle and a fizzing sound and the ceiling light went out. The wall light was on, so she could still see, but it wasn't bright enough to work by. She'd been telling Jim for years he ought to improve them. She had a spare light bulb in the wardrobe. She stood up and felt the desk chair. Yes, it was sturdy enough and the ceilings were so low, she'd easily be able to reach. It wouldn't take a moment, and she must have changed hundreds, if not thousands, of light bulbs over the years. And made thousands of beds. And set thousands of breakfast trays. And cleaned a *million* lavatories. She must count them all up one day, it could be amusing.

She took a scarf off the end of her bed to unscrew the hot bulb. Opening the wardrobe door to give herself something to hang on to, she climbed up onto the chair. As she did, the chair shook slightly. She turned to grasp the wardrobe door but misjudged the distance. The chair tilted some more and she felt herself falling. She put out both arms to stop herself but it was too late. Her head knocked sharply against the wardrobe door and she fell to the floor.

The break was nearly over. Everyone was milling back in from the bar next door, complimentary beer and wine in hand. At their table in the corner, the three sisters were flicking through the forms.

Bett glanced down her list. Many of the names had enthusiastic ticks beside them. 'What did you think, Carrie?' She was quite surprised how easy it had been tonight to make conversation with her sisters. Then again, Lola's ban on difficult subjects was still firmly in place.

'I thought there was plenty of talent. And these here, see. What about them for the lead roles? Anna, who have you picked out?'

Anna moved her hand. Her sheet of paper was blank, apart from a few swirling doodles.

Bett bit back a smile. 'Anna, it's an amateur musical, remember. We're raising money for a new ambulance, not going for the Tony Awards.'

'But if we're going to do it, we may as well –'

'Do it well,' the other two chorused. The times they'd heard Lola chant that.

Anna sighed heavily, then flicked through the forms again. 'Have we heard this Daniel Hilder audition? He filled out the form and he'd be the right age for the Jack-the-Lad character, wouldn't he?'

Bett stiffened. 'Daniel Hilder's here?'

'The photographer?' Carrie looked up. 'I didn't see him. Will I go and ask him to audition?'

'No.' Bett spoke louder than she intended.

Anna and Carrie looked surprised. 'You don't want him to audition?' Anna asked.

'No, I mean I'll go and ask him.' Bett stood up, taking her glass of wine with her. What would Lola have said to her? Face your fears. You are thirty-two. What happened was years ago, embarrassing and all as it was. Exactly. Of course she could handle this.

She did a circuit of the room, then spotted him walking in from the bar, a drink in hand.

'Daniel?'

He turned. As she came near him, someone behind her stepped back suddenly, bumping her elbow and sending her glass of red wine flying. She stood there with red wine dripping from her chin to her knees and all down the front of her dark-blue dress.

For a split-second she was tempted to run out of the room. Then she had a brainwave. React as if you are Anna, not Bett, she told herself quickly. It worked. 'I'm going to ignore the fact that even happened,' she said coolly.

'Are you?' He seemed surprised. 'All right, then. So will I.'

She stared straight at him, trying to ignore a glint of amusement in his eye. 'I was wondering whether you wanted to audition, because if you do there's still time.'

He nodded, but didn't answer.

'Well?'

He smiled. 'I'm sorry, Bett. I really am trying to ignore that little accident, but it's a bit hard when you've got red wine dripping down your chin.'

She clung desperately to her new cool persona. 'Well, we can't have that.' She reached for a serviette, and wiped it away. 'Would you like to audition? I noticed you'd put your name down, but we didn't get to hear you.'

'I got called out for an hour,' he said. 'An urgent phone call. I missed my slot.' He gave a surprisingly shy smile. 'I thought it might be something different to do.'

How come he was being so normal? Did he have one-night stands all the time or something? Or had he blanked it out? Bett had been trying to but all day she'd been tormented by memories from that night. She tried to block them out again. He's got a live-in girlfriend, remember that. Possibly even married. Possibly even seven or eight children. A Labrador. Halitosis. Alopecia. Fungal toenails. It wasn't helping. She was noticing only good things about him. The dark eyes. The laughter lines. The kind face. The shaggy dark hair. The faded jeans and casual shirt, hanging loosely, sexily, on him.

She opened her mouth, needing to say something about their night together, trying to find the words for it, when she heard a voice behind her.

'Hi, Daniel. I'm Carrie. I don't think we've met.'

'Hello, Carrie.'

Carrie looked from one to the other. 'So are you two ready to get down to it?'

Bett blushed. She didn't look at Daniel. 'Pardon?'

'The audition?'

Yes, the audition. 'Of course. Ready, Daniel?' Bett discovered you could look just to the right of someone's face and it almost seemed as though you were looking directly at them.

He smiled. 'Ready when you are.'

Bett followed them back to the piano, surprised the candles on the tables weren't melting from the heat coming off her face.

In her room, Ellen woke up. 'Mummy?' No answer. 'Mummy?' Then she remembered. Her mum was doing the musical and Lola was looking after her. She'd told her to come to her room if she wanted anything.

Ellen climbed out of bed.

Anna was businesslike. 'Okay, Bett, Daniel, when you're ready.'

Daniel was standing by the piano, looking down at her, ready to sing. She had to blink away another memory of kissing him. If she was remembering his body, was he remembering hers? She sucked in her stomach.

'Bett?' Anna's voice a little louder.

Concentrate, Bett, she told herself. Easier said than done. How had her life come to this? Sitting at the piano in the Valley View Motel about to play the backing music so that Daniel Hilder could audition for a musical Lola had written. She'd have been less surprised to find herself strapped to the nose cone of a space shuttle. She stared at the sheet music. Hands poised over the piano, she glanced up at him, nodded and played the first note.

A loud shrieking filled the room.

They all turned. Ellen was in the doorway, dressed in her pyjamas, tears pouring down her cheeks.

'Mummy, Lola's dead.'

Chapter Eleven

Bett pressed her cheek against the wall of the hospital corridor, feeling the coolness as she spoke into the public phone. 'No, you don't need to come back, Dad. She's in hospital. It's all under control.'

'Are you sure? We can catch a flight and be there in a few hours.'

'Seriously, you don't need to. She's a bit shocked, but it's just a broken wrist and a bad cut on her forehead. She wasn't even unconscious when Ellen found her. It's just Ellen got such a fright.'

Nothing compared to what Ellen's words had done to the rest of them. The auditions had been forgotten, Daniel Hilder had been forgotten, as Bett, Anna and Carrie ran to Lola's room. The first sight was the worst, seeing Lola sprawled across the floor, the chair upended beside her, her left wrist bent at an awkward angle.

'Lola, no,' Bett heard herself scream. Anna reached for her right wrist to feel the pulse, then nearly leapt out of her skin as Lola spoke. 'Hello, darling.'

'You're not dead?'

'Not unless heaven looks like the motel.'

Bett was on the floor beside her in seconds, gently touching her. 'Are you hurt? What happened?'

'The stupid light bulb. I told your father to buy better-quality ones.'

'Lola, we've told you not to change those bulbs.' Anna said crossly. 'You're eighty, too old to be climbing up on chairs like this.'

Lola rallied. 'One minute you're crying because you think I'm dead, the next minute you're telling me off. Talk about fair-weather friends.'

Crouched on the floor beside her too, Carrie put a hand on her own chest. 'Oh God, Lola, at least you're okay. I nearly died of the fright. My heart is still racing, you should feel it.'

'*Jesus*, Carrie.' Bett was shocked as a surge of fury hit her. 'Do you have to be the centre of attention all the time?'

Carrie's eyes widened. 'I wasn't, I was just –'

'You were so. You always –'

'Stop it, Bett, for God's sake.' Anna snapped. 'You're as bad as each other.'

Bett glared at her. 'Don't you start on –'

'I will start on you. Leave Carrie alone and ring an ambulance, would you?'

'I was about to, before she –'

'Darlings, please.' Lola's voice came from between them. Her head was against Carrie's shoulder, her eyes closed. 'Don't fight over me. And, Bett, please don't blaspheme like that again. You know I don't like it.'

Her words set them into motion, even as they avoided any further eye contact. Bett called for an ambulance. Carrie stayed with Lola while Anna moved to the door, asking the crowd that had gathered to please move back. 'She's fine, she'll be fine. She's not dead at all.'

'Mummy?' A familiar little voice came from the back of the group. Anna turned as Richard Lawrence came into view, holding Ellen by the hand.

He brought her forward. 'I found her crying in the function room.'

Anna pulled the little girl into her arms. 'Ellie, I'm so sorry. I'm so sorry to leave you behind.' In the rush to find Lola after Ellen's announcement they had run straight past her. 'You're such a good girl, you might have saved your great-grandmother's life, do you know that?'

Bett was about to suggest a cup of tea, something warm and sweet for Lola, when she saw headlights approaching. She crouched down beside her grandmother again and gently took her good hand. 'Here we are now. The ambulance is here.'

It wasn't the ambulance but an ordinary station wagon. Daniel Hilder got out and walked over. 'I thought it might be as quick for me to bring Lola in to the hospital. The ambulance could be a while yet.'

'You see how important this musical is?' Lola said, rousing again for a moment. 'I told you this Valley needs another ambulance.'

'Lola, are you sure you're okay to move?' Bett asked. 'You're not hurt anywhere else? Your back or your legs?'

'I'm fine. It's just my sore head and this stupid wrist.' She was shaking violently.

Carrie was on one side of her, Bett on the other. Bett turned to Daniel, businesslike, serious, in no need of an inner-Anna now. 'Daniel, we'll accept, if you don't mind. Carrie, you and I go in with her. Anna, you'd better stay here with Ellen. Lola, can you stand?'

Daniel stepped forward. 'I can carry you to the car, Lola, if you need it.'

'So kind of you, Daniel,' Lola managed to be gracious. 'But I'll walk. Where's my little Ellen first?' Ellen came forward and Lola touched her gently on the cheek. 'Thank you, my little darling, for doing exactly the right thing.'

Bett had felt her eyes well up with tears at the sight of Ellen's face, filled with pride. After that it had been all action, getting Lola to the hospital, into the waiting room. Daniel Hilder had been there, gentle, helping, then he had gone before Bett had a chance to thank him.

On the phone, Jim Quinlan sounded relieved. 'You're absolutely sure you don't need us there, Bett?'

'I'm sure, Dad. She's sleeping now. We're going to go home too. I'll call you first thing in the morning.'

As she hung up, she saw her hands were shaking. Nurses were moving swiftly up and down the hospital corridor. Carrie was in a chair down a little way, making a call on her mobile phone. To Matthew, Bett presumed . . .

'Bett?'

She turned. It was Daniel.

'Is everything okay? Is Lola all right?'

She nodded. 'She's going to be fine, they think. It looked more serious than it was.' She glanced up at the clock. Nearly two hours had passed since they had arrived, the time speeding past in the flurry of doctors' visits and X-rays, before Lola was finally settled into a small ward. 'Have you been waiting all this time?'

'I didn't mind. I had a book with me. I thought you and your sister might need a lift back to the motel.'

She was too tired to be embarrassed or to feel nervous with him. She just gave him a big, grateful smile. 'Thank you.'

Ten metres away, Carrie was talking into her mobile phone. '. . . so they'll keep her in overnight. God knows what would have happened if Ellen hadn't found her. She was so shocked she hadn't been able to get up off the floor.'

'What was she doing up on the chair in the first place?' Matthew said. 'Don't tell me, swinging from the light fittings?'

It was nice to laugh. As soon as she'd heard from the doctors that Lola was going to be all right, she had wanted to ring Matthew. He had been wary when he first answered, but his tone had changed as soon she told him what had happened. Just hearing his voice helped calm her, too. Until he suddenly changed the subject.

'I want to come down, Carrie.' He paused. 'Not just for Lola, but also to see Bett. I think I need to. I've been thinking about her a lot.'

Something chilled in her again. She thought of the photo she'd found. 'No, you can't.'

'Carrie, come on.' He sounded cross, impatient again. 'What do you think will happen? That I'll decide I made a mistake and go back to her?'

So the thought of that had been in his head already. 'I don't know what would happen and I don't want to find out.'

'Carrie, don't hang up. Can't you see –'

She didn't want to see anything else that night. 'The doctor is coming back, Matthew. I have to go. I'll be in touch.'

'Carrie . . .'

'Goodbye.' She hung up first, once again. Composing herself, she walked over to Bett and Daniel.

At the motel, Anna was kneeling beside Ellen's bed. She stroked the hair back from Ellen's face and tucked the sheet in close around her shoulders. The child was nearly asleep, stirring now and again to ask another question. 'Lola will be all right, Mum, won't she? They're not taking her to be put down, are they?'

Anna stopped herself from laughing. Their neighbour's cat in Sydney had been run over and had needed to be taken to the vet to be put down. Anna thought she'd explained the situation to Ellen well when it happened, telling her the truth, that the cat had broken so many bones and was in such terrible pain it was kinder to end its life than try to fix it. She stroked her forehead again. 'Of course not, Ellie. The doctors and nurses know exactly what to do and she'll be back home before we know it.'

Ellen's eyelids fluttered, then closed, and in seconds her breathing was slow, measured. Anna waited a moment longer, then leaned forward and kissed her on the forehead and whispered. 'I'm just going to turn all the lights off in the motel and then I'll be right back.'

As Anna came out of her room, she jumped as a figure appeared in front of her. It was Richard. She noticed the bar and function room were already in darkness.

He came closer. 'I hope you don't mind, I wanted to do something, so I closed up for you. I've been here so long I know where all the light switches are.'

'Thank you,' she said, surprised and touched.

'And Lola will be all right?'

Anna nodded. 'I'm sure she will. It's us who nearly died of the shock.'

Richard looked concerned. 'Anna, can I make you a cup of tea? Or perhaps a hot chocolate? I know my way around the kitchen, I think. Would you like that? You must have had a terrible fright tonight.'

'Yes. Yes, I have. Thanks, Richard. That would be really kind of you.'

Then she burst into tears.

The blue station wagon pulled up in front of the motel.

'Thanks, Daniel,' Carrie said from the front passenger seat beside him.

'Yes. Thanks, Daniel,' Bett said from the back.

'I was happy to do it. You're both okay from here?'

'We're fine, thanks.' Bett managed to get in first.

'And will you tell Lola I was asking after her?'

'Of course.' Bett hesitated for a moment, wondering if this was the opportunity to speak to Daniel. She had to mention something about their night together, or the tension at work would be too much. But she couldn't do it now. Not with Carrie in earshot. Her sister already seemed to be taking what seemed like hours to undo her seatbelt and get out of the front.

They finally got out at the same time, standing side by side to wave as Daniel drove off. There was a long, awkward silence. Bett felt uncomfortable. Did she ask Carrie to stay for a cup of tea? Give her the chance to talk over the night? Surely she was feeling as shocked as Bett was?

Carrie took the decision away from her, reaching into her bag for her car keys. 'Anna's turned off the lights, I see, so I'll leave you to it.' Her voice was very brisk.

'Oh. Okay. Goodnight, then.'

'Yes. See you tomorrow.'

Bett walked to her room. Carrie walked to her car. Neither of them turned around, or noticed that the light was still on in the kitchen.

Chapter Twelve

'Fusspot.'

Anna grinned. 'Lola, I'm not a fusspot. I'm doing what the doctor told us to do, checking on you all the time.'

'Much ado about nothing, if you ask me.'

'Taming of the shrew, more like it.'

Anna stood by Lola's bed, looking down at her grandmother, sitting up against the pillows, her arm in a sling made from a wildly patterned silk scarf. Her bed jacket was a bright-yellow satin. There were bunches of flowers all over the room – they'd been arriving all day as word got around that Lola was out of hospital and back at the motel. She was wearing full makeup, the foundation applied around the bandage on her forehead. Anna could see she'd missed her mark slightly, a smear of blusher heavier on one cheek than the other, the lipstick wobbly. Lola had been keeping up a brave front since the accident, although her doctor had called Anna aside and told her to keep an eye out for delayed shock. So far there'd been no sign of it, though. Lola had spent the afternoon reading to Ellen and would still be at it if Anna hadn't prised them apart and put Ellen to bed.

Anna gently tucked the sheet in around her grandmother. 'Are you sure I can't get you anything before I go to rehearsals?'

'I'm fine, darling. Stop looking at me as if I'm some museum specimen.'

Anna sat down beside her and took her hand. 'You frightened us, you know.'

'I frightened myself.'

'Don't die, Lola. We wouldn't like it.'

'All right, darling, I promise I won't. Now, off you go to those rehearsals and make your poor sick grandmother proud of you.'

Anna had been gone only a minute or two before Carrie knocked lightly on the door and came in. 'Is everything all right, Lola? Do you need anything?'

'I couldn't be happier, darling. I should have done this months ago. All this spoiling, it's marvellous.' She patted the bed. 'Now, enough about me. Let me interrogate you for a quick minute. Are you coping with all the motel business while your parents are away? Do you need any extra help?'

'Everything's fine. No problems at all.' Carrie was enjoying it, in fact. It was giving her the opportunity to try out a few of her own ways of doing things.

'And how are things with Matthew?'

'They're fine,' she lied smoothly, picking up one of the Get Well cards on Lola's bedside table, concentrating fiercely on the greeting inside. It was from the ladies in the charity shop, wishing her a speedy recovery. Beside the cards was a large basket filled with fruit, chocolate and crossword puzzle books. Jim and Geraldine had sent it. 'He sends his love. Says he would have brought you a bunch of grapes if he'd been here.'

'If he'd been allowed to be here, you mean. Carrie, I've been thinking about the ban and I've decided it can be lifted. I think it would be all right now if he visited here again. In fact, I think Bett would like to see him.'

Carrie's head shot up. 'Has she said that to you?'

'No, but she doesn't need to. I know her. Has Matthew said anything?'

'He said he'd like to see Bett again too.' The words tasted awful in her mouth.

'Good. I'd hoped as much. I'll leave it up to you to arrange it. The sooner the better, I think.'

Carrie turned away before Lola saw her expression.

Lola had just gone back to her crossword after Carrie's departure when there was another knock. A dark curly head poked around the door. 'Lola? Are you okay?'

Lola smiled at her. 'Bett, darling, shouldn't you be at the rehearsal too?'

'I'm on my way. I got delayed with a late arrival at reception. I just wanted to check if you needed anything or if you wanted to come up and watch.'

'I couldn't bear the pain.'

'Oh, you poor thing. Shall I move one of the big armchairs in from the bar? You could rest your arm on that, if you liked.'

'Not the pain in my arm, the pain of seeing you all massacre my masterpiece.'

Bett relaxed. 'Very funny. You might be surprised. We've actually got a pretty good cast lined up.' Anna had spent the day after Lola's accident on the phone, handing out the parts as well as reporting on Lola's condition.

'Lola couldn't have timed it better if she tried,' she'd confided to Bett. 'People didn't dare say no to any of the parts, not knowing it was Lola's life's work. You don't suppose she did it deliberately?'

For once, Bett was sure she hadn't. She'd seen real pain and shock in Lola's eyes that night.

Anna had gone on. 'I asked that Daniel Hilder if he wanted to come and audition again, but he said no, unfortunately his circumstances had changed. Shame, he'd have been about the right age for that Jack-the-Lad character.'

'Yes, that is a shame,' Bett had said casually, relief flooding through her.

Lola was leaning back against her pillows, content. 'I can hardly wait until opening night. Tell me, Bett, are you ready to see Matthew yet?'

'You're asking me just like that? Haven't you got a little bell you can ring to warn me you're bringing up something personal?'

'Do you want to see him? I think you should. Get it over and done with. It will clear the air between you and Carrie.'

'Carrie and I are fine. All things considered.' They weren't, actually. Things may have been thawing between her and Anna, but they were definitely still covered in snow with Carrie.

'No, you're not. Not yet. Think about it, Bett. Remember my two rules.'

'Face your fears and tell the truth. Yes, I remember.' She leaned and kissed her grandmother. 'You know, you're lucky I love you so much or I'd call you an interfering meddlesome old bag.'

Lola laughed and returned to her crossword.

Anna smiled at everyone in the function room. There were fifteen people sitting in a circle of chairs all around her. Carrie was on one end. Bett sat nearby, at the piano, the sheet music piled beside her.

'So you've all got your scripts now? Good. And you're sure which parts you're playing? Yes? No more confusion over who's playing the General MacArthur role?' Two of the men studiously avoided looking at each other. 'Terrific. To get in the mood, I'd like you all to call each other by your characters' names while we're in rehearsals, okay? So we'll start today with a read through of the opening scene with you, Mrs MacArthur, and your son Arthur beside you.'

Mrs MacArthur, formerly known as Len the butcher's daughter Kaylene, smiled broadly at everyone. The thirteen-year-old boy playing the part of the four-year-old Arthur didn't look quite so happy. But a part was a part and he needed all the experience he could get if he eventually wanted to go to drama school. Or so his mother had told him.

Anna moved her chair to face them. 'As it says in the script, you are with your husband and father, General MacArthur, in a plane flying from the war in the Philippines on your way to Australia. A storm is raging all around you. There'll be the sound of gunfire as well as thunder and lightning, so it will be very dramatic.' She hoped it would be, anyway. Her first meeting with Len about the stage set hadn't filled her with confidence. She'd had to gently explain to him they would need more than clashing saucepan lids and glass jars filled with rice to make the storm effects.

'So, Mrs MacArthur, your young son hasn't been well and is feeling frightened, so to ease his terrors, you start singing "My Favourite Things" to him. Would you like to try that scene?'

Mrs MacArthur cleared her throat and looked down at the page.

'Poor-Arthur-you-must-be-scared-of-that-noise-don't-worry-I-know-how-to-put-a-smile-back-on-your-face.'

Anna had heard more animation from the speaking clock. 'That's a great start. But perhaps it would help if I could talk through some of the motivation with you.' She paused, thinking hard. 'Imagine the scene. You've been travelling with your husband and ill son for weeks, bombarded by war, homesickness, longing for the familiar, feeling cut off from everything you know and love – your home, your family.'

She stood up and started pacing the room, drawing on her own experiences as she'd been taught at drama school, thinking back to the latest angry phone call with Glenn. 'Is this what you wanted when you first got married, you ask yourself? Did you go into it with your eyes wide open? Or were you seduced by the thought of glamour and travel and social standing and allowed that to take over? Has your marriage become a shell? Your friends abandoned you because they are sick of the two of you fighting all the time? Is your child suffering?'

'Anna?'

'Do you cry yourself to sleep some nights through loneliness and fear and the pain of broken hopes and dreams?'

'Anna?'

Anna came to as Bett said her name even louder. The group was looking at her in some alarm. She steadied herself and briskly tapped the script. 'Or another simpler way of looking at it would be a mother singing her scared son to sleep. Bett, when you're ready. "My Favourite Things" from the top.'

At the break, Bett brought a glass of water over to her sister. 'Anna, are you okay?'

'Fine. Couldn't be better.'

Bett hesitated. There had been some uncomfortable echoes in Anna's words about Mrs MacArthur. Echoes from the big fight the night she had found out about Carrie and Matthew, when she had turned on Anna, and said terrible things about Glenn, about Glenn and Anna's marriage. Some of it almost word for word what Anna had said. Ever since Lola's accident she'd had an urge to talk about it all. To bring everything out in the open. To stop all this stepping around each other. 'It's just . . . what you were saying about Mrs MacArthur . . .'

Anna waited.

'Was it only about Mrs MacArthur?'

'Of course.' She gave a light laugh. 'My directors were always telling me off for going overboard with my motivation exercises.'

'Really?'

'Really.' Anna busied herself making notes on her script.

Say it, Bett, say it. 'You weren't talking about you and Glenn? It's just some of what you said . . .' She trailed off as she saw Anna visibly sit up straighter and her chin lift.

Bett backed off immediately. 'Never mind. I'll leave you to it.'

That night, Carrie was in the office when she heard a knock at the door. It was Bett. Carrie was surprised. So far they had done their best to avoid being alone together. 'Is everything all right? Lola's okay?'

'She's fine. Watching TV, complaining that her gin and tonic levels are way down and that she's going to have to get drunk for a week to bring them up again.' Bett hesitated. 'I actually wanted to talk to you about something else.'

'Oh. Okay. Come in.'

Bett took a seat and tried to choose the right words. Perhaps that was where she'd gone wrong with Anna earlier. She'd said it too bluntly. She tried to feel her way now. 'It's about Matthew.'

Carrie stiffened.

Bett couldn't help noticing. 'Carrie, I've been thinking about this a lot. I need to see him.'

'What do you mean "need"?'

'I think the three of us need to get together. Maybe Lola was right at the start to ask you to keep him away, but I'm staying on and, with the musical and everything, I think it's important.'

'You've been talking to Lola, haven't you?'

'Yes. But it's what I want, too.' Couldn't Carrie even meet her halfway on this?

'He's away for work,' Carrie said shortly.

'Then when he's back on the weekend.'

'He doesn't come back every weekend.'

'Well, on the weekend he does come back.'

Carrie was looking down at her paperwork again. 'I'll think about it.'

'I don't get it,' Bett whispered to Anna several minutes later. On the way back to her room, Bett had seen Anna's light on, and on the spur of the moment knocked gently on her door. Anna had seemed surprised, but beckoned her in, her finger on her lips. Ellen was asleep in the single bed. A book lay open on Anna's bed. 'What does she think I'm going to do, hurl myself at him when I see him? Manacle myself to his legs?'

'That would make sheep crutching a little tricky for him. You dragging around in the dust at his feet,' Anna whispered back.

'So much for Lola's advice,' Bett said, her voice still low. 'It's all very well to say face your fears but what if your fears don't want to be faced? I actually thought Carrie would want to get it over and done with too. But it's like she doesn't want me anywhere near him, in case I burst into tears and try and steal him back or something.'

'And you wouldn't, would you?'

'Wouldn't what?'

'Try and steal him back.'

'Sorry?'

'You wouldn't want him back, would you?

Bett tensed. 'I don't know.' A pause. 'I'm not sure how I'll react until I see him.'

'Still avoiding the truth after all these years, Bett?' Anna's tone was joking, but her eyes were serious.

Bett looked away. She didn't want to spoil this new fragile friendship with Anna. 'I mean it. That's why I need to see him.' She rushed to change the subject. 'So how did Ellie enjoy school today?' The little girl had started at the local school that week. They had all gathered to see her go off in her school uniform the first day, waving as if she was their own daughter.

Anna hesitated, then accepted the change of topic. 'Fine. She hasn't said much yet. It takes time to settle in, though. You remember what it's like, arriving at a new school in the middle of term.'

Bett nodded. The tension was definitely back between them. What did she do now? Try and break through it again? Ask about Glenn, when he was one of the main reasons she and Anna hadn't spoken in three years? She imagined Lola in the corner of the room, urging her on. 'How's Glenn, Anna?' The words came out sounding half chewed.

'He's fine,' Anna answered.

Bett knew her well enough to know that was the most Anna would say about it tonight. She watched as Anna went to the fridge, took out a bottle of wine and reached for the corkscrew. She didn't look like the mother of a seven-year-old, Bett thought. She looked amazing, in fact – the sleek straight hair, the perfect makeup, the thin, tanned body, not an ounce of extra flesh on her at all. And that cool poise she had, the keep-your-distance kind of elegance that

Bett knew she could never have, not in a million years. It suddenly seemed important to Bett to compliment Anna, to let her know how great she looked, to be the first to start building bridges. As Anna came over to the bed with the opened bottle and two glasses, she smiled up at her. 'Anna, you really are amazing.'

Anna's brow creased. 'Pardon me?'

'You look incredible. The perfect figure, perfect clothes, perfect hair, perfect skin, the perfect marriage, gorgeous little daughter, all so effortlessly.' Bett laughed, pleased with how it was all sounding. 'I'm sure the day will come when we're reading about the Anna Quinlan range of home and beauty products. Martha Stewart, watch out.'

To Bett's amazement, Anna wasn't amused. And she certainly didn't take it as a compliment. 'You think it comes easily? Effortlessly?' Her voice was still low but her eyes were furious. 'You think I am skinny by accident? No, Bett. It's called discipline and sometimes it's called starvation. Think my hair looks like this naturally? No, it costs a fortune once a month. And my perfect marriage?' Anna took a breath, ready to tell all – wanting to tell all, sick of the charade. 'Oh, yes, Bett, it is so perfect that I am –'

'Mummy?'

They both turned to see Ellen tossing around under her sheet, talking in her sleep or having a nightmare, Bett wasn't sure which. Anna put down the wine and moved swiftly over to her daughter, talking gently, stroking her forehead until she settled again. When all was quiet, she moved silently back.

Bett stood up, her voice almost a whisper. 'I'll go. I'm sorry to interrupt –'

'Bett, stay, please.' Anna looked very tired all of a sudden. 'She'll be fine. Please, don't go yet.'

They sat awkwardly for a moment, neither of them speaking. Bett shifted on the bed, wanting to apologise. She had been silly to assume things would fall into place so quickly. Two steps forward, one step back. She took a breath. 'Anna, I'm sorry for what I said about the way you look. It wasn't a dig, I promise. I know you work hard at it. I meant it as a compliment, really. It just came out wrong.' She seemed to have chosen exactly the right words for once. In front of her eyes, tension slipped out of Anna's body, the tight look around her mouth disappeared.

Anna gave an embarrassed smile. 'I'm sorry for snapping at you, too. I'm just really tired, I think. Ellen had nightmares again last night and I didn't sleep well.'

Bett gladly took up the change in subject. 'Does she have them often?'

'Not as often as she used to, but now and then still. She's reliving the attack, I think. And then she won't sleep until I read to her, or cuddle her or she hops into bed with me. Which means she sleeps like a log but I don't sleep at all. She favours the horizontal approach in bed, rather than the vertical.' She smiled again.

'She's been very brave. It must have been hard for her.'

'It was. It was hard for all of us.'

A shaft of guilt went through Bett. She should have been there to help.

Anna stood up, retrieved the wine and poured two glasses, passing one to Bett. 'If we're going to be whispering in the dark like old times, we may as well be drinking in the dark like old times too.'

Bett took the glass, surprised and pleased. 'Do you remember how furious Lola was that night?'

'We were under-age, I suppose. And it was Dad's best bottle of red.'

They sat in silence for a moment, before Anna spoke. 'So London was good? And Dublin?'

'It was, yes.' There it was, three years summed up in one sentence.

'You were working in a record company?'

Bett nodded. Lola had definitely acted as a conduit of news about each of them. 'And you're the voice behind every second ad on TV these days, I believe.'

Anna shrugged. 'Not exactly the Royal Shakespeare Company, but I enjoy it.' Another pause and then Anna spoke again. 'Bett, can I ask you something personal?'

Bett stiffened.

'Did you meet anyone in Dublin or London? Any men, I mean?'

Bett shook her head. On the plane she'd harboured a wish to invent a fantasy husband, a fantasy family, a whole family life to make this homecoming easier. She'd decided against it, knowing only too well Lola would demand photographic proof and all the intimate details. The sad truth was she hadn't met anyone she liked, or anyone who had liked her, either. She decided to keep her answer light. 'No. Still on the shelf. Destined to stay on the shelf, I suppose.'

'Bett, please don't talk like that. I'm sure you'll meet someone, when the right person comes along. Maybe even a nice country boy.'

Bett laughed softly, suddenly exhilarated by the pleasure of talking to Anna again. It was almost like old times – if she ignored the dozens of subjects they couldn't approach. 'That'd be ironic, wouldn't it? I spend three years in Dublin and London and all the time my dream man is waiting in my home town.' She'd been joking, but someone came to mind. 'Do you know who is nice? Richard, the Englishman here at the motel. I sat next to him at Lola's party and he's good company. Really witty. And have you seen when he smiles? It's like a transformation. His eyes get all sparkly. Anna, should I ask him out for a drink, do you think? Tonight, even?'

'I think he's out.'

'No, he's not. I saw him go into his room earlier. We said hello.' Bett stood up. 'Do you know what? I think I will. I'll ask him if he wants to go into town and have a drink with me.'

'No, Bett.'

'Why not?'

'I think there's a motorbike rally on in town. The pubs are jammed. It'll be terrible.'

'Oh.' Bett sat down again. 'Well, perhaps I'll have an early night.'

'Good idea. You look a bit tired. You look good,' Anna said hastily, 'just a bit tired.'

'I am, actually.' She stood up. 'Maybe I'll ask Richard out for a drink tomorrow night.'

'Go to bed, Bett.'

'All right.' She hesitated, then leaned over and kissed her. 'Thanks. It was very good to talk to you again.'

'I liked talking to you too.'

Bett let herself out, quietly closing the door. Anna sat down on her bed and breathed a slow sigh of relief.

Chapter Thirteen

In his room, Richard typed one more paragraph, then pressed the save button on his laptop computer. Good, he'd managed to get a lot done and still leave himself time to get ready.

As he stretched he looked with pleasure at the growing pile of paper beside him. It had been a good idea to come here. He was easily imagining his characters in the same landscape more than one hundred and fifty years earlier. The Clare Valley was like a wilder version of Tuscany, he'd decided. Rolling hills, vineyards, olive groves, old stone buildings and that incredible wide blue sky, day after day. He'd explored the towns and villages, and a good few of the wineries. He'd soaked up the scenery – the wooded hills, the gum trees silhouetted against the sky and the willow trees edging the dry creek beds. At sunset he'd watched the pink-chested galahs swoop in great flocks. He'd even started noticing the different smells, the gum leaves, the native flowers and the earth itself, baked hot under months of sunshine. The sounds were distinctive, too, the warbling of the magpies and the loud laughter of the kookaburras. It was all helping him get the details just right.

He had talked about writing a book for years, always expecting when he got down to it that it would be a long dark night of the soul. Instead, he'd discovered an interest – and a talent, if the responses from agents to his early chapters were anything to go by – for rollicking, fiction-based-on-fact adventures. He was basing his story on the life of an English petty criminal who had been shipped to Sydney, then escaped to the Clare Valley, where he'd hitched up with an Irish servant girl. The pair of them had gone on to quite a life of crime, before disappearing, either to new lives under assumed names, or to their deaths in the desert. Not exactly Bonnie and Clyde but not a long way off, either.

He said another silent thanks to his aunt, his father's only – and very wealthy – sister, who had died a year earlier, leaving Richard and his two sisters more than thirty thousand pounds each in her will. The money had come through six weeks after he had split with his long-term girlfriend, a reporter on the same newspaper in London. It had spurred him into making some big decisions – to get out of journalism, get out of London and make a real attempt at writing the novel.

He'd spent a month in Sydney before deciding to base himself in the Clare Valley. Not only would it give him a feel for the novel's other main setting, he'd decided it would be cheaper and have fewer distractions, too. He'd found the Valley View Motel on the Internet, liking the idea of a motel room overlooking a picturesque valley view. The motel hadn't quite lived up to its name, he thought with a grin. More Part of a Hill View than Valley View. But what had been happening as expected recently? He certainly hadn't thought he'd want to stay in the Clare Valley for this long. He hadn't expected to uncover such fascinating research material from the local history group. Or to come across such a character as Lola Quinlan. And he certainly hadn't expected to meet anyone so beautiful, or so fragile, or so entertaining as Lola's granddaughter.

There was a knock at the door. He opened it and smiled. 'Hello.'

'Hello.'

He turned and gestured extravagantly towards the small table set with a bottle of wine and two glasses. 'Please, come in.'

Anna smiled. 'Thank you. I'd love to.'

Out at the farmhouse, Carrie was lying in the middle of the double bed, wide awake. After she'd got back from work, she'd scrubbed the whole house and cleaned out the fridge. But she still wasn't tired and she still couldn't get her conversations with Bett and Matthew out of her head.

She'd taken out the photo of them again and looked at it for a long time. She'd thought about burning it, then told herself off for being childish. It wasn't going to change things if the photo didn't exist, was it? Matthew would still want to see Bett. Bett would still want to see Matthew.

From her position on the bed, she noticed a T-shirt had fallen between the wardrobe and the dressing table in the corner of the room. She hadn't noticed it before. She was over to it in a moment. It was one of Matthew's.

She didn't think twice. She stripped off her nightie and pulled his T-shirt over her head, breathing in his smell, feeling the cotton against her skin, trying to imagine how he felt when she hugged him.

It made her feel a bit better.

Anna let herself quietly back into her room. She went straight over to Ellen and kissed her gently. The little girl was still fast asleep.

She walked into the bathroom and started taking off her makeup. What an unusual night. And what an unusual man. She hadn't felt under any pressure. He hadn't made a pass at her or made her feel at all uncomfortable. They had just enjoyed a glass of wine and talked. The same way they had talked so easily the night of Lola's accident, when he had made her the hot chocolate. He was just so interested in everything, in what she did for a living, in what had happened to Ellen, in how long her parents had owned the motel.

'Are you a detective?' she'd asked him.

'No, I'm not. I'm a journalist trying to become a novelist.'

'That explains the questions. But why are you so nice? Are you gay?'

He laughed. 'No, I'm not gay either. Why are you so suspicious?'

'In my experience, people don't ask so many questions unless they're after something.'

'I'm interested because I'm interested in people. And I'm especially interested in people with such beautiful speaking voices.'

She had actually blushed.

'I've also discovered there's nothing to fuel the imagination like hearing other people's stories,' he said. 'So it's not so much curiosity as cannibalism. I'm feeding off you so I can write my own book.'

'Oh, in that case, that's fine.'

He'd understood completely when she had slipped away several times to check on Ellen, a few rooms away.

'Everything all right?' he'd asked each time.

'She's fast asleep,' she'd been able to answer.

'So you can stay a bit longer?' At her nod, he poured her some more wine. 'Then tell me some stories, Anna Quinlan.'

'About what?'

'Well, let me think. An easy one to start with. Tell me why there is so much tension between you and your sisters.'

'You noticed?'

'It's a little hard to miss. I don't think I've seen the three of you so much as have a cup of coffee together since you all got here. My own two sisters spend their entire time in a huddle whispering, so I was just curious . . .'

She hesitated. 'We had a bit of a fight three years ago.'

'About . . . ?'

She decided she wanted to tell him about it. 'Have you ever heard that song "Sisters" from the film *White Christmas*?'

He started to sing it, note perfect.

She raised an eyebrow. 'You know musicals off the top of your head? Are you sure you're not gay?'

He grinned. 'No, I just like old musicals. I can cook, too. So it was a mister who came between you and your sister?'

'No, not between me and my sister. A mister came between my two sisters. Well, moved from one of my sisters to the other, anyway. If you know what I mean. And married her instead.'

'Ah, I see. So that explains them. But what about you? How did you get caught up in it?'

Anna didn't want to spoil the mood by going into it. She was enjoying this gentle atmosphere too much. 'That's a story for another time. It's your turn to tell me some stories. Are you really writing a book or is that a cover story for something much more sinister?'

'I'm really writing a book. Trying to write a book, at least,' he'd said. 'And this is the perfect place to do it. The scenery is beautiful. The wine is delicious. And all the people I've met seem very interesting too.' He paused. 'One in particular, actually.'

'Really?' A look had passed between them. 'That's good.'

She smiled as she finished taking off her makeup and moved quietly back into the bedroom. She'd been flirting with him, she realised. And not only that, she'd enjoyed every minute of it. She kissed Ellen again and climbed into bed. The room was quiet for a few minutes and then she actually laughed out loud. She'd just caught herself lying there smiling into the dark like a teenager.

In her room next door, Bett couldn't get to sleep. First she'd been too hot, and then when she'd turned on the airconditioning, it had been too cold. All the noises outside seemed too loud – guests arriving back late, doors opening and closing in nearby rooms, the murmurs of night-time conversations.

Her mind was filled with thoughts of her sisters. It was strange to think that Anna was just metres away, Carrie a few miles away, home alone in the farmhouse that Bett still hadn't seen. The three of them were managing to work on a musical together, help run the motel together, yet the tension still hummed away between them. Bett knew that Lola was watching their every move, listening in to all the conversations she could, trying to gauge how things were going between them.

Bett had tried her best tonight. She'd broached the subject of Matthew with Carrie. She'd spoken to Anna about Glenn. But she wasn't feeling any better. She turned in the bed again. What else could she do to get rid of this tension between them? Challenge them to a duel?

She lay back, kicked at the sheets, then tugged at her pillow. She turned it over, feeling the cool side. She paused for a moment, then took the pillow in her hands, lifted her legs into the air and balanced the pillow across her feet. She glanced over at the clock and started timing herself. Less than a minute later her leg twitched and the pillow slid off. A very bad performance. She'd obviously lost her touch.

Perhaps that was the solution, though. She could invite Anna and Carrie into her room for a re-run of the Pillow Balancing

Competitions they'd enjoyed as children. She lifted the pillow onto her feet again, remembering the first time they played it, at a different motel but on a hot summer night just like this one. They'd been forced for space reasons to share a dormitory-style room. The windows had been left wide open and the girls were lying in bed dressed only in T-shirts, trying to keep cool. It had been too hot to sleep, too hot to do much at all.

Bett, fourteen at the time, had turned her pillow first one way, loving the brief feeling of coolness against her face, then turned it back. Before a few minutes had passed, it was warm again. 'It needs a constant supply of air on it,' she said out loud.

'What?' Anna said, engrossed in a book. In the bed between them Carrie was asleep.

'Nothing,' Bett said, preoccupied now. She gave up on turning the pillow and instead wriggled down in the bed and stuck her legs straight up in the air. Then she reached up and balanced the pillow across her feet. A few minutes later she was still like that and very pleased with herself indeed. 'Anna?' she whispered again.

Anna didn't look up. 'Mmm?'

'Bet you I can balance a pillow like this for ages.'

That earned a glance from Anna. 'Well, that's really going to get you a place in the Moscow Circus.'

'It's harder than it looks. You try it. It actually takes great staying power and balancing skills.'

'How long do I have to do it for?' Anna said, grunting a little as she reached up and put her pillow in place. Hers wasn't as firm as Bett's, and hung saggily over her feet. 'Hold on. It's not an even competition yet.' Leaning over, she pulled out Carrie's pillow with a tug.

'Ow, what?' Carrie opened her eyes, face crumpled, as if she was about to cry. 'Anna, give that back.'

'I can't, sorry. I need it for equipment.'

Carrie looked around blearily, noticing Bett with her legs sticking upright, a pillow atop of them, and then Anna, getting into position to do the same thing. 'What are you doing?'

'It's the Annual Quinlan Pillow Balancing Competition. First heats start today,' Bett said matter-of-factly. 'And I am winning by a long shot. I'm miles ahead of you.'

Carrie reached over and snatched the spare pillow off Anna's bed, putting it on her feet.

Anna moved the lamp onto the floor and angled the clock so she could read the time. 'Okay, starting in ten seconds. Pillows in position. Go.'

They lay like that for several minutes before Carrie spoke up. 'It's a bit boring.'

'It is not,' Bett's voice was as indignant as possible in her physical position. 'It's a combination of balance and concentration. You just can't stick it.'

'Can so. It's easy.'

Bett shot her a glance. Carrie was looking remarkably relaxed. 'It's easy for you. Your legs are shorter, so there's less muscle to ache.'

'Yours have got more fat, and fat rises, so it should be easier for you.'

Anna quickly stepped in. 'Carrie's right. It is a bit boring. Let's make it more interesting.'

'I know,' Bett said, trying to take back control of her game. 'You have to do something while you're balancing the pillows.'

'Like what?'

'Like, I don't know, doing something revolting with your face. See, like this.' Bett pulled her eyes down with one hand and grimaced, pushing her nose up with the other hand.

Anna looked at her blankly. 'I thought you were going to do something revolting with your face.'

'I am,' Bett said in a voice muffled by the contortions.

'You look the same to us, doesn't she, Carrie?'

'Just the same,' Carrie agreed happily.

'A little prettier than normal, if anything. Are you wearing makeup, Bett?'

Bett just poked out her tongue. 'Go on, Anna. You do something if you're so smart.'

'Okay, then.' She thought for a second. 'Right, I'll be a bat. Listen.' She started making a high-pitched noise, the noise getting louder and louder, unrelenting, ignoring Bett and Carrie's protests until Bett finally threw a book at her. Anna's pillow toppled, with Carrie's tumbling seconds afterwards.

Bett leapt up, holding her pillow above her head. 'I win. Champion of the Pillow Balancing. Out of my way, vermin, and let me take a victory leap.' She leapt from her bed onto Carrie's, badly misjudging the distance and landing square on Carrie's leg. Carrie set up a terrible wailing.

Anna hissed at her. 'Carrie, shush. You'll get Lola in here.'

Carrie didn't shush. 'I don't care. She's broken my leg, the big fat pig.'

'I have not broken it.'

'You have. It was like a ton of bricks fell on me.'

Stung, Bett turned on her sister. 'It was not. If I'd meant to do it, you would have felt it, believe me. Like this.' With that, she leapt onto Carrie's bed again, this time deliberately and twice as firmly landing on her sister's leg.

Carrie set off a squealing to rival any high-pitched bat noise of Anna's. The door flung open and the light switched on. Lola was standing there. 'For heaven's sake. What is going on here? Your parents could probably hear you from the bar. Carrie, would you shut up? You're behaving like a baby over there.'

'Bett stepped on me,' she said through the tears, her voice shuddering. 'She nearly broke my leg.'

Bett was now in bed, all innocent eyes. 'God, Carrie, stop exaggerating all the time.'

Lola wasn't interested in either side of the story. 'I don't care how it happened. Shut up and go to sleep, all of you. I shouldn't have to remind you you've got a concert tomorrow. You're supposed to be having an early night. Anna, you're the oldest. Try and get them to behave, would you?'

The light snapped off and the three lay still.

'I'll get you for that, Bett,' Carrie hissed, the sobbing miraculously over.

'I'll get you first for dobbing on me, you big baby. I'm going to ask Mum to put the cot back in the room for you. You're obviously too young to sleep in a bed yet.'

'Anna, make Bett stop picking on me.'

'Shut up, the pair of you. I need my beauty sleep.'

'Pig.'

'Baby.'

'Pig.'

'Baby.'

The taunts had gone back and forth in the dark bedroom until one or the other of them had finally fallen asleep.

Bett turned over in bed again. It was a strange thing. She wasn't actually sure whether the memory of those times together made her feel good or bad. In the past few weeks it had been getting harder to tell the difference.

Chapter Fourteen

Sitting on a comfortable chair in front of her room the following morning, Lola closed her eyes in the sunshine, feeling like a tired old cat snoring on a windowsill. A tired satisfied old cat, at least. Broken wrist and banged head aside, things were going well. She'd managed to get the musical underway, send Geraldine and Jim off on holiday, and get the girls working together in the motel. There was the little matter of getting Matthew back on the scene, getting the reunion out of the way, but that day was drawing closer, Lola knew.

So now what did she do with herself? The best way to keep the mind alert was to keep it occupied, her doctor had said. She needed another project, something else to do. This morning she'd been reading her new copy of *Ireland's Treasures*, the magazine sent airmail to her each week, hoping that might spark some idea. It had arrived the previous day, along with a postcard from Geraldine and Jim in Alice Springs. The pair of them sounded like they were having the time of their lives.

She winced at a sudden wailing noise of a fire siren coming up the valley from the town. So much for the tranquillity of living in the country. If it wasn't the siren, it was the gas guns keeping the birds away from the vineyards, or the tractors or the tankers rumbling up the roads.

Perhaps this was a false alarm or perhaps some poor devil had gone and set his house on fire. She'd drop into the charity shop that morning, find out what she could. The son of one of her co-workers was one of the fire service volunteers. 'Do they actually respond to the noise of that siren?' Lola had asked once. 'What if they're in the middle of something, a good movie or nice sex, for example? Can they pretend they didn't hear anything?'

'Lola!' The woman had been shocked. 'Of course they can't pretend. It's calling them. They have to answer it.'

Such a good method, Lola thought again now, looking down the road seeing several cars speeding into town, either volunteers or sticky-beaks on their way to the fire station. She'd often wished she had something similar to sound when she had a good idea, or wanted to tell the girls something. Or indeed, wanted them home after too late a night out. Not a screechy wail, though – perhaps a blast of Cole Porter or the opening notes of Glenn Miller's 'In the Mood'.

A shout from Carrie broke into her thoughts. 'Bumper, come here! Come here, you brat.'

Oh dear, Lola remembered. She'd forgotten to tie Bumper up again yesterday. She and Ellen had been leading him around from one new patch of grass to another.

'Bumper, you stupid sheep, come here.'

This sounded entertaining. Lola slowly rose out of her seat and walked around the corner of the building just in time to see Carrie chasing after Bumper. The sheep was well and truly spooked, ramming blindly into the crates of beer bottles and rubbish bins in the back of the motel. Carrie called out as she caught sight of her. 'This is your fault, Lola.'

'No, it's not. I didn't invent sheep.'

'You know what I mean. You know how crazy he goes when he hears loud noises.'

'I didn't know there was going to be a fire.'

'Well, help me tie him up, will you? Before he does any more damage.'

'I'm far too old and frail to be chasing sheep.'

'Can I help, Auntie Carrie?' Ellen had heard the fuss from her room. 'Bumper likes me, doesn't he, Lola?'

'He certainly does, darling.'

Carrie winced at the sound of more crashing bottles. 'Sure, Ellie. Give it a try. God knows I'm sick of chasing the silly animal.'

Ellen moved closer to the bottles and loudly and clearly started calling out to the sheep. 'Bumper, come here to me. Here, Bumper.'

Carrie started laughing. Ellen was not just imitating Lola's calls but also her Irish accent.

Ellen was oblivious. 'Here, Bumper. Everything's all right. Come here to me now, my darling.'

Carrie wasn't sure whether it was Ellen's cooing or the fact that the fire siren had suddenly stopped, but Bumper calmed down enough for Ellen to lay her hand on his back and take hold of his collar. With his hooves making little clacking noises on the concrete, she led him over to Carrie. 'There you are,' she said, a smile lighting up her entire face.

'Ellen, you are a genius.' Carrie shook her head in amazement, before taking Ellen by one hand and holding the sheep firmly in the other.

The fun over, Lola returned to her seat in the sunshine and picked up the magazine again, stopping to read a fascinating article about the Lisdoonvarna Matchmaking Festival in County Clare.

An annual event, when bachelor farmers would come down from the hills and meet young ladies in the genteel surroundings of tea dances and elegant lunches. So civilised. One of the matchmakers spoke proudly of his track record – hundreds of marriages, nearly as many engagements. He didn't mention any separations or divorces. It sounded like good fun, Lola thought. Perhaps she could suggest to Geraldine and Jim that they start up something similar here in the Valley. There were already plenty of connections between the town of Clare and County Clare in Ireland. They already exported wine from Australia to Ireland. Perhaps Ireland could ship over a few dozen bachelors in return?

She put down the magazine as Richard Lawrence walked towards her, dressed in shorts and a T-shirt. Lola waved and beckoned him over. He was quite the fitness fan, it seemed. Back from the gym again. Almost as bad as Anna. No wonder he had been so snake-hipped at the party. It had been good to see him and Bett chatting away too, the couple of times she had looked over. They had a lot in common – journalism, London . . .

'Morning, Richard,' she said as he came closer.

'Good morning, Lola.'

'It does the heart good to see a fit young man like yourself out in the air.'

'Young man?' He grinned. 'Don't make me worry about your eyesight now, will you?'

'Oh, you're just a child in my eyes. Tell me now, will you pop in a little later? I've a bottle of gin that I need help opening. Those caps are very tight these days. Around four? Perfect.'

She waved him off as a blue station wagon came up the drive. Lola watched as Daniel Hilder climbed out with a load of newspapers. Bett had chosen her one-night stand well, she thought with a wicked smile. He certainly wasn't fashion catalogue handsome, but there was something so attractive about him. A pair of laughing eyes took a man a very long way, she'd always thought. She had so enjoyed their little chat the other day. If there was one thing she liked, it was a young man with a bit of wit about him. He'd shown such interest in the photos she'd taken out for him, as well. He'd also done a very efficient job of straightening the shower rose and re-hanging the painting. Too efficient, really, for her purposes. She had a feeling there was a bit more there to discover.

She'd recalled afterwards that she had seen his mother in the charity shop now and then in the early days. Making donations, not shopping, of course. The distinction was important for some people. She remembered Mrs Hilder as a well-to-do woman. Very well-spoken, always elegant, beautifully turned out. One of the matching shade of lipstick, nail polish, bag and shoe women. How they did it, Lola just did not know. She glanced down at that day's outfit, her culottes and tunic ensemble. About fifteen different colours fighting for prominence, none of them winning. What had one of the charity shop women said to her once? 'Lola, you always look so different.' 'I suppose you mean different as in terrible,' she had replied, to the woman's horror. Lola laughed at the memory.

Bett came into view, pushing the cleaning cart loaded with soaps, teabags and fresh linen. Lola watched as she took out the master key and let herself into one of the rooms to do her share of the cleaning. Dear girl, it was so good to have her home again. She had been so rocked by the business with Matthew. In Lola's opinion, it had been a narrow escape. Funnily enough, she had always felt Carrie and Matthew made a much better pair than Bett and Matthew. She had held her tongue on the matter for once, though. She'd held high hopes that Bett would meet someone in Melbourne, or Dublin, or London. Someone with a bit more spark than Matthew. But it hadn't happened. Bett was still single. Madness. What were the men of the world thinking letting a fine woman like her run free?

Moments later Daniel Hilder stepped lightly down the front steps and climbed back into his car. Lola could see him checking something in a folder beside him. In a few minutes he would drive right past her room, on to the next delivery.

She re-read the quote from the matchmaker. 'It's a simple process. We interview all the single men and then we interview all the single women, and then we decide who would be best suited to who. We don't rush into it, either – it's a matter of getting to know people, assessing their suitability before we bring them together.'

She started to smile. The Valley View Motel Matchmaking Festival might not have the same ring as Lisdoonvarna, but the principles were the same, surely? Find a single man who suits your single woman and bring them together. Her smile broadened. She'd already arranged to talk to Richard this afternoon. If she got Daniel now, that would be the two of them done in the same day. Very efficient. As for Bett, well, she didn't need to interview her, did she? She already knew her granddaughter inside out.

Rising as swiftly as her old bones would allow, she moved inside, picked up the cane she used occasionally for walking and knocked the painting off the wall, wincing as it crashed to the floor. Just as well their budget hadn't stretched to glass frames. As the sound of a car started up, she returned to the doorway, waving madly with her good arm.

Daniel slowed the car to a stop beside her, wound down the window and smiled. 'Lola, hello. You're looking very well again.'

'Pulling the devil by the tail, as we say at home. Daniel, you're heaven sent without a doubt. That blasted painting has fallen down again. Could you spare a moment, do you think?'

She smiled to herself as he turned off the engine. This might be even more fun than writing the musical.

The next day, Bett was driving back to the *Valley Times* office with Daniel. They'd spent the afternoon following one of the Valley's young winemakers around his small winery, as he showed them the process from grape to bottle. At the end of the session, Daniel had handed over the digital camera and watched as she flicked through his shots. They were good, a bit quirky, with plenty of action and interest in them. Rebecca would be very pleased.

Bett was pleased with herself, too. So far today she'd managed to stay quite composed in his company. She'd tasted a glass of the new shiraz without spilling it everywhere. Even better, she'd had several conversations with him without turning bright red. Perhaps deep down she actually was a mature grown-up.

The car radio was playing the new single from the country's latest manufactured pop band. He turned it up. 'Great, one of my favourites.'

'You're kidding.'

He had a glint in his eye. 'To tell you the truth, I can't decide between this lot and the all-girl band formed after that supermarket reality show.' He pressed the button to change stations. A screaming punk song filled the car. Bett winced.

Daniel noticed and turned it down. 'I take it you weren't ever a punk?'

She shook her head. 'Why? Were you?'

'For a whole six months. I even changed my name.'

'You didn't.'

'It was written in studs on the back of my best denim jacket. Danger Hilder. I was extremely scary for a twelve-year-old.' He grinned. 'So you were never spiky-haired? Covered in safety pins?'

'No. Unfortunately I reached my teenage years in time for fluorescent socks and sweat bands.'

'Ah yes. I think I may have seen a photo from that time.'

Had he been at Lola's birthday party? No, she was sure he hadn't been. Colour raced up her neck into her face. There was only one other way he could have seen them. 'Has Lola shown you the Alphabet Sisters photos?'

He nodded solemnly. 'Quite a lot of them, actually. She's very proud of you, isn't she?'

'That's it. I'm going to break into her room and burn them.'

'You'll never find them. She had them hidden in books and under boxes all over her room. "I have to hide them or the girls would have them spirited away in seconds."'

She had to laugh at his good impression of Lola. His mobile rang before she could say anything more. He pulled over to take the call and she took the opportunity to have a good look at him. He was probably thirty-five or thirty-six by now, she guessed. She thought she remembered him celebrating his thirtieth birthday just after she'd first joined the *Valley Times*. They had only worked together on a few jobs, but she'd occasionally spoken to him in the pubs, or in restaurants around the Valley. He'd had a girlfriend at the time, hadn't he? One of the high-school teachers, if memory served her right. And she had been going out with Matthew. Engaged to Matthew, even.

Back then, she'd always found him easy to work with. It had been the same today. Bett had interviewed the winemaker while Daniel strolled the property taking photographs, like a normal journalist and photographer team. The only difference being they'd had a night of wild sex three years ago and not mentioned it since. She decided she had to bring it up today. Get it out of the way. Into the open, as Lola would advise.

He finished the call, from one of the other reporters on the paper setting up a photo shoot for the next day. 'Sorry about that,' he said.

'No problem.' She decided to launch straight into it. 'Daniel, before you start the car, I think there's something we need –' She was interrupted by the ringing of his mobile again.

He glanced at the display screen. 'Sorry, Bett. I'll need to get this.'

It was obviously a personal call. He got out of the car and walked a short distance away. Her window was already wound down and snippets floated in. He was soothing someone by the sound of things. Listening a lot and then reassuring the caller. She wasn't close enough to hear any more. 'I'll see you tonight. Okay. Bye.'

He got back into the car. 'Sorry, Bett. You were about to say something?'

She noticed his mood had changed, become more serious. She lost her nerve. 'It doesn't matter.'

'Are you sure?'

'Sure.'

He started the car and they had driven for a little while before he spoke. 'That thing you were about to say. Was it about that night in Melbourne, by any chance?'

'Yes. Yes, it was.' Was that squeak really her voice?

'I wondered which of us would bring it up first.' He was still serious. 'Bett, it's all right. I'm a grown man. I got over it.'

'You got over it?' Had it been that bad? Something that had to be got over?

'Of course,' he said. 'It wasn't the first time and I'm sure it won't be the last time.'

That he had a one-night stand? 'Really?'

'Yes, really. Honestly, don't give it a moment's thought.'

She was feeling worse, not better. 'I thought I had to mention it, at least. You know, now that we were working together. In case you were thinking . . .' she trailed off. In case you were thinking that I was an old slapper who would jump into bed with you at any opportunity. She couldn't say it.

They were coming into the town now. 'Bett, it's okay. I got the message in Melbourne. So please don't feel awkward working with me.'

What message? She hadn't left him a message. She'd been so embarrassed she'd crept out without even waking him.

His phone rang again and he answered it without pulling over. 'Hi, Rebecca. About five minutes away. No worries. I'll drop Bett at the office and head straight out there.' He turned to her. 'Sorry, Bett. Do you mind? That fire out at the old quarry has flared up again. Rebecca wants me to go straight there.'

'Of course.' They were silent as they drove up the main street of Clare. He deftly pulled in behind one of the tall trees sending out splashes of shade onto the hot bitumen.

'See you later, then.'

'Yes, see you.' She got out of the car so quickly she nearly tripped.

The following night the cast was once again gathered in the function room. Bett's hands were folded in her lap. She'd given up playing any of the songs. Carrie was in the middle of the group, looking mutinous. Anna was in front, extremely unhappy.

'General MacArthur, have you actually looked at the script since our last rehearsal?'

'I intended to, Anna, I really did. But I had trouble with the dam at the end of the bottom paddock, and I ran out of time.'

'And what about you, Mrs MacArthur?'

'I looked at it. But the school fair was this week, and I had to choose between making three dozen fairy cakes or learning my lines.'

Anna looked from one cast member to the next.

'The dog ate my script.'

'The cat weed on my script.'

'I got called away to fight a fire at the old quarry.'

Anna sighed, put her hands on her hips, exasperated. 'I bet a million dollars Andrew Lloyd Webber never hears excuses like this.' Everyone laughed. That was the whole problem, she realised. No one was taking it seriously. What would Lola do if she was here? Whatever was necessary, she guessed. She'd have to do the same.

She stood up, composed herself, mentally searched through her voice repertoire until she found the most cajoling one and then coughed politely to get everyone's attention. Speaking persuasively, she started talking about General MacArthur, about what he had meant to people during the war. She reminded them all about Lola's dream, about the need for a new ambulance, about the highs and lows of acting, about pride, belief in your work, determination.

Good heavens, Bett thought. She felt a verse of 'Climb Every Mountain' coming on.

Carrie wasn't listening. She'd learnt her lines days ago. She'd had nothing else to do in the lonely house once she got home from work. She and Matthew had tried to have another conversation on the phone that afternoon. It had ended in disaster again. Another row. More shifting blame. It was getting to the stage where they nearly hung up before they said hello to each other.

She shot a glance at Bett. They'd hardly spoken a word to each other since that night in the office. It was all very well for Bett to say she wanted to see Matthew. What was she supposed to do? Produce him out of a hat? Say, 'Here, Bett, have him back?' She longed to ask Lola's advice, but that would mean telling her the whole story of their separation. She couldn't bear the shame of it. If only there was some way of making things all right between her and Matthew again. She turned away as Bett looked up and caught her eye. She stared rigidly at the script, pretending to be concentrating on Anna's speech.

'So, please, all of you,' Anna said passionately, her voice husky by this stage. 'Please have your lines and the words of your songs learnt before our next rehearsal. We've only got a few weeks to put this together, remember. And I want to say again how much it would mean to my elderly grandmother to see her dream brought to the stage.' She lowered her voice. 'You all know about the accident, and it does worry me how frail she has become, that she is losing her already tenuous grip on life. I think it would give her a real boost and I hope you'll all give it your best shot.'

She gazed around. Was that woman on the left crying? Oh dear, perhaps she'd gone a little too far. 'So, Bett, let's try "Chattanooga Choo Choo", from the top.'

In her room at that moment, Lola took a long sip of her gin and tonic and pointed the remote control at the CD player. She did love singing along with those old show tunes. There was nothing like them to buoy the spirit. But now it was break over and time to get back to work.

Settling herself more comfortably in the armchair, she put on her glasses and studied the two rather wobbly handwritten lists on the page in front of her. She wished she'd thought of doing this years ago. Who'd have thought there could be such entertainment in the little matter of getting two people together?

She had followed the matchmaker's guidelines to the letter. First, draw up a shortlist of available suitors. Hers was short, just the two names. Then draw up a list of their attributes. She'd done that too, based on her interviews, formal and informal, over the past little while. They were similar in some ways. Both seemed very kind, with lovely senses of humour and the necessary glints in their eyes. They both had a bit of life experience behind them, too – always a good thing. They'd both lived in the city, but had chosen to be in the country for the time being – also a good thing.

Now all she had to do was make her final choice. It was hard enough, with both of them having so much going for them. She read the lists again. It was close, certainly, but she was veering towards the one on the left. Yes, she decided firmly. He was the one.

All her project needed now was a name. It finally came to her and she wrote it carefully on the folder.

Operation Richard and Bett.

Chapter Fifteen

At home in the farmhouse two nights later, Carrie poured a glass of wine and moved from the living room to the bedroom, then back into the kitchen, trying to decide where to do it. It didn't help that there were traces of Matthew everywhere – a pair of boots in the hallway, his Driza-Bone jacket on the back of the door. And memories in each of the rooms too. The painting they had bought in Adelaide not long after they were married. The lamp she had admired in an antique store up north one weekend they'd been away, which Matthew had gone to such trouble to get for her as a surprise, driving three hours there and back. The hall cupboard the two of them had spent weeks sanding back, only to find the wood underneath in such bad condition they'd had to paint it all over again.

She finally settled on the kitchen. She pulled a chair up to the wooden table, reached into her bag and took out the magazine. She'd seen it in the newsagents in town that morning, its glaring coverline talking directly to her – *How To Save Your Marriage.* She'd bought a whole selection of other items to pad all around it – pens and writing pads, even a *Your Garden* magazine – so the woman behind the counter, whose wedding she had helped organise, wouldn't guess.

'You looking for a new man, Carrie?'

She had nearly leapt out of her skin. 'No, Matthew's fine. He's just away for work for a while.'

'Don't want him to catch you looking at that, then.'

'No.' She was flaming red by that stage. It was only when she'd got into the car she realised what the woman was talking about. *Fifty Most Eligible Bachelors. Tasty touch-me-now photos inside!*

She skimmed past the perfume ads, the fashion pages and the eligible bachelors until she reached the *How to Save Your Marriage* article. Please let it be a matter of mixing up a quick potion of pomegranate seeds and vinegar, or chanting over an old photo of the two of them, she thought. She realised a little guiltily that most of their photos were in a bag in the shed where she had thrown them after the last row. Still, at least she hadn't ripped them up. She corrected herself. At least she hadn't ripped all of them up.

She skim-read the introduction to the article. *Do you feel the gloss has gone out of your relationship?* Not just the gloss. The relationship had gone out of the relationship. *Don't know where it went wrong?* She shifted uncomfortably. Next question. *Have things really changed for the worse?* That was easy.

Then try this exercise to get in touch with your feelings. Sit quietly, and recall the early days of your relationship. Think about everything that first attracted you to him, and him to you. Remember your first touch, your first kiss, the first time you made love. Let the memories wash over you. Let go of any anger you may feel now. Let go of any hurts or misunderstandings. Take your mind back to your early days, remembering the wonderful first moments of attraction.

Carrie moved the chair further back from the table, shut her eyes and concentrated. She opened an eye, and read the last line again.

Take your mind back to your early days, remembering the wonderful first moments of attraction. That she could do, at least. It had been the first night she met him, when she got home from her overseas trip. At first, in all the fuss of arriving, her luggage everywhere, the talk and the chat with her parents and Lola, he'd just been Bett's fiancé – medium height, sandy brown curls. Solid looking. But later, in the pub where Bett had insisted on taking her, something had happened between them.

Jetlagged, exhilarated to be home, she remembered being in teasing form. 'Normally, Matt – I can call you Matt, can't I? I mean, we're practically brother and sister. Normally, Matt, I'd have got to know you slowly, vetted you to make sure you were good for my sister, but I'll just have to do a crash course now. You're studying to be a vet, I believe. That's good, a steady job. Now, let me see. What sort of a physical specimen are you? Should I check him out, Bett?'

'Go right ahead,' Bett had said, laughing at her.

She patted him down, commenting all the while. 'Yes, fine shoulders, a lovely broad chest, oh yes, good, a flat stomach too.' Bett was enjoying it, Carrie thought. 'And he's got terrific legs, Bett, hasn't he?' She touched them as well, felt firm muscle under the dark denim. Did her hands brush against his upper thigh deliberately? 'Yes, he's gorgeous, Bett. He'll do very well.'

All laughter and joking, standing there arms around one another, Bett in front of them. But as she sat down, just for a moment there was an exchange of glances between her and Matthew. The laughter had gone out of his eyes and there was a flash of desire. She saw it. She felt the same thing in herself. A tiny spark, the quickest of flickers between them. And then some other friends came up and the night changed, became casual.

Except she remembered it the next day. It was probably jetlag, she told herself. Or the pleasure of touching a man again. She'd gone travelling with a boyfriend through Asia but they had broken up in Vietnam, after fighting in Laos, making up in Cambodia and spending three months rowing as they travelled through Thailand. In Bali she'd had a brief affair with a practised Portuguese man, who had certainly taught her a few bedroom tricks as well as some filthy Portuguese words, but that had been months ago.

In the first few weeks the tension between her and Matthew masqueraded as simple teasing between a brother-in-law- and sister-in-law-to-be, encouraged by the whole family. But it was more serious than that, even from the start. There had been genuine interest in one another, wanting to talk to each other. If Matthew came to collect Bett to go somewhere, he always made a point of seeking Carrie out, just for a few moments of conversation. If she heard his voice, she too would find herself going to him, wandering in almost casually, teasing, joking, on the surface.

Once or twice there was casual physical touch – when Matthew was holding a door open for her, or passing something to her at a family dinner. Just the swiftest whisper of skin against skin. With another person she might not have noticed. With Matthew it was as if all her senses had sprung to attention. Nothing was said, but the contact became something they would engineer. At a family picnic, when Anna, Glenn and Ellen were home one weekend, they all piled into one car. Bett was driving. In the back, Carrie needed to sit on Matthew's knee, Anna, Glenn and Ellen squeezed in beside them, Lola in the passenger seat in front. Had any of them noticed the effect the physical contact had on her and on Matthew? The touch was like exquisite pain to Carrie, feeling his thighs beneath her, the brush of his hand against her bare arm. He slowly moved his left arm so it was almost around her waist. Just as slowly, she lowered her hand so it was on top of his arm. She felt the sunshine on it, her breathing change. Everyone's attention was on Ellen, three years old at the time, and delirious with too much soft drink and attention, squealing each time they turned a corner, their bodies moving from side to side with the momentum. Carrie felt a slow burning between her and Matthew with each motion. When they finally arrived back at the motel, she climbed out quickly. There was just a quick glance between them, loaded with meaning.

He felt the same way, she learned afterwards. It got to the stage that she knew he was in the motel, somewhere nearby, a sort of tingling, humming between them. But he's Bett's fiancé, she told herself.

Remember your first kiss . . .

It happened the day he drove her to the agricultural college with him. She'd been trying to decide whether to do a course, and it was Bett who suggested she make the trip with Matthew. She was aware of dressing more carefully, choosing the pale-blue dress that looked good against her brown skin and blonde hair, the strands even lighter after the long hot summer. Bett waved them off.

They drove for an hour perhaps, not even halfway there, the teasing conversation rippling between them. She felt intensely conscious of her own body, the hem of her dress lifting a little as she moved her legs, crossed them once or twice, knowing Matthew was noticing. She had a bug to thank for the first contact. Feeling hot, she had wound the window down. An insect had blown in, right at her face.

'Oww,' she said. 'Something flew into my eye.'

He pulled over right away, their car the only one on the long straight road. He unbuckled his seatbelt, leaned across. 'Let me see.'

His hand was on her face, his face closer than it had ever been.

There was a moment when all the tension between them seemed to tighten and contract until they were no longer apart but lips on lips, bodies pressed as close as possible.

She pulled back first, reluctantly, eyes wide. 'We can't.'

Matthew didn't answer her, just looked at her in a way she had never been looked at before. Her stomach turned somersaults, and she didn't say anything as he leaned towards her again, the kiss softer, more exploratory, but deeper and sexier than the first one.

A car went past, the driver honking the horn at them. It broke the spell. He pulled away. Looked ahead.

Carrie looked ahead too. 'I'm sorry.'

He made a noise somewhere between a laugh and a sigh. 'I am too.'

They kept looking forward.

'We should keep driving.'

They did, silently for ten minutes, and then his hand came off the steering wheel and crossed the seat, meeting hers. His voice was soft. 'Carrie, I have never felt about anyone the way I feel about you.'

She understood what he meant.

'I don't feel about Bett the way I feel about you.'

'It's wrong. You're Bett's fiancé.' It was hard to say, when the touch of his hand was sending what felt like sparkling explosions into her bloodstream. She placed his hand on her thigh, and heard the little intake of breath. She thought of Bett again, and then consciously, forcibly, blanked her out. This wasn't about Matthew and Bett any more. It was about the two of them and what was happening here.

'You feel it too, don't you?'

She nodded.

'We need to talk about this.'

Ahead there was a sign pointing to a camping ground just off the main road. He turned in. The park was sheltered, too early in the morning, even on a hot day, for anyone to be there. He got out. She got out after him. They stood against the railing, looking down into the dry creek bed, not speaking, the only sounds the crackle of wind through the peeling bark on the gum trees, the warbling of magpies. The sun was hot on her skin.

She touched his arm and he flinched as though it had burnt him. But the movement had set the tension buzzing between them again. She felt her own body respond, felt her breasts strain against her clothes, wanting to touch him again. This had to be right, this had to be real, Bett or no Bett.

He moved first, running a hand gently from the shoulder strap of her dress down her arm. She breathed in deeply. Closed her eyes. He moved his hand, repeating the touch. She felt every nerve-ending in her skin respond. She didn't move, just breathed, as he traced the neckline, his hand brushing against her breasts.

And then she did the same thing to him, ran her hand down the length of his arm, then his other arm, touching the skin, feeling the little hairs. Then her fingers moved from the neckline of his T-shirt, down over his chest, his stomach, and lower, enough to hear a sharp intake of breath.

It became a slow, intense trade of pleasure, taking it in turns, not speaking. He moved towards her, touching her dress, tracing her breasts through the material. It was all she could do not to push herself against him.

Staring into his eyes, she was intensely aware of all the sensations around her, the heat of the sun, the slightest of breezes, the hum of insects. She touched his body again, running her hand over his stomach, over the denim of his jeans, watching the response in his eyes, a darkening of his pupils as she cupped him, stroked him gently.

'We can't. We have to stop this,' she whispered, as he held her hand against his jeans.

'I know,' he said, shutting his eyes in pleasure as she took one of his fingers into her mouth and gently sucked it.

The sound of a car behind them called a halt. Carrie knew she had been seconds from taking off her dress, from undressing Matthew, from making love there, in the open. It was a family, a man and woman with three small children, parking just metres from them, and immediately unloading chairs and barbecue equipment.

'Lovely day for it,' the man called out.

'Sure is,' Matthew answered.

They returned to the car and sat for a few moments, before Matthew started the engine and headed back onto the main road. She wasn't surprised when he pulled into a side road a few kilometres down and turned to her again. Some reason had come into her mind by then – the shock of nearly being caught, the shock of realising she had been about to have sex with Bett's fiancé. And the shock that she still wanted to.

Another hot, deep kiss until she pulled away first. 'What about Bett?' she whispered again, barely able to speak.

'I don't know what to do about Bett,' he answered.

For four weeks they resisted it, trying not to spend time with each other. But it was like a fever, an addiction. The tension between them increased. There were phone calls, three, sometimes four, a day. He wrote her letters. All the while, sexual tension hummed between them.

Lola noticed something, Carrie knew. And perhaps Bett

suspected something. She tried not to spend too much time with her sister, needing to keep the distance. She had one awkward conversation with Matthew about her.

'Are you still sleeping with her?'

Matthew looked uncomfortable. 'I can't. I want it to be you. It wouldn't be fair.'

It made her feel better, for herself, even while she felt sorry for Bett. But it just seemed out of her control, out of their control, as though it was fated, and destined and all the magical things.

Matthew felt the same way, he told her. 'It's different with you, different than it has ever been. With Bett, it seemed easy, like we drifted into it. But with you . . .'

Carrie was torn between wanting to know about his relationship with Bett, and feeling it was best she knew nothing about it. 'We can't talk about her. We have to put her out of our minds when we're together, until we work out whether this is real or not.'

He rang her the night before they were due to go to the agricultural college again. 'I've made a decision, Carrie. I'm going to break it off with Bett. I can't live like this, feeling one thing with you, talking about the wedding with her, feeling like I'm lying.'

'Are you sure?'

'If you are.'

'You know what it will mean.'

'I'm still sure.'

Remember the first time you made love . . .

That conversation had been the turning point. The next morning he collected her from the motel as usual. Bett had left for the newspaper office early. Carrie was glad of it.

They barely spoke as he drove, but she found herself unable to take her eyes off his hands on the steering wheel, feeling the lightness of her own dress against her thighs. He turned into the forest clearing they had first visited five weeks earlier. There was no one else there. The air was as hot and still, the sky as cloudless. They climbed out of the car. He took her by the hand and they started the slow, erotic dance again, his hand tracing her body, her hand tracing his, no words being spoken until they were both nearly faint with desire. 'Are you sure?' he whispered.

She nodded.

From that moment they wouldn't have cared if there had been rows of cars around them. He slowly undid the buttons of her dress, exposing her breasts in the bra she had chosen so carefully that morning. She unbuttoned his shirt, touching the brown skin, the muscles on his arm, then unbuttoned his jeans, moving her hand until she was touching him at last.

He kissed her again. The kiss went on and on, his hands holding her body tight against his. They moved up against a table and had fast, passionate sex, both of them still partly clothed, the sweat covering their skin, their hard, fast breaths and moans the only noise around.

Carrie knew she shouldn't have done it. She knew it the moment they had finished, the moment the tension passed and the two of them were holding each other close, his head against hers. But then he held her even tighter, whispered, 'Thank you,' and she felt that it had been the right thing. And that they would be able to face Bett together. Which was exactly what they did that night. Matthew called her, arranged to meet in the motel. They had both broken the news to her . . .

Remember your wedding day.

Quiet, without fuss, everyone trying to ignore the fact Anna and Bett weren't there.

Think back to the early days of married life.

The first two years they lived in a rented unit in one of the smaller towns in the Valley. Carrie worked in the motel, Matthew finished his study and started working in the vet practice in the town. On weekends they met friends, looked at houses, occasionally went away when her days off allowed them, or he wasn't on call.

It was in the past twelve months it had started changing. She started noticing things about Matthew that either hadn't been there before or had just become apparent. He wasn't exactly mean with money, but he seemed interested in every little thing she spent. 'It would make more sense if we cut down on things like that for the first few years when we're saving for a house,' he said one night, when she arrived home with three bunches of expensive flowers.

'Matt, come on,' she laughed. 'You're running this marriage like it's some kind of business.'

'It is, when we're talking about buying a house. See, Carrie, look at these figures.' She gave them a glance, trying not to stifle a yawn too obviously.

He was the same about the flowering plants she bought for the garden. She'd come home with a car boot full and spent an afternoon planting them, delighted with the effect. He came home late, left early the next morning. It was the weekend before he was able to see them. She blindfolded him and took him outside.

He wasn't impressed at all. 'How much did they cost?'

She gestured vaguely. 'A fair bit, but isn't it worth it? See how brilliant they look.'

'They're all flowering though,' Matthew frowned. 'They won't last. You'd have been better off buying seedlings or seeds. Otherwise it's a waste of money.'

She stood there, debating whether to burst into tears or make a run inside. In the end, she did a combination, stalking to her car and driving off in a temper of showering gravel, making sure he could see her crying face. She drove straight to the motel, looking for sympathy.

Her mother stopped preparing the salad, patted her on the hand, then went back to her lettuces. 'It's part of married life, Carrie. We all have rows.'

Her father asked how much the flowers cost and then laughed when she refused to tell him. 'Too much, then, by the sounds.'

Lola listened to the whole story, then said, 'I see. Now, go home and say sorry.'

'Why should I say sorry? It's his fault I'm upset. He should have been pleased I did the garden.'

'Perhaps he would have been if he'd had a say.'

'He's not my keeper. I won't apologise.'

There was a three-day stand-off, until the night he came to the motel, walked into the kitchen, took her by the hand and practically dragged her out to the car.

Outside, he said just one thing. 'I miss you.'

It was all she needed to hear. 'I miss you too.'

'Will you come home again?'

She nodded. He was driving home when he took a turn off to a park they both knew. Without words, they re-enacted their first time together. In the hot night of a summer, they stood in the open air and made love.

The passion lasted between them for nearly two years. Longer than most, from what Carrie could gather from talking to her friends. One girlfriend said that once their three kids had come along she and her husband had both lost interest. 'Honestly, if he wants to go off and have a mistress, it's fine with me. Between the kids and work, I haven't got time for sex.' Another friend had warned her even before they were married. 'The spice will go out of it now, you know. Now you can actually do it whenever you want. So don't be surprised when a TV program seems more interesting than his crotch.'

Carrie pretended to be shocked. The same friend, a little later that evening and a lot drunker, had gone further. 'Can I ask you a blunt question?' How much blunter could she get? Carrie wondered. 'Has Matthew ever compared you and Bett? You know, said anything about what you were both like in bed? Don't look so outraged, Carrie. He must have thought it. Haven't you ever been curious?'

Of course she had been. But of course she had never asked. She'd told her friend to mind her own business and tried not to think of it again herself. And there had been plenty of consolation in their lovemaking – surely it hadn't been like this for Matthew and Bett, or he would never have left her.

Can you pinpoint when things started going wrong?

Easily. When Lola started obsessing about having Anna and Bett home again. When Carrie started feeling guilty about the marriage. Started wondering whether perhaps it hadn't been a love match written in the stars. Started noticing more things wrong with Matthew. Started picking on him, deliberately wanting him to fight with her, to prove that he loved her. Except it had backfired, hadn't it? She'd picked on him so much he'd been glad to leave.

Are you sure things are as bad as you think?

She realised she was crying, and roughly wiped away a tear. They were, but she wished they weren't. She missed him, really missed him. Their talks at the end of the day. The funny impressions he used to do, especially the ones of Frank Spencer and Basil Fawlty. She loved hearing his plans for the house, going furniture-hunting with him. She loved being in bed with him . . .

Sometimes it can be as simple as sitting down and talking about things. Don't be afraid to be the first person to say sorry.

Sorry? To who, though? Matthew? Bett? Anna? Lola? What was she supposed to do – hire a stadium and make a PA announcement? Get it over in one fell swoop? Stupid magazine. Didn't they realise things were never that simple? She was about to hurl it across the room when the phone rang and her heart leapt. Matthew? She snatched it up. 'Hello?'

'Hello, this is the *Sports Weekly* subscription service calling from Sydney. Is your husband at home please?'

She burst into tears. 'No, he's bloody well not.'

CHAPTER SIXTEEN

IN ANNA'S room the following night, Lola and Ellen sat side by side on the single bed, both wearing dressing-gowns. They had towels wrapped as turbans on their heads and their feet were soaking in basins filled with steaming, fragrant water.

'So, Madame Lola, you'd like which treatment today?' Anna said in an excellent French accent.

'The full works, thank you. I'd like to look twenty years younger by eight p.m.'

'No problem at all, madam, even if it will involve a little plastic surgery. I have a very sharp knife and I enjoy using it. And you, little madam, what would you like done? The full treatment?'

Ellen nodded. 'I would like to look twenty years older, please.'

Lola hooted with laughter. 'We'll meet in the middle yet.'

Anna gently tucked in the turbans around both their faces, giving Ellen a little stroke on the nose for good luck. 'What I shall be doing today is applying my finest products in the most gentle way, giving you both the full pampering treatment. So sit back, relax, and let Anna of the Magic Fingers do her best work.'

She had applied the first of the creams to their faces when there was a knock at the door. Bett poked her head in. 'Anna, message from – Good God, what is this? A cult meeting?'

Lola and Ellen looked out at her through faces covered in thick white cream, their eyes panda-like. 'We're seeking eternal youth and beauty, as supplied by Madame Anna of the Magic Fingers,' Lola said. 'Would you like to join us?'

'I'd need a full construction team, not Anna of the Magic Fingers.' She sat on Anna's bed so she had a full view of the proceedings. 'A message from Len the butcher for you, Anna, to say that the set designs are nearly finished and he'll have the last one done by this weekend.'

'All those years of cutting up chops have finally come into their own,' Lola said.

'Enough talking, thank you, Madame Lola,' Anna said. 'You are supposed to be relaxing.'

'How can I relax when my musical is at such a crucial stage? Tell me again, I know Carrie is Juliet, but who is playing Romeo? And the man playing General MacArthur – are you sure he has the right gravitas?'

'What's gravitas?' Ellen asked, her voice muffled as Anna started wiping away her first layer of cream.

'It's another word for seriousness,' Bett said, as she picked up a magazine from the bedside table.

'Ladies, please,' Anna stepped back. 'I won't be held responsible for the consequences if my attention is diverted.' She pretended to remove Ellen's nose. 'Please, a little quiet.'

'A little gravitas,' Ellen said.

'Exactly. Oh, Anna, I can feel the years slipping away,' Lola purred like a cat as Anna gently stroked the cleansing cream away with soft cotton wool and sure fingers.

There was quiet for a little while and then Ellen spoke up. 'Mum, is it true that Lola was raised by the fairies in Ireland?'

'Of course I was, Ellen,' Lola murmured.

'Lola, tell Ellen the truth.'

Lola crossed her feet in the water bath and gazed across at Ellen, all shiny-faced. 'Once upon a time . . .' Then she stopped. 'I can't tell a story and have a facial at the same time. Bett, can you tell it for me? That way I can hear it too.'

'Of course.' Bett put down the magazine and made herself comfortable on the bed, sitting cross-legged. 'Your great-grandmother was born in Ireland, Ellie, on the other side of the world. Over there they have counties, and she was born in a county called Galway. Her father was a businessman, and her mother was a very elegant lady and they lived in a beautiful big old two-storey house covered in ivy, with a long drive leading up to it, surrounded by fields and streams and black-faced sheep.'

'Did you have a pet sheep there when you were a little girl, Lola?'

'Hundreds of them, Ellie.'

Bett continued. 'Lola went to boarding school, where they taught her to be a fine lady, and how to ride horses and arrange flowers and be gracious and good and kind. And then in the school holidays she would come home and have parties and they would dance and listen to music. At one of these parties she was introduced to a handsome young man called Edward, who was the son of a friend of her father's. Before six months had passed, Lola and Edward were engaged to be married. How am I going so far, Lola?'

Lola's eyes were shut. 'Perfect, darling. Keep going.'

'Edward's father had business interests in Australia, and to Lola's great excitement, he suggested that Lola and Edward spend a year in Australia. Within four months of their wedding the two of them were living in Melbourne.'

'Did you fly in an aeroplane, Lola?'

'Oh no, Ellie. In those days we travelled by ship. It took four weeks to get here, imagine that.'

'Edward's job was to keep an eye on the wool and the wheat and other crops that were being produced on his father's farms, and while he did that, Lola stayed in Melbourne, making the house beautiful.'

Anna stopped applying the second cream, waiting for Bett to tell the next bit of the story.

'Around this time World War II broke out and Edward, your great-grandfather, volunteered to join the Australian Army. He trained to be a soldier, only getting to see Lola once every few months, before he was sent away with the rest of the troops. And then something very sad happened. Edward was killed on the very first day of fighting.'

'He was killed?'

Lola had told the lie so many times the words came easily. 'That's right, Ellie. The soldiers told me afterwards he had been very brave. That I should be proud of him.' Far better than the truth – that her husband had not been a brave soldier but a weak, bullying drunk.

Bett took over again. 'And two days after Lola got word of that, Ellie, she discovered that she was having a baby. And that was James, your grandfather.' She had always found it so heartbreaking that Edward had died without knowing he was going to be a father.

Beside her, Anna was quiet. She always imagined Lola, so young, away from her family and her own country, discovering she was not just a widow, but about to become a mother too.

'Why didn't you go back to Ireland, Lola?' Ellen asked.

'I wasn't well enough to travel and it was wartime. There were no ships available for passengers like me. And by the time the war was over I had started up the guesthouse, and Jim was nearly ready for school. I decided I liked Australia. I loved the sunlight and the birds and the plants. So we decided to stay.'

'Wasn't that brave of her, Ellie?' Bett said. 'All the way across the other side of the world, with a little son to look after?'

'If you had gone back to Ireland, would I be an Irish girl now?'

'I don't know, Ellie. Because if I had gone back to Ireland, your grandfather might not have met your grandmother, and they might not have had three daughters, and you might have been born into another family altogether.'

Ellen seemed to take all that in. 'And have you ever been back to Ireland?'

'No, I haven't. My own family are gone now and it's too far away for a creaking old woman like myself.'

'But I visited Lola's house when I was in Ireland, Ellie,' Bett said.

Anna looked over. She hadn't known that.

'And were there still sheep and ponies and parties?' Ellen asked.

'None that I saw, but there might have been some behind the walls.'

'What did it look like?' Anna asked.

Bett remembered the day she had gone across to Galway on a day trip from Dublin. She had rung Lola the night before to get directions, surprising her. 'Would there be family left that I could speak to?'

'Oh no, Bett. The family would be long gone,' Lola had said.

It had taken Bett a whole morning to find the house, following Lola's directions. It had been different to what Bett had imagined, much smaller, the drive not as curvy as she remembered Lola telling them. The front entrance has been spoiled by a small clump of pine trees, she thought. She had taken a roll of photos and sent them back to Lola. She'd been a little disappointed with her reaction, she remembered. Lola had seemed grateful, but not all that interested. As she described it to Anna and Ellen now, the thought that had been niggling at the back of her mind since the slide show at Lola's party came back. It was about the trees.

'Lola, that slide you showed at the party, that was of your house, wasn't it?'

'It was.'

'And what tree was out the front?'

'A huge oak tree.'

Bett clapped her hand to her forehead. 'I can't believe it. How stupid was I? You know how I got so lost that day I went looking for your house, trying to follow your directions? That weekend I went to Galway to see if I could find anyone who remembered you and Edward? I was sure I'd followed your directions perfectly, but the house I went to had pine trees out the front, rows of them, not an oak tree. No wonder I couldn't find anyone who knew you. I was at the wrong house the whole time, wasn't I?'

'Yes, Bett, you were,' Lola said honestly.

'Oh, Bett, you silly sausage,' Ellen said.

The three of them burst out laughing. Bett turned to Lola. 'Why didn't you tell me when I sent you those photos, Lola?'

'I didn't want to embarrass you, Bett.'

She clapped her hand to her forehead again. 'Idiot. My one chance to uncover the mystery that is Lola Quinlan and what do I do? Go in the wrong direction completely. Sorry, Lola.' No wonder she hadn't been that interested, trying not to hurt Bett's feelings for turning up at the wrong house.

'It doesn't matter at all, Bett.' Time to change the subject, Lola thought. 'So that brings you up to date, Ellie. Time now to concentrate on the beauty treatments.' She leaned back and shut her eyes, glad of the silence. She had always hated lying, even though sometimes it had to be done. She especially hated lying to Bett.

Chapter Seventeen

It was Bett's turn to walk Ellen to school the next day. She waited in front of the motel as Ellen ran over to say goodbye to Bumper the sheep. She'd already taken ten minutes to say goodbye to Lola and Carrie. It was probably as well Anna had left early that morning for her voice-over work in Sydney, or they would have been delayed another twenty minutes while she said goodbye to her.

'Ready?' she called as the little girl ran over, her school bag bumping on her back, one sock already down at her shoes. She had been going to the new school for nearly two weeks, and the goodbye routine each morning seemed to take longer every day.

Ellen nodded.

'Sure? You don't want to say goodbye to that magpie over there?'

'Which magpie?'

'Forget it,' Bett said laughing, as she reached and took her hand. It was a beautiful summer morning, the front gardens in the main road lush with growth, the air crisp, the sky already a deep blue. As they walked, Bett started singing 'Oh What a Beautiful Morning'. 'There you are, Ellen. A little taste of the Alphabet Sisters for you.'

'Did you and my mum and Auntie Carrie really travel all around the country singing?'

'We did, indeed. Your mum stood on the left, then me in the middle, then Carrie on the right. And we'd sing songs and sometimes we'd even dance a little bit.'

'Do you still do it now?'

Bett laughed at the mental image. 'No, we're probably a bit old for it, I think.'

'And why did you stop?'

'It's a long story, Ellie. I'll tell you one day.'

'Does that mean you don't want to tell me? Mum says that sometimes, even when we've got plenty of time.'

'It must run in the family.'

'What does that mean?'

'It means that we do things the same way. We might all look a bit the same, or like the same things, or be good at the same sorts of things.'

'So I could be a singer too?'

'Would you like to be up on stage?'

Ellen shook her head. 'No. I don't really like people looking at me.'

'I don't like it all that much either.' They walked on a little way, swinging their hands. Bett pointed out a tall gum tree with a fork in the middle. 'See that tree up there, Ellie? Your mum got stuck up one like that one day when she was a bit older than you, when we were living in a different motel. We had to wait three hours before we could get her down. Dad, that's your grandpa, had to call the fire engine in the end. And even then she'd only get down if they sounded the siren.'

Ellen laughed. 'Tell me another thing about my mum.'

'She borrowed all of Lola's makeup once, and dressed the three of us up thinking that no one would notice. Except we were all even younger than you, covered in lipstick and eye-shadow.'

'I borrowed Mum's lipstick once. And Julie let me use some of hers once too.'

'Julie?'

'Dad's friend. She's really nice to me.'

'Your dad's friend?'

Ellen nodded. 'She keeps his secrets too.'

Bett stopped. 'Sorry, Ellie, who is Julie?'

'She works with Dad. In his office.'

Bett got it then. God, for a minute it had sounded like this Julie was Glenn's girlfriend or something. 'Julie is Glenn's secretary, Ellie, is that what you mean?'

Ellen nodded again. 'He's in Singapore with her at the moment. Mum doesn't like it.'

'Your dad being away? No, I guess she wouldn't. She must be missing him.'

'I miss him too. But he rings me every night.'

'Does he? Oh, that's good,' Bett said, keeping her tone neutral. Ellen didn't need to know what she thought of Glenn. They reached the school gates and Bett knelt down in front of her niece, checking her shoe-laces were tied and the ribbon was straight in her hair.

'There, you're perfect. So, have you made lots of friends already?'

Ellen looked at her feet. 'Not yet.'

Bett reached over and touched her cheek. She knew only too well that feeling of starting in a new school. 'You will, Ellie. Don't worry. These things just take time.'

Ellen nodded.

'Good girl. So have fun and I'll see you after school, okay?' She gave her a big hug and watched as Ellen ran off to her classroom.

It suited Bett to walk her niece to school and then get into work early. To be efficient, she told herself. To be hard at work by the time Daniel Hilder arrived, was the truth. Rebecca had picked up something and challenged her about it the day before.

'We're old friends, aren't we?' Rebecca asked.

'Sure.'

'Can I ask you a favour, then?'

'Of course.'

'Go easy on Daniel Hilder for a while.'

'What do you mean go easy?'

'Be nicer to him.'

'I am nice.'

'Bett, you're not. You go all stiff and weird. And he changes when you're around as well. I don't know what's between the two of you, but he could do with a bit of support.'

'Is something wrong?'

'It's his story not mine, but things are tough for him at home, let me say that.'

'With his girlfriend?'

'His girlfriend?'

'He's living with someone, isn't he? Someone he met in Melbourne?'

'No, they split up months ago, I think. He came back on his own. Bett, for a journalist, you're not very up to date with the facts.' Rebecca was looking intently at her. 'What's going on? Did you and Hildie go out together years back? Before I got here? Have a messy break-up?'

'No.' If she concentrated hard she could keep the blush from rising. 'No, we didn't. I was going out with Matthew when Daniel was here before.'

'Ah yes, you and Matthew. I never did get to the bottom of all of that business either.' Rebecca's phone rang. She grinned. 'Saved by the bell, Bett. I'll keep that interrogation for another time.'

In Sydney that afternoon, Anna was speaking in a low, measured voice. 'Take the condom carefully in one hand and slide it over the erect penis.'

Bob's voice came into her headphones. 'Sorry, Anna. Can you do that last bit again? Problem with the tape there.'

Anna stepped close to the mike again. 'I suppose you think this is funny, Bob? How come we managed to do the entire section about childbirth without any problems but we've had to do this bit how many times now? Three?'

'It's that husky voice of yours. You know it drives me crazy.'

'One more time, Bob. Or I'm reporting you and your faulty recording equipment to Actors' Equity.'

'Okay, tape rolling, vision coming up now.' A picture of a woman fitting a condom onto a model of a penis appeared on the small TV screen in front of her. Just a model, Anna noticed. It seemed these school educational videos weren't that far advanced yet. She matched the script to the visuals, nearly knowing the words by heart she'd read them so many times that day. 'Be sure to tie the end of the condom and ensure there is no spillage of the sperm. Carefully dispose of the used condom. Do not flush it down the toilet.' Do not hurl it out the window of a car, like most teenage boys of her acquaintance had done.

Bob's voice in the headphones again. 'Perfect, thanks. Though, could we try that bit about oral sex one more time?'

'Your mind is a sewer, Bob. One more crack like that and I'm ringing your wife and claiming sexual harassment.' She knew Bob's wife well.

He grinned through the glass at her. 'Okay, half-hour break, I think. You're starting to sound a bit breathless, or perhaps that's wishful thinking on my part.'

'Very funny.'

'See you back here at three for the joys of teenage pregnancy. How about that? I'm a poet and I didn't know it.'

Outside the sound booth, Anna made a coffee and took it onto the little balcony. She leaned her head against the warm brick wall and shut her eyes, surprised by a sudden longing for a cigarette. She'd given up eight years before, when she was trying to get pregnant, but even now she had the occasional urge. More so recently. She blamed it on all the tension at home. Once upon a time she would have dismissed anyone who said emotional problems had an effect on a person's health. Now she wasn't so sure. She was either tired all the time and wanting to sleep, or so wired she couldn't sleep at all. And she was getting short of breath now and again. She'd been noticing it more in the past week or two.

On her way to the airport in Adelaide the previous day she'd seen a sign for a medical clinic. No appointments necessary. On the spur of the moment she'd gone in. The surgery had been busy, four or five different doctors coming in and out. She'd almost convinced herself she was over-reacting and had been about to leave when her name was called.

The doctor was in his mid-sixties, she guessed. Red-faced, cheerful. She'd run through her symptoms. Feeling tired. Feeling short of breath. Loss of appetite.

'Could you be pregnant?'

She and Glenn hadn't had sex in months. 'No, no chance.'

'I see your home address is Sydney? But you're living here? Can you tell me a little of what's going on in your life?'

The doctor started smiling sympathetically midway through Anna's reply. 'I think we've found our answer. Your daughter's accident alone could be the cause of this. You would have unleashed enough adrenalin that day to fuel you for a year. Do you get a tight feeling across your chest, as if it's hard to breathe. Yes? And any nausea?'

She nodded. 'All of those things.'

'It sounds to me like you are having panic attacks. Also known as anxiety attacks. It happens when a person is especially stressed. You subconsciously hold your breath, so then your lungs have to work twice as hard, and your heart as well, which explains the breathlessness. And loss of appetite is often another sign of stress.' He glanced at Anna. 'You're very thin already. You really do need to keep an eye on that, make time to eat.'

He checked her blood pressure, her eyes, her tongue. All fine. 'And your age is on your side, too. Thirty-four? Prime of life. Tell me, can you take life a bit easier? Slow down a little?'

Anna laughed and decided not to mention the fact she was in the middle of producing a full-scale amateur musical. 'Not really. Not at the moment.'

'Then can you spoil yourself a bit? Is there something you enjoy doing that you haven't had time to do recently? Someone you like being with? A place you like going to? Somewhere that makes you feel good and relaxed and happy? Often that's as good as any tablets or meditation exercises I could give you.'

She made a follow-up appointment for a few weeks' time. But the doctor was reassuring. 'Slow down, Anna,' he said. 'Don't forget to enjoy life while you're rushing through it.'

Her booking agent, Roz, a calm, older woman, had been just as reassuring when they'd had lunch that day. 'So let me get this straight, Anna. You've been feeling tired? A bit anxious? Breathless now and again? Now, why would that be, I wonder. It's not as if you've got any stress in your life, is it? A daughter in and out of hospital for the past year. A husband in and out of his secretary's bed, the dirty old dog. Don't look so shocked. You know I've never liked Glenn. And now you're back home with your two estranged sisters for the first time in years and directing an amateur musical at short notice. No, from my expert reading, I'd say you should be feeling light as a feather with all that going on.'

Anna started to laugh. 'Well, when you put it like that.'

'I do put it like that. Anna, don't worry. Of course you're stressed. That doctor's right. You just need a break and I hereby give you one. Once you get this school health project out of the way, of course. I want to get my commission out of you first.'

Anna had laughed, feeling more relaxed immediately. She was enjoying the work, too. The only difficulty was the voice-overs weren't being recorded in order, which was making things a little confusing. The young actors in the documentary had met at a disco, then swiftly had a child together, then had sex and now the girl was about to have her first period. No wonder the poor things were so upset.

A memory came to Anna out of the blue, of the day her own first period arrived. It was one afternoon in the summer school holidays, when she was thirteen, before they'd moved to the Clare Valley. She knew exactly what it was. She had been keeping a lookout for months, reading up on it all, supplementing the slap-dash school sex education program. She went to her mother in the kitchen, whispered the news in her ear and was rewarded with five glorious minutes of her full attention. 'Are you okay?' 'Do you know what to do?' 'Have you got any cramps?' There was even a brief hug, before the phone rang and something on the stove boiled, and her mother left her to it.

Feeling on top of the world, she walked over to the manager's house and into the bedroom she shared with both sisters.

'I'm a woman now,' she said to Bett, who was lying on the bed reading.

'What were you before, an iguana?' Bett answered, not looking up.

'No, I mean I've got my first period, which means I am physically officially a woman.'

'You're disgusting. I don't want to know about it.'

'What's disgusting? It's perfectly natural. You'll be next.'

'I'm not interested.'

'What? You're going to stop it happening, are you? Take boy pills? Start playing football perhaps? Hang upside down . . .' Anna poked Bett with her foot.

Bett swiped at her. 'I mean it. I'm not interested. Bleuch.' She gave a shiver of disgust.

Anna looked at herself in the mirror, staring at her face, convinced that, yes, she even looked different. Not exactly more mature, but more knowing. As one of the books had said, she was now privy to one of the great female secrets of the universe. She smoothed her hair, and looked at Bett in the reflection. 'Apparently once you and Carrie get your periods there's every chance we will all start having them at the same time.'

Bett was now lying on her stomach, face buried in her pillow. 'Shut up, shut up.'

Anna hadn't realised it was going to be this much fun. 'It's to do with the moon,' she said, coming over to her, leaning in close. 'All of our wombs are linked, with the sky and the sea, in tune with nature. The three of us will be able to dance naked, creatures of fertility and womanhood. Once a month under the moon.'

'Shut up. I'm not listening. You're disgusting.'

'You're just jealous.'

'Jealous of what?' Carrie came into the room.

'Of me. Because, young Caroline, I, Anna Mary Quinlan, officially became a woman today. I'm having my first period.'

'Really? Cool. I can't wait. Are you using tampons or those pad things?'

Bett had groaned and covered her face with her pillow. 'You're both disgusting.'

Twenty years later, the memory still made Anna laugh. Bett had always been so funny about anything to do with becoming a woman, much to her and Carrie's entertainment. So easy to tease, too, about boys or sex or relationships. She guiltily remembered the time she and Carrie had been asked to the school social, but Bett hadn't. She should have sympathised more, Anna thought now, been supportive. But she'd been so excited at her own date, getting ready, applying makeup, that she hadn't noticed how forlorn Bett was. She and Carrie went off in one car, bright, dressed-up, not even worrying about Bett, who had chosen to stay home with Lola. Anna felt a ripple of shame, thinking of how she would feel if Ellen wasn't asked out. It must have been hard for Bett sometimes – the two of them fighting off attention from boys, but not Bett. She remembered another time she and Carrie were getting ready to go out. Bett had been reading, pretending not to be watching, not to be interested. Carrie, with the know-all confidence of a thirteen-year-old, had taken it upon herself to give Bett some advice. 'You could look quite nice if you did something with your hair. And I can teach you how to put on makeup if you want me to.'

Anna had seen the flash of anger, just before Bett lifted up her book. 'I don't want your help.'

'Well, don't blame me if you never get asked out,' Carrie said before flouncing out.

How could they have been so cruel? Anna wondered. That hadn't been the only time, either. Was it too late to apologise now? Surely it was never too late. She had a sudden urge to ring Bett, to say sorry for everything, not just those awful teenage years, but for all they had said to each other that night of the fight. She took out her mobile and switched it on. She'd had it turned off during the recording. It beeped, telling her she had two messages. The apology to Bett was forgotten as she listened to the first one.

'Anna, hello, this is Mrs Harold from Ellen's school. Would you please be able to come and collect Ellen? She's very upset and I think it's best if she goes home for the rest of the day. Can you call me as soon as possible?'

The second message was also from her. 'Anna, Mrs Harold again. Can you call me as soon as you get this message?'

Anna checked the time. Both calls had been left in the last fifteen minutes. She pressed the speed dial on her mobile and didn't bother with greetings when Mrs Harold answered.

'It's Anna, Ellen Green's mother, Mrs Harold. Is she sick? Hurt? What happened?'

'Hello, Anna. No, it's just there's been a bit of an incident in the playground.'

A rush of panic up her back again. 'Not another dog?'

'Nothing like that,' the voice soothed. 'But it would be better if we talk about it face to face. Ellen is here in the office with us. Could you come in as soon as possible?'

'I'm sorry, I can't. I'm in Sydney. For work.' Anna waited for the disapproval, the change in tone, and was amazed when it didn't come.

'Is there anyone else who could collect her? One of your sisters? Lola?'

Anna gave a little prayer of thanks for small towns. Of course they all knew the set-up. 'I'm sure one of them can. I'll give them a call now. Can I talk to Ellen first?'

The woman's voice was lowered. 'She's fallen asleep. It might be best not to wake her for the moment.'

'Of course. Right. I'll call home straight away.'

Ten minutes later it was all sorted. Bett had been back at the motel for lunch and had answered the phone, listening closely as Anna explained the situation. 'Of course, I'll go and get her now. I'll ring you as soon as I get back.'

Hanging up, Anna realised that the back of her neck was damp with sweat and the churning feeling in her stomach had returned. Ellen in trouble and here she was hundreds of kilometres away. Thank God for families. What did people do when they didn't have sisters they could call on to help? Then she remembered. Exactly what she'd done for the past three years. Felt desperately alone.

Anna felt the phone vibrate against her leg just as she was voicing the segment about the different methods of pregnancy testing. It was her turn to stop the tape. 'Sorry, Bob. I'll be right back.'

She answered it outside. 'Bett? Is she all right?'

Bett's voice was low. 'No, she's really upset. Crying a lot. She's with Lola at the moment. She's trying to put her back to sleep.'

'What happened?'

'The kids were picking on her. A gang of them.'

'What were they doing?'

Bett paused. 'Calling her scarface.'

Anna had never felt such rage. 'The little fuckers. The mean little fuckers. That's it, I'm taking her out of school. Can you tell her I'll be home tonight, as soon as I can get a flight, but she's not to worry, she'll never have to go back there again.'

'Lola said –'

'I don't care what Lola said. She's my child, Bett, and she's not going back to that school again. Put Lola on.'

A minute went past, then Lola's Irish voice came on the line. 'She's sleeping now, Anna. Poor little mite. She was very upset.'

'Of course she was. And she's not going back there again, Lola. I'm getting a flight tonight, and she'll stay home with me tomorrow. I'll teach her from now on myself if I have to.'

'I thought you'd say that. But what about your work? Didn't you say it was three days' worth? You don't have to rush back. We're all here. She's fine with us. We'll spoil her rotten tonight and then tomorrow I'll take her to school myself.'

'Lola, didn't you hear me? She's not going back to that school.'

'It's the best thing to do. She has to face her fears.'

Anna lost her temper. 'Don't you tell me about facing fears, Lola. I have seen that child face more fears than you and I ever had to face. I've seen her face nearly ripped away by a dog's teeth, and those little, those little fuckheads at the school dare to tease her about it.'

'They are seven-year-old children, Anna. They don't know they're being cruel. It's just the way kids are. And that's why she needs to go back, to show them they haven't won.'

'It's not a matter of winning or losing. I just don't want her to be hurt any more. She's not going back, Lola. I'll be home as soon as I can, no matter what you say.'

'Anna, I know you're upset but please don't talk to me in that way. Stay there. Bett and I are here with Ellen. She'll be fine tonight. I think you're wrong but if you don't want her to go to school tomorrow, then that's fine, she won't. I'll keep her here with me. But don't cancel your trip, or rush home yet. You said this job was an important one.'

The tension was draining from her. 'It is.'

'Then finish it. And I will watch over Ellen like she has never been watched over before, I promise. I'll get her to ring you when she wakes up. And you can ring her again tomorrow. All day long if you want.'

Anna realised she was right. 'I'm sorry, Lola. Sorry for swearing.'

'That's all right, darling.'

Lola let Ellen sleep for an hour or so, gave her a sandwich, then decided it was time for a little walk and a little talk. 'You and me and Bumper need to spend some time together, I think.'

Hand in hand, with Ellen holding Bumper by his lead, they set off slowly along the perimeter of the motel. Lola pointed out different trees, a galah on a branch, curling bark, even a lizard sunbaking on a rock, before heading over to the bench Jim had set up especially for her. Halfway up the hill, it had a wonderful view over the vineyards. The bench looked almost golden with the late afternoon light streaming onto it. Lola sat down with Ellen beside her, Bumper in front of them, safely tethered, slowly pulling on shoots of grass from under the bench, making little tugging sounds. Lola had always found sheep one of the world's most relaxing creatures to be near. She gave him an affectionate scratch on the head. 'If he was your sheep, what would you call him, Ellie?'

'Mike,' she said without hesitation.

'Mike the Sheep. Well, that's an interesting one. Now, my dear little Ellie, I've been thinking about what happened this morning and there's some things I'd like to say to you. Would you like to hear them?'

A tiny nod.

'Ellie, do you know why the kids at school were teasing you?'

'Because I'm horrible. Because I'm ugly, and I've got a horrible scar.' The tears started coming again.

Lola pulled her close with her good arm, held her tight and waited for the tears to quell again. 'No, that's not the reason. They teased you because they're scared of you. Because you look a bit different. And people have always been scared of people who look different. Do you know what a scar actually is, Ellie?'

'It's what happened when the dog –' The rest of her words were lost in a shuddering sob.

Lola waited a moment again, and then turned Ellen around so they were face to face. 'A scar is a sign that you've survived something, Ellie. That something happened to you but your body was so strong and clever it joined itself up again. Have you told the kids at school what happened?'

A shake of the head. 'Mum says to just ignore them.'

'Well, most times Mum is right but sometimes it's good for people to know the whole story.'

Ellen twisted away. 'I don't want them to know the whole story. I don't want them to know anything. I never want to see them again.'

'Good idea. We'll run away together, will we?'

Ellen went still. 'What do you mean?'

'If those children are being mean to my beautiful great-granddaughter, then I never want to see them again either. We'll run away together. Where shall we go?'

A shrug.

Lola continued. 'Good. I'll decide, then. We're going to go to a land where everyone is a little bit different, and that way we won't stand out. What do you say to that?'

She had Ellen's complete attention now. 'What land?'

'Well, let's think about it. I'm really old and I get called things like "dear" and "poor old thing" and spoken to in a strange voice and I don't like it much. Do you know what I heard a young man in the charity shop call me last month? An old wrinklehead. Isn't that rude? So I want there to be lots of wrinkled old people there so I don't stand out. And I think we should have lots of really tall people there too, because they get called names too, don't they? And overweight people, because they get called Fatty and Chubster, don't they? And people with red hair get called names. And people with no hair. And people with glasses.'

'And people with big noses,' Ellen said in a little voice.

'Yes. And tiny chins. And big bottoms. And bad teeth. Or no teeth. Or teeth that are too big. Or people with broken bones like me. People in wheelchairs. Heavens, it's getting pretty crowded in that land, isn't it?'

'No one with scars like me, though.'

'Of course there will be. There'll be lots of people with scars. Don't you think you're going to be the Scar Queen there, young lady. You can be the Princess of Scars perhaps. So let's see. We'll start with Harry Potter, will we? He's got a terrific scar across his forehead.'

'He's not real.'

'It's our land so we can have whoever we like, whether they're real or not. I've got a scar, you know. On my leg, from when I was kicked by a horse when I was a little girl.'

'I didn't know that.'

'I'll show you one day, when I'm not all trussed up in support tights. I'll probably have a scar on my head, too, when this silly thing heals.' She touched the small bandage on her forehead. 'Your mum has got a scar too. Did you know that?'

'Has she?'

Was Ellen too young to learn that she'd been born by Caesarean section? Perhaps. 'That's a very special scar, and you should ask her about it one day, get her to show you. Your grandfather's got a scar, too. I'll get him to show you when he comes home. On his knee. He took a terrible tumble down some stairs once when he was a little fellow. Auntie Bett probably has one, too, from when she fell off her bike once. I think Carrie's got one as well. We'll have to form a scar club in this land we all live in.'

Ellen was giggling now. 'When do we get to go there?'

'We're already here.'

'At the motel? This is it?' She sounded very disappointed.

'Not just here, Ellie,' Lola said matter-of-factly. 'It's here in the Valley, here in Australia, here in the whole world, with all sorts of different people who look different in all sorts of ways. Because no one is perfect, darling, not a single one of us. We all have something a bit different about us, scars or big noses or small feet or crooked teeth. And that's not going to change no matter where we go to live. What we have to do, you and I, is work out the best way for you to get by here, as happily as you can.'

'But not at that school.'

'Not for a day or two perhaps. Not yet, anyway.' Lola had had another idea, but it was probably too soon to mention it to Ellen. 'But I hereby promise that we'll do all we can to make things as good for you as they can be. And that is enough about that for now.' She stood up with an exaggerated groan. 'Come on then, Princess Scar. Will we go in and see what they're planning for dinner?'

A little sparkle was back in Ellen's eyes. 'Yes, Granny Wrinklehead.'

Lola squeezed her hand. 'It's Great-Granny Wrinklehead, you scallywag.'

The following morning Lola let Ellen sleep in. If she had been her child, the little girl would definitely have been back in school the next day. But Anna had insisted. So a day off it was.

They spent the morning together. She and Ellen had their breakfast in the motel kitchen, then Ellen helped the cleaners do a couple of the rooms, carrying in fresh linen and new packets of biscuits. Ellen seemed bright enough, Lola thought, watching her playing, but there was a tight quality about her. Tension, imminent tears.

Anna arrived home late that afternoon, driving at great speed into the carpark. Ellen had been listening out for her. Lola watched with interest as she changed moods in an instant. One moment she had been playing very happily with her dolls – some complicated scenario involving one set of dolls trying to book into a motel the other set of dolls were running, but not liking the rooms. Lola had started to lose track. Then, at the sound of Anna's car, she started crying and ran out to her mother, wailing at the top of her voice. 'Mummy, Mummy.'

Anna pulled her tight and held her close, the two of them staying like that for some time. They ate dinner together, Ellen still teary, needing to be fed like a toddler. The evening before she had used a knife and fork without any problem, Lola recalled. She nearly needed to tape her mouth shut to keep the comments in. Ellen was Anna's daughter. It was up to Anna to raise her as she saw fit, she told herself. But what if there is another, possibly better, way to approach this? she also asked herself.

Once Ellen was in bed, a tortuous enough exercise, with more tears and tantrums, Lola made a pot of tea and took it into the bar, where Anna was alone, curled up in one of the big chairs, looking at the TV, but in a dazed way. She was still a picture, Lola thought, but so slender these days, fragile even. 'Anna, darling, some tea?'

Anna smiled gratefully. 'You've come to lecture me, haven't you? Tell me where I'm going wrong with Ellen. What a bad mother I am. That I've made the wrong decision taking her out of school.'

'I think you're a wonderful mother. I think Ellen is a wonderful child. But there might be other ways to approach this situation.' She told Anna about her conversation with Ellen the previous day. As she expected, Anna wasn't happy.

'Lola, I don't want you to call her Princess Scar. It's not funny.'

'It's not meant to be funny. It's a new psychological treatment. The more you expose someone to something, the less frightened they are of it. I read about it in the paper. They do it with spiders, slowly expose someone to –'

'I don't care if you have the backing of the Harvard Medical School. I don't like you calling my daughter Princess Scar.'

'What about Scar?'

'Fine. You call her Scar and I'll tell her to call you Great-Grandmother. Old Grandma. The Old Bag.'

Lola smiled. 'All right. I'll stop calling her Princess Scar. But I mean it, Anna. You can't keep taking her out of situations each time they get tricky for her. So you take her out of this school, move her to a new one and the same thing happens there. Then what? You take her out of there as well? Try another school? What will that do to the poor little girl, being moved in and out of schools like that?'

'You and Dad did it to the three of us all our lives.'

'Touché,' Lola smiled. 'But every few years is not the same as every few weeks. And Ellen is facing different things than you three had to put up with. You need to make her stronger, braver, not more cowardly.'

'My daughter is not a coward.'

Lola held up her hand. 'No, she is most definitely not. But she knows how to cry when it suits her, and she knows how to upset you.'

Anna was silent.

'She'll get through this, Anna, she will. But you need to help her, make her brave. You can't protect her all the time.'

Anna opened her mouth, wanting to tell Lola everything – about Glenn, about their marriage being over, about the hundreds of things she wanted to protect Ellen from. But it was too much and the words stuck in her throat.

Lola was watching, waiting, then moved over to her. 'I am an interfering old woman, Anna, but I think I am right. I think Ellen has to go back to school, face them again. It'll be for the best, you wait and see.'

'All right,' Anna's voice was low.

'Are you sure you're up to the rehearsals tonight? I can cancel them if you want.'

Anna smiled, a little shakily. 'You know yourself. The show must go on.'

Anna walked Ellen to school the following day. She was called back before eleven a.m. to collect Ellen once more. The other children had been teasing her again.

After she'd put Ellen to bed, Anna confronted Lola. 'Oh, that really made her brave. Not just Scarface today, but Chicken as well, because she hadn't been to school yesterday. And then they finished it with Crybaby, when she started crying. Shall we send her back again this afternoon so they can really finish her off, Lola? I'll kill them. Little bastards.'

'Do they actually know what happened to her? Know why she has that scar?'

'Oh, yes. I went in and sat every single one of them down and explained that Ellen had been attacked by a dog and that things had been very rough for her and that they should be admiring her, not attacking her. Of course they don't. Do you think I wanted to draw any more attention to her than she needed?'

'I think that's exactly what you should do. I think you should go in and sit down and tell everyone of those little bastards, as you call them, what happened to Ellen. Show them the photos. Let them ask Ellen questions. And then see what happens.'

'What good will that do?'

'I think it will help them understand.' Lola could see Anna's hurt, and could also see her desperation. 'Trust me, Anna.'

Lola rang her friend the principal that afternoon. They had a long discussion and set a time and date. She found a letter and some photos she had received from Anna several months after Ellen was attacked, showing what good progress she had made. Lola rang Frank in the electrical shop and asked him to make up several more slides as quickly as he could. Then she sat down with Anna and Ellen and put her suggestion to them.

Three mornings later, Anna stood in front of a classroom of seven-year-olds, more nervous than she had ever been on stage or in a recording studio. The teacher hushed the children then introduced her.

'This is Anna, Ellen Green's mother. She wants to talk to you about what happened to Ellen and I'd like you all to listen and watch closely.'

Anna told the story simply. She showed a slide of Ellen before the attack, then explained what had happened with the dog on the day in the park. She showed slides of Ellen in the hospital, straight after the attack. Several of the children gasped. She showed another slide of a close-up of the wound. The dog's toothmarks were obvious. She didn't need to point them out. She showed slides from the next month or two, as Ellen went through surgery, stitches, plastic surgery, in and out of hospital.

'That's why Ellen has the scar on her face. It's a sign that she survived a horrible attack from a very large dog, and I am so glad she did, because she is very precious to me, and to her father, and to her aunties, and grandparents and great-grandmother. I wanted to tell you this today so that you will understand and I hope you will be kind to her. She is a very nice little girl.' Anna's voice cracked slightly and she coughed to cover it.

The teacher went outside and fetched Ellen, who had been waiting there with Lola. They had explained to her exactly what Anna would tell them, and that she would come in afterwards and rejoin her class. She was very pale as she took a seat next to Anna in front of the students, nestling close, her hair in front of her face.

The teacher smiled at her, then turned to the class. 'So then, children, any questions for Ellen or her mother?'

A little boy held up his hand. 'What happened to the dog?'

Anna answered truthfully. 'It had to be put down. That means the vet had to give it an injection to make it die, in case it did something to another child, something even worse.'

That satisfied the little boy. Another boy put up his hand. 'Was there a lot of blood when it bit Ellen?'

Ellen nodded.

'There was,' Anna said. 'Ellen lost so much blood that the hospital had to give her some more.'

'Did Ellen get to go in an ambulance?'

Ellen nodded again, still silent.

'Cool.'

All the questions were now being directed to Anna. 'Will she always have that scar on her face?'

'We're doing laser treatment on it at the moment.'

'Laser? Like in *Star Wars*?'

'Not quite, but they shine a special light, a laser beam, onto Ellen's face to break down the scar tissue bit by bit. So when she's older hopefully it won't be so obvious.'

'Is Ellen scared of dogs now?'

To Anna's surprise, Ellen answered. 'Not all dogs. Just big dogs.'

'So you can't have pets, then?'

'I've got a sheep called Bumper Baa. My Really-Great-Gran gave it to me. It's got something called lanolin in its wool which makes your hands soft.'

The teacher was trying not to smile. 'Bumper Baa? That's a very good name for a sheep, Ellen.'

'It's my Really-Great-Gran's idea. She's outside, but she told me she'd have her ear pressed against the door so she could hear everything we're saying. She's very old, but I heard my grandfather say she still has hearing like a bat. And my grandmother said, "Yes, an old bat".'

They all clearly heard Lola's laughter through the door.

Anna was waiting at the school gates at the end of the day. She stood back a little from the other school mums, though she knew they were watching her and probably knew who she was. The principal had sent out a note to all the parents, explaining that Anna would be giving the talk, and why, asking for their help in stopping the children calling Ellen names.

The bell went and the children came streaming out. Anna recognised a couple from the class, but there was no sign of Ellen. She finally appeared, on her own. Around her there were little groups of girls and boys, in pairs and trios. Anna searched her face for tears. Nothing. 'Hi, Ellie. How was the rest of the day?' She kept her tone breezy and light.

'Good, thanks.'

'Lunch was good? And recess?'

Ellen nodded. 'But I'm still hungry. Can I please have an ice-cream when we get home?'

'I think you can today.' No mention of the talk that morning. Anna decided not to push it either, not to ask if any of the other children had talked to her afterwards, or if they had picked on her during the breaks, even though the words were burning a hole on her tongue.

They were nearly at the car when a little girl ran over, her mother a few metres behind. 'Ellen, can you ask your mum now?'

Anna stopped. 'Ask me what?'

The little girl spoke before Ellen. 'Ellen and I were wondering if I could come and play at the motel and see the sheep one night?'

Ellen looked up at her. 'I can show Hannah round, Mum, can't I? Patrick and Samuel wanted to come too, but I said I thought they would have to wait their turn. That was the right thing to say, wasn't it?'

Anna leant down and tucked Ellen's hair behind her ears, smiling at her. 'That was the perfect thing to say.'

Hand in hand they walked over to talk to Hannah's mother.

Chapter Eighteen

'So how are rehearsals going?' Daniel asked.

Bett and Daniel were in the car on their way back from Martindale Hall, a nineteenth-century Georgian-style house near the small town of Mintaro. Bett had spent the morning roaming through the lavish rooms, imagining herself living in such glory and grandeur.

'Good,' she lied. No, they weren't. The way things were going there was more chance of Lola appearing on the cover of *Vogue* than her musical being ready for its gala premiere in mid-March. 'Actually, no they're not. You might have had a lucky escape.'

'I don't know. I'd like to have got up on stage again, as it happens.'

'Again?'

'You're not the only child performer in this car, you know.'

'You were a child performer?'

He nodded. 'Briefly. As a twelve-year-old. In my Danger Hilder days. But I wasn't a common-or-garden variety street punk rocker. I had my own band.'

She saw that glint in his eye again. 'Really? What were you called?'

'Promise you won't laugh?'

'No.'

'We were called Dangerous.'

She smiled. 'Talk about scary. Did you get many gigs?'

'One.'

'Oh. Well, I suppose kindergartens don't have big budgets for live bands at their end-of-year shows.'

'It was on a TV show, actually. A talent quest.'

She turned fully in her seat. This was getting better and better. 'Did you do a cover or an original?'

'Bett, I was an alternative artist. An original, of course.'

'Would you sing it for me now?'

'No.'

'It's a shame videos weren't invented back then.'

'They were, actually.'

'You've got a tape of it?'

He nodded.

'Can I see it?'

He laughed. 'Of course not.'

'Daniel, please.'

'No.'

'I beg you to let me see it.'

He raised an eyebrow. 'You beg me?'

'You're going to tell me you've lost it, aren't you?'

'No, it's at home.'

'In Melbourne?'

'No, home here. In my mother's house. I'm staying there at the moment.'

'I really would like to see it.'

He hesitated, then grinned. 'All right. Have we got time now?'

'Now?'

They were a few kilometres south of the Valley town of Sevenhill. 'My mother's house is over there.'

It was a big old stone house, with a verandah running around all four sides, the roof clad in corrugated iron, painted red. They walked up a path of flagstones, well-cut grass to the left, a well-tended vegetable patch on the right. Bett noticed corn, tomatoes, watermelon, the leaves lush and green, the fruit hanging heavy. 'Your mother's a good gardener.'

'She used to be. That's my patch these days. Six months of back-breaking work in that. To think I could go and buy it in the shop in less than five minutes.'

He opened the door and she followed him inside to the living room. It was a bright cheery area, full of feminine touches – bright cushions, light curtains, women's magazines, and family photos on lots of the cupboards. He switched on the overhead fans, sending a cool breeze through the warm room.

'You're sure you want to see this?'

'If you're sure you want to share it.'

'I bet I'll regret it, but yes.' He smiled. 'I'll get the tape.'

While he was gone she studied a photo on the TV, an old black and white shot of a man and a woman with a baby. Daniel's parents, she guessed. His mother was very elegant. The house was obviously her work as well. Looking around, she noticed several unusual touches. There were coloured lines on the floor, and locks on the cupboards. Like a kindergarten crossed with a *Home Beautiful* centrespread.

He returned with the tape. 'Unfortunately I was able to land my hands on it straight away.'

She put down the photo, hoping he hadn't minded her looking. 'Are you an only child?'

'No, I've got a younger sister. Christine. She's away studying in New Zealand at the moment.'

'Oh, right. And has she got children?'

'No.'

She didn't think he had children, either. She was puzzled. The house looked like it had been well and truly childproofed. Maybe his mother did child-minding. She'd liked to have asked more questions, but he was now crouched in front of the television and video recorder. She looked at his long back, lean under the T-shirt, and had to blink away a clear memory of kissing it.

He pressed play and then pause so that a shimmery stilled image appeared on the screen. 'You realise I'm only doing this in the interests of fairness. After me seeing those photos of you and the Alphabet Sisters.'

She took a seat on the sofa and nodded. 'I understand. The "I show you mine and you show me yours" principle.' In light of their Melbourne meeting, it suddenly felt like the wrong thing to have said.

His lip twitched. 'That's right.' He leaned against the door frame behind her and pointed the remote control.

She was laughing out loud in just moments. It was a low-budget TV talent show from the early 1980s. The set appeared to be made of tinfoil and plastic cartons. Dangerous were on third, after a woman singing a fast and off-key version of 'Love Me Do' and a dreamy-looking harpist playing a Scottish air, also very fast. The host introduced Dangerous with mock fear, warning viewers that the following scenes might disturb.

She recognised Daniel immediately, a smaller version of himself, with black kohl around his eyes, black lipstick, spiky hair and ripped clothes. Skinny white arms poked out of his torn T-shirt and he'd perfected a good snarl that obviously amused the director. There were at least six close-ups of Daniel pulling a face at the camera. The lyrics were straightforward, about being tormented with nightmares about rats and spiders and snakes.

She was still laughing by the time Daniel pressed pause. She had to wipe her eyes, sure there was mascara all over her face. 'So did you win?'

'No, and to this day, I don't know why. I think we were much better than the harpist. Did you like the lyrics? I can write them down for you if you want.'

'No, thanks anyway. What was that rhyme in the chorus again, snake with awake? Very inflammatory.'

'Don't mock a twelve-year-old. It was hard to talk about bringing down the government when you couldn't spell the word. I stuck to what I knew. The girls at school were terrified of me.'

'You're lucky Lola hasn't seen this. She'd have written a part in the musical especially for you. You beat the Alphabet Sisters hands down.'

'Oh, I don't know. What was it you won? Third prize in the Miss Indooroopilly Talent Quest of 1978? Even though you were the only entrants?'

'Lola told you about that as well?'

'No, you told me. That night in Melbourne.'

'I did?'

'Don't you remember? When we left the party and went to that little Italian bar. You told me all about the Alphabet Sisters. I hadn't laughed so much in a long time.'

'I did? You hadn't?'

He gave her a long, thoughtful look. 'Bett, do you actually remember much of that night?'

She'd spent three years trying to forget it. 'Um, yes, some of it.'

A pause. 'Do you mind telling me which parts?'

'I remember meeting you at the club.'

'Yes.'

'And I remember . . . going to the bar. And then to your flat, talking, and then, um, going to bed with you . . .'

A glimmer of a smile. 'Good.'

Something about the way he was looking at her made her want to tell him the truth. 'But mostly I remember waking up and being so embarrassed at my behaviour I crept away as quickly as I could.'

'Embarrassed? Why?'

'You know,' she said feebly. She couldn't say the rest of it. Because I seemed to have got it into my head I was a sex goddess. Because I didn't so much throw myself at you as hurl myself at you . . .

'Bett, don't be embarrassed. I enjoyed it. All of it.' He gave a slight shrug. 'That's why I was disappointed that you'd gone when I woke up. Before we'd had a chance to swap numbers. I went back to the bar we met at a couple of times, but I didn't see you there again.'

'You did?' She hadn't gone within a two-mile radius of the place after that night.

'I was going to ring the motel here, to see if they had a number. But I thought because of all the problems with your sister and your fiancé that might be a bit awkward.'

She cringed inside. Had she shut up for a single moment all night?

'And then I figured if you'd wanted to see me again, you would have left a note. Look, as I said the other day, I was disappointed you didn't want to see me again, but I got over it. I don't want you to feel awkward about this.'

'That's what you meant last week when you said you'd got over it?'

He looked puzzled. 'What did you think I meant?'

'That you'd got over the night. Got over how terrible it was. And then you said that it wasn't the first time and it wouldn't be the last time. I thought you were talking about having one-night stands.'

He threw back his head and laughed. 'Oh, yes. Danger Hilder rides again. No, Bett. I actually don't make a habit of one-night stands. Not that we were a real one-night stand, anyway, were we? Don't one-night stands have to be between strangers?'

'I'm not too sure of the official definition. I haven't made a habit of them either.'

'No?' There was a sparkle in his eye. 'You're very good at them, for a novice.'

'You're one to talk.' She could hardly believe they were joking about this.

His phone beeped and he checked the text message. 'I don't know why I thought country papers would be quieter than city ones. We'd better get back.'

They were pulling into the carpark behind the *Valley Times* office when she felt she had to mention it one more time.

'Daniel, thank you for being so nice about it today.' She hesitated. 'And three years ago.'

'It was my pleasure, Bett.'

Bett knew he was remembering exactly what she was remembering. 'Good. Great. Well, see you later, then.' Once again, she nearly tripped as she climbed out of the car.

Chapter Nineteen

'Welcome, General MacArthur. Can I offer you one of our finest lamingtons?'

Anna sighed. Still no good. So much for her pep talk the previous week. Yes, some of them had learned their lines, and yes, some of the songs sounded a bit better, but the acting was still atrocious. There was no other word for it. This was the fifth run-through of the scene featuring the CWA president, Mrs Smith, greeting the newly arrived General MacArthur at the Terowie Station and it was getting worse, not better.

'One more time? With perhaps a little bit of enthusiasm?' The woman sounded as though she was offering him a plate of snake heads instead of cakes.

Mrs Smith put her hands on her hips. 'I can't help it if I don't like lamingtons. Have you ever tried to make them? You get chocolate icing and coconut all over the place and the cake always crumbles.'

'Well, could you pretend you like lamingtons? Just for this scene?'

'Can't I offer him a cheese sandwich or something simple like that?'

Anna kept her voice calm. 'An American General has survived

days of fierce battles, has travelled on a train for hours and hours to your tiny town in the middle of nowhere and you want to offer him a cheese sandwich?'

'He might like cheese sandwiches. We might have heard from one of his people that he likes cheese sandwiches. Sometimes the simple things are what people want. I read in a magazine once that Princess Diana used to get sick of all that fancy food and would long for a night in front of the TV eating cheese on toast.'

Anna tried counting to ten. Then to twenty. It didn't help. What had got into them all tonight? She looked around the room. Romeo and the American GI were playing an improvised game of table tennis in a corner of the room. The musicians from the high school were reading pop magazines instead of rehearsing their songs with Bett. General MacArthur was sending text messages. The plumber playing Jack-the-Lad had disappeared, muttering something about a burst pipe in one of the pubs in town.

Things had been as bad earlier, too. Kaylene had at least learnt her lines, but was insisting on speaking them in an English accent.

'Kaylene, you can't,' Anna had said. 'She's American.'

'But she doesn't sound posh enough. Can't she be English? I love doing English accents.'

'If we were doing *My Fair Lady*, yes. But you're Mrs MacArthur. Mrs Married-to-the-American-General-and-an-American-herself MacArthur. So will you please speak in an American accent?'

Kaylene folded her arms. 'There's no need to get huffy about it.'

Things had gone no better with Kaylene's father, either. Len had arrived with the first of the set panels that evening. His painting of the railway station at Terowie looked more like the interior of a submarine. He had been telling her for days how well the train was going and then had produced it in a shoebox. It was five inches long.

'Len, I don't know if this is going to work on the stage. It's a bit small, don't you think?'

'This is the model, Anna.' He roared laughing. 'As if this would be the real one.'

'It's just you've spent days making it and I'm a bit worried we're running out of time.'

'It's the detail that takes time. See, Anna, take a look. I've even painted tiny people in the carriages. Have a look.'

Anna looked. Yes, so he had. A row of faces grinned wildly out of one of the little carriages. Marvellous. Splendid. Especially if she was planning on staging this musical in an ant farm. What was she supposed to do – give everyone in the audience a pair of binoculars?

'So can it be a cheese sandwich, Anna?' the CWA woman asked stubbornly now. 'Maybe even a cheese and tomato sandwich?'

Anna stared at her. 'Can you please excuse me?'

She marched out the door, across the carpark and knocked politely on Lola's door.

'Come in.'

Lola was in bed, a folder of papers on her lap. 'Anna, darling, how are things going?'

Anna opened her mouth, screamed, then shut her mouth again. Feeling much better, she turned on her heel and returned to the rehearsals.

The next morning in his room, Richard Lawrence took a break from his writing and picked up the latest edition of the *Valley Times*. As he flicked through the pages, an article on page five caught his eye.

Auditions Unearth Valley's Hidden Talent

Auditions for the forthcoming fund-raiser musical *Many Happy Returns* unearthed a surprising amount of local talent, musical director Anna Quinlan said this week.

All seven lead roles have been cast, with a large chorus also assembled for the 1940s-style musical, written by Anna's grandmother, Lola Quinlan (80).

The musical is loosely based on the true story of General Douglas MacArthur's wartime visit to the small town of Terowie.

It will be staged at the Clare Town Hall on March 20, the anniversary of General MacArthur's visit to Terowie. All proceeds will go to the Buy a New Ambulance Fund. Tickets are available from the Valley View Motel.

Richard smiled. Anna had told him she'd given a diplomatic interview to the local paper. She had called over for another drink after rehearsals the evening before. She was such good company, full of stories about plays she'd been in, voice-overs she'd done, but filled with questions for him as well, about London, about his work. She'd also been keeping him hugely entertained with stories of the rehearsals, five-inch trains, stubborn actors and all.

'It's not too late for you to join in, you know,' she'd said. 'I'm sure I could find you a part. General MacArthur even.'

'No thanks. I'm happy to save myself up for the opening-night audience.' He'd already extended his stay for another fortnight so he could be there.

His mobile rang, and he hoped briefly it was Anna calling from Adelaide. She'd told him she was going there early that morning to hunt down some costumes for the musical. She'd thought it was safely in Len's hands and then discovered his idea of an army uniform was a spray-painted ice-cream container helmet and a broom stick as a gun – with the bristles still attached.

The name Charlie came up on the phone display. Charlie Wentworth, a university friend currently travelling around Australia producing an offbeat cable TV travel series. 'Charlie, hello.'

'Mr Lawrence, how are things with you? That book of yours still coming along?'

'Couldn't be better. How about you? Still headed this way?' He settled back, preparing to be entertained as his friend filled him in on the latest batch of items he'd been filming. The program specialised in quirky 'Did you know?' stories. Last time they'd spoken Charlie had just finished a segment on Australia's oversized tourist attractions – the giant fibreglass pineapples, koalas, lobsters and oranges dotted around the countryside.

Charlie had just as many stories this time. Richard laughed as he heard of a filming disaster in the Flinders Ranges the previous week. Charlie had tracked down a camel that made a sound uncannily like the tune of 'Jingle Bells' when it brayed. The animal had upped and died the morning they arrived.

'How very inconsiderate, leaving a hole in your schedule like that.'

'Who are you telling? Keep an ear out for stories for me, would you? I'm desperate, to tell you the truth. Any sort of Australiana you can lay your hands on.'

Richard picked up the newspaper beside him. 'All right, then. Did you know that in 1942 General Douglas MacArthur, yes, as in the song "MacArthur Park", caught a train from Alice Springs, stopped at a tiny outback town and made one of the most famous speeches of the war?'

'Is there a plaque marking the spot? A MacArthur plaque?'

'Very funny.'

'What's the place? I've never heard of it.'

'Terowie,' Richard read from the newspaper. 'I think that's how you pronounce it. It's not far from where I am. Less than an hour, anyway. You could drive through it on your way here, check it out.'

'Rich, you might have saved my bacon. Are there any locals who'd remember it? Anybody I can get to talk about it?'

'I don't know. The only expert on the subject I know is an eighty-year-old Irishwoman here in Clare who's written a musical based on it.'

'An eighty-year-old Irishwoman who's done what?'

Richard filled him in. He could nearly hear Charlie thinking it through. 'Could we film a bit of it, do you think? Just enough to add a bit of colour and movement to the station footage?'

'Let me check and I'll call you right back.'

He dialled the number of a phone just two rooms away. 'Lola, hello, it's Richard. Something very interesting has come up. Would you have a moment to talk about it?'

Ten minutes later, Lola hung up the phone and beamed from ear to ear. God had been smiling on them the day Richard Lawrence came to stay at their motel.

'Would I like to be interviewed on a TV program? Would I like my musical to be filmed? Richard, has Elizabeth Taylor got any jewellery? Was Fred Astaire light on his feet? When? Now? All I need is five minutes to pop on a bit of makeup.'

Richard had laughed down the phone. 'It won't be for a couple of weeks, Lola, if it happens at all. They're still working out their filming schedules. It's just a possibility, an idea, but I wanted to check with you first, to see if you minded.'

'Such manners, Richard. You're one of the world's gentlemen.

Let me say loudly and clearly, we would love to appear on the program. Just say the word and I'll have them all primed and ready.'

'I'll call my friend back, then. He'll probably want to talk to you himself as well, if that's okay?'

'Oh, darling, it would be my pleasure.' She was thinking quickly. 'But it might be best to keep it a secret from everyone else for the time being, from my granddaughters as well as the cast, don't you think? Just in case it doesn't come off. I'd hate to disappoint anyone.'

'That's probably good advice,' he'd said.

Which Lola had no intention of following herself. She ran her eye down the cast phone list in the folder beside her, trying to decide who would be the best one to tell. Who had the biggest mouth, to put it bluntly. Of course, Len the butcher. Plant a little seed with him and before long it would have turned into a big oak tree. And if Lola knew human nature as well as she thought she did, Anna might find her problems at rehearsals magically disappearing.

She dialled the number. 'Len, it's Lola Quinlan, up at the motel. Oh, I'm absolutely grand again, not a bother on me. I've had a bit of news about the musical, and I'm bursting to tell someone and I know how involved you are in it, but will you promise me you'll keep it to yourself?' She lowered her voice to a whisper. 'It looks like a British TV company is going to come and film a documentary about us. I'm not sure when, soon. Yes, isn't it wonderful? The only thing that's worrying me is everyone might not have learnt their lines by then, or the set won't be ready and we'll be the laughing stock of the United Kingdom. Or of the world, if they end up showing it on all the cable channels. Oh, I'm absolutely serious. The producer is a mad fanatic about General MacArthur, apparently. He couldn't believe his luck when he heard about it. Don't tell anyone, though, will you? And it's especially important that you don't tell my granddaughters. Even if you happen to let it slip to someone else, as long as they don't find out. I want it to be a real surprise for them.'

She hung up, pleased with herself. She waited and then tested her hunch, ringing Len's number. It was engaged. Good. She had a feeling it would be engaged for the rest of the night.

At the rehearsals three nights later, Bett turned away from the piano, amazed. Anna and Carrie came over.

'Has someone put something into the town water?' Anna asked.

'It's bizarre, isn't it?' Carrie whispered.

Every single cast member knew their lines, and the words to the songs. They had all arrived on time. There was an air of excitement about them as well, faces made up, clothes a little more flash. Kaylene looked like she was on her way to a nightclub.

'That pep talk you gave them really had an impact,' Bett said.

Anna smiled proudly. 'It must have. Whatever it was, I'm not questioning it. If this keeps up, we might get there yet.' She clapped her hands to end the break. 'All right, everyone, from the top once again.'

Chapter Twenty

It was one week later. Lola lay back further against her pillow and yawned delicately. 'It's a terrible thing, but since I've turned eighty I seem to be feeling tired earlier each night.'

'Is it your arm? Do you need any pain-killers?' Bett turned from the wardrobe where she was hanging up Lola's clothes. The three of them had been taking turns dressing and minding Lola since she had broken her wrist. Tonight Bett was on duty. Carrie was on a night off. Anna had gone to Adelaide again to collect the last of the costumes. Ellen was already tucked up in Bett's room for the night.

'Not at all. It's not giving me any bother at all. You're the ones it's bothering, having to come in here every morning and night to dress me. And don't think I'm not noticing that you're trying to change the clothes I wear, because I am.'

Bett smiled innocently.

'What do you think of that Richard Lawrence, Bett?'

Bett didn't blink at the change in subject. 'He seems nice.' He seemed very nice, actually. But she still hadn't invited him out for that drink. Life seemed to have suddenly got too busy, between the musical, and work in the motel, and the assignments with Daniel around the Valley . . .

'He has an excellent sense of humour, you know.'

'He seems to have, yes.'

'I wish I'd known at your age that a sense of humour is worth far more than a bulging wallet or a bulging –'

'Stop it, Lola.'

'Truly, a shared sense of humour is all you need to get you through.'

'Was Edward funny?'

'No.'

'He didn't make you laugh?'

'He might have once, that time he tripped over the fence wire. Yes, that was very funny.'

'Why did you marry him, then?'

'Things were different in my day. And especially with my family.'

'It was an arranged marriage, do you mean?' Lola had never been so forthcoming.

'A suitable marriage would probably be the correct term.' Lola wasn't in the mood to talk any more about that right now. She yawned widely, covering her mouth in a mannerly way. 'As a matter of fact, Richard was asking about you today.'

'Was he?'

Actually, he hadn't been. Lola hadn't seen him today. 'Yes, he asked me if you were single. He also said he thought you had the most beautiful eyes he'd seen.'

'What?'

'And the creamiest skin. Is that how he put it? No, sorry, he said milky-white skin.'

'Richard said that? He's hardly spent any time with me. How would he know what my skin is like?'

'He mentioned how much he enjoyed your company the night of my party. How entertaining you were.'

'Did he?'

In Lola's experience, nothing made someone more attractive than to think they found you attractive. And Richard may well have thought all those things about Bett. Perhaps he was too shy to mention them.

A knock at the door. Richard poked his head around. 'I'm ready when you are, Lola. Oh, good evening, Bett.'

'Hello, Richard.' Her smile was very broad.

Lola yawned extravagantly. 'I'm so sorry, Richard, but I just seem to be overcome with tiredness this evening. And so suddenly.' She turned to Bett. 'Richard was saying today how curious he was about the whole MacArthur story and kindly invited me out for a meal so he could pick my brains.' Another yawn. 'Richard, my dear Bett knows the story as well as I do, if not better, and she'll have that journalist's way of giving you the concise story, whereas I would be inclined to ramble all over the place. Or nod off mid-sentence, the way I'm feeling tonight. Bett, would you mind at all taking my place as Richard's dinner guest tonight? Richard, I promise she's sparkling company.'

Richard handled it all very smoothly. 'It would be my pleasure, of course. But I wouldn't like to deprive you of a night out, Lola. We can reschedule for another night when you're not so tired if you like.'

'I seem to be tired every night these days.'

Bett glared at her. It was only tonight she'd been complaining of this sudden tiredness. 'I can't go out, Lola. I'm minding Ellen tonight.'

'Is she asleep yet?'

Bett shook her head.

'Then bring her in to me and I'll mind her myself. We'll both be asleep before eight o'clock, I should think.'

Five minutes later Ellen had been transferred into the double bed beside Lola. Bett had hurried back to her room, changed into a new skirt, run a brush through her curls and applied mascara and lip gloss.

She poked her head into Lola's room. 'You're not up to anything, are you?'

'How could I be? I'm too tired. I look tired, don't I, Ellen?'

Ellen was propped up with several pillows, in imitation of Lola. 'Yes, you look very, very tired.'

That sounded suspiciously rehearsed to Bett. 'Goodnight, then.'

'Have fun,' Lola called.

'Have fun,' Ellen echoed.

Lola waited until Bett had definitely gone, then brought out a packet of chocolate éclairs from under her pillow, pointed the remote control at the TV and grinned at her great-granddaughter. 'Make yourself comfy, Ellen. You're going to love this.'

As the opening credits of *Mary Poppins* came up, Lola smiled to herself. *Operation Richard and Bett*, we have lift off.

Richard had made the dinner booking at Lorikeet Hill, a small winery-restaurant south of the town. The food was delicious, the Irish music playing in the background soothing. The wine relaxed Bett's mood and loosened her tongue. Richard seemed genuinely interested in so many things. Not just the General MacArthur story, but in Lola, Anna, Carrie, herself – all of them.

He refilled her glass. 'So you went to journalism college a couple of years after you left high school?'

'That's right.'

'And Anna went to drama school around the same time?'

She nodded. 'She always said that the Alphabet Sisters had given her the edge. Not many people have spent six years touring the country by the time they're nineteen.'

'And she met her husband in Sydney?'

'That's right.' She pulled a face. 'Unfortunately.'

'You don't like him?'

'Sorry, that was very childish.' And alcohol-induced, she realised. Bett tried to find the words. 'If Glenn was an animal, he'd be a bear. If he was a vehicle, he'd be a bulldozer. But he adores Anna, and I suppose that's all that matters at the end of the day.'

'He adores Anna?'

'He idolises her. Worships the ground she walks on.' It had given herself and Carrie the creeps, in fact. Glenn had a way of looking at Anna, of talking about her, as if she was his latest acquisition. 'This is my new car, this is my big house on the harbour and this is my beautiful actress wife.'

Richard was looking at her closely. 'And how long since you've seen Glenn and Anna together?'

'It's been a while, actually.'

'A while?'

'More than three years,' she admitted.

As the waiter came up and removed their plates, Bett realised how much she'd been talking. He must have been a skilled journalist, she guessed. She should be taking tips from him, not spilling her soul. She waited until the waiter left before she spoke again. 'You're not about to write an unauthorised biography of the Alphabet Sisters, are you? I don't know if there's enough scandal for a book.'

'Oh, I don't know about that.'

She caught something in his tone and narrowed her eyes. 'You know, don't you?'

He gave a slightly sheepish smile. 'A little.'

Bett cursed Lola inside. Of course she would have told Richard all about it. 'Can I ask exactly what you were told?'

'That you had been engaged to a man here in Clare but then he met your younger sister and fell in love with her instead. And that there was a row between you and Anna and Carrie, and that you hadn't spoken or seen each other from then until Lola's party.'

'Well, that's it in a nutshell, I suppose.'

'That must have been terrible for you.'

She took a sip of wine. 'Yes, it was. It's been hard. I've missed them a lot.'

'Them?'

'Anna and Carrie.'

'I actually meant it must have been terrible when your fiancé left you for your sister.'

Bett blinked. 'Yes. Yes, it was.'

The waiter came then with their main courses. Bett was glad of the interruption, taking the opportunity to steer the conversation back to safer ground. They spoke about the musical, about Lola, and then Richard moved on to the Alphabet Sisters again.

'Do you miss those days? All that adulation? The tours? The motel rooms?'

'Well, we'd grown up in motel rooms, so that was never a luxury for us.'

He laughed. 'No, I suppose not. What did you demand? That the promoters give you a three-bedroomed suburban house to stay in?'

'Exactly. And you should have seen our backstage requests. Bottles of lemonade. Comics. Barbie dolls.'

'Now we're getting down to the nitty-gritty.' He grinned. 'I think I always wanted to be a showbiz journalist. You know, sniffing out the stories behind the stories, the truth behind the public image.'

'Oh, we were squeaky clean, I promise. Except for the time Anna and I stole a bottle of Dad's wine. And Lola told Carrie off for swearing a few times, but I think she apologised afterwards.'

'So why did it come to an end?'

Bett thought about it. She could wave it away. Or she could tell the truth. 'Because of me.'

'You?'

'I finished it. I refused to do it any more.'

'Why?'

Because of their awful final performance at the local music society Christmas show. The real number one on her embarrassing stories hit parade. 'It's a long story.'

'Tell me,' he said.

She took a sip of her wine, gathered her thoughts, then started to talk.

They'd been too old for it, really – Anna eighteen, Bett sixteen, Carrie nearly fourteen. The three of them had stood in age order, as always. Lola had gone all out on their outfits, dressing each of them in red satin, with a green tinsel hat. In the mirror, Bett had been aware that her dress was tighter on her than Carrie's and Anna's were, but Lola had just hugged her, told her she was gorgeous and sent the three of them out onto the stage.

Midway through 'Sisters', their opening number, she looked out into the audience and noticed the three cool boys of the town. Her heart gave a leap, as she veered from self-consciousness to excitement. She looked away, then looked back. The three of them were actually looking at her, concentrating on her for once, not Anna, not Carrie. She had a rush of confidence, stood straighter, sang louder, smiled wider.

Then one of them shouted, 'Piggy in the Middle.'

The people in the front of the hall heard. She noticed neighbours leaning and asking what he'd said and then stifling a laugh themselves. The three boys kept it up as a sort of chant, under their breaths. She tried to keep singing, knowing her cheeks were fiery red, feeling as though her skin was about to burst. They nudged a few of their other friends into it as well then, a row of them mouthing the chant 'Piggy in the Middle'. Anna hadn't noticed or, if she had, hadn't cared – too busy striking an aloof pose, always the lady. Carrie had probably been too busy revelling in the fact she was attracting most of the admiring glances, people nudging each other and whispering, 'Isn't that little one cute?'

Somehow she got through the other three songs. But she was in tears when they came off stage. Lola was waiting. She had noticed everything. 'They're just stupid, silly boys, Bett. Ignore them, do you hear me?'

In Lola's arms, Bett was almost comforted. Then from behind her came Carrie's voice. 'Maybe you could lose a bit of weight, Bett, if you don't mind me saying. We probably would look better if we were all the same sort of size.'

Her tears stopped abruptly. She felt as though iced water had been flung over her. 'What do you mean by that? I spoil the look?'

'Not spoil it. But if we are going to do this thing seriously, keep up the Alphabet Sisters, then maybe you do need to think about losing some weight.'

Bett turned to her other sister. 'And what do you think, Anna? Do you think I should lose weight?'

Anna gave a shrug. 'Carrie's got a point, yes. But it's your choice how you look.'

Bett refused to sing with the Alphabet Sisters from that moment on. There had been three more performances booked after the Christmas one, but she point blank refused to do them. Lola tried talking sense. Anna tried to apologise. Carrie was sent in, pleading, eyes filling with tears. But it was too late for Bett. The Piggy in the Middle taunt had lodged itself firmly in her brain. She was never going to perform with her sisters again.

Anna didn't mind too much. She'd already set her heart on getting into drama school and treated the Alphabet Sisters as a joke by this stage. But Carrie was very upset. One of the performances was going to be televised on the local TV network. She'd been looking forward to it for weeks. She kept trying to talk Bett around.

'Please. You have to do it, Bett.'

'No, I don't. I told you, I'm never singing with you again.'

'But I apologised.'

'Only because Lola told you to.'

'But I really am sorry.'

'You should have thought before you spoke.'

'You're spoiling it for everyone else. Not just me. For Lola. For the TV people.'

'I would have thought you and Anna would love to have the stage to yourself, without me spoiling the perfect look.'

Carrie had lost her temper. 'I didn't call you Piggy in the Middle, it was those boys. But you are behaving like a pig now. A selfish pig. And I'll get you back for this, I promise.'

Bett didn't tell Richard this, but the truth was that her sisters' lack of support had hurt far more than the taunts. It had been the start of a horrible period of her life. From that moment on it seemed as though Anna and Carrie had been set adrift from her, into a world of romance, dates, boys and confidence. Bett had felt like Cinderella and Bessie Bunter rolled into one – overweight, unhappy, finding pleasure only in food and books and her piano.

'And that was the end of it,' she said to Richard. 'We just stopped.'

He had been listening closely. 'They always say it's the people closest to you who know how to hurt you the most.'

'I suppose so.' She tried to lighten the mood. 'That'll teach you to ask me a question when I've had half a bottle of wine. You should have shut me up.'

'I didn't want to. I was very interested. And I'm sorry, Bett. Being a teenager's not much fun for anyone, but that must have been hard on you.'

'Yes. Yes it was, actually.'

'And is that why you think Carrie made a play for Matthew? To get you back for something that had happened years before?'

'I'm sorry?'

'You said that Carrie told you she was going to get you back for it one day. And then years later she broke up your engagement and married your fiancé. Do you think it was connected?'

Was he mad? Carrie and Matthew had genuinely fallen in love. Bett had always known that. She'd seen how they were with each other. It had been an almost instant attraction.

She stared at him as she realised what she'd just admitted to herself. Behind his glasses, Richard was assessing her closely. Kindly, but still closely. She decided then she'd definitely had enough of talking about herself.

'No, I don't think it was connected at all. In fact, I'm sure it wasn't.' She made a point of picking up the water jug and refilling his glass until it was nearly overflowing. 'So, enough about me.' She was pleased with how firm her voice sounded. 'This book of yours, Richard. It's set in the 1850s, did you say?'

Chapter Twenty-One

Anna glanced at the dashboard clock as she drove through Auburn, the town that marked the start of the Clare Valley. She was making good time. She noticed her hands on the steering wheel. They were actually quite relaxed, not gripping it like it was a lifeline. In Sydney she'd often caught herself driving like that. Then again, in Sydney lots of things had been different. Up there her thinking time had been filled with jagged thoughts of Glenn, memories of rows past and premonitions of arguments they were sure to have in the future, a constant barrage of angry voices and disagreements. But since she'd been in the Valley there had been softer images in her mind. Nicer things to think about.

The musical, for one. It had surprised her how much she was enjoying it. Not just the rehearsals, but all the production side as well. She'd had a very productive trip to Adelaide today, collecting the final props and costumes from different fancy-dress shops around the city. Everything was slowly coming together.

She was even feeling a bit better. Not quite so tense. She'd tried to explain exactly that to the doctor that morning, when she'd called in to the surgery for her follow-up appointment. She'd expected to get the cheerful red-faced older man again, not this serious-faced woman, who looked less than twenty-five and seemed determined to find out the cause of every scratch or bump she'd ever had in her life.

'Look, I'm sure it's probably just stress,' Anna had said to her. 'As your colleague said a few weeks ago, I needed to slow down a bit.'

'I don't like the sound of that breathlessness. How many weeks now?'

'A month, maybe two.'

'And it's getting worse?'

'I've been stressed,' she repeated. 'It's probably just panic attacks. And things are getting much better at home.' Not just with her sisters, either. She'd even managed to have a normal phone conversation with Glenn in Singapore. Short, but at least neither of them had hung up.

'You've never had asthma?'

'No, I haven't.'

'Anna, I'd like you to have a scan. Just to ease all our minds.'

'Is that necessary? It's just I've a lot on, and it means coming down to the city again. I live two hours away.' She gave the young doctor the look which usually stopped other people in their tracks. Not this time.

'I think it's very necessary, to put my mind at rest as much as yours. That's why we have all this technology, to show us what's not there as well as what might be there.' She made several phone calls, while Anna sat fidgeting.

The doctor put down the phone and smiled. 'We can get you in at the end of next week. They've had a cancellation.'

Anna scribbled the date and the address in her diary. It was two days after the musical. She'd be down in Adelaide anyway returning the costumes. 'Fine, thanks.'

As she walked back out to the car she'd taken her mobile from her bag and checked her messages. There was just one, from Lola, asking her to call. There'd been a little incident with Ellen at school today, but it was nothing to worry about.

Anna had called the number immediately, her heart beating faster. 'What is it, Lola? Not more trouble?'

'Hello, darling. No, I wouldn't say it's trouble exactly.'

How could Lola sound so calm? Amused even? 'More bullying? Or no, not another dog?'

'No, a sheep. Bumper the sheep, to be precise.'

'Bumper?'

'Ellen took Bumper to school today. For show-and-tell. I had a phone call half an hour ago from her teacher to ask if I could come and collect him.'

Anna had felt a bubble of laughter start deep inside her. 'How did she get him there without anyone seeing? I thought Bett walked her to school this morning.'

'She did, bright and early. Then it seems Ellen walked back to the motel, untied Bumper and headed back to school. Along the back roads, you'll be pleased to know.'

'And her teacher didn't mind?'

'The teacher didn't know until it was Ellen's turn to stand up in front of the class. She apparently said, and I quote, that she had to "slip outside for a moment and fetch something". She'd tethered him to a tree at the end of the playground.' Lola was laughing now too. 'You probably also should know that she's invited everyone in her class back to the motel for her birthday party. And they've all accepted.'

'But it's not her birthday for months.'

'I don't think she specified a date. She seemed more interested in outlining what the food and entertainment would be. Prawn cocktails, hide-and-seek in the motel rooms and rides on Bumper's back featured quite prominently, I believe.'

Anna had been laughing properly by then. 'Oh, Lola, I'm sorry. Can you sort it out for me or do you want me to drive back right now?'

'Sort it out? What's there to sort out? I'm going to take lessons from her.'

Anna grinned again at the thought of it. Being in the Valley had been so good for Ellen. She had noticed her daughter growing more confident every day. Happier. More relaxed. The way a child should be.

As she drove past more vineyards, getting closer to Clare, Anna started thinking of someone who made *her* feel good and happy and relaxed. Richard. She thought of the late-night glasses of wine and conversations they'd shared. He was so curious, courteous. He had a way of resting his head slightly on one side, like an owl, she'd thought at first, but then it became more endearing than that. He wore glasses, which he adjusted a lot, especially when he was talking passionately about something. He liked cricket, and didn't like it when she told him how bad the English team were these days. He also disagreed with her opinions on Harold Pinter, Neil Simon and David Hare, but completely agreed with her in regard to Shakespeare, Beckett and O'Casey. That had led to her telling him all about her unsuccessful acting career and how it had led to her new very successful voice-over career.

He had turned on the small TV in the room and made her sit with him until one of her ads came on. They hadn't had to wait long. He sat in silence as the ad played. Afterwards he took her hands and kissed her on each cheek. 'You were marvellous, darling.

Such a combination of pathos and urgency. It was a truly bravura performance.'

The ad was for brake fluid and she had been the voice of the car. She'd inclined her head, accepting the praise, trying not to laugh. 'I do actually think that was one of my best moments.'

'Can I get a video? I'd love to see it again. I'm sure there were some subtleties of your performance I missed.'

She smiled now, remembering the teasing. Fun teasing, not the sneering way Glenn had often spoken about her work. They'd talked for hours that night. He'd told her more about his life in London. He'd talked about the three-year relationship he'd had with a fellow reporter, until she had ended it the year before. It was another reason why he had decided to leave London. And so she had told him about Glenn, and Glenn and Julie, and Glenn and Julie and Singapore.

She felt warm, good, thinking about him. And the more time she spent with him, the sexier she was finding him, too. Not in the confident, macho way she had found Glenn sexy. Richard was more quietly confident, slow burning rather than white heat. She found it even more attractive that he hadn't made a pass at her. He just listened. Seemed so interested. When it was time to leave he walked her to her own room, five doors down. 'Sleep tight,' he'd said, before kissing her on the cheek, gently touching her arm at the same time. She had never felt quite so cared for in her life.

They'd arranged to meet for a glass of wine when she got home tonight. He was taking Lola out to dinner, he'd told her the night before, but expected to be home by eleven. It was half past ten. She couldn't wait to see him.

Bett and Richard stood in the motel carpark.

'Thanks, Richard. That was a lovely night.'

'You're welcome, Bett. I enjoyed it too.'

She wondered whether she should invite him in for a glass of wine. Or would he invite her in for a glass of wine? But there was no spark between them, she'd realised. She liked him, enjoyed talking to him, even if she had told him too much. But that was all.

'Well, goodnight.'

'Goodnight.'

Inside her room, she sat on the bed and pulled her knees under her chin. Her conversation over dinner kept echoing in her mind.

'It's been hard. I've missed them a lot.'

'Them?'

'Anna and Carrie.'

'I actually meant it must have been terrible when your fiancé left you for your sister.'

She went into the bathroom and stared at herself in the mirror, not liking what she saw. She wiped her hand across her lips, smearing her lip gloss. She leaned in closer and saw her mascara was already smudged. How many years had she stared at that face, felt cross, felt angry, felt powerless? When was maturity going to kick in? When would she get the ability to deal confidently with everything life sent to her?

She decided to have a shower, needing to stand under the stream of water, wash away some of the troubling thoughts. She turned the shower tap on full blast, wanting to fill the room with steam before she got in. As she went back out to the bedroom area to get her dressing-gown, she heard a car pull up next door, the headlights momentarily coming through the thin fabric of the motel curtains. Anna arriving home from her trip to Adelaide, she guessed. Five to eleven, a late enough night for her. Bett undressed, stepped under the streaming water and shut her eyes.

After carrying the costumes into her room, Anna simply turned off the light again, shut the door after her and walked five doors down. She knocked lightly, two little taps.

He answered immediately. 'Anna, welcome back.' His smile was as warm as his voice.

'Hello, Richard.' She took in every detail of him.

'Anna? Are you all right?'

'I'm fine.' She was more than fine. She was happy, she realised. She was home at the motel. She knew Ellen was safe in Lola's room. There had been a note on Anna's bed in Ellen's best handwriting. 'I love you Mummy', with a picture of Bumper the sheep and the two of them in bright colours. Anna felt light after months of heaviness. She spoke softly, but surely. 'Richard, I know I should be coy. And that we should spend more time together first. And have dinner, and go for walks, and get to know each other better. But I don't want to wait that long. I want to go to bed with you.'

'Now?'

'Yes.'

'Right now?'

'Yes.' She faltered slightly.

'Will you at least give me time to make the bed?'

She smiled. 'No, I won't.'

'Never mind, then. We'll have to manage.' He took her by the hand and drew her inside his room.

Bett sat on the edge of her bed, wrapped in a towel. Her mind was leaping all over the place. From the dinner with Richard tonight to her conversation with Anna the other night. '*Still avoiding the truth after all these years, Bett?*'

She hadn't been avoiding it. She'd known for years, in fact. It's just she had chosen not to tell anyone, to let the rift go unhealed between them, for three long years. But why? Because she wanted to keep the rift going? Because she was glad to be away from her sisters?

Yes.

That night of their fight she'd felt a hot high flame of anger that she'd never felt before. In the days and months that followed she had easily found other fuel to keep it burning. Some of it had surprised her. Memories of Anna doing things first – learning to ride a bike, wearing a bra, wearing makeup – and feeling jealous, that she always had to wait her turn. Being equally jealous of Carrie, who had been born with all the right accessories for life success – a mop of blonde curls, a small frame, even a slight lisp as a child, like some modern version of Shirley Temple, without the saccharine sweetness.

She had a sudden urge to talk to Anna about it all. About everything. To apologise for the terrible things she had said about Glenn. She'd had no right. Anna loved him and Glenn loved Anna. Their marriage was their business. The remorse lasted for a moment, then she started remembering things about Glenn. His arrogance. The way he could be so condescending. It was no good. She couldn't pretend she liked Glenn. But she could still apologise for saying such mean things about him.

Bett pulled on her dressing-gown, slipped outside and headed to Anna's door. The lights were out. She knocked gently.

'Anna?' she said softly.

No answer. She must have gone straight to sleep.

Bett looked down the row of rooms and saw a light on in Richard

Lawrence's window. Perhaps she could start with him instead, use him as a trial run. She imagined it. 'Hello, Richard. You don't know me that well, but I need to make another confession, if you don't mind.'

As she watched, his light went out. She felt a sudden frustration. Why had everyone decided to have an early night? She waited a moment, then turned and went back into her own room, pulled back the sheets of her bed and climbed in.

In his room, Richard traced a finger across Anna's face in the light from the moon coming through the curtains. 'Do you know, I'm not sure if we got that quite right.'

'I'm not too sure either,' Anna answered, just as solemnly. 'Perhaps we could try it again?'

'What a great idea.' He leaned down to kiss her again.

Chapter Twenty-two

By the time dawn came, Bett still wasn't asleep. It was a combination of the wine she'd drunk and the conversation with Richard, she decided. It seemed to have unleashed memories she'd kept well locked away for more than three years. Uncomfortable memories.

The motel room felt very claustrophobic. She needed to feel her limbs moving, hoped that would calm her mind. She pulled on tracksuit pants, a light windcheater, laced on her sneakers and crept out of her room as the sun was coming up over the gum trees on the hill across the road. She started walking out of the town, headed north past the vineyards, the early autumn colours of red and yellow appearing on the edges of the leaves, still heavy with fruit.

Walking usually soothed her. She'd been walking for an hour a day most days, since the year after she first started working on the newspaper. Lola had got her started, in her usual blunt way. She had come into Bett's room one afternoon, pulled a chair beside the bed Bett was lying on and looked very serious. 'Bett, we need to talk.'

'About what?'

'Do you remember that Piggy in the Middle jibe that upset you so much all those years ago?'

Bett had put down the bag of chips she was eating. 'Yes.'

'You might want to be careful or someone will call you that again.' She ignored Bett's shocked expression. 'I'm not the body police, but I don't like to see someone letting themself go, and that's what you're doing.'

'I've got every right to be as fat or as thin as I like. And you can hardly talk about clothes.' Stung by Lola's remarks, she'd wanted to hurt her back.

'I'm happy with what I wear, Bett. And if it makes you happy, you can be as big as you like and wear shapeless clothes for the rest of your life. But you're not happy, are you?'

For a moment her temper had flared. She had started to deny it. And then she had let the defences down, confessed all to Lola. No, she wasn't happy. She was extremely unhappy. Everything had been getting on top of her and the only comfort had been food. Sitting for hours studying or working at her desk, she'd consoled herself by eating biscuits and cakes and chips. And she was wearing baggy clothes because that was all that fitted her these days.

Lola had listened and then waited for the tears to pass. 'You have two choices, Bett. You can do something about your weight. Or you can stay as you are and decide not to let it bother you.'

'It does bother me. Of course it does. But what do I do? I'm useless in a gym or those aerobics classes. And I really love food. I don't want to live off cabbage soup for the rest of my life.'

'What are those two things hanging off your waist there?'

'They're my legs.'

'And what can they do?'

'Hold me up. Walk.'

'Walk. Exactly. From today I want you walking an hour a day, in rain or shine, fog or mist. Or, more likely, seeing as it's summer, in blazing sunshine day after day.'

'Walk?'

'Walk. The world's best exercise. The world's best calmer. No one ever regrets a walk, Bett. I'll be your trainer. I'll make you do it.'

'You'll walk with me?'

'On these old legs? I'd collapse in a moment. No, I'll drop you off somewhere and then I'll drive to the end of the walking trail and pick you up an hour later. And that way I'll know how far you've gone, and if you get to me any quicker I'll also know you've hitched a lift. And I can sit in the car and listen to classical music, which will calm me down at the same time the walk is calming you down. Is it a deal?'

Bett shook her grandmother's hand. 'It's a deal.'

So she had started it, walking for an hour every day, along the dusty roads at the back of the valley. Lola would drop her off and then head off in her small white car, driving past her, sitting upright in the car like a meerkat as she went past. The girls had always laughed at Lola's style of driving. Bett walked until she met Lola waiting some miles away, reading the paper, doing a crossword or sometimes dozing, classical music or a tape of musical highlights playing loudly from the car. Three months later Bett had summoned up the courage to go clothes shopping. She'd dropped only a size, but her body shape was different, firmer. She wasn't skinny – she'd never be skinny – but she was fitter and had definitely found a figure that she was comfortable with.

She'd met Matthew not long afterwards. He had moved to the Valley as a junior vet, while he was studying at the nearby agricultural college. She had interviewed him on his second day for a feature on new arrivals in the town. As an interview subject, he hadn't seemed eligible, so she hadn't been as nervous of him as she would have been if she met him in a bar or somewhere social. When he mentioned he didn't know anyone locally yet, she'd invited him for a drink up at the motel bar. Her father had poured him beers and asked him lots of questions, while Bett sat beside him, joining in, enjoying the fact it was her, not Anna or Carrie for once, sitting beside a good-looking man on these bar stools. Carrie had been on her overseas trip at the time. Anna was in Sydney.

The next weekend she and Matthew met again, this time in one of the three pubs in town. Again, she'd had no nerves. She felt relaxed with him. They met the weekend after that. It had become a regular thing, so stress-free, so easy that people in the town had started calling them a couple before they had thought too much about it themselves.

He'd kissed her on their fifth date. By the seventh date it had progressed to his hands touching her body. She'd decided six weeks into the relationship that she was going to sleep with him. She had gathered early on that he was more experienced than her. He'd had a number of girlfriends in Perth, he'd told her. On a weekend away, two months after they'd met, they'd had sex for the first time. It had been nice. Not earth-shattering, not painful, not even especially passionate, but comfortable. Easy. Gentle. It had continued that way, too. She was still self-conscious, not liking to make love in full light, feeling a bit awkward in the sexy underwear he started buying her. But the relief she felt outweighed any of that.

Because the truth was she had been a virgin when she started going out with Matthew. At twenty-eight years old. There had been several near misses, one or two very close encounters, but something had stopped her each time. She hadn't told Matthew. He hadn't guessed either. And she'd certainly never told Anna or Carrie. To the two of them, losing their virginity had been straightforward, pleasant. Just a matter of them getting it out of the way, was how it had seemed to Bett.

After five months she and Matthew had fallen into an easygoing relationship – meeting for drinks once or twice a week, dinner one night a week, after which she would usually go back to the house he was sharing in town. Sometimes they would make love, sometimes they wouldn't. Then one night, out of the blue, he asked her to marry him. They were on their way back from a friend's wedding. All night long the two of them had been teased, been asked when their big day would be. 'A wedding begets a wedding, you two, remember.' The speeches had been very moving, the couple talking of their love for each other, the importance of their families, how they couldn't wait to set up home together, start their own family.

On the way back to Clare, Matthew told her more about his own childhood, how his parents had separated when he was young, and how he'd shifted around a lot. 'I don't want the rest of my life to be like that, Bett. I want to stay in one place. Have children. Make them feel safe.'

It had moved her almost to tears at the time, thinking of him being so lonely as a child, wanting to make sure that his own kids didn't go through what he'd been through.

'You understand, Bett, don't you? You know exactly what I mean.'

At the back of her mind, Bett wanted to disagree. She'd quite liked all the shifting they had done as children. But that night the champagne had taken over her emotions. 'Of course I understand. And I think you'd be a great dad, make a great husband and father.'

He stopped the car, took her hands. 'Bett, do you want to get married? You and me?'

She felt a warm, comforting feeling. Even a sort of relief again. She wasn't a failure, someone loved her enough to want to marry her. They drove straight to the motel to tell her parents and Lola. That night, Carrie happened to ring from her travels and they told her the news too. Word whipped around the town. Rebecca came into work with a bottle of champagne. It was a very happy time.

But had it felt like it was something they both were destined to do, couldn't live without doing? No. If anything, the pressure came from people around them, their friends, who were all busily planning their weddings and buying their first houses.

They didn't rush into any wedding planning. They set a date, booked the church for a year's time, to be sure of a place more than anything. Bett started thinking about her wedding dress. But, mostly, life settled down – Bett with her work at the newspaper, Matthew with his work and his study, both living separately. The fact that they were engaged was a nice link between them, but nothing momentous, life-changing. Again, that thought – comforting. Which had started to feel like boring.

Bett recalled coming at the subject in a roundabout way during a phone conversation with Anna. 'Did you ever have doubts about Glenn before you married him, Anna?'

Anna got to the point immediately. 'Why, are you having second thoughts about Matthew?'

'No.' A pause. 'But it stands to reason, doesn't it, that you'd start to see faults in someone, especially after you've been going out with each other for a while?'

'You and Matthew, you mean? You've only been together for less than a year, though, haven't you? I think that's still officially known as the honeymoon period. What sort of things are you talking about?'

'Well, with Glenn, for example, do you ever, um, I don't know, run out of things to talk about? Find yourself sitting there wondering what to say next?'

'No, I don't think so.' Anna laughed. 'If we're not talking, we're usually fighting about something, so communication isn't usually the issue. Have you run out of things to say to Matthew?'

Bett had, but she'd hedged around it. 'Maybe we've just been too tired to talk. Things have been pretty busy work-wise for both of us.'

'But you must have things in common you can talk about, even if you are tired. Do you like the same things? The same sort of books or music?'

Bett grimaced. She and Matthew couldn't be further apart in their musical tastes. He was strictly John Cougar Mellencamp. He listened to the rock stations, she preferred the alternative ones. He liked listening to her play piano, but now she thought about it, only when she was playing the sing-a-long Top 40 ones, not the musical numbers or classical pieces Lola had taught her. Matthew didn't read much, either, apart from veterinary magazines, whereas Bett always had two or three books on the go.

'Um, no, not really.'

'Does he make you laugh?'

She had to think. Occasionally he did. But his main party piece was his impressions of Basil Fawlty, Frank Spencer and Elvis Presley, and the truth was she'd never found them funny. A bit embarrassing, if anything. 'Sometimes,' she said to Anna.

'What about his work?'

It had been interesting enough to begin with. But she had never been that keen on animals – well, she liked cats, but she wasn't that keen on their inner workings, not to the extent of talking about intestinal worms over dinner most nights. Carrie was the animal fiend in their house, the one who collected photos of dogs and horses and stuck them on her schoolbooks and on the wall above her bed. She'd even had an imaginary horse for a few years, called Plink for some reason, on which she would gallop around the motel carpark, to the amusement of their guests.

Bett remembered thinking that the music Matthew listened to was the same sort of music Carrie had liked. That she wasn't a reader either. That even the way he looked was more to Carrie's taste than Bett's. Carrie had always liked the rugged outdoor type.

She and Anna had talked about it some more, before Bett deliberately moved the conversation on to other matters. Four days later, she got a letter from Sydney.

Dear Bett,

I've been thinking a lot about our phone call last night, and rather than ring again, I decided to write this to you. First up, it's none of my business, so there's the disclaimer out of the way – if you take my advice, I won't be held responsible for the consequences. But what seemed to be coming loud and clear through everything you were saying is that you have serious doubts about marrying Matthew. You kept asking whether I'd had the same sorts of doubts about marrying Glenn, but as I said last night, Glenn and I are completely different to you and Matthew. It's a different combination, a different situation. The problems we have are not the problems you and Matthew might be having or would have.

Can I ask you a very blunt question? Why are you marrying him? I'm not too sure you love him, as you're not too sure yourself, but do you even like him all that much? It worried me when you said that you and he don't have all that much in common. It worried me even more when you said that you weren't getting any younger, and besides all your friends were getting married. As Lola would say, if all your friends jumped off the roof, would you do that too?

While I'm on the subject, why does Matthew want to marry you? He sounds like the world's greatest romantic, but has he got a sense of you? Is he interested in you, as Bett, rather than as a woman he can marry? It just sounds to me as though the pair of you have drifted into something and don't know how to drift out of it again.

If you are still reading this, then you are probably thinking I should mind my own business. But you are my sister and I love you dearly and what you do is my business. I worry about you, worry that sometimes you stick your head in the sand, pretend everything's okay when it patently isn't, just to avoid confrontations. But it would be a lot less messy to get out of this engagement than it would be to get out of a marriage. It sounds like the two of you get on okay, and maybe you would make better friends than lovers, or better acquaintances than husband and wife. You said a telling thing last night, that because Matthew was your first serious relationship, you had nothing to compare him to, so you were just assuming that being bored, being annoyed, was normal. I don't think that's a normal comment for someone a few months away from tripping up the aisle.

I'll shut up now, I promise. I just wanted to say that I'm worried about you and I hope you'll think about this carefully. Everyone makes mistakes. It wouldn't be the end of the world if you called it off.

Never forget how much I love you, even when you are driving me up the wall.

Anna xxx

Anna had come back to the Valley not long after to see Carrie, but Bett hadn't mentioned the letter or her doubts to her again. There'd been so much fuss about Carrie's return that it had been easy to avoid the subject. Bett had loved the novelty of having a boyfriend to show to Carrie. She'd enjoyed the feeling of going to the pub with them that first night, watching as Carrie jokingly road-tested him for her, patting him down. She hadn't minded at all when the two of them often became the three of them, Carrie joining them for dinner, drinks in the pub. When Carrie was around, Matthew seemed to have lots more to talk about. It had been easier to have the three of them. There were none of the long silences there had often been between her and Matthew. Carrie bubbled into the space, brought out a different side of Matthew. They had kept finding things in common – music, antique shopping, even clothes shopping. It was Bett who had suggested Carrie go to the agricultural college with Matthew and sit in on some lectures, when she'd seemed so interested in his vet stories. Bett had a clear memory of that day. 'Matthew and Carrie should be together, not Matthew and me.' She had actually thought that.

She stopped walking, alone on the path, the early-morning air crisp around her, cool against her skin. Her memory jumped to the night Matthew had told her about Carrie. He had called her at the office, his voice sounding strange, asking if he could meet her after work. He said he had something very important he needed to tell her . . .

Fury, hurt and anger had propelled her through the next few months. Then the ticket overseas had turned out to be a lifeline. A chance to start afresh, leave the mess that was her life in the Clare Valley, her relationship with her sisters, far behind her.

It had been frightening but it had been a chance to be herself, to stop measuring herself against Anna and Carrie. Except she hadn't been able to leave them behind, had she? All the memories had come with her.

And they were still there.

Chapter Twenty-Three

Several days later, out at the farmhouse, Carrie pointed the remote control at the TV and turned down the volume. Lola had insisted she take the night off from the motel. 'You've been working too hard, darling. Have a break. Prepare yourself for the musical, with lots of relaxing, lots of good food, lots of snuggling up to Matthew.'

Some chance of that. She was too stressed to relax, there was no food in the house and the only snuggling she'd been doing was with the sofa cushions. She'd spent all afternoon watching imported American confrontational chat shows on TV. It was so much easier for Americans, Carrie thought. They were so good at that 'come on TV and let it all hang out' approach. She didn't think her own Irish-Australian heritage stretched to the same candidness. The program credits came up, with a contact number if you needed a family matter sorted out. Would the producer's budget stretch to flying the entire Quinlan family over to America? she wondered. They could start small and work their way up, she supposed. Just fly her and Matthew over for a start.

If only it were that easy. What would the producers do? Make them talk about their true feelings? Insist they were honest? Carrie could almost hear herself telling Matthew how sorry she was for all the fighting. How much she missed him. How she wanted to give it another go.

She sat upright.

She did. That was exactly how she felt. But what would Matthew say if she told him all that? If she asked him to come home again?

She realised there was only one way to find out.

Anna ran her hands down Richard's body, stretching herself so she was full length against him, skin against skin. He smiled into her eyes, leaned forward, kissed her on the lips again. There was just a white cotton sheet covering them, the one lamp throwing a soft light into the room. There had barely been time to draw the curtains when she had called to his room that evening before they had undressed one another and started kissing for a very long time. Luxurious, gentle lovemaking had given way to more conversation, whispered confidences, shy offerings of what they thought of one another, which had led to more lovemaking.

Anna felt wrapped in warmth, in compliments, in his admiration. She loved the touch of his fingers on her body, his lips on hers, the sound of his voice telling her stories, asking her questions, showing interest in her like she hadn't felt in years. She'd felt the same intense curiosity about him, wanting to hear all about him as well. She had never had this with Glenn, simple lying under the sheet together, talking, their bodies entangled, the memory of lovemaking fresh on their skin and in their minds, the promise of more to come in the stroking of fingers on bodies, the look in each other's eyes. She felt reckless, like a naughty teenager again, staying out late, comforted by the thought of Ellen safe with Lola.

He had just told her some of the conversation from his dinner with Bett several nights before. She was struck equally by his gentleness and his curiosity, as if he was trying to understand her, and her sisters, and the feud between them.

'I can understand why Carrie and Bett might have fought, but why did you and Bett fight about it all?'

'Oh, not just me and Bett. Me and Carrie too.' She smiled. 'We were never a family to do things by halves. I fought with her straight after I'd fought with Bett, actually.'

'Tell me about it.'

'You really want to hear?'

'I do. I love hearing you talk.'

Anna had been in Clare on a quick weekend visit, while Glenn had taken Ellen to visit his parents in Queensland. She was in her room when Bett burst in, wild eyed, her mop of curls more unruly than usual. She spilled out the story in moments, before Anna sat her down and made her go through it again, slowly and in detail.

Bett took a deep breath. 'Matthew had some news, he told me. Something urgent he needed to talk to me about. So we met here, in the bar. I thought it would be about a job move or something about work, but no . . .' A pause, as Anna could see Bett was trying not to lose control. 'No, he said he needed to call off our wedding.' Bett told Anna that she had scarcely mouthed the word 'Why?' before Matthew had delivered the answer. 'He said: "Because I've fallen in love with Carrie."'

And then into the bar walked Carrie. A glance between her and Matthew, Bett said, and she had known. Carrie felt the same way about Matthew.

'You should have seen them, Anna. The two of them sitting there, holding hands, telling me how hard it was for them, for *them*, but that they'd thought it best if they broke the news to me together.'

Anna winced. 'They were holding hands in front of you? Being that open about it? So they've been lovers? Already?'

'I don't know. They must have been. Of course they have.' Bett was very distressed. 'Carrie kept going on about how they had tried to fight it, but it had been too strong, too *passionate*, between them to ignore.'

'I can't believe Carrie would do this. And what is Matthew playing at? Creeping from your bed to Carrie's? What has he got, some kind of sister fetish?'

Bett shifted uncomfortably. 'Matthew and I . . . hadn't actually been . . . well, not for a while.'

'Since before Carrie got back or after?'

'Before. I don't know, between everything, all the wedding plans, and my work and his work, there hadn't been time.'

Hadn't been time? Anna was puzzled. Wasn't sex something you made time for – especially when you were in the first flush of love? 'Bett, things really hadn't been okay with you and Matthew before this, had they?'

'Of course they had,' Bett said quickly. 'Things were perfectly fine, until this. That's why I just can't believe it.'

Anna frowned. 'Really? You don't remember calling me about Matthew, saying that you were worried you weren't suited? That you didn't think he had enough get up and go in him?'

'I didn't think he'd get up and go to my sister, though, did I?' For a moment they both nearly started to laugh, then Bett started pacing the room again. 'I can't believe it.'

'Bettsie,' Anna used the pet name, 'come on. Remember our phone call? The letter I wrote that you never acknowledged? You know you weren't feeling sure about Matthew. You told me as much. Maybe this was the chance to have told him. To bring it all into the open.'

There was no answer.

'Oh, Bett, please.' Anna gave a quick laugh. 'Don't deny it. You must be the only journalist in the world who makes a habit of changing the facts to suit yourself.'

'You're one to talk. You're hardly broadcasting from the Palace of Truth yourself.'

Anna abruptly stopped laughing. 'And what is that supposed to mean?'

'Forget it.'

'Bett . . .'

Bett lifted her chin. 'You and Glenn.'

'What about me and Glenn?'

'Why do you stick with him? Are you happy together? Do you really love him? Does he love you? Or is it because of Ellen? Or your social standing?'

'Don't do this. Don't try and change the subject.'

'I'm not changing the subject. I'm saying that people in glass houses shouldn't throw stones.'

'And sisters who come seeking help shouldn't turn into complete and utter bitches.'

'Bitch? Excuse me? I have been completely humiliated and you turn on me.' She stood up, her eyes blazing. 'Fine. Brilliant. Off you go to Carrie, then. Tell her how delighted you are. Tell her what a wonderful success she has made of her life. The two of you again, Miss Perfect and Miss Even More Bloody Perfect. No need to worry about me cluttering up your perfect space again. Just as you've always wanted it.'

'What the hell are you talking about?'

Bett gave a rough laugh. 'It's the same old story again, isn't it? You and Carrie together, doing it properly, like you always said. Not making a mess of things, not spoiling the look – that's how you both put it, isn't it?'

'For God's sake, that was years ago, we shouldn't have said –'

'Yes, you should have. If you've both always thought that I lowered the tone, ruined the perfect picture, then of course you should have said it. Let's bring everything out into the open, shall we? Carrie's done it again tonight. You both did it years ago, so it's my turn now.'

'Bett, calm down.'

Her eyes were glittering. 'No, I won't. Enjoying life up there in the ivory tower, are you, Anna? Good. Great. You're welcome to it, though I'm sure Carrie and Matthew will enjoy popping in for a visit now and again, if they pass muster, don't spoil your décor.'

Anna only just held her temper in check. 'Stop it, Bett. You're upset. You're not seeing things clearly.'

'Oh I am, Anna. I'm seeing things more clearly than I have ever seen them before. What was it you and Carrie said to me that day? That I spoiled the look? Well, not any more. I should thank Carrie and Matthew. They've given me the exit I always wanted. Goodbye, Anna. I wish I could say it's been a pleasure being your sister but quite frankly it hasn't.'

Anna was now furious herself. 'Taken an overdose of your melodramatic pills, have you? Calm down, for God's sake. I told you I'm on your side.'

'You are not. You never have been. It's only ever been about you. We saw through it, though, you know that. No one likes Glenn. I mean, all right, marry for money if you have to, but couldn't you have picked someone who was a little more like a human being?'

'That's enough.'

'Good thing Ellen is so pretty, I suppose, though God help the poor girl if she ever puts on a gram of excess weight. I can see it, you'll have her down at the Kiddy Gym, in at the beauty parlour, applying layers and layers of fakeness. Like mummy, like daughter.'

'You bitch, Bett.' Her own fury rose like a geyser. 'I wanted to help but you're beyond it. Forget it. Go. Good riddance. You're on your own now.'

Bett stared at her coldly. 'Maybe I have been for years, Anna.' She walked out, slamming the door behind her.

Anna barely had time to catch her breath when the phone on the bedside cabinet rang. It was Carrie.

'Annie?' She only called her Annie when she was upset. 'I need to talk to you. Are you alone?'

Anna noticed then that her hands were shaking. 'Yes. Bett's just left me.'

'Can we talk to you? Will you come to my room?'

So 'they' had become 'we' already. A united team. Quelling her angry feelings towards Bett, trying to be calm – someone had to be the voice of reason in this situation, surely – Anna went straight to Carrie's room. Inside, Carrie and Matthew were sitting side by side on the bed. Carrie was crying. Beside her Matthew had his arm around her shoulder, awkwardly stroking her, looking embarrassed, stopping, then stroking again. Anna found it very distracting.

'So it's true,' she said, looking at them both.

Two nods, Matthew a little shame-faced, Carrie more defiant. 'Is Bett okay?'

Anna gave an almost laugh. 'Okay? Well, no, I wouldn't say she's okay.'

'We couldn't help it, could we, Matthew? It just happened.'

Anna looked from one to the other. 'And you're sure?'

Matthew nodded.

Carrie looked at him and nodded too. 'We are. Hurting Bett was the last thing, the very last thing, I ever wanted to do. She's my sister, but this became bigger than both of us. As if all the choice was taken from us.'

Between Bett's histrionics and now Carrie's mea culpa act, Anna had suddenly had enough. 'All right, Carrie. You don't have to lay it on too thick.'

The crying stopped. 'What do you mean by that?'

Anna put it to her straight. 'You know you and Bett have circled each other for years. I'm not saying you deliberately made Matthew fall in love with you, but be honest with me if not with yourself. At the start was there not a bit of playing with fire, flirting, to annoy Bett?'

'Are you saying I deliberately made this happen?'

'Subconsciously, maybe. I don't think you thought it would come to this though, no.'

Carrie's lower lip was quivering. 'Yes, you are. That's exactly what you're saying. That I made this happen to hurt Bett.'

Anna laughed. She couldn't help herself. Carrie looked like a sulking five-year-old. How could she have a proper fight with her sisters when the pair of them carried on like this?

Carrie turned stony-faced. 'It's not funny. You've always taken Bett's side. It's always been the two of you, ganging up on me.'

'What?'

'You know it has been. You both always hated me tagging along behind you, getting in the way.'

'Carrie, what are you talking about? Stop behaving like a child.'

'That's it exactly. You've been saying that to me for years. Well,

I've had enough. Enough of you and Bett telling me what to do and lording it all over the place. It's always been like this, since the school fair that time.'

'What school fair?'

'That one before we moved to the Valley and Mum and Dad said you and Bett had to take me and you didn't. You paid that girl to look after me.'

'Carrie, that was twenty years ago. You were eight years old. We didn't want you hanging around.'

'Exactly. You didn't want me hanging around. How did you think that made me feel?'

'Like an eight-year-old who had been left behind by her older sisters. Like every single eight-year-old with older sisters in history, I expect. Carrie, are you actually listening to what you're saying? You are linking the fact you have broken Bett's heart by running off with her fiancé with something that happened when you were eight?'

'It's symptomatic.'

'What the hell does that mean?'

'Patterns. Recurring events. Here it is again. Matthew and I have made an adult decision. We love one another and yet here you are sticking your nose in and meddling when it's none of your business.'

Anna's hackles hadn't just risen, they were now practically visible, sticking out in sharp points from her shirt. 'Caroline, you need a slap. You're the one who has made all this happen.'

'I'll tell you something, then. I'm glad it has.'

'You're glad?'

Carrie looked uncomfortable for only a brief moment. 'If this is what it took for you and Bett to see I'm not a child any more, then, yes, I'm glad.'

'Sorry, Carrie, can I get this clear – you're glad you've broken up Bett's engagement? I hope to God you're joking because if you're not you are a much sadder case than I already thought.'

Matthew leaned forward then. 'I have to step in here, Anna.'

Anna didn't look at him. 'Shut up, Matthew. Mind your own business. This isn't about you any more.'

Carrie gasped. 'Don't you dare talk to him like that.'

Anna was beyond reason now. 'What? I should keep it sweet with him in case he gets sick of you and wants to make a play for me? He's going for the hat-trick, is he?'

Now Matthew and Carrie looked outraged. 'That was uncalled for, Anna.'

Inside, Anna knew it was exactly that. But the pair of them, sitting there, all smug and wound around each other, had suddenly annoyed the hell out of her. Carrie with her hand on his thigh, Matthew stroking Carrie's arm, the physical attraction between them so obvious. When was the last time Glenn had stroked her in public like that? In private, even? She blocked the thought and concentrated on the two angry faces glaring at her.

'I apologise for that remark. But I don't apologise for anything else I said. It's time you grew up, Carrie.'

'I grew up? At least I'm being honest with myself, going into a relationship for love, not gain.'

'How dare you! First Bett and now you. How dare you both cast judgement on me like this.'

'Bett told you what she thought of Glenn as well? Good. Isn't it time we said something? Rather than keep up any pretence that we like him? Well, we don't. And I don't like you when you're with him. You changed when you went to Sydney, Anna. Got airs and graces. Too good for us any more.'

'Shut up, Carrie.'

'It's true. How come it's all right for you to march in here and tell me off, but you won't listen to a few home truths about yourself?'

'You self-centred, selfish little –'

'I don't care what you think of me, actually.' Carrie's lip quivered again. 'Come on, Matthew. This is pointless. Let's go.'

'You can't go,' Anna had said, suddenly exhausted. 'You're in your room. I'm the one who has to go. And I'm happy to, believe me. Goodbye, Carrie. Goodbye, Matthew. Good luck whatever happens to you both in the future, but I'll tell you something – I don't want anything to do with it. '

'Good. Because I don't want you to have anything to do with us either.'

And with that Anna had slammed the door.

Richard shook his head in amazement. 'And where was Lola in all this? I can't imagine her sitting back and letting it happen.'

'No, she didn't.'

There had been a family conference, Geraldine and Jim, Anna and Lola, with a number of phone calls made to Carrie on her mobile phone. She had left the motel and gone to stay with Matthew in his house on the other side of the town. Bett had left too. Got in her car the next morning and just driven away. She had phoned Lola to tell her she was safe, that she was in Melbourne, and had then turned off her mobile.

Jim Quinlan had been sure it would all blow over. Lola had put him right on that. 'Darling, you haven't noticed any of this going on, have you?'

'Noticed what?'

Lola had shaken her head. 'Geraldine, what about you?'

Anna remembered her mother looking a little uncomfortable. 'It's been so busy here, Lola, I thought they were all getting on so well.'

'They were indeed,' Lola had laughed. 'Just in the wrong combination.'

They'd all agreed what to do next. The wedding would have to be called off, the church booking cancelled, any engagement presents returned and word carefully put around a few key information-brokers in the town. Lola volunteered to do it all.

Anna had left the Valley the following day, still furious with Bett and Carrie. 'They've shown their true colours, Lola – Bett lives in fantasy land and Carrie is a selfish little cow, and I don't care how long it is till I see them again.'

'Now you're being childish.'

'Don't you start with the insults. I had enough from those two. I don't care if I never speak to either of them again.'

'Ah, so that's it. Not just disgust at their behaviour, you didn't like what they had to say either? And what's all this dramatic nonsense about never speaking to each other again? Of course you will. This situation will all blow over soon.'

'It won't, Lola. I saw a side to Bett and Carrie that I didn't like one bit. I'm not running to them, I'll tell you that. If they find it in themselves to apologise, well, we'll see, but I'm not making the first move.'

'When did you get so haughty? It must have happened when you were in Sydney because I certainly would have put a stop to it if I'd seen it happening here.'

'I am not haughty. That's a terrible thing to –' She'd stopped there at the sight of Lola laughing.

'Don't fight with me as well, darling, or you'll have no relatives left at all. All right, you're not haughty and you're not too proud either.'

Anna coloured, hating being caught out. 'I need to calm down, like the whole situation needs to calm down. And then I'll see how I feel.'

One month later she was still cross, and she'd heard nothing from Carrie or from Bett, who had now decided to stay in Melbourne. Well, if they weren't going to apologise for their behaviour, she wasn't either. The one-month silence between them grew to two, then to twelve.

Anna heard via Lola that Bett had gone travelling overseas. Carrie married Matthew, a very small affair in Adelaide – neither Anna nor Bett was invited. Lola attended with Geraldine and Jim, and sent a photo and a report to each of them, with a note of disgust at the end: 'This should have been a fun, happy day for the whole family. I am still ashamed of the three of you. It will only take one apology to get the ball rolling, you know . . .'

Anna put the photo away and turned all her attention to Glenn, Ellen and work, returning home to the motel just once a year, timing it to coincide with Matthew and Carrie's annual holiday away. One year became two, became three years, when the attack on Ellen happened, and took precedence over everything else.

'And that's how things were between us,' she said to Richard. 'Until Lola's party.'

'You've been through a lot lately, haven't you?' he said.

She lay looking into his eyes. 'Yes. Yes, I have, I think.'

She felt the touch of his fingers on her arm, on her bare skin. 'Too much to go through on your own. I wish I'd known you then. I'd like to have helped.'

She moved closer, moulding her body against his, feeling an

answering reaction from him, his fingers tracing her body. 'You're helping now,' she said. His lips met hers once again.

At that moment, in the vet's quarters of the Red Hills sheep station, Carrie was kissing Matthew's lips, then his chest, going lower and lower.

'Carrie . . .' he murmured.

'Shh,' she said. 'I told you, I'm tired of talking. We're not to say a word.'

'We have to talk.'

'Matthew, if you say another word I'm getting back in my car and driving straight back home.' Once she'd made her decision it had been simple. She loved Matthew and she was going to fight for him. She'd changed her clothes, packed a bag, and driven for two hours without stopping. He'd been in his quarters when she knocked on the door. She'd given him no chance to protest, no explanations, just moved into his arms and started kissing him. It had taken him only a second to respond.

She unbuttoned his jeans, lowered his boxer shorts, did exactly what she knew he loved and was rewarded with his groans of pleasure above her. She stopped abruptly, slowly took off her clothes and stood before him in her transparent pale-pink lace underwear.

'I've missed you so badly.' His voice was nearly hoarse.

She held herself a little away from him. 'And you don't regret marrying me?'

'No, I don't.'

'You don't want to go back to Bett?'

'No.'

'Are you sure?'

He pulled her close. 'Carrie, can you shut up about Bett for one minute and come here so I can . . .' He finished what he was going to do in a whisper in her ear.

Carrie shut up.

Chapter Twenty-Four

The phone rang as Bett was passing reception. It was her turn to mind the bar and the phone. Carrie was on a night off and Anna had said she wanted an early night. Ellen was in with Lola again. She'd decided her favourite sleeping place was her great-grandmother's double bed. Bett had checked on the pair of them a little while before. They'd both been asleep, books strewn on the bed around them.

Bett picked up the phone. 'Valley View Motel.'

'Hello, could I speak to one of your guests please.' The caller had a well-bred English accent. 'Mr Richard Lawrence.'

'Certainly, sir. I'll put you through to his room.'

She tried it and got the engaged tone. 'Can I take a message? I'm afraid I can't get through at the moment.'

'I've been trying for the past two hours and it's been constantly engaged. And his mobile is turned off too. Is that a small motel?'

'Reasonably small, yes. But it's a good motel.'

He laughed. 'I'm sorry. I'm not asking for economic reasons. It's just it's urgent I speak to Richard this evening. Would it be possible for someone to knock on his door in case he's accidentally left the phone off the hook? I need to check something with him urgently.'

'Of course. Who can I tell him is calling?'

'Please tell him it's Charlie. It's about the filming.'

Bett walked over to Richard's room. The curtains were drawn but she could see the faint outline of a bedside lamp. She knocked softly at the door. 'Richard, I'm sorry to disturb you. There's an urgent phone call.'

She heard moaning.

'Richard?'

Another kind of deep sigh.

Good God, was he all right? 'Richard?' She tried the handle.

The door swung open just as Richard and Anna reached orgasm together.

Bett was back at the reception desk in record time. 'Hello? Um, Richard is a bit tied up at the moment. Can I take your number and get him to call you back?'

'Are you sure he didn't want to be disturbed?'

'Pretty sure.' She didn't know who had looked the more startled, them or her.

'Could I speak to Lola, then?'

How did he know Lola? 'She's asleep, I'm afraid.'

'Damn.' He sighed. 'I'll just have to leave a message, then. Can you tell him we need to change the filming arrangements? Can he have everything set up for the day after tomorrow rather than next week? He'll know what I mean. And could he ring me as soon as possible to confirm?'

She took his details, and tucked the note in her pocket. There was no way she was going to go back to Richard's room with the message. Not yet, anyway. She was completely shocked. How long had this been going on between them? What about Glenn? What about Ellen?

She was in the kitchen making up the breakfast trays for the morning when she heard the door open behind her.

'Bett?' It was Anna. 'I think we need to talk.'

Bett didn't turn around. 'Anna, you don't have to explain anything. Seriously. What you do is your own business.' Bett picked up the next order form – one cereal, bacon and eggs, eggs hard not runny, underlined five times. And honey, not marmalade please. Also underlined.

'Bett, I want to explain.'

Bett picked through the box of preserves, searching for a little sachet of honey. 'You don't need to.'

'I still want to explain. I don't want this to cause another rift between us.' She hesitated. 'I know you were a bit interested in Richard.'

Bett kept busy with the tray. 'It's hardly the same situation, is it? I mean, I was engaged to Matthew when Carrie slept with him. All I'd done with Richard was tell you I might like to have a drink with him.' An awful thought occurred to her. 'Were you laughing at me? You and Richard? Laughing that I was going to invite him out?'

'No, Bett, we weren't. I promise we weren't. Richard doesn't even know you were going to ask him out. Please, Bett. Please put down that bloody honey and listen to me.'

Bett turned. Anna was dressed in a silk dressing-gown. Bett was struck by how tired and fragile she looked. 'So how long has this been going on between you?'

'Not long. A week or two.'

'And what about Glenn?'

'Glenn and I have been over for a long time, Bett. He's having an affair.'

'He's *what*?'

Anna walked over, shut the kitchen door and started talking.

Forty minutes later, Bett was holding her crying sister close against her. 'Oh, Anna, I'm so sorry for you. I didn't realise it had been so bad. Why didn't you tell us?'

'When? How? We weren't talking.'

'But what about telling Lola? I can't believe you've been through all this on your own.'

'It was pride. I knew if I told Lola, she'd tell you and Carrie. And I decided I could bear the life, the silences with him, more than I could bear the two of you telling me you'd been right. That he wasn't right for me. That I shouldn't have married him. All the things you both said that night.'

'Does Ellen understand what's going on?'

'Some of it. She's picked up the tension, and the fact he's away so much. Even though he'd try and get back in time to take Ellie to school most mornings.' Glenn would come in, freshly showered from Julie's bathroom, to be sitting there in the kitchen when Ellen woke up, for all the world the perfect father. 'That's the only good thing. He adores her at least. And she adores him. And he's wonderful with her.' It was a simple fact. 'It's the two of us . . .' She stopped, started crying again. 'It's been a mess, Bett. A horrible, awful, lonely mess . . .'

Bett held her close until the tears stopped again. 'And this thing with Richard?' she asked softly.

'I don't know. All I know is that he is kind and he listens to me and he makes me laugh. It might last a day or a week but it's what I need now. Do you understand?'

Bett thought of her night with Daniel three years ago. 'Yes, I do.'

'I'm sorry. I should have told you the night you were going to ask Richard for a drink. Told you that he and I were becoming friends.'

'I don't mind at all. Really, I don't.' She smiled. 'But you might want to think about locking the door from now on.'

Anna hugged Bett close again. 'We needed to talk. Years before this. Why has it taken this long?' She took a step back. 'Bett, I'm so sick of having secrets from each other. Please, can't you and Carrie sort things out too? Have you talked to her about Matthew yet?'

Bett shook her head, wary again.

'Please, Bett. You have to. She thinks you're still in love with him, I'm sure of it. You need to –'

The door opened behind them. It was Richard. 'I'm sorry to interrupt. I'll come back –'

Bett was relieved. She moved away from Anna. 'It's fine, really.'

He looked uncomfortable. 'Bett, I must apologise. I'm sorry if that put you in an embarrassing position.'

Her lip twitched. Actually it had been him in the embarrassing position. 'It's fine, Richard. And I'm very sorry for barging in on you like that.' She took out the note from her pocket. 'I had a message for you. Someone called Charlie rang to tell you the filming will have to take place the day after tomorrow not next week. That you'd know what he meant but could you call him back.'

'The day after tomorrow?'

Bett nodded.

'Is something wrong?' Anna asked him.

He gave a slightly awkward smile. 'I think there's something I'd better tell you both.'

As she drove into the Clare Valley that night, Carrie knew that everything had changed for the better. She loved Matthew and she knew he loved her. He had actually cried in her arms.

'Carrie, I stopped loving Bett when I met you. I don't know any more if that was what I felt for Bett. We got on well, but –'

'But she loved you so much. She was so upset when you split up.'

'I know. I'm so sorry, but I couldn't do anything about it. I had to be with you.'

They talked about the past few months, about the fighting and the separation. 'You changed when Lola started talking about Bett coming back.'

'I got so worried that you'd decide you'd chosen the wrong girl.'

'Of course I wouldn't. But it felt like you were trying to push me away. So I went. But I missed you, really missed you.'

'It was other things too. You started talking about money all the time.' She paused, then forged ahead. 'You stopped talking about having a baby.'

He had held her close. 'Carrie, I didn't think we could afford to have a baby yet. I want one as much as you do, but I want us to have some security first. I'm not qualified yet. The house isn't finished. I want it to be all ready when the baby comes.'

'So you do want one?'

'Of course I do. I tried to explain that's how I felt, but I couldn't get through to you.'

Carrie recalled heated conversations, flaring into rows, which generally ended in her storming out, back to the motel or over to a friend's house. That was what he had been trying to tell her, she realised guiltily. She'd heard 'I don't want a baby', when what he had been saying was 'I don't want a baby yet'.

That morning over breakfast he had agreed to come back to the Valley to meet Bett. He would come the day after tomorrow, in fact. Carrie kept driving, straight to the motel. It was after ten but she was determined to speak to Bett that night, to arrange a time and place for the meeting.

All the motel lights were on. She was surprised to find both her sisters in the office. Anna was on the land line, Bett on the mobile phone. Bett was finishing a call just as Carrie walked in.

'Carrie, you're back early. That's great. Can you –'

'In a moment, Bett.' She couldn't let herself be distracted. 'I'm sorry to get right to the point but we need to talk about something.'

'In a minute, Carrie. Something's come up. We need to ring –'

'It's important.' Her tone surprised them both. 'Matthew is coming back to the Valley and he wants to see you. And I want him to see you. Do you still want to see him?'

Bett blinked at her. 'Sure. Yes. Fine. Can we worry about him later, though?' She thrust a list of phone numbers at her sister. 'We've got a musical emergency on our hands.'

By eleven o'clock the following morning the cast and a hastily assembled crew were in the Clare Town Hall. Len was directing a small group of men, who were moving paint pots, set panels and ladders noisily across the wooden floor. The piano had been transported from the motel in the back of a refrigerated truck, sandwiched between twenty boxes of ice-cream. They were just waiting on the arrival of the forklift from the local supermarket to help lift it onto the stage.

Richard was worried. 'It's not a full-scale documentary, Anna. It's just a short segment. Maybe only a few minutes long. I'm worried you're going to too much trouble.'

Anna lowered her voice. 'I think your friend Charlie is doing me a favour, actually. We'd never have got this done on time otherwise.'

Bett had phoned her editor, Rebecca, to see if she could come and lend a hand too.

'Are you going to ring Daniel?' Rebecca asked. 'Can you tell him if he needs someone to look after his mother, I'll do it. He'd probably be more use to you than me.'

'What do you mean look after his mother?'

'Well, not look after. Sit with. Listen, I'll save you the bother and ring him myself and you can get onto the others. Should I tell him to come straight to the town hall? Okay, see you.'

Lola, her arm still in its sling, was watching all the activity from a chair to the side of the stage. It was an excellent vantage point. In a corner of the hall, three of the ladies from the charity shop were organising the costumes onto racks. Bett was at the piano, frowning a lot but otherwise looking in control of her little band of musicians, who had been summoned straight from the high school, still in their uniforms. Len was moving set panels. As Lola watched, Daniel Hilder arrived and started helping him. Up on the stage, Carrie was practising her solo dance scene, striking quite an elegant pose. One thing puzzled Lola. Anna's behaviour with Richard Lawrence. Were eyes deceiving her or was there a lot of flirting going on there? More than flirting, in fact. Little hand touches. Glances. Quick conversations.

She made her way over to Bett and sat down on the piano stool beside her. 'Hello, darling.'

'Hello, Lola,' Bett smiled distractedly. Some of the songs weren't working, now that she had seen them performed on stage. The tempo or the length was wrong. She was going to have to cut a verse out of 'Oh What a Beautiful Morning' and quicken the tempo of

'I Could Have Danced All Night'.

'Bett, can we have a word about Richard Lawrence?'

'Mmm?' Bett had her pen in her mouth, sheet music in one hand and was trying out a chord with the other.

Lola lowered her voice. 'Have you and he had another dinner or a drink or anything since the night I was so tired?'

'Me and Richard?' Bett took the pen out of her mouth. 'Oh no, Lola. Richard's having an affair with Anna. Anna and Glenn's marriage has broken up, too, by the way. Months ago. He's been having an affair with his PA. I only found out last night. Sorry. I know Anna would have told you too but all this took over.'

Lola didn't even blink. 'Oh. I see. Well, I'll leave you to it, then.' She returned to her chair and sat for a moment taking all that in. Anna and Richard. Who would have thought? She turned slightly so she could see them, standing on the edge of the stage. Anna was smiling at something he was saying. His expression was courteous. Mindful. And very affectionate. Still waters ran deep, as the saying went. As for the break-up with Glenn – was she surprised? Not particularly, she realised. She actually quite liked Glenn, with his bristling energy and booming voice. He'd always been so good with Ellen, too. But possibly hell to be married to. No, perhaps Anna was better off with a gentle man for a while. Yes, she quite approved, she decided.

Len's voice sounded through the hall. 'That's it, Daniel. No, sorry, a bit to the left. Now right. Forward. Forward. No, back again. To tell you the truth, I think it might be upside down.'

Lola watched as Daniel Hilder and Len stood in front of one of the Terowie Railway Station set panels and determined that, yes, it was indeed upside down. They carefully lowered it to the floor again. Lola put on her glasses and took the opportunity to assess Daniel one more time. He was good-humoured, that much was obvious. Anyone who could work with Len for more than ten minutes without throwing up their arms and running shrieking from the room was definitely good-humoured. And patient. He could do with a haircut, though. And he would look a bit neater if he tucked his shirt in every now and again. But that casual, unstructured look was quite the fashion, according to a TV show she'd seen the night before. Yes, he'd do fine. A worthy second choice.

Operation Bett and Daniel sounded so much better, anyway.

Chapter Twenty-Five

Charlie arrived at half past nine in the morning, sweeping into the town hall with his film crew. He was as flamboyant as Richard was quiet, long hair tied back in a ponytail, hugely amused by everything and everyone. 'Anna, it's a pleasure. I've heard great things about you. And Bett, I'm charmed. And you must be Caroline, is that right? But where is the magnificent Lola, whose phone calls have been entertaining me so hugely these past few days?'

'I'm right here.' They turned around. Lola was dressed in a brightly coloured combination of a long red satin overshirt, wide-legged paisley trousers, glittering costume jewellery, teased white hair and bright-red lipstick. Her sling was of gold lamé. She had wound a coloured ribbon around her walking cane.

Charlie bowed deeply. 'Lola, it's an honour. I don't suppose you could do that entrance for me again? On film this time?'

She gave him her most dazzling smile. 'Darling, I'll come somersaulting in if you want me to.'

An hour later Anna had nearly chewed her bottom lip to pieces. It had taken three takes to get 'My Favourite Things' right. The train stalled midway across the stage in the first verse of 'Chattanooga

Choo Choo'. General MacArthur forgot his lines and said 'I might return' instead of 'I shall return'. Mrs MacArthur defied Anna and started speaking in her English accent as soon as the camera was rolling. Carrie's solo version of 'I Could Have Danced All Night' was beautiful until two of the dancers gave a yelp behind her. They'd trodden on each other's toes.

But Charlie was delighted. Not just plenty of material for his own program, he'd whispered to Richard, but some perfect footage to sell on to one of those video blooper shows. Especially when the front of the train took off, leaving the engine driver standing behind on an empty stage. And the marching scene when the two soldiers missed their step and clashed, forehead to forehead, into each other.

Charlie strode into the centre of the hall and clapped his hands. 'Wonderful job, everyone, just wonderful. If we can have the three granddaughters up here singing "Sisters" together, we're done for the day.'

Bett turned from the piano. Carrie stopped in the middle of the stage. On the hall floor Anna stepped forward. 'Sorry, Charlie, that's not part of the show.'

'But it's in the script.' He waved his copy.

Anna noticed he had a copy of Lola's original version. 'No, we took it out.'

He frowned. 'But that's the charm of the whole story. I had the whole thing edited in my head. Shots of Terowie, the MacArthur plaque at the railway station, snippets from the musical, an interview with Lola, the three of you singing, finishing up with Lola coming in proudly behind you.'

Lola stepped forward. 'Would you want me to be smiling, Charlie, or would you prefer I had a tear in my eye?'

'We'll try both, Lola, I think. So you'll do it, girls? Terrific.' He didn't give them a chance to protest, turning to call to the cast and his crew. 'All right, everyone. Thanks for a great morning's work. We'll have a break and be back in twenty minutes with the three sisters on stage together.'

Bett sat at the piano, fighting a rush of memory and self-consciousness. Back with the three sisters on stage together? Oh no, they wouldn't be. She couldn't do it. Not in front of all those people. In front of Richard. In front of Daniel. All of them thinking the same thing that boy in the audience had thought all those years ago . . .

'Bett?'

She turned. Anna and Carrie had come up to the piano. Anna seemed exhilarated after the filming. 'What do you think? Will we do it?'

'No,' Bett said automatically. She said it to Anna, trying not to look at Carrie.

'Come on. It'll be fun.'

'I really don't want to, Anna. Thanks anyway.'

Anna noticed then that Kaylene was standing nearby and blatantly eavesdropping. Anna spoke loudly and deliberately. 'Let's go backstage, then, will we? See if we can remember all the words.'

They followed her into the long dressing-room behind the stage, past rows of stacked chairs, trestle tables, coat racks and a makeup mirror covered in fly spots. Anna checked that they had it to themselves, then turned to Bett again. 'This isn't because of that Piggy in the Middle business, is it? Bett, that was more than fifteen years ago, for God's sake. Carrie apologised to you. I apologised to you. Can't you leave it all behind?'

Bett felt a ripple of temper start inside her. 'It's not always that simple, Anna.'

'Of course it is. Is it really going to kill you to get up on stage again? You know how much it would mean to Lola. And it would mean a lot to me, too. We can talk about it all again now if we have to. Apologise again if we have to. Can't we, Carrie?'

There was only silence from Bett and Carrie.

Anna lost her temper. 'Fine. Brilliant. More silences. Well, I've had enough of it, do you hear me? All this tiptoeing around each other. All the things we won't talk about. Well, not any longer. I'm going to start talking about all the things the three of us have managed to avoid so beautifully the past month. How long is this going to go on otherwise? Another three years?' She was having trouble getting her breath, and had to pause for a moment. 'I hereby put it on the record that I hated that stupid fight we had. I hated getting caught up in it. I hated the fact you both came running to me to try and fix it and I ruined it. Do you think I liked not talking to you both? Liked having my marriage crumble around my ears and not having anyone to talk about it with, or –'

'Marriage crumble?' Carrie was shocked into speech. 'But Glenn worships you.'

'No, he doesn't, Carrie. Glenn and I are getting divorced. And in the new spirit of openness, here's another piece of news. I'm having an affair with Richard Lawrence and loving every minute of it.'

Carrie turned to Bett. 'Did you know about all this?' At Bett's nod, she lost her temper too. 'Of course you did. Fine. Perfect. The two of you, ganging up on me again, like you always have.'

'What? What are you talking about?' Bett was furious now as well. 'It was never me and Anna. It was always the two of you, doing it all so well, managing everything so perfectly. I was always the one who was left behind.'

'Stop it, Bett,' Anna snapped. 'Stop changing the facts to suit yourself. You did it with Matthew three years ago but I'm not going to let you do it again now.'

Carrie tensed. 'What do you mean she did it with Matthew? Did what with Matthew?'

'Changed the facts. Didn't you, Bett? And I still don't understand why.'

'Anna, stop it –'

'No, Bett. I've been trying to talk to you about this since we got here. You know exactly what I'm talking about and it's time Carrie knew too. Time we brought all of this business out in the open so we can get on with our lives and –'

'I've been trying,' Carrie interrupted. 'I've asked Matthew to come and see Bett. I know I should have done it before now, but it's been very difficult –'

'It's not just about seeing Matthew again, Carrie. Is it, Bett? It goes back further than that.'

Bett's face was burning. 'This is wrong, Anna. This is the wrong way to do it.'

'Then what is the right way? Because I don't know any more. All I know is I've had enough of secrets and rows and the three of us not talking about things. We were lucky to have each other and now it's all ruined.'

'It's not ruined.' Bett stared at Anna, remembering all her sister had been through with Glenn and Ellen. On her own, because Bett had been too proud to admit the truth to Carrie, to try to heal the rift between them.

'It is ruined.' Anna seemed defeated. 'Okay, then, forget it. I tried, but I can't make you do it. I'll go and tell Charlie we won't be singing together because we're never going to be friends again, so there's no point.' She was nearly at the door when Bett spoke.

'Anna, wait. Please.' She took a breath. 'I'll tell her.'

Carrie was looking back and forth between the two of them. 'What? Tell me what?'

'About Matthew and me. About what happened three years ago.' Bett could feel Anna's eyes on her, willing her to tell the truth. 'I was going to split up with Matthew, Carrie. I didn't want to marry him.'

Carrie went still. 'I don't believe you. You're just saying this now.'

'It's the truth. I'd been talking to Anna about it. Telling her things weren't going well with us.'

Carrie looked at Anna. Anna nodded. 'What do you mean not going well?'

Bett wavered. How honest could she be about the man who was now her sister's husband? 'I'd realised we weren't suited to one another. I don't know if we ever had been.'

Carrie seemed genuinely shocked. 'Then why did you get engaged?'

Bett told the truth. 'Because I thought he would make me feel better. Stop me making mistakes. Help me to fit in. I thought that once I had a boyfriend everything would be all right.'

'So were you ever in love with him?'

She paused. 'No, I don't think I was.'

'But I don't understand. You were so upset when . . . when he fell in love with me.'

'I was hurt. Of course I was. And shocked. But I was just as upset with you. And then with Anna as well. It was the way you both reacted. You, Carrie, as if it was your right. You didn't even seem surprised that Mathew would have fallen in love with you. It was as if you expected it to happen. All this dreamy talk, that it was written in the stars, that it had swept you both off your feet. And it was the way you told me, as if I could never hope to understand, that it was something way out of my reach. The way it had always been.' The words were pouring out of Bett now. 'And you, Anna. When I came to you after Matthew and Carrie told me, all I wanted was your sympathy. And you just stood there, all cool and collected, making me feel like I had made a mess of everything yet again.'

'I didn't, Bett. I just wanted you to admit that you'd been having doubts about him. Because you had been. But you just lost your temper and started attacking me instead.'

'I couldn't help it. It just seemed that you were criticising me, judging me again. And I couldn't bear it.' She felt tears in her eyes and roughly wiped them away. 'It just seemed like the final proof, that I was stuck in the middle, that I'd never be as good as either of you.'

'But how did you think it was for me?' Carrie said passionately. 'I fell in love with him, and you wouldn't stay long enough to let me tell you that it was genuine. You wouldn't listen to us, even though we wanted to try and explain. And when I went to you, Anna, you just attacked me too, asked me was I sure that it wasn't just infatuation. You just spoke to me as if I was a child, like you always had.'

'I couldn't win, could I?' Anna said. 'Caught in the middle, yet again. I told Bett she should admit the truth, to you and to Matthew, and she just flew off the handle. And then you flew off the handle too, Carrie. You told me to mind my own business, told me that you were an adult, that you could do what you wanted. And I thought, well, to hell with the pair of you.'

'So did I,' Carrie said. 'That's exactly what I thought. To hell with the pair of you. I wanted to live my own life.'

'Me too,' Bett said. 'That's exactly what I wanted to do. As far away as I could.'

Carrie turned to her. 'That's why you went away? Not because of me and Matthew?'

'It was about you and Matthew at the start. I couldn't stay here, with everyone talking and whispering about us.'

'So why didn't you come back, though? Why did you stay away?'

Bett hesitated. 'Because once I'd got over the shock and got through the first few months in Melbourne, I realised I liked being away from you both. I liked the freedom. I liked being just me, not Bett, sister of Anna, or Bett, sister of Carrie. I had to get away from you both. I couldn't take it any longer.'

The words came haltingly as she tried to explain further. How sometimes it had been the best thing in the world to have a sister on either side, protected, surrounded. But how other times it had felt like she was being suffocated and squeezed. The oldest did it first, the youngest did it sweetest. What had been left for the one in the middle? She'd had to go away, hadn't she? Or she'd never have found herself, found what she was capable of . . . She slowly came to a halt. To her surprise, Anna and Carrie didn't look hurt. They looked – what? Relieved? As if they understood?

'I felt like that too,' Anna said suddenly. 'To begin with, anyway.'

Bett stared at her. 'What was there for you not to like? You always ruled the roost with us.'

'But I was so tired of it, Bett. Tired of sorting out your fights, tired of giving you both advice when I had my own life to live, tired of the two of you passing remarks about Glenn. Not just the night of our fight, but ever since I'd met him. It was getting to the stage I didn't know what I thought of him myself. I kept getting confused with what you both thought about him.'

'I was glad at the start, too.' Carrie said in a low voice. 'It had always been the two of you ahead of me, getting all the grown-up attention, while I was just the silly little sister. And it was the same that night we fought about Matthew, Anna. You made me feel like I'd been sneaky and devious. And I hadn't been, really I hadn't. We both hated the fact it was going to hurt you, Bett. If there had been any other way of telling you –'

'Why didn't you say that to me, then?'

'You wouldn't listen. You just went running off as soon as Matthew told you. And then we were all fighting and . . . and it was just a mess. And the next morning you were gone before we had a chance to talk to you again.'

'I had to go. I had to get away from everything, from all of you. I wanted to be me for a while. Just me. Not one of the Alphabet Sisters or even one of the Quinlan sisters any more.'

'And do you still feel like that? Now?' Anna looked very serious.

Bett shook her head. 'I haven't felt like that for a long time. I got so lonely without you both. Once the novelty wore off. Once I'd proved to myself I could live away from you, that I could do things on my own, even live overseas. That I wasn't a disaster area. I wanted the freedom, I loved the freedom, but –' her voice wavered. 'I missed you both so much. And then Ellen was attacked, and, Anna, this is a terrible thing to say, but one part of me was glad, because it was a reason to write to you. So I did. I sent that letter. But then I didn't hear back so I thought, well, you didn't want contact again.'

'Me too,' Carrie said. 'I wanted to go to Sydney, but Lola and Mum got in first. I rang and talked to Glenn, left a message. But then I didn't hear anything back either.'

Anna remembered receiving Bett's letter, reading it once, then putting it away. She remembered Glenn passing on Carrie's message and then doing nothing about it. 'I couldn't contact either of you. I'm sorry. I didn't have any room for anyone but Ellen. I was so angry with everyone at that time, at myself for letting it happen, at Glenn for blaming me. I couldn't handle anyone else. I'm sorry.'

There was silence and then Carrie spoke. 'Do we all have to tell the truth now?'

'It might help,' Anna said.

'I think you both should know that Matthew and I have been separated for a while.'

'*What*?' Anna and Bett spoke in unison.

'We've been separated for a few months. We only decided to get back together yesterday.'

'So we were fighting about the two of you and you weren't even together?' Bett said.

'We were at the start. But everything went bad for a while.'

'Oh, Carrie, why?' Anna asked.

'Misunderstandings about all sorts of things. And I got guilty. I thought it was because of the way we got together. That I was being punished for taking Matthew away from Bett.' She wasn't looking at either of them. 'And I wasn't sure if Matthew was over Bett.'

'Carrie, he was. I'm sure he was.' Bett had seen the wedding photo. She knew Matthew had never looked at her the way he looked at Carrie in the photo. 'I'm sorry. I'm sorry for not telling you before, Carrie. And I'm sorry that you had to go through everything on your own, Anna. It had just gone on for so long, and even though I wanted to I just didn't know how to fix it.' She was embarrassed to feel her eyes filling with tears. 'It was easier to keep away, to keep blaming the two of you, rather than myself.'

'It doesn't matter now, does it?' Anna asked. 'We're talking again, aren't we?'

They both nodded.

'And we'll keep talking, won't we? No matter what?'

Another nod.

There was a warm silence for a moment and then Carrie turned. 'Bett, am I allowed to ask you something personal?'

She tensed again. 'I might not answer it, but ask, sure.'

'Is there something going on with you and Daniel Hilder?'

Bett looked up in surprise.

'It's just I noticed he looks at you all the time in a particular way. Doesn't he, Anna?'

Anna nodded enthusiastically. 'Like this.' She put on a pantomime adoring glance, all big eyes and amused smile.

'He does not.'

'He does, Bett. But it's more like this.' Carrie put on an even more exaggerated look, soft smile and indulgent expression.

'Stop it. You're imagining it.'

Carrie grinned, then turned her attention to Anna. 'And you and Richard are really an item?'

Anna nodded.

'Wow. So I should give him a discount on his room, then? Or will he be moving in with you?' She laughed. 'Just joking.'

Anna smiled. 'And you and Matthew, Carrie?'

Carrie's expression softened. 'It's okay. It's very good again, actually.' She hesitated. 'You really don't mind, Bett?'

'I don't mind at all, Carrie. I honestly don't mind one bit.'

They moved unselfconsciously towards each other, into a long, warm hug. Then Carrie stepped back.

'Do you want to meet him again, Bett? Now?'

'Now?'

'Matthew's here. He came down this morning. He's outside. Will I get him?'

Bett hesitated, then nodded.

Carrie was nearly at the door before she turned and came back. 'This is a bit awkward, but . . . well, do we need to tell Matthew that you were going to break up with him? It's just I'd hate to hurt his feelings.'

Bett nearly laughed out loud. But of course Carrie wanted to protect Matthew. 'Perhaps he doesn't need to hear it right now.'

Carrie nodded, relieved. 'I'll be back in a moment.'

Anna waited until she was gone before she spoke. 'Do you want me to go, to leave the three of you alone?'

Bett shook her head. 'No, all for one, one for all, don't you think?'

'I'm glad you told her, Bett. I'm sorry I had to force it.'

'I'm glad you did.'

They heard noises from the hall, as the camera crew finished its break. Set panels were being dragged across the stage again. They heard a faint hum of traffic from the main street. A car door shutting. Footsteps and the glass door opening. Bett turned and there he was, with Carrie a few feet behind.

'Hello, Bett. Hello, Anna.'

'Hello, Matthew,' they said in unison.

Bett took in every detail of his appearance. The sandy hair, the curls now cropped short. The square, kind face. The work clothes. The stocky body. It was like looking at someone she had been at school with years before.

He looked uncomfortable. 'How are things, Bett?'

'They're fine. It's good to see you again.' And it was. Nothing more and nothing less.

'You too.' Matthew gave an embarrassed laugh, looking from one to the other. 'Bett, I'm sorry for what happened. With me and Carrie. For hurting you like that.'

For one moment she was tempted to tell him the truth. That she should never have gone out with him in the first place. That it had been for all the wrong reasons. Then she looked at Carrie, standing proudly beside him, and realised that this definitely wasn't the time for the truth. 'It's fine, Matthew.'

He didn't seem convinced. 'If Lola was here she would probably use her truth stick, I suppose. Make us all say how we're really feeling.'

'You know about the truth stick?' Anna asked.

Matthew nodded. 'And the Alphabet Sisters stories. Lola used to like telling us them, didn't she, Carrie?' He gave another self-conscious laugh. 'Not that Lola ever used the truth stick on me. It was more a family thing, wasn't it? Very handy sometimes, though, she said.'

'It was, yes,' Anna said. She turned to Bett. There was challenge in her voice, even though she was smiling. 'If Lola was pointing the truth stick at you now, what would you say, Bett?'

Bett answered honestly. 'I would probably say I'm feeling a bit uncomfortable but I'm also very relieved to finally see Carrie and Matthew together. And I think they make a good pair. And I'm so sorry it's taken this long for me to tell you both how I felt. And you, Anna?'

'I'd probably say I've been feeling sick about all of this for weeks – no, years – too. And I'm glad it's over and I hope we won't ever have a fight like this again.'

Carrie was gripping Matthew's hand. 'And I would say I'm sorry for any hurt we caused you, Bett. And you, Anna. And I hope you forgive us.'

'And I would say about bloody time.'

It was Lola, standing in the doorway. 'That's the thing about swear words,' she said, smiling broadly. 'Use them sparingly and they always have much more impact, don't you think? So, all set to do the "Sisters" song for Charlie?'

Oh hell, Bett thought. She'd forgotten all about that. 'I'm sorry, Lola, but I can't do it.'

'Why ever not?'

'I've forgotten the words.'

'If she has, then so have I,' Anna said.

'Me too,' Carrie added.

'Oh, I'm sure it'll come back to you once you get started. It's that one about the mister coming between the sisters. No? Then it's just as well I brought these.'

She passed over three sheets of lyrics. They were cornered. 'Come on, then. Charlie and his cameraman are waiting. He was just saying again how this is going to be the centrepiece of his segment.' Complete lies, of course. Charlie had no interest or intention of using any of this footage of the Alphabet Sisters. He had staged that little scene earlier purely as a favour to Lola. She had explained the whole situation to him on the phone the day before and he had been highly amused and happy to oblige. And, by the looks of things, it had worked.

'Come on then, girls. Time's money and I'm short of both.' She started shooing them in front of her, one by one. Then she stopped. 'And you too, Matthew. I've had the very amusing idea of using you as well.'

Half an hour later, Charlie strolled over to where Lola was sitting, watching all the action. She took his hand and smiled up at him. 'Thank you, Charles darling. You're quite an actor yourself.'

He bowed deeply. 'A pleasure to be of service. You never know,

I may end up using the footage yet. They were rather good, weren't they? Some wonderful harmonies.'

'Once they stopped laughing, yes, they were. That was always their problem. They didn't take it seriously enough.'

'Matthew was a good sport, to stand there like that while they sang that "Sisters" song around him.'

Not so much a good sport as terrified of what might happen if he didn't do as he was told, more like it. 'Wasn't he just?'

'I'll send you a tape of it all anyway. For your records.'

'My records. What a marvellous phrase. Thank you, I'd love that.'

Lola gazed around. Anna, Bett, Matthew and Carrie were in a corner of the room with Richard and Daniel, the group of them laughing. Well, thank God. If the feud had gone on one day longer she was going to go simply and utterly mad.

'So what's your next project going to be?' Charlie asked.

'Well, I have the little matter of our gala world premiere, of course. But after that?' She smiled up at him. 'A musical adaptation of *One Flew Over the Cuckoo's Nest*, I think.'

Their parents arrived home that night. There was an hour debriefing about their holiday, an hour hearing about the musical, ten minutes on Lola's accident and then Jim Quinlan was back behind his bar, sorting bottles, and Geraldine was in the kitchen organising the freezer.

Lola watched the three girls vying for their mother's attention and had to stop herself from shaking Geraldine. She'd managed to restrain herself for many years. She could manage for another few, she decided.

In bed that night, Jim and Geraldine were talking about their holiday and homecoming.

Geraldine took off her glasses and reached out to turn off the bedside light. 'The girls seem to be getting on very well again, don't they?'

'Remarkably well. I was sure there would have been at least one row or something while we were away, but it seems not. Perhaps that's all it ever needed, just getting them back under the same roof again.' He chuckled. 'I take my hat off to Lola.'

Jim didn't see Geraldine's expression. 'They're grown girls. I knew they'd sort it out eventually themselves.'

'Of course they would. Goodnight, darling.'

'Goodnight, Jim.'

He put his arm around his wife and shut his eyes.

Chapter Twenty-six

Bett woke up with just the slightest hint of a hangover. She and Anna and Carrie had stayed up talking and drinking red wine until very late. Richard and Matthew and Lola had joined in at first, before stealing away one by one, leaving the three girls on their own. They had taken over the small motel bar, shamelessly helping themselves to glasses of wine from their father's fine cellar of local reds, leaving increasingly scrawled notes to him.

'He won't mind, I know he won't,' Carrie had said as she opened one of the oldest bottles of shiraz. 'Anyway, it's not as if he can sack us, is it?'

Another time, after that much wine, Bett might have woken with a headache, a sense of the dreads. But not this morning. There was nothing to cringe about. She didn't feel that she had said anything stupid, or talked too much. She could remember every word, every joke, every laugh they had shared, even though it had been nearly two a.m. by the time they went to bed, practically pouring a giggling Carrie into the taxi they had called.

Bett stretched, enjoying the feel in her muscles, the look of the sunlight streaming in through the thin curtains, the sound of the birds outside. She had a glorious, light feeling inside her, that things were going to be okay again. That things were okay with Anna and Carrie again. She hadn't felt so good in years.

She checked the time. Eight o'clock. She'd better get up and get ready. She had two more assignments with Daniel that day, and they'd arranged to meet at the office at nine thirty.

There had been more teasing about him from Anna and Carrie the night before.

'You must have noticed something, Bett,' Anna had insisted.

'Picked up the *vibes* from him,' Carrie had added, in a bad American accent.

'You're reading too much into it,' Bett protested. 'We just get on really well. It's nothing more than that.'

'No?'

'No. Stop it, you two.'

'You really, genuinely, sincerely don't have any romantic feelings towards him?'

'No, I don't,' she said, fighting a little voice in her head that was suggesting something quite different.

'Then let me ask you a few simple questions.' Anna winked over at Carrie. The two of them were really enjoying this. 'Does Daniel make you laugh?'

'Yes. A lot.'

Anna was ticking them off on her fingers. 'Do you think he's good-looking?'

'Yes.'

'A-ha!' Carrie said. 'The giveaway.'

'I'm just stating a fact,' Bett said quickly. 'He is.'

'In what way is he good-looking?'

Bett took a sip of wine and thought about it. 'He's got gorgeous eyes, all kind of crinkly, and that lovely sort of dark shaggy hair, and he wears great clothes, I reckon.' She stopped. 'What? What are you both laughing at?'

'Nothing,' Anna said, quite straight-faced. 'So you've noticed all these things about him. You admit that you get on really well. He doesn't take his eyes off you. But you still don't think anything's going on between you?'

'It's not.'

Anna turned to Carrie. 'It's sweet that she's managed to keep her innocence for so long, Carrie, don't you think?'

'Remarkable really, in this day and age.'

'Stop it, you two. Leave me alone.' Bett had been laughing too by this stage. She was also thanking her lucky stars that she had stopped herself just in time from telling them all about her one-night stand with Daniel. God only knows what they would have made of that . . .

She hadn't minded the teasing one bit, though. It had been good fun. Not like old times all over again, either. Much better than that. It had been the start of new times between them.

Getting ready that morning, she chose her favourite dark-green shirt, her favourite vintage skirt and the Italian shoes that people always remarked on. She applied a bit of mascara. And while she was at it, she popped on a bit of lip gloss, too. She was going to be out and about doing these two interviews, so she may as well look presentable, she told herself.

'You look smart, Bett,' her father said as she walked into the kitchen for a coffee. 'Have you got something special on today?'

'No. Just doing a couple of stories for that tourism project.'

'With Daniel?' Lola piped up from her chair.

'Yes, actually.'

'Marvellous!' Lola beamed.

Lola didn't have to have looked quite so delighted, Bett thought as she walked into the newspaper office a half hour later. Her grandmother's face had lit up as if Bett had said she was heading off to elope to Gretna Green. What had got into everybody suddenly? She and Daniel were becoming good friends, that's all. Men and women could be friends, couldn't they? She and Daniel just got on well. They worked well together. They made each other laugh. Quite a bit, in fact. And yes, perhaps they'd had a night of pretty terrific sex three years before, but that was in the past. All it meant was . . . She stopped there. All it meant was if they were to have sex again, it would probably be just as great.

'Morning, Bett. Ready to get going again?'

It was Daniel.

The colour whooshed into her face.

She was a little awkward with him to begin with, she knew she was. As they spent the morning at an art gallery tucked away in the hills south of Clare, she was more businesslike than she'd been on any of the previous assignments. Brisk even. She noticed him glance at her once or twice.

'Everything okay with you, Bett?'

'Fine,' she said cheerily, cursing Anna and Carrie for putting the idea into her head.

After the art gallery their next stop was Sevenhill Cellars, the Valley's oldest winery.

'We've a few minutes before they're expecting us,' Daniel said, glancing at his watch. 'Do you mind if we take the scenic route? The light's good today for a shot I want to take over the hills.'

'No, I don't mind at all.'

Daniel smiled his thanks and then turned the car off the main road onto the bumpy dirt road.

Her reply echoed in her mind as she watched him stop and start the car at different spots along the road, choosing scenes where the sunlight filtered through clumps of gum trees, sending dappled light onto the rows of vines, or near the dry creek beds, lined with water-smoothed pebbles of different shapes and sizes. No, she didn't mind at all if she got to sit on the bonnet of the car in the sunshine and watch him at work. She didn't mind at all seeing him concentrate on finding the best picture, walking along the road looking for the right angle, sending her a grin when he took a shot he was happy with. She didn't mind at all if they got to spend a bit more time in the car together. She didn't mind, in fact, if they spent the rest of the day in the car together, talking and laughing.

The realisation came on slowly and surely throughout the day. She found herself watching him more closely, being more conscious of him than she ever had before. She was acutely aware of him walking close behind her as they were taken on a tour of the cool stone winery building, breathing in the rich smells of the wooden barrels of wine around them. As she interviewed the winemaker and spoke to the people at the cellar door, she knew Daniel was nearby. She watched him deftly take the cameras out of the bag, check settings and switch lenses. She noticed the casual, assured way he put light meters into his pockets, the way his body moved so lithely as he walked around, looking for good angles, trying for unusual shots. She noticed his manner with the people he was photographing, how quickly he put them at ease.

They drove back into Clare in the early afternoon. The sight of his lean, brown hands on the steering wheel was beginning to have quite an effect on her. The way he tapped his long fingers gently in time to the music on the radio. The way he changed the gears so skilfully. She dragged her eyes away from his hands, then found herself noticing his thighs instead, how good they looked in the jeans he was wearing. As they stopped at an intersection, he pushed back the rolled-up sleeve of his shirt to check the time. She noticed every detail in an instant. The brown skin of his arm, the golden hairs, the muscles. She nearly leapt out of her seat when he reached over suddenly to catch a brochure that kept sliding back and forth along the dashboard.

He sent her a puzzled look. 'Bett, are you sure you're okay today? You seem a bit distracted. Jumpy.'

'Do I? Am I? Sorry. I must be coming down with something.'

They started talking about the work they'd done that morning, and then the dress rehearsal for the musical. He casually referred to the fact that Matthew had been there and they were all getting on just fine, and she just as casually remarked that it was good to see Carrie and Matthew so happy together.

'I'll be able to die a happy man now too. I actually got to see the Alphabet Sisters perform.'

She pulled a face. 'I did warn you. We weren't exactly The Supremes.'

'Oh, I don't know. I just wish I'd seen you in your heyday. When you were really at the height of your powers.'

'Count your blessings that you didn't.'

He was laughing as he pulled into a shady spot in the main street, a hundred metres or so down from the *Valley Times* office. 'So did you have a triumphant last performance? The audience in tears, waving cigarette lighters at the three of you?'

'Not quite.' She hesitated for only a second. 'It was awful actually. Three boys shouted Piggy in the Middle at me when we were on stage one day and it ruined it for me from then on.'

'They called you Piggy in the Middle?'

She nodded.

'How ridiculous.'

'Ridiculous?' She didn't understand.

'Well, Pretty Girl in the Middle I could understand.'

She went still.

'Or Bright-eyed Girl in the Middle.'

She held her breath.

'Or Great Fun To Be With in the Middle.'

She was smiling now.

'But Piggy? No. They were three blind boys, obviously,' he said, very matter-of-fact. 'Three blind stupid boys. Three blind stupid boys who wouldn't know a world-class singer and performer if she came up and –' he foundered for a moment.

'Grunted in their faces?' she helped him.

He grinned. 'Well, I was thinking more along the lines of yodelled.'

Later that day Rebecca called her into her office. 'Everything go well today?'

'It did, thanks. Just the Drover's Experience story to go next week and that tourism project is all done.'

'You and Daniel getting along okay?'

'Yes, thanks.' She couldn't read the expression on Rebecca's face. 'I have been going easy on him, I promise. Like you asked me to.' She was still puzzled by what Rebecca had meant by that. Daniel hadn't let on that anything was wrong at all.

Rebecca was trying not to smile. 'I know. I suppose I was wondering what your definition of going easy on him might be.'

'Why?'

'It's just I had two calls today from people wondering why my reporter and my photographer were sitting in the company car in the main street for nearly an hour talking and laughing their heads off. Was it a stake-out, they wondered? Were we on to a hot story?'

Bett gave a strange-sounding laugh. 'God, this town. They just make up gossip if they can't find any, don't they?'

'Do they?' Rebecca smiled mischievously. 'You tell me. You've lived here longer than I have.'

Chapter Twenty-seven

Opening night arrived. The last tickets had been sold that morning. It was a full house.

Lola had pulled out all the stops, raiding not just her own wardrobe, but Carrie's, Anna's and Bett's as well. It had taken everyone some discipline not to gasp or laugh too loudly when she first stepped out of her room, ready to be driven to the town hall by Jim. After seeing her, Geraldine had decided to drive down a little later.

Lola now stood, dressed in full splendour, at the front door of the town hall. Her floor-length orange taffeta skirt clashed with the purple tunic, which clashed with the gold wrap. It all clashed with her makeup. She had a rose and a fabric butterfly pinned in her hair, and nearly rattled as she walked from all the jewellery. Beside her, in a much more low-key outfit but just as bright a smile, was Ellen. She'd been put in charge of handing out programs as people came in.

Lola was shining, accepting compliments and handing them out just as enthusiastically. 'Mrs Gillespie, you look marvellous.' 'Yes, I am as proud as punch. It's a wonderful night for all of us.'

Ellen greeted every one who passed her with the same message. 'Good evening. Enjoy the show, won't you?'

Backstage, Anna was moving back and forth, checking on

costumes, makeup and sets. She was glad and relieved to feel the adrenalin coursing through her, giving her the energy and buzz she had always loved before a performance. She'd had a very bad night's sleep, tired but unable to sleep, feeling the tightness across her chest again. Perhaps that scan the young doctor had mentioned was a good thing, she'd thought as she lay there in the dark, thinking the worst. She'd confided in Richard, and been comforted by his matter-of-factness.

'It's probably asthma, by the sound of things. But the doctor's right. You're just as well to get it checked out. When is the test?'

In Adelaide, two days after the musical, she'd told him. She was going to return the costumes at the same time. She'd been surprised by his next words.

'Would you like me to come with you? I can help you carry things, wait while you do the tests and then take you somewhere really splendid for lunch. To celebrate the musical. And to celebrate you and –' he had stopped there. 'Well, just to celebrate.'

She had been very touched. 'I'd love that,' she'd said.

'Anna! Anna!' She turned as Len ran in, a panicked expression on his face. 'One of the wheels of the train has jammed. Has anyone got any oil?'

Anna swiftly produced a bottle from a basket by the window. She'd brought oil, nails, sticking plasters, double-sided tape, needle and thread, ready for any eventuality. There was even an industrial-sized upholstery stapler that Lola had produced from somewhere.

'Deep breath, now, Len. Everything's all right. Everything's going to be fine.'

'Damn right it is,' he said loudly, cheery again. 'Thanks, Anna. Break a leg, everyone.'

At the edge of the room, leafing through her music for the tenth time, Bett overheard and grinned. Probably not the best thing for Len to say, even if it was a theatrical tradition. Knowing his ability to create chaos, the entire cast breaking a leg each was entirely possible. She was loving this part of the evening, all the excitement before the show began. Carrie was beside the mirror, applying makeup to all the cast members, who were lined up in a row like laughing clowns at a fair. Lola's ladies from the charity shop were making last-minute adjustments to the costumes. In the middle of it all was Anna, calm, in control. As Bett caught her eye, Anna smiled then mouthed something.

'What?' Bett called.

Anna's voice came over clearly. 'Break an egg, Bett.'

Bett laughed. She'd completely forgotten the Alphabet Sisters' own version. 'Break an egg, Anna,' she called back. Carrie looked up and grinned too.

Bett tucked the music under her arm and went up onto the stage, nervous and excited. She peered through a gap in the curtains into the hall. It was now nearly filled. There was a warm, bubbling noise of conversation, mixed with the sounds of chairs scraping, people finding their seats and greeting friends. It was fifteen minutes to curtain up.

Bett made her way down the side stairs out into the little musical pit they had set up at the foot of the stage, the area marked out by trestle tables standing on their side. One wobbled as she went past. Len's work again, unfortunately. Such enthusiasm, but he had a mind like a dragonfly, jumping from one project to another before the first was finished.

The other members of her small band were already seated: a sax player, a guitarist and a drummer, each of them dressed in dark trousers and white shirt. She greeted them warmly, noticing their flushed cheeks, their bright eyes. From their excitement, it could have been Carnegie Hall, not the Clare Town Hall. She took her seat and nodded, and they began playing the first of the introductory tunes, Glenn Miller's 'In the Mood'. Looking up from the keyboard, her fingers so familiar with the notes, she spied Rebecca in the audience, with a gang of people from the newspaper. Daniel was at the end of the row. He winked at her as she caught his eye. She grinned and winked back.

The noise in the hall changed as Lola started making her way to the stage through the centre aisle. She climbed the stairs, then paused dramatically in the middle of the stage, just as Bett finished the last notes of Vera Lynn's 'We'll Meet Again'.

'Ladies and gentlemen, boys and girls, thank you all very much for coming tonight. My name is Lola Quinlan.' She gestured flamboyantly. 'Welcome to the world premiere of *Many Happy Returns*!'

At interval, Anna went out to the hall to say a quick hello to Richard and Lola. She couldn't get near her grandmother. Lola was standing in the middle of an admiring crowd, holding court. 'The idea first came to me in the middle of the night about twenty-five years ago . . .'

Anna smiled as Richard came up to her. 'So? What do you think?'

'It's wonderful.'

'Wonderful?' Anna pulled a face. 'I don't know about that.' She lowered her voice, started ticking things off on her fingers. 'General MacArthur forgot his lines again. The train got stuck. The dancing wasn't in formation. Some of the singing was flat . . .'

He caught her hand and squeezed it in his. 'And it's still wonderful. Look at the mood. Everyone's having a great time.'

She grinned. 'They are, aren't they?' The audience had cheered

Lola when she got up at the start. There had been some singing along with 'My Favourite Things' and 'Oh What a Beautiful Morning'. Len's trick with the corn – where the sheaves suddenly came up through the stage – had almost worked. They'd risen about three inches, at least, which was better than nothing. Kaylene had veered between her English and American accents, sounding vaguely South African by the final scene of the first act, but she had put across the right emotion.

Back at the piano, five minutes before the end of interval, Bett felt a touch on her arm. It was Daniel. 'Congratulations. It's hilarious.'

'Hilarious? It's supposed to be serious drama, not great fun.'

'Sorry. Of course it is. That's what I meant to say. It's hugely dramatic. The whole gamut of human emotions.'

'Careful. We have an audience participation spot, and I have connections with the director.' The bell sounded to indicate the end of the interval. 'Are you staying on for the party?'

'If that's okay. Len invited me, but I wasn't sure.'

'You were last-minute crew and nearly cast. Of course you should be there.' She wanted him to be there.

He smiled. 'Great. I'll see you later, then.'

'See you.' Bett was smiling too as she turned back to the piano. Lola was right. There was something very attractive about a man with a glint in his eye.

In the middle of the next act she heard a faint crying from the audience, like a child, but rising louder and louder. She turned her head slightly, to see Daniel help an elderly woman out of her seat and towards the back of the hall. The crying faded to a little whimpering sound. Were the war songs reviving sad memories? Bett brought her attention back to the stage as Kaylene did her best to reach a high note but unfortunately failed. Bett played extra loud to try and cover up for it.

They all crowded into the backstage area afterwards. The noise was deafening.

'We got five curtain calls! Five!' Carrie exclaimed. Not only that, she'd been applauded wildly after her rendition of 'I Could Have Danced All Night'. Lola had received another huge cheer and then called the three of them up beside her to receive enormous bouquets of flowers. Backstage it was all excitement, backslapping, relief, re-enactments of moments when scenes hadn't worked, overlaid with compliments and praise. Some of the cast took their makeup off and changed into normal clothes. But as the after-show party got underway, Bett noticed many of them were still in their costumes and stage makeup. They looked happy to stay in them forever, in fact. Lola was beaming as though lit from within, brighter even than the night of her party.

Bett was surprised by a sudden big hug. It was Rebecca. 'Congratulations, Bett. It was fantastic. I don't know how you all did it. What next, the West End?'

A face popped in between them before she had a chance to answer. Len the butcher. He kissed each of them on both cheeks, nearly spilling a glass of champagne. 'Bett, Rebecca, a night for celebration, don't you think?'

Bett clinked glasses with him. 'It was fantastic, Len. Thank you so much for all the hard work.'

'Well, I think we all contributed.' He leaned forward conspiratorially. 'You weren't put off by poor old Mrs Hilder's crying, I hope? Daniel was very good to bring her out, though, don't you think? His sister's the same, takes her out everywhere. Can't imagine my girls bringing me out if I lost my marbles like that. They'd have me locked in a home before I knew what had hit me.' He gave a loud roar of laughter, then raised his glass to them again. 'See you later, then, ladies. On the dance floor, perhaps?' He gave a little twist of his hips, then moved away.

Rebecca shook her head after him. 'And the prize for the most sensitive man in the Clare Valley goes to Len once again. Daniel would hate it if he heard his mother being talked about like that.'

'Is that the trouble at home you spoke about?'

Rebecca nodded. 'Seeing as Len has introduced the subject so delicately, yes, it is. Daniel's mother has Alzheimer's. That's why he came back to Clare, to look after her. He and his sister have been taking it in turns staying with her. But it got to the point that Mrs Hilder was beyond staying at home. They had to move her into Lilac House a week or two ago. You know it? The care house next to the hospital?'

Bett nodded.

'He only told me about it because there were times he'd need to leave work to go to her.'

'Why was it such a secret?'

'I don't think it was out of secrecy. It was more loyalty, a way of protecting their mother. You don't remember her?'

Bett shook her head.

'It's so sad. She was the most elegant, proper woman. You know the sort? Everything perfect, under control. And she just had a complete personality change the worse her condition became. She started swearing, going down the street in unsuitable clothing. The one good thing was she wasn't aware of what she was doing, but it was heartbreaking for Daniel and his sister, Christine. I think that's why they tried to look after her at home for as long as they could.

You know, getting carers, installing all sorts of things to stop her from hurting herself and to keep her occupied.'

Bett thought of the coloured lines, the signs on drawers and the locks on the cupboards she'd seen the day Daniel showed her his Dangerous video. They weren't for any grandchildren but for Mrs Hilder herself.

'Oh, the poor things. That must have been so hard for them all.'

'It has been, I think.'

'You wouldn't know it from Daniel, though, would you?' Bett said. 'He's so good-natured, so lovely all the time.'

Rebecca gave her a knowing look. 'Yes, he is, isn't he? He just gets on with it, I think.' She glanced around. 'I thought he might have come back after he took her back to Lilac House, but no sign of him. His poor mum must have got quite upset.'

Bett had already noticed he hadn't come back. She'd been keeping an eye out for him.

Rebecca hugged her again. 'Enough of such serious talk on your night of triumph. Come on, musical director, help me find a fresh bottle of champagne.'

Midway through the party, there was a sudden, loud clapping of hands. Someone was trying to get everyone's attention. Slowly the talk died down, and the music playing from the stereo was lowered. Lola stood in the middle of the room, with a glass of champagne in one hand. 'Thank you all. I promise I'll only be a minute. We've all got a lot of celebrating to do tonight and far be it from me to put a halt to your gallop.' There was laughter. 'Some weeks ago, when my three granddaughters reunited for my eightieth birthday, I said something to them that I meant from the heart. And I'd like to say it to all of you tonight as well. I never dreamed this would happen in the way it did. Thank you, each and every one of you. You've made an old lady very happy.'

There were cheers, and more applause. Then from the back someone shouted. 'Give us a song, Lola.'

She gave an imperious wave. 'Oh no, I'm far too old for that. I'm an observer these days, not a performer.'

'Oh come on, Lola. We all did it. Now it's your turn,' General MacArthur called.

At different spots around the room, Anna, Bett and Carrie started smiling. Anna wished Ellen was here to see this, but her daughter, so tired she had been drooping, had just been taken back to the motel by Geraldine and Jim.

'Yes, come on now, Lola. You can't let everyone down,' Carrie called out, egged on by Matthew beside her.

'You're only as old as you feel, remember,' Anna added.

'She taught us everything we know, you know,' Bett said to Rebecca.

'Really? In that case you can be her backing singers.'

Someone overheard. 'Yes, bring on the Alphabet Sisters as well!'

This time there was no hesitation. There was a tumble of movement and laughter, as Lola was lured into the middle of the room, and the three girls made to line up behind her, like an old-fashioned backing group, standing sideways. Everyone was laughing.

'So what do we sing?' Bett said. She wished again that Daniel was there. She knew he would have enjoyed this.

'It has to be Lola's choice,' Anna said.

'One of your favourites, Lola,' Carrie added.

Lola was thinking hard. Then she beckoned the girls in, told them her choice. There was more laughter, and a huddle of heads as they all checked they knew at least some of the words. Then Lola stepped forward and bowed dramatically. 'Ladies and gentlemen, boys and girls. It gives me great pleasure to introduce myself, and my three granddaughters, for your listening pleasure tonight.'

And in a voice that threatened to shatter every piece of glass in the building, Lola – backed very badly by a laughing Anna, Bett and Carrie – warbled her way through her own unique, high-kicking version of 'There's No Business Like Show Business'.

In bed that night Lola stretched one leg, then the other, did her facial exercises, then gave up. She didn't want to do exercises. She wanted to just lie there and grin all night long. She wanted to savour every minute, rewind it all, relive it second by second, from Bett's music, to Anna's direction, to Carrie's singing and dancing. Had she ever felt as proud in the Alphabet Sisters days as she had that evening, standing there on stage with her three girls, her son, Jim, and granddaughter, Ellen, smiling up from the audience at her? Even Geraldine had been smiling, had actually hugged her afterwards.

And had she ever felt as good as she had at the party afterwards? All those people coming up, showering her with praise, firing questions. Were they going to stage it again? What about a tour? Had she thought about sending the script to a professional company? What about next year's project? She had laughed them all away, insisting tonight was no night for future plans, it was for savouring a triumph.

But lying there, she did have a thought. Richard had put it in her mind, with all his research into English convicts and Irish servant girls coming to the Clare Valley in the 1850s. What a marvellous storyline that would make. She could follow just one of them, or no, perhaps two, even three sisters, on their journey from Ireland to

South Australia. It could involve one or two scenes on a ship. After Len's triumph with General MacArthur's train, surely building a ship would be no bother to him. And all those lively Irish jigs and reels. Such scope for a plot, too. One of the servant girls could fall in love with her cruel, handsome master . . .

Lola sat up and reached for the notebook she kept on her bedside table.

CHAPTER TWENTY-EIGHT

FORTY-EIGHT hours later Bett was sitting beside a campfire near a clutch of gum trees, watching the flickering fire, experiencing first hand the Drover's Experience. This would be the final article for the tourism supplement. This time next week she'd be back on court reports and police articles.

She had a notebook filled with quotes from the drover himself, craggy-faced, brown-skinned, laconic. The perfect face for a man with his job. 'Straight out of Central Casting,' Daniel had whispered earlier as he set up shots of Fergie with his sheep and the blue sky behind him.

They'd eaten dinner by the campfire – damper bread, billy tea, stew in a pot, exactly as the tourist groups would enjoy it in the months ahead. Their tents would be pitched in a circle around the campfire too, logs of wood acting as seats, under the huge night sky. Tonight there were just the three tents, one for Fergie, a long way back from the main camp site – 'I snore,' he'd explained succinctly – and one each for Bett and Daniel.

Fergie had told Bett some of the tales he'd be sharing with the tourists. He knew the whole story of the area, from its Aboriginal history to the early pioneer days. He'd spent most of his life working in shearing sheds and had plenty of stories about them as well.

Bett took down the final details and then put her notebook away. 'This isn't for the article, but tell me, do you ever get sick of sheep?'

Fergie laughed. 'No. If I do, I get a whole fresh bunch every spring, remember. That's the wonder of nature.'

Daniel came back to the campfire. He'd been taking photos from a distance as the final light faded around them. 'We'll take a few more in the morning, Fergie, if that's okay.'

'I'll be up at five, Dan, with my best smile on.' He pulled an exaggerated face and they both laughed. 'Early to bed for me, anyway. Dan, you'll sort out the fire, won't you? Goodnight to you both.'

Bett stretched out her legs towards the fire, alone for a moment while Daniel went to his tent to put away the camera equipment. Her mobile rang, the noise incongruous in the surroundings. She read the name on the display. 'Lola? Is everything all right?'

'Everything's fine, darling. Your parents are in the bar with a couple of guests, swapping stories about train journeys. Carrie is home with Matthew, and little Ellen is staying over with them for the night. Anna is in Adelaide returning the costumes. Richard's gone with her for the trip. Do you suppose they'll be staying in separate rooms tonight?'

'You're too old to be thinking things like that.'

'What is the tent situation like there, darling?'

'We have one each, Lola.'

'Really?' A pause. 'You know that if it gets cold, the best way to warm up is through body heat?'

'I'll tell Fergie that, will I?' She had discovered earlier that Lola and Fergie knew each other from some years back. 'That will be a surprise for him in the middle of the night. A little visit from me.'

Lola laughed. 'Goodnight, darling. Have a nice night.'

Bett glanced up as Daniel came back to the fire. He nodded to the phone. 'Everything all right at home?'

'Everything's fine. And you?' She had seen him talking on his mobile phone too.

He took a seat on the other log next to her and stretched out his legs. 'Not so bad.'

Bett hesitated. 'Rebecca told me about your mother, Daniel. I'm sorry. It must be very hard on you and your sister.'

'It has been. But worse for Mum, of course.' He picked up a long stick and broke it in pieces, throwing the bits into the fire. 'I'm sorry about the night of the musical, Bett. One of the songs distressed her. That's the sad thing about it, it's so unpredictable. It could have been a voice that sparked a memory, as easily as a song. But we don't want her to never go out. She's very healthy apart from that. It's her mind not her body that's been affected.'

'You and Christine have been very good to give up your lives for her like that.'

'We don't see it like that. You just do it for family. You'd do it for Lola, wouldn't you?'

'In a shot.'

'You just need her to slow down enough so you can look after her, I guess?'

She smiled, then was serious again. 'If there's ever anything I can do for you or for your mother, just ask, Daniel, won't you?'

'Thanks, Bett.'

There was a long pause before he spoke again. 'So are you going to stay on in the Valley, now the musical is over?'

'I don't know yet. I'll see what happens.' She took up a stick too and poked at the embers, watching sparks fly into the air. 'So did you get some good shots today?'

'I think so. A good subject always helps.'

'It's not just that. You're a very good photographer.'

'Thank you.'

'So is that what you always wanted to do? When you were growing up?'

'Always. I had a box brownie as a teenager. Before that one of those homemade ones from cardboard.' He grinned. 'I had to draw my own photographs, but it was a start.' He threw another bit of wood into the fire. 'And what about you? Did you always want to be a journalist?'

'Not always. It was a choice between something to do with music and something to do with writing, and writing won. And now I really love being a journalist.'

'You do, don't you? What about it, exactly?'

She realised he was genuinely interested. She thought about it for a moment. 'I like watching something happen and turning it into a sentence, or a story. Capturing it, I suppose.'

'And you don't miss the music? You can't do both?'

'I tried. When I was in London, I wrote about music and bands but it wasn't for me in the end.'

'No? What happened?'

She told him stories from her time in the record company, encouraged by his laughter. It did seem ridiculous from this distance, coaching teenage pop stars, telling them what they thought. She laughed too. 'You see what a mess the music industry is in? Where were you, Danger Hilder, when we needed you most?'

He smiled and reached down to the bottle of wine. 'More?'

'Yes, please.'

The sounds around them became distinct. The slow glug of the wine into her glass. A quiet crackle from the flames in front of them. A bird far off in the trees. Faint rustling noises and low bleats from the sheep in the distance.

'So was it hard to leave London?'

She shook her head, remembering the day she'd decided to resign. 'Once I'd decided, it was the simplest thing in the world. I knew this was where I wanted to be.'

'It's easier for women in lots of ways, don't you think?'

'What's easier?'

'Life. Decisions, everything.' He waved an arm. 'Women seem to know how to do it. You always seem so confident, assured. You know what you want, how to make things happen.'

'Women generally? Or me? Because I haven't a clue.'

'What are you talking about? That was one of the first things I noticed about you, how confident and alive you are, how comfortable you are in your own skin.'

'No, I'm not.' Bett was astonished. 'I'm a walking disaster area.'

'You are not. I used to see you in Clare, when I was first here. You'd be talking away to people, interviewing them. And I'd see you in pubs and restaurants with Matthew, telling stories, always so confident.'

'You should have looked closer, then.'

He gave a soft laugh. 'I was probably too busy worrying about my own appearance.'

'But men don't think like that, do they? Get worried about what people think of them? I mean, I haven't got any brothers, but I thought you all knew exactly what you wanted, how to act, how to –'

'Of course we don't. I can't speak for the entire male population, but I get scared and worried about things. That I'll make a mess of something, choose the wrong moment, misread a situation . . .'

She was speechless.

'I'm scared now, for example.'

'Of what?'

'You.'

'Scared of me?'

He hesitated. 'Of what you'd do if I asked you if I could kiss you.'

She blinked. 'You want to kiss me?'

'I've wanted to kiss you for weeks.'

'Why haven't you?'

'In case you slapped me. Told me to go away. Told me you didn't like me in that way.'

'Oh,' she said. A warm glow had started deep inside her. 'And how were you planning on going about it?'

'I was thinking of coming over and sitting beside you, and perhaps putting one hand on your cheek. And then if that went okay, I was probably going to lean down and kiss you. That was when I was worried that you might slap me.'

'I see.' She thought about it for a moment. 'I don't think I would.'

'No?'

'I don't think so.'

'Should I check?'

She nodded.

He moved towards her. She sat, her face turned up at him, nervous but also excited. She'd had one glass of wine, not the quantities she'd drunk last time they'd kissed. She'd had a good, busy, interesting day, not weeks of frenzy and turmoil. Her breath caught at the touch of his lips against hers, soft, exploring. She felt the touch of his hand on her face.

'Aphrodisiac qualities, those campfires, I've always found.'

They both jumped at the voice. It was Fergie, coming out of his tent. They separated, embarrassed, and stared into the fire again until Fergie returned from the tree he was visiting. He gave them a cheery wave from the opening of his tent.

A moment passed, and then they turned back to one another. This time she met his lips halfway. They kissed, long, slow kisses that tasted like red wine. He kissed her eyelids and the lobes of her ears and the side of her neck. She kissed the side of his face, the corners of his lips. Did she put his hand on her breast or did he do it himself? Bett wondered. She touched the side of his body, his back, their lips soft against one another all the while, the kiss continuing. They both stood up. He pulled her in against his body and she could feel his arousal, feel herself pressing against his body, her breasts full, aching to be touched.

A huge sneeze from Fergie's tent resounded in the air. She could feel Daniel laughing, even as she laughed herself.

'The cry of the wildebeest,' he whispered, kissing her again. He moved his hand down her body. Without realising it she started to tense.

He pulled away. 'Do you want me to stop?'

She shook her head. Tell the truth, she heard a voice inside her say. 'I'm just a bit nervous.'

'Of me?'

She shook her head. 'Maybe not nervous. Maybe self-conscious.'

'But you're perfect. And I should know. I've been staring at every inch of you for weeks. I could draw you from memory, you know.

This curve here,' he brushed her thigh. 'The curve of your arm.' He touched her arm. 'Your breast.' Her breathing faltered as he slowly stroked her breast. 'These curves here.'

He laughed at the expression on her face. She laughed too, relaxing, feeling his hands on her, not minding at all now. She touched his back, feeling the skin under his shirt. There was another long, luxurious kiss. She pulled back again, needing to say something. 'I'm sorry about last time. That time in Melbourne. I don't know what got into me. I was very drunk.'

'You needed to be drunk that night?'

She nodded.

'Can I get you a glass of wine now? A bottle?'

She laughed, then it became serious. 'I don't think I need to be drunk tonight.'

He touched her cheek. 'Are you sure?'

She reached up, kissed his lips, felt his body against hers. Then they stopped talking and started kissing again, different, deeper, sexier kissing. Somehow they moved from the campfire to his tent, to the sleeping bag on the ground, as warm flickering shadows from the fire played against the canvas. She loved the feeling of his hands on her body, her breasts, between her legs. And she loved the feel of his body, lean and silky to touch. Was there touch memory, she wondered. Did her body remember what it had felt like to have Daniel against her that night? Because it was responding now as though it couldn't wait to repeat itself . . .

Bett woke up as sunlight was coming into the tent. She felt stirring beside her and turned towards Daniel.

'Good morning.' His voice was soft.

She smiled. 'Hello.'

'Did you have a good night's sleep?'

He knew full well she hadn't. Nor had he. They had been making love most of the night. 'Not really. To be honest, I'm a bit worried.'

She felt him tense. 'What about?'

'My article. Do you suppose I can promise this experience for every woman doing this camping trip?'

He relaxed. 'I could have a word with Fergie. It could be a handy sideline if I lose interest in the photography.'

She laughed, closing her eyes as she felt his fingertips brush her bare skin. His voice was quiet. 'So if you were writing an article about what happened last night, what would you write?'

She thought for a moment. '"Local reporter Bett Quinlan announced today that she was a little bit embarrassed to be waking up naked in a tent with Daniel Hilder but said she didn't regret a second of the previous evening's shenanigans."'

'Shenanigans?'

'Shenanigans. Your turn.'

'"Photographer Daniel Hilder today admitted that he had fancied local reporter Bett Quinlan for some time." Have I got the tone right?'

'Yes. Yes, that's very good.'

'"When questioned, he said that he had always been a sucker for a shock of brown hair and a pair of cheeky eyes, and Ms Quinlan fortunately was endowed with both." Am I still getting it right?'

Bett's head was on his chest, her eyes closed as he stroked her skin. 'It's very good.'

'"When asked about Ms Quinlan's murky past, Mr Hilder gave an insouciant" – I'd have an asterisk there and at the bottom of the page the translation – relaxed, okay? Anyway, "gave an insouciant shrug and said, 'The murkier the better, as far as I'm concerned. The more dirt there is the more we have to talk about.'" I think I've got the hang of this now. Can I go on?'

She nodded.

'"When asked about his future plans, Mr Hilder gave another insouciant shrug, clearly being short of gestures that day, and said, 'It's up to Ms Quinlan, really. Loath as I am to resort to clichés, in this case the ball is in her court.' The press corp then gathered around Ms Quinlan seeking her reaction."'

She could feel his fingers all the way down her back now. '"Ms Quinlan responded to reporters' questions by first checking what the time was –"'

Daniel lifted his wrist. 'Six thirty.'

'"And then wondering aloud if it would be possible for Daniel Hilder to make love to her so beautifully one more time before they left the tent that morning."'

He moved closer, then kissed her lips. His fingers caressed her body again. It seemed it was a yes.

Bett deliberately didn't turn on her mobile for the journey home later that morning. It was a one-hour drive along curving roads, the yellow stubbled paddocks stretching out on either side. They talked and laughed, easily, eagerly. He stopped the car once, didn't speak, just reached over to kiss her. She met him halfway again.

It was early afternoon by the time they arrived at the Valley View Motel. They had taken the slow way home. He pulled into the drive in front of the reception area and turned off the ignition. Bett smiled at him. She felt like just sitting here and smiling at him all day.

'Can I see you tonight?' he asked.

'Again?'

'It's fine if you don't want to.'

'I'd love to. Let me just check in with everyone, make sure nothing's happened while I've been gone.' She'd only been away one night, she laughed to herself. Back here motel life would have gone on as normal, yet it felt like her life had changed completely overnight.

'I'll call in and see my mother too. But I'll ring you afterwards? About six?'

'Perfect.' She waited on the steps of the motel until he had driven away, then turned. She felt like she was radiating happiness. 'Hello?' she called as she came into reception. There was no answer. She checked the bar. It was empty too. She'd already noticed Anna's car wasn't in its usual place. She and Richard must still be in Adelaide. There was no one in the function room either. Or in the kitchen. 'Hello? Where is everybody?' She went outside and heard her name being called.

'Bett?' It was Carrie, coming from Lola's room. She was crying.

'Cancer?'

Bett looked at the faces in front of her. Lola was ashen. Carrie's eyes were swollen. Her mother and father were tightly holding hands.

Jim Quinlan repeated what Anna had phoned and told them. She had called from the hospital. 'She had an MRI scan this morning. There's a tumour in her lungs. A very large tumour. They admitted her straight away.'

Bett stared at him. 'But I don't understand it. She hasn't had any symptoms.'

'She has. It's just they were mistaken for other things. Stress. Exhaustion. Anxiety attacks. And she's always been so thin, so even the weight loss wasn't too out of the ordinary.'

'But what made her have the scan? Why didn't she tell us?'

'A young doctor in Adelaide arranged it.' Jim's voice was dull. 'She didn't want to worry anyone, she said. Not with so much else going on.'

Bett tried to take in everything as her father kept talking. The doctors had told Anna she may have had the tumour for months, even years. It was only now that it had grown so large that it had started causing her problems.

It was as if the world was slightly off kilter. As if voices were not in tune, the colours not right, as if she was several steps behind. She wanted to blink, to start this again, to get out of Daniel's car, come in the door and see Lola reading in the bar, her parents working, Carrie in the office, Anna and Ellen playing Scrabble. Not this gathering.

Someone was missing. 'Where's Ellen?'

'She's in her room playing. Anna spoke to her on the phone but she's asked us not to tell her too much yet. Not until we all know more ourselves.'

'So can we go to Anna? Ellen, all of us? Now?'

Geraldine shook her head. 'She said there was no need to come down tonight. They're giving her sleeping tablets. She'd be asleep before we got there. Richard's with her in the hospital. They're starting radiation treatment first thing in the morning.'

'So it's treatable? So she's going to be all right?' Bett looked around again, knowing she hadn't been the first to ask that question in that room tonight.

No one would answer her.

CHAPTER TWENTY-NINE

TIME STARTED moving at a different pace, as though they were in slow motion, in a bubble of their own, while outside things continued as normal. Anna's treatment started immediately, a team of people working with her – a specialist, a doctor, nurses. Bett felt she was always two steps behind what was happening, barely taking in the news that Anna had cancer in the first place, before they were talking about doing a biopsy, operating or not operating, chemotherapy or no chemotherapy.

Geraldine and Bett were the first to go to Adelaide to be with Anna. Richard returned to Clare. They took it in turns talking to Anna's doctors, getting reports, phoning back to the motel. Everyone had questions and no one was satisfied with the answers they were getting. 'What do they mean it's an aggressive tumour?' 'If they hadn't found it now, what would have happened?' 'Will she lose all her hair when they start the treatment?'

There was test after test. Anna spent most of every day in bed, already exhausted from the X-rays, the scans, the drugs, the shock. Bett and her mother sat beside her, reading, talking a little, watching her while she slept. Bett couldn't reconcile that this already more frail-looking Anna was the same woman who had been smiling up on stage just a few days before. She was still bright and cheerful at first. But the mask dropped when the two of them were alone for the first time. Geraldine had left the room to get coffee.

Anna reached for Bett's hand. 'I'm scared, Bettsie. I'm really scared.'

'We all are, sweetheart. But we'll know more soon, won't we?'

'I don't know. The specialist said I could be in here for weeks. What about Ellen? Who'll look after her if I'm in here for that long?'

Bett squeezed Anna's hand. 'All of us. We're fighting over who gets to look after her. Don't worry about Ellen.'

'Will you ring Glenn?'

None of them had even thought of telling Glenn.

Bett called him in Singapore that night. She could hear the shock in his voice. 'I'll come back as soon as I can, to help look after Ellen. I can be there by the end of the week. She's going to be all right, isn't she? What about the hospital? Is it the best one? Money's no problem, Bett.'

She could tell he was truly concerned. It made it easier to talk to him, to put her anger towards him aside. Did some love survive at the bottom of all failed marriages? she wondered. 'It's a very good hospital. They're doing every test, every scan. We can't get near her for doctors and nurses.'

'What does Ellen know?'

'We don't know what to tell her yet. She knows Anna is in hospital, but we just said it was for a day or two, that she'd be home soon.' Lola had sat with Ellen and explained that Anna wasn't feeling very well, that there was a germ in her body the doctors were trying to get rid of and that fighting the germ sometimes made Anna very tired. They would bring her down to visit Anna very soon. In the meantime, Ellen was talking to Anna twice, sometimes three times a day on the phone.

'And will Anna be home soon?'

Bett had told him the truth. 'We don't know.'

'And you're sure there's nothing I can do, Bett? Nothing you need brought down to Adelaide? Nothing I can do at the motel?'

'I'm sure, Daniel, honestly. But thank you anyway.' She'd called him from the public phone in the hospital corridor. It was the first time she'd spoken to him at length since they'd spent the night together. They had spoken briefly when he had phoned her, the night they had learnt about Anna. She'd been barely able to talk, in deep shock. She had asked him to tell Rebecca the news. Rebecca had rung the next day, offering help as well, with everything from making beds to driving the family to and from Adelaide. 'Don't even think about work, Bett,' she'd said. 'Just stay close to your family. Will you ring me if there's anything any of us can do? It doesn't matter how small.'

There was someone waiting to use the phone. 'I'd better go, Daniel.'

'Of course.' He hesitated. 'I'm thinking of you, Bett.'

'I'm thinking of you too.' She hung up and went back into Anna's room.

Lola and Carrie came down several days later. They brought Ellen with them. They'd told her the truth – that Anna needed to stay in hospital for longer than they expected, while the doctors did more tests on her. Ellen seemed to take it all quite calmly. As Lola said, she was used to hospitals.

Bett drove her mother back to the motel, lost in her own thoughts as she passed the car yards and housing developments of the city's outer suburbs, the scenery gradually changing to open countryside, farms and small towns the further north she drove. Her mother made calls on her mobile throughout the journey, speaking to cancer support agencies, arranging for information to be sent to them, returning phone calls from friends in the Valley enquiring about Anna, offering their help. Her manner was direct, matter-of-fact. Things to be done, practical issues to be organised. Geraldine specialised in those, Bett thought.

She had seen her mother walking down the corridor with Anna the previous night. All around them were other families, some of them in even worse situations, one or two older women in distressed tears. Geraldine had held herself erect, composed. She'd helped Anna get back into bed, hadn't flinched when Anna's gown had lifted slightly and they had seen just how thin she was. She had been almost businesslike when the nurse had come in and expressed concern about how little Anna had eaten of her evening meal.

But an hour later Bett had gone in search of a cup of tea. She had been about to turn on the light in one of the side sitting rooms when she'd heard a noise. Standing still, she had seen a figure in one of the armchairs in the corner of the room. It was her mother, staring out of the window, softly crying.

Bett had hesitated, about to go in and comfort her, when her mother had noticed her first. Geraldine had stood up immediately, briskly wiped away the tears. 'A cup of tea, Bett? Let me get one for you. And Anna too?'

Neither of them mentioned her tears.

Anna and Lola were alone in her room. Lola had been reading to her, picking out bits of ten-year-old gossip from a magazine she had found in the waiting room. Midway through an article about the cast of some since-axed soap opera, Anna put her hand on Lola's arm. 'Lola, I'm so scared.'

The magazine was put away. Lola took both her hands in hers. 'Darling, of course you are. You don't know what's going to happen. That's always scary.'

'Come with me. I want you to come with me and help me.'

'I would if I could, darling.'

'What's going to happen to Ellen if I don't get better? How is she going to cope without a mother? It's not fair, she's suffered too much already.'

'Anna, you mustn't think like that. And you must never worry about Ellen. She'll never be on her own, Anna, I promise you that.'

There was a knock at the door. It was Glenn, in his suit, straight from the airport.

Lola stood up and moved aside immediately. As she shut the door she saw him reach down and hold Anna tight.

Carrie refused to talk to Glenn. She ignored the concern he was showing, the offers of financial help, the offer – gently declined by Anna – to move her to a private hospital in Sydney. Outside, in the waiting room, Carrie railed at Lola.

'It's his fault. This wouldn't have happened if it wasn't for him. I read all about it on the Internet. Stress can cause cancer and that –' she searched for the insult, 'that bastard caused her so much stress and pain. How dare he come here like this? How can you even let him stay here, Lola?'

'It's not Glenn's fault. It's no one's fault, Carrie. It's just happened.

We can't waste time blaming someone, fighting amongst ourselves. We have to think of Anna.'

Carrie was in tears. 'I know. I'm trying to, but I'm so mad, Lola. And I feel useless and I feel like there's nothing I can do. It's all happening too quickly.'

Their lives started revolving around visits to Adelaide, taking it in turns to sit with her, talk to the nurses, listen to the doctor, wait for the specialist. They spent a lot of time in Anna's room, talking, reading, or sitting quietly while she slept, exhausted from the latest round of treatment.

Her room was on the second floor of the hospital, looking out over the parklands. A glass office block stood to the left. The day-to-day movements of the workers, dressed in suits, behind desks, drinking coffee or talking on their phones seemed more and more ridiculous to Bett as each day passed. The hospital waiting room seemed more real, with its scuffed plastic seats, misspelled signs about canteen opening hours, even the empty drink can lying underneath the soft-drink dispenser.

Carrie was with Anna when the specialist came to talk to her, two weeks after she'd been admitted to the hospital. Coolly, succinctly, he explained the situation. It was a very aggressive tumour. They had discovered some secondaries, but so far they were confined. Surgery wasn't an option at this stage. The tumour was too large. There was more treatment to try – more radiation, some new drugs.

'And if the new drugs don't work?' Anna's voice was as calm as his. Beside her, Carrie was tightly holding her hand.

His tone softened. 'Then we're looking at a palliative care situation.'

Bett arrived back at the hospital several days later with more cards and letters from people in the Valley. Word had quickly got around. Each day at the motel there had been calls from people offering to help mind Ellen, to cook for the motel guests if Geraldine needed to be in Adelaide. Prayers were being said for Anna. Len the butcher had dropped off a folder of information he had gathered from the Internet on miracle cures. Bett had left that behind in Clare.

She was shocked at the change in Anna. Her sister was sitting up in the bed, pillows propped all around her, like a tiny bird in a white nest. She was even thinner and her skin seemed to be changing in texture and colour. Her breathing was changing too, becoming more laboured.

She managed a big smile, though. 'Hello, my darling. You've come to admire my new nose jewellery?' Anna had two plastic clips in her nostrils, carrying oxygen into her system. She wasn't able to breathe fully without it any more.

Bett managed a grin too. 'It's very fetching. Does it come in a range of colours?'

'Horrible clear and even more horrible white, I think. I did tell them white wasn't my colour but they can be very obstinate in here. It'll be all the rage next year, you mark my words.'

Bett sat in the chair beside the bed and took Anna's hand. They were touching her constantly now. Whoever was sitting beside her would be stroking her arm, or holding her hand, or just resting their fingers on her. 'Can I get you anything? Do you want the radio on? Any tapes?'

Anna shook her head. 'Tell me about Ellen this week.' Ellen came down to the hospital three days every week, but stayed in the Valley, going to school the rest of the week. The doctors had advised them to keep things as normal as possible for her.

Bett told her the latest stories. Ellen had invited two of her friends over to play after school. Lola had caught them tying hats to Bumper's head. They had been rehearsing their own mini musical, for when Mum came home.

'She'd better hurry it up, then.'

'What do you mean?'

'I've made a decision, Bett.' Her voice became serious as she explained what the specialist had told her that afternoon. That there was still another course of treatment ahead of her. More radiation. Another course of tablets. Still in the experimental stages. 'I agreed, Bett. What did I have to lose?'

'But isn't it dangerous?'

'What? Might it kill me?' She laughed softly at the expression on Bett's face. 'I can joke about it, Bett. It's me who's dying of cancer.'

'You're not dying of cancer. There's still lots of things they can try.'

'I'm too tired. That's the worst thing about it. If I wasn't feeling so sick I'd be interested in thinking about it and talking about it. But if I wasn't so sick I wouldn't be dying, would I?'

Bett was shocked by a sudden flare of temper. 'That's not what I meant. How can you joke about it? Why aren't you angry? Why am I the cross one? Why aren't you raging against the light and the night or whatever it is you're supposed to be raging about?'

Anna was calm. 'I am, Bett. I don't want to die yet. I've no intention of dying yet.'

'Then don't be so bloody passive about it. Fight it.'

'You don't think I am? You really think I want to bow out here and now, slip off, leave all this? Bett, I hate this. I hate every tiny thing of it. Lying here like this, being pumped full of this drug and that drug, getting X-rayed, feeling my lungs trying so hard. All my life I was never conscious of what my body was doing to keep me alive, and now it's as if I can hear every cog turning, every cell doing its job. Of course I hate this. I see a sunrise, or a bird or the smallest beautiful thing and I treasure it and I want it forever and I can't have it. I might not have any of it for much longer.'

'What would you like? If we could get you anything, make anything happen for you before you went,' Bett stumbled on the word. 'What would you want?'

'It's not the obvious things. It's not seeing Ellen walk up the aisle, or holding my first granddaughter. It's the ordinary things. I want mornings in a coffee shop with her when she's about twenty-five. I want her rushed, saying, "I can't stay long, Mum, I have to go and meet someone."'

'What else?'

'I want more drunken nights with you and Carrie and a call from you the next morning to tell me I was all right, that I hadn't been badly behaved. I want you to ring and not introduce yourself – you know, you never do that, you always launch straight into a conversation. And I want to hear all those stories again about your misadventures. Please, Bett, tell me the one about you falling off the treadmill again? I love that story.'

'You're very cruel.'

A smile, vivid in the pale, thin face. 'I know. Shall I start you off? Once upon a time, you were in a gym and . . .'

'The new drugs haven't worked. It's spread even further.' Geraldine spoke as soon as she walked into the kitchen two weeks later.

Jim, Lola and Bett stopped what they were doing. They had known Geraldine was ringing Adelaide and talking to Carrie, who'd been in with Anna for the previous two days. They had known that crucial X-rays were taking place that morning, to check on the growth of the tumours. All day each of them had kept busy, filling the hours. The bar was cleaner than it had ever been. The kitchen had been completely reorganised. Bett had got down on her hands and knees and scrubbed the showers in all fifteen rooms, playing the bedside radio at top volume in each, blasting sound into the air to keep her thoughts from pummelling her.

Geraldine spoke as if she was reading from a list, her voice expressionless, her eyes distant. 'The radiation hasn't worked either. It's spread into her lymph nodes. And her spine.'

A few weeks ago Bett hadn't known what a lymph node was. 'Did Carrie talk to Anna's specialist? About what Anna's decided to do?'

A nod. 'He said that if that was Anna's decision, he fully supported it. He told Carrie afterwards that he felt it was the right option.'

Anna had made her decision three days before. If the latest, more intrusive attempts to stop the cancer hadn't worked, she was going to stop all the radiation, the scans, the invasive procedures.

Jim spoke. 'So she's coming home?'

Geraldine nodded. She didn't need to spell it out. Anna was coming home to die.

Chapter Thirty

Her favourite room in the motel was prepared. They hung bright curtains in the windows. Lola chose a colourful bedspread and a new rug for the floor. Ellen picked fresh flowers and put them in vases. Lola had tried to explain to her that Anna was still very sick, but Ellen hadn't seemed to take it in. She'd been too excited by the fact that her mother was actually coming home. Jim went to the garden centre and bought plants and trees in pots, arranging them outside the room, to give Anna something green and restful to look at from bed. Bett scoured every surface, washed the windows, wiped down the walls, until she had touched every inch of the room.

She smiled at Richard as he carried a box of Anna's favourite books into the room. She was helping him arrange them on a shelf when he spoke, his voice low.

'I should leave, Bett. This is a time for close family.'

She was struck by the deep sadness in his expression. 'No it's not, Richard. It's a time for anyone who loves Anna to be close to her.' She touched his arm. 'I know it's been very hard on you. When things had only just started between you. But you make her very happy.'

'I'd like to have made her happier. For longer.'

Bett blinked away tears which had suddenly come into her eyes. 'So would we,' she answered softly.

Anna arrived home the next day in the car with Carrie and Geraldine. She'd travelled in a nest of pillows, fragile from the treatment and the illness, but refusing to make the trip in an ambulance. She was even thinner, her hair a dark little cap around her face, now even more gaunt. 'I know my hair's a mess, but at least I've still got it. You should have seen some of the bald heads in that ward,' she tried to joke.

She had to be helped into the room. The oxygen came everywhere with her, pushed on a small trolley beside her. Her voice was changing, becoming weaker, but she was still bright, interested.

'Ellie, did you do those drawings for me? They're gorgeous.' She leaned and kissed her daughter, who was clinging tightly to her hand. 'And all the flowers. And look at that bedspread. It's beautiful, everyone. Thank you very much.'

As Anna was settled, Ellen skipped around, unable to stay in one place, running up to her mother, hugging her, then running away again. She sidled up to Bett, as she stood outside Anna's room, arranging a chair and table for the times Anna felt able to sit up, outside in the morning sunshine. It had been Richard's idea.

'My mum is very sick, isn't she?'

Bett stroked her hair. 'She is, Ellie. She's very sick.'

'When she gets better, Daddy and Mum and I are going to go on a holiday.'

'Did he say that?'

She nodded. 'He said he would take me on a long trip, maybe even to Disneyland.'

'That'll be fun,' Bett said, keeping her voice bright. She knew what Glenn had been trying to do. She also knew Anna wouldn't be going with them.

The days fell into a pattern. Anna had more energy in the mornings. She could sit and talk with one or other of them, eat a little, before needing to go back to bed again. Now and then she managed to go for a short walk, or would let them push her in a wheelchair, in the cool of the morning, or after dusk, when the heat of the day had passed. The palliative care nurses visited twice a day and monitored her pain. They showed Bett, Carrie and their mother how to measure the morphine, answered their questions, calmed and soothed them.

Anna slept a great deal. When she was feeling strong enough, she came into the kitchen in a brightly coloured silk dressing-gown and sat in a corner, watching all the activity around her. Ellen continued going to school, but ran in each afternoon, with a new drawing, or a love note, which Anna would exclaim over and put into her pocket.

When Anna was too tired to get up, they all took turns spending time with her in her room. Geraldine was there the most, tidying the room, counting the tablets, straightening the curtains or just sitting quietly by Anna's bed. She seemed to know when Anna was feeling any pain, when she needed more oxygen, what she might like to drink or eat, almost by instinct. No one remarked on it, but everyone noticed.

'Can I get you anything, love?'

Anna looked up from the bed. Ellen was tucked in beside her, asleep. The two of them had been watching cartoons together. 'No thanks, Dad.'

'A cola? A squash? A rainbow drink?'

'A rainbow drink? Now you're talking. Not for me, but for Ellie when she wakes up.'

'You're not thirsty at all? Or hungry?'

She shook her head. Her appetite had almost gone now.

He had turned to go to the bar to make Ellen's drink when she called after him. 'Dad, can you make Ellie's drink later?'

'Yes, of course. Is there something else you want done instead?'

'Would you just sit here with me for a while?'

He sat down in the chair beside her bed, taking her hand in both of his. 'Of course, sweetheart. For as long as you like.'

Lola carefully draped the scarf over Anna's bedspread, then stepped back and looked critically at it. 'It will do for the moment. I've got my eye on a rather nice pink one down at the charity shop. I think I'll put in a bid for that and bring that home for you as well.'

Anna smiled up at her. 'I love you, Lola.'

Lola stopped still. She gazed down at Anna, then gently, slowly, lifted her hand and stroked the soft cheek. 'Not as much as I love you.'

'Do you believe in heaven, Bett?'

'I want to. I want to know that you are going somewhere special, somewhere that you'll love, and that you'll get a good spot ready for us when we arrive.'

'I will, I promise. Sun or shade?' She was trying hard to sound bright.

'A bit of both, I think.'

'Bett, will you do something for me?'

Her voice was getting weaker. Bett had to lean in to hear her. 'Anything.'

Anna reached under her pillow and took something out. 'Would you look after these for me?'

It was an envelope, filled with small pieces of paper, each neatly folded. 'What are they?'

'They're birthday cards for Ellen. Little notes. Until she turns twenty-one. I was going to ask Glenn to give them to her, but I'd love you to do it instead. If you don't mind.'

'If I don't mind? I'd love to give these to her.' She realised she had a lump in her throat. 'I'd be honoured.'

'And you'll help him look after her, won't you? Even if it's hard sometimes. I know you and him haven't always –'

'Of course I will. We love her dearly, Anna. You know that. I love her dearly.'

'And, Bett, will you tell her about me? Please? I don't know how much she'll remember.'

Bett blinked away tears, so used to them now she barely noticed them. 'Of course I will. I'll tell her how beautiful and how kind and how brave –'

Anna's smile was frail but full of mischief. 'Well, you don't have to get too carried away.'

Richard moved the chair in close to Anna's bedside and reached into the box beside him. 'I've Jane Austen or Seamus Heaney or even a bit of Ian Fleming.'

'Don't read to me. Talk to me instead.'

'What about?'

'Anything you like.'

'Anything? Then in that case I want to talk about you.'

Anna didn't speak, just kept looking at him.

He started, haltingly. 'I want to talk about how unfair this is.

And how much I wish this wasn't happening. But that would all be about me, not about you.' His face was very sad.

'I'd liked to have made you so happy, Anna. I'd liked to have gone travelling with you. I'd liked to have made you laugh, and heard more of your stories. I'd liked to have got to know Ellen. For the three of us to have got to know each other.' He paused. 'I'm sorry, it's about me again, not you. What I would have liked. But it's the truth. All I would have wanted was to be with you. Making love, on orange bedspreads in motels all around the world. Drinking wine and talking all night. Telling you how much I loved you, every day, until you got tired of hearing it.'

Tears formed in her eyes. 'I wouldn't have got tired of hearing that. I'd have liked that.'

He gently wiped away the tears. 'I'd also liked to have spent one entire week doing nothing but lying in bed and listening to your voice.'

'You wouldn't have let me sleep?'

'Not a wink.'

'I'd have liked all of that,' she said softly.

He didn't say anything more then, just picked up her hand and pressed a kiss against her palm. Then, still holding her hand, he quietly started reading to her.

Carrie learned she was pregnant a week after Anna was brought home from Adelaide. Bett was in the room with her when she told Anna. 'It's still early, only a few weeks. But I wanted to tell you.'

'Carrie, that's fantastic news.' Anna's smile was almost luminous now in her thin face. 'That lucky little baby. I've so many clothes and toys of Ellen's in storage in Sydney. I'll make sure to ask Glenn to send them down to you.' Because she wouldn't be needing them.

All the things that didn't need saying any more. 'And you're feeling okay? Not too sick? Oh, you're lucky. I was sick every morning. I actually lost weight in the first few months. The first time I wasn't dieting in years. The freedom of it. Enjoy every minute of it, Carrie, won't you?'

Carrie kept the smile fixed on her face. Anna was now virtually skin and bone, her face gaunt, her eyes large, yet managing to laugh about not having to go on a diet.

'If you get morning sickness, dry bread is supposed to be good, but only if someone brings it to you. Is Matthew being good? Obeying your every command?'

'He's great. It's apparently not even the size of a clothes peg yet, but he keeps telling me he can feel the baby moving.'

'Oh, that's sweet.' She shut her eyes.

Bett moved closer to her. 'Anna? Are you in pain?' They had given her morphine an hour before, but they could give her more if she needed it.

Anna opened her eyes. 'No, I was just remembering when I was pregnant with Ellen. It's a wonderful time, Carrie. Write it all down, so you'll remember it. You'll tell yourself there's plenty of time to do that, because there's no way you'll forget something like this, it's so amazing. But then an even more amazing thing will happen, and then another, layer on layer of them. When you first see them, and when they look at you, and when you're feeding.'

It was the most she had spoken in some days. 'Ellen used to go cross-eyed when she was feeding sometimes, just from the concentration. We used to laugh and laugh at her. And when she first started walking, one of her feet would turn in a little, like a rolling gait. And do you remember, when she first started talking, she'd always repeat the last two words you said to her? I remember Glenn saying it was like having a performing parrot in the house.'

She looked from one to the other. 'You'll make sure Ellen gets to see her cousin a lot, won't you? You'll go up to Sydney or ask Glenn to fly Ellen down here?'

Carrie hadn't dared ask. 'She'll stay with Glenn after . . .'

'After I'm not here.' The smile again. 'I'm lucky in a way. He loves her so dearly and she loves him just as much. It will be hard at first, I know. I've asked him to make sure Ellen spends as much time as she likes here with all of you.'

'She can live with us if she wants to. I'll adopt her.'

'I will too,' Bett said.

Anna gave another gentle laugh. 'Glenn loves her and she loves him. But will you both help him look after her for me?'

Carrie's eyes filled with tears. Anna was talking about Ellen more and more. 'We will, Anna, we promise. She'll come here to us as often as she wants, and we'll go and see her in Sydney or Singapore or wherever she is. We'll do everything we can for her.'

Bett reached for their hands and held them tightly. 'I'm so sorry. I'm sorry for taking three years away from all of us. For taking so long to tell the truth about Matthew. If I had done it earlier –'

'It wasn't just you, Bett. It was just as much my fault.' Carrie was as upset. 'I should have rung, should have tried to –'

'Stop it.' Anna sat up a little, her voice surprisingly strong. 'Don't. Don't do this. Don't waste all this time wishing that you'd done this or done that. Please. It's not worth it. It's what happened. And maybe we're better with each other now, because of that.'

'But I'm sorry –'

'Stop it. I mean it, Bett. I don't want to waste time talking about it.'

Carrie managed a smile. 'You were always so bossy, you know that.'

Anna's head was back on her pillow. 'I'm the oldest. I'm allowed to be. And soon Bett will be the oldest so you have to let her boss you.'

She didn't get any further. Bett and Carrie were crying too hard.

Bett was bringing a new jug of water into Anna's room the next day when she heard voices inside. Anna and Ellen together. She stopped, not wanting to interrupt and also needing to hear.

'Ellie, do you know how much I love you?'

Ellen's voice was as melodic as her mother's. 'One hundred times?'

'More.'

'One thousand times?'

'More.'

'A million times?'

'Even more than that.'

Ellen started to giggle. 'A million billion trillion hundred thousand times.'

'Not even close.'

'More than that? Is there a number bigger than that?'

'Well, there'd better be. Because that's how much I love you.'

Bett walked away as silently as she could. She couldn't bear to hear any more.

'All right, everyone, smile!'

It was Richard who had suggested they take some photos. It hadn't occurred to any of them, too busy caring for Anna day to day.

'I have a decent camera with me,' he had said to Bett that morning. 'It just might be good for Ellen, especially . . .'

She had been too overcome to speak for a moment. 'We hadn't even thought. Thank you.'

It became a joyous afternoon. Lola brought in all her scarves and beads. Geraldine filled vases with flowers and autumn leaves. They took it in turns, sitting on the bed beside Anna, in different combinations. Anna's voice was stronger than it had been for some time, directing them.

'If she makes us start singing, I'm out of here,' Matthew said. 'She's very bossy, isn't she?'

'Always has been,' Bett and Carrie said at the same time.

They took photo after photo. Anna with Lola. No one commented that it was Anna who somehow looked older. Yet her eyes were still bright.

Anna with Bett. She gently got on the bed beside her sister and held her hand. Ellen was put in charge of decorations and darted forward with a flower for Anna's hair.

Jim and Geraldine sat on either side of Anna. Geraldine's eyes were over-bright. Bett saw that she was holding Anna's hand as tightly as she was holding Jim's.

Carrie and Matthew stood on one side of the bed. Anna reached up and put her hand on Carrie's stomach.

The next one was Bett, Carrie and Anna together. 'Give us a song, Alphabet Sisters,' Matthew called, trying to be cheery. They shook their heads, without needing to even look at one another. They couldn't have done it.

Richard took about ten shots of Anna and Ellen together, pulling faces at each other, hugging one another. He took one of the two of them with their faces pressed cheek to cheek, looking directly at the camera, solemn-faced. Everyone in the room held their breath, until Ellen moved, and the moment passed.

Then Ellen became over-excited, insisting on being in every photograph from then on, bursting into tears and having to be soothed. 'She's my mummy who's sick in bed, so I have to be in every photo.'

'Of course, Ellie.' Anna patted the bed beside her. She was exhausted from the activity, her eyelids starting to flutter. 'Hop up here, sweetheart. Will we have one big family one to finish? All of us together?'

'I'll take it,' Matthew and Richard said as one.

Carrie looked over at Matthew, beckoning him over. He shook his head. She understood. This one was for immediate family only. They moved in around Anna's bed, surrounding her. Lola on a chair beside her, Ellen tucked in next to her, Jim and Geraldine on either side. Bett and Carrie sat where they could.

Bett was struck with a memory of people at airports, crowding around the person who was heading away on a long journey, wishing them well, sending them love.

'Smile, everyone.'

They did their best.

A week later, Bett and Daniel walked down the tree-lined road behind the motel. There were vineyards on one side and paddocks of grazing sheep on the other. Sunlight flickered through the trees, sending shadows, then flashes of light in front of them. Since Anna had come home Daniel had called by every few days, dropping in just for a few minutes with flowers for Anna or a bottle of wine for the rest of them. Each time he had invited Bett to go for a walk or a drive with him, or for a meal in one of the local restaurants. The first few times she had said no.

'Go, Bett,' Lola had finally insisted. 'You have to have some time for yourself. Otherwise you'll have nothing left to give her.'

'But what if . . .'

'Take the mobile and I will ring you if there is any change. But there won't be. You heard the doctor as clearly as I did. He said weeks not days.'

As if that made a difference, Bett thought. Oh, we've got weeks with her and there was me thinking it was only days, silly old me. She was so angry and so sad, all at once, and it was massing in her, settling inside her.

From then on she started walking with Daniel several times a week, out on the quiet back roads behind the motel, or along the walking track that followed the path of the old railway line through the Valley. The walks began to mean a great deal to her, brief breaks from the slow heartbreak of seeing Anna fade away a little more each day, seeing the weight disappearing from her, the alertness dulling bit by bit, as she ate less, slept more. Daniel visited Anna briefly and was able to nod in understanding when Bett spoke of the light in Anna's eyes, the warmth of her smile. They spoke about his mother too, both of them painfully conscious of the difference in their situations. Mrs Hilder was physically healthy but fading mentally, already long gone from Daniel and Christine. Anna was still herself, the personality still strong in the failing body.

That morning had been particularly bad for Anna. She hadn't been able to eat anything at all and they'd managed to get her to sip only tiny amounts of water. The morning dose of morphine had finally eased her. She had been sleeping, with Geraldine and Lola by her bedside, when Daniel had come to collect Bett.

They walked for some distance before Bett was able to talk, to find the words for what she was thinking. 'I always thought it was good to know lots of things, Daniel. To experience lots of things. But I don't know if that's true any more.' She stopped and looked up at him. 'I know words I don't want to know. Like palliative care.

Metastases. I know how to give Anna morphine. I know that when her breathing changes it's because the tumour is pressing on her lungs. I know that oxygen comes in tanks not just in the air. And I don't want to know any of those things.'

As they started walking again he put his arm tighter around her.

'She's not even dead yet, and I miss her, Dan. And sometimes I go into the room and she's asleep and I think, oh she's died, as if it will be some simple thing like that. But I know it won't be. And I can't bear that she's suffering. But the thing is I just don't want her to leave us.'

Her tears came in a flood. He took her in his arms and held her close for a long time.

Glenn came to stay at the motel full time. He and Richard circled each other for a day or two, before there was a silent acceptance of each other. They took their turns at Anna's bedside.

Walking past the kitchen one afternoon, Bett heard Glenn's low tones, followed by her parents'. She walked in. It looked like a legal meeting. She excused herself and was about to walk away, when Glenn beckoned her in.

'Bett, please, it's all right. We're talking about Ellen.'

Bett waited.

'I was just explaining to your parents that Ellen's going to come to Singapore with me to begin with, after . . .' his voice seemed to catch. 'Afterwards. But you'll always be her family as well. I want you to know that. I want her to come here as often as she can, I want you to feel you can all come and see her as much as possible. No matter what the situation might be, or where we are.'

Bett needed to bring everything out into the open. This was no time for secrets. 'Will your girlfriend be all right with her?'

She saw her parents' heads shoot up. She would have to

explain it to them later.

'She and Ellen get on very well,' he said simply. 'And she knows Ellen will always come first to me.'

Bett knew he meant it. He was trying as hard as he could. 'Thank you, Glenn.'

Then Geraldine spoke, her voice very soft. 'Ellen needs to know that it's not going to be long now. We need to tell her. Prepare her.'

There was a pause before Glenn spoke again. 'Anna and I talked about it last night. She's asked me not to tell Ellen in front of her. She said that it would –' that break in his voice again. 'It would be too hard for them both.'

Bett had never seen Glenn look so vulnerable. 'Can I help, Glenn? Do you want me to be with her when you tell her?'

He nodded. She could see he was now fighting tears too. 'Yes please.'

She knew he was thinking what she was thinking. How on earth did they do it?

The moment came the following afternoon. Ellen had spent the morning lying on the bed beside Anna, chatting away as normal. When the palliative care nurses arrived, she'd only gone a little way away, sitting outside Anna's room, drawing with chalk on the footpath. She was still there when Glenn and Bett went to find her.

Hand in hand the three of them walked over to Lola's seat overlooking the vineyards. Ellen clambered up onto her father's knee, waiting, as if she knew something important was happening. Glenn cleared his throat. 'Ellie, we have to tell you something very sad about your mum.'

'I already know.'

'You know?'

'She's not going to get better, is she?' Her voice was very matter-of-fact.

Glenn and Bett exchanged glances. 'How did you know that?'

'I heard the ladies talking about her. They said they thought she might not have more than a few weeks to live.'

Bett took her niece's hand then. 'Ellie, do you know what that means?'

Ellen nodded. 'It means she's going to die.'

Another shared glance. Bett could see Glenn was struggling.

'And do you know what that means?'

Ellen shook her head.

Bett tried to find the right words. 'It means that this time we have with her now is very special, Ellie, because after your mum dies –' She lost her way for a moment. 'Ellie, after she dies that means we won't be able to see her any more.'

Ellen looked puzzled. 'But she doesn't go anywhere, does she? Doesn't she just stay in the bed even after she dies? And we keep on visiting her?'

'No, Ellie. It means she's going to go away from us.'

'But where is she going to go? Why can't I keep seeing her?'

Bett couldn't speak any more. It was left to Glenn to try and answer. He held Ellen tight against him, pressed his face against her hair, tried to hide his tears. 'I don't know, Ellie. I don't know.'

Anna started sleeping most of the time, so thin now there seemed almost nothing of her beneath the cotton sheet. The days revolved around the visits from the doctor and the nurses, or coaxing her to eat a spoonful or take a sip of water.

Somehow, around all this, the motel kept running. Geraldine and Jim worked like automatons, spending every spare moment with

Anna. Guests were dealt with efficiently, briskly, checked in and checked out in record time. Lola spent hours in Anna's room, reading snatches of poetry, arranging tiny bouquets of autumn leaves, late flowers, or coloured pieces of silk for Anna to look at. Richard read to her, or just sat with her. Glenn kept close to Ellen. Carrie started to show her pregnancy but didn't mention the nausea, or the tiredness, her own discomfort nothing compared to Anna's. Ellen moved from confusion to understanding, then back to confusion. Bett cleaned the motel rooms in the morning, spent all afternoon with Anna, then waitressed in the evening, a forced smile fixed on her face. Daniel called by every day, but they had stopped going for their walks. She needed to stay close to her sister.

They all took turns sitting with her, watching her sleep, the sound of her breathing more ragged each day, the effort of getting air into her lungs racking her body. She spoke rarely, but her eyes were bright, her smile still her own.

Four weeks after Anna had come home from the hospital, Bett was woken by a knocking at her door. She hadn't been in bed long. All of them had been around Anna's bed until after midnight, talking a little, praying a little, mostly just quiet in their own thoughts. They were now keeping a vigil at her bedside. Bett was due to be back with her in just three hours' time.

At first she confused the sound of the knocking with the sound of the rain that had been pelting down on the roof when she had gone to bed. It had been wet for five days running. Then she heard a voice and was out of bed before Lola opened her door. She knew by the expression on her grandmother's face before Lola had a chance to tell her.

Anna was dead.

CHAPTER THIRTY-ONE

ANNA'S FUNERAL took place on a perfect autumn day. The sky was blue. The air was crisp and clear. The rows of vines around the church and the cemetery were vivid reds, browns and oranges.

They all dressed up. Lola, Carrie, Geraldine and Bett put on makeup, did their hair, getting ready quietly and calmly, moving from room to room at the motel. The men shaved carefully, polished their shoes, wore good suits. Ellen wore her favourite clothes, the pink dress and matching hat she had worn the night of Lola's party.

They took up the entire front pew of the church. Lola. Jim. Geraldine. Bett. Daniel. Carrie. Matthew. Glenn. Ellen. Richard. There wasn't quite enough room, but they couldn't be separated, needing the touch of another each time they sat down. Ellen had hardly let go of her father's hand since Anna had died.

Several feet away from them, in the middle of the aisle, was Anna's coffin.

The church was crowded. The service was simple, the readings and music beautiful. Lola had produced a sheet of paper the day after Anna died. It was a list of the songs she wanted played, the readings she loved. She had dictated it to her grandmother several weeks before.

They had all been sitting around the kitchen table in the motel when Lola had shown it to them. Numb with shock, Carrie and Bett had found it irrationally funny, nearly falling into each other's arms in hysterics, a raw mixture of laughter and tears. 'She's still telling us what to do? Even now?'

After the funeral mass, after the time in the cemetery, everyone came back to the motel.

'I'm so sorry.' 'We're so sorry for you all.' 'Please accept our sympathies.'

The mood was dull, subdued. There was talk, but not a great deal. Cups of tea. Sandwiches. Bett felt removed from everything. She kept expecting to turn and see Anna in a corner of the room. The old Anna, not sick Anna. She kept expecting to see that glossy dark hair, that tall, straight back. She wanted to hear her voice.

She saw her father in the corner. He was pouring tea, his head bent low to hear what an elderly lady was saying to him. He looked ten years older. Her mother was on the other side of the room. Her face was like a mask. Carrie was standing with Matthew. He had his arm tightly across her back. Richard was in a corner, in conversation with the local priest. He seemed dazed, as though he wasn't taking any of it in. Glenn was holding Ellen, so tightly it was as if he never wanted to let her go.

'Bett?'

She turned. It was Daniel. 'Is there anything I can do?'

In that moment it seemed to hit her. There was nothing he could do. There was nothing anyone could do. He opened his arms and she moved soundlessly into them.

Glenn and Ellen left a week later. The departure was heartbreaking for all of them. Ellen kept going to Anna's room, as if expecting her to be there. An hour before they were due to leave, she disappeared. It took them nearly thirty minutes to find her. Bett reached her first. Ellen was tucked up behind the shed at the back of the motel, holding tightly to Bumper by his lead.

'Ellie, you need to go, sweetheart. Daddy's nearly ready.'

Ellen wouldn't look at her. 'I don't want to. I want to stay here.'

'You can come back here whenever you like.'

'I want to be here now.'

Glenn came up behind her and took in the situation. He got down to Ellen's level. 'Ellie, I promise you can come back very soon. I want you to come home with me for a while first, though. I need your help.'

She shook her head.

Bett realised this was a moment for father and daughter. She silently slipped away, back to where Lola and her parents and Carrie and Matthew were waiting. There was still the jolt at Anna's absence. The gap where she should be. The terrible reality of all of them gathered without her.

Ten minutes later Glenn and Ellen came towards them, hand in hand. Ellen was subdued. She said goodbye to each of them very solemnly, hugging them around the neck. Each one of them had the same farewell message. 'See you soon.' 'We'll see you soon, Ellie.'

Then each of them hugged Glenn goodbye as well.

Richard left three days later. Bett had gone for a drink with him the evening before. He was as sad these days as they were.

He was going back to London again. For a few months anyway. He'd been offered work at his old newspaper. 'I'll be back, I hope. In a while. I just can't seem to finish anything here at the moment.'

'Will you keep in touch with us?'

'If you'd like me to.'

'We'd like it very much.'

They all hugged him goodbye as well.

Carrie and Matthew came for dinner at the motel most nights. They were trying to fix up one of the rooms of their house as a nursery, but Carrie was finding it very difficult. 'I'm so scared something will happen to the baby, that it's bad luck. I keep thinking about everyone dying. We'll have to go through this again and again, with Lola, with Mum and Dad, with you, with . . .' She was crying. 'I want her back, Bett.'

'I want her here so she can tell me off. I wouldn't even mind if she yelled at me for a week.'

There was a kind of laughter those nights, but it was fragile, like glass.

Two weeks after Anna died, a videotape arrived addressed to Lola from Richard's friend Charlie Wentworth. It was the complete version of the program he had been making, as well as all the rough footage he had shot the day he was in the Clare Valley with them.

He had enclosed a note. Richard had told him about Anna. He explained that the program had gone to air in the UK and Ireland a fortnight before, but that he thought they might like the extra footage just as much. 'I am thinking of you all at this time of great sadness,' he'd signed.

They watched it together, on the video in Lola's room, in virtual silence. Another time the scenes would have caused much hilarity. They would have set the video up on the bar TV, ordered drinks for everyone, watched the tape over and over, laughing at everyone's expressions. Not this time.

The segment about General MacArthur's visit to Terowie took up just a few minutes of the program. There were shots of the MacArthur plaque at Terowie Railway Station, then a shot of the Valley View Motel, followed by Lola sweeping in and pretending to work at her desk. The voice-over explained she had emigrated from Ireland sixty years previously and considered this musical her life's work. There were several scenes from the musical itself. It was fun, snappy.

The extra footage Charlie mentioned contained image after image of Anna, up on stage with Carrie and Bett, attempting to sing 'Sisters', first accompanied on stage by Matthew, then on their own. There was a kind of joyousness, laughter, a lightness between the three of them. It had taken four attempts, but they had finally got their harmonies right, standing in a row with their arms around each other, singing and laughing. The camera kept rolling afterwards, long enough to capture Anna firstly hug Bett and then Carrie, giving them flamboyant two-cheek kisses, actor-style.

It was like watching something from another century.

Bett went back to work at the newspaper three weeks after Anna's death. At first it was as if she was sick. People kept a distance from her, wary, in case she burst into tears. Only Rebecca was normal, and Daniel.

She went to his house for dinner the weekend after that. It was the first time she'd been out at night in the weeks since Anna died. She hadn't been able to go too far from any of her family. He made a simple meal of pasta and salad, opened a bottle of wine for her. Afterwards, she sat in his arms on the sofa, watching TV.

She tried to concentrate on the program, but the dialogue didn't make any sense and the people looked ridiculous, all made up, wearing glamorous clothes. As if any of that really mattered in the end.

She felt Daniel kiss the top of her head. Another kiss on the side of her face. She turned, met his lips, a soft, gentle kiss. His hand went lower, skimmed her arm, touched the side of her breast. She felt the stirring of feeling, a slow melting feeling begin and then the sadness roared in at her again. She couldn't do this. Not with Anna dead.

She sat up abruptly, and moved away from him. 'I'm sorry, Daniel, but I can't.'

'It's okay, Bett.'

It wasn't okay. 'I'm sorry. It's not you, I promise. It's me.'

'Bett, it's fine. I understand.'

It suddenly seemed urgent to explain it to him. To tell him exactly how she felt. 'I need you to know that I love it with you. I love being with you.' She meant every word. She did love him. 'It's just –' she was struggling now, 'something is different at the moment. Lola keeps telling me it will get better eventually, that it won't always hurt as much as this. But I'll understand if you can't wait. If you want to stop seeing me.'

'Bett, please, come here. Come closer to me.' She moved and he met her halfway, holding her tightly in his arms. 'I'm not going anywhere. And I don't want you to go anywhere either.'

One night in the motel bar, Jim, Geraldine and Bett were shocked into silence by the sound of Anna's voice. It took them a moment to realise it was coming from the TV.

They sat staring at it, hearing her voice warmly extolling the virtues of a new range of baking products.

Geraldine started crying. Jim turned off the TV.

Bett went to Lola's room each night to say goodnight, to check she was okay, to make sure she had everything she needed. Lola had changed too. She seemed older. When Bett hugged her now or when she curled up beside her on the bed like now, she felt that the spirit that had driven Lola had dimmed somehow. Nothing felt quite the same.

'It hurts so much, doesn't it, Lola?'

'It does, darling.'

'Was it as bad as this for you when Edward died?'

There was a long pause. 'It was different.'

'Does it really get better?'

'You get used to it, Bett. It becomes a part of you, like everything that happens to you in life becomes a part of you.'

Lola stopped talking then, just stroked the head on the pillow beside her until Bett fell asleep.

Chapter Thirty-two

'Enjoy your stay, won't you?'

It was six weeks after Anna's death. Bett was at reception, checking in some late-night guests. Carrie had gone home for the night. Bett had handed them their room key, explained how to order breakfast, where the dining room was and the opening hours for the bar. She'd felt like a liar, a fake, the entire time, as she smiled and tried to talk normally to them. She wondered if any of the guests noticed there was something not quite right with the family in charge of this motel. Could they see that their smiles weren't real? That they seemed to move more slowly than usual? That the life had gone out of all of them?

She had never expected it to hurt this much. She'd never expected to feel grief like a physical pain. But it was. She would be walking along and she'd feel the reminder of Anna's death like a punch, a blow from nowhere. She felt exposed to the world, over-sensitive, anxious, as if she had lost several layers of protective skin. She wanted to stop complete strangers, tell them that her sister was dead. That her beautiful thirty-four-year-old sister had died and that they had been given only weeks to say goodbye to her. Her heart ached for anyone who had lost someone suddenly, in a car accident or from a heart attack. She at least had had some time to say goodbye, to tell Anna how much she loved her. How much worse would it be if they hadn't had that chance?

She hadn't ever thought it was possible to have so many tears. To wake up every day with the same feeling in her chest. But she was a different person now, Bett realised. They all were. Her parents had changed, too. They worked as hard and the motel kept running, but there was a different rhythm to their movements. The same heaviness that Bett felt in herself.

Bett closed the registration book and found the day's mail lying underneath it on the desk. She started opening it: bills, circulars and several cards in pale cream envelopes. Word of Anna's death had filtered through to her acting friends, advertisers she'd worked for in Sydney, clients, neighbours and mothers of Ellen's friends. The cards had come in a rush the first few weeks. Even now, weeks after, they were still arriving in twos and threes each day, some addressed simply to the Quinlan Family, some to her parents, some to Lola, or Carrie, or her. She opened them automatically, reading the messages, simple and heartfelt. 'We are thinking of you in your great sorrow.' 'She was a beautiful woman, we loved her and will miss her very much.'

Bett noticed the airmail sticker on the final envelope as she slit it open. There had been quite a few cards from Anna's overseas friends, actors working in Los Angeles or New York, or in different parts of Europe. This one had an Irish postmark. She opened the card and read the message. Then she sat down and read it one more time, trying to make sense of it.

Dear Lola,

I write this tentatively, hoping that you are the same Lola Quinlan, originally from Leixcraig House, Kildare, Ireland, whom I knew more than sixty years ago.

I saw a program called 'Did You Know?' on the Discovery channel last week, featuring you and a musical you had written on General MacArthur. Would you be the same woman who married my brother Edward and then emigrated to Australia with him just before the war?

I am sad to write that Edward died five years ago, leaving behind no family. After he left Australia he continued to travel, spending some years in America, before returning to Ireland and the family home in Kildare. He died at home, aged 78. May he rest in peace.

Edward never explained the whole story of your separation but I wish you no ill will, Lola. If you find it in yourself to contact me, I would be pleased to hear from you.

Yours truly,
Margaret Hegarty (née Quinlan)

Bett walked as if she was in a dream, through the motel, out to the yard, along the row of rooms until she reached Lola's door. She knocked once, twice. A soft voice called her in.

Lola was at her writing desk. 'Bett? More cards? People are very kind.'

Bett couldn't speak.

Lola was puzzled. 'Bett? Are you all right?'

She handed the letter over to Lola without a word. She watched as Lola started to read, watched Lola's hand creep up to her neck. Heard as if from a long way away Lola say softly, 'Oh, dear God.'

Bett found her voice. 'So Edward didn't die during the war.'

Lola looked up. Her hand was still at her neck. 'No, Bett, he didn't.'

Bett wasn't angry or upset. Not yet. She just needed to understand. 'So who was Dad's father?'

'It was Edward. He just didn't know that I was pregnant when I left him.'

'You left him?'

'I had to. If I had stayed with him I –'

'You would have given Dad a father.' Bett was stunned. Confused. 'Lola, I don't understand. We had a grandfather all this time, and we didn't meet him. He didn't meet us. Me, or Carrie, or –' her voice faltered, 'or Anna or Ellen.'

'I'm sorry, Bett.'

'Sorry for what? For leaving him? Or for not telling us the truth?'

'Only for not telling the truth. I couldn't stay with him. He was not a good man. We shouldn't ever have been together. And I didn't realise it until too late. Until we were married and here in Australia.'

'But why the lies? Why say he was dead? Why not say you had left him?'

'Because this was the 1940s, Bett. Because a month after I left him I discovered I was pregnant with your father. I was a young woman in a new country at wartime. What choice did I have? It was better if people thought I was a tragic widow. A widow was respectable.'

'But I can't understand why you didn't ever tell us the truth.'

'How could I? Tell Jim that the father he thought was long dead was in fact very much alive? And then what? Try to find him? Trawl every bar in the country? The truth is, Bett, I didn't ever want to see him again. I didn't know what would happen if he found out he had a son and I didn't want him to find out. He hit me once, one night he returned from a drinking binge, and that was enough for me. I didn't want his family or mine getting their hands on Jim.'

Bett took back the letter, trying to make sense of everything she was hearing. She read the address. 'She's writing from Kildare. Is that where Edward was from? Where you were from?'

Lola nodded.

'That day I went to take photos. You sent me to completely the wrong place, didn't you? Not just the wrong house, but the wrong side of the country.'

Lola was very calm. 'I had to.'

'Why? Because you thought I'd find out the truth? Find him?'

'I panicked, I admit it. I was worried that you would go to the right house and possibly even find Edward living there. And I didn't want you to have that shock. You might never have come back home, then.' Lola glanced down at the letter again. 'But it seems he was dead by then. You wouldn't have met him then either.'

'This will devastate Dad, you know that.'

'Only if he finds out.'

'You're not going to tell him? Show him that letter?'

'No. There's no point now. What he knows is enough. It was my decision years ago and it's one I've stuck with, even if it has been difficult.'

'But how can I keep a secret like that from my own father? From Mum? And Carrie? Ellen? Don't you see they have to know?'

'No, I don't.'

'You'd let the lie continue? You, who spent your entire life telling us to face our fears and tell the truth?'

'This is different.'

'No, it's not. Lola, can't you see this changes everything? It's like everything you've ever told us has been a lie.'

'It changes nothing, Bett. I am the same person, you are the same person, all the things we have ever done or said to each other are the same.'

Bett stared at her. 'I think you're wrong. This changes everything.'

She left the room, shutting the door behind her. She ignored Lola's call to come back.

Bett returned to the reception desk. She updated the booking register. Set out the last of the breakfast trays. She sent her parents to bed, and closed down the rest of the motel herself, switching off the lights one after the other.

She walked across the carpark to her room, pausing for a moment to look up at the clear sky, the Milky Way and the Southern Cross easily visible. She opened the door quietly and then nearly leapt out of her skin as she saw Lola, sitting in the armchair in the middle of the room.

'You won't do this to me, Bett. I won't have it.'

Bett was speechless.

'I won't have you walk out on me like that, or ignore me, or stop talking to me because of this. Do you hear me?'

Bett had never seen Lola so angry. 'I'm not ignoring you. I'm trying to take it all in. I can't hear something like that, and just let it wash over me.'

'Of course you can. That's exactly what you have to do with it. With any news. Let it wash over you, let it soak into you, and then get on with it. Nothing has changed, Bett. I still want you to face your fears and tell the truth. Even if your fear is that the family is ruined and that you hate and despise me forever. But at least you would have been courageous enough to say it.'

'I was trying to work out what I thought about it.'

'So tell me now. How do you feel?'

Lola didn't need to mention a truth stick. Bett could feel it being pointed at her without being told. 'I'm shocked.'

'Why?'

'Because I discovered my grandfather was alive all the time I thought he was dead.'

'Yes, that would be a shock. What else?'

Bett hesitated. 'I'm disappointed.'

'Why?'

'Because the grandmother I idolised for years was lying to me for years.'

'A little melodramatic, perhaps, but all right, accepted. What else?'

'I'm sad, Lola.' The truth burst out of her. 'Sad, sad, sad. And I can't take any more of it. Any more bad things. Any more shocks.'

'Yes, you can. And you'll take a lot more before you're dead yourself. There'll be more deaths, more disappointments, more people will let you down.'

'I can't, Lola. I can't take any more hurt.'

'You can and you will. Because there won't just be hurt, Bett. There'll be great happiness and moments of joy and lightheartedness and pleasure. Because that's what life is like. Multicoloured, not black and white. Stop judging people. Stop judging me. Step outside of yourself for one moment and think why I would have done what I did. Why I chose not to tell you.'

'I don't know.'

'Then try harder.' A long pause. 'Perhaps I was wrong. But I thought I was right. I had to believe I was right, to go on. There was a time, when your father was small, when things were very hard, when it would have been easier to go back to Edward, to Ireland, to take that life, take back the security. But I couldn't do it. I wanted more, for me, for Jim, for my life. I wanted freedom and I wanted adventure and I wanted a life. I was trapped in my family, Bett. You can't know how that feels, having all the freedom that you and your sisters had. I had none of that. It was rules and regulations and expectations and it was suffocating me. And marrying Edward and going to Australia seemed like a lifeline. But I knew within weeks that I'd made an even bigger mistake. He wasn't what I thought he was. I wasn't what he thought I was.'

'I can understand that. What I can't understand is why you didn't tell us the truth.'

'I've wanted to. For years. But there just never seemed the right time. I wasn't sure who to tell. Even how to tell it. And these were lies out of necessity, not out of malice, or trickery. There is a difference. And the lies became real to me. I began to think of Edward as dead. Began to think fondly of him in a certain way. Because when life puts you in those situations you have to go on, you have to make something of yourself. I started living life pretending I was a brave young widow and so I had to become a brave young widow.'

'But it wasn't true.'

'No, it wasn't. And I can't force you to forgive me. But I can ask you to use your imagination, the imagination I have done my best to feed over the years. I want you to imagine yourself in my place, to see how it might have been for me. You know me. And I know you. Don't disappoint me.'

'You've disappointed me.'

'No. What I've done is show you one more bit of truth about me. And that is something you would rather not see. In fact, you've disappointed me.'

'What?'

'I would prefer you were the perfect understanding granddaughter just as you would prefer me to be the perfect faultless grandmother. But I'm not perfect. I never have been. I never will be.'

'You were perfect. You were the most wonderful grandmother.' Bett started to cry. 'You still are the most wonderful grandmother.' She found herself in Lola's arms. 'I'm sorry, I'm so sorry. It was your life. You had to do what you had to do. Of course I know that. But it's one more hurt, Lola. One more person gone, one more thing changing.'

'You wouldn't have liked him.'

'That's not the point. I might have liked him.'

'Really, you wouldn't have.'

Bett was suddenly crying and laughing. 'But I wanted the choice.'

'We don't always get a choice. We don't always get what we want. I wanted a good husband, not an awful drunken old bully. I wanted lots of things I didn't get.' She held Bett close. 'I also got things that I never wanted or expected.'

'Like Anna dying.'

'Anna dying. But also the life I've had with all of you. Because the real truth is that I have never loved anyone in my life like I love your father and the three of you, and now Ellen too. And if I had to do it all over again to give you a better life, I would. Do you understand that? Because you have all been the most wonderful thing that ever came to me. More than I ever imagined I would have. We don't get a list that we can tick off, Bett. I've learned that. Some things we can make happen, other things happen to us, other things surprise us, other things sneak up. We just have to keep going, whatever happens.'

'I can't. I just hurt too much.'

'It will all become a part of you. I promise you that. This news. Even Anna's death. You might think I am just a mad old woman, but I've seen a few things in my day.'

'I just want her back, Lola.'

'We all want her back, darling. All of us.'

Bett cried then as if it was the first time since Anna died, until her body hurt from it. Lola held her tight until it passed, until Bett's breathing calmed, the shaking stopped. She spoke again, her head buried against Lola's chest, her face wet with tears. 'I'm so sorry, Lola.'

'It's all right.' She kissed Bett's forehead, tucked a lock of hair behind one of her ears.

'I would never have stopped talking to you.'

'I know. I wouldn't have let you.'

'And I won't tell Dad or Mum or Carrie. It's not for me to tell them any of this.'

'You can if you want to. It's up to you. I can't stop you.'

'What good would it do?' Bett hesitated. 'Are you going to write back to Edward's sister?'

Lola shook her head. 'There's no point. I think it's best that I don't.'

'But is it wrong for me to have a secret from the rest of my family? That you and I know, and the others don't?'

'A family without secrets is a very boring family. And I don't think we want to be a boring family, do we?'

Bett shook her head.

'Come here to me.' She took Bett's face between her two hands. 'I'm sorry I hurt you, too. Because you are very precious to me. I want you to know that. And I'm glad you know. I'm glad it's you who found out.'

Bett mirrored the action, her hands against Lola's soft, powdered skin. 'I'm glad it was me, too.' She stared at the older woman's face, the blush, the lipstick. 'But you've been very bold, you know that.'

'Very bold, yes. But what else am I?'

'You're my darling.'

'That's right. Now go to bed, Bett.'

'No.'

'You're disobeying me?'

'Yes. I want you to talk to me about it. I want to hear everything. About what it was like for you. How you found the first guesthouse to manage.'

'It was an ad in the newspaper.'

'How you managed to buy that first one.'

'I saved. I saved and scrimped until I had enough.'

'And were you ever frightened? Did you ever think you'd done the wrong thing?'

'Many times. I cried myself to sleep many nights. But I kept telling myself that it could only get better. That it was better than what I'd had before. And that I would get through, for Jim's sake and for my sake too.'

'But even though you were scared and it was hard and there were bad times, it worked out in the end for you, didn't it?'

'In most ways, yes.'

'I need to hear that, Lola. I need to hear that things can be bad but they can also get better.'

'I promise you.'

'You never saw your parents again, did you?'

'I didn't, no. I wrote for a while but then it got harder to make it up, to explain why I never mentioned Edward. So I wrote less often, until –'

'You lost contact.'

'It wasn't unusual in those days. Letters took a long time to arrive. People didn't expect to see their sons or daughters again after they went to Australia.'

'Did you miss them?'

'To begin with. But things were different back then. We didn't expect to be close to our parents.' They exchanged a look.

Bett sat on the bed beside Lola's armchair, picked up her hand and started turning the ring. 'This isn't from Edward, either, is it?'

'No. I bought it for myself.'

'I want to hear where. I want to know why you bought that particular one.'

'Why do you want to know all that?'

'I just do. I want to hear all your stories. The real ones.'

Lola smiled. 'You sounded just like your niece then, do you know that? Can I get my gin and tonic first?'

'Will you get me one as well?'

'At last. A drinking partner. I've been waiting for the day. Would you like ice? Lemon?'

'Yes, please.'

Lola was nearly at the door when she turned. 'It's going to be a long night, isn't it?'

'I hope so,' Bett said.

'Shall I fetch the whole bottle?'

Bett smiled at her grandmother. 'I think you may as well.'

Epilogue

Anna's grave was on the high side of the cemetery, overlooking a sweep of vineyards curving in lines along the contours of the hills, tracing the edge of the dam. It was a cool, crisp May day, the sky blue and grey, the air fresh. They parked their cars at the bottom of the hill, walked up past the other graves, gravel and fallen gum leaves crunching under their feet. They had been preparing for two days, working from the detailed list. Everything they needed was now packed neatly into two baskets.

Glenn, Matthew and Jim carried the chairs, arranging them around the gravestone, looking out over the hills. Geraldine and Bett laid the fold-up table with a linen tablecloth, champagne glasses and the plates of food. 'And orange juice for Ellen. Did we bring the orange juice?'

Ellen held it up. 'It's here, Lola.'

'Good girl.'

Once everything was organised, Lola stood up. 'Now, we have to do exactly as she says. Just a moment, I can't read my own writing. Oh, well done, Anna. What a perfect way to begin.' Leaning on her stick, she started reading aloud from a piece of paper, written in her own hand. Anna had dictated the words to her three weeks before she died.

'"First of all, pour champagne and orange juice and drink a toast to each other and to me." The champagne is a gift from Richard, by the way. The finest French, he told me.' Richard wrote to Lola every month or so. He was still at the newspaper in London, but he'd started working on the novel again, he'd told her. Lola shook her head, laughing softly. 'Do you know Anna even dictated stage directions? "You are all to lift your glasses into the air – joyfully." Not too joyfully, everyone, or you'll spill it.'

Anna had left exact instructions on how they were to mark the first anniversary of her death. Carrie had laughed as she read through it several days before. It was like a mini play, filled with stage directions, a cast list ('my family'), what props they'd need, and the setting: her graveside at lunchtime.

'Is this joyful?' Ellen asked, moving her glass of juice vigorously from side to side.

'I'd say that's more enthusiastic than joyful,' Bett said, stepping out of the way as drops of juice flew through the air. 'Slow it down a little. That's it, Ellie, perfect.' She turned in time to see Carrie juggling her baby daughter on one hip, a bottle in one hand, a glass in the other. 'Carrie, are you okay there? Do you want me to take her?'

She pulled a face. 'Would you, Bett? Just for a second? Until I grow another arm?'

Bett took her five-month-old niece, moving her head back as a little hand made a grab for one of her earrings. She'd been christened Delia Anna three months earlier. 'Her name had to start with the letter D, didn't it?' Carrie had said. 'We had A for Anna, B for Bett, C for Carrie and then a jump to E for Ellen. This way she's a bridge between us. She joins us all up again.'

'Ready, everyone? You all have your glasses?' Lola called out the toast. 'To us and to Anna.'

'To us and to Anna,' they echoed. The clinking of glasses was loud in the clear air.

'And now to the food,' Lola said gloomily. They all stared down at the array of dishes on the table. No one moved.

'It's a bit hard to know where to start, isn't it?' Jim said.

'I just wish I hadn't been pregnant when Anna asked me what my favourite food was,' Carrie said, looking balefully at her plate piled high with sardines.

'I certainly wouldn't have said mashed potatoes if I'd known what she was up to,' Geraldine said, looking just as bleakly at the large bowl. 'Bett, will you share your chocolate pudding?'

'Only when you've finished your potatoes. You know the rules, Mum. No dessert until your plate is clean.'

Jim squeezed Geraldine's hand. 'You can have some of my cake, love.'

Glenn took a tiny spoonful of Beluga caviar and said nothing. Ellen was also perfectly happy with her plate of donuts. Matthew was already halfway through his ham and pineapple pizza.

'Are we allowed to top up the glasses, Lola?' Glenn asked. Lola checked Anna's instructions. 'She didn't say, but as the matriarch, I'll make the decision. Of course you can. Have as much as you like.'

'Will I give Mum a glass of champagne?' Ellen asked. 'She liked champagne, Dad, didn't she?'

'She sure did.' He poured a glass and they watched as Ellen balanced it on the gravestone.

'I was talking to her last night,' Ellen said as she came back and settled herself on her father's knee. 'I asked her how things were and told her about the flight from Singapore and how Dad and I are going to Disneyland next week.'

'And did she say anything back?' Bett asked, keeping her tone light.

Ellen gave her a pitying look. 'No, of course not. I say her bits for her. Like when we do plays at school, and I play more than one part. So I told Mum that we were going to Disneyland and she said, "That's wonderful, Ellen."' Ellen lowered her voice and for a minute sounded very like Anna. '"Have lots of fun, won't you? But don't eat too much ice-cream before you go on the rides or you'll be sick."'

Lola peered up into the sky. The blue was nearly gone, darker clouds coming in their direction. 'I think we should move on to the entertainment section of the afternoon. You've all been rehearsing, I hope? Bett, we'll start with you.'

Bett stood up and took a sheet of lyrics from her bag, remembering the moment she had unknowingly chosen her song. She had been sitting beside Anna's bed, answering her soft-voiced questions about her days in London, when, midway, Anna had stopped her and said, 'Name a song, Bett, quick. The first one that comes to mind.'

'"London Calling" by The Clash,' Bett had answered, surprised. 'Why?'

'Just wondering. Go on, you were telling me about your boss Karl and the punk bands . . .'

Bett finished her song and took a bow. Carrie was next, with a stirring version of U2's 'I Still Haven't Found What I'm Looking For'. Anna had asked her to name a song while she was searching through the pile of magazines on Anna's bedside. Ellen sang 'Don't Sit Under the Apple Tree'. Lola, Bett and Carrie joined in on the chorus. Geraldine followed her with 'Sadie the Cleaning Lady'. She'd been washing the windows in Anna's room. Glenn had been at the airport when Anna phoned and asked him. He did a very enthusiastic version of 'Leaving on a Jet Plane'. They all laughed as Jim sang 'Bob the Builder'. He had been looking out at the house being built on the hill opposite the motel when Anna asked him. Lola sang 'Lola' – she and Anna had been reminiscing about the eightieth birthday party. Matthew sang 'Baa Baa Black Sheep', doing his best through everyone's teasing. 'I'd just come from work when I visited her. What did you expect me to say? Nellie the Elephant?'

Lola applauded. 'Beautiful, everyone. You should be proud of yourselves. And now, another message for all of us.' She unfolded the last piece of paper and started reading, her voice strong and clear in the afternoon air.

To my darling family,

If it is possible for me to be watching you today, I promise you I will be. If you notice some champagne missing from your glasses, that will be me who has taken it, too. This note won't be the Gettysburg Address, and I can't think of anything as memorable as General MacArthur's 'I shall return'. All I want to say is that I love you all very much, and thank you for all you did for me and for my beautiful Ellen, during my life. I have been very, very lucky. Thank you for being so obedient today and don't worry, I'm not going to make you come back here year after year. It's up to each of you how you remember me from now on, but please keep eating your favourite things, drinking champagne, talking to each other and singing good and bad songs, even if I'm not there to boss you around.

With all my love,
Anna

Lola held up her glass. 'Another toast, I think. Just to Anna.'

'Just to Anna,' they all echoed.

Everything was packed up into the baskets again and the chairs folded by the time the first spatters of rain started falling. Geraldine, Jim, Glenn, Carrie and Matthew walked ahead, Delia in Matthew's arms. Behind them, a little more slowly, came Lola, Bett and Ellen.

'I miss my mum every single day,' Ellen said.

Bett squeezed her hand. 'I do too, Ellie.'

They reached the bottom of the hill and started walking to the wrought-iron gate at the entrance.

'What would Mum have done if we hadn't been obedient today?' Ellen asked as they reached it.

'Haunt us, probably,' Lola said.

'What's haunt?'

'It's when someone keeps appearing all the time to keep an eye on you, making sure you're okay,' Lola explained.

'Like Daniel does with Bett, you mean?' Ellen said.

Lola smiled at Bett. 'A bit like that.'

Arm in arm, the three of them walked back to the carpark where Daniel was waiting for them.

One year later

Bett looked up as the screen door snapped shut. 'Is everything all right?'

'It's fine,' Daniel said. 'She just rang to say they're running a bit late. Mum's insisting on wearing something pink, apparently, and

Christine said she couldn't decide between the dark pink or the light pink. They'll be here soon, though.'

'That's great. There's no rush, anyway.' It wasn't a formal lunch, just a barbecue and some salads. Everything was ready to go, the barbecue coals heating, the table already set in the garden. They'd been lucky with the weather, blue and clear, with no sign of the rain they'd had the previous year. It was just as well. It would have been very crowded in their small living room. Bett checked the time. There was still an hour before Ellen was going to ring from Singapore. Everyone was sure to be there by then. Bett had promised Ellen, and Glenn, that she would be able to say hello to them all, even if she wasn't with them on the actual date of Anna's second anniversary.

Two years on, Bett had realised that it wasn't the date that made them think of Anna, in any case. Thoughts of her flowed freely between all of them, no matter where they were or when it was. There were memories and conversations that made them sad, memories that made them laugh. It helped them all when Ellen came to stay, or when they went to visit her and Glenn in Singapore. Ellen was so like Anna physically it still surprised them to see her each time, yet they could see her own personality getting stronger. Sometimes they would share their thoughts of Anna with her or with each other. Other times the memories were more personal, private. It was as Lola had said. Anna's life and Anna's death had become a part of them all.

Bett shifted up a little so Daniel could sit on the high-backed swing seat beside her. They both put their feet up on the verandah rail. Daniel went back to the book he'd been reading when the phone had rung. She returned to the last few pages of hers.

They had moved into this house together nearly a year before.

It was a stone cottage in the hills behind the motel, right on the northern edge of Clare. The town was on one side, gum trees, bare paddocks and vineyards on the other. The intention had been to renovate the house themselves, but they'd been rapidly losing interest. Reading was much more fun than scraping paint, they'd discovered.

'Bett?'

'Mmm.'

'What about Fred?'

Bett gave it some thought. 'No, I don't think so.'

'Florence?'

'No.'

'Flossy?'

'If we have a pony instead of a baby, sure.' She turned. 'Daniel, the name doesn't really have to start with an F.'

'Yes, it does. I love the idea of it.' He put down the battered copy of *1001 Names for Your Baby*. 'And we have to get in quick, before Carrie and Matthew have another one, and we get stuck with G.'

Bett laughed. 'Can we get the wedding out of the way before we worry about the baby's name? I'm not even pregnant.'

'Not for want of trying. Have we got a few minutes now to give it another go, before the others arrive?'

'No, we haven't. Anyway, what if we can't have children?'

'Then we'll get lots of pets and treat them like our children.'

She smiled and went back to her book. She was on the second to last page when he spoke again.

'Bett, how do you feel about having eleven children? Or eleven pets?'

'Pardon?'

'I've just worked it out mathematically. If you and Carrie

spend the next eleven years having a baby a year, you and I will end up with Z. Isn't that great? I've always liked the name Zelda, or Zephaniah if it's a boy. Or we could try for quadruplets. That would speed it up a bit. But maybe that's asking a bit much. What about going as far as Yvonne?'

'That's a lovely offer, Dan, but no, I don't think so.' Bett stood up as Carrie and Matthew's car turned off the main road and started up the dirt road to their cottage. She could already see Lola waving majestically from the back seat. Not far behind them she saw her parents' car.

Daniel stood beside her, his arm across her back. He leaned down and brushed his lips against her ear. 'Xanthes?'

She shook her head.

He lowered his voice even more. 'Wilhelmina?'

She started to laugh. 'No, Dan.'

'Violet? Ursula? Thomasina? Please, Bett, can't we have a Thomasina? You'd grow to love her, I know you would. And Saxon. And Rhiannon. As for Quincy, and Peony . . .'

She turned in his arms. 'All this time we've known each other and I never realised you knew your alphabet backwards.'

'I can juggle a bit too. I could teach the children. We could go on the road, pick up where the Alphabet Sisters left off. All of us juggling together. Little Olaf, and Nero and Magenta. Leopold. Klaus . . .'

Carrie and Matthew's car came to a halt at the end of their garden.

Bett looked up at Daniel and smiled. 'Have you finished?'

'Nearly,' he said, a sparkle in his eye. 'Jefferson. Indigo . . .'

She was laughing again as she walked down the steps to greet her family.

Family Baggage

For Maura and her buachaillin Xavier

Acknowledgements

My love and thanks to my (baggage-free) families in two hemispheres – the McInerneys, Lemms, Johnsons, Gallifords and Meaneys in Australia and the Drislanes in Ireland and Germany. A special thank you to my sister Maura for her help just when I needed it.

Thank you to Angela Harman, Max and Jean Fatchen, Hugh Ponnuthurai, Aoife and Imacus Ling, Maeve O'Meara, John Allen, Jill Kirby, Danny Coholan, Karen O'Connor, Bart Meldau, Eveleen Coyle, Helen Peakin, Jean Grimes, Kristin Gill, Noëlle Harrison, Melanie Scaife, Simon Lawlor, Laura Cochrane, Karen Wilson, Kylie Tyack, Ben Redden, Kathryn Black and Nicola Black. A big thank you to Col Cooley and Greg Cooley for the Mr Douglas-isms. My special thanks to Eileen in Dublin for sharing her insights and memories.

Thanks to my publishers: everyone at Penguin Australia, especially Clare Forster, Ali Watts, Anne Rogan, Cathy Larsen, Bridie Riordan, Sally Bateman and Daniel Ruffino; Imogen Taylor, Trisha Jackson, Daniel Watts and all at Pan Macmillan in the UK, and Alison Walsh, Michael Gill and the Tivoli team in Ireland. Thank you to my agents: Fiona Inglis and everyone at Curtis Brown Australia, Jonathan Lloyd and Kate Cooper at Curtis Brown in London, Christy Fletcher in New York and Anoukh Foerg in Munich.

And, once more, all my love and thanks to my husband John.

Chapter One

It was all coming back to her, Harriet Turner realised. The key to being a successful tour guide was to think of herself as a duck. A mother duck, to be precise. A thirty-two-year-old mother duck in charge of twelve elderly excited ducklings.

She glanced back over her shoulder, doing a quick headcount of her tour group. Good, all twelve were still in sight, obviously tired but upright, at least. They'd followed her obediently as she led the way off the plane, through passport control and here into the baggage collection area of Bristol Airport. Ten grey-haired women, two balding men, none of them under sixty-five years of age, all in comfortable clothes and sensible shoes. Each sported a large 'Turner Travel: Tours Tailored Just for You' nametag on one shoulder and a homemade 'I'm on the *Willoughby* Tour!' badge on the other. Some looked bedraggled from the long journey, but more than half were still smiling. The excitement of arriving in England had obviously lifted their spirits. Harriet was glad to see it.

Her protective feelings towards them had grown with each step of the journey. She'd arrived at Melbourne Airport two hours early so she could greet each of them personally. On the plane she'd regularly checked whether they were too warm or too cool and if they needed anything to eat or drink. During their overnight stopover in Malaysia, she'd kept a close eye when they crossed roads, walked across bridges or ate anything that might have bones in it. All the simple rules of being in charge of a group had come flooding back. Of course she could do this, she told herself for the hundredth time since her brother's surprise phone call. The tour would be a success. She'd do everything she could to make it a success.

They were among the first passengers from their flight to arrive at the baggage carousel. Harriet found a prime position, near the start of the conveyor belt and close to the exit. She was taken aback when the group clustered in a circle around her, looking up with big smiles and expectant expressions. It took her a moment to realise what they were waiting for. The customary Turner Travel welcome speech. James, her eldest brother, had begun the tradition, marking the start of each group tour with a little poem or funny speech beside the baggage carousel. He was usually so organised he had copies printed to hand out to the group members as souvenirs. Harriet's mind went blank. She had been brought on to this tour at such short notice she'd hardly had time to learn the itinerary let alone write a funny ditty.

She looked around at them again. Twelve faces looked back. Pushing embarrassment to one side, she smoothed down her official Turner Travel uniform, gave a big smile and threw open her arms.

'Welcome to England!' she cried.

It wasn't enough. They needed much more than that. She could see it in their eager expressions. She tried to ignore the curious looks from the other passengers coming into the baggage area and racked her brains. A rhyming game she used to play as a child with James and her other brother Austin sprang to mind. She'd have to give that a try. She threw out her arms again, hoping she looked confident and theatrical rather than weird and scarecrow-ish, and said the first lines she could think of:

'Here we all are on the Willoughby *tour*
Through Devon and Cornwall, across several moors
I hope you'll all have a wonderful time
And quickly forget this very bad rhyme!'

She cringed inside even as they rewarded her with a burst of laughter and applause. 'She's definitely James's sister,' she heard one of them whisper. She was saved from attempting an even worse second verse by the sound of the conveyor belt starting up with a metallic groan. Everyone sprang to attention, their eyes fixed on the emerging luggage.

As the first bags trundled past, Harriet felt a tug at her sleeve. She looked down. It was Miss Talbot. At seventy-three, she was the oldest member of the tour party. At four foot eleven, she was also the tiniest.

Her soft wrinkled face was all smiles. 'That was a lovely poem, Harriet. You hit the nail right on the head.'

'Oh, thank you, Miss Talbot,' Harriet said, smiling back. She had known Miss Talbot for as long as she could remember and was very fond of her. The little white-haired woman not only ran the Country Women's Association craft shop in Harriet's home town of Merryn Bay but also knitted most of the contents. She specialised in yellow matinee jackets and small knitted penguins with crocheted orange beaks. She was also well-known in the town for buying her clothes from children's wear shops. Harriet glanced again at Miss Talbot's travelling outfit of pink tracksuit and matching shoes, trying not to look too obviously at the Groovy Chick logo embroidered on the front. 'How are you feeling? Not too tired, I hope?'

'Oh no, Harriet. I snoozed like a bug in a rug the whole flight. And those little meals on trays were just delicious, thank you so much.'

'You're very welcome, I'm glad you liked them.' No matter how many times she'd tried to explain, Miss Talbot remained convinced that Harriet was responsible for every single thing that happened on the trip, the meals included.

Miss Talbot gave another happy sigh. 'I just can't believe we're here at last. All these years of seeing Willoughby on TV and tomorrow we're actually going to meet him. I know I'm old enough to be his grandmother, but it really is so exciting. He's such a dreamboat.'

Harriet grinned at the old-fashioned term, fighting an urge to pick up Miss Talbot and give her a cuddle. She wasn't actually sure whether Willoughby was a dreamboat or not. She could never admit it to Miss Talbot – or any of the others in the group – but she only had a dim recollection of the *Willoughby* TV series on which their entire trip-of-a-lifetime was based. All she knew was it featured a dark-haired detective disguised as a postman solving crimes in beautiful seaside villages in Cornwall.

Her brother James, lying in his hospital bed, had tried to assure her it wouldn't matter.

'You'll never know the series as well as the tour group, anyway. You know where the word fan comes from, don't you? Short for fanatics. And that's what the *Willoughby* fan club members are.' He'd lowered his voice. 'More *Willoughby* weirdos than fans, some of them, if you ask me.'

A bright blue suitcase decorated with a gaudy yellow ribbon came trundling past. 'That's mine, that's mine,' one of the tour group called. Harriet leaned across and retrieved it. In the pre-travel information pack, each member of the group had been advised to attach a distinctive ribbon as well as the Turner Travel label to their suitcases so they would be easy to spot on the carousel. They had certainly taken up the challenge, Harriet saw, as more of their bags appeared. They were decorated with everything from tartan bows to shiny red ribbons and chiffon scarves. It looked like they'd been on holiday in a haberdashery.

Another suitcase came towards them, decorated with the Turner Travel label and a bright pink pompom. It belonged to Mrs Dorothy Lamerton, the official president of the *Willoughby* fan club. English-born, wealthy, polished, a widow, she thought of herself as the social Queen Bee of Merryn Bay. Harriet thought of her as the High Queen of the *Willoughby* weirdos. She had a matching pompom around her wrist. Harriet leaned forward and lifted her suitcase off the carousel too.

Mrs Lamerton gave an imperious wave. 'Thank you, Harriet. Those conveyor belts go by far too quickly, if you ask me.'

A simple thing like collecting their clients' luggage off the carousel was just part of the Turner Travel personalised service, but Harriet still got a little glow inside at the thanks. Harriet's late parents, Neil and Penny Turner, had prided themselves on delivering personal touches. They had started the business thirty years previously in the small coastal town of Merryn Bay, two hours from Melbourne, after emigrating from England as part of the 'Ten Pound Pom' assisted passage scheme. The business had started slowly but grown successfully, with its emphasis on tailored tours and, latterly, themed tours like this one for the *Willoughby* fan club members. Harriet didn't have to try hard to be able to picture the handwritten list of Turner Travel official rules her father had pinned to the wall of the staffroom:

- *Always be punctual.*
- *Help our clients in any way you can.*

- ✶ *Check passports and tickets twice.*
- ✶ *Confirm everything and then confirm it again.*
- ✶ *Be sure to memorise everyone's names.*

Neil Turner had once drawn up an unofficial list, too, only half in jest, one Friday night when they were all sharing a bottle of wine after work.

- ✶ *Remember the quietest ones are often the most trouble.*
- ✶ *Beware the domino effect – repair all problems as quickly as possible before they cause more.*
- ✶ *All bus drivers are peculiar, the only difference will be in what way.*
- ✶ *Drink and jetlag never mix – for guides or clients.*

The most important rule, her father had always insisted, was the simplest one to remember.

- ✶ *Expect the unexpected.*

Even as it came to mind, the conveyor belt gave a jerk and came to a halt. A voice over the PA announced a slight delay with the rest of the luggage. Harriet took the opportunity to check the itinerary one more time. She flicked over the cover page showing the new brightly coloured logo of a suitcase with wings and their slogan – Turner Travel: Tours Tailored Just for You. She turned past page two: *Welcome Aboard the* Willoughby *Tour. Follow in the footsteps of one of TV's best-loved detectives in this special*

Turner Travel tailored tour of Devon and Cornwall! She stopped at page three, where the real business of the tour began. *Day 1. Arrive at Bristol Airport. We'll be greeted by Lara Robinson, our on-site guide, and then travel by bus to our hotel for the night!*

There it was in black and white. *We'll be greeted by Lara Robinson.* James had hastily had it added to the revised itinerary. That's what was supposed to happen. They were supposed to walk out into the arrivals area any minute now and be greeted by Lara, who would then lead them to a waiting bus and get them to their hotel, so they could all be tucked up asleep in their beds before eleven o'clock.

So if Lara was waiting for them just metres away on the other side of the baggage area wall, why wasn't she answering her mobile? Why hadn't she been answering it for the past four hours, in fact?

Harriet had rung her first from the airport in Paris, when she'd heard there'd been a delay with their connecting flight to Bristol. She'd got her voicemail and left a brief message. 'Lara, it's Harriet. Just to say if you're not already at the airport, there's no rush. Fog in Paris, so we'll be a bit late.' Businesslike. To the point. The only way they spoke to each other these days.

She had overheard several members of the group talking about Lara during the flight from Paris. Some of them were Merryn Bay locals and had taken Turner Travel theme tours before. They were cheerfully filling in the details for the others. Harriet heard every word. It was one of the advantages of travelling with people with hearing problems. What they thought were whispers were often almost shouts.

Mrs Lamerton in particular was holding court. As well as being the head of the *Willoughby* fan club, she had also appointed herself the Turner Travel and Lara expert. Harriet tried not to listen as her family's private business was shouted across the cabin. '. . . Yes, it's one of the last family-owned travel companies in the state. Started by the children's parents, Penny and Neil Turner, may their souls rest in peace. Marvellous people, emigrated to Australia to start a new life and just took the bull by the horns and started their own business . . . Actually, the *Willoughby* tour was my idea, well, mine and Lara Robinson's . . . Yes, she's meeting us at Bristol, she's at the end of a three-month study program at a tourism college in Bath . . . Yes, part of an international travel industry exchange program, she told me all about it . . .'

One of the other women managed to interrupt her. 'Is Lara married?'

'No, and nor is Harriet, for that matter.' Mrs Lamerton lowered her voice, but only slightly. 'They're both in their early thirties, too. One of the drawbacks of living and working in a small town like Merryn Bay, I suppose. Not a big catchment area for eligible males. They'd want to start getting a move on.'

Harriet had to force herself not to lean over the seat and explain that in fact she had been living with a man until quite recently and that Lara had also had several serious relationships over the years.

The other woman hadn't pursued that subject anyway. 'So why is Lara's surname Robinson not Turner? I thought you said all the Turner Travel tour guides were family members?'

Mrs Lamerton sounded almost triumphant with her knowledge. 'Lara grew up with them, and she's always worked with them, but she's not a real Turner. The Turners took her in when her own parents were killed in a car crash. She was only eight years old.'

'Oh, how tragic. So she's not related to them at all?'

'No, I understand both families emigrated from England to Australia at the same time. They all met on the ship, I believe.'

'So what do we call her? Harriet's foster-sister or stepsister or —?'

A PA announcement from the captain had drowned out their voices after that. Harriet wondered what Mrs Lamerton's answer would have been. Lara's title had always been a bit confusing, for all of them. Not a stepsister, or foster-sister, or even half-sister. An almost-sister, perhaps? Harriet remembered her brother Austin asking Lara once what she wanted them to call her. The four of them had been down on the Merryn Bay beach together, trying to sail a homemade raft Austin and James had built. It was about five months after Lara had come to live with them permanently. James was seventeen, Austin was fifteen, Harriet and Lara had recently turned nine. It had been a hot day. They were all dressed in shorts and T-shirts, sweating under their sunhats.

Austin had brought the subject out into the open. 'It's up to you, Lara. If you want me to call you my sister, I will.'

'I don't mind.' She'd said the same thing to Harriet when she asked.

'In that case, I'll choose a name for you myself.' Austin thought about it. 'Got it. I'm going to call you my blister, rather than my sister.'

'Blister?'

'Blister. Because you arrived suddenly but you've grown on me.'

Lara had given her sudden sweet smile. 'In that case, I'll call you my bother, instead of brother. Because you're almost my brother but you drive me a bit mad, so you're a bother.'

Harriet had always wished she'd thought of that. She'd often felt a few steps behind Austin and Lara, especially once the two of them started firing off each other.

She thought about phoning her brothers now, just in case Lara had been in touch with them to say she'd been delayed. No, the timing was bad. It was too early in the morning for James in Australia. Austin was at least in the same hemisphere, but he was probably on stage right at this moment. A percussionist with an opera company, he was currently in Germany midway through a European tour. She wondered if he had been told she'd taken over the *Willoughby* tour. It had all happened so quickly, so possibly not. She was still finding it difficult to believe herself.

It had started with a panicked phone call just four days before from James. He'd been calling on his mobile phone from an ambulance on the way to hospital, with a suspected broken leg. He'd fallen off a ladder while cleaning gutters at home. He got straight to the point. 'Harriet, I'm in trouble. I need you to take over my *Willoughby* tour.'

'The fan club tour? The one to England? The one that's leaving tomorrow?' Her voice rose in pitch with each question.

'I know it's short notice. And I know you haven't toured for ages. But please, Harriet, you know how important it is. And how much they've been looking forward to it. I'm begging you.'

Her heart started beating faster. Was she up to it? After nearly a year of saying no to even the smallest of the company tours? After everything that had happened the last time she led a group? She opened her mouth to automatically say no, of course she couldn't do it, when something stopped her. A split screen image appeared in her mind – one side showing the old her, out on the road, getting to know all the group members, loving the excitement of travelling; the other side showing herself recently: deskbound, suffocated by paperwork and unspoken pity, feeling more trapped each day. It was like being at a crossroads. The longing to be her old self again was overwhelming. There was a moment's pause and then she heard herself answer decisively, strongly.

'Of course I can do it, James. No problem.'

'Really?'

'Really.'

He'd given a loud whoop. The painkillers had obviously just kicked in. 'Harriet, you're a bloody saviour.'

She'd driven up to the Geelong hospital from Merryn Bay that night, feeling the excitement rise throughout the hour-long trip, almost cancelling out the doubts and fear. She was going back on the road. And not next month, or next year, but the next day!

James had been pale, but pain free, tucked up in a bed, his red hair and freckled skin vivid against the white of the sheets and the pillows. He was nearly forty years old, eight years older than her, but he still looked boyish. Harriet had heard her other brother, Austin, once describe James as looking like a ventriloquist's dummy, and the awful thing was she had been able to see the likeness for herself. She loved both her brothers but was the first to admit that James had missed out in the looks department. Austin had got the good looks in the family. His height, fine features and glossy black hair gave him a dashing appearance, like a pirate, Harriet had always thought.

She was neither pirate queen nor ventriloquist's dummy, but something in between the two. Her short black hair was a less dramatic version of Austin's dark locks – her hairdresser had breathlessly called his latest cut 'my own twist on the Audrey Hepburn elfin look'. Her skin was pale but without James's freckles. She was taller than average for a woman, nearly five foot seven, but still small beside her brothers. Their taste in clothes was different too. When he wasn't wearing his Turner Travel corporate suit, James unfortunately favoured check shirts and baggy jeans, adding to the ventriloquist-dummy look. Harriet preferred simple, unfussy clothes – jeans or cotton skirts; coloured T-shirts, usually in bright shades of reds, blues and greens, worn with one or two pieces of jewellery: the opal bracelet she always wore and perhaps a striking necklace or eye-catching earrings. Austin was the real follower of fashion, his lean frame the perfect clotheshorse for linen shirts and designer suits. He liked handmade leather shoes, too, when he could afford them. The only thing all three really had in common was their large dark brown eyes. Their mother's eyes.

Harriet kissed James on the forehead. She gave him a large supply of cricket magazines, grapes, crossword puzzles and chocolates, adding them to the pile his wife Melissa and daughter Molly had delivered earlier that day. At his invitation, she lifted up the cotton sheet and peeked in at the large wire cage protecting his plaster-covered leg.

'Wow, look at all that room. You could keep a few rabbits in there.'

'If they give me any more morphine I'll be seeing rabbits.' He got down to business, wincing as he leaned across the bed to pass her the itinerary and information folder. She could see extra handwritten notes on some of the pages. He'd been busy since he rang her. 'Harriet, you're a lifesaver, you know that? These international theme tours are going to be the future of the company. It would have been a disaster if we'd had to call this one off.'

She knew how deeply James cared about the family business. Since their parents had died and he and Melissa had taken over, he had thrown himself completely into making it as big a success as possible, working long hours, extending their range of tours into themed trips like this *Willoughby* one. The work was paying off. Turner Travel had nearly doubled its profits in the past year. Melissa hadn't let any of them forget it.

The *Willoughby* tour would be very straightforward, he assured her. Melbourne to Malaysia to Paris then on to Bristol. They'd have one night in a hotel and then drive the next day to their base in St Ives, where they'd meet up with their special guest, the English actor who had played Willoughby in the program. They'd spend the next five days visiting locations from the TV program. After that she was to escort the group to Bath for a handover to another company for two of their themed tours, an *All Creatures Great and Small*-flavoured visit to Yorkshire, followed by a *Monarch of the Glen* tour of Scotland.

'No need to completely reinvent the wheel,' James explained. 'We've set up a good working relationship with some of the UK companies. We link in with some of their tours, and they'll send people over for our *Neighbours* and *Thorn Birds* tours down the track. And that's it. You collect the group in Bath on their return and then bring them home safely. You'll be away two weeks all up.'

She'd been scribbling page after page of notes as he spoke. She looked up to find him studying her with a look of concern and affection.

'I'm throwing you in the deep end, Harriet, but you'll be okay, I know it. You were a great guide before all that stuff happened and you will be again.'

She was surprised at how much his words meant. James rarely spoke about personal things like that. She was about to thank him, when he leaned back against the pillow.

'And you won't be on your own with them once you get to

England,' he said. 'I've asked Lara to meet you at Bristol Airport and travel with you for the first couple of days. Just until you really find your feet again.'

'Lara?'

James didn't notice her tone of voice change. 'Don't you think it's a brainwave? The tourism college she's doing that course at is in Bath, practically down the road from Bristol. And the *Willoughby* tour's her baby really. She knows it all inside out. Better than me, even. She said it was no problem, she could take a few days off from her course to give you a hand. I rang her as soon as you said yes.'

'But you just said you knew I could handle it.'

'I do, but Lara's so close, it makes sense for her to help you out. It's all organised. She'll meet you at the airport, stay with you in the hotel nearby the first night, and then travel down in the tour bus to St Ives with you the next day.' He gave her a smile. 'The two of you will just have to toss a coin to see who gets the guide seat and the microphone.'

Harriet gave a half-smile back, trying hard not to let her feelings show. The excitement at the thought of going back on the road had abruptly faded. She twisted the bracelet she wore on her left wrist. It was a new habit. She'd only started doing it in the past few months. It hadn't occurred to her that she would be meeting up with Lara, let alone travelling with her. What could she have said to James, though? 'I'm sorry, James, but I'm not sure I can do the tour for you after all. I don't think Lara and I can work together any more.'

What would he have said in return? 'But why not? I always thought you were the greatest of friends. What's happened? Something you did? Something she did?'

Something Lara had done. But James hadn't noticed her reaction or given her time to explain to him how she felt. He'd finished his briefing, she'd driven back to her flat in Merryn Bay, hurriedly packed and now here she was, less than seventy-two hours later, in England, in charge of a group, just minutes away from meeting Lara again.

Mrs Lamerton came up beside her at the baggage carousel. 'The hotel's not far from the airport, I hope, Harriet, is it? We're all very tired.'

Harriet glanced at her watch. It was getting late. 'It's just down the motorway, Mrs Lamerton. I'll have you there as soon as I can, I promise.'

She stepped back out of Mrs Lamerton's earshot and surreptitiously tried Lara's mobile again. Still no answer. Where was she? Had she had an accident on the way to the airport? Or was it something as simple as losing her mobile? And if she wasn't there, should Harriet wait? Or get her poor tired group to their hotel as quickly as possible and then worry about Lara?

She felt a slow rising of anxiety and tried to ignore it. Another of her father's travel rules came to mind, also a duck metaphor, she realised. *A good tour guide is like a duck on a pond – serene on the surface and paddling like mad underneath*. He was right. Her job was to keep calm and show leadership, to stay serene in the face of all difficulties. She tried to imagine herself gliding across a pond but the only creature that came to mind was an agitated cat, eyes dilated, back arched, fur bristling. She imagined the group's reactions if they were to turn and see their tour guide down on all fours, hair standing on end, hissing and spitting beside their suitcases. She tried some deep breathing instead.

The conveyor belt started again and the last pieces of their luggage came past. She added them to the trolley and did a quick count. It was all there. Another step of the tour successfully completed. She decided it was a sign. Of course Lara was waiting for them outside. She would be friendly and Harriet would be just as friendly back. And yes, the next few days together would be difficult – very difficult – but they would work through it. They had to work through it. It was what her parents would have wanted . . .

Gathering her twelve ducklings around her, pushing a laden trolley in front of her, Harriet took another deep breath and stepped through the door into the arrivals area.

In Berlin at that moment, Austin Turner stood poised, watchful. He was dressed in a formal black suit and immaculate white shirt, with his dark hair slicked back. The music swirled around him, building to a crescendo. On the stage to his right the heavily made-up woman was kneeling, face wretched, voice pure, as she mourned the loss of her husband, only seconds from seizing a knife and plunging it into her own body.

Austin felt the wood of the hammers in his hands, running his thumbs along the smooth surface as the music surged. He watched the conductor, waiting. The sound of the violins and cellos was building, quickening, as the drama reached its height on the stage. The soprano's voice and the orchestra's music intertwined, rising and falling. Austin didn't need to look out into the audience to know that every person was sitting still, their eyes wide, caught in the story, seduced by the sounds. He focused on the conductor, waiting. The nod came, at last. Austin hit the hammer against the cymbal, the noise like a thunderclap, sharp, sudden. Again. Again. He kept one eye on the conductor, almost sensing the movement of the knife in the soprano's hand in the corner of his vision, matching his sounds to her actions. Again. Then his two hands a blur, rolling and hitting against the sides of the drum, the echoes of sound layered with the other instruments, a cacophony of swirling and building up and then —

Silence.

A faint panting from the soprano.

And then like a wave of sound, the applause, rushing at them. Austin bowed his head. Ten years of study, no money, constant travel, waiting for what seemed like hours every night for his short time in the limelight, when the only sounds filling the hall were the ones he was making. It was worth it, every time.

There was one curtain call. Then a second. As he was turning to the audience for the third bow the mobile phone in his pocket vibrated. Just as well he'd put it on mute before he'd come into the pit. The bassoon player had been bawled out in front of the whole orchestra at rehearsals last week when his mobile went off midway through the tower scene. It hadn't helped that he'd answered it, of course. Strictly speaking they were all banned from keeping their mobiles on them. But they all disobeyed. The violinists couldn't get away with it, under the nose of the conductor, but it was easy enough for Austin, tucked away to the side, surrounded by kettle drums and percussion instruments. Sometimes entire scenes went by and he didn't have a thing to do. He'd taught himself to text without looking, which filled some of the time. The messages were often even more misspelt than usual, but that was the whole fun of texting anyway. And he needed something to occupy his time. He'd become bored enough of the opera storyline by the fiftieth time he'd seen it.

He waited until the conductor had left the stage and the other musicians had filed past him before he checked the new message. It was from Harriet. One word.

HELP!

Chapter Two

Harriet's bedside digital clock clicked over to midnight. Outside her door, the hotel corridor was quiet. Fifteen minutes had passed since she'd last heard the nearby lift being used. She knew the tour group members were safely in their hotel bedrooms, probably fast asleep already. Most had been so tired they'd started to fall asleep in the bus on the way from the airport. They'd only needed to be guided gently up to their rooms, although Mr Fidock, one of the two men, had insisted on being guided gently into the bar.

'Watch him, Harriet, won't you?' James had warned her. 'Mr Fidock treats these tours like lonely hearts club outings. He had poor old Mrs Kowalski in tears at the end of the *Man from Snowy River* tour two years ago. She fell for him, hook, line and sinker.'

'Mr Fidock? The short bald man? But he's more than seventy years old.'

'And so is Sean Connery, as Mr Fidock will tell you over and over again.'

Harriet was still wide awake. She'd changed out of her Turner Travel uniform into soft brushed-cotton pyjamas and her favourite red socks. She was now sitting cross-legged on top of the bed, facing the TV in the corner of the bedroom. Before she got started she took off her glasses, polished the lenses and put them back on again. She'd taken her contact lenses out after she'd spoken to

Austin, finding the routine task oddly soothing.

He'd replied to her text message within ten minutes, phoning as soon as he got off the stage, but it had taken a while to get him to take her seriously. It was often hard to get Austin to take anything seriously.

'Lara's gone missing?' he'd said. 'That's taking the *Willoughby* plot theme a bit far, isn't it? She's run off with some Cornish smugglers, has she? She's hiding in sea caves as we speak, drinking rum with pirates?'

'Austin, please, listen to me.'

Harriet ran through all that had happened: the unanswered mobile phone calls; Lara's non-appearance at the arrivals gate; the waiting for another half-hour before she decided to get the group to the hotel, trying Lara's numbers all the while. Once in her own hotel room she had tried Lara's flat in Bath yet again, and finally got an answer. Not from Lara, but from her flatmate, Nina. Harriet had texted Austin as soon as she'd hung up from her.

Austin's light-hearted mood changed as Harriet filled him in on the conversation.

'According to Nina, Lara's gone away for a while and it's nothing to do with the *Willoughby* tour. She seemed surprised I didn't know anything about it. She said Lara packed a suitcase and left this afternoon.'

'But left for where? She's supposed to be with you.'

'That's what I said. But Nina was positive that's what Lara told her. Lara handed her a month's rent in advance, asked her not to let out her room and then left.'

'Nina didn't misunderstand? She's sure Lara wasn't on her way to meet you?'

'Absolutely sure. Nina said she actually asked Lara what had happened with the *Willoughby* tour. She'd obviously been talking about it. Lara told her there'd been a change of plan and she wouldn't be doing it after all. That she had some other family business to take care of.'

'What family business? We're her family business.' Austin started firing more questions at her. Yes, Harriet had also checked with the local police and hospitals and no, there hadn't been any reports of accidents. No, Lara hadn't left any messages for her, either. She'd checked at the airport information desk, at the hotel, under her name, James's name, Turner Travel, everyone. Nothing.

'Did Nina say Lara seemed upset? Different in any way?'

'She said she was as calm as she always is. Focused was the word she used.'

Austin was quiet for a moment. 'It's weird. Really weird,' he finally said. 'This isn't about a man, is it? She hasn't mentioned meeting anyone to you?'

'No, she hasn't.' That wasn't surprising. In the few times they had spoken on the phone since Lara had left for England they had barely talked about the weather, let alone their social lives. 'What do you think I should do, Aust? Do I call the police? Go and look for her?'

'What could you say to the police? That she's left voluntarily? People do that all the time. The police will just laugh. And you can't go looking for her, can you? Not with a tour group trailing behind you. You can still go ahead with the tour, can't you, even if she's not there?'

'I think so. I mean, of course I can. I have to. They're so excited, there's no way I'd call it off.'

'Where did you tell them Lara was tonight?'

She knew he was thinking of another of their father's rules.

Never tell clients anything they don't need to know. 'I said she'd been unavoidably delayed. I'll think of something for tomorrow. Sudden study commitments perhaps. They've already had one change of tour guide, I don't want to unsettle them any more.' Her mind was racing now. 'And I'll just have to try and answer their questions about *Willoughby* as best I can. Change the subject as quickly as I can.'

'Change the subject? When the whole subject of the tour is *Willoughby*?'

'It'll be fine,' she said, hoping he couldn't hear the uncertainty in her voice. 'I'll just have to bluff it.'

'Aren't you forgetting something?'

'What?'

'Willoughby himself? Isn't the actor joining the tour too? He's the one they'll be asking questions of, not you, surely?'

'Oh my God, the actor!' Harriet laughed with relief. 'Austin, I love you. I'd completely forgotten about him. Let me check he's where he should be. Can I call you right back?'

She quickly dialled their hotel in St Ives, two hundred miles down the north Cornwall coast. If all had gone to plan the actor was in his hotel room at this moment, waiting for their arrival tomorrow afternoon. Yes, the young receptionist reported, Mr Patrick Shawcross had arrived safely that evening. Yes, the welcome basket of fruit had been delivered to his room. He had asked not to be disturbed but if it was urgent . . .

'No, no, that's fine, I just wanted to check he was there. Thanks very much.' She called Austin back and reported the good news.

'There you are. That'll take some of the pressure off you at least,' Austin said. 'Did you ever see any of the *Willoughby* programs? I'm not much help, I remember the theme tune after the news every Sunday night, but those slow motion shots of the actor always put me off.'

'I've got the videos with me. I didn't get the chance to watch them before I left.'

'Can you have a quick look at them tonight? Fast-forward through a couple of them if you have to. If nothing else they might put you to sleep. And in the meantime, leave Lara to me. I'll start making some phone calls. See if I can find out what's going on.'

'Are you sure? Have you got time?'

'I did have a date with one of my adoring fans tonight, but she'll just have to wait. Treat 'em mean, keep 'em keen, as the saying goes.'

'Austin, stop it,' she said, automatically. It worried her how cavalier Austin was about women sometimes. He always said he was too young to settle down or that he travelled too much to be a good catch.

'Relax, Harold,' he said, slipping into his childhood nickname for her. 'I respect my female fans. They adore me. It's a win-win situation. Have you told James what's happened, by the way?'

'Not yet, I didn't want to wake him. You're the first person I've rung.'

'I do have you well trained. No problem, I'll call him in a little while. It'll do him good to wake up early.'

'You know he's in hospital?'

'I do. My basket of grapes must have gone missing in the post.'

'He's a nice man, Austin.'

'He is. It's not his fault he's married to a she-devil. I'll ring him and then we'll get onto Lara, too, keep trying her mobile until we find out what's happened. We'll worry about her, you just worry about the tour group. Promise me.'

'I promise. And thanks, Aust.'

'Any time. And Harriet, I mean it, relax. It'll be fine. You'll be fine. You know and I know James wouldn't have let you within a hundred yards of one of his precious tours if he didn't think you were up to it. He's been trying to get you back on the road for months, hasn't he?'

'How did you know that?' The last she knew, Austin had told Melissa he didn't want to receive any updates or monthly reports about Turner Travel. He'd been extremely forceful about it. Something about Melissa sticking her overbearing, patronising, self-aggrandising reports somewhere the sun doesn't shine, if Harriet's memory was accurate.

'I pay Glorious to spy for me.' Glorious was his nickname for Gloria Hillman, Turner Travel's long-time office manager and a close family friend. 'Someone has to keep an eye on my inheritance. Now seriously, relax, little sister. Repeat after me: "I will be fine. I can handle this if I just take it step by step." Better than handle it. You'll do it really well.'

Behind his joking tone, she knew he really was serious. Austin knew better than anyone how important this tour was to her. He was the one who'd come to her rescue nine months earlier after that last disastrous trip. She smiled into the phone. 'You're actually very nice underneath everything, aren't you?'

'Talented and handsome too. It's a devastating combination.'

He'd cheered her up, as always. Calmed her down too. And despite the light-hearted tone, his advice had been good. Just the matter-of-factness of going down to the reception desk to ask about the use of a video player had helped. The receptionist, hair tied back so tightly she nearly looked plastic, had hardly blinked at the request. A video viewing at this time of night? 'No problem at all, madam. I'll have the equipment delivered to your room. Would you like tea and sandwiches delivered while you work?'

Harriet thanked her stars they were staying in a business-oriented airport hotel for their first night in England, and not a homely B&B. Within half an hour she had been set up, the stack of *Willoughby* tapes on the bed beside her. She also had a cup of tea in one hand, a remote control in the other, a round of sandwiches on a plate by her elbow and the tour itinerary on her lap. She forced herself to put the troubling thoughts about Lara to one side and pressed play, willing her brain to take in every detail of the program.

The screen flickered into life to a soundtrack of faint music and the barking of a dog. A man appeared on screen, walking across a very green field. He looked to be in his early thirties, tall, his dark curly hair ruffled in the wind. He wore a duffle jacket over black jeans. His face was craggily good-looking, interesting rather than handsome, his eyes dark, shadowed. As he kept walking, the blue of the sea became visible behind him. The music grew louder, a cross between folk music and something orchestral. The shot widened to include a farmhouse, beyond it a jutting cliff, further still a lighthouse. Lettering appeared.

PATRICK SHAWCROSS
as
Willoughby

More barking filtered in through the music. The man stopped, turned. A black and white dog came running towards him. The two kept walking along a cliff path, a spectacular bay in the background, all soaring cliffs and blue water. The shot changed to an aerial view of a red post-office van making its way down narrow tree-lined roads. A montage of shots followed, as other cast members appeared on screen against a backdrop of harbours, old churches, farms and moorland. Harriet pointed the remote control at the television, pressing the fast-forward button. There wasn't time to watch the opening credits. What she really needed was *Willoughby* in pill form.

She watched most of the first episode, pressing fast-forward again whenever the action slowed. The plot involved the arrival of Willoughby in the town of St Ives under mysterious circumstances, shots of several curious villagers watching him unpack his few belongings from a battered old Rover, and then a dramatic shot of him standing looking out over a cliff, talking to himself. It quickly moved on to the theft of some valuable paintings from a country-house hotel clinging to the hillside of a picturesque village nearby. The setting was magnificent, with spectacular views across the sea. Harriet remembered it was one of the first stops on their tour.

She flicked through the itinerary on her lap and read the activity description James had written. '*Let's go walking in Willoughby's footsteps in beautiful Lynton on the north Devon coast, better known to the true fan as Ecclesea! We'll also visit the very hotel that played host to the action in several episodes, including "The Case of the Stolen Sketchbooks" and "The Case of the Mournful Model".*'

She leafed through the other notes James had given her, feeling like she was cramming for a 'Trends in TV Light Entertainment' exam. *Willoughby* was like a cross between the Agatha Christie *Miss Marple* series and *All Creatures Great and Small,* she decided.

She'd already gathered that Willoughby – it was never explained if that was his first or last name – was a postman with a mysterious past, possibly involving a career with Scotland Yard and a nervous breakdown, now living on the north Cornwall coast, delivering mail to farms and villages and managing to solve crimes along the way.

Among the press clippings James had given her she found a serious magazine article from several years previously, trying to explain the show's continuing popularity in Australia. It had lasted for only two runs on the BBC, but in Australia it was repeated year after year, tucked cosily in its Sunday evening slot, after the news, alternating between reruns of *Fawlty Towers* and *To the Manor Born*. English migrants loved it, the magazine noted, and so did plenty of Australians not of English descent or origin, happy to be reassured by its safe, comforting messages.

'Emigrants look back at their homeland through increasingly rose-coloured glasses. For some, the sentimental outlook is supplied by music. For others, TV programs. *Willoughby* has managed to combine the two with its snapshot or capsule form of English life.

All the elements are there – the mysterious man with a past and a handy penchant for sleuthing, the job as postman a convenient cover, allowing him to travel the length and breadth of south-west England. His co-stars, a simple but wise farmer, a member of the upper class and the ordinary postmasters and mistresses at surrounding rural post offices, supply additional colour.

The glorious Cornish countryside plays a role too, with scenes of fishing villages, wild coastline and chocolate-box farms featuring prominently. Even a dog – so beloved in English society – has a part to play.

The plots might be predictable, the crimes old-fashioned, the acting uneven, but it somehow feeds right into the heart of a nostalgic viewing population.'

The whole tour had actually been sparked by another magazine article, Harriet remembered. They had all been at their desks late one morning when Mrs Lamerton swept in. Mrs Lamerton did a lot of sweeping in to shops in Merryn Bay. Settling herself in the waiting area until Melissa was free to take her to lunch, she had started leafing through the pile of magazines. On the top was a collection of old English magazines that Lara had found in a junk shop. She'd added them to the pile for novelty value.

Harriet had been working at her computer, updating the monthly newsletter they sent out to each of their clients. The job had been given to her when it became clear she wouldn't be able to go back on the road again for a while. Perhaps Melissa had been trying to put it to her nicely, but it had come out all wrong. 'We're hoping it's a nice simple job for you, Harriet. But if it gets too stressful at any stage, if you feel that little problem of yours coming on, you just let me know and we'll put you onto something else in a whisker.'

'Oh good heavens!'

They'd all turned at the gasp from Mrs Lamerton in the waiting area.

She was waving one of the English magazines at them. 'Where did you get this from? I used to get this magazine every single week. In fact, I remember this very issue. I read everything about *Willoughby* I could get my hands on.'

Mrs Lamerton sighed as Lara and James came over to her. 'We were still living in England when they showed the first episode. I'll never forget it. It was the night we decided to emigrate. We were so thrilled when we arrived here to see it on Australian TV too. It's still my favourite program, you know.'

Lara had looked at the magazine article while Mrs Lamerton gave James a detailed commentary, explaining that the series was set in fictional villages along the north Cornwall coast but in reality had used different aspects of a number of real towns and locations in Devon and Cornwall: the cobbled streets and long beaches of St Ives; the wild Bodmin Moor scenery; the village green of Widecombe-in-the-Moor; the harbour at Port Isaac; cliffside country hotels in Lynton. The magazine had full-colour photos and poetic descriptions of each setting.

'And would all these places still be there?' Lara asked, glancing up from the magazine.

Mrs Lamerton made a tchy sound. 'They've stood the test of time for hundreds of years, Lara. Of course they'd still be there. You have to remember, Australia hadn't even been discovered when these places were celebrating their sesquicentenaries.'

Harriet tried not to smile. Mrs Lamerton always had the unfortunate habit of talking about Australia as if it were a misbehaving toddler.

'I'm ashamed to say I've never been to Cornwall,' Mrs Lamerton continued. 'It's one of the few parts of England Timothy and I didn't visit.' Timothy was her late husband. He had died ten years previously, three months after he and Mrs Lamerton had retired to Merryn Bay. He had been something in the army, or the navy, no one had ever found out exactly what. It was often hard to get a word in around Mrs Lamerton. 'Though of course I feel I know it like the back of my hand from watching *Willoughby*. Such a beautiful place. And of course having a handsome young man like Willoughby stride through it gave it extra appeal too.' She gave a surprisingly girlish giggle.

Nothing was said at the time, but over the next few days Harriet noticed Lara looking up English websites. A guide to Devon and Cornwall appeared on her desk. So did photocopies of the

Willoughby magazine article. She revealed it all at the next planning meeting, standing up to make her presentation. Her uniform was so crisp it could have been freshly ironed, her shoulder-length blonde hair shining, her make-up flawless. Across the table Harriet wished she'd thought to redo her lipstick before the meeting, too. She bit her lips so much while she was working her lipstick was usually eaten off before morning tea.

It was a very impressive presentation. Lara had put together a full itinerary for a *Willoughby* tour of Devon and Cornwall, taking in all the locations from the TV series. She'd discovered that there were dozens of *Willoughby* fans in the Merryn Bay area. She'd put the word around and already had firm interest from eight people. She knew there would be no problem getting that up to twelve. She'd done costings, timetables and market research. It was extremely viable.

'Lara, you are a gem,' Melissa said, beaming. 'I couldn't have done it better myself. Absolutely full steam ahead with it, I say. Well done. Now Harriet, what about you? Any ideas for new tours?'

Harriet stammered an answer. 'No, I'm sorry, nothing concrete yet.' She'd felt unable to think about a shopping trip to Melbourne at that time, let alone plan an international tour.

'No? Never mind.' Melissa looked like she did mind. 'But you're happy enough with your workload? Not too much for you?'

'It's fine, thanks,' Harriet said as brightly as she could. It wasn't fine. It was hard and scary and suffocating, all at once. She sometimes felt that she had no right to still have a job there, that all the others were carrying her. Lara especially. It was like they were on a seesaw, she realised. Lara flying high, Harriet falling lower and lower.

Over the next few months, Lara methodically set about organising the *Willoughby* tour. The clincher had been the discovery that Patrick Shawcross, the English actor who had played Willoughby, was alive and well and living in Boston. It had taken Lara some time to discover the fact, sending emails and faxes to the ABC in Sydney, the BBC in London and to actors' agencies in the UK before she was given a contact number for a large American agency in New York. She'd sent two emails without reply and finally decided to phone them, coming in early one morning to make the call.

Lara had told the story over morning tea, twisting her blonde hair as she spoke, her habit when she was amused about something. 'I said I was hoping to speak to someone about one of their clients, a Mr Patrick Shawcross. And the receptionist said, "I'm sorry, his name again? Parma Shorkle, did you say?"' Lara was laughing now. 'I ended up spelling it three times. I had to tell her that he'd starred in a program on English TV called *Willoughby*. I heard a click of keys again and then she said, "I'm sorry, ma'am, we don't represent anyone called Willoughby, either."'

She had been passed from person to person until she had found someone who thought she knew who he was.

'I think she was on work experience from their French office. "You want him to do what? Why?"' Lara had explained they had seen the article about *Willoughby* in the magazine and wanted to base a tour around it. '"When? And you would pay his expenses? And a fee?"' Lara did an excellent impersonation of a French accent. 'It was surprisingly reasonable. It sounds like he doesn't do much work with them any more so she was probably quoting from the last job he did. But I think we have him. I faxed over the magazine article to her and the dates we'd need him in Cornwall, and she said she'd come back to me as soon as she'd been in touch with him. If he says yes, I send all the flight details and a fee to her, they take their commission and we have our tour.'

Less than a week later, a fax had arrived from the agency. It was good news. They'd all gathered to hear Lara make the call.

'Mrs Lamerton, I'm calling about the *Willoughby* trip. What would you say if I was to tell you that not only is a tour to all the locations from the series possible, but our special guest would be Patrick Shawcross, the actor who played Willoughby himself?'

They had all heard the squawk of delight.

Harriet remembered James's words the night of the handover in the hospital. He was right. The tour really had been Lara's baby. Which made it even stranger that she would abandon it like this. Simply announce to her flatmate there had been a change of plan. Just up and leave . . .

Another episode ended and the closing credits played. Harriet sped through the opening credits of the next episode, then paused while she checked James's itinerary notes again. He had become very fond of exclamation marks in the past year, she noticed. '*Here in Marazion near Penzance is the dramatically stunning island castle of St Michael's Mount, used as the setting for those calamitous wedding scenes in "The Case of the Titled Temptress"! En route to Marazion keep a look out for the police station, scene of the hilarious confrontation between Willoughby and Sergeant Carling in episode eight, "The Case of the Hunted Hounds". The sergeant certainly met his match in our Willoughby, didn't he?!!*'

Harriet pressed fast forward again and Willoughby sped around the town in his red mail van, hopping in and out with amazing dexterity, before driving down a tree-lined lane and through some tall gates. She released the button and let it play normally again, as he pulled into the driveway of a large mansion, the gravel sounding under the wheels of the car. He climbed out and stood, broodily good-looking, against the van. The front door opened and a well-groomed blonde woman came down the steps and slowly made her way towards him. She was wearing a trim, pale-blue suit, high heels and a lot of jewellery for that time of the day.

'*Willoughby*,' she drawled.

'*Lady Garvan*,' he said. The shots were now full close-up. '*You know why I'm here*?'

She moved forward and stroked his cheek. '*I know why I hope you are here*.'

He didn't react. The camera pulled even closer and Harriet pressed pause. The actor certainly looked the part of a man with a mysterious past, with his dark hair and dark eyes. Would he have aged well? Fifteen years had passed. She leafed through the information pack but there were no photos of what Patrick Shawcross looked like these days. According to the brief biography, he had been living in America since the series ended, 'pursuing his acting career and other interests', whatever they might be.

She fast-forwarded again. As always the crime was solved and analysed in a scene between Willoughby and his best friend, George the farmer, sitting in their favourite pub in St Ives, enjoying a pint of bitter and shaking their heads.

'That's people for you, George.'

'Aye, Willoughby, so it is.'

Mr Douglas and Mr Fidock, the only two men in the tour party, had acted out that same scene at the airport. And on the plane. And in the hotel lobby. They were surprisingly good mimics, Harriet saw now. They had the Cornish accent with its rolling r's just right. She sped through the opening credits of the next episode as well, nearly laughing out loud as the black and white collie went tearing across the fields. Had Lara and James thought about tracking down Patch the dog as well, Harriet wondered. She pictured a sort of old pets' home, full of ageing animals from different TV series, sitting around in their luxury, pastel-painted kennels and hutches, reminiscing about their favourite scenes. The rabbits from *Watership Down*. The cat from the opening credits of *Coronation Street*. The pigs from *Babe* . . . She blinked hard, forcing herself to concentrate.

An hour later she had fast-forwarded through all of the episodes and felt slightly more familiar with the show. As long as everyone in Cornwall did everything at twenty times the normal pace she would be perfectly fine. She stood up and stretched, first one arm, then the other, her bracelet sliding down her arm as she lifted her left hand into the air. She had worn it every day for the past year. It had belonged to her mother, a present from Harriet's father the year they arrived in Australia. It was made of ten opals, each gem a swirl of blue and red fiery colour embedded in gold rectangles, simple but striking. As a child, Harriet had loved to sit on the Merryn Bay beach beside her mother and move her wrist up and down so the blue of the opal was lined up against the blue of the sky. 'That's it, Mum. Leave your hand there. It's exactly the same colour as the sky, isn't it?'

Harriet had a flash of wanting to be on that Merryn Bay beach right now. A longing to be taking an early morning swim, with the sea to herself. She and her niece Molly used to laugh about the fact that Molly did all her swimming in the chlorinated swimming pool, while Harriet stuck to the sea.

She decided on fresh air in the absence of water and went over to her hotel window. It opened only a little way, looking out over the car park, to darkness beyond. Her face was reflected back at her, her skin pale, her hair a black cap, spiky in places from where she had been running her fingers through it. She didn't have to look closely to know there would be an anxious expression on her face.

The five days stretched out ahead of her. She thought of the daily trips to the different *Willoughby* locations, the problems that might crop up with traffic delays, bad weather. There were bound to be personality problems, too. There always were on these group tours. The only variable was how quickly they happened and how she reacted. *Expect the unexpected.*

As the list of possible black spots grew longer in her mind, she felt a shimmer of the frightening feeling inside her. No, she nearly said aloud. Not here. Not now. Think positive. Look on the bright side. She shut her eyes and did the breathing exercises she'd been taught. Talk to yourself, Harriet, she said as she breathed. It won't happen again. You will be fine. You are fine. Breathe in, breathe out. Centre yourself.

Slowly, gradually, the panic subsided. Don't be afraid of the feeling, her doctor had said. Understand it and where it comes from. The more you know, the less you'll fear it.

That was the trouble. She knew more about it than she wanted to. She could pinpoint exactly when her panic attacks had started and she also knew exactly what had caused them. She was reminded of it every day. Their empty chairs in the office, their voices missing from conversations, the daily task of explaining to people ringing Turner Travel asking to speak to Penny or Neil Turner. The knowledge that her parents no longer lived just metres away in the house that adjoined the Turner Travel office, her childhood home. Reminder after reminder. Even after the tour went wrong, after she had got out of hospital and come back to work, the deep sadness, the desperation had stayed with her.

She remembered her first week back at work, when it had all seemed so hopeless and overwhelming. Lara had come in early and left a little vase of jonquils on her desk, Harriet's favourite flower.

'Harriet, if I can help, will you just ask?'

She'd been very moved, as she had easily been at that time. She'd looked up and smiled gratefully. 'Thanks, Lara.'

'I mean it. With the tours, or any itineraries.'

'Thank you.' Even through her sadness, Harriet had noticed Lara's self-assurance, her elegance. Her clothes were immaculate, her hair tied back in a stylish ponytail. Even her nails were manicured. How did she manage it, Harriet had wondered. She felt like she was falling apart, inside and outside.

In the background, Melissa answered the phone. 'Oh, I'm sorry, you can't have heard the news,' she said as loudly as ever. 'Mr and Mrs Turner passed away earlier this year. Yes, both of them. No, not together, one after the other. Yes, it was tragic. Very hard on the children. They were with them, thank God. Well, all except Harriet.'

She and Lara were looking at each other as Melissa spoke. Harriet had replayed that moment many times in the past three months. She had seen the grief and the hurt in Lara's eyes, as she knew Lara would have been able to see it in hers. But what else had she seen in Lara's eyes? A flicker of guilt? Or had she imagined that afterwards? Wanted to see it?

'Yes, it's very tragic,' Melissa had said again. 'We miss them every day.'

Every day, every hour. Harriet hadn't needed Melissa's words to remind her how she felt. Every detail was only ever moments away from being recalled. It was like having something on loop tape, always on her mind, there for her to review, replay, time and again, wishing for a different ending, wanting to make it different, wishing with all her heart that it could be. Even standing here, in a motorway hotel in England, it was the same. All the memories, as clear as if it had happened the day before, not the year before.

Chapter Three

Harriet called into the travel agency just before closing time the day her father would die. Her parents always worked the half-day on Saturday, insisting the children had the weekends off. She and her boyfriend Simon were on their way to Melbourne for the day on a shopping trip. He'd lost his mobile phone and was going to buy a new one, while Harriet wanted to browse in the bookshops. She had a cup of tea with her mother and collected measurements for some curtain material she wanted Harriet to buy from a department store in the shopping centre they were visiting.

She didn't see her father. He'd finished up early in the office to get ready for golf. She poked her head through the door that joined the travel agency to the house and called out loudly. 'See you later, Dad.'

His voice came down the hallway. 'See you, love. Drive safely.'

Three hours later she had a bag of new books and was walking around the department store, carrying the curtain material, hoping she'd chosen the right pattern. She didn't know where Simon was. They had arranged to meet at five o'clock, in two hours time. If they still felt like it, they were going to see a film. 'Don't be late, Harriet,' he'd said. 'If I don't find the mobile phone I want, I won't be able to ring you to remind you, remember.'

'I won't be late, I promise.'

'Harriet, you're nearly always late. You'll come dashing up, saying you couldn't help it, you got talking to someone who told you the most amazing story about being stopped in the street by a man in a giraffe suit —'

She didn't like it when he talked to her like that. 'I've never met anyone who said that.'

'I bet you will one day. So I'll see you at five o'clock. Will I write it on your hand?'

She softened and smiled. 'I'll shock you one day by turning up on time.'

'Yes, you will.'

She decided she'd shock him today. She was determined to be waiting there when he arrived. She'd be twenty minutes early, to make doubly sure. She checked her watch. Not even three o'clock. She had plenty of time yet.

When her mobile phone rang she thought it would be him on his new phone. She checked the display screen as she kept walking. No, it was Austin.

'Hi, Austie,' she said brightly.

'Harriet, it's Dad. He's had a heart attack on the golf course.'

She stopped in the middle of the shopping centre. Two people nearly ran into her.

'He's in hospital. You'd better get back as quick as you can.'

'He's alive? He's all right?'

'Get back as quick as you can.'

She couldn't get back. Simon had the keys to the car. There was only one bus a day to Merryn Bay and the bus station was miles away. 'Aust, I can't get there.'

He misunderstood. 'Harriet, I think you'd better. It's serious. Hurry. I have to go, I'm trying to get James and Lara as well. I'll call you back as soon as I can. Hurry up and get here.'

She ran from one side of the shopping centre to the other looking for Simon, trying to spot his sandy blond hair, the striped shirt he'd been wearing. Was it a striped shirt? Or had he been wearing a T-shirt? She suddenly couldn't remember. There was no sign of him in the mobile phone shop. What else had he said he was looking for? Sports shoes? There seemed to be twenty sports shops. She ran up escalators. She called his name into shops. She went back to the car park, in the vain hope he had got bored and was sitting in the car. He wasn't anywhere. She tried all the coffee shops and cafes. Where could he be? Where else could she look? She was getting desperate. She stumbled on the information desk. It hadn't occurred to her, but of course, she could get them to make an announcement.

The woman behind the counter made the call in a smooth, clear voice. 'Would Mr Simon Baxter, Mr Simon Baxter please come to the information desk as soon as possible. Mr Simon Baxter.'

Harriet waited. Nothing. There was no sign of him. She looked at every man his size and his age in the centre, but none was Simon. None of them was headed towards her. The woman was keeping an eye on her. She guessed before Harriet had a chance to ask. 'Shall I try again? The music is loud in some of the shops. Perhaps he didn't hear the first time.'

One more time. Again. Harriet couldn't stand still. 'If he does come, can you ask him to wait. Or to ring me?'

'Of course.'

'Where else would a man in his thirties shop in here?'

The woman answered as smoothly as if Harriet had asked for directions to the ladies toilets. 'Menswear on levels two and three; sportswear, videos, DVDs and CDs on levels five and six.'

'Thank you.'

As she ran down the side of the escalator, dodging people, her mobile phone rang. Austin. 'Harriet, where are you?'

'I can't find Simon. I don't know how to get there.' Her panic was rising. She was trying not to cry. 'Aust, how is he?'

'We're all here, at the hospital. Mum's in the room with him. He's had another heart attack, Harriet. Since they brought him in.'

She was more than two hours drive away. 'I'm getting a taxi.'

It would be several hundred dollars but Austin wouldn't have told her to hurry if he didn't mean it.

The first driver turned her down. He was nearly at the end of his shift. So did the second. 'You're only paying me one way. Who's going to want a fare back to Melbourne?' She hadn't been able to find the words to convince him. The third one hardly reacted, just nodded. She got into the back seat. He slowly put on his seatbelt, slowly put the car into gear, slowly indicated.

She leaned forward. 'You've got to hurry. Please. You have to do everything faster.'

'What?'

'My father is dying.' Her voice was shaky. 'He's in hospital. Please, can you hurry.'

He did his best. He shot her glances now and then as they made their way out of the city into the countryside. She stared at her mobile phone. If it didn't ring, it meant her father was all right.

'Black spot here, love. No signal for the next twenty miles or so.'

She didn't take her eyes off the phone, willing Austin to call with good news. Of course her dad was all right. He was in intensive care but he was all right. She'd arrive and he'd be sitting up, looking weak, a few tubes coming out of him and he'd be wearing one of those white gowns, of course, but he'd be all right. 'I hope you didn't rush,' he'd say. 'Didn't I tell you this morning to drive safely?'

The phone rang. It was Austin. 'Harriet?'

'Don't tell me.'

'Harriet.'

She knew before he said it. 'Don't tell me.'

'He's gone.'

'No, Austin.' They were still more than an hour away.

'They tried everything. We were all with him. Lara, James, Mum.'

But they hadn't all been with him. She hadn't been with him. She couldn't talk any more. She said goodbye. She said she'd be there as soon as she could. She cried, stopped crying, started crying again. The taxi driver kept driving.

They had just arrived at the hospital when the phone rang again. She stared at it. She didn't recognise the number. It kept ringing.

'You'd better get that, love.'

She pressed the connection.

'Hello.'

'It's half past five, Harriet. A joke is a bloody joke. Where are you?'

It was Simon. She couldn't answer him. She passed the phone to the taxi driver as she climbed out.

Simon arrived at the hospital at nine o'clock that night, coming in to the room, pale faced, where they were all gathered. Harriet's mother was inconsolable. She kept saying the same things, over and over. 'But he was healthy.' 'He exercised every day.' 'He was only sixty-three.'

He had been dead for one hour and thirty-three minutes by the time Harriet saw him. She'd walked into the hospital and been met by Austin.

'Harriet, I'm sorry. I'm so sorry.'

She moved into his arms, tears flowing down her cheeks. 'Where is he, Austie? I need to see him.'

It hadn't been her dad. It had been his face, his body. She had been right about the hospital gown. But there had been no sign of the smile, the soft accent, the teasing look in his eyes. She spoke to him. She touched his hand. She was overwhelmed by emotion, barely able to stand. Her dad was dead and she hadn't been able to say goodbye to him.

Austin was beside her. His hand was on her back. She turned to him. 'Austie, did he know I wasn't here? Did he know I was trying to get here as quickly as I could? Did he know?'

'Harriet —'

There was a noise at the door behind them. They turned. It was their mother. Lara was on one side of her, James on the other. They were both holding her tightly.

'Mum . . .'

'Oh, Harriet. Harriet.'

She needed her mother to come over and hold her, to make it all right, to make it better, but she stayed with Lara and James. Austin had moved over to them too. The four of them were holding on to each other.

Harriet looked at them. 'Were you all here? Was I the only one who wasn't?'

'Harriet, it was so quick,' Austin said. 'You couldn't have known.'

She didn't answer him. She needed to know exactly what had happened. 'Where were you when you heard, Lara?'

'I was in the office.'

'On a Saturday? Only Mum and Dad work on a Saturday.'

'I was working on that new tour.'

'Where were you, James?'

'At home. With Melissa and Molly.'

Austin came over and touched her arm. 'Harriet, stop it. It doesn't matter.'

'Yes, it does. It does matter.'

'Harriet? Come here, love.'

She turned. Her mother opened her arms. Harriet moved into them and cried until it hurt.

They closed the travel agency for two days. Gloria volunteered to keep it going, but they wanted her with them. Having her in their midst made it easier, held them together, stopped the shock from completely overwhelming them. She and Melissa quietly and methodically organised what needed to be done. Their mother was too distraught. The rest of them were too shocked.

Simon kept apologising, over and over again. It was his fault she had been in Melbourne. His fault for losing his mobile phone so she hadn't been able to ring him. She was calm with him. 'I wanted to go. It's not your fault.'

Gloria noticed something was wrong. She seemed to guess it was to do with Harriet not being there when her father died. 'I know it's hard, Harriet. But would it have been better if none of you were with him? If he had died on his own on the golf course? Would that have made you feel better?'

'No, of course it wouldn't.' But why did it have to be me who was missing? She didn't say that out loud. She felt so guilty, so terrible even thinking it, but it came from somewhere deep inside her. She should have been there.

Gloria moved closer, taking Harriet's hands in hers, squeezing them. 'Harriet, you can't change it. That's the way it was. That's what happened. It would hurt no matter how and when your dad died, or who was with him. It's awful, but it's the truth.'

They all wanted to speak at his funeral service. Austin and James went first. They spoke simply, briefly. They had loved their father very much. Harriet was supposed to be next, but she wasn't ready. Austin touched Lara on the arm. She glanced at Harriet, as if seeking permission. Harriet watched through her tears as Lara walked from the pew to the altar, adjusted the microphone, so calm, so collected. Her speech was brief. 'Neil welcomed me into his home as if I was his own daughter. I loved him for that, and I loved him for his kindness and his humour, and for all the parts of him that were special. I loved him dearly and I will miss him so much.' She cried then, but she managed to finish her sentence.

Harriet wasn't able to get past her first line. She had been up until two a.m. trying to write her tribute. Trying to put into words what her dad had meant to her. Trying to reduce thirty-one years of being loved and cared for and encouraged into three minutes. 'I loved my dad.' It was the past tense that got her. When he was alive she had been able to say to him 'I love you, Dad.' Now he was dead. Now he was in that coffin, in the middle of that aisle, and all she could say was that she had loved him. Because she hadn't been able to say 'I love you, Dad, please, Dad, get better. Please, Dad, don't die,' like the others had in the hospital room. If she had been there, would it have made the tiniest bit of difference that his spirit might have needed?

She started crying and she couldn't stop. Her mother didn't speak either. She broke down on her way to the altar.

Two months later, unbelievably, horribly, it happened again. They had all gone back to work, still numb with the hurt and grief, their father's empty desk a reminder every day of their loss, yet none of them wanting to sit there or move it out.

It had been a normal day: the phones ringing, customers calling in to book holidays or to show photos from a previous tour. A new set of company brochures arrived from the printers on the outskirts of Melbourne, two hours away. Harriet was the first to notice there was a problem with the photographs on the front page. The colours were out of alignment. Normally, that was something her father would have sorted out, quickly and easily. He'd have jumped in his car and driven there, and been back within the afternoon.

It was as if all their reactions had slowed when he died. Harriet knew her mother was still dazed. Time after time she had looked up and seen her staring out the window, not hearing phones ring, not realising someone had asked her a question. She had aged in just a few weeks, as if the spirit had gone out of her. Harriet noticed it again that day. Her mother was staring at the brochures as if she didn't know what they were.

Harriet needed to help. She desperately needed to try and make things better. 'Mum, do you want me to take them back to the printers?'

Her mother's smile was childlike in its relief. 'Oh, Harriet, would you?'

'Of course. Do you want to come with me? For a drive?'

Gloria looked up. 'Penny, you've got that lunch today, do you remember? Out at the golf club? And then Austin's arriving after lunch?'

'Oh yes, I'd forgotten. I'd better be here when he arrives too.

Harriet, thank you anyway. I would have liked that. We'll do it another time.'

Harriet was about to ask if there was anything else she wanted her to do while she was there, when the memory returned of asking about the curtains the day their father died. Instead, she picked up the brochures and her car keys. 'I'll be back as soon as I can.'

She planted a quick kiss on her mother's head. Her mother briefly touched her arm. 'Thank you, Harriet. I don't know what I'd do without you.'

Afterwards, the words had swum round and round Harriet's head. Is that what she'd said? Without you or without you all?

She had driven the two hours to the printing plant and spent nearly an hour with the production manager, trying to sort out the problem. She'd stayed calm, not even getting annoyed when he took a personal phone call on his mobile midway through, laughing for five minutes while he set up a football outing with a friend. How could that bother her? Her father had died. What could be worse than that? She was walking out of the printworks when her mobile phone rang. James.

Afterwards she couldn't remember whether she had said hello or whether James had started speaking first. She vaguely remembered getting into the car, turning it around, ignoring the angry blast of someone's horn and then driving back to Merryn Bay. She needed to stop for petrol halfway. She got out of the car, filled the petrol tank, went in and paid, like a robot. The whole time James's voice replayed in her mind.

'Harriet, thank God I got you. Mum's in hospital. Quick, get back as soon as you can.'

She drove straight to the hospital. She was too late. At the bedside she listened, staring at her mother's lifeless face, as James,

Austin and Lara told her what had happened, over and over, needing to give her the details, as if they could make sense of it that way themselves. Lara had been driving back from dropping train tickets to an elderly client outside the town when she found their mother slumped at the wheel of her car beside the road to the golf course, the car engine still running. The ambulance had been called. She'd had a second stroke soon after she was admitted to hospital. A fatal one.

Her funeral was held in the same church. She was buried next to their father. His grave was still a mound of earth. They hadn't been able to face organising his headstone yet. The wake was held in the same hall.

The whole family was devastated. The aftermath was as traumatic: the changes in the company, James and Melissa and their daughter Molly moving into the family home, the shifting and changing as the family came to terms with what it all meant, personally, professionally.

Everyone had felt the hurt and the grief. Harriet knew that. But underlying everything for her was one desperate, unassuageable fact. She was the only one who hadn't been able to say goodbye to her parents. The only one who hadn't been there with them when they died. Not just once, but twice.

The grief, the hurt and the shock at their deaths twisted into anxious feelings deep inside her, a constant watchfulness that something like that could happen again with someone else, without warning, without the chance to prepare or say farewell.

It began as a constant nagging unease. Over the following days and weeks it grew into something as pervasive as a migraine or a toothache, an anxiety, dark and encompassing, deep inside her mind, seeping into every part of her life.

She began to worry from the time she woke up until she went to bed. About small things at first. Checking and then having to double-check if she had enough petrol or if the brakes in her car were working. Having to go back home in case she'd left the iron on, left a tap running or the front door ajar. She started worrying about other people, especially people travelling anywhere by car. She kept imagining burst tyres, rogue truck drivers changing lanes without warning, faulty railway crossings. She started insisting her family, Simon and her friends phone her when they arrived at their destination so she would know they had got there safely.

The anxiety spilled into her working life. When she was typing up tour itineraries, she couldn't stop imagining catastrophic events. Bus drivers having heart attacks and crashing off the road. Viewing platforms on the edges of canyons or cliffs collapsing, taking groups down with them. Planes crashing. Trains derailing. Food poisoning outbreaks. She decided it was an omen of some sort, that she had to make doubly sure to check all the tours were properly organised, and that every possible safety measure was in place.

Everyone started to notice. James insisted she take some time off. She protested. Gloria was drafted in to take her home and put her to bed. She couldn't sleep. The worry turned from work to her personal life. She sat up, three nights in a row, thinking about Simon. He was away on a week-long conference. They had been together for four years, and had lived together in his rented flat for the past twelve months. They had started to talk about getting married, buying a house together. She inspected their relationship from every angle, made lists, went over every moment of their time together, paced the house. She didn't answer the door, or any phone calls. She was clear in her head when she rang him at the conference at six o'clock in the morning to tell him she was very sorry, but she had realised there was no future between them and she had decided it was best if they split up. She was as kind as she could be to him. She felt genuinely sad but she knew she couldn't give him any hope for a future reconciliation. He was extremely upset. Her family were shocked. Despite the anxiety, she knew it was the right thing. She moved out of the flat they shared, found a small house for sale four streets back from the beach on the opposite side of Merryn Bay, put down a deposit, all in the space of a few weeks. She ignored any advice that she was moving too quickly, acting irrationally. There was an urgency, she realised. She had to move quickly before anything else bad happened. She had to try and keep one step ahead of it.

She worked longer hours so she didn't need to go home to her empty house. She volunteered to do any extra tours going. She worked weekends. She did anything she could to try to block the anxious thoughts crowding into her brain.

Two weeks before she was due to take a group on a five-day tour of the Flinders Ranges in outback South Australia James took her aside.

'Harriet, are you sure you're up to this? I can take over, or Lara can, if you're not.'

'I'll be fine. Why? Who said I wouldn't be?'

'No one said anything. It's just you've checked all the arrangements at least six times already. The hotel in the Flinders Ranges rang me. They're worried we don't think they're up to scratch.'

'I was making sure of everything, the way we're supposed to, the way Mum and Dad taught us to.'

'Harriet, we've been staying in that hotel for more than ten years. You know they're good.' He paused. 'The helicopter company rang too. They said you've been querying their safety record.'

'I have to do my job. I can't take people up on a sightseeing flight if I don't have faith in the company.'

'Harriet, you've rung them every day this week too. I think you might be taking this all too seriously. Maybe it would be better if —'

'No.'

'Just this once. Maybe you need a break. You've been working flat out since Mum and Dad died and maybe —'

'No, James. We're all in this together. We're all sad. We've all been working hard.'

'Yes, but not all of us have ended a relationship and moved house in the past two months too.'

'Everything's under control, James.'

'Look, if you're sure. But if you change your mind, if you want to be taken off the tour . . .'

'I can do it.'

'Okay.'

It had gone wrong from the start. The group was a party of middle-aged car yard managers and their wives. They wanted the back-to-the-bush experience, and had asked Turner Travel to put together a tailored tour, combining luxury travel with some outback adventure. Harriet had organised short bushwalks through Wilpena Pound, the crater-like mountain visible on the desert horizon for hundreds of miles. She'd arranged for meals of emu pâté and kangaroo steaks in a luxurious pub at the end of a long dirt road. A scenic helicopter flight. One night of camping in luxury tents, the rest in an authentic bush hotel. Authentically renovated, anyway, to a four-star standard.

The bus driver was a sixty-year-old called Des. They'd used him several times before. He was brusque, but fine. Taciturn – they couldn't rely on him to add any local information or colour – but he knew the roads.

For the week before the trip Harriet had trouble sleeping. She was in her new house on her own, so at least she didn't have to worry about Simon making comments all night long. 'Come back to bed, Harriet.' 'What are you doing up, Harriet?' 'Can't you forget about work for a minute?' She would try to sleep but each time she lay her head on the pillow a detail would come to mind that she hadn't checked off. What if there was a vegetarian on the trip? What if Des got sick and they were out in the desert? Would she be able to drive the bus? Should she check if any of the group had heavy-vehicle licences, just in case?

The group met at the airstrip near Wilpena Pound and drove to the hotel for the first night. She had to go back to the airstrip twice to check they'd picked up all the luggage. The first time Des didn't mind. The second time he was cranky. 'I counted the bags, I told you. They counted them, too. It's their luggage, why couldn't you believe them?'

'I had an idea I'd left something behind.'

She worried about the seating arrangements on the bus and kept trying to move them around. They told her to relax. 'Harriet, we're old friends, we don't care where we sit.'

She was up all night, checking the map Des was using against an older one she'd found in the hotel reception area. She knew outback roads were often washed out by sudden rain storms. It wasn't the wet season but flash floods happened out of nowhere. Everyone knew horror stories of people camping in dry creek beds and being woken in terror by a ten-foot wall of water sweeping them away in the middle of the night. She woke Des at five the next morning to see if he would think about changing their route, just in case.

'No.'

'I'm worried about flash flooding.'

'No way, if that first no wasn't clear enough. You've got problems, missus.' He shut the door in her face.

She'd hammered on the wood until he answered. 'I'm worried about the wellbeing of the group. About something happening to them.'

'If anything happens to them it'll be because you woke me up too early. I'm going back to bed.'

She became fearful of hygiene problems and started checking the kitchen before and after each meal. The chef complained, and suggested if she wasn't happy she should move somewhere else.

She cancelled the helicopter ride, upsetting the group.

'But that was going to be the highlight,' one of the men said. 'It's a perfect day.' It was, too. Clear, blue. They would have been able to see for miles.

'I had a dream that it crashed.'

'You had a dream?' The man was incredulous. 'You cancelled our thousand-dollar flight because of a dream? Then you'd better have another dream that the helicopter takes off.'

He rang James. James rang the helicopter company. Then he rang Harriet.

'Harriet, what's going on? You can't cancel things like that. What's this nonsense about a dream?' She started to explain how real it had seemed. She'd seen the helicopter fall from the sky, crash and burst into flames. She'd heard the screams. She had woken up drenched with sweat, terrified. James spoke over her. 'Look, it was a dream, okay. It's not going to crash. That flight is the high point of their trip and it's going ahead, Harriet. This afternoon. Promise me.'

'I can't go, James. I won't be able to watch.'

'Are you getting enough sleep? Sounds like you were up all night with those nightmares.' When she admitted she was sleeping badly, his tone changed. 'Harriet, take the afternoon off. Go to bed. I'll get Des to take the group to the helicopter pad by himself. You take it easy and you'll be right as rain tonight.'

The group returned later that day, exhilarated from the helicopter flight. They talked about seeing hundreds of miles of red earth, deep gorges and dry river beds; wedge-tailed eagles, kangaroos, emus and camels; Wilpena Pound looking like an ancient bowl. None of it eased her worries. She managed to have dinner with them, hear all the stories, even put up with the teasing. 'See, Harriet, we survived.' But she was barely able to eat, and didn't join them in the bar afterwards. She couldn't sit there, talking and laughing. The feeling of dread had multiplied, except now she didn't know where the horror was going to come from.

She paced the room all night. They were supposed to be going camping the next night and all she could think of were flash floods, spiders, snakes. Her clients writhing in agony. Des sick at the wheel of the bus, shouting that she'd have to take over. Two of the men doubled over in pain, brushing away spiders. A woman screaming that a snake had crawled into her sleeping bag, that Harriet had to come, quickly. And what if the camp fire wasn't put out properly? A flicker of flame would spark on to a dry gum branch nearby, smouldering, sending out tendrils of low fire across the desert floor, towards their tents . . . Something bad was going to happen, and there was nothing she was going to be able to do about it.

She didn't come out to breakfast the next day. The group assumed she was in her room, or in the office making phone calls. They met Des at the minibus outside the hotel at nine o'clock, as arranged, but there was no sign of her. It was Des who came to her room.

The door was locked. She was inside, in the corner, the quilts and pillows bundled all around her. She had pulled the curtains across and locked the door, now so frightened she couldn't bear any light or the thought of someone being able to come in. His knocking sounded like bellows, shouts. 'Harriet? Are you in there?'

After a while he went away. She curled up tighter, trying to slow her heartbeat, feeling her nails pressing into her palms. She'd be all right, they'd be all right, she just had to be sure they didn't camp near any rivers, and check for spiders and snakes and . . . The waves of terror took her again. She couldn't help it. She screamed when the knock came at the door again. Des, and someone else with him. She saw the door handle turn. They were trying to get in.

'Harriet? Harriet?' It felt like they were screaming her name. She managed to crawl across the floor, still bundled in the quilt, and push a chair under the door handle to keep them out that way. She checked the bolt. Please, please, please let it be strong enough. She knew the window was already locked. She'd done that in the middle of the night. She'd locked the bathroom window too. She put another chair against the bathroom door, but it didn't make her feel any safer.

She heard a female voice and for one moment thought it was her mother, but it was one of the women in the group. More knocking. 'Harriet, are you all right? Please, answer us.'

She curled up tighter, as tightly as she could. If she spoke softly to herself, if she kept up a sort of murmuring, she discovered she couldn't hear their voices. She tried counting, repeating numbers over and over again, in order first and then at random, trying to fix them in her mind, something solid and normal like numbers . . .

It took the local policeman nearly half an hour to break down the door. By the time they got inside, she was so terrified she was screaming the numbers. They called the doctor. Austin flew up that night. She was taken to a clinic outside Melbourne. An anxiety state was diagnosed. A nervous breakdown. A severe grief reaction. She was given different names for what had felt like a boiling mass of fear and hurt and deep, endless sadness.

She'd discharged herself from the hospital after three weeks of treatment, rest and medication, and returned to work. She'd thought she was okay. But then James asked her if she would be able to lead a three-day tour to the Riverland. The idea terrified her. Lara had taken it instead. She was offered another one two weeks later. Again, she'd turned it down. Then another. James stopped asking her. It went without saying that she wasn't up to it. She was moved into the administration side of the business, while James and Lara spent nearly all their time out on the road with the tour groups. Yes, she was fine again, she told people. Yes, absolutely. No, she was perfectly happy being in the office. It was a nice change, not to have to do all that packing and unpacking. Oh, she'd go back on the road again, one day, just not quite yet, she said as brightly as she could. She'd been trying to convince herself as much as them.

Harriet turned away from the hotel window and the darkness outside. It was quiet now, barely any noise from the motorway. It could be anywhere out there – England, Australia. She knew the same thoughts would have been in her mind wherever she was. She'd learnt that from all her years of travelling. You didn't leave your memories, your worries, your problems behind when you got on the plane. They came with you, whether you wanted them to or not.

It was the slow aftermath of her parents' deaths that still shocked her. There had been the initial grief, the everyday wallop of feeling, when she would realise over and over that they were gone and that she wouldn't ever be able to see them or speak to them again. That rawness had faded, changed in shape, but something else was emerging. The sharpening picture of how life would be now.

It wasn't only the physical details that were painful: her parents' absence in the office, at family gatherings, in Merryn Bay, or the fact that James, Melissa and Molly now lived in the house where they had once lived. It hurt in her heart and mind, too. She had never realised how often every day she naturally thought of her mother and father, wanting to tell them something, remembering something one or the other had said, a flash of childhood memory, an idea, or the beautiful comfort of a memory of conversations with someone she loved and who she knew loved her. Thoughts like that which had once brought warm feelings now produced a sharp little stab of grief.

It was as if all the safety nets she had never even known existed around her had been snatched away, leaving nothing to buffer her from what could be so frightening about life. Pain, grief, shock, sadness – she found it hard to believe she had made it to the age of thirty-one without truly knowing how any of those emotions felt. Her childhood seemed idyllic now, bathed in a glowing light of safety and familiarity. Even Lara's arrival all those years ago had started fading into that golden state of memory, as if she had simply imagined that things were tricky at the start. It felt like she'd had two lives: the one before her parents' deaths, when the world seemed full of promise and good things; and then afterwards, when it felt as if the ground beneath her feet was unsteady, prone to sudden chasms and gaping holes.

As she started preparing for bed, washing her face and brushing her teeth, Harriet made herself focus on the present, on the tour. She talked herself through all the positives of the situation. She had tomorrow morning to do some final checking before the bus arrived to take them to St Ives. Out of consideration for the age of most of the group and the long journey, James had scheduled a late start. Once they got to St Ives she could sit down with Patrick Shawcross and talk through the itinerary, before his first official meeting with the tour group, an informal cocktail party at the hotel itself. All straightforward. All manageable. All of it under control.

All except for Lara's disappearance.

'I'll do what I can from here to track her down,' Austin had repeated before he hung up. 'I'll ring James for you as well. He can get Melissa and Gloria on the job. Between all of us we'll find out what's going on with her. It'll be something simple, you wait and see. So don't worry about her. Your job is to worry about the tour.'

She knew what he was trying to do, and she loved him for it, but what he was asking was impossible. Did he truly think she could block Lara out of her mind? Simply switch off the part of her brain that had worried about Lara for as long as she could remember? She had spent twenty-four years wondering if Lara was okay, if she was happy, and just as long being puzzled and confused by Lara's behaviour in return. It had become second nature to her.

Except this time it felt different. Since she had come out into the airport and there had been no sign of Lara, she had gone through a whole range of reactions. Worry. Concern. Confusion after she'd spoken to Nina, Lara's flatmate. But if she was honest with herself now – in a way she never could be with Austin, or even Gloria – the more she was admitting to a strange kind of relief.

Perhaps Lara was feeling the same way, wherever she was. Perhaps that's why she had gone away, not only to England in the first place, but away this afternoon, abandoning the tour. She'd realised what she had done to Harriet was so inexplicable that she couldn't face her again either.

The thoughts went round her head, as they had been doing for three months, ever since the night she had learned the truth from Lara. Harriet was still no closer to understanding it. She climbed between the white cotton sheets, turned off the bedside lamp and tried to sleep. Don't worry about Lara, Austin had said. It was so much easier said than done.

CHAPTER FOUR

On the other side of the world, Gloria Hillman moved across the bedroom of her Merryn Bay cottage, carrying a tray and listening to the rattle of the cup in the saucer. It always woke her husband up much better than any alarm clock could. 'Morning, darling.'

'Hello, my sweet.' Kevin sat up in the queen-sized bed. He'd greeted Gloria that way each morning for the past thirty-five years. She placed the cup in the same spot on the bedside table she used every day, then perched on the end of the bed watching, but not helping, as Kevin reached and felt for the saucer. He was sixty-three years old, a bit older than her, but still fit-looking. Tanned, too, from all the outdoor work he'd done as a roofer over the years. He even had a full head of hair still, even if it was more grey than brown these days. He took a long sip. 'Thanks, love. Did you sleep well?'

'Like a dream.'

'Any big news?'

'Nothing earth-shattering.' Gloria always delivered the seven o'clock news headlines with the morning cup of tea. 'Industrial action on the ports. Election campaign due to begin next week. And two goats from Melbourne Zoo seen making a run for it down Flemington Road.'

'Good for them. And the weather?'

'Blue. Sunny. Twenty-eight degrees, if you can believe a word any of them say.'

Gloria stood and pulled back the curtains. Their house was set back from the road, but if she leaned in a certain way she could get a glimpse of the sea through the pine trees, and a good view of the sky. It was cloudless so far. April was her favourite time of year. All the summer crowds had left and they had the small town back to themselves. Merryn Bay's normal population of five thousand swelled to nearly twelve thousand for a few months, the holiday shacks and caravan park down the end of the beach crammed to bursting point. People were drawn to the simple beauty of the town, with its curving bay, secluded beach, little wooden jetty and the view across the water to bare hills and other small towns, invisible in the day, twinkling lights at night.

Strolling around at lunchtime in the summer, down the only shopping street in the town, she'd often overhear conversations between holidaymakers from Melbourne, remarking on how well set up the town was, with its banks, hairdressers, clothes shops, supermarket, 'Look, even a travel agent,' one would usually say. 'Let's sell up and move down here. It's a big enough town, and we'd be beside the sea all the time.'

She was always surprised at how protective she felt, as if it all belonged to her – the changing colours of the water, the long beach path lined with imported pines, the big sky, blue and hazy in the summer, dramatic in winter. She didn't want it teeming with crowds all year round. She liked it the way it was.

'Any clouds, love?'

She turned back to her husband. 'Not that I can see. Blue skies ahead. Do you want the radio on? Your book, or anything, while I get ready?'

He shook his head. 'I'm fine. You look after yourself.' As she left the room, she watched as Kevin reached confidently to the back of the bedside table and switched on the radio. A Beatles song filled the room, too loud. Without hesitation, Kevin found the right knob and turned the volume down.

He smiled. 'Sorry. Bit early for a disco.'

'Just a bit,' she said. That was one of the advantages of it having been a slow decline in his sight. There had been time for him to prepare, to make almost a mental imprint of not only appliances like the radio and the CD player, but also the arrangement of the house. He'd been able to learn his way around before his sight went completely. The girl from the Institute for the Blind in Melbourne had been wonderful. They would never have thought of doing the things she'd suggested.

'The mind is amazing, it can remember more than you think possible,' she'd said. 'If you practise things before your sight goes, Kevin, it won't be as frightening when it happens.' She'd given some examples. The teacup and radio on the bedside table. The position of his knife and fork and glass of wine at meal time. 'You never know. You might find this opens up far more experiences than you thought possible, once you get over the shock.'

She'd been so honest about it. It was going to happen so they may as well be practical about it. Other people gave them false hope or avoided the subject altogether. She had helped Kevin, and Gloria and their three sons, come to terms with it in many ways.

Honesty was always the best policy, in Gloria's opinion. She remembered arguing with Penny Turner about it. Penny had been shocked at the way Gloria spoke so openly about it when Kevin was first diagnosed. The words had sounded so ominous: macular degeneration blindness. The lay term – the slow erosion of the retina – had sounded even worse.

Penny had been just as shocked to overhear a conversation between Gloria and one of their more tactless customers. The woman had asked after Gloria's health before leaning forward and lowering her voice, 'And how is that poor husband of yours?'

Gloria hadn't skipped a beat. 'Like a pig in muck. He has me running around after him from dawn to dusk. Says he should have gone blind years ago.'

'He's very courageous,' the woman said, unabashed. 'And so are you. It can't be much fun caring for an invalid in your home like that.'

'Oh, we have lots of fun,' Gloria had said cheerfully. 'We play hide and seek most nights. It's great. I always win.'

One evening, over their usual end of the working day cup of tea in the back room of Turner Travel, Penny had brought up the subject. 'Gloria, I think you're wrong to talk about this so bluntly. Kevin might get better and you're talking as though his sight has already gone. If you don't have hope, what's left?'

'Confusion,' Gloria had said. 'Disappointment when the inevitable happens. He is going to go blind, Penny. Kevin knows that, I know that, we talk about it, so his mind is already adjusting to the idea even before it happens.'

Penny had never liked facing up to the nasty side of life. If she didn't like something, she'd either pretend it wasn't happening or gloss over it. She called it being sensitive. Gloria called it being blinkered. It was the one thing they had always argued about, in all their years of friendship. Gloria and Kevin had often spoken about it too. 'Think about it, Kev. It must have had an impact on the kids. Penny did it with Lara's arrival, never wanting to acknowledge that there might be some repercussions on the others, especially Harriet. She chose not to see that Austin spent all his spare time teasing James. Is it any wonder James found a fierce woman like Melissa to protect himself with?' Penny had done it in another way, too. Trying to protect Lara from something. The one thing in thirty-five years of marriage that Gloria had never been able to speak to Kevin about.

In the early lean months with the travel agency, though, when anyone else might have given up or decided they had made a mistake, Gloria had been forced to admit it was Penny's attitude that had kept them all so cheerful. 'Our time will come. I know it will. We just have to stick at it.' She had been right. The terrible shame was that Penny wasn't there to see the agency these days, when it was doing better than they could ever have imagined.

'You know, I think I'm missing Penny and Neil more as time passes, not less,' Gloria said to Kevin now, as she came back into the bedroom to pick up her work jacket – her uniform, as she had to learn to call it – and do a final check of her hair and make-up in the wardrobe mirror. Not that she bothered too much with that side of getting ready. A quick brush of her now greying curls, perhaps a dab of lipstick, and she was done. Her sixty-year-old skin had seen too much sunshine over the years to be saved by any make-up now. Besides, she knew practically everyone who came into the travel agency and they'd get a shock if she started dolling herself up. 'I've been thinking about them so much lately for some reason. It would be great to have one more of those nights of good conversation with them, wouldn't it?'

'Good conversation? Good arguments, you mean.'

'No, not arguments. Spirited discussions. Remember that's what Penny always called them?' She glanced at her watch. 'Quarter to eight. I'll be late.'

'Run, Gloria, run. You'd better be careful or Melissa will sack you.'

'An old piece of the furniture like me? She wouldn't dare.'

'No, of course she wouldn't. That place would crumble if you left.'

'Once upon a time, perhaps. Not under this new regime.'

'Melissa's still on the warpath?'

'She was born on the warpath. But it's Melissa they have to thank for things turning around, as I keep telling Austin. If she hadn't come on the scene they would be bankrupt by now, whether Penny and Neil were still alive or not.'

'To which Austin replied, if my memory serves me right, it would have been better to be bankrupt than bullied to hell and back by the Evil One.'

Gloria laughed. 'He really is far too wishy-washy about her, isn't he?' She finished her tea, and leaned and kissed Kevin goodbye. 'I'll see you at lunchtime, love.'

'Good, because I won't see you.'

It made her laugh every day. Even better, it made him laugh. Picking up her bag and sunglasses from the bench beside the sink, she pulled the door shut behind her and walked down the path to the front gate.

At her desk in the Turner Travel office, showered, made up and in the full Turner Travel uniform, Melissa Turner hung up, cursing the nurse in the Geelong hospital. How dare she refuse to go and wake James up, especially after Melissa had stressed how important it was.

'Yes, Mrs Turner,' the nurse had replied in an infuriatingly calm voice. 'You said that last night as well. And the night before. It's not good for your husband to be woken in the middle of the night, you know.'

'But it's nearly eight, not the middle of the night. And I should know, I've been awake since five a.m. It's an important family matter.'

'Family? Close family?'

Melissa thought for a split second about inventing a problem with Molly, their fifteen-year-old daughter, before changing her mind. She had heard Molly come in from swimming training already and the adjoining wall between the office and the house carried sound so well there was every chance Molly would hear her and protest. Melissa told the truth. 'It's about his sister. His foster-sister, at least. Lara.'

'Has she been in an accident?'

'Well, no —'

'So it's not a life and death situation?'

'No, but —'

'Then I'm sure it can wait until after your husband's had his breakfast.'

Melissa had hung up, loudly. Perhaps it was a shame she had called so late the night before, pretending it was a family emergency. One of the nurses had obviously reported her. It had been important, though. She'd had an idea for revamping their coach tours to the Gold Coast. James told her he hadn't minded at all. He was always understanding about being woken in the middle of the night. She often had her best ideas then. And as he said many times, it was her middle-of-the-night ideas that had got the company back on track.

She'd been in a terrible state since Austin called two hours before with his bombshell about Lara not turning up to meet Harriet and the *Willoughby* group. He'd made it clear he'd only rung her because he hadn't been able to get past the ward gatekeepers to James either. They'd had a terse conversation – she and Austin had never got on and even an emergency such as this wasn't enough to forge bonds between them. She was desperate to talk to someone about it, to start putting a rescue plan into action. Thank God Gloria would be in soon. She could share the burden with her.

Melissa tried Lara's mobile number again, making sure she was dialling the correct international codes. It had been working perfectly two days ago, the last time she and Lara had spoken. A quick call, to confirm that the hotel in St Ives had a lift. Lara had sounded fine, businesslike as ever.

She tensed as Lara's recorded voice filtered down the line. She knew from Austin that Harriet had left several messages. She decided to leave another. Just in case.

'Lara, it's Melissa. We need to talk. I don't know what's going on, but I hope you're not in any trouble. Ring me, please. Or send an email. We'll sort it all out, all right?' She thought perhaps that she sounded too cross and hastened to make up for it before the space for messages was filled. 'I mean it, that I hope you're okay. So call us, will you?'

It was so odd. What could have got into her? Had she met someone and fled to a love nest? Discovered she was pregnant and run away to do something about it? No, that wasn't Lara's style. Not organised, under-control Lara. Organised, under-control Lara who had just left nervy, basket-case Harriet in charge of a group of twelve people. Melissa felt her temper rise. She should have known something like this would happen. Hadn't she told James it was a mistake sending Harriet back on the road? She should never have let him talk her into it. He'd sat there going on and on about

Harriet needing her confidence built up again, that she was much better again, she had been one of their most popular guides, all the groups had loved travelling with her, Melissa only had to read the comments book, they all said how kind and sweet and fun she was, blah blah blah, on and on until Melissa had eventually pleaded a headache and given in.

Not for the first time Melissa wished James had several other sisters, preferably six or seven, each with business and tourism management degrees, instead of just Harriet and Lara. Not that Lara was strictly his sister, of course, and one had to make allowances for Harriet since her breakdown, but it really did sometimes feel as though she, Melissa, was the only one keeping the business on an even keel.

What she found hardest about working with the Turner family was the ripple effect, she decided. Something happened to one, and it affected all the others. Like when Neil and then Penny had died. Of course it was sad, but that was the natural order of things, wasn't it? Parents died, children took over. You got on with it. Not that she was that close to her own parents, in fact she rarely saw them these days, but they were happy enough in the old folks' home, she knew. And she would only unsettle them unduly if she was to start calling in each Sunday the way some people's relatives did. The monthly visits worked well for them all. If they were to die, of course she'd be sad, but she would get on with it. Not like the Turners. James had gone so serious. Austin had become even more impossible. Harriet had fallen to pieces. Even Lara had gone strange, announcing out of the blue she was going to study in England. How were they supposed to work productively together in these kind of circumstances?

She checked the time on the airplane-shaped wall clock above the front door. Ten to eight. She'd have to pop her head in to the house soon and make sure Molly was ready for school and had remembered to have her breakfast. At least she was still eating properly, and doing her homework, and behaving normally, not like some other fifteen-year-olds around town she'd heard about, getting up to no good, going off the rails. And Gloria would be in any moment, too. Thanks heavens for one non-family employee, even if she possibly should have retired years before.

Melissa turned to her computer. She'd try and distract herself with work while she was waiting for Gloria. Beside her was a pile of books on the archaeological settlements of Sweden. Axel Dortmund, the owner of one of the guesthouses on the Merryn Bay beach, had come into the travel agency a month ago, offering to lead a study tour to Viking settlements in his native country. An early listing on the Turner Travel website calling for expressions of interest had yielded an encouraging number of inquiries.

There was no accounting for taste in travel, Melissa thought for the hundredth time since she and James had taken over the running of Turner Travel. And thank heavens for that.

Chapter Five

In her bedroom at the back of the house adjoining the travel agency, Molly Turner was nearly ready for school. She'd been up since six-thirty. She had crept out of the house and cycled, half-asleep, to the pool, barely spoken to the other members of her swimming club, swum her usual twenty laps and been back home and showered by seven-thirty.

Sometimes her dad was up when she got back, making coffee or sitting at the table reading the paper, but not this morning. Poor old Dad, stuck in hospital, she thought. Silly old Dad, falling off the ladder. She hoped he was missing them, stuck in Geelong. She and her mum had been to see him at the weekend and were hopefully going again this evening, after she'd finished her afternoon swimming training. He'd looked funny in the bed, with his leg all plastered up, a cage under the covers making him look five times bigger. He'd been as lovely as ever, though. Some of her friends complained about their dads, and she did her best to join in, but the truth was she really liked her dad. It was her mum she had problems with . . .

She went out into the backyard and slung her towel, bathers and damp tracksuit over the clothesline, pegging them haphazardly. It was a beautiful autumn day, the sky blue and clear even this early in the morning. She picked a late plum off the tree by the back door as she came in and bit into it, the juice already warm from the morning sun. Passing through the kitchen, this time she noticed the signs of life, the toaster out, the dishes drying in the rack. Her mum must have gone into work early. Gloria wouldn't like that, Molly thought. She'd heard her say many times how much she liked that quiet morning time in the office on her own.

Molly went into her room to dress. She was still wearing her summer school uniform, a knee-length blue cotton dress, but once the winds started up in May they would all switch to the longer blue winter skirt and jumper. She tied her still damp strawberry blonde hair back into its usual long thick plait, adding a glittery hair slide for that touch of glamour, as her friend Hailey called it. She rubbed moisturiser into her bare brown legs and applied the barest minimum of tinted moisturiser to her face. Proper foundation was banned, but she and her friends had discovered this was the next best thing. She found her lip gloss and put it in her pocket. That was also banned but they all still wore it anyway. She'd apply that on her way to school. Next, her earrings – simple gold studs, anything showier was also banned. Finally, she strapped her watch on, a small oval face and a blue leather strap. The school even had strict guidelines about what sort of style the band could be. Nothing too showy that might cause envy, apparently. It was stupid, she thought. All these rules and regulations, piled one on top of the other. If the teachers only knew what the kids got up to. Which reminded her . . .

She put her hand under the mattress, rummaged inside the little hole she had made in the stuffing and pulled out the packet. She pressed out the pill, swallowed it and hid the packet again. It was the only hiding place she'd been able to think of. Her mother still tidied her room and put her clothes in her drawers, even though

Molly had tried to make her understand she was happy enough to do it herself.

'You're still my little girl,' her mother had said, ignoring that at five foot five Molly was now nearly a head taller than her. 'I don't mind doing it one bit.'

Molly's friends couldn't understand why she complained. Their mothers insisted they clean their own rooms and do their share of the housework. Jacinta and Hailey even had to do their share of the washing – and so did their brothers.

'When does your mother get time to do this housework, Molly?' Jacinta's mother had asked, after overhearing the conversation in the car one afternoon. 'She works full-time, doesn't she?'

'She gets up early,' Molly said. 'And she does some of it at lunchtime.' It had got worse since they moved into her grandma and grandpa's house. At least in the old house, a couple of miles away from the main street, her mother hadn't been able to nip in and out during the day. Now there was only a door dividing the travel agency from the house. Molly couldn't leave anything lying around in the morning. She never knew when her mum might be popping in and out of her room, doing a spot of tidying, as she put it.

'So when does she relax?' Jacinta's mother had asked.

'She doesn't.'

Mrs Symons had laughed, but Molly hadn't. It was true. Her mother didn't relax. Not even when they went on holidays together. She would be checking out the hotel or the caravan park, or all the local tourist attractions. Molly always had to try out all the attractions for children, too, and give full reports.

'It was okay,' she'd say, in answer to her mum's questions after she climbed off a funfair ride or came out of a museum.

'What do you mean it was okay?' her mum would say, pulling out her notebook.

Molly hated those questions. 'It was just okay.'

She'd mentioned it once to Lara, the day before they were going away on another research holiday, even though she felt a bit guilty complaining about her mum. Lara had got it immediately. She worked with her mum every day, Molly supposed, so she knew what she was like. She'd given her some good advice. 'Okay isn't that descriptive a word, Mollusc. Think about it as if you were telling one of your friends what a place was like and use that word. Your mum wants to know what it will be like for kids, so that would be really helpful. One good, juicy word should do the trick.'

Lara had been right. Molly had described the next set of attractions as awesome, scary, wild. Her mum had been really happy and had got off her back. Molly had texted Lara straight away. It workd. U r genius. She'd got one back minutes later. No, u r. L xxx

Molly checked her mobile phone now, where it was recharging by the chest of drawers. She'd been keeping half an ear alert for it all night, hoping to get the reply text from Lara. Usually she came back to her quickly, as soon as she got one of Molly's messages, even if it was to say Stop Txting & Get Bk 2 Work! There were no messages, though. There hadn't been any for nearly two days now. It was a bit weird.

Maybe her latest message hadn't got through, she thought, even though she knew it had. She had waited and watched for the Sent sign to flash. But maybe it had gone astray on the way. It was a long way for a few words to travel, from Australia to England. It wouldn't hurt to send it once more.

She had to type it all out again. She hadn't dared to leave the message in her outbox. Her mother had started occasionally picking up her mobile phone and reading her saved messages and Molly had already had to explain a potentially embarrassing text she had sent to one of the boys in her class. Luckily her mum hadn't known what some of the abbreviations were, but she'd been suspicious. 'Your mobile phone is for communication not for flirting, Molly, remember that please.'

She had to be joking. They all used their mobiles to flirt. She tapped on the keys. L, Nd sm advce. Boy stuff. Cn u cll me? Lol M xxxxxx

She pressed Send. Waited. Message sent appeared. She crossed her fingers Lara would call her back soon.

Molly had thought it would be fine, Lara being away for these three months. She'd been excited for her, too, getting the chance to study in England. She'd gone to the airport to see Lara off, and they'd been texting and phoning each other while she'd been away. But she still really missed her. Things weren't the same when Lara wasn't around. She knew some people thought Lara was a bit stuck-up, but she really wasn't. She was quiet and calm, but underneath she was really good fun and she always seemed to understand how Molly was feeling about things.

She was great with fashion tips too. Molly really liked Lara's clothes and the way she wore her hair. Lara was always really happy to let her borrow anything, too, or to show her different ways to style her own hair, like in plaits or French twists, or once even using chopsticks in a sort of bun. She'd even spent a whole afternoon helping Molly get ready for a school dance, when she was going in fancy dress as a pop star, helping her tease her hair and put on loads of make-up until she looked exactly like someone on MTV. It had been great fun, a real laugh, like being with a really cool older friend or big sister rather than an aunt.

Molly had gone out a couple of times with her other aunt Harriet since Lara had gone away, once to see a film, the other time to do some shopping, and it had been good but they just didn't have the same kind of friendship as Molly had with Lara. Harriet had changed so much. She used to be great fun, always ready to mess around and have a laugh, but then all that stuff had happened on that tour, and for ages after she'd seemed to be really quiet. Molly's dad had taken her aside one day, asked her to be extra kind to Harriet, that she was finding life tough, ever since her mum and dad had died. That was fair enough, Molly thought. It had been awful, especially when it had been one after the other like that, but how come everyone else hadn't fallen to pieces the same way? She'd asked her mum once, really casually, but she'd been no help. So she'd asked Gloria. Molly was actually a bit scared of Gloria, the way she sometimes seemed to know what you were thinking before you knew it yourself, and the way she would speak her mind. But at least she always told you the truth.

Gloria had thought about it for a little while and then said she thought it had been extra hard for Harriet because she hadn't been able to say goodbye to her parents, the way Austin and James and Lara had.

Molly found that a bit hard to understand. 'She was at their funerals, though. She said goodbye then. Everyone did.' The church had been packed both times.

'I meant when they died, Moll. Harriet was the only one of the kids who wasn't with them when they died.'

Molly still didn't really understand why that would have made Harriet go funny. It wouldn't have changed things even if she had been there, would it? Her grandpa would still have died of the heart attack and her grandma would never have recovered from the stroke. She'd heard lots of people say it at her funeral. That it was better she had died, that she might have been paralysed if she'd lived, in a wheelchair or in hospital all the time.

She still wondered if that's what Lara and Harriet had been talking about that night out in the garden, the night of Lara's farewell drinks party. It had definitely been about Grandma but she hadn't heard enough to know exactly what. It hadn't been a big party, mostly their clients, friends of Lara's and Harriet's, people they knew from around Merryn Bay, friends of the whole family. Even Austin had come down for it, even though it was just a few weeks before he was going on that big tour of Europe and probably catching up with Lara anyway.

Molly had enjoyed it. She got to be waitress at these family or Turner Travel parties, which meant getting to move around as much as she liked and not getting stuck in boring conversations with clients like that scary lady Mrs Lamerton, who lectured all the time about how things had been in her day. Molly had run out of clean glasses and her mum had asked her to go and get some more from the boxes outside. She'd gone out and nearly jumped out of her skin when she heard voices in the garden, until she realised it was Lara and Harriet. She was about to go over to them when something stopped her. They weren't talking. They were fighting. But in a strange way. She'd never heard Harriet speak in a voice like that, either before or since. She wasn't shouting. Neither of them was. That's what Molly thought about afterwards. How quiet they had both been, but how strange Harriet had sounded. Lara had been standing still, not reacting at all. Harriet had been asking her something. 'Lara? Is that true? I have to know, can't you see that?' Molly hadn't been able to hear the rest of it or what Lara said in reply. She'd heard a murmur, and then Harriet's voice again, soft at first, then louder, sounding like she was really upset but trying not to cry. 'I can't understand. How could you have done it?'

They hadn't seen or heard her, Molly was sure of it. She slipped back inside as quickly as she could. Not long after, Lara came in, looking really strange, and then Harriet ages after, all strange-looking too, pale like she always was but like she was in shock. What had they been talking about? What had Lara done or not done?

Molly spent a lot of time in the office after school, folding brochures and helping out with filing and she hadn't once heard Harriet have a proper phone conversation with Lara in England since that night. Lara phoned fairly often but Harriet barely talked to her, just transferred the call or took a message as if it was a stranger, not Lara, practically her sister. Lara didn't ever ask to speak to Harriet, either, any time Molly answered.

One day, when Molly was talking to Lara on the phone, she asked her about it, out of the blue. 'Have you had a big fight with Harriet?' Lara reacted really funny, too, she thought. 'Why?' That was all she'd said. Molly had murmured something vague about just wondering and quickly changed the subject.

She'd nearly, *nearly* said something about it when her mum told her that Harriet was going to be travelling with Lara on this *Willoughby* thing now instead of her dad. But there'd have been a big fuss, she knew. 'What do you mean they had a fight? What about? What did they say?' And Lara didn't like fusses, Molly knew that. No, better to keep quiet.

'Good morning, darling!' A voice sounded outside. Her mother, poking her head through the adjoining door from the office. 'Come on, Molly, breakfast please. You'll be late.'

Five minutes later, she was rinsing out her cereal bowl and about to go and clean her teeth when her mobile phone beeped to say she had a new text message. 'Let it be Lara, let it be Lara,' she said under her breath. It wasn't. It was her friend Hailey asking her to remember to bring in the magazines she had loaned her last week.

NW, she texted back. It was short for 'no worries'.

She checked the time. Three minutes to eight. She'd have to hurry. She brushed her teeth then called out a goodbye to her mum through the door. 'See you later, Mum.'

'Bye, darling. Do you want to come and see your dad tonight?' her mum called out.

'Yes, please.'

'Leaving at six.'

'Okay. See you.'

Her phone beeped again as she was a little way down the street, letting her know another new text message had arrived. Perfect timing. She didn't like being home when this text came in. It was too special to read at the kitchen table. She stopped and checked. Not from Lara, she knew. Even better than Lara. And right on time, as always. His message came every day at eight a.m., on the dot. I l u. I love you.

She wrote the message she sent back every day. I l u 2. Then hitching her backpack on to her shoulders, she walked on to school.

Gloria picked up their mail from the post office and then stopped at the deli two doors from Turner Travel, taking a carton of milk from the still-to-be-unpacked delivery by the front door. The verandas on each shop in the main street gave plenty of shade, and kept the milk cool, which was especially fortunate in the hot summer months. Gloria had collected the Turner Travel milk from this step every morning for the past thirty years, paying for it at lunchtime. She looked across the road and saw Molly on her way to school. They waved to each other, as they also did every morning. Molly was getting so tall, Gloria thought. Almost a woman not a schoolgirl these days. And getting quite beautiful, in that long-limbed teenage way.

As she reached the Turner Travel glass front door she noticed the lights were already on inside. She could see them through the edge of the blind she had pulled down the night before. She felt a flicker of alarm. Had she forgotten to turn them off last night? Or, oh God, not burglars. She was trying to decide whether she should call the police when she saw Melissa emerge from the staffroom, with a large pot of coffee in her hand.

Gloria unlocked the door and pulled the blind up with a snap. 'You're up bright and early. You nearly frightened the life out of me.'

'I've hardly slept. Thank goodness you're in early.'

'I'm always in early,' she said, put out to see Melissa. She treasured the early-morning peace in the office, straightening all the brochures in their racks, dusting all the framed travel posters on the walls and then writing up her travel fact on the blackboard they placed on the footpath outside. It had been her job since the agency opened. She already knew what today's was going to be. *Did you know it took 1400 men eight years to build the Sydney Harbour Bridge? (Great bus/rail packages and guided tours to Sydney available now.)* Afterwards she would enjoy a slow cup of tea while she sorted the mail, sometimes even playing some opera or listening to the news programs on the office radio. Not today . . .

Melissa paid no attention to the tone in her voice. 'You know I'm not one to exaggerate, Gloria, but we've got a disaster on our hands. I've made you a coffee, here. Please, take a seat.'

Ten minutes later Melissa had filled her in on Austin's phone call and the situation with Lara, Harriet and the *Willoughby* tour. She put her cup down with a bang on the table. 'Which brings us to the serious question of our next step. How to rescue the situation. I don't suppose you could go?'

'Go where? To England?'

'Yes, to England.'

'Why would you want me to go? Or anyone to go for that matter?' Gloria was genuinely puzzled.

Melissa gave an impatient laugh. 'To stop the tour turning into a complete disaster, of course. You don't think Harriet's going to be able to cope on her own, do you?'

'Of course. Why wouldn't she?'

'You know why. The first sign of trouble, the littlest hitch, and it'll all be too much for her. It'll be harder to come to her rescue when she's on the other side of the world. At least she was only a few hours away last time.'

'Harriet will be fine. That was nearly a year ago. It's time you forgot about it.'

'It's taken nearly a year for me to get those people back travelling with us again. I've put a lot of work into it, regaining their trust.'

'I'm sure they coped.' Gloria noticed it was about the work Melissa had put into it, not how hard Harriet had worked to overcome her problem.

'I'm serious, Gloria. Would you be able to go there? Would Kevin be able to cope on his own?'

Gloria sat upright. 'Sorry, Melissa, let me get this straight. Quite apart from you knowing I hate long-haul flights, you're asking would my blind husband be able to cope on his own while I flew to the other side of the world to rescue Harriet from a situation that she doesn't need any rescuing from? In fact, a situation that might be just what she needs to build her confidence up?'

Melissa had the grace to colour. 'Look, I know you're fond of Harriet —'

'It's got nothing to do with me being fond of Harriet or not.' Gloria was surprised how angry she was. Perhaps it was the extra cup of coffee this early in the morning, but for a second she felt as though she was channelling Penny Turner, defending her daughter. 'Harriet has a great deal of ability. She has a lovely warm way with people. She gets things done, sometimes in her own unique roundabout way, but she still gets them done. All she needs is the confidence and the feeling that people believe she can do it. You are not to think for a minute about sending someone over to rescue her.'

'But it's one of our international theme tours. It's important to the company, to our future direction.'

'So was the *Lord of the Rings* tour of New Zealand that James ran last year. The one that got flooded out for two days. Did you send in anyone to rescue him?'

'No, but that was James. He's done dozens of these tours. And besides, the clients loved it. They were talking about it for days. Some of them were even on the TV news.'

'And the disastrous *Mutiny on the Bounty* trip to Norfolk Island? The one you were leading?'

'I wasn't to know there would be a pilots' strike.'

'No, but between us all we managed to organise other transport, didn't we? And your clients were fine. Leave Harriet alone, Melissa. You bully her enough as it is.'

A gasp. 'I do not bully her.'

Gloria suddenly didn't care what she said. 'No? What do you call it then?'

'I help her. And my number one priority is always the clients, Gloria. Which is how it should be in any business.'

'It's a family business. Family plus me. It should be us first, and then our clients.'

Melissa didn't have anything to say to that. Gloria knew it was her part shares in Turner Travel, the ones that Penny and Neil Turner had left her in their wills, that infuriated Melissa. She knew that Melissa, and to a lesser degree James, disliked having to come to her to float ideas, to pass any expansion plans. She had been as surprised as the rest of the family when the will was read out, but she had been able to imagine a conversation with Penny about her reasoning behind it.

'Will you keep an eye on all of them for us, Gloria? Not just the three children and Lara, but Melissa as well? Just to stop them fighting?' Penny had been asking her to do that since the early days. And she would have said yes, she knew.

She kept control of the conversation. 'Surely the tour is the least of our worries, in any case. The main worry is Lara. Where she is. How she is.'

'Yes, of course it is.'

Gloria suspected Melissa had completely forgotten about Lara. 'Have you got any idea why she might have done this? Has she seemed different to you? Worried about anything?'

'Not that I noticed.' Melissa was sulking now. 'But Lara isn't one to spill her secrets in any case, is she? I've always found her secretive, if anything.' She paused. 'Perhaps we should ring Austin back. He might have some ideas. And at least he's on the right side of the world.'

Perhaps *we* should ring Austin back? Chance would be a fine thing, Gloria thought. She knew perfectly well that the last thing Melissa would do was ring Austin again. The devil got into her, though. 'That's a good idea. You won't mind talking to him again?'

Melissa's chin lifted. 'I've never minded talking to him. It's Austin who doesn't like talking to me. He's got this idea in his head about me and James and the business, and he refuses to see or hear sense.'

Gloria had to bite her tongue again. Austin's idea that Melissa was putting ideas into action without checking with the rest of the family. Not so outlandish really.

'I'll ask James to phone him,' Melissa said, busying herself with a pile of papers and not looking at Gloria.

Gloria softened. This was about Harriet and Lara, not Melissa, after all. 'Would you like me to ring him? It might be difficult for James in the hospital.'

'Would you mind? I've got a lot more on than you today, so that would be helpful.'

Gloria only just kept her temper again. Fighting an inclination to pour what was left of her cup of coffee over Melissa's head, she checked her watch and did a quick calculation of the time difference. Morning in Australia meant it was after midnight the night before in Europe, a good time to ring Austin. She knew from his tales of past tours that the members of the orchestra didn't go to bed until at least two a.m. after any performance. He'd said in his last email that the orchestra was performing every night this week. 'No problem, I'll do it now.'

'Thanks, Gloria. I appreciate it.' Melissa didn't look at Gloria as she spoke. She'd already turned to her computer and was scrolling through the morning's emails.

CHAPTER SIX

Gloria decided to call Austin from the phone in the staffroom, preferring to be out of Melissa's earshot. She dialled his mobile phone number and was disappointed when it went straight to his voicemail. She left a brief message. 'Austin, it's me. Can you call me back as soon as you can? I think you know what it's about.'

She took the opportunity to make a pot of tea, hoping that would dilute some of the effects of the morning's coffee. As the kettle boiled, she gazed around the room. A stranger would assume the pattern on the walls was old faded wallpaper – rows and rows of little multicoloured suitcases, apt for the staffroom of a travel agency. In fact, each suitcase had been stamped individually, over the thirty years Turner Travel had been in business.

It had been Gloria's idea, a way of marking their bookings in the early days, when things had been slow and they needed all the encouragement they could get. She'd presented Neil and Penny with a custom-made stamp in the design of a suitcase, and different coloured inkpads, suggesting they stamp the wall each time they got a booking. In the first few months there hadn't been much stamping. Ten a week if they were lucky. That had gradually changed. The proof of it was on the walls now, hundreds and hundreds, thousands even, of tiny suitcases, thirty years worth. The rows of suitcases were in different coloured inks, each colour representing a new year. The one colour that hadn't changed was the green for group tours. There were hundreds of those, sprinkled all over the walls.

'Imagine all the stories each of those suitcases would hold,' Penny had enthused one afternoon, just two years ago, when they were all sitting in the staffroom. It had been either Lara or Harriet's birthday, Gloria remembered. They were both in May, so her memories of their parties sometimes got confused. There had been cake, anyway, and a bottle of champagne. It had been a happy afternoon, she remembered. Lots of talk, teasing, laughter. And a lot of reminiscing, too, of the early days, when the staffroom wall had been more paint than suitcase stamps. Neil had started to count the suitcases and quickly given up, not even reaching the first thousand.

'What about the suitcases that went missing en route?' Austin asked. He had been home for a few days, not working but hanging around getting under everyone's feet. 'All the lost luggage? Should we paint over some of the stamps in memory of them?'

'Turner Travel lose clients' luggage? Never!' Penny had said. 'I couldn't live with myself if that happened.'

That day Penny and Neil had started talking about the trips they'd like to take, if and when they ever retired. Harriet, or perhaps it had been Lara, had leapt up, gone into the office and returned with a big bundle of brochures about great cruise journeys of the world. There was a lot of discussion about which would suit their parents best. Harriet chose the one around the Mediterranean. James preferred the more adventurous one to the Antarctic. Lara argued enthusiastically for two weeks in the Caribbean.

'You're all just trying to get rid of us,' Neil said.

'No, of course we're not,' Harriet said quickly. 'You don't have to go anywhere. You know we don't want you to. You're the ones who mentioned retiring. If it was up to me you'd work here forever.'

Penny laughed, pink-cheeked from the champagne. 'It's all right, my pet, we're in no hurry to go anywhere, are we, Neil?'

'Of course not. How could we leave Turner Travel in the children's hands? Austin would have it sold and be off to Bermuda on the profits before the others knew what had hit them.'

Austin rolled his eyes, pretending to sigh heavily. 'Thanks, Dad. You gave the game away. Surprise was my number one weapon.'

'So you're not thinking about retirement yet?'

Gloria could still remember Melissa asking the question. She wondered was it only her who had thought the question was being asked in great seriousness. In any case, Penny hadn't noticed any undercurrent.

'No, not yet.' She'd gazed around the room, up at the walls. The champagne had made her sentimental. 'Not until the day we've stamped ten thousand suitcases. Then we'll think about calling it quits.'

Gloria picked up her cup and took it over to the sink. They'd all had such optimism back then, such a naïve belief that it was all in their control, that they had a choice about what happened. But they hadn't, had they? Neil had died suddenly a year later and Penny just two months after that. Everything had been different since then. Melissa – with James in the background – had somehow taken charge. The suitcase stamping had virtually stopped. Only Gloria thought to do it now, once a week, and she wasn't sure how accurate her numbers were, not now when so many of their bookings were made on computer and spoken of in terms like PAX and Clientele or Groups A, B or C, rather than customer names. Melissa had never been interested in the idea of the stamps, in any case, Gloria knew. She looked at balance sheets, not stamps on a wall, to measure their success. Things had changed in so many ways since Penny and Neil died. The new regime had taken over, as Austin had put it. There was no time for frivolous things like stamps. No time for enjoyment. It was a serious business these days. Even the monthly meetings, which had once been good fun, were now regimented to the last minute.

Gloria thought of the last one Austin had attended. Melissa had been in top form, making pronouncements, producing flowcharts and pie-charts as though they were discussing a major economy, not a travel agency. She had reported on new tours, travel trends and where Turner Travel was placed in the market. She also announced a new company rule. There had been no discussion about it. All clients, both in the office and on tour, were to be referred to as Mrs, Mr or Miss, or, in extreme cases, Ms. She'd quoted from a recent study that good manners in business dealings had a greater impact on customer relations that any other aspect of communication.

Gloria had decided to herself she'd be having no part of it. Most of their clients were Merryn Bay locals and there was no way Gloria was going to start calling a woman she had known since she was five years old by a formal title. She said nothing, though. She'd already learnt the art of passive protest.

Melissa stood at the top of the table, tapping her hand on a pile of paper in front of her. 'I think our older clients – the greater part of our business as I don't need to tell any of you – will find formal titles particularly respectful.'

'That's a fantastic idea, Melissa,' Austin declared, falsely bright. 'Let's start with me. From now on, I'd like all of you to call me Lord Austin.'

'Don't be ridiculous, Austin, please.' Melissa was barely able to hide her impatience.

'Why not? Have you got the monopoly on ridiculous behaviour? Actually, now I think about it, it seems you have.'

'Austin, give it a rest, would you?' James snapped, his face flushed red.

Austin fell quiet and left the meeting soon after, as Melissa finished presenting the quarterly figures. He hadn't spoken, simply stood up, gathered his papers and headed for the door. 'Austin?' James was the first to speak. 'Where are you going?'

He stopped, and gave them all a long look. 'Do you know, I'm not sure. Somewhere a long way from here.'

Harriet tried to stop him. 'But you need to be here. It's a family meeting.'

'She's right,' James said. 'Sit down, would you?'

'It's not a meeting. A meeting is a discussion of ideas, shared thoughts. This is a dictatorship and your charming wife,' Austin bowed at Melissa then, who was growing as red-faced as her husband, 'our self-appointed dictator. I don't recall that part of Mum and Dad's will, do you, James? Harriet? Lara? My understanding was they wanted us to carry on as a family business. With you as well, Gloria, of course.' He nodded courteously in her direction.

Harriet coloured. Lara went still. James straightened in his chair. 'Melissa is family, Austin. She's my wife. We come as a package and I think you are being bloody arrogant not to listen to her ideas. It's all right for you, sailing around the world, playing your drums, breezing in and out as it suits you.'

Gloria winced inwardly. Austin didn't just 'play drums'. He was the lead percussionist in one of Australia's best-known orchestras.

James kept going. 'What would you prefer, that we'd have shut up shop after Mum and Dad died? That we'd go on as we had for years, the same tours, the same profits, year after year? Well?' He looked around for support. 'What about you, Harriet? What do you think?'

Harriet hesitated for too long. Gloria knew what would be going through her mind. They had talked about it often enough. She thought that both her brothers were right, that was the difficult part of it. Melissa and James had practically taken over, but if they hadn't been there after their father and then their mother had died, who knew what would have happened. 'I think it's worth listening to what everyone thinks,' she'd finally offered.

Across the table Lara spoke. The three Turners were pink-cheeked, their dark brown eyes flashing. Harriet's hair was in tufty spikes from where she had been anxiously pulling at it during the meeting. Lara had looked as serene as usual, her blonde hair smooth, her blue eyes clear, no spots of angry colour on her olive skin. 'Aust, come back, please,' she'd said, quietly, firmly. 'James is right. I think Melissa's got some great ideas. Let's at least talk about them.'

He'd refused. He hadn't attended a meeting since.

The phone rang. Gloria snatched it up. 'Turner Travel, Gloria Hillman speaking.'

'Glorious, hello.' It was Austin. 'You've heard about Lara then?'

'First thing this morning. What's happened, Aust?'

'I haven't a clue. I told Melissa everything I knew. Harriet arrived with the group and there was no sign of Lara. She rang her flatmate and was told that Lara had announced there'd been a change of plan and she wouldn't be doing the tour after all.'

'That's it?'

'That's it.'

'How did Harriet sound to you?'

'Thrown at first, of course, but no more than anyone would be if they got to an airport and the person they'd expected to meet them hadn't turned up.'

Gloria leaned forward and checked through the half-open door whether Melissa had left her computer. No, she was on the phone herself. 'You didn't get any sense that Harriet was going to —'

'Fall to pieces on us again? No, if anything, I think she wants to prove something to everyone. She only texted me for help after she'd got the group to the hotel and sorted out their rooms. She's worried, but I think she's got it under control.'

'Of course she has. Melissa however has just asked me if I would like to pop over to Cornwall and help her out.'

Austin gave a short laugh. 'Dear, thoughtful Melissa. What did she suggest you do with Kevin? Drop him off at a Holiday Home for the Blind for a few days?'

'Thank you, Austin. I knew I could rely on you to say the unsayable.'

'Melissa seems to bring out the best in me. So what do you think's going on with Lara? I played it down as much as I could with Harriet, in case she got too worried about her, but it's weird, isn't it?'

'Completely. Lara sounded fine last time we talked. It was a quick call, mind you. She wanted me to fax over some information for a project she was doing at college.'

'I spoke to her last week. I've got a few days off next month and we were seeing whether there was any chance of meeting up, either in Bath or somewhere else. And she rang me quickly the day James had his accident. It was just a quick call but she sounded fine then too.'

'You're in touch with her a lot?'

'We ring a bit, and text. She nags me about my wild life, asks me when I'm going to settle down; I nag her about her perfect life, ask her when she's going to loosen up. No change there.'

Gloria slipped into their usual banter without even thinking. 'She's got a point, Austin. God knows, time's marching on. Late-thirties, still no sign of settling down . . .'

'If God wanted me to settle down he wouldn't keep putting all these beautiful women in my path, would he? What am I supposed to do, Gloria, pretend I can't see them? Ignore their pleas to be asked out? Ignore their shining, hopeful eyes?'

Another time Gloria would have kept up the teasing. But something had just occurred to her. When she first heard that Lara was going to England, she'd anxiously waited for Lara to come to her, to ask if she knew anything about her parents, to ask if Penny and Neil had given her any more details about them. It would have been the most natural thing in the world, surely, for her to go looking for her parents' homeplaces in England while she was in the same country. And perhaps also the most natural thing in the world to want to visit where they had died. But she hadn't asked Gloria anything. There had been no mention of them in any of her emails or postcards either. She'd sent weekly reports from the tourism college, enthusiastic about how much she was learning. She mentioned Penny and Neil, as she did often and naturally, but not her own parents. Gloria had found it strange, but also a relief. The closer Lara came to the end of her studies, the better she'd felt, too.

She hesitated and then made herself ask him. 'Austin, has Lara ever mentioned anything to you about her mother and father? Whether she was going to go and visit the towns they were from, anything like that. Go to where it happened . . .'

'No. No, she didn't. It actually puzzled me that she didn't. I would have, in her position. But you know Lara, she wouldn't necessarily tell me even if that was what she was thinking of doing. She might already have done all of that, tracked them down, without telling us about it.'

Gloria had an uneasy feeling.

Austin continued. 'Look, I've been thinking about this since Harriet rang. Maybe I should fly over to England this weekend. See how Harriet is doing in Cornwall. Then go across to Bath and have a chat with Lara's flatmate. Just in case there's more to it. Because something's odd. This isn't like Lara, is it?'

It was as if he had read her mind. She'd been about to ask him if there was any way he could do exactly that. 'There won't be a problem with the orchestra?'

'No, not once I explain what's happened. Anyway, we've got a break from the public performances after tonight. It might get me out of a very dull embassy event and two school workshops. I should be thanking Lara and Harriet.'

They had a quick exchange of business, checking he had enough money for the air fares – he did; checking that he had Lara's address in Bath – yes; that he knew where Harriet and the tour group were staying in St Ives – he hadn't known, but took down the details. 'And you're okay to sort out the flights yourself?' Gloria asked, finally.

'You're talking to the son of a pair of travel moguls, remember? I think a bit of it might have rubbed off.'

'Sorry, I'm getting forgetful in my old age. I'll leave you to it, then.' She hesitated. 'But will you tell her we love her when you see her?'

'Tell who? Lara or Harriet?'

'Both of them. But especially Lara.'

'Why do you say that?'

'I don't know. In case she's feeling . . . Just in case.'

'I will.'

'And everything's okay with you, Austie? The opera tour's going well?'

'No. It's a disaster. Every time I hit a cymbal a woman on the stage plunges a knife into herself. Do you think I should take it personally?'

'Good heavens, yes. Your drumming's always had that effect on me, too.'

She hung up and came into the office to report back to Melissa. The other woman was in her glass office, still on the phone, facing the wall. Gloria guessed she was talking to James.

'. . . I can't believe it. How could Lara do this to me? She knows how busy I am, and then she leaves us in the lurch like this . . . No, please don't go on about Harriet again, she's going to have to handle it, isn't she, whether she can or not . . . Yes, she's here, she knows, she's talking to Austin at the moment.'

Gloria suspected she'd be called in to give James a full report on her conversation with Austin any moment. While she waited she took the opportunity to finish her morning tidying, straightening the photo pinboard that had hung on the side wall since the early days. Under a handwritten sign 'Turner Travel: We go further for you!' were dozens of photos of the Turners and Lara with groups in front of landmarks all around Australia and, recently, some overseas ones as well. It was out of place in Melissa's newly painted and remodelled office, but even she hadn't dared to take it down.

A recently arrived photo caught Gloria's eye. Lara, with a group of fellow students from the tourism college, the Royal Crescent in Bath behind them, grey English skies above them. Lara stood out, even in a group shot like this one. She'd always had a certain presence, even in a photo.

Gloria had tried to describe Lara and Harriet to Kevin once. He had a memory of them as children and teenagers but not as adults, as they were now. Gloria had tried to use words that would give Kevin more of a picture. He already knew that Harriet had dark hair and those big brown eyes that all the Turner children had, and that Lara was blonde, with eyes halfway between blue and grey. She'd thought about it for a moment.

'Harriet's still all movement, you know, she laughs easily and she uses her hands when she speaks, and she's eager. Do you remember the way she was as a child, wanting to be helpful and look after people? But still ready for mischief at the same time? And the way she would follow Austin around, like a little sorcerer's apprentice?'

Kevin smiled. 'That's right, so she did. Lara did too, didn't she? He had a harem even back then. And what about Lara now? What's she like?'

That had taken more thought. Gloria started hesitantly. 'Lara is . . . she's like a gum tree.' She laughed at her own description. 'That's flattering for her, isn't it?'

'There are hundreds of different species of gum trees, aren't there? Which one do you mean?'

'Oh, aren't you the expert. She's like a particular type of gum tree. Do you remember out on the north road, Kev, the Melbourne road? There was that old farmhouse with a group of trees planted to the side of it, a whole collection of them, and there was that one on its own?'

Kevin was nodding.

'She's like one of those gum trees. Those slender grey ones that just sway in the wind, even when it's blowing a gale. That stand out, even in the middle of other trees. That's what Lara is like.'

Gloria looked at Lara's photo again and invoked Penny, as she had often done since she had died. She hadn't heard any answer yet, but it was still a comfort to talk to her old friend. She missed Penny and Neil very much. She missed the old days of Turner Travel too. Penny had joked one day that the agency was like a hippy commune, with the three Turners and Lara in and out from the adjoining house every day, and Gloria's three boys calling in after school until hanging around an office lost out against surfing and playing football. All three of Gloria's sons now lived in Melbourne, married with families of their own, but they still felt comfortable enough to call in, help themselves to tea or coffee, sit behind one of the desks, as if it was their family business as well. Penny had known all about Gloria's three boys in the same way Gloria knew all there was to know about Penny and Neil's family. More than she had wanted to know sometimes . . .

'Is it about her parents, Penny?' she said softly. 'Is that where she's gone?'

Still no answer.

'Gloria?' Melissa's loud voice cut into her thoughts. Gloria winced. If only it was possible to turn down her volume sometimes. If only it was possible to make her disappear sometimes. If only it had been possible for James to have met someone else he wanted to marry . . .

'Gloria? I've got James on the line. He wants you to fill him in.' The voice, even louder. 'Gloria?'

'Coming.' She turned from the photo board and walked out into the main office again.

Chapter Seven

The noise of planes coming in to land at the nearby airport woke Harriet before seven o'clock. She'd slept fitfully, but enough to set her up for the day, she hoped. She threw open the curtain and got her first daylight glimpse of England. The hotel was for business or international travellers like themselves, not far from the airport, on the edge of a village. Harriet was looking out over green fields, all so neat, with trimmed hedgerows on each boundary. There was a smattering of daffodils here and there. The sky was blue, but a watery, soft blue. She'd left autumn leaves and changeable skies behind her in Australia.

She fiddled with the window lever and pushed it open as far as it would go. There was the smell of bacon frying. She must be near the kitchen vents. She could hear traffic sounds from the nearby motorway. But she could also hear birds, snatches of conversation and surely that was the sound of a lamb or sheep? She heard an Australian accent and leaned forward. Yes, it was two of the group, chatting as they took a pre-breakfast stroll. It was a good sign that they were up so early.

An image of Lara came into her mind. She'd been her first thought on waking. Where was she at that moment? Waking up in a hotel somewhere else? With someone? On her own? Happy? Unhappy? If Lara had been at the airport as planned, what would the two of them have been doing now? Would they have been sitting here in Harriet's room, going through the itinerary together, as James had imagined? Laughing? Would they have swapped stories of tours they'd been on, the way they used to do? Once upon a time, perhaps. Not now. Harriet knew they wouldn't have been able to. There would have been too much wariness. Too much tension humming between them.

She heard Austin's voice in her mind, telling her to leave Lara to him, to concentrate on the tour. He was right. Her job this week was to make sure the tour group and Patrick Shawcross had everything they needed, wanted, or thought they needed or wanted.

She checked her watch. Time to get dressed and then go to the breakfast room and greet the tour party. She opened the closet and took out her uniform, glad to see any creases had fallen out overnight. She could hear Melissa's voice, extolling the fabric's virtues. She had produced samples at one of the meetings, passing them around the table. 'It'll make a difference for all of us,' she said. 'It's not only convenient to have a uniform, but time-saving too. I'm assured the material is virtually uncreasable and uncrushable.'

'Not to mention unspeakable,' Austin had muttered.

Harriet dressed quickly, pulling on the stockings, skirt, shirt, jacket and the scarf, which was patterned with dozens of tiny versions of the Turner Travel winged suitcase logo. Melissa insisted they added a jaunty yet feminine touch. She looked at herself in the mirror for the briefest possible time, cursing Melissa yet again for her choice of colour, fabric and style. Harriet was slim from all the swimming she did, but the design couldn't have been less flattering. Even Lara looked awful in this outfit. The only person it suited was, astonishingly, Melissa. She had the right trim little body, blonde hair and brown skin that the style and colour needed.

The day she produced the uniforms, Melissa had made a speech about how proud Mr and Mrs Turner would have been of them all, for keeping things going, for making the Turner Travel name live on. Harriet had wanted to stand up to her, to make her admit that all of these expansion plans were nothing to do with her memories of Mr and Mrs Turner and everything to do with Melissa's own ambitions. But she'd said nothing. It had been too hard to put up a fight against Melissa's bulldozer tactics when she felt as fragile as a paper doll, as if one tiny puff of aggression, argument, even a strong opinion from Melissa, from anybody, would send her spiralling, fluttering into the sky, never to be seen again.

But not any more. She turned away from the mirror. That was the old her. She had to try and forget about that uncertain Harriet, and find the Harriet who had loved being on tour, who had faced any problems, dealt with difficult groups, managed anything that was thrown at her. She knew exactly what she needed to help her confidence. She reached for her bag, opened her purse and took out a small envelope. Even holding it in her hand helped her feel better.

Gloria had given it to her. She had come into the Turner Travel office late one night, a month after Harriet had discharged herself from hospital. She'd found Harriet at her desk, not working, just staring at the screen, her eyes filled with tears. Gloria had said nothing at first, just come over and taken her in her arms, holding her tight.

'What is it, lovie?' she'd asked. 'Tell me.'

'I can't do it, Gloria. James asked me again if I could lead one of the tours and I told him I'd think about it, but I know I can't do it. I'm going to have to tell him tomorrow. I'll have to leave. Resign. It's not fair on everyone else – him, Melissa, Lara, you.'

'It's a family business, lovie. I don't think you can resign from your family.'

'You know what I mean. I can't keep asking everyone to carry me like this.'

'Why can't you? If your family can't carry you when things are tough, then who can?'

'We're not a normal family.'

Gloria smiled. 'No, I'll grant you that.'

'We're a business family, I mean. That changes everything.'

'You're a family before you're a business. That will never change.' Gloria glanced at the itinerary on the desk in front of her. 'This is the one James has asked you to consider?'

Harriet nodded.

Gloria read through it quickly. 'It's one you've done before. Only two nights away, only ten in the group.'

'But I wouldn't be able to look after them properly, Gloria, I know I wouldn't. All I keep seeing is things going wrong and people dying and bad things happening to everyone.'

'Then it's too soon for you and you shouldn't go. It's as simple as that, Harriet. There's no rush, is there? James just asked you if you were ready, didn't he? He didn't put any pressure on you?' She looked closely. 'Don't tell me. Melissa is putting pressure on you.'

'Melissa's thinking about the business, I know. And she is trying to be kind . . .'

'Kind? Perhaps, though I'm not sure she knows what the word means.'

'But she's right. I have got ground to make up. I know I ruined that group's holiday. Embarrassed the company —'

'You did not embarrass the company. And Melissa is out of line telling you you ruined that group's holiday.' She held up her hand.

'No, perhaps she didn't say it in so many words, but I know what she's inferred. I've got a large pair of flapping ears, remember. Harriet, you probably made those people's holiday. Think of the stories they've been able to tell. It's not every day a tour guide —'

'Cracks up?'

'Has a breakdown. Don't make it sound worse than it was. You had anxiety attacks and then you had a breakdown. Harriet, you have to be more gentle on yourself. You have been through a bad time. Losing one parent is hard; losing both within weeks of each other is even more traumatic, especially the way it happened for you. Of course you had to react to it.'

Just the mention of it . . . 'I miss them so much, Gloria. Everywhere I look, everything I think about —'

'I know you do, lovie. We all do. But that's all right, we're allowed to. You loved them very much. Of course you should miss them.'

'But James and Austin loved them and miss them and they didn't crack up, did they? They lost their parents too. Lara lost them. Molly lost her grandparents. You lost your oldest friends. You all miss them as much as I do.'

'But there's no rule book saying we all have to react in the same way. We've all been affected too. I talk to your mother the whole time, did you know that? First sign of madness, but it helps me. James has thrown himself completely into work. Austin has been touring non-stop, taking any job going, hardly been home. Lara only applied for that overseas study course after Penny and Neil died. She never even mentioned going to England before that. That's how everyone else is coping. In their own way.'

Harriet sat silently.

Gloria squeezed her hand. 'Harriet, what happened to you is

completely understandable. And it doesn't matter whether it happened in public with a tour group or alone; what you felt was what you felt. No wonder you feel scared. No wonder your world feels unsteady and scary and uncertain. But it will change, I promise.'

'It won't, though, will it? It can't.'

'No, your parents won't come back but you won't always feel as bad as you do now. And all the solid things you had, and all the things you were able to face before this happened won't have changed. You are still you, underneath the fear and the panic attacks. You just need to believe in yourself again.'

'I'm too scared of everything, Gloria. I feel like I'll never be able to manage anything again.'

'But you will, Harriet. Not yet but one day. I've known you since you were just a little girl. I've seen for myself all the things you know how to do. Do you want me to remind you? No, tell you what, you remind me instead.'

'What do you mean?'

'Tell me some things you can do. Can you drive a car, for example?'

That brought a faint smile. 'You don't remember teaching me? After Mum and Dad gave up?' They'd tried to teach her and Lara the year they turned seventeen but the combination of a parent sitting beside her and a constantly stalling or kangaroo-hopping car had left Harriet helpless with giggles during each lesson. Eventually Gloria had stepped in. Harriet and Lara had managed to pass their tests on the same day.

'How could I forget? The day I got my first grey hair.' Gloria reached over the desk for a pen and paper and passed them to her. 'Come on now. Remind me of some other things you've done. Write them down so you can't forget.'

Harriet's mind seemed blank. 'I can't think of anything else.'

'Well, that's nonsense for a start. You got dressed this morning by the looks of things. Unless you've started sleeping in the beautiful uniform Melissa chose for us, have you?'

Harriet smiled properly that time. 'No, wearing it for eight hours a day is bad enough.'

'Write it down, then. *I can dress myself*. No, not good enough? Will I help you remember some better things?'

Harriet looked up at Gloria's so-familiar face, her sun-worn skin, her clever eyes, her mop of grey hair. She couldn't remember a time without Gloria. She'd come to Gloria for years, bringing news, asking questions, seeking comfort, liking being around her and her husband Kevin almost as much as her own parents. 'You're my extra mother, aren't you, Gloria?' she'd said to her once as a child. The thought sent a ripple of that grief through her again. And guilt, for calling on Gloria again. Time after time. 'Gloria, I shouldn't be keeping you. Kev will be worrying where you are.'

'Kev knows very well that if I'm not home responding to his every whim and at his beck and call then I am here in the office. He'll cope. Absence makes the heart grow fonder. Now, don't change the subject. Tell me something else you've done or know how to do.'

Slowly Gloria coaxed a list of things out of her, with difficulty at first, and then eventually even through some laughter. They were written in no particular order, here and there over the page.

I have worked and supported myself for more than fifteen years. I am buying my own house. I have travelled all around Australia. I have led hundreds of tour groups. I can touch type. I know how to cook Thai food, Italian food and Malaysian food, make jam, chutney, and tomato sauce. I have grown my own tomatoes, sweet corn, parsley, coriander and pumpkins. I once made dinner for ten people on a camp fire. I can drive a car and a tractor and, in an emergency, a minibus. I know how to replace a fanbelt, change a tyre and put up tents. I can row a boat. I once killed a snake. I can almost surf. I can swim thirty metres underwater. I taught my niece Molly to swim thirty metres underwater. I can say hello and how are you in German, French, Spanish, Japanese, Italian and Dutch.

'Now we're getting somewhere,' Gloria said. 'More please. What else have you done?'

'I lived with Simon for four years. Is that an achievement?'

Gloria's lip twitched. 'Depends on what you thought of Simon, I suppose. I liked him. So did Lara, I think.'

'Then you were the only ones who did. Mum and Dad were only polite to him, I know. James barely noticed him and Austin hated him.'

'Your parents thought he was a fine young man who should have asked you to marry him, not live with him. James has barely noticed anyone since he barricaded himself behind Melissa and Molly. And of course Austin hated Simon. He's always guarded you like a hawk. You and Lara, actually. In any case, Simon was too ordinary for Austin. Too ordinary for you, too, I always thought.'

'Too ordinary?'

Gloria nodded. 'I'm not putting him down. But he wanted less out of life than you do. And he'll be much happier with that new girlfriend of his. You know the word is they're about to get engaged?'

Harriet nodded. She'd heard. All she'd felt was glad that Simon was happy again. She hadn't had any pangs at all.

'In fact, Harriet, difficult as it was for you, I'm glad you broke up with him.'

'You never said that before.'

'It wasn't my place. I'm the faithful old family servant. Silent and loyal.'

'Silent?'

Gloria winked. 'Don't change the subject. Go on, add Simon to the list. He's part of your life. I want you to write down all the big things you've done. In fact, let me remind you of another big one. You welcomed Lara into your family. You made another little girl feel wanted when she was probably feeling the way you are feeling now, scared and alone. That was a very important thing to have done and you did it. Not only shared your bedroom and your friends with her, but also shared your parents and your brothers. I was very proud of the way you did that.'

Harriet opened her mouth as if she was about to say something and then shut it again.

Gloria kept talking, leaning over and taking back the list. 'I'll write it for you. *I welcomed Lara into the family*. There. And that's just for starters, Harriet. All true, and none of it has changed. You've done all those things. You will be able to do those things and more again.'

Harriet tried to make light of it, embarrassed now. 'I'd rather not kill a snake again, if it's all the same to you. It was a bit messy.'

Gloria smiled at her. 'That's fine. No snakes.'

'And I don't know if I'll ever live with anyone again.'

'No, I'd say you'll end up on the shelf. Poor Harriet, condemned to a life as Austin's housekeeper.' Gloria folded the piece of paper, reached over for a small envelope and put it inside. 'Stop that nonsense as well. You'll meet a man when you're good and ready and when he's the right man for you. Now, keep that list. Use that as a reminder if you ever feel an attack coming on. It might help.'

Harriet leaned across and gave Gloria a hug. 'Thank you, silent and faithful family servant.'

'You're welcome, sweetheart.'

'How have you put up with us all these years? Don't you ever get Turner overload?'

'Not yet. I'll let you know if I do. You're like a spare family to me, you see. When my own three boys used to drive me crazy I pretended you lot were mine. You've actually been quite a comfort over the years.'

Harriet had come in the next day with the biggest bunch of flowers she could get from the Merryn Bay florist. She hadn't made a fuss, simply got a vase and put them on Gloria's desk.

'What's this about?' Melissa had said, sounding a little put out that she hadn't been informed. 'It's not her birthday, is it?'

'No, it's National Thank Her for Everything Day,' Harriet had said.

Gloria had just smiled. 'Any time, lovie,' she whispered.

Harriet read the list again now. It didn't always work, but most of the time it did. It was like a voice of reason when everything threatened to overwhelm her. She could almost hear Gloria's voice. 'One more thing to add, Harriet. Go on. *I led the tour group from Melbourne to Bristol via Malaysia*. You did it and nothing went wrong.' She'd rung Gloria the night James had asked her to take on the tour. She had been just as calm then. 'Of course you can do it, Harriet. You're more than ready.' Gloria was right. Austin was right. She could do this tour. Nothing would go wrong. She was going to manage. All she had to do was remember all the things she'd done before: driven a bus, killed a snake, cooked over a camp fire, changed a tyre . . . She stopped there, and actually laughed out loud. No need to get too carried away. She was here to be a tour guide not a stuntwoman, after all.

She put the list back into her bag and did as she had been taught to do every morning – took a chair by the window, sat herself neatly, straight backed, feet together on the floor, arms by her side, not clenched in front of her. Eyes shut, breathing slowly, deeply . . .

Her eyes snapped open once, as she realised she still had to confirm the tour bus. She forced herself to close her eyes again. Back to the breathing. Keep the mind clear. Five minutes later she was ready. Only then did she ring the tour bus company. It was too early to ring the office, so she rang the emergency mobile number listed. A weary-sounding woman answered. Yes, she said, the bus was booked. Yes, the driver knew which hotel to collect them from. Yes, he was one of their most experienced drivers, Mr Clive Tillon, who had done many group tours over the years. Everything was under control. She'd just hung up when she remembered another question. She dialled the bus company again. Yes, the woman confirmed, now sounding more cranky than weary, the bus was fully equipped with a microphone, guide's seat and video player.

A news jingle played from the radio beside the bed, followed by a deep-voiced man announcing the news headlines from the BBC. Harriet checked her watch was telling the right time. Turner Travel rule number seven. Yes, eight-thirty. A good time to ring Patrick Shawcross in St Ives and welcome him to Cornwall. She was about to ring his hotel when she remembered she hadn't checked the number of seats on their tour bus. She dialled the bus company's mobile number again, confirming quickly that the bus that would be arriving shortly was a sixteen-seater. She hung up and rang the St Ives hotel next, introducing herself and asking to be put through to Mr Patrick Shawcross's room.

'Of course, Ms Turner. We're looking forward to welcoming you and your party here later today. One moment please.' There was silence, then the soft burr of the dial tone, over and over, until the call switched back to reception.

'I'm sorry, there doesn't seem to be any answer. Can I take a message?'

'Yes, please. If you could just say I called, and that we'll be on our way to him shortly?'

'Of course, oh, excuse me,' Harriet waited as she heard the receptionist have a brief conversation. 'Ms Turner, my colleague spoke to him briefly this morning. She said he was on his way down to the beach. Are you sure I can't get him to call you when he comes back?'

'No, that's fine,' she said. 'If you could tell him everything's fine and I'm looking forward to meeting him this afternoon.'

Harriet didn't think her first conversation with him should be over a mobile phone on the bus. She had a bit of explaining to do. James had told her they would fax the actor's agency with the change of details, explaining that it would be Harriet Turner and Lara Robinson he would be travelling with, but now that had changed as well. It wasn't a conversation she wanted to have with him in front of the group. Not when there was every chance Mrs Lamerton would snatch the phone out of her hands and pass it around to everyone.

She had overheard them in the minibus from the airport the evening before. They were a-twitter, there was no other word for it, at the idea of meeting Patrick Shawcross. Mrs Lamerton was making it clear she considered him her property. It had been her idea for the *Willoughby* tour, after all. Harriet half-expected Mrs Lamerton to have that line tattooed on her forehead or made into a T-shirt slogan. It would save her repeating it over and over again. 'As I mentioned to Lara when I first mooted the idea of this *Willoughby* tour.' 'When we first started planning this *Willoughby* tour . . .' She reeled off facts about Patrick Shawcross like a *Mastermind* contestant. 'Born in Penzance, you know. The only son of Irish parents. That would explain those Celtic good looks,' she'd gushed. 'Originally wanted to be a dentist – a dentist!' Mrs Lamerton had trilled. 'Imagine the queues to get into that surgery!' He'd been talent spotted in a college amateur dramatics society staging of *Macbeth*. Appeared in three episodes of *Doctor Who*. Brief marriage to Caitlin Moore, a Welsh actress, no children. Second marriage to Alicia de Vries, one stepson. He'd played the part in *Willoughby* for the two series before the show was axed. None of the women in the group seemed too up-to-date with him after that. They didn't seem to care much, either. Their attention had turned to other favourite TV programs.

'I always liked that Richard Briers,' Mrs Pollard said. 'Something kind-faced about him. He'd bring you a cup of tea in bed each morning, I bet.'

'No, too easy to boss around if you ask me,' Mrs Hart said. 'I liked the one in *Yes, Minister*, what was his name? Geoffrey someone? Or was it Nigel?'

'Sir Humphrey, do you mean? No, too sarcastic. And you'd never see him, all those long hours he'd have to work. Wasn't he in another program too? You know, the one set in that hobby farm?'

'No, that was Richard Briers as well, wasn't it? With that blonde lady with the sweet voice? Felicity Kendal?'

'She was voted Rear of the Year, you know.' Mr Fidock interjected.

Mrs Lamerton ignored him. 'Aren't you thinking of *To the Manor Born*? That was Penelope Keith, wasn't it?'

'No, that was *The Good Life*. What about that pretty American waitress in that one about the hotel? The one with John Cleese and Prunella Scales?'

'Fawlty Towers, you mean? Harriet, will we be able to see the hotel in Torquay from *Fawlty Towers*? St Ives isn't that far from Torquay, is it?'

She'd done her best to explain that as far as she knew the hotel didn't actually exist, but certainly, if it turned out they had time, she'd see what they could do.

She made sure she was downstairs in time to greet the party and do a headcount as they came into the breakfast room. Several years before, James had done a count of one of his parties – a sixteen-strong group, average age seventy, exploring the sights of Sydney – and realised one was missing. After checking the foyer, the car park and the lounge room of the hotel they were staying in, he'd finally asked at reception for a spare key to check the room. The missing man had been found in his bed. Dead, unfortunately. Natural causes, the doctor had declared. Since then, all the Turners had been very particular about their morning headcounts. Harriet was pleased to see all her twelve had survived the night. They were, in fact, looking quite bright-eyed this morning. She moved quickly from table to table, hearing a complaint or two about lumpy pillows, and assuring them the pillows in the St Ives hotel would be far superior and if they weren't she'd do her best to get first-class replacements.

Three times in five minutes she was asked if she was absolutely sure Mr Shawcross would be waiting for them in St Ives. They had obviously been more shaken up by Lara's non-appearance the evening before than she had realised. 'Yes, I've called the hotel and he arrived safely last night,' she told them. 'He's there waiting for us right now.'

'And how is he?' Mrs Lamerton asked, practically elbowing her way across the room to Harriet. 'Did he sound excited about the tour?'

She didn't think it right to tell them she hadn't spoken to him in person. She nodded and smiled, hoping that wasn't quite a lie, then moved purposefully out into the foyer before they had an opportunity to ask any more difficult questions. A bus pulled up in front of the glass double doors. Renwick Hire. Their bus.

The driver's door swung open and a small, tanned man jumped out, wearing a khaki shirt, khaki shorts, long white socks up to his knees and very white shoes. He strolled in, blew a kiss to the receptionist then turned in Harriet's direction. As he came closer, she guessed he was probably in his mid-fifties. Not much more than five foot four in height. She stepped forward and held out her hand. 'Clive Tillon? Hello, I'm Harriet, from Turner Travel.'

He shook it. His grip was tight. 'You're the nervy one who's been ringing the office all morning?'

Her voice faltered. 'That's right.'

'Leave it to me, now, love. There's nothing I don't know about the roads around here, or buses, so if anyone is to do any worrying, it's me. So fill me in. What have we got here? How many and what for?'

'I beg your pardon?'

'It's a tour group, isn't it? We do dozens of them, everything from walkers to TV fans. What's our poison this time?' He peered past her shoulder, into the area of the foyer where her group was assembling. 'That your lot? The oldies? It'll be a nostalgia trip then, I suppose? A trip down memory lane before a trip to the cemetery?' He gave a monkeyish laugh, showing a row of very white teeth.

Harriet wasn't used to bus drivers taking an interest in the tours.

On the ones she'd run in Australia, the driver usually started yawning when he met the group, yawned all the way through, dozed at the wheel while they did any sightseeing, and yet somehow still managed to form an alliance with at least one of the women on the trip, often two. It was a travel industry phenomenon, Gloria had remarked once. Bus drivers were notorious lady-killers. She was convinced it had something to do with the uniform.

Clive barely reached her shoulder and his uniform was for a man a size or two bigger, so she wondered would it work its magic this time. She tried to imagine Mrs Lamerton clutching him to her breast ('Clive. Oh, my Clive') and failed. He was still waiting for an explanation of the trip.

'We're a tour group from Australia,' she said. 'We're visiting the locations of a TV series called *Willoughby*.'

He frowned. 'That one about the postman? Solving crimes? From years ago?'

'That's right. Are you a fan yourself?' She brightened. It would be a real help if the driver knew some of the episodes.

He made a snorting sound. 'Biggest load of rubbish I ever saw. All the actors were terrible, none of the plots made sense and when's a postman going to find the time to solve crimes? There's a lot more to delivering mail than pushing bundles of letters into slots, you know. It's all systems, organisation. My brother worked as a postman for a while, and the stories he used to tell. I didn't know the half of it until he told me. It's a science, dividing up the regions, the way they place the bundles in the bag, so they're in the right order geographically. Think about it – what did you say your name was?'

'Harriet.'

'Think about it, Harriet. You post a letter in, let's say here in

Bristol, and it has to be in London by the next day, and somehow it is. It gets there. In pristine condition, too. That's a science.' He stopped. 'What's with the gear by the way? You in fancy dress?'

They both looked down at her clothes. Her bright yellow skirt and shirt. Her bright yellow stockings. Her yellow scarf. Every single inch of it was a glaring shade of the colour. Melissa's idea again. She'd read a study that it would stand out best against all other colours in an airport. She was right. Harriet had a feeling it would be visible from the moon. 'It's the Turner Travel uniform.'

'You look like Big Bird.'

He was right, she realised in horror.

He must have seen something in her expression. He gave her several hard pats on her yellow-sleeved arm. 'Don't take it as an insult, love, will you? That's just my way. I say it as I see it. Now then, let's get this show on the road and have a look at all of this.' As he spoke he started rifling through the notes in the folder he was holding. 'Are you it from the tour company? I thought there was going to be two of you?'

She nodded. 'There was. But there's been —' What? 'A change of plan. I'm in charge on my own for now.'

He whistled between his teeth. 'That's a shame. Easier on everyone if you can share the burden and believe me, I know what I'm talking about. I've done dozens of these elderly group tours. By the time the fights start, and the moaners start moaning away, you'll wish you could swap places with me, at the wheel, my own boss. That's not even taking into account the possibility of one of them dropping dead, or having a heart attack. I said all that to your colleague, what's her name, Lara? When she rang last week to check a few details. Some story about your brother falling off a roof and you coming instead, was that it? I thought she was bad enough, until we got all your calls this morning. You two need to relax.'

'You spoke to Lara last week? On the phone?'

'No, love, via morse code. Of course on the phone.'

She ignored his sarcasm. 'And how did she sound?'

He shrugged. 'Like an Australian girl sounds on the phone. Why? Who should she have sounded like? Gina Lollobrigida?' He made the snickery monkey-laugh sound again.

Harriet was conscious that Mrs Lamerton was approaching again. She lowered her voice. 'She didn't sound worried about anything?'

'No? Why, what did she have to be worried about?'

'Harriet, good morning again.' The imperious voice, right behind her.

Harriet turned. 'Hello again, Mrs Lamerton.'

Mrs Lamerton was wearing a flowered dress that fitted a little too snugly over her matronly frame. She favoured bright nylon dresses, generally decorated with bold patterns of flowers, and underpinned by what she must surely have called foundation garments. Her bosom was remarkable, there was no other word to describe it, though Austin had suggested one or two rude alternatives over the years. She was also wearing one of her brooches. She had a wide selection of them, most of which depicted large insects, such as grasshoppers or ladybirds, their colours picked out in glass stones. Today there was a gold spider with emerald eyes and a matching emerald stone at the end of each of its eight legs pinned to her left shoulder. It made quite a contrast to the poppies decorating the fabric of her dress.

'Still no sign of Lara, I see.' As she spoke, Mrs Lamerton was fingering the corners of her mouth, checking for lipstick residue.

Harriet wondered if she should tell her there was a mark of her too-red lipstick on her front teeth. She decided against it. 'I'm afraid not.'

Clive ignored Mrs Lamerton and spoke directly to Harriet. 'She's looking for her too? Who is this Lara? Lord Lucan's daughter?' Another cackle and another flash of the white teeth.

Mrs Lamerton gave Clive a haughty glare, before Harriet hurriedly introduced them. Mrs Lamerton's manner defrosted. The uniform working its magic again, Harriet realised. 'Lara and I formulated the *Willoughby* tour together and I am greatly puzzled, and still unsatisfied, as to why she isn't here. In fact, it's a disappointment. I thought she would have put the tour first, before any other commitments that may have arisen.'

'That's a good point. So where is she then?' Clive looked back and forth between the two of them.

Harriet felt like glaring at him. With his brown skin and brown eyes he suddenly reminded her of a monkey. A nosy monkey. 'She unfortunately couldn't make it. Something else came up. At the last minute.' She couldn't say they didn't know where she'd gone or what had happened. 'I think it had something to do with the tourism course she's doing in Bath.'

'Bath's only a couple of hours from St Ives,' Clive said. 'She could nip over and join us when she's finished, couldn't she?'

Now the pair of them were staring her down. Harriet tried to stand her ground. 'That might be unlikely. She asked me to apologise on her behalf.'

'So you've spoken to her?' Mrs Lamerton leapt at the news.

'Not exactly. She left a message.'

That tchy sound again.

'Well, it all sounds queer to me,' Clive said cheerfully. 'Come on then, Mrs Lamerton. First here, first served, let me help you on to the bus.'

'I'm sure I can manage.'

'Of course you can. I'm just looking for an excuse to put my arm around you.'

Once again, Mrs Lamerton surprised Harriet with a girlish giggle. Perhaps her fantasy of Mrs Lamerton clutching Clive to her chest wasn't that far-fetched, she thought, as she watched them head for the pile of luggage.

Chapter Eight

By one o'clock the tour party was only halfway along the coast road from Bristol to St Ives.

It had taken Harriet nearly an hour to get everyone onto the bus. Mrs Lamerton had been first, settling herself into the front seat with a loud sigh. Harriet had been reminded of a large cruise ship docking. Mrs Pollard had been next. It had taken two people, one in front pulling and one behind giving her a gentle push, to get her up the steep steps. As she said loudly several times, it wasn't that she was overweight, it was more her problems with the arthritis. Mr and Mrs Douglas – the only couple on the tour, and keen world travellers – insisted on trying out every seat on the bus before settling on a pair right in the middle, the first ones they'd tried. In the Turner Travel office, Mr Douglas was known as Mr Been – as in Been There Done That. He had a fund of stories and they had all heard most of them, several times over. It was Gloria who had first noticed his habit of getting his words mixed up. Since then, an unofficial competition had been underway for the best Mr Douglas-ism. Harriet's personal favourite had been his account of a safari trip to Kruger National Park in South Africa.

'There we were,' he'd told them as he leaned over the office counter, 'sitting on a rocky outcrust, looking at the wilmerbees.'

As she listened now, she heard him and his wife talking to Mr Fidock in the seat behind them.

'You've got a bit of a cold, love, haven't you?' Mr Douglas was saying, patting his wife on the arm. 'She often picks up a cold on these long-haul flights, don't you, pet? We'll have to stop off at a chemist, get a few of those euthanasia tablets for you.'

'Echinacea, dear,' Mrs Douglas absently corrected.

Harriet smiled a welcome at the last few members of the group as they made their way onto the bus. Miss Talbot, dressed in denim, carrying a bag in the shape of a heart. Mrs Biggins, who'd undertaken five conquer-your-fear-of-flying courses in the past two months so she could come on the tour. Mrs Pennefeather and her twin sister Mrs Hart, both widows. They did two Turner Travel tours together every year. They also did a lot of whispering and giggling. Mrs Kempton – married to one of Mrs Lamerton's cousins, and another long-time fan of the *Willoughby* series – came aboard next, followed by Mrs Randall. She smiled shyly at Harriet as she took her seat. All the Turners knew her, too. She was famously quiet. Austin called her Rowdy Randall.

The last to arrive was Miss Boyd. She had read about the *Willoughby* tour in the local paper six months previously and had phoned Turner Travel almost daily since. She was on and settled within moments, practically swinging herself on board and then proceeding to start sucking noisily on a barley sugar to stop herself getting 'travel-motion sickness' as she called it. The noise reminded Mrs Kempton that she had an awful feeling she had left her supply of anti-travel sickness tablets on the cupboard beside her bed upstairs.

'Or perhaps I packed them, Harriet, do you think? Would I be able to check in my luggage?'

Harriet had already seen Clive load the last of the luggage into the compartment, heaving Mr Fidock's bag on top of the large pile. She just knew that Mrs Kempton's case would be right at the back. There really wasn't time to unload and check, not if they wanted to keep to their schedule.

'Could I offer you one of my anti-nausea tablets, Mrs Kempton?' she asked. James had insisted she take the company's large first-aid kit with her. He'd phoned through a detailed tour of the contents the morning she left. If the plane had crashed on a desert island Harriet had enough knowledge and supplies to open a small hospital. 'I'm told they're the best on the market. I'm sure they'll do the trick if you do start to feel queasy.'

'No, mine are a special brand,' Mrs Kempton said, looking teary. 'From a Chinese doctor.'

Behind her, Clive was hefting himself up into the bus and caught the last few words. 'Not into that herbal medicine business, are you? A man I know did that, spent all his time boiling up bags of sticks and leaves. The house stunk of it.'

Harriet shot him a look. 'That's fine, Clive, thanks. I'm sure Mrs Kempton is happy with her doctor and her tablets.'

'Could I please check in my bag, Harriet?' Mrs Kempton asked. 'Or could someone check upstairs for me? Just in case I left them behind. I've been getting forgetful of late.'

Clive was watching with interest, arms folded, leaning against the driver's seat. 'One tablet is like another, you know. It's probably a placebo, or whatever the Chinese word for that is. Made from sugar or something. Not that sugar helps motion sickness. It just gives you something to do with your mouth, rather than think about getting sick. I read a study last year that —'

'Clive, please.'

'Just trying to help.'

Harriet herself had gone back into the hotel, explained the situation, been given the key to Mrs Kempton's room and, to her great relief, found her Chinese pills on the bedside table. She also found a pair of spectacles in the bathroom, a raincoat in her wardrobe, her book (a James Herriot novel) on the floor, and an umbrella on the hook on the back of the door.

Back on board, Harriet took the microphone and, after one false start with the on switch, welcomed everyone, urging them to settle back and enjoy the scenery or doze, whatever they liked. James had made a handwritten suggestion in brackets on her itinerary (*You could sing 'We're All Going on a Summer Holiday' to get everyone in the mood.*) Yes, or she could just smile and sit down as quickly as possible. A bad poem at the airport was one thing. She didn't want to break the bus windows with her singing. She switched off the microphone.

The itinerary for the first day was deliberately light, with brief stops at just two of the *Willoughby* locations en route to St Ives. Harriet knew there had been a lot of discussion in the Turner Travel office about how to plan the trip, taking into account the age of the group. The number one concern of elderly travellers was getting enough to eat and drink, and their number one pet hate was packing and unpacking every day or two. She remembered Lara suggesting they base themselves in St Ives, which was not just beautiful but also where Willoughby had lived in the series.

'We can do day trips from there, all over Cornwall,' she'd suggested during her presentation. 'The distances aren't great, and that way our clients won't get too exhausted.'

Harriet felt a tap on her shoulder. It was Mrs Lamerton, sitting squatly in the first seat again, with her bags piled on the seat beside her.

'Harriet, have you decided yet where Mr Shawcross will be sitting each day? When we're doing our bus tours?'

She realised then why Mrs Lamerton was sitting in that seat and also why the seat beside her was piled high with bags and scarves. 'I don't really know yet, Mrs Lamerton. I suppose I thought I'd leave it up to him.'

Miss Talbot leaned over from the adjoining row. 'But he will move around, won't he? He won't sit in the same seat each day?'

Mrs Pollard leaned forward too. 'Yes, we'll all get a go at sitting next to him, won't we?'

'Are you ladies fighting over that actor? A bit young for you all, isn't he?' It was Clive, loud from the driver's seat. He turned back, taking advantage of the fact they were stopped at a red light. 'If you're looking for a bit of action, I'm right here. Much fitter than I look, too. You wouldn't mind, Big Bird, would you? All part of the service, heh heh heh.'

Miss Talbot gasped. Miss Boyd gave a giggle. Harriet realised she had to put her foot down. 'Thank you for that, Clive. Perhaps you could concentrate on the road and keep your comments to yourself?' She winced inside at her prim school-mistress tone.

He shrugged. 'Who is this Shawcross bloke anyway? A local fella, is he?'

He couldn't have asked a more welcome question. As a chorus of voices sent information to the front of the bus about his birth in Penzance, his Irish parents, his plans for dentistry, Harriet took the opportunity to put down the itinerary and take in the scenery instead.

Beyond the traffic and the motorway, the fields were very green, with neat, trimmed hedges around them, cows and sheep grazing, daffodils in clusters underneath trees. April was a good time to be here. The sky was blue, the air crisp. The light was softer than she was used to in Australia.

They passed a house called Owl Cottage; farm shops selling cider, vegetables, strawberries and clotted cream; signposts for villages called Chapel Allerton, Bradley Green, Wootton Courtenay. Everything looked so English. As they drove further down the coast towards Cornwall the scenery was becoming wilder, higher cliffs and sweeping bays instead of the neat fields and small farms of Devon. Harriet was waiting for some rush of recognition, some feeling that she was in her ancestral homeland, but so far it hadn't come. Not that her parents were from this side of the country. Her father had been born in Manchester, her mother in Leeds, with both their families coincidentally moving to Watford when they were children. They had been childhood sweethearts. They'd gone to school there, married there, and had James and Austin there, before making the decision to emigrate to Australia, where Harriet had been born.

She had addresses if she wanted to see where her parents had lived back then. She wasn't sure how she felt about that yet. The previous year James and Melissa had made a trip to the UK, and James had visited all the family places. He'd been planning on doing it again at the end of the *Willoughby* tour, as well, when he had a few spare days. It was different for him, though. He had childhood memories of Watford, even one or two schoolfriends that he'd looked up. Harriet tried to imagine standing outside the house where her parents had lived. It would be one more reminder that they were gone from her life, a reminder of all the gaps in her knowledge of them, as well. It had been a whole new hurt, a new layer to her grief, when she realised there were things about them, about her own history, that she would now never know. All those years she could have asked them about their early years in England, or why they had emigrated, or the early days in the migrant hostel, and she had never thought of it. Now they were gone, she would have given anything to ask them thousands of questions, to hear every tiny detail of their lives. She had taken the addresses from James, murmured something about thinking about it and then pushed them to the bottom of her bag.

She wondered if Lara had made any plans to return to her own parents' home places. Harriet didn't know a great deal about Lara's mother and father. She'd only met them once, when she was little. She remembered overhearing discussions about them over the years, and the yearly memorial day her mother had instigated to help Lara get over losing them so tragically like that, but it was all shadowy. She knew a few vague facts, that Mr and Mrs Robinson had left for Australia from Watford under that same 'Ten Pound Poms' scheme, emigrating on the same ship as her own parents, which was how they had met. She thought Lara's father was also from Watford, but she knew Lara's mother had been born in Ireland, then grown up in England. It meant Lara had three homelands in a way: Australia, Ireland and England . . .

'— and she said, "Over my dead body, Colonel!" '

Harriet registered too late that Clive had turned on his microphone and was treating everyone to a selection of bawdy jokes. The two men in the group laughed, two of the women tittered, the others looked scandalised. Harriet managed to interrupt him just as he introduced another one about a barmaid, a bishop and a monkey.

'Clive, please!'

'Just sharing some of that famous English humour,' he said, still speaking into the microphone. 'We're going to be together for the next five days, ladies and gentlemen, so no point standing on ceremony. Any of you have any jokes at any stage, hold up your hand and I'll get Big Bird here to pass back the microphone and we'll have a good old laugh together, all right?'

She needed to lay down some ground rules, Harriet realised. Her chance came an hour later, at their first scheduled stop for the day, the cliffside village of Lynton, home to the hotel featured in several early episodes. Clive announced he was going to stay in the bus and read his newspaper. Once Harriet had led the group safely inside to the tearoom and left them exclaiming over menu descriptions of piping hot tea, warm-from-the-oven scones, homemade strawberry jam and thick clotted cream, she seized the opportunity and went back out to the bus.

'Clive?'

He was reading a newspaper, opened on a page showing a topless young woman. He didn't look up. 'Mmm?'

She cleared her throat. 'Clive, I don't like to cause problems between us, but I am having a few difficulties with your manner.'

'What manner?'

That was it. He didn't have any manner. 'I think you're being a bit informal. Interrupting. And some of your comments have been a little blue.'

'The others like it. That bald fellow didn't stop laughing. You're too formal, that's your problem.'

'I'm in charge of the tour, I have responsibility for everyone in the group and your comments aren't helping me.'

'Just trying to lighten the load.'

'Really? By singing the theme from *Sesame Street* each time I stand up?'

'Not loudly.'

'It's a small bus. And you used the microphone.'

'But you do look like Big Bird. Not that you're big.' He looked her up and down. 'You've got a very nice figure, in fact. Pretty face, too. It's the yellow. The yellow legs especially.'

Harriet was going to kill Melissa as soon as she got home. And she was definitely going to stop wearing the yellow stockings. Melissa would never know.

He swung his legs around the seat and gave her his full attention. 'Do you change colour with each season? It being spring, you go for yellow. Do you go orange in autumn?'

'No, I'm yellow all year round. Clive, please don't change the subject. I'm serious.'

'I know. As I said before, that's half your problem. You're the most tense person I've ever met. And I've met a lot of Australians. Lived out there myself for nearly fifteen years.'

She thought she'd detected the trace of an Australian accent in his voice. 'You did? Where?'

'In the mines, in Western Australia. Worked as a driver in a place called Pannawonica. Picked it because the name made me laugh. Made a fortune but nearly went mad with the loneliness. And the heat. How the hell do you all stick it out?'

'It's not that hot where we live. It's a seaside place.'

'I'd have given my left ba—,' he stopped himself just in time, flashing her his monkey smile. 'Sorry, thought I was back in the mines for a minute there. I'd have given anything for a day by the beach back then. It was the homesickness that got me in the end. That and the minor matter of a family left back here.' He made that snickering sound again.

'You're married?'

'Yep, for my sins. One wife, two grown sons, four grandchildren.

Don't know how the missus puts up with me. She runs a B&B back in Bristol nowadays. Good company for her, I'm on the road most of the time.' As he was talking he was wriggling around in his seat. 'Do you know there was a study done once into whether bus drivers had fertility problems on account of all the sitting we do. No one asked me any questions, I could have told them a thing or two, though. Sheepskin is the key.'

'I'm sorry?'

He lifted himself up off the seat and she saw the sheepskin cover under his bottom. 'Keeps me cool in summer, warm in winter and lets plenty of air circulate. Now then, you wanted to say something?'

'Yes, Clive, before the others come back, I do need to clarify that —'

'Yes, yes, that you're in charge. Of course you are. But it's like that nanny business, really. The hand that rocks the cradle rules the world. The hands that drive the bus rule the tour. Har, har!' His laugh was like a motorbike starting up.

She wondered whether the best thing to do would be to ring the bus company and ask for a different driver. It was as if he read her mind. 'You're lucky you got anyone to drive this bus, you know. The most awful dose of gastro has been doing the rounds of our drivers the past few weeks. One of the drivers had it without realising. Before he knew it, he'd passed it on to the entire tour group. Imagine those pit stops!'

That answered that, then. What would James or Lara do in this situation? It was best not to think that way. It had to be her decision. She decided to give in for the time being. Sometimes that was the best option. 'The poor things. And you're feeling all right?'

'Couldn't be better.'

She swallowed again. 'Well, I'm glad we had this chat. And if you could help me a little more, Clive.'

'I'll do my best, BB, I'll do my best.'

She smiled weakly and went back inside to pay for the scones.

It was nearly three by the time they reached the second stop, the seaside town of Bude, over the Devon border into Cornwall. As they drove into the town, Harriet read from James's prepared script: '*Here in Bude is the grand hotel dating back to the 1790s that was used as the setting for the ballroom scene in episode two, "The Case of the Titled Temptress". That ball was, of course, also where our dashing hero Willoughby first met the beautiful yet wily Lady Garvan, who was to prove more than his match in subsequent episodes!*'

James's writing was getting more colourful as it went along. He'd either been getting further into the swing of it or further into a bottle of wine. It gave her a glimpse of a different James. If he hadn't been so responsible, so obliging, so barricaded behind Melissa and her ambitions, he might have chosen a different career, she suspected. He'd always loved writing, she knew. As a teenager, when he wasn't watching cricket, she remembered him scribbling away in notebooks, coming up with ideas for his own comedy skits or writing funny poems. But he'd been so loyal to his parents; there had never been any talk of him going to work anywhere but the travel agency. He'd been one of their hardest working guides and he worked even harder now as the general manager.

Perhaps that was the downside of a family business, Harriet thought. It brought a guaranteed income and a job for life, but it wasn't necessarily the job you would have chosen for yourself. Writing the notes for the itineraries was probably James's only creative outlet these days, she realised. It explained a lot. It also helped her forgive his more colourful phrases. She read on, much more cheerfully.

'*An extra five minutes with Patrick Shawcross to anyone who can remember what Lady Garvan was wearing the night of the ball!*'

The subsequent discussion – it came down to a choice between an off-the-shoulder green taffeta dress or a silver sheath with long white lace gloves – kept the group occupied throughout the twenty-minute stroll through the town.

They arrived in St Ives right on schedule. The whole bus – even Clive – fell silent as they drove down the coast road, past rows of terraced houses and hotels, tantalised by quick glimpses of blue water now and then.

The view suddenly opened in front of them. It was a glorious sweep of bay, beaches and sea, edged by a jumble of hilly streets crammed with whitewashed and stone-fronted buildings. The late afternoon sun shone down on the long curving stretches of sand, creating sparkling spots of golden light on the blue sea. They couldn't have timed their arrival better. There were white sails against the blue water, and along the shore line, families playing on the sand.

Clive leaned over to her. He'd been almost well behaved since their chat, having told only one vaguely ribald joke about a goose and a nun. 'The roads are clear enough. Do you want me to take a quick run along the seafront before we go to the hotel?'

'That would be great, thanks.'

Clive slowed the bus almost to a crawl, and they peered up cobblestoned laneways at the vivid splashes of colour from window boxes and pots of geraniums. There were art galleries, cafes, sweet shops, fish restaurants and old-fashioned seaside shops with buckets and spades, umbrellas, beach chairs and jaunty sunhats hanging outside. A sign by the road pointed to the Tate St Ives and the Barbara Hepworth Sculpture Museum.

Harriet turned on the microphone and read from the script, editing out James's more breathless passages as she went along. '*Over the years many famous artists have made St Ives their home, drawn by the natural beauty and the unusual quality of the light. We'll have plenty of time to explore over the next few days and to visit not just the cottage whose exterior was used as Willoughby's home, but also the lighthouse featured in episodes three, ten and fifteen and the post office featured in episode six.*'

'Episode seven,' Mrs Lamerton interrupted. '"The Case of the Mislaid Mail".'

'Sorry, episode seven.' She had misread it. They'd definitely be keeping her on her toes. '*But now let's go to the hotel, check in and then all meet for cocktails with our special guest, Mr —*'

'Patrick Shawcross!' Three of them finished her sentence for her. Someone – was it Mrs Lamerton or Miss Talbot? – even gave a cheer.

Chapter Nine

'It's so homely,' Harriet heard Miss Boyd say as they all filed into the hotel foyer.

'My grandmother had that very same wallpaper,' Mrs Pollard remarked.

'It reminds me of that guesthouse we stayed at in Canada, Doris, do you remember it?' Mr Douglas asked his wife. 'It was so beautiful, with such wonderful views. The bay was still as a milkpond.'

'Millpond, dear,' she said wearily.

The hotel was in a perfect position, right on the cliff, looking down over Porthminster Beach and across to the lighthouse. The décor was a bit old-fashioned – overly patterned carpets, a mixture of chintzy and flock wallpaper, and big baskets of artificial flowers – but the tour members were delighted.

Mr Fidock came in from his exploring, rubbing his hands together. 'There's even a seaview bar, ladies and gents. Bring on happy hour!'

The hotel staff ferried bags up and down the stairs, leaving the old gated lift free for the tour party. Harriet made sure everyone was settled in their rooms, for the time being, at least. She knew there would probably be the usual complaints about itchy bedding, dirty windows, faulty bathroom lights and/or slow-boiling kettles over the next few days, but for now everyone seemed happy. She darted up to her own room. It was one of the smaller ones at the back of the hotel, in the same corridor as Mrs Lamerton, Miss Talbot and Mrs Kempton, but looking out over the road and several other hotels rather than the beach. It was the usual arrangement – she and Clive would have the equivalent of servants' quarters, leaving the good rooms for the tour guests.

There'd been an awkward moment at reception, when the woman in charge asked in Mrs Lamerton's hearing whether Lara would be checking in later.

Harriet had lowered her voice. 'I'll come back to you on that, if that's okay?'

'So she might be turning up?' Mrs Lamerton had still managed to eavesdrop.

'I'm still hopeful,' she'd said, before taking refuge in a pretend call on her mobile phone. She'd also slipped back to reception after Mrs Lamerton had gone upstairs, and asked if there was any chance of getting a TV and video machine installed in her room. It would be no problem at all, she was told. She'd have it within the hour.

Now, in her room, she called reception again and asked to be put through to Patrick Shawcross's room. She listened to the soft burr of the dial tone, her mind drifting as it went on and on. She jumped when it was finally answered.

'Good afternoon!'

It was an American man. A cheery American. Harriet was taken by surprise. 'I'm sorry, I must have the wrong room.' She hung up and dialled reception again.

'Hello, this is Harriet Turner again. Could you put me through to Mr Shawcross's room?'

'I'm sorry, Ms Turner, I thought I just did. Let me try again.'

The phone was answered quickly. 'Good afternoon again. And let me check, yes, it's still a beautiful afternoon.' It was the same man.

'Mr Shawcross?'

'That's right.'

'Oh, Mr Shawcross, hello. This is Harriet Turner. I'm so sorry for hanging up on you before.' Harriet had been expecting a Cornish accent, her head so full of *Willoughby* episodes she was imagining a Patrick Shawcross of fifteen years ago. He'd been living in Boston for years, of course he would have picked up a bit of an American accent. Had Lara mentioned that? Then she remembered Lara hadn't spoken to him while setting up the tour. Everything had been arranged via the French assistant in the talent agency in America, mostly by fax and email.

'Hello, Harriet. That's no problem.'

She tried to sound as businesslike as possible. 'I hope your room is fine, and that you had no difficulties getting here? And that you got my messages?'

'I did, thank you. Everything is fine. And your basket of fruit couldn't have been more welcoming, so thank you for that as well.'

'Oh, good.' He sounded so friendly. So normal. She took a breath and started delivering the explanatory speech she had been rehearsing all day. 'Mr Shawcross, I need to fill you in on one or two things. There's been a slight change in arrangements. We did fax your agents with this news, but you may have been en route already and not heard all of it. You were originally going to be travelling with my brother James, but unfortunately he had an accident, so I've taken over his role. My apologies also that neither Lara nor myself were able to phone and greet you last night as we expected. I'm afraid our flight was delayed, and then unfortunately Lara was unable to meet us . . .' she trailed off. He didn't need to know everything immediately, did he?

'It's a real family affair by the sound of things. No problem at all. I'm sure you and I will get on just as well.'

He sounded completely relaxed about it. Perhaps that came from the acting background. Presumably film sets and TV studios were unpredictable workplaces. Harriet gave a relieved laugh. 'Thanks so much. We've had a few unexpected ups and downs so I wanted to be sure that was all fine with you.'

'It's absolutely fine.'

'Perhaps we could meet for coffee before we go and have a cocktail? Have a general chat about the tour before we get started?'

'That's an excellent idea. Will I meet you downstairs? I'll carry a newspaper so you know me. Either the *Times* or the *Guardian*, I'm still trying to work out which political camp I'm in now I'm back in Britain.'

'You won't need to bother with the newspaper. I've been watching the videos of your show for the past while, so I'm sure I'll know you.' She was warming to him more and more. 'So how long is it since you've been home?'

'Home?

'Here, in Cornwall.'

'I come back to England quite regularly, but, oh, I haven't been in Cornwall since we filmed the series. So it's nearly fifteen years.'

The more they spoke, the more she could hear his English accent coming through. Mrs Lamerton and Mrs Pollard had been particularly keen on hearing that voice of his in real life. She'd heard them talking about it the night before. They'd been competing to see who could describe it the best. Like warm treacle, Mrs Lamerton had said. No, deep and rich, like toffee, Mrs Pollard had insisted. They were both right. It was a warm, deep voice.

'And have you still got relatives in Penzance?' He might like to call in to them while they were so near.

'In Penzance? No, not that I know of.'

'Really? Oh, I thought you were born there. Your biography said —'

'You were given the Penzance biography? I'm sorry, please don't believe a word of it. My first agent and I made that up one night over a bottle of whiskey. I was actually born in London. Stoke Newington, to be precise. But my agent thought Penzance sounded far more romantic.'

'But your parents are Irish?'

'No, English. From London, too, though they're living in Spain these days. I've just come from visiting them, in fact.'

The image she had of him was crumbling away piece by piece. 'So you weren't ever planning on becoming a dentist, either? Before you were talent spotted?'

'It says that too? We really did get carried away. I'm sorry about that. No, I'd always wanted to try acting.'

Harriet mentally ran through the facts. He wasn't born in Penzance. His parents weren't Irish. His path to acting wasn't a romantic one . . . *Expect the unexpected*, she thought warily. What else would be different about him? An image of a prematurely old, wrinkled grey-haired man flashed into her mind. Quite a few years had passed, after all. She had to ask. She had to know before she saw him, so she had time to prepare herself if the news wasn't good. 'Mr Shawcross, getting back to what we were talking about a few moments ago . . . just so I'm sure I recognise you when we meet downstairs . . . ' How did she put this? She decided to try the roundabout approach. 'Would you say you've changed much in appearance since the *Willoughby* days?'

'Have I changed much?' She heard something in his voice, but she wasn't sure if it was amusement or annoyance. 'Well, now, there's a question. Tell me, do you look anything like you did fifteen years ago?'

'I hope not,' she said emphatically. Fifteen years ago she'd had braces on her teeth, puppy fat and a peculiar pair of spectacles that Austin and Lara had picked out for her. They'd insisted they were very cool. It was only years later, after she'd switched to contact lenses, that they'd admitted they'd picked the awful ones as a joke.

'It was that bad?'

'It was that bad.' She was kicking herself. Why couldn't she have waited until she saw him to find out for herself? 'I'm sorry, it's fine, I'm sure I'll recognise you —'

'No, you're right, it's a perfectly reasonable question. Fifteen long years have passed since then. Lots of water under the bridge. Lots of hair loss, too, unfortunately.'

'Hair loss?' Was this why there hadn't been a photo of him in the notes?

'Bald as a badger, I'm afraid. Oddly enough, I'm also finding it takes me longer to get around these days. My old legs seem to tire so quickly. Will we be able to stop now and again for a cup of tea and a bun, do you think?'

Another mental picture appeared, with more detail this time. An elderly bald man limping across green fields, a flask of tea in hand, an elderly lame dog limping behind him. She blinked it away. 'Yes, of course we can.'

'And I hope you don't mind but I decided to ask my doctor to travel with me, too. There'll be no problem with the expenses, will there? I've booked him into the room next to mine.'

'Your doctor?'

'I've had a couple of angina scares lately, so I thought it better to be safe than sorry.'

'Oh. Well, no, of course that's fine. I'm sure we can make room for him.'

He laughed then, a warm sound. 'Harriet, it's all right. I'm teasing you.'

'Pardon me?'

'I'm teasing you. You were being so diplomatic I couldn't resist it. It was only fifteen years ago, not fifty. I promise you I haven't changed that much since the series. And I promise my doctor isn't with me, either.'

She sat down, a mixture of embarrassed and relieved. 'Mr Shawcross —'

'Please, call me Patrick. We're going to be travelling together, we can't be standing on ceremony. Let's just enjoy ourselves. Isn't it a matter of us driving around beautiful Cornwall for a few days together? A few photo sessions? Interviews over dinner each night?'

'Interviews?'

'You're right, that's too formal. Let's call them conversations. We could probably have had it all done in a day, but that's neither here nor there now, I suppose. The two of us can take it easy.'

'The two of us?' It was her turn to be amused. 'You mean the fourteen of us.'

'Sorry?'

'There's fourteen of us on this trip, remember. Fifteen if I include the bus driver. And he's a handful, I don't mind warning you.'

'Very funny.'

'I wish I was being funny.'

'And don't tell me, the other twelve people are a handful as well?'

'Yes, I think they might be.'

'All right, Harriet, I think we're even.'

'Even?'

'I teased you and you teased me. So, to get back to this article . . .'

'Article?'

'The magazine article you're writing about me.'

'But I'm not writing an article about you. I'm leading a travel group. That's what I meant about the group of fourteen people. There are twelve in the tour party, plus you and me.' Things had turned very odd. 'This is the actor Patrick Shawcross I'm talking to, isn't it? The one who played Willoughby?'

'Yes, but we are talking about the same trip, aren't we? The trip down the *Willoughby* memory lane? Organised from Australia?'

'Yes, but Mr Shawcross, I'm not from a magazine. I work for Turner Travel. It's my family's travel business based in Merryn Bay, just outside of Melbourne. We specialise in leading themed tour groups, like this *Willoughby* one.'

'You're with a tour group?' His amused tone had now completely disappeared. 'But I was told this whole trip was for an Australian magazine article, one of those "where-are-they-now" features. Your colleague Laura —'

The back of her neck was prickling. 'Lara.'

'Lara faxed over a copy of a magazine feature I did here in England years ago. Sophie at the agency said it was all going to be based on that.'

'It is. That was the starting point for the whole tour. But we only faxed the article to give your agent an idea of the places we'd be visiting. Didn't you get the itinerary? The one we faxed last month? With all the notes about the tour?' Harriet had seen James fax it to the agency himself.

'No, I've been travelling in Spain the past few weeks, visiting my family. The only itinerary I saw was a list of dates and places, months ago, when I first got the invitation. I have it here.' There was a pause and then he returned. 'It's from a Lara Robinson to Sophie in the agency. "Dear Sophie, As discussed, the following is the suggested itinerary for Patrick Shawcross's trip." And then a list of placenames and suggested dates, St Ives, Boscastle etc., etc. "I look forward to hearing from you. Lara." Sophie sent it to me when she first got the invitation; I said it all looked fine. That's all I knew until I collected the tickets and details of this hotel at the airport.'

Harriet knew the fax he had mentioned. It was the interim one Lara had prepared. And he was right, there hadn't been any mention of a tour party on it. She was now extremely worried. 'What about the one we asked the hotel to deliver with your fruit basket?'

She heard him take a look. 'There's a card, but no itinerary.'

She tried to keep the alarm out of her voice. 'Mr Shawcross, I'm so sorry about this. We really need to talk, as soon as we can.'

'Of course we can talk about it. But Lara —'

'It's Harriet.'

'Sorry, Harriet. As I'm sure you don't need me to tell you, a tour group is a different kettle of fish to a magazine article. I'm not sure I can —'

'*No!*' She couldn't let him say it. She couldn't even let him think about pulling out. 'I mean, please, Mr Shawcross, don't make any hasty decisions. Not until we've spoken face-to-face.' She knew she sounded desperate. She was desperate. She could feel the colour rising in her cheeks. 'Could you tell me your room number?'

'Thirty-nine. On the third floor.'

She knew it was one of the rooms with a seaview balcony, but on a separate floor from the tour party. 'I'll be there as soon as I can.'

She quickly ran to the bathroom to splash some water on her face. As she turned on the old-style tap, a gush of water splashed out of the sink, all over her shirt and skirt. She swore out loud. She couldn't go up and see him like this, or wait for it to dry.

Within three minutes she had thrown off her uniform, opened her case and changed into the first outfit she could find – jeans and a simple red T-shirt. She pulled them both on and glanced in the mirror. Both a bit casual, but stylish enough. Jewellery would help, perhaps. She was already wearing her blue opal bracelet and added a pendant around her neck, a simple resin circle in a striking darker blue. She quickly took out her make-up bag and reapplied some red lipstick, mascara, a smudge of golden brown eyeshadow and a touch of blush, all in record time.

She was nearly out the door when she caught sight of her feet. She'd put on her Turner Travel court shoes again without thinking. It was a very bad look. Another scrabble in her case for some high-heeled boots. They were on in seconds. She checked from all angles that they looked okay and that the jeans hadn't got tucked up in the boots like jodhpurs. They had. She quickly fixed them up. There was only time for the quickest restyle of her hair – a matter of running her fingers through the short black strands and perking up the fringe – and a check that her lipstick was still in place. It would have to do. And at least her own clothes gave her more confidence than the Big Bird outfit. She gave herself one last glance in the mirror and then she was out the door, her heart pounding.

Chapter Ten

He answered at her first knock. It was definitely the man from the *Willoughby* videos. The same dark curly hair. The dark eyes. He was taller than she'd expected though. At least six foot. But apart from that he could have stepped straight off the set. It was a huge relief. She beamed up at him. 'Oh thank God. You look just like Patrick Shawcross.'

His lips twitched. 'Well, yes. That's because I am Patrick Shawcross. You must be Harriet.'

'Yes, I am. Hello, Mr Shawcross.' She couldn't take her eyes off him. It was like Dorian Gray. It was remarkable how little he'd aged. It had to be plastic surgery.

'No, actually it's not.'

Her hand flew to her mouth. She'd said it out loud. How rude. She blamed the jetlag, even though she'd been denying to herself she had any. 'I'm so sorry. You look much younger than I expected, that's all.'

'Oh, well done. Wrap an insult up in a compliment like that and you'll go straight to the heart of any actor, lapsed or otherwise.' He smiled then. 'You really do have quite a thing about age, don't you?'

'Not usually, no.' She was very embarrassed. 'I somehow got it into my head that you were in your seventies, grey-haired, one foot in the grave.'

'Not quite. I've just turned forty-five and I'm fit as a fiddle. I have my passport here if you'd like to check my birth date?' His face was serious but there was a definite sparkle in his eye.

'No, I believe you, I promise.'

'Then we're off to a good start.' He smiled at her again. Very nicely. 'Please, come in.' It was a suite, twice the size of hers. A lounge area with a table and chairs, leading on to a full length balcony with a stunning view over the beaches. Through a door she could see a double bed. She was pleased to see the large fruit basket on the side table.

As she followed him across the room, she got the scent of his aftershave. She loved the smell of aftershave. His was distinctive, something lemony, with musk or something deeper underneath.

'Can I offer you tea?' he asked. 'Coffee?'

'No, neither thanks. I thought it might be better if we got straight down to —'

'Business? Absolutely. Let me take a look at the itinerary and we'll see if we can get to the bottom of this.'

They had just sat down when a mobile phone on the table between them rang. He checked the number. 'Harriet, I'm sorry, but I've been expecting this call all day. Would you mind?'

'Of course not. Would you like me to wait outside?'

'No, please don't. I won't be long, I promise.'

He answered the phone, moving over to the open balcony door as he spoke. He was obviously pleased to hear from the caller. She heard a snatch or two, the talk punctuated with low laughter, his English accent coming through more obviously the longer she heard his voice. 'That's great news, well done. Fill me in . . . Four weeks worth? . . . No, I'll check the script when I'm back . . .' It sounded like he was lining up work.

As he leaned against the balcony rail looking out over the water, she took the opportunity to study him even more closely. It was odd to see him in the flesh after spending so long looking at him on the videos. He really had changed very little. It was like looking at Willoughby's older brother, she decided – his just as good-looking older brother. He was dressed in dark jeans and a white shirt, the sleeves folded up over his brown arms. A tan from his time in Spain, she presumed. He somehow didn't look the type to go for sunbeds. He was a solid build, but fit-looking. He turned back towards her then, saying his goodbyes. As he came closer, she noticed more details. There were traces of grey in his hair, at the temples. And perhaps a few more lines, especially around his eyes. She saw them again now as he sat down and smiled at her.

'I'm sorry about that. I'm all yours now. You're sure I can't get you coffee? Tea?'

'No, thanks, I'm fine.' There wasn't time. The cocktail party was due to start in less than two hours. They needed to get this sorted out quickly. She passed him the itinerary. 'Please, take a look.'

She watched his face as he read the cover page. Then he turned to the next page. Today's program. He started reading it aloud. If she wasn't feeling sick to her stomach she would have quite liked listening to his voice.

'*The tour really starts tonight with your first opportunity to meet and mingle with our SPECIAL GUEST! Patrick Shawcross, yes, Willoughby himself! Have you got your questions ready??! And go on, try an exotic cocktail, while also enjoying a buffet selection of the finest local produce in the comfortable setting of the hotel. The bolder ones among you might even like to kick on afterwards with a nightcap in the stunning seaview bar and lounge! But don't forget our early start tomorrow, now, will you??*'

He looked up at her. She saw his eyes weren't dark brown but in fact a dark blue. 'Did you write this?'

'No. No, I didn't.' She had a feeling that was just as well.

He turned the page and read aloud again. '*A day of* Willoughby *treats is in store for all of us today! We're off in the bus to the harbour villages of Boscastle and Port Isaac, the settings for episodes nine, twelve and fifteen, passing some of Cornwall's most spectacular coastal scenery en route. There'll be ample opportunities for photographs and, even better, plenty of chances to hear Patrick Shawcross's reminiscences of his* Willoughby *filming days. There's sure to be a few surprises!!*' He turned the pages and read some more. Kept turning. She watched his face. No reaction. Finally he turned to the last page, then closed the folder. He was silent, slowly patting it against his hand. Harriet was reminded of the flicking tail of a lion. An unhappy lion.

'I wish Sophie had shown me this.'

Harriet swallowed. 'Yes, so do I.'

'I'd have turned it down.' He gave it back to her. 'Harriet, I'm sorry, but I can't possibly do it.'

She couldn't hear him say that. She wouldn't let him say it. She tried to keep her voice calm. 'I can certainly see why you might think that. But Mr Shawcross, you're here now. We're all here. Surely the easiest thing would be to go ahead?'

'I can't. Harriet, that *Willoughby* series was fifteen years ago. I can barely remember it. What I agreed to do – what I thought I had agreed to do – was a simple "where-are-you-now" magazine feature, photos of me at all the different locations, you know, standing next to the church at Widecombe-in-the-Moor, recreating the scene from the opening credits —'

'Widemouth Bay.'

'They've moved the church to the Bay?'

'No, the opening credits started with you at Widemouth Bay and then went to the Widecombe-in-the-Moor church.'

'That's right, so they did. I'm sorry, but you must understand that being interviewed for a magazine article is a long way from being paraded from one part of Cornwall to the other like a prized pet.'

'We've called you our special guest, not a prized pet.'

'I'd feel like a prized pet.'

'But we thought you'd jumped at it. Sophie told Lara that you accepted immediately.'

'I did. I knew I'd be on holiday this month so the timing was good. I liked the idea of seeing Cornwall again.' He smiled. 'I also thought I'd better get in quickly, before you tracked down someone from *Poldark*.'

She gave a guilty smile. 'That isn't quite as popular in Australia as *Willoughby*.'

'It really is still a hit there?'

Harriet nodded.

'Amazing. I've had fan mail from Australia occasionally, passed on months after it's been sent, usually. I don't do much work with that agency any more, so I'm small fry to them these days, I suppose.' He sounded surprisingly relaxed about it. 'We didn't ever expect *Willoughby* to take off at all, you know. My suspicion always was that it had been made as a sort of tax dodge. It was the most ramshackle production. No one seemed to know what they were doing. Not only the cast but the crew as well. Not that I complained. It was a dream first job.'

If she wasn't on the verge of losing him as her special guest she would be enjoying hearing all this. Her curiosity got the better of her. 'How did you get the part?'

He seemed just as happy to talk, crossing his long legs in front of him. 'Three things, really. One, I was an unknown so I was cheap. Two, the way I looked. The director had a specific idea in his head and I happened to match it. And three, I was sharing a house with one of the producers. I've always had a sneaking suspicion that was the clincher.' A flash of that smile again. 'And TV back then was nothing like it is now. If anything, it was embarrassing to admit you'd done a TV show. The real actors stayed in repertory theatre.'

'That's why you went to America? To go back to stage acting?'

'No, I actually got a part in a very bad soap opera over there.'

'Really?'

'Really bad, do you mean? Oh yes, on every level. The writing, the sets, my acting.'

She was surprised again at how honest he was. Where was the big ego she'd been expecting? 'Would I have seen it?'

'I hope not, for your sake. I played the heir to a huge oil fortune who was making pornographic films to bring disgrace on his family. My name was Roger Hardwick. Imagine. I'm sure the scriptwriters thought it was hilarious.' He shook his head. 'I was thinking about it on the flight over. If I thought *Willoughby* was bad . . . Mind you, it made for some excellent dinner party stories over the years. All soft focus and cardboard sets. I also had to wear a large fake moustache.' He laughed again.

'So no one recognises you, at least?'

'No, luckily. That's being grateful for small mercies, isn't it?'

She was about to ask him another question when she remembered why they were both here. 'Mr Shawcross, perhaps we should get back down to business . . .'

'That actually sounds like a line from that very soap.'

'I'm sorry, but we really do need to sort this out. If I could just explain —'

He held up his hand to stop her. 'Please, Harriet, you don't need to. There's nothing to explain. It was a simple mix-up. I've had a nice flight over, a good night's sleep, a morning swim. It's been a pleasure to see St Ives again after all these years. So no harm done. I'm more than happy to refund you any of your expenses, and please, give my apologies to the tour group.'

An icy feeling shot down her spine. No. He had to stay. Harriet knew Mrs Lamerton was put out enough about James and Lara not turning up. She would *kill* her if there was no Patrick Shawcross. 'Please, Mr Shawcross, can't you give it some more thought? The group have all been looking forward to it so much. They've been doing nothing but watch *Willoughby* videos for weeks in preparation.'

'Really?'

She nodded.

'The poor things.'

She blinked.

'It really was a terrible program, you know,' he said. 'None of the plots ever made sense. There was one where the vicar's wife was murdered, and supposedly it was the jealous gardener who did it. Yet if you traced it chronologically there was no way possible it was him.'

She had watched that program the evening before. Series one, episode three: 'The Case of the Green-eyed Gardener'. 'That's what I thought. It all tied up too neatly in the end. It would have made far more sense if it was the visiting professor, the one who had rented the holiday cottage, who had been behind it.'

'Yes, exactly.' He smiled. 'That's funny. I haven't thought about that episode in years.'

She glanced at her watch. It was getting very late. There was no time for reminiscing. She had to plunge in again. 'Mr Shawcross, what would it take to convince you to stay? Because I'll do whatever I can.'

'Harriet, are you sure you didn't see that soap opera I was in? You seem to be quoting it back at me, line for line. I remember a casting couch scene just like that.'

'No, I didn't. And I didn't mean to sound —' she searched for the word and chose the first one that came to mind, 'racy.'

'Racy?' He laughed again, a deep, rich sound. 'What a wonderful word. And look, you're actually blushing. How lovely. I didn't think anyone blushed any more. Do you know, I was at an Actors' Equity dinner in Los Angeles last year and there wasn't a blush or a frown to be found in the entire room. They'd all had either plastic surgery or Botox injections. Women and men.'

'Really? You've had it yourself?'

'Good God, no. You know it's made out of a virus that causes paralysis? An actor friend of mine at home in Boston told me he is waiting for the day when all the side effects cut in and ninety-five per cent of the actors in America drop dead. "Think of the work we'll get then, Pat," he told me. "They'll come begging for us. The only standing actors in the world."'

'So you're not working as an actor much these days?'

'No, not much.'

He didn't seem worried about it. Her mobile phone beeped in her bag. Melissa checking up on her? The thought chilled her. She let it go to voicemail.

He stood up. 'I'd better not keep you. It's been a pleasure talking to you, Harriet, but as I said, I don't think —'

No. She couldn't let him go. She stood up too, glad her heels gave her some extra height. He was nearly a head taller than her as it was and she needed all the authority she could gather.

'Please, Mr Shawcross. Won't you at least come to the cocktail party tonight? I can't tell you how much it would mean to the group. It really wasn't their fault there was this mix-up and they'd be devastated if they didn't get to meet you.' She noticed something in his expression as he looked down at her. A wavering? She started talking at record speed. It seemed important to tell him everything. 'They've so many questions they want to ask you. And they're dying to show you their impersonations. Two of them want you to watch them act out their favourite bits from the series. And one of the ladies has even made you a jumper. With a little embroidered Patch on the bottom right-hand side.'

'Really?'

She nodded.

'Who was Patch again?'

'Your dog. The black and white dog.'

'The dog?' He frowned. 'So who was it I had the beer with at the end of each show?'

'That was George. The farmer from the adjoining property to your cottage.'

'Oh yes. "*That's people, isn't it, George?*" '

' "*Aye, Willoughby, so it is.*" ' Harriet answered without thinking. She rushed on. 'Could you see it as a challenge to you as an actor? I could help you. Feed you all your lines. I've got all the videos of the show here. You could watch them all, get a refresher course.' She gazed up at him, crossing her fingers behind her back, trying to stay calm, imagining a duck paddling madly under the water.

His next words gave her some hope. 'Tell me again how the tour was supposed to start?'

She knew the itinerary by heart. 'Tonight, officially. With a cocktail party here in the hotel so they could all meet you. Then we had trips planned for every day, to different locations from the program. The group helped us put the itinerary together. They even did a vote of which were their favourite locations.'

'Oh? Which one won?'

'It was a toss up between the smugglers' cottage in episode four and the historic hotel where you first met Lady Garvan and accused her of dealing in counterfeit artwork.'

Another puzzled look.

'When you kissed her, and she slapped you and said she didn't mess with commoners. And then you took her to bed.'

'Did I? Good Lord. Did I enjoy it?'

'I think so.' The program had been surprisingly sexy for its time. Lots of groans and flashes of bare skin in that scene, before it faded to out-of-focus and then came back to them both in bed, puffing away on cigarettes.

She had to make one more effort to convince him to stay. Her words came in a rush. 'Mr Douglas has even bought a digital camera to take photos of you. He's going to set up a *Willoughby* website for everyone when he gets home. And little Miss Talbot has hardly been able to sleep with the excitement. It's the trip of a lifetime for everyone. Please don't go. I'd hate to let them all down.'

'Harriet, that was so heartfelt. Have you ever thought of taking up acting yourself?'

She could see the amusement in his eyes. He wasn't only smiling at her, she realised. He was practically laughing. She couldn't bear it. If he'd had any idea how hard the past year had been, stuck behind her desk, doing nothing but filing, and computer work, feeling nothing but scared and a failure. This time tomorrow he'd be home in America, while she'd still be trying to explain to the tour group and James and Melissa why the trip was a disaster before it had begun. And that didn't even begin to take into account why Lara had decided not to show up.

She was suddenly furious. With him, with James for landing her in this mess, with Melissa for all her bullying, with Lara for disappearing, with Clive and his Big Bird remarks, all of them . . . 'No, I haven't. And never mind. I understand. I'm sorry to have brought you all the way here for nothing. If you can give me an hour or so I'll get on to the airline and organise your flight back home to London or Los Angeles or —' Oh, damn it, now she'd forgotten where he lived, 'Silicon Valley, wherever it is you want to go.'

'Silicon Valley? Because of the plastic surgery?' He laughed out loud. 'Very droll, Harriet. And please calm down. I'm not going anywhere.'

'You're not?'

'Apart from a strange ragbag of *Willoughby* locations, it seems.'

A tremor of hope. 'You'll do it?'

He put his fingers on his temples and shut his eyes.

'Mr Shawcross?'

He opened his eyes. Blue mischief looked at her. His voice was low, deep. It filled the room. '"*There are some mornings when I wake up and see the blue of the sea and feel the freshness of the wind and I know I'm home.*"'

She knew the line by heart. It was from the beginning of episode one, 'The Case of the Prodigal Postman', setting the scene when Willoughby first returns to his home place. He had it word for word. And he'd spoken in a perfect Cornish accent.

She couldn't stop the big smile. 'Oh. Oh, thank you. You won't regret it, I promise. We'll spoil you rotten.' It was all she could do not to hug him.

Back in her room five minutes later, she had to stop herself somersaulting onto the bed. She'd managed it! She'd pulled the tour back from the brink! It was going to be okay! The sound of the mobile phone interrupted her victory lap of the room. She snatched it up.

'Harold? Is everything okay? I rang your mobile before and only got your voicemail.'

It was Austin. 'I was in doing a briefing with Mr Shawcross.' She loved how normal it sounded.

'Oh, right. And everything's fine with him?'

'Absolutely fine, yes.' She kept her voice even, but inside she wanted to shout the words. She wanted to leap in the air and click her heels together it was so fine.

'Harold, I've decided to come over to Bath as soon as I can, to have a word with Lara's flatmate. I've checked out the airports. I'm going to fly to Plymouth first, come and see you in St Ives and then drive up to Bath. Talk to Lara's flatmate, some people at her college, see if they've noticed anything out of the ordinary.'

'You're coming here?'

'It'll just be a quick visit.'

'You don't need to on my account. It'd be great to see you, but I'm fine.'

'It's no trouble. Besides, I need to pick your brains about Lara some more. She's obviously upset about something and between the two of us we might be able to figure it out. Work out where she's gone. Get her back on to the tour as soon as we can.'

She sat down abruptly. 'But what if she doesn't want us to find her?'

'What?'

The words felt like they were bursting their way out of her. 'What if she doesn't want us to know where she is?'

'What's got into you? She's our sister, Harriet. Aren't you worried about her too?'

'I suppose I'm playing devil's advocate,' she hedged. 'If she did want us to know, then wouldn't she have told us where she was going? Maybe she does just want some time on her own.'

'If that's what she'd wanted, if everything was all right, then you know as well as I do that Lara would have rung one of us, told us what arrangements she was making, kept us all up-to-date and then gone away. You know how organised she is. And she would never leave a tour group in the lurch like this. Or you, of all people. I think we need to find her, to make sure she's okay. Then if she wants to be left alone, we'll leave her alone.'

'You, of all people.' She had to tell him. She needed to explain to someone what had happened between her and Lara. She'd just begun to speak when she heard him have a brief conversation with someone near him.

He came back on. 'I have to go, Harriet. See you in a couple of days. I'll find her, don't worry.'

'Austin, wait, please . . .' She was too late. He'd already gone. Her words were left hanging in the air.

Chapter Eleven

Harriet was eight years old when Lara first came to stay with the Turners. James was sent out by his mother to round up her and Austin so they could hear the news. He found Austin in the back garden of the house and travel agency, lying reading in the hammock strung between the plum tree and the clothes-line post. He gave it a push, nearly toppling Austin out onto the ground. 'Mum wants to talk to us.'

'I'm busy.'

'She said it's important.'

'This is important. I'm sleeping. It's an important activity for fourteen-year-olds. We do most of our growing while we're sleeping, so if I interrupt the growth spurt now there's every chance I'll have halted it mid-cycle and I'll never grow another inch.'

'Austin, I don't give a rats myself but Mum wants to talk to you.'

Austin stood up and stretched. 'When I'm a parent I'm going to let kids do whatever they want.'

'And then you'll know the torment you've put me through.' Mrs Turner had come out and overheard. 'Where's Harriet?'

'In her room.' Austin said, yawning. 'Locked inside her jigsaw puzzle prison.'

'Go and get her, Austin, would you?'

He headed inside, picking a plum on the way and throwing it, with perfect aim, at James. He found Harriet in her room, bent over a card table their father had set up for her. A cardboard box with a picture of three kittens peering out of a wicker basket was propped up in front of her. She was frowning, her black hair in little tufts from where she'd been pulling at it as usual.

'Harold, Mum wants a meeting.'

'I'm nearly finished.'

'Now.'

'Help me find the middle one's tail first. I thought I had it but it was his ear.'

He found it within seconds, slotted it into place and she reluctantly followed him outside, bringing the lid of the puzzle with her.

Mrs Turner waited until they were sitting down, James at the top of the table, Austin on the bench against the wall and Harriet on the chair beside her mother. 'Thanks, Harriet. I promise you can get back to your kittens in a minute. I want to give you all some news first.'

Harriet put up her hand. 'Are we getting another kid?'

'Child, not kid, Harriet, please. And you're at home, darling. You don't need to put up your hand to speak. What made you think we're getting another child?'

'Bernie at school. She said that every time her mum and dad tell them they have some news they get a new baby.'

Mrs Turner bit back a smile. The Kellys were up to seven children already. She reached across and kissed Harriet's head, smoothing down her tufty hair at the same time. 'No, I'm not having a baby. But it's a bit like that. You're going to have a new sort of sister. An instant sister. Just for a little while.'

Three blank faces looked at her.

'Boys, do you remember Rose Robinson? My English friend from the ship? And in the hostel?'

'A bit,' James said. Austin thought he vaguely remembered her. Harriet wriggled. She didn't like it when they spoke about the days on the ship from England or in the migant hostel. She'd heard all the stories and almost convinced herself she could picture the early days in Australia, but they weren't her own memories. All she knew for sure was she had been born in one of the tin huts at the migrant hostel, eight and a half months after her parents and two brothers arrived in Australia. Her mum had told her there hadn't been time to go to the hospital. 'You were in such a hurry to arrive, Harriet.' 'You should have called me Hurriet, then,' she said. It was her first ever joke. She was really happy when everyone laughed and after that first time she said it as often as she could until Austin told her to put a sock in it. She had to ask him what 'put a sock in it' meant.

Mrs Turner was explaining. 'Rose was pregnant while she was on the ship too, and she had her own little girl just a few days before you were born, Harriet. You've even seen a photo of her.'

Harriet nearly remembered. There were lots of photos of the other families. Pale people blinking into the bright sunshine.

'She and her husband moved up to Queensland and we lost touch with each other,' she told them. She explained that Rose had since moved back to Melbourne to live, seen an ad for Turner Travel with a photo of Penny and Neil and got in contact again. She had been writing and telephoning often since then.

'That's who you've spent all those hours on the phone to lately?' James said.

'Things have been tough for her and she hasn't been well. She's needed someone to talk to.'

Austin rolled his eyes. 'So go tell it to the marines, Rose.'

'I beg your pardon, Austin?'

Austin looked embarrassed. 'Sorry. I'm not sure what I mean, to tell you the truth. I heard it on a film. As long as you don't neglect us for some troubled woman from your past.'

'I won't, I promise.' She told them the rest of it. Rose needed a break for a few weeks. She'd thought of the Turners, and remembered that their daughter was the same age as her own. She'd wondered if it would be possible for Lara to come and stay with them for a short while. Just until she was better.

'Where's her dad? Why can't he look after her?' James asked.

'Lara's mum and dad don't live together at the moment. Her dad still lives in Queensland, but Rose and I thought it might be better for Lara to come and live with a family like ours. So she can keep going to school.'

'Will she go to school with me?' Harriet asked.

'I think so. I'm talking to your principal about it tonight, and it looks that way.'

Harriet quite liked the sound of that. A brand-new friend to show around. 'But who do I say she is?'

'You tell the truth. Say she's Lara and she's come to stay with us for a while.'

'But she's not a relative, is she?'

'No, but that doesn't matter. You can tell your friends she's the daughter of a friend of mine. Which is what she is.'

'Where will she sleep?'

'In your room, with you, if that's okay with you?'

There was nowhere else, really. The house behind the travel agency was compact. Three bedrooms, one for her parents, one for James and Austin and now one for Lara and Harriet. She nodded. She didn't mind one bit.

'We'll move that spare bed out of the shed into your room, and hopefully you can make room in the chest of drawers for her clothes as well as yours. It's going to affect you more than anyone, Harriet, but I know you'll be able to rise to the occasion.'

That sounded so grown up. 'I'll be really kind to her.'

She forgot about the jigsaw puzzle for the rest of the day. It was much more interesting to help prepare a room for a motherless child. She said as much to Austin as she helped him and James move the bed in to her room.

'She's not motherless, Harold. She just can't live with her mother for a while.'

By the end of the afternoon she was ready. 'Mum, come and look.' She had piled all her toys on top of the spare bed. 'I thought Lara might like them.'

'That's very kind of you, Harriet, but I think she's bringing some of her own toys with her.'

'But I thought she could have a loan of these too. In case she's feeling homesick. And I've put some tissues beside the bed, in case she starts crying and missing her mum.'

She found herself bundled up in her mother's arms. A kiss was pressed firmly into the top of her head. 'You are a lovely little thing, Harriet Turner, and no mistake.'

Two nights later she was doing her homework at the kitchen table when the phone rang. She ran to answer it before James or Austin got there.

'The Turner house, hello.' That was what her mother said when she answered the phone.

'Is that Harriet?'

'Yes.'

'Harriet, this is Rose calling. Your mother's friend.'

'Hello, Rose.' She thought she should say something else. 'I hope you are feeling better.'

'Better?'

'Mum said you hadn't been well which was why you wanted us to look after your daughter for a while.'

'Oh. That's actually why I'm ringing. Is your mum there?'

'Yes, I'll get her.' She didn't want to get off the phone yet. 'I have the room all ready for her. I've got the bed by the window but if Lara really wants it she can have it. And I've put lots of toys and dolls out for her too. They're dirty but I said to Mum it wasn't worth washing all of them yet, that it was better to wait until Lara got here and then we can wash the ones she likes.'

'Thank you, Harriet. That's really kind and thoughtful of you.'

Harriet thought she sounded funny, like she had a cold or was trying not to cry or something. Her mother came in through the door then. Harriet put her hand over the mouthpiece as she had seen her mother do, as well. 'Mum, it's Lara's mum.'

Mrs Turner came over, her hand outstretched to take the phone. 'I didn't even hear the phone ring. Thanks, Harriet. Rose, how are you?' There was a pause as she listened for a minute or two. Sitting back at the kitchen table, ears straining, Harriet could hear the murmur of Lara's mum's voice. She sounded like her own mother, except she spoke much more quickly. Harriet concentrated fiercely on the page, wishing she had been able to keep talking to her herself.

'Has he? No, I understand. Of course. No, of course not,' her mother was saying down the phone now, her first words, apart from a few murmurs, in some time. 'Hold on, Rose, would you?' She put her hand over the mouthpiece. Harriet was pleased to see she'd had it right when she did it herself. 'Harriet, would you mind giving me some privacy for a little while? I need to have a quiet chat with Rose.'

Harriet got up happily enough. But an hour later her mum was still talking to Rose. She crept into the kitchen after a while to get her homework off the table. Her mother nodded, to let her know it was okay. She took as long as she could to gather her pencils and books. It sounded like Rose was doing all the talking and her mum was doing all the listening. She wanted to stay longer but she noticed her mum's hand going towards the mouthpiece and got out quickly before she was told to.

She was up in the lounge watching *Candid Camera* with her dad, Austin and James when her mum finally reappeared. Harriet had already filled them in on who was on the phone.

Her father looked up at her mother. 'Long session?'

Mrs Turner nodded, holding her hand to her ear. 'It's burning hot.'

'Can I feel it?' Harriet asked. Her mother leant down. She was right. Her ear was warm to touch.

'Everything okay?' her dad asked.

Harriet looked back and forth between her parents. Austin and James were oblivious, eyes glued to the man on the screen trying to prise off a fifty cent piece the *Candid Camera* people had glued to a footpath.

'She says so.' Her mother lowered her voice. 'He's come back. A new start and all of that. But I don't know. She sounded terrible, tears one minute, laughing the next, saying it was for keeps this time, that it was a fresh start, they mean the world to each other . . .'

Her father spoke as quietly. 'She said that the last time, didn't she?'

'And the time before.'

'She says he promised her it won't happen again . . .'

What wouldn't happen again, Harriet wondered. She knew not to ask. She lay quietly, pretending to watch TV but listening intently.

'So what about —?'

'No. Rose wants the three of them together.'

Harriet understood that. She kept quiet but had to pretend to be surprised when her mum told her, James and Austin in the next commercial break that there had been a change of plan and that Lara wouldn't be coming to stay after all.

Harriet was genuinely disappointed. 'Should I put all the toys back? And will the boys put the bed back in the shed?'

'We might leave it there for the time being. She might come. But I'll let you know.'

'Give me plenty of warning, won't you?' She'd heard Austin use the phrase and had liked it very much.

Her mother had given her another one of those nice smiles. 'I'll give you plenty of warning, Harriet, I promise.'

Two months passed. School was nearly over for another year. Six weeks of summer holidays would be theirs to play in. Soon it would be Christmas. The cards had already started arriving from their mum and dad's friends back in England. Harriet loved opening them, seeing the pictures of snow-covered fields, robins, mistletoe and fireplaces, presents and stockings bundled all around them. She and her mother had gone out shopping, trying to pick the best Australian Christmassy ones they could send in return. Oddly, all the Australian cards had the same northern hemisphere pictures, Santas in full regalia, plum puddings and winter scenes, even while the skies were blue and the sun beating down outside.

Harriet volunteered to make their Christmas cards instead. For two weeks she stayed inside, away from the beach, her fingers getting increasingly multicoloured from felt pens, as she drew Santas in shorts on the beach and drawings of her whole family with captions in her best handwriting underneath, 'Mum, Dad, Austin, James and Me', with a sun big and yellow over their shoulders, the rays nearly covering the page. She added a red starfish to every card. It was her favourite thing to draw. She liked the way starfish had five pointy arms, one for each member of her family.

Gloria loved her drawings. 'Will you come and do one on the blackboard for me, Harriet? Once a week?'

'On your special blackboard?' She looked at her mum.

She smiled. 'If Gloria says you can touch the special blackboard then you can.'

Each Monday she went in after Gloria arrived and drew a summery picture in the corner of the blackboard. Sometimes Gloria had already written her special travel fact by the time she got there, in which case she had to fit her drawing around it. Other times the blackboard was still bare, and Harriet had more freedom. Once she drew a picture so big – of a tropical island, with palm trees and coconuts and a trio of monkeys – there was no room for Gloria's fact.

Gloria was impressed. 'I love your drawing. We can give my fact a miss this week.'

'Oh no,' Harriet said, already rubbing it off. 'Mum says that you and your facts are the goo that holds this place together.'

'Did she really?' Gloria looked like she was trying not to laugh.

'Something like that.' Harriet had overheard it, and wasn't sure if she'd got it right.

'We'll compromise then. You do the same drawing, just smaller, and I'll think of the smallest fact I can.'

That morning she came out to the kitchen after helping Gloria to open up. Austin and James were silently eating their toast. Austin was reading a section of the newspaper. James was scribbling something in the notebook he always carried round with him. Her father was dressed for work, standing up, finishing a cup of tea. He seemed in a hurry.

'Where's Mum?' she asked, as she settled herself at the table and helped herself to a bowl of cornflakes.

'She got called away early this morning,' her father said, finishing his toast and quickly drinking his tea. Harriet thought she had heard the phone ringing during the night, but had gone back to sleep. 'She'll be back as soon as she can. Austin, James, look after Harriet, won't you? I've got to go into Geelong this morning for a meeting, so don't forget to eat something at lunchtime if I'm not back. And call in to Gloria if you need anything.' All of this was delivered as he shrugged into his suit jacket and collected his keys. 'I'll see you all later.' He paused long enough to plant a kiss on Harriet's forehead.

They called out after him.

'Thanks, Dad.'

'Okay, Dad.'

'Thanks, Daddy.'

'Thanks, Daddy,' Austin mimicked Harriet after their father had gone.

She looked up, stung at the teasing. 'He is my daddy.'

'Daddy-waddy.'

'Stop teasing me.'

'Austin, give it a rest.' James didn't look up from his notebook.

'What, Jamesy-wamesy-pamesy?'

'I'm ignoring you. But leave Harriet alone.'

'Oh, poor Harriet-larriet-carriet.'

'Shut up, Austin,' James said, still writing.

'Make me.'

Harriet dropped her spoon with a clatter. 'Stop it, both of you. Stop it.' She hated it when they fought. It made her stomach feel funny. She had to fix it, quickly. She took the notebook away from James, ignoring his protest. 'Come on. Take me to the beach. Or for a picnic.'

'Later, Harriet. Let me finish my breakfast first.'

She didn't care if they went to the beach or not. But it had worked. She'd stopped the tension. Austin gave a loud yawn and then started beating out a rhythm with his fingers on the edge of the table. He was always doing that. He'd told her once he heard music in his head all the time.

James had overheard. 'That's because you're mad, Austin.'

'Better to hear music than have moths flying around in a great blank emptiness, like in your head, James,' he had snapped back.

She pulled at Austin's sleeve, getting in before James said anything about his drumming. 'Come on. Let's go to the beach now. You said you'd teach me bodysurfing this holidays.'

'Harriet, you're eight years old. I'm too cool to be seen with someone like you.' Austin was now tapping away at the table with both hands, the way he did when he was especially bored.

'Can you stop that noise, please? It drives me mad.' James spoke again without looking up.

'You're just jealous.' Austin kept up the tapping, adding cymbal crash noises for good measure. 'No natural rhythm, that's your problem, James.'

'All rhythm, no brains, that's your problem, Austin.'

'Stop it, you two. Dad said you're not to fight.'

'We're not fighting. We're just bored. You really are a little anxiety bag of a child, Harriet, aren't you?'

'I am not a —' She'd forgotten the insult. 'What did you say I was?'

James and Austin both laughed.

'An anxiety bag of a child,' James said helpfully. 'It's all right, Harriet, relax. We're not going to kill each other. Not yet.'

'Mum's away,' Austin said, stopping his tapping. 'Dad's in Geelong. Gloria's busy. Don't you think it's time we played the game?'

Harriet looked up and felt the shiver of excitement. The Game? Austin's Game?

The three of them had been playing the game for two years now. Austin had first had the idea for it in winter, but the locals knew them too well and weren't so easily taken in. Summer, however, brought hundreds of families with children to the small seaside town. Plenty of potential victims. It wasn't something they could play every day, though. The conditions had to be right. In other words, both their parents had to be away.

Harriet loved Austin's game. It was so funny when it worked. 'Yes, please,' she said.

Austin stood up and stretched, lazily. 'James, you in?'

James pushed back his chair. 'Why not? Nothing better to do.' But Harriet knew he was as pleased as she was.

Austin got what he needed from the cupboard and then the three of them went outside. Weather-wise, things were perfect. Dry, hot, the sort of day that brought plenty of kids from the caravan park up the road past their house on the way to the beach.

Austin went to the shed and got his bike while James and Harriet took up position on the roof of the house, climbing first onto the low wall, then swinging up from the veranda railing, until they landed on the rainwater tank. From there it was just a step across the tank to the roof. It was the best place to get a view of any approaching kids. Down below they could see Austin getting ready.

'Three coming, from the caravan park end,' James called. 'Go, Austin, quick.'

Harriet didn't have to watch Austin to know what he'd be doing. She kept her eye on the road. The three kids – all boys, Harriet could see now – were coming closer. They looked older than her, ten, eleven maybe. She had to put her hand over her mouth to stop herself from making any sound as they came closer, noticed Austin lying in the middle of the road, his bike tipped on its side next to him. They started quickening their step. Austin was motionless, his arms and legs spreadeagled, pools of red all around him.

'Oh yuk, look, is that blood?' one of the boys said.

'He must have fallen off his bike.'

'Is he dead?'

James nodded at Harriet. From their position on the roof, they'd clearly heard the conversation. They sprang into action, leaping from the roof to the rainwater tank, then swinging down from the veranda railing. That was always Harriet's favourite bit.

'What's going on here?' James said in a gruff voice.

The boys looked horrified. 'We don't know,' the oldest one said. 'We found him like this.'

None of them heard the car coming up the road behind them.

Just then, Austin stirred. The three boys jumped. 'He's alive!' one of them shouted.

Austin made a gurgling sound. 'Barely. I don't know how much time I have left.' He reached out a hand to the three boys. 'You saw it. Will you tell the police when they start their investigation?'

'But we didn't see anything.' The older boy sounded panicked. 'Shouldn't we call for an ambulance?'

'I think it's too late for that,' Austin said, dramatically. 'The agony. A searing pain shoots through me.'

Harriet felt a shiver of delight. Austin was so good at this. He caught her eye, prompting her with an expression. Whoops. She'd nearly forgotten her line.

'Have you got a final message for all of us, Austin?' she said, as he had taught her.

Behind them, a car door shut. Then another.

Austin raised himself on one arm, addressing the three boys. 'I want to say to all of you, if I die here today, that knowing you, even for this brief time, has meant the world to me . . .'

'What's going on here? Austin? James? Harriet?'

They all spun around. Mrs Turner stood by her car, with a little girl beside her. Harriet noticed immediately they were holding hands.

The oldest of the three boys stuttered his answer. 'There's been a terrible accident. He fell off his bike . . . '

Mrs Turner walked over. The little girl came too. Harriet saw she was wearing a nice red dress and shoes that matched. Shoes with buckles. 'Yes, it looks fairly terrible,' Mrs Turner said. 'There's a lot of blood, anyway. Or a lot of tomato sauce, at least.'

The boys looked again. 'It's tomato sauce?'

'A whole bottle, by the looks of things.' Mrs Turner smiled at them, even while she glared at Austin, now sitting up and looking in much less pain. 'Get off the road, Austin Turner, and apologise to these poor boys immediately.'

'It's just a bit of fun, Mum. You know how the school holidays drag.'

'Do it now, Austin.'

'So it's a joke?' the oldest of them said, looking relieved.

'Yes, hilarious, isn't it? Austin, apologise please. James, you should know better. Harriet, stop snickering.'

Austin leapt up, wiping off the excess sauce on his shorts. He put out his hand. 'Thanks, kids, you were good sports.'

Mrs Turner apologised to them once more. 'I'm so sorry, I promise you it won't happen again. Don't let them put you off going to the beach, either.'

The older boy and his brothers took off. They didn't look convinced.

Mrs Turner looked down at the little girl standing beside her, still clutching her hand. She gave her a big smile. 'Not quite the introduction I'd have liked, but never mind. Austin, James, Harriet, let me introduce you. This is Lara.'

While Lara was unpacking her small brown suitcase – Harriet had seen she also had a plastic bag of toys with her – James, Austin and Harriet gathered around their mother in the kitchen.

'I'm sorry there wasn't much warning, but I wasn't sure until I got to Melbourne whether or not she'd be coming home with me. So please, the three of you, be kind to her. You know how we've talked about other people not being as lucky as we are? Well, Lara and her mum and dad have had some bad luck and that's why we're helping.'

Harriet liked the idea of that. It sounded mysterious. It made Lara even more interesting, she decided. She was going to be really, really kind to her.

In her bedroom soon after, Harriet was very interested in the way Lara had taken all her clothes out of her suitcase and refolded them into five neat piles. She had counted them. One for underwear, one for tops, one for shorts, one for dresses and one for jumpers. Lara was now neatly putting them away into the third and fourth drawers of Harriet's chest of drawers, as Mrs Turner had shown her. It had taken Harriet a while to decide whether to give her the top two or the bottom two drawers. In the end her mother had made the decision, hurriedly moving the contents to allow Lara the use of two spare drawers.

'Mum, they're all crumpled now,' she had protested.

'No more or less crumpled than they were to begin with. We'll tidy them up later. I'll give you a hand. You're a good, kind girl, Harriet, thank you.'

Now, Harriet perched on the end of her bed and watched Lara empty the contents of the plastic bag.

'How old are you?' she asked.

'Eight.'

'Me too.'

As she watched her unpack, Harriet decided it was as if one of the black babies she sponsored in Africa had come to live with them. Things took on a rosy glow. Lara could be her new project. Her 'be kind to less fortunate children' project, the way the teacher had said last year at school, when they were doing their fundraising. Harriet had loved it. They'd saved up their pocket money and sent it away in a small cardboard box to the missions and then a few weeks later they'd got a letter back with strange stamps and a polite note. 'Thank you for your kind and gracious generosity. We now have a new water tap in our village and we think of you every time we see the clean, fresh water.'

'Will you be coming to school with me?' Harriet asked her. 'And to swimming?'

Lara sat neatly on the side of the bed. 'I don't know. I suppose it will depend on how long I stay here.'

Harriet was a bit surprised by her. Lara didn't seem nervous at all. If Harriet had been a little kid arriving out of nowhere like this she would have felt really sick, she thought. Perhaps Lara felt bad inside but was good at hiding it. Harriet felt really sorry for her then and tried to think of the most kind thing she could do, like her mother would want. 'Which bed would you like? I always sleep by the window, but if you would like that one, I don't mind.' She had her fingers crossed as she said it. She did mind. She minded badly.

'I'd love to sleep by the window. Thank you.' Lara picked up her plastic bag and went to the bed by the window.

Harriet blinked and uncrossed her fingers. That hadn't gone how she'd expected. She tried again to be friendly. 'When's your birthday?'

'May 14.'

'Mine is May 17.'

'I was born early,' Lara said. 'My mother said that for a little while they worried that I wouldn't live.'

'Were you sick?'

'No, just really small.' She showed how small, holding her two hands about a foot apart.

'How do you know how small you were?'

'My dad did a drawing of me once.'

'Oh.' Harriet didn't know what to say about that. She knew her Dad sent lots of people away on holidays but she didn't think she'd ever seen him do a drawing.

There was a noise at the door. It was Harriet's mother. 'Hello, girls, are you getting on? Good. Now, how about something nice to drink? Lara, what's your favourite drink?'

'Chocolate milk,' she said.

How could Lara be so sure? Harriet never knew what her favourite of anything was, if anyone asked her. How could she choose between Coke and lemonade and orange juice?

'We'll have to take a walk down to the shop to get some, then. Harriet, would you like chocolate milk too?'

She was amazed. Not only was Lara going to get chocolate milk – even though there wasn't any in the house – her mother was going to take them to the shop to buy it. This never happened. It wasn't a matter of being asked what would you like either. There were the options – lemonade or water. Quick, make up your mind.

'It's nice here,' Lara said as they walked along the beach path. The sea looked very blue. There were people on the beach, paddling, building sandcastles, setting up umbrellas.

'The sea air is good for you too,' Harriet said. She'd heard her dad say that the week before.

Lara looked up at Mrs Turner. 'Mum says she always thought that until she had a month of it on her way here to Australia.'

Mrs Turner laughed. 'Your mother didn't like that ship much, did she?'

Harriet started feeling even more bewildered. This girl had arrived out of nowhere and yet she and her mother were talking about things she had never heard of. And how did her mum know whether Lara's mum had liked it or not? 'Where is your mum?' she asked Lara, wanting to make her look at her for a change, instead of her mother all the time.

'At home.'

'Is she sick again?'

'No.'

Harriet knew her mother was giving her The Look. She deliberately glanced down so she was out of its firing range.

'Where is home?'

'Melbourne.'

Harriet nodded. She knew where Melbourne was at least. 'We lived there when we first got to Australia. Before I was born.'

'I know. My mum and dad and your mum and dad lived in the same place. We've got photos in our kitchen.'

That was too much. 'Mum, how come we don't have photos?'

'We do. Lara's mum and dad came out from England on the same ship as us.'

'The *Plymouth Wanderer*.'

'That's right, Lara. The *Plymouth Wanderer*.'

'Were you named after the captain too?' Harriet asked.

Lara didn't smile. 'The captain was a man.'

'I know. But I was named after him.'

'Harriet's a funny name for a man.'

'No, not Harriet. His name was Harold. But Mum thought I was a man, I mean a boy, so she promised she'd call me after him because that's where I was made, on the ship, wasn't I, Mum?' It seemed urgent to be the one doing the talking, the one having the proper conversation with her mother. 'That's why Austin calls me Harold sometimes.'

'Which one is Austin?' The question was directed at Mrs Turner, not Harriet.

'The middle one. The naughtiest one. Here we are.' They'd reached the milk bar. 'So, chocolate milk for you, Lara. And what about you, Harriet?'

'Chocolate milk,' she said firmly. Even though she hated it.

Later that afternoon Mr and Mrs Turner were in the garden. While Mr Turner weeded the edge of the path leading to the corrugated iron shed, Mrs Turner spoke to him in an urgent whisper.

'Of course some warning would have been better, Neil. But what could I do? She was begging me. Tears one minute, shouts the next. She was in a complete state. Her husband rang while I was there and you should have heard the screaming match. And the house was a mess. Chaos. It was no place for a child.'

Inside, at the window of the laundry, Harriet stood still, listening to everything.

'The whole place in a mess, except for Lara's little room. She had it as neat as can be. And her bag all packed in minutes. She nearly broke my heart.'

'She didn't mind going? Leaving her mother?'

'She seemed to understand. I asked her about it on the trip back and she said her mum had told her she needed to go and get her dad. And that it would be easier if she could travel on her own.'

Harriet strained to hear. Luckily her father's voice was louder than her mother's. She heard him clearly.

'I keep thinking of all the beers we had on the ship together. He seemed like the nicest of fellows. Not the type to do this.'

'That's what I thought. I asked Rose why she puts up with it and she started crying again and went on and on about how much she loves him, that he's the centre of her universe, that he can't really help himself, that he —' Her mother's voice was drowned out again by the sound of a passing car. When Harriet could hear again it was her father talking.

'So how long does she want us to keep the little one?'

'A week, two weeks perhaps. You don't mind, do you?'

'No, of course not. She'll be company for Harriet, anyway. Let me finish that up, if you want to go and make up the beds or get her settled.'

'Thanks, love.'

Harriet slipped away up the hallway as the back door opened and her mother came into the house.

Lara only stayed five days the first time. A phone call came after dinner one night. Mrs Turner had another conversation. Harriet came in at the end in time to hear the arrangements being made. 'Are you sure? I can run up with her. No, lunchtime is fine.'

She scooted back into the lounge room where they'd been watching TV so she'd be there for the announcement from her mother.

Mrs Turner came in and touched Lara gently on the head. 'That was your mum, Lara, love. They're coming to collect you tomorrow.'

Harriet glanced at her. Lara's expression didn't change. 'Thank you.'

That night in bed she had a feeling of excitement, as though they were her parents coming to get her. 'What's your mum like?'

She almost heard Lara's shrug in the darkness. 'She's shorter than your mum, and she's got brown curly hair.'

'And what about your dad?'

'He's taller.'

'And you really haven't got any brothers or sisters?'

'No.'

'Do you get lonely when you're home on your own?'

'No.'

'I would.'

'You get used to it.'

They arrived at the Turners' just after one o'clock. Harriet's mother and father were both there. The table had been set. There were sandwiches, egg and lettuce, ham and mustard, and cheese and pickle. There were two sorts of cakes. It was all under white netting cages, used as flyguards. It was Harriet's job to put them on and take them off. She knew it was important to make sure there were no flies trapped underneath when she put them on.

They were all in the kitchen as their mother got things ready. 'Wouldn't that be terrible, Mum?' Harriet said, trying to get her attention as Mrs Turner moved back and forth between the fridge and the sink. 'If you had put them on to stop the flies getting on the sandwiches and the whole time there was a fly trapped under there.'

'If I was a fly that's what I'd do,' Austin said. 'Sit there quietly, my wings whirring a little bit, while the sandwiches were being made. And then, in that split second, after the sandwiches had been made and the human was reaching for the —'

'Not a human. Me.'

'All right, Harold. When you were reaching for the flyguard, I'd set my wings whirring to five hundred miles per hour and just as the guard was about to go down, whiz in underneath and there my feast would be.'

'That wouldn't work,' Lara said.

Austin turned to her, an eyebrow raised. 'No? Why not?'

'The noise. Flies make a lot of noise. What I would do is sneak in under the plate. Flies can run really fast, as fast as they fly, but without the noise. They could go in under the plate and sit there. There would have been plenty of time too, while the sandwiches were still being made and the human was walking back and forth to the fridge.'

'You know, Lara, I think you're right.'

'So when the guard came down, even if the human —'

'Me,' Harriet said. 'I'm the one with the guard.'

Lara was still looking at Austin. 'Harriet wouldn't see us, because we'd be hidden under the plate. And we could wait until the coast was clear and then crawl out and eat everything we wanted.'

'Smear our germs all over the bread.'

'Climb inside the sandwich and have a sleep,' Lara said, grinning now.

'We could dance on the crusts.'

'No,' Harriet said too loudly. 'No, you couldn't. I'm in charge of keeping the flies out and I would kill you both.'

'You wouldn't,' Lara said. 'You wouldn't know we were there.'

'Lara's right,' Austin said. 'We tricked you, Harold.' He held out a hand and shook Lara's vigorously. 'Well done, team. The flies win.'

'The flies win,' Lara echoed.

After that, Harriet wasn't so keen to meet Lara's parents. She deliberately went into the lounge room and started watching television. She pretended she didn't hear the car arrive, or her mother calling out hello over the fence or her name being called.

James came up after a while. 'Harriet, lunch is on. Lara's mum and dad are here. Come on.'

'I don't want to meet them. I just want her to go.'

James shrugged. 'Mum wants someone to take off the flyguards. No problem, she'll ask Lara to do it instead.'

Harriet was up in a moment. 'That's my job.'

'Then come and do it, would you? I'm starving.'

She sidled into the kitchen, staying close to the wall. Her mother was saying something about the travel agency being busy but stopped as she noticed Harriet in the corner. She gestured to her.

'Here she is at last. Rose, Dennis, this is Harriet. Harriet, this is Lara's mum and dad, Mr and Mrs Robinson.'

She felt shy. She hated it when adults all stopped and looked at her like this. 'Hello.'

'Hello, Harriet. We spoke on the phone the other night, didn't we?'

She nodded. Lara's mother did have brown curly hair. She also had a bruise under her left eye. It was either coming or going. Lara's father had gone back to talking with Harriet's father. He was tall, smiley. He had something in his hair that made it shiny and wavy. Mr Perrotti at Mass had hair like that, Harriet remembered. She always wanted to touch it, or put a marble in one of the waves, to see if it would run down. If she and Lara made jokes with each other, she would have joked to her about that.

Lara was sitting beside Austin on the bench by the wall where Harriet usually sat. Since she had arrived she had been sitting in the guest's chair. Where she belonged. That side belonged to family.

'That's my chair, Lara.'

Mrs Turner's smile stiffened. 'Harriet, don't worry about that. Say hello to Mr Robinson.'

'But Lara is in my chair. I always sit next to Austin.'

'Today's different, because we've got guests so we are all sitting wherever we want to.'

That ripple of something hot and uncomfortable went through her again. Lara had gone back to talking to Austin. They were playing rock, scissors, paper. It was Harriet's favourite game. She knew it wasn't right, but she wanted to spoil it for everyone, the way it had been spoiled for her. She turned back to Mrs Robinson and thought of the rudest thing she could ask.

'Mrs Robinson, why have you got that bruise under your eye?'

'Harriet, please. Don't be nosy.'

Mrs Robinson gave a loud laugh and reached up and touched the mark. 'It doesn't matter. It's nice to meet a curious child. I was a silly-billy, Harriet. At our house in Melbourne we have a big apple tree and last week we were pruning it – do you know what pruning is?'

Harriet shook her head, hating that her question was now being answered, while beside her Lara and Austin kept playing their game. She didn't like Lara's mother's voice either. It was too high and she kept looking over at her husband when she was talking instead of looking at Harriet. She kept doing twitchy things with her fingers too. If Harriet had been at school doing that she would have been told off for wriggling.

'It means cutting back the branches and dead wood, so that all the new spring growth can come and there'll be plenty of apples. I pulled down a big branch and thought I had it and it went ping,' another laugh, 'well, not so much ping as splat. It hit me right in the eye and sent me flying.'

She was torn between her curiosity and wanting to join in with Lara and Austin. 'Is that why Lara came to stay with us? Because of the tree?'

'Harriet, please.' It was her mother.

'I couldn't see for a couple of days and I had to go to hospital,' Mrs Robinson explained. 'And my neighbours were away. Your mother was a wonder to step in when she did.' That smile again, directed right at Mrs Turner.

'Why didn't Lara's dad take care of her?'

'That is enough, Harriet.'

Mrs Robinson was now answering the questions directly. 'He wasn't there.'

'I work interstate.' It was the first time he'd spoken. He had an accent like her own father's.

'But you said *we* were pruning.'

'You've got a detective on your hands here,' Mr Robinson laughed.

'Or a lawyer.'

'We were. Me and Lara. Lara called the ambulance for me, didn't you, Lara?'

Lara nodded. 'Mrs Turner, can I please have a sandwich?'

'Of course you can. Dennis, Rose, you must be ravenous. Now, sit down everyone and help yourselves.'

The flyguards were whipped away without ceremony.

'Watch out for flies,' Harriet said to no one in particular.

Chapter Twelve

Three months later, James, Austin and Harriet were in the living room watching *Gilligan's Island* on TV after school when their mother came to find them. Austin was stretched out on the sofa. He was getting so tall he hung over the end of the cushions. James was in the beanbag, also stretched out. Harriet was lying on her beach towel on the carpet. She'd got it for her eighth birthday and liked using it all the time. She loved the colours, the feel of the material and especially the fact that her mum had got someone to sew HARRIET'S TOWEL in curvy letters on the bottom.

'Harriet, boys, I need to talk to the three of you about something important. Can I turn the TV off?'

They sat up immediately.

'It's about Lara. You remember Lara?'

They all nodded. As Austin said afterwards when they were alone and talking about it, of course they remembered Lara. How often did their mother think strangers came to live with them out of the blue for a few days?

'And you remember her mum and dad?'

More nods.

'I don't know quite how to tell you this, but something terrible has happened.' She paused and took a breath. 'Lara's parents were killed yesterday. In a car accident in Ireland.'

Austin and James were straight in with the questions. How? Where? When? Harriet just sat there. There was shock but there was also a kind of excitement. She had met two people who had been killed in a car accident! It was only afterwards she thought how sad it must have been for her mother, that her friend Rose had been killed like that.

'What were they doing in Ireland?' James asked.

'Rose's mother was Irish. She died a month ago and Rose and her husband went back to Ireland to sort out her things.'

James wanted all the details of the crash. 'Was it night? Or was it bad conditions during the day?'

'I don't know, James. I don't know the whole story yet.'

'Were they killed instantly?' Austin wanted to know.

'I think so. I hope so, for their sakes.'

Harriet still couldn't speak, her mind filling with images of a car slipping and sliding on a road and then Lara's mother and father being dead, just like that.

'Is Lara all right?' Austin again. 'Has she been hurt?'

'She's fine. She wasn't with them. She's away on a school camp in Melbourne.'

That made it even sadder in Harriet's opinion. Would she have been killed if she had been with them? Austin got in first with the question. 'So does she know yet?'

Mrs Turner shook her head. 'I'm driving there this afternoon. The police contacted me. They want me to tell her.'

Austin frowned. 'The police in Ireland contacted you? How did they know where you were?'

'They got in touch with the Australian police who contacted me.'

'But how did they know to contact you?'

'Because Rose asked me if I would be the contact person while they were away. She didn't know many people in Australia, and she knew we'd be close by if anything happened.'

'It's as if she had a premonition,' Austin said.

'What's a premonition?' Harriet asked.

'A feeling that something bad was going to happen. Maybe even that the car was going to crash.'

Harriet knew from the tone in Austin's voice that he was feeling that same excitement. It was awful but it was also thrilling.

Mrs Turner stood up. 'We don't know all the details yet, but what it means for now is that Lara will be coming to stay with us again. And it could be for longer than a few days.'

Harriet felt a bit funny about that. She didn't remember every detail of Lara's brief visit those months ago, but she knew it hadn't all been good. That she had wanted to be kind but it had backfired on her.

'Your dad is driving up to Melbourne with me to get her. Gloria will be in soon, she'll stay here with the three of you while we're gone. Harriet, would it be all right if Lara stayed in your room again?'

'Yes, Mum.' She decided she did want to be kind again. She liked how it felt when she was. But this time she wasn't going to offer Lara the bed by the window. All her books were on the windowsill there and she liked the feel of a cool sea breeze on her face on hot nights. But maybe they could take turns. If Lara really wanted the bed by the window she could have it now and again . . .

'She's going to be very upset,' Mrs Turner said. 'So I need you all to be kind to her, all right?'

'Is she an orphan?' Harriet asked.

'Yes, Harriet, she is.'

Gloria arrived with an overnight bag. There were more whispered adult conversations in the kitchen, and then their parents drove away.

When Lara arrived with Harriet's mum it was immediately obvious she didn't care where she slept. Harriet, James and Austin stood back as she came in. She was pale, her eyes red-rimmed. She was clinging to Mrs Turner.

They had talked to Gloria about what they should say to her.

'Do we say "sorry about your parents"?'

'Or "we're sorry you're an orphan"?'

'Just say you're sorry. Leave it at that for the time being.'

Harriet tried when she arrived. 'I'm sorry, Lara.'

Lara turned and Harriet was frightened by the look in her eyes. She looked like she was a long way away, even though she was there in front of her. Harriet wanted to say more. She glanced at Gloria. Gloria gave a nod.

'About your mum and dad.'

That blank look again. She noticed Mrs Turner was holding her close. Even when Harriet came back into the room a few minutes later, after her father had asked her to get some milk from the kitchen, her mother and Lara were still holding hands. Harriet wondered if they had been like that for the whole drive. Would they have sat in the back of the car, side by side, or would her mum have sat in the front while her dad did the driving? If that's how it was, then Lara would have been in the back on her own. That wouldn't be fair. Not for hours in a car when your mum and dad have just been killed in a car crash.

She needed to find out. She went over to her dad, who was

sitting at the table. 'Did Lara sit in the front or in the back with Mum?' she whispered.

'What, love?'

'On the drive, who sat where?'

'Harriet, does it matter?'

'I just wondered.'

'Not now, Harriet.'

Lara slept in the bed by the door from the first night she arrived. Harriet was relieved. She had been prepared to let her have the window bed the first night, but she was glad it hadn't come up. Mrs Turner tucked both of them in, and then sat beside Lara on the bed stroking her head until she fell asleep. Harriet waited for her to come over to her next, but instead she blew a kiss from the doorway.

'You were nice and kind to Lara tonight, Harriet, thank you,' she whispered.

'But I didn't do anything.'

'I thought you did. You were very welcoming.'

She hadn't really been. She had got Lara a glass of cold milk but that was only because her dad had told her to. 'I feel sorry for her,' she said. It was the best she could do.

'It's going to be a difficult time for her, Harriet.' Mrs Turner came over then, even though the room was nearly in darkness. Only the light from the living room was spilling in, giving her a path to follow. She crouched beside the bed and Harriet waited for her forehead to be stroked too, but her mother's hands stayed on the edge of the bed, smoothing down the sheet. 'I know it will be tricky for you, too. But we'll all make it as easy for her as we can, won't we?'

She wasn't sure what her mother was talking about but nodded anyway.

'Good girl. Night night.'

'Night night.'

She got a kiss on the head. Not as good as the stroking on the forehead Lara had got but then her mum and dad hadn't just been killed in a car crash.

Lara stayed home for the first week. Harriet had to go to school, but she didn't mind because she got to tell all her friends about Lara, the orphan who was now living with them.

'What does she look like?' her friends asked.

'Like a normal person,' she admitted. Her friends seemed disappointed. Harriet was a bit, too. In her books orphans all wore rags and had black circles under their eyes.

'So if she lives with you forever, does that mean your mum and dad adopt her?'

She didn't know. She asked them one night. Lara had gone down to the beach with Austin. Harriet had been torn between spending time with them and having her parents to herself for a while.

'Are you going to adopt Lara?'

'We don't know yet.'

One afternoon she saw Lara go into the garden with her mother. They stayed there for a long time. Harriet wandered out after a while and tried as casually as she could to get close enough to hear.

'Harriet, love, what are you doing?'

'Having a look at the garden.' She leant down to touch one of the rose bushes to back up her story.

'Pet, can you leave me and Lara alone for a little while? We're having a talk about a few things.'

Harriet deliberately didn't look at Lara. 'Do you want to talk to me about it as well? I might have some good ideas.'

'In a while perhaps. But for now it's between Lara and me. So be a good girl, won't you, and go back inside?'

She stayed in the kitchen. There was a good view out to the garden from there. Her father came in.

'Harriet, come and help me wash the car?'

She couldn't say she had to stand at the window and keep watch. She turned away, reluctantly.

That night after tea her mother called Harriet, James and Austin together and told them the news. Lara was going to be living with them all the time from now on. 'Isn't that great?' their mother said.

Harriet nodded. Austin and James asked a few questions, but seemed relaxed about it. Afterwards they all went back into the living room where Lara was sitting watching TV with their father.

As Harriet came in she gave Lara the kindest smile she could produce. Unfortunately, Lara wasn't looking at her when she gave it.

Over the next few months it felt like there were many new layers to the household. Before it had been Harriet and James and Austin, and then her mum and dad. There was the travel agency, the main street, Gloria, school, the house and the beach. They roamed freely back and forth and everyone was where Harriet expected them to be. Now it was all different. Everywhere it had been only her it now seemed to be her and Lara.

People in the town knew all about them. 'Is this your new sister, Harriet?' they would ask when they saw them walking back from school together, or going down to the beach. Harriet wasn't sure what to call Lara. If she was asked that, she would nod and smile, to be polite, which was what her mum and dad said she had to be as much as she could.

'Do you want me to call you my sister?' she asked Lara once.

'I don't mind,' Lara said.

Lara called her mum and dad Penny and Neil, like Gloria and Kevin did. Harriet didn't feel good about that when she first heard it. She asked Austin what he thought.

'She has to call them something, doesn't she? And Penny and Neil are their names, after all. Would you rather she called them Mum and Dad?'

'No.' She was sure about that. They weren't Lara's mum and dad.

She heard the man in the shop next door ask her mum if she was going to adopt Lara. She heard bits of the conversation, words like guardian and legality, that she didn't understand. She went to Gloria again. 'If Mum and Dad adopt Lara, does that mean she can call them Mum and Dad too?'

'She could if she wanted to. But I think she likes calling them Penny and Neil.'

'Would I call her my real sister then?'

'I think legally you'd call her your stepsister. But you could call her your sister now, if you wanted to. I don't think they're going to formally adopt her, though, are they? Your mum said that they'd decided on a legal guardianship, which is almost the same thing.'

'I don't know. No one tells me anything around here.'

She nearly caught Gloria laughing. But then her face went serious again. 'Here, Harriet, help me put these brochures in these envelopes, would you?'

As they stuffed them – glossy pamphlets advertising the islands off Queensland and Fiji resort holidays – Gloria asked her about school. About her jigsaw puzzles. And about Lara.

'So how are you and Lara getting on, Harriet?'

'Fine.'

'Are you in the same class at school?'

'We were at the start but she's better than me at reading and maths, so they moved her into a different one.'

'And are you okay about that?'

'She is better. I don't like maths much.'

Lara also played with different girls at recess and lunch, but sometimes they all played in a big group. At home, they all did things together – ate their meals, watched TV, went to the beach. At least her mum and dad got Lara to do the dishes and sweep the floor, too. Harriet had been worried she would get out of it, but her mum and dad seemed to be treating her like another kid. Austin and James did too. Sometimes they teased Lara, sometimes they ignored her. Just like they did with Harriet. She wasn't sure how she felt about that.

Lara started having nightmares about six months after she arrived. Night after night, Harriet was woken up by Lara talking in her sleep. Once or twice she would scream or wake up crying. The first time Harriet tried to help her, but it scared her. She started running into her parents at the first noise.

'Ah, Lara, you poor little mite.' Her mother would cradle Lara, do that thing where she stroked her forehead until she fell asleep again. It lasted for more than a week sometimes, night after night. Harriet would hear the screaming and go and get her mother. Each time, her mother would come, hold Lara tight. Once she stayed for more than an hour, murmuring to Lara in a voice too soft for Harriet to hear.

There was a break of three nights and then it happened again. Harriet had had enough. She put her pillow over her head and tried to block out the crying. It wasn't until Lara was sobbing very loudly that her mother came in.

The next morning her mother sat down next to Harriet at the kitchen table while she was having breakfast. It was the weekend, so there was no school. Lara was outside with Austin, filling the bird feeder that hung on the plum tree. 'Harriet, why didn't you come and get me last night when Lara was crying?'

She kept eating her cornflakes. 'I didn't wake up.'

'You must have. Please, Harriet, come and get me if Lara's upset. You know we have to be kind to her.'

That was too much. She put down the spoon. 'I am being kind. But you and Dad love her more than you love me now.'

'Harriet, we don't.'

'Then you love her as much as you love me. And she just got here and I'm your real daughter and it's not fair.'

She got up and ran away. She only got as far as the beach path. The sea scared her in wintertime. The waves sounded too noisy and sometimes people would appear, just when you thought the beach was empty. Some of the kids at school said there were even people who lived on the beach. She stood for a while by the grass path, near the swings and the barbecues.

She waited for more than ten minutes but no one came to look for her. When she slowly made her way back she saw her mum was now out with Austin and Lara, moving the bird feeder to a new place.

They hadn't even noticed she was gone.

The first anniversary of Lara's arrival came around. Their mother made an announcement over lunch a few days before. 'I want Lara to have a special way of remembering her parents. So we're going to have a little ceremony.'

'At church?'

'No, not at church. Here, in the garden.'

She knew then that Lara and her mum had already talked about this. The decision had been made. 'What will we do?'

'Lara thought she'd like to say something, and then I will say something about her mum and dad, and so will your dad, and then we will think about them, and how sad we are that they're not with us, but how glad we are that Lara has been able to stay with us and become part of our family.'

'What date will it be?'

'We talked about that, too, didn't we, love?' Her mother smiled over at Lara, who was sitting quietly. 'And we thought maybe the day Lara came to live with us, rather than —' she hesitated, 'rather than her parents' anniversary. So we remember something good at the same time as we remember something sad.'

Harriet liked the sound of this. 'Can I do something?'

'I think this first one is for Lara, Harriet. We'll see how we go after that.'

'But I could do the flowers or help with the prayers. I'm good at prayers.' She'd got a star last week at school for the prayer she wrote about wanting the weather to be good for sports day. She had rhymed *keep the rain away* with *on our sports day*.

'Not this time, Harriet.'

Harriet got up and walked away then. It wasn't until ages after that her mother came out to find her. She'd had to start dropping plums from the tree she'd climbed up to draw attention to herself.

'Harriet, please don't be like this.'

'Lara gets to do everything.'

'Harriet, this isn't a treat. This is a way for Lara to remember her mum and dad, and for her to know we remember them too.'

'But it's not fair. You're always *asking* her to do things. You *tell* me.'

'What do you mean?'

'You say to her, "Lara, would you like to go into your room and finish your homework." And you say to me, "Harriet, go and do your homework."'

Her mother was silent for a few seconds and then nodded. 'You're right. I have done that. I'm sorry, Harriet, I didn't realise. We're trying to make it as easy for Lara as we can, to be as kind as we can to her. Do you remember, we talked about being kind to her?'

'But she's okay now. She hardly cries at all any more. She doesn't even have those nightmares.'

'That doesn't mean everything is okay, though. She's still very sad inside.'

'How do you know?'

'Because I know what it feels like when your mum and dad die.'

'That was different. You said your mum and dad were old when they died.'

'It's still sad, whenever it happens. Come down from there, Harriet, come and help me. And you'll have your own special days down the track, I promise you. This one is for Lara and her mum and dad memories.'

Harriet climbed down. She didn't really need her mum's help but it felt nice to take her hands and jump into her arms like she used to do when she was little. 'What's she calling it? It's not a birthday or Christmas Day, is it? What's the name of this day?'

'It's an anniversary, of when she came to stay with us, and a day to think about her parents.'

'Can she call it Memory Day?'

'You can ask her if you like.'

Harriet asked her as soon as they went inside. Lara thought about it and then shook her head. 'No, thanks anyway, Harriet.'

'But Memory Day is a good name. You can remember your mum and dad and remember when you first came to live with us.'

Mr Turner patted her on the head. 'Harriet, I don't think Lara wants to call it that.'

She couldn't do anything right. Anything. 'It's always about Lara in this house!' she shouted, as loudly as she could. She slammed the door after herself, ran into her room and threw herself onto her bed.

Her mum didn't come to find her that night. She eventually fell asleep. When she came out the next morning she was told off, by her mum and by her dad, for being so rude.

Chapter Thirteen

The St Ives hotel had set aside a corner of the bar area for the *Willoughby* cocktail party. Harriet checked with the manager that all the preparations were in place. They were. He told her Lara had faxed through a detailed running list and everything she'd asked for was organised. Harriet checked the date. Three days previously. It was so peculiar. If Lara had known she was going to leave them like this, would she still have been checking that the buffet and wine were going to be in place?

Harriet glanced at her watch. Twenty minutes to seven. She had promised Patrick Shawcross she would meet him in his room and escort him down to the cocktail party. It was a way of keeping things in control. It was also for his own safety, but she hadn't told him that. She didn't like to imagine what Mrs Lamerton might do if she happened upon Willoughby on his own in the hotel corridor.

She made one last check of her appearance. She'd washed and blowdried her hair and applied night-time make-up – darker eye-shadow and a bolder shade of the red lipstick she liked. It was how she looked from the neck down that was the problem. After spending the afternoon in normal clothes she was back in her now dry Turner Travel uniform. Another one of Melissa's rules – full uniform to be worn at all group functions, as well as during travel-ling days. It made the tour leaders easy to spot across rooms, as well as in airports. She had three attempts at tying the scarf before deciding it would have to do. Perhaps Miss Talbot would show her how to tie it again. She had seen her itching to get her fingers on it in Malaysia during the stopover and eventually given in. Those nimble knitter's fingers had proved equally skilled at twisting and tying a silk scarf. If she'd had time she would have called in to Miss Talbot's room and asked for her help. She suspected there would be a flurry of activity in all the rooms already though, especially those of the women. From what Harriet had seen so far, they all took a lot of trouble to dress up each evening.

As she put her key in her bag she realised she had run out of peppermints. She liked to have a supply with her on tour, more for her clients than herself. Gloria called them the tour guide's secret weapon. As they had all discovered over the years, there was nothing more upsetting for groups of people travelling in close quarters than someone with halitosis. She decided to nip out quickly to the chemist she'd seen down the road when they pulled in. She glanced out the window and saw dark grey clouds had covered the sky. There was even a smattering of rain on the window. She took her own, non-Turner Travel red macintosh off the hook and slipped it on over the uniform.

Ten minutes later she had a new supply of peppermints and a beating heart. There had been a queue in the chemist and she was late getting back to the hotel. There wasn't time to take her mac back to her room. She smiled at the receptionist and darted into the room where the cocktail party was being held. Everything was set up. The bar was open, its wooden shutters pulled aside. There were cocktail glasses and bowls of glacé cherries, pineapple chunks on sticks and a giddy arrangement of paper umbrellas and twirly straws. It looked like something from a cruise ship. Across the room two uniformed waitresses were arranging the buffet dinner. They had ordered a simple selection of poached salmon, cold ham and salads, with plenty of warm bread rolls and dishes of butter curls. Nothing too spicy, nothing too exotic. Elderly stomachs had a habit of 'playing up', as their clients often delicately put it, when on tour. Most of the group were already there, more than ten minutes early. Their faces lifted in expectation when she opened the frosted glass doors and then fell again when they realised she was on her own. She gave a big smile and promised to see them again shortly.

'With the guest of honour?' Mrs Lamerton said, sharply.

'The man himself,' Harriet said with a smile.

She went up the stairs to Patrick Shawcross's room, catching sight of herself in the mirror at the end of his corridor. A little wind-blown but not too bad. And at least the red of the macintosh suited her, which was more than could be said for the yellow uniform. She knocked on his door at ten to seven, as they'd agreed. There was no answer. Another knock.

'Mr Shawcross?'

Nothing.

'Mr Shawcross?'

She tried the door. It opened. She walked in, just in time to see him step in from the open balcony. 'I'm sorry to just come in like this. I knocked but . . .' She stopped. He looked terrible. Pale, with beads of sweat on his forehead. There was no sign of the amused, relaxed man she'd seen earlier.

'Harriet, hello.'

'Mr Shawcross, are you all right?'

'I think so. I will be.' He gave a weak smile. 'Just a bit queasy.'

What could it be, food poisoning? Or perhaps he had an allergy?

'I'm so sorry. I can call a doctor, we could maybe get you some emergency medication or —'

'I'll be fine. Well, not fine, but you don't need the doctor.'

'But if it's food poisoning —'

'It's not food poisoning. It's nerves.'

'Nerves?'

'Stage fright.'

'You mean about the cocktail party?'

He nodded.

'But you can't be nervous of them. It's twelve old people.'

'I'd be nervous if it was four toddlers.'

'But you've been working as an actor for years, haven't you?'

'Yes, and I've been sick with nerves beforehand for years too.' The colour was coming back into his face. 'I know it's ridiculous. And I know I'm hardly on the brink of stepping out into the Royal Albert Hall, but a performance is a performance.' He gave her a shadow of his usual smile.

'But you'll be great. You will be. They're all beside themselves at the idea of meeting you. They've been talking about it non-stop. Like teenagers . . .' She regretted her words immediately as she saw the blood rush out of his face again. But she couldn't pretend the group wasn't excited. She tried again. 'Once you get to know them you'll be all right, I promise you. And you will get to know them, over the next few days. They'll be like family by the end of it.' A particularly deranged family, but it wasn't the time to tell him that.

He still looked pale. 'I shouldn't have said yes to this.'

'Of course you should have.' There was no way she was letting him escape now. 'Please don't worry, Mr Shawcross. Really. I know you'll be terrific.'

'Harriet, I won't be, you know. I told you, I could have bluffed a magazine article, but this? I'm hardly the world's best actor, am I? Known for what? A long-forgotten role in a bad TV detective series?'

He was like a different man, not the confident, amused man she'd met earlier that day. He had seemed like something from a celebrity magazine then, all jokes and good looks and accents. Now he seemed like a normal human being. A nervous normal human being. The peculiar thing was that the more nervous he seemed, the more her own nerves were subsiding. She felt perfectly calm. It all seemed straightforward. 'But that's exactly who they want you to be. That's why they're here and why they wanted you to be here. It's not really Patrick Shawcross they're interested in. It's who they think Patrick Shawcross is. Which is Willoughby. So all you have to do is pretend to be Willoughby again. Or at least a sort of Willoughby.'

He stared at her.

She thought that might have been hurtful and stepped closer, hurrying to correct the impression. 'I mean, of course they'll be interested in you, Patrick Shawcross, your life and all of that, but I think deep down they just want you to be like Willoughby the detective.'

He came close and, to her astonishment, took her face in his hands and kissed her forehead. She got a faint scent of mint mouthwash and that nice aftershave again. 'You're a genius, Harriet. It's that simple, isn't it? It's got nothing to do with me at all. I just have to start acting from now on, don't I?' He sat down at the table. 'The only problem is I can't really remember much about Willoughby.'

Harriet could have done a PhD on Willoughby. 'He was moody.

Mysterious. Charming. Enigmatic. All those kinds of things.' He was sexy, too, but she didn't say that.

'Did he have any catchphrases?'

'Sorry?'

'Like Dirty Harry said "Go ahead, make my day" and Kojak had "Who loves ya, baby?"?'

'I don't think so. Only that line at the end of every program. "*That's people for you, George.*"'

He answered her distractedly. '"*Aye, Willoughby, so it is.*" That's right. But no, that wouldn't work in a crowd situation. We don't have time to watch the video now, do we? To refresh my memory?'

She checked the time. Five minutes to seven. They were already cutting it fine. She wouldn't have been surprised to hear slow hand-clapping coming up from the cocktail lounge. 'I'm sorry, no.'

'What did he wear?'

Harriet had a mental picture immediately. 'Thick sweaters. Dark blue shirts. I think that was supposed to be his postman's uniform. And in the opening credits, he wore a sort of baggy white shirt, with a dark duffle jacket over it.'

'That would help.' He went to the cupboard, unbuttoning the blue shirt he was wearing as he moved. 'A white shirt like this?'

She saw dark hair on his brown chest as he turned back from the wardrobe with the new shirt. She also noticed his toned body. A swimmer's body. 'Just like that,' she said.

He did up the shirt quickly, rolling the sleeves up over his elbows. He had well-shaped hands, too, with long fingers. He flicked through the cupboard again. 'No, nothing even close to a duffle coat. Would this do? It's not too casual, is it?'

She looked at the jacket he had taken out. It was a dark blue corduroy one. It felt strangely intimate, advising him on his appearance like this. 'No, that looks perfect.'

He tried it on and looked over at her again. 'It's okay?'

'You look great. You look like you should. Just like Willoughby.' He did too.

'I don't suppose you could get me a black and white dog from somewhere? A stand-in Patch? To complete the look?' He shot her a grin. He was starting to relax again.

'I think the hotel has rules about dogs. Except guide dogs, but that might not be quite the right look,' she said, straightfaced.

'No, perhaps not. Another, smaller animal perhaps?'

'I did see a cat outside the kitchen earlier, if you want me to try and catch it for you?'

He pretended to consider it. 'What colour was it?'

'Ginger, I think.'

He shook his head. 'No, the colours would clash. But thank you anyway.'

'My pleasure.' Harriet bit back a smile. The mischief was back in his eyes again. She was surprised at how much she was enjoying this. And how relaxed she was feeling. As if this was a perfectly normal way of spending an evening, watching a stranger get dressed, talking about cats and dogs. She checked her watch. Nearly seven. They were cutting it fine. She stood up. 'I'm sorry to rush you, but I think we'd better get going.'

'Of course. I'm ready now. And thanks, Harriet. You've been very understanding.'

'I'm glad I could help.' She waited in the corridor as he closed the door. They walked side by side down the carpeted corridor to the lift. 'It really will be informal, I promise, but as I said, everyone is quite —' she stopped there, as the word hysterical came to mind.

She didn't want to make him feel nervous again '— excited about meeting you. If it gets too much, please just signal me to help out and I'll do what I can.'

'Signal? Wave wildly across the room at you, do you mean?'

She smiled. 'Well, that's one way.'

'Something more low-key, perhaps?' They were waiting for the lift. 'We need a code word. Something I can drop casually into the conversation that will let you know I need rescuing.'

'That's a good idea. What did you have in mind?'

'Armadillo,' he said, as they moved into the lift. 'If I happen to slip the word armadillo into a sentence, you'll know I need rescuing.'

'Armadillo? Won't that be a bit obvious? I don't think there's going to be much chance of you spotting one wandering across the room.'

'That's my challenge. So do you agree? Armadillo it is?'

'Armadillo it is.' He was quite mad, she decided.

The lift stopped at the ground floor and the door slowly opened. He held it open but didn't make any move to step out. 'Can I ask you one more thing before we go in?'

'Of course.' She had stepped forward and was standing closer than normal to him.

'Would you please call me Patrick? This Mr Shawcross business is really making me feel like a schoolteacher.'

'I'm not supposed to. It's one of our company rules, particularly with a special guest.'

'Even if I command you? In my best Willoughby voice?'

'Well, perhaps. But only in private.'

'Then I'll have to make sure we're in private together as much as possible.'

Was he flirting with her? She shot him a glance but he looked innocently back. 'I can probably make the occasional public exception, too.'

'Thank you, Harriet.'

'You're welcome, Patrick.' She stopped around the corner from the cocktail party. 'Here we are. They're all waiting. I'll introduce you and please feel free to say a few words too, if you want, but it might get a bit —' like a rugby scrum, she suspected, '— hectic, after that.'

'I'm ready for anything, I promise. Me and my armadillo.'

She realised she was still wearing her red macintosh. She quickly unbuttoned it and folded it over her arm as they came to the closed doors. Beside her, Patrick Shawcross came to an abrupt stop.

'Harriet, what on earth are you wearing?'

She turned back, puzzled. 'My company uniform.'

'You've started working for a banana exporter since I saw you this afternoon?'

First Big Bird, now this. She gave a weak smile. 'No, it's the Turner Travel uniform.'

'Your family did this to you?' That amused look in his eyes was well and truly back. 'That's grounds for legal action, surely?'

The clock in the hall chimed. Seven o'clock. She decided to ignore his comments. 'We'd better go in. You're sure you're all right?'

He chose to misunderstand her, touching her briefly on the back as she moved to open the door. 'I think so. But will you promise to stay out of any bright lights? I've left my sunglasses in my room.'

Chapter Fourteen

Harriet had once read an article in a wildlife magazine in which a safari guide described how it felt to be almost trampled by a herd of buffalo: 'They came rushing towards me, and for a minute I thought this is it, this is the end.'

As she escorted Patrick Shawcross into the cocktail room, she knew the sensation.

Ten minutes earlier, when she had called into the room to check all was fine and everyone had made it there safely, the tour group had been normal human beings. The women had been a little overdressed, perhaps, Mrs Lamerton like a peacock in full plume in a purple trouser suit, with a bright dragonfly brooch securing a mauve chiffon scarf around her neck. Beside her, Mrs Pollard, Mrs Hart and Mrs Pennefeather were in smart pastel twin-sets. She'd overheard them talking during the journey. Nylon was perfect for travelling, they'd all decided. It didn't crush and was so versatile. She'd noticed both Mr Douglas and Mr Fidock were wearing cravats. Their accents had changed too, she thought. Both of them had been living in Australia for many years, and while they hadn't lost their English accents entirely, there had certainly been nothing like the House of Lords plums they now seemed to be speaking with.

All their clothes and accents were virtually a blur, though, as they surged past her now towards Patrick. Harriet barely had time to say, 'Good evening, everyone, may I introduce our special guest, Patrick Shawcross,' before she had to step out of the way. She'd warned Patrick they were eager to meet him but she hadn't prepared him to be mobbed. About to rescue him, she watched as the crowd parted. Patrick appeared again. Harriet was reminded of Moses and the Red Sea.

'Ladies and gentlemen, thank you so much for that enthusiastic welcome.' His voice had a deep, rich tone, with just the right hint of soft Cornish accent. He glanced over at Harriet and she was sure he gave her the slightest of winks. 'Now, please, there's no rush. We have four days together and I know there is going to be an opportunity to talk to each of you and for all of us to get to know each other very well indeed.'

They were visibly calming. Mrs Lamerton still seemed to be trembling, but she was at least keeping a normal distance. The group had somehow arranged themselves in a circle around him, as though in some pagan ritual. Any trace of the nerves Patrick Shawcross had shown earlier had disappeared. They must have been part of his preparation, to get himself into the mood and get the adrenaline rushing, Harriet realised.

'Now, let me get myself a drink.' He had barely uttered the word and one was thrust at him. 'Oh, thank you, Mrs —'

'Lamerton, Dorothy Lamerton,' Mrs Lamerton said, her voice cracking. 'It's Guinness. I read that it's your favourite.'

'And it is. Thank you, Mrs Lamerton. Here's to your excellent research abilities.'

There were peals of laughter.

He held up his hand again and looked around at them. They fell silent. 'Let me say first and most importantly how delighted I was to be invited on this tour. My *Willoughby* years were among the happiest of my life and I'm truly touched,' he put his hand on his chest, Harriet observed with some amazement, 'that the program still means so much to all of you, despite the years that have passed. Since the invitation arrived from my friend Harriet over there . . .'

Harriet felt Mrs Lamerton bristle beside her. Uh oh. She should have filled him in on the whole story of the trip, and particularly Mrs Lamerton's role in it. There hadn't been time, though. She suspected he would be hearing it from the horse's mouth soon. She stared fixedly at Patrick, ignoring Mrs Lamerton's pursed lips beside her.

He was now completely relaxed, the pint of Guinness in one hand, the other hand leaning casually on the antique dresser beside him, the white shirt and dark curls painting the perfect Willoughby picture. ' . . . I've found so many memories have come rushing back. There's a lot to making a series like *Willoughby*. Not only the scripts, and the location hunts, but all the laughs, the dramas, the sheer bloody hard work,' (there was a ripple of oohs at the carefully placed swear word) 'as well. It will be my pleasure to go walking back down the *Willoughby* memory lane again with all of you.'

He smiled and threw out a hand. 'And that's it for the formalities. Please, enjoy yourselves and feel free to approach me at any time. I promise I won't bite.' There was more laughter. He held up his pint. 'Here's to wonderful times and travels ahead.'

There was a loud burst of applause, a raising of glasses and then another surge forward. Harriet was impressed. Who would have thought twelve elderly people could move so quickly, or make so much noise? Their comments were flying around the small room. Several of them were speaking loudly, as if Patrick Shawcross was still on television and not able to hear them.

'He's so charming, isn't he?'

'That voice of his nearly makes me melt.'

'His mother must be so proud of him.'

'I think he's even better-looking than he was on the TV. Do you think he's had plastic surgery?'

The final remark sailed through the room.

Patrick Shawcross gave a wry smile. 'Well, if there's something I've learned about Australian tour groups today, it's that there is no beating around the bush. So you deserve an honest answer. No, I promise I haven't had plastic surgery, lip implants or taken any performance enhancing drugs.' There was more laughter. 'But if any of you would like to come closer to check for scars, please feel free.' He caught Miss Talbot's eye. 'Perhaps I could ask you to check on behalf of everyone, Mrs —?'

'It's Miss,' she said in her high, bell-like voice. 'Miss Emily Talbot.'

'Would you like to check, Miss Talbot?'

To whoops from Mr Fidock and Clive, who had just sidled in from the front bar, a now pink-cheeked Miss Talbot marched up and took Patrick Shawcross's face firmly between her little hands. He had to lean down and she had to stand on tiptoes but she made a thorough inspection.

'No, all clear,' she said, stepping back and smoothing down her red velvet pantsuit. Harriet recognised it from the front window of Tina's Teen Wear in Merryn Bay. 'And I can also tell you he smells lovely!'

The room soon filled with questions, laughter and conversation. Harriet remembered as a child desperately trying to get Austin or James to include her in their ball games, jumping up and down, calling 'Kick it to me! Kick it to me!' The same urgent tones sounded all around her now. 'Mr Shawcross, come and have a drink over here!' 'Mr Shawcross, can I get you a drink?' 'Mr Shawcross, look at me! Talk to me!' She checked to see if he was all right. He was more than all right. He was in his element.

Two hours went past before Harriet felt a touch on her arm. After his speech she had started circulating around the room, making sure everyone had drinks, that there was plenty of food and no trouble with spillages or allergies. She kept a close eye on Patrick Shawcross. There had definitely been no mention of an armadillo, or any animal at all, when she had been near enough to listen in to the conversations he was having. She had spoken to every member of the tour group, but she realised they weren't at all interested in talking to her. Not tonight, anyway.

At one stage, she and Clive stood back from the group, watching it all. Clive had changed from his bus driver shirt and shorts into quite a natty suit. His manner was the same, though.

'He seems like a nice enough bloke,' he said, too loudly. 'But how come I've never heard of him since *Willoughby*? He's hardly set the world on fire with his acting, has he?'

Clive was jealous, Harriet realised. She felt a need to defend Patrick Shawcross. That protective instinct kicking in again, she realised. 'Actually, Clive,' she whispered, 'he's hugely famous in America. We had to ring ahead to check that there weren't any Americans staying in the hotel, or he wouldn't have got any peace at all.'

'Really?'

'Really.'

He still didn't look convinced.

Harriet had just fetched Miss Talbot another Fluffy Duck

cocktail from the bar ('Oh, would you, Harriet?' she had said. 'They're so pretty and they make me feel so nice inside.') when she felt the touch on her arm. 'Harriet, could I have a word?'

It was Patrick Shawcross. She hadn't noticed him escaping from the scrum. 'Of course.'

'That outfit of yours really does have its uses, doesn't it? I'd have spotted you a hundred miles away.'

'That's the idea. Is everything okay? No sign of any, um, armadillos?'

'An extremely large armadillo, unfortunately.'

She lowered her voice. 'You'd like to go?'

'As soon as you can manage it.'

'Of course. I wasn't sure if you were enjoying yourself or not.' Talking in whispers like this, standing close to each other, she had the strangest sensation that they were a long-married couple deciding whether it was time to go home.

'More than I'd thought possible. I'm not being sarcastic, I promise. I have enjoyed it. It's just been a little more . . .'

'Overwhelming?'

'Exactly.' He smiled. 'Overwhelming than I expected. Could we go? And could you come up to my room with me? I need to talk to you about something.'

She didn't like the sound of that. 'Of course. Let me just say goodnight to everyone.'

She clinked a glass to get their attention. 'Hello again, everyone. I'm sorry to interrupt your conversations. I wanted to let you know that Mr Shawcross needs to take his leave of us now.' Had she actually said 'take his leave'? Somehow it fitted. Everyone in the room seemed to be speaking in heightened English this evening. 'Thank you so much for making him so welcome. Please continue to enjoy yourselves and I'll be back down with you soon.' Not that they would miss her for a second.

Beside her, Patrick paused, waiting until he had everyone's full attention, not speaking over remnants of conversations and glass shifting as she had. All the stage tricks were obviously coming back to him. 'Thank you, Harriet, and thank you, everyone, for that warm welcome and all the fascinating conversations I've had with many of you already tonight. I'm looking forward immensely to the next few days together.'

They left the room surrounded by applause, walked down the corridor in silence and into the small lift. She waited for him to speak, but there was someone else in with them. He obviously wanted them to be alone. She dreaded what it was he needed to talk to her about. Please don't let him say it was all too much. Or that he'd changed his mind about staying on. It would be even worse now if he left, now that the group had had a glimpse of him, brushed against him. It would be like so much promise being snatched away.

She started talking as they left the lift and walked along the corridor but he touched her arm, nodding at a guest standing outside his door further down. He spoke in a low voice. 'Can we wait? Just until we get to my room?'

'Of course.'

They were barely inside when he turned to her. He was very serious.

'Harriet, they are all mad. To the last person, completely and utterly mad.'

Oh, thank God, she thought. That's all that was wrong. 'No, they're not. Not really. Not all of them, anyway.'

'Harriet, they are. They know more about me than I know

myself. I've heard of fan conventions but this lot are in a league of their own.'

'I'm sorry, I did want to warn you . . .'

'I need a crash course in not only *Willoughby* but in my own biography, fake or not. Why did I agree to do this again?'

'Because you didn't want to let everyone down.' She was struck again by the difference. He had been larger than life downstairs. Now he seemed . . . he seemed normal again. Worried, even. She rushed in to help. 'It's not an examination, I promise. It's pure enthusiasm. They just love the show so much. And when we knew we had you as our special guest, Mrs Lamerton started holding *Willoughby* information evenings. That's why it's all so fresh in their minds.'

He ran his hand through his dark curls. 'I'm going to have to do something about this.'

Did he mean make a complaint? About her? 'Oh, please, don't do that. It wasn't anyone's fault. I mean, it was more a chain of things, James falling off the ladder, and then Lara deciding to go away like that, and maybe faxing the magazine article didn't help in the first place, I can see how that might have been confusing, but —'

'Harriet, I'm sorry, but what are you talking about?'

'I'm trying to explain how it all went wrong. I can see how you might want to make a complaint, but it's just there is an explanation for everything —'

'I'm not going to make a complaint. I meant I'm going to have to do something about this, before I really do let everyone down. Did you say you had tapes of the *Willoughby* series?'

'Two series.'

'We made two series?' He shook his head. 'I'd forgotten that too. Of course we made two series.'

'Twenty episodes. Half an hour each.'

'Do you have the itinerary?'

She reached into her bag. She carried it with her everywhere. 'Right here.'

He took it from her and glanced through the pages. Harriet knew what he would be reading. The list of locations they'd be visiting and the episodes they had featured in. It was there, in great detail, with James's extra handwritten comments alongside.

He handed it back. 'Harriet, I'll need your help. Can you watch some of the *Willoughby* episodes with me? Two heads will be better than one. Then if I forget you could nudge my memory?'

'Now?'

'If that's all right?'

'Of course. I just need to say goodnight to everyone first.'

He checked his watch. 'It's nearly nine-thirty. That's not too late for you?'

That mixture again of actor confidence and regular courteous human being behaviour. 'No. Anything to make the tour go well is fine by me.'

'While you're doing that, I'll call the front desk to see about a video player.'

'I already have one. It's set up in my room.'

'You're a mind-reader as well? That's great. I'll come to you, then.' He glanced at his watch. 'Is fifteen minutes okay?'

'That's fine.' She gave him her room number, trying to remember how much mess she had left behind. She'd have to quickly tidy it before he got there.

Downstairs, the tour group had barely noticed she'd gone. Everyone was swapping stories on what they had said to Patrick Shawcross, what he had said to them, what they planned to say to him tomorrow. As expected, Mrs Lamerton was holding court.

'As I said to Mr Shawcross . . .'

Harriet coughed politely in a bid to get everyone's attention. It was difficult over the hubbub. A clink of a spoon on a glass again worked much better. 'Hello again, everyone, and thank you all for making Mr Shawcross so welcome.' At the mention of his name the room quietened completely. 'If you'll all excuse me, I need to say goodnight myself and go and check some of our arrangements for tomorrow. Please enjoy yourselves and I look forward to seeing you all at breakfast in the morning.'

Mrs Lamerton gave Harriet one of her imperious waves, spilling her bright pink drink as she did so. 'Harriet, I've ordered another round of cocktails for everyone. I assured the young lady behind the bar that was all right.'

Harriet decided not to worry. It was the first real night of the tour. They were excited. Turner Travel could wear the expense. 'That's no problem at all, Mrs Lamerton. Goodnight, everyone.'

But, just in case, she went to the bar manager on her way upstairs and asked her to close the tab.

She had time to hastily tidy her room before his knock came. The room was compact, and the addition of the TV and video player on their stand made it even more crowded. There was only one armchair, as well. He could have that. She would have to sit on the edge of the double bed.

As he came into the room, she saw he'd changed his clothes. He was now wearing a dark blue sweater and a pair of dark jeans.

He was very relaxed again. 'Thank you so much for this, Harriet.'

'It's no problem at all. You don't want to watch all of them tonight though?'

'No, it's an episode or two a day, in a way, isn't it? Taking in several locations, is that right?'

She nodded.

'I think the best thing is if we watch the right episodes the night before each trip. I can learn the lines again, refresh my memory, come up with a few anecdotes.' He shook his head again. 'Did you know those two men can do the dialogue from all the final summary scenes? Twenty programs' worth?'

She nodded. She'd heard them do it often enough.

'And that lady with the blue hair —'

'Mrs Lamerton.'

'She could describe every outfit every female character was wearing. Down to the jewellery. I heard her telling that tiny lady, the one with the white hair and the funky clothes —'

Harriet's lips twitched. 'Miss Talbot.'

'Miss Talbot. The pair of them were swapping facts about Willoughby's girlfriends and who was better suited to him. In all seriousness.'

Harriet wasn't at all surprised to hear it. She knew Miss Talbot had been keen on Willoughby ending up with Lady Garvan, whereas Mrs Lamerton felt she was nothing more than an upper class gadabout, to use her term. 'They have taken their research seriously.'

'They were like vultures, Harriet. I was a rotting set of bones in that cocktail room.' He looked at her and once again surprised her with a deep burst of laughter. 'I'm taking it a bit seriously, aren't I?'

She smiled. 'A little bit.'

'It's only a television show, isn't it?'

'A very popular TV show.'

'Then we'll just have to beat them at their own game.' He sat down on the end of the bed and patted the cover beside him. 'I'm ready when you are.'

She sat next to him, conscious that she was perched on the end of her bed in a tiny room next to their guest of honour. She pointed the remote control and sat back as the theme music started to play and the opening credits began.

Several times over the next hour she shot a glance at Patrick. Once she was sure she saw him wincing, at a particularly emotional moment between Willoughby and Lady Garvan. And he was definitely smiling – laughing softly even – at a scene involving Willoughby and one of the postmasters from a neighbouring village. She referred to the itinerary notes a couple of times, checking what had happened at each of the sights, a small fishing village, a police station, a cliff lookout point. Lara and James had really done their research. All sorts of locations had been picked out for the group to visit, from houses and churches to scenic lookouts and harbour pubs.

In the break between episodes she made him a cup of tea, boiling the plastic kettle on the cupboard. He took it with a smile and then they turned back to the TV. Towards the end of the second episode her phone beeped to alert her to the arrival of a text message. She checked it. It was from Austin. She quickly read it. Still no word on Lara. Flights booked. Arriving day after tomorrow. See you then. A x

Patrick Shawcross pressed pause on the remote control and stood up. 'I'm sorry, I'm probably keeping you from work business.'

'No, it's fine. It's a message from my brother.'

'That's probably enough for tonight in any case.' He seemed

distracted now. 'That's been very helpful. I'll cast my mind back and see what stories I can remember from those filming days.'

'I know they'll appreciate whatever you can tell them.' She turned to the video player, finding it disconcerting to be standing so close to him. It had to be the change from staring at him for so long on the screen to finding him standing beside her like this.

As he went to leave, she half-expected him to kiss her on the forehead again or give her a flamboyant actor hug. Instead, he gave a formal nod of his head. 'Thanks again, Harriet. I'll see you in the morning.' He looked down at the itinerary, then read aloud in an excitable voice that exactly matched James's tone and exclamation marks.

'*We'll be reliving Willoughby's dramatic altercation with Sergeant Kendall, the corrupt policeman, at the harbour in Boscastle, followed by lunch in the restaurant near the old mill!! Perhaps they'll even have those famous crab claws on the menu from the lunch scene in episode six, "The Case of the Crooked Chef"!! Yum!!*' He glanced at her. 'You're sure you didn't write this?'

'I promise you I didn't.'

A flash of that grin of his again. 'Thanks again. Goodnight.'

Chapter Fifteen

Molly Turner was outraged. 'Lara's gone missing? Why didn't you tell me?'

She had come in to the Turner Travel office after swimming training and overheard her mother on the phone to her father. Her mum hadn't realised she was there. Molly heard the whole thing. 'No, James, not a word yet. It's like she's disappeared into thin air. Austin's on the case with her flatmate. No, apparently Harriet's doing fine on her own. Well, no dramas yet but it's early days. I'm sick with worry about it. I don't think she's told them anything much, no. What's she going to say, in any case? "Sorry it's just me in charge, Lara's mysteriously gone missing"?'

Molly had barely let her mother hang up before she demanded an explanation.

Melissa turned around. 'Molly, calm down. She's not missing. We just don't know where she is.'

'That's missing, isn't it? Is she all right?'

'Of couse she is. She's probably just got some personal problems she wants to sort out on her own.'

'So why are you so worried?'

'We're not worried.'

'You are. I heard you talking to Dad.'

'Of course we're concerned. It's a lot to ask of Harriet, her first tour in months. We were expecting Lara to be there to help her.'

'Lara said she'd be back at the end of May. In six weeks.' Molly was counting down the days. She wanted Lara to be home in time to help her plan her sixteenth birthday party.

'And I'm sure she will.'

'Why don't you ring her and ask her what's wrong?'

'We did. She hasn't answered.'

'She'd answer me. We've been texting each other the whole time she's been away.'

'Have you heard from her in the past few days?'

'Well, no, but I thought she might have got busy.'

'Would you write her a quick text now?'

Molly nodded, reaching into her pocket for her mobile phone. She nimbly pressed buttons. Hi L. R u ok? Worried about u. L Mol xxx Send. Message sent. 'She'll text me back now. I know she will.'

'When she does, could you ask her to give us a call? As soon as she can.'

'Of course.' Molly hesitated. 'Are we still going shopping tomorrow, Mum? You and me? Even though Lara has —' What? Disappeared? Gone missing?

'Of course, Molly.' She leaned over and gave her a kiss. 'You know how much I like our trips. I wouldn't give it up for anything.'

Molly tried to smile. It sounded good, but it wasn't true. Her mum cancelled week after week. 'Sorry, Molly, I need to finish these bookings or poor old Mr and Mrs Jennings won't get to have their holiday and wouldn't that be terrible?' 'I'm sorry, Molly, but I completely forgot I'd agreed to help out at the golf club luncheon. Did you have to get anything urgent, or will it wait until next week?'

No, Mum, it won't. I need to talk to you. I want to talk about what feeling in love is, and check if that's what's happening to me. I need to talk to you about having sex or not. She loved her mum, she really did, but she made it hard sometimes. Come back, Lara, Molly said to herself as her mother turned back to her computer. Lara never cancelled on her. She always listened to her, too.

Once when Molly was about thirteen she'd had a crush on a boy at school. One of her friends had told him and it had been horrible, because the boy had wanted nothing to do with her. It had been so awful, she had felt like her heart was breaking in two, and she had felt so stupid as well, knowing that he and his friends were probably laughing at her. Lara had heard her crying in her bedroom and had come in and been so quiet and gentle about it that Molly had told her everything. She thought that Lara would probably have said, 'Oh, don't worry, Molly, you'll get over it,' but Lara hadn't. She had said that yes, of course it hurt. If you loved someone and they didn't love you back then that wasn't a nice feeling, but the thing to do was be patient and wait for the person who did feel the same way about you. And she'd told Molly that there were so many special things about her and it was a good thing to wait for the person who saw all those things. It had really helped.

Molly went back into the house and into her bedroom. She sat on the bed and took out her mobile phone again. It was getting urgent. Maybe she should send Lara a long text, spell it out, so Lara would know why it was important. She wrote it out in full, seeing the words appear on the tiny screen. She knew there was only enough space for 500 letters. She kept it as short as she could.

Drst Lara. Hav got sm big news. Am going out w my new swimng coach. Yes, ther is age difrence, but doesn't mattr, he loves me & I love him, 2. No, havn't had sex. But he wants to & so do I. He wants me to tell M&D I am at swimng camp for w-end but insted we going 2 motel 2gethr. Shld I?????? I think I want to do it. Am on pill, in case, but I'm just not sure. Help!!!!! Love Molly xxxxxoooo

She hesitated, her thumb poised over the Send button. It looked a bit funny written out like that, but she really needed to talk to someone about it. It had nearly come up at school today. Sitting around at lunchtime with her girlfriends, Hailey had been making a big deal about the fact she and her boyfriend Jake had been caught kissing on the sofa by his parents. 'I was mortified,' she said. Hailey was always mortified about something. That was her favourite word. The others had all shrieked about it for ages. Molly had got annoyed with them in the end. That was one of the problems. The other girls were all so immature, and hers was an adult problem.

She imagined if she had told them. 'Do you remember that trainee swimming coach I had?' She pictured them screwing their eyes up, trying to remember. 'The student teacher?' she'd prompt. 'Dean?'

'Oh, him. Yes. Why?'

'We've been going out for the past two months. He's invited me to go away for the weekend with him. Just him and I, in a motel.'

Would she say it as simply as that? And what would they say back?

'But he's a teacher!'

She had her arguments ready, even in pretend conversations. 'It would only matter if he was a teacher at my school. And school is only for a few hours each day. The rest of my life I'm me, and Dean is a man, not a teacher.'

'But he's so much older than you!'

'Not really. He's only just turned twenty-six, and I'm nearly sixteen, so it's only about ten years. That's nothing.'

'Just tell your parents it's a training camp, Molly,' he'd said last time they met. 'I'm going crazy not seeing you. Imagine what it would be like. Just you and me, together. The whole weekend.' He'd leaned down and kissed her lips, her neck. She'd got that incredible feeling again, of being scared and excited and thrilled, somewhere deep inside her body.

She knew he was talking about having sex. They'd had enough lessons about it. There'd been one particularly embarrassing video the previous term. Two actors pretending to be lovers, stopping and starting at different points. Kissing. Touching. Him touching her breasts. Every now and then words would flash up on the screen in red letters. *Stop if you feel uncomfortable! It's your body! Say no if you want to!*

Those videos always made it sound as though sex was like fighting off an army or something. What they hadn't told them was how good it felt to be kissed and cuddled and caressed the way Dean did it. It was the same with the magazines. They warned you about diseases and getting pregnant and being called a slut and all the reasons why you shouldn't have sex until you were sixteen, or even older. But if it was so wrong to do all those things, how come it felt so right with Dean?

Just thinking about him gave her that lurching, tumbling, breathless feeling again. It wasn't anything like the few times she'd kissed any of the boys from school, not that she had done very much of it. Or even the story Hailey had been telling, being caught kissing Jake like that. It didn't feel bad, either. They'd all been warned about chat rooms on the Internet. About being with strangers. The teachers carried on sometimes as if there was a whole tribe of perverts lurking in a shadowy ring outside the school. That there were dirty men out there waiting for them to let down their guard, to smile too brightly, or offering them lollies or rides into town in exchange for something dirty.

It just hadn't been like that with Dean. It had happened so

naturally, as if it was meant to be. That's what Dean always said, too. And her swimming had improved, as well. Because apart from the talking, and the drives they took together, and the kissing, he really had been helping her to swim better.

She reached up to the shelf above her bed and took down the photo. It had been taken at her last swimming carnival. Her mum and dad had wanted to come, but there had been an association of travel agents' dinner in Melbourne that weekend. To Molly's delight, Harriet and Lara both came along instead.

Lara had brought her camera, the one with the long lens, and had taken all sorts of action shots. One of Molly diving off the blocks, and one of her winning her race. She'd even taken one with a sort of slow exposure that had made the water look all silky, like it was carved marble. Molly had framed that one and put it up on her bedroom wall. There were the victory photos too. One of Molly standing up on the top step of the podium. Best of all was this one, the only photo she had of her and Dean together. It had been a natural one for Lara to take, too – the swimmer with her coach. Both Lara and Harriet had been so proud of her. 'Come on, arms around each other. The winning combination.'

Molly touched Dean's face in the photo. The cropped blond hair, that beautiful smile. He was all muscly, too, but in a nice way, not like a bodybuilder. She really liked his body. She felt different in her own body, too, since she and Dean had started seeing each other. He'd told her so many times how beautiful it was, and that he loved how she looked. He often whispered that he especially loved her breasts, that she shouldn't try and hide them like she used to do under baggy windcheaters and T-shirts. 'Not that I want you showing them to anyone else. You won't, will you?'

She'd shaken her head.

'And you haven't told anyone about us?'

'I won't.' She'd affected a casualness. 'What, and have you get into trouble for interfering with an underage girl?'

'I'm serious, Molly.'

'I'm joking.' She'd wanted to kiss him, kiss that line of worry away from his face. But they had made a rule that they never touched in front of other people. They had to be so careful. He'd told her it was enough to have him thrown out of teaching for ever. Maybe even a prison sentence.

'No one would understand the truth of us, Molly. They wouldn't believe that I tried to fight it. I did. But I knew that it was something special between us.'

She could replay all the things he had ever said to her. Sometimes in bed, when it had been a while since she had seen him – they tried not to make it longer than two weeks, but sometimes his training commitments made it hard – she made up plays in her head, reliving the whole thing.

It had been special from the start. She thought so, at least. Sometimes she wasn't sure if she had slightly rewritten his arrival in her life, made it more dramatic than it might have been, because of what had happened afterwards. But it didn't matter either way. It still felt the same now.

It had been a normal training session, straight after school. Her coach Mr Green was there. They called him Greenie. Beside him that day was a young man, dressed in a tracksuit. They were all quickly introduced. 'This is Dean, down from Melbourne. He's going to be my assistant coach for the term.' She shook hands with him, then went into the changing room. He told her afterwards, when they were together, that he had noticed her straightaway. 'How couldn't I, you were so beautiful.'

She had wrinkled her nose. 'I was in my training suit, in my cap and goggles. You couldn't tell what I looked like.'

'You're wrong. I saw what was important.'

It was just like Lara had said. She'd been patient and someone who loved her for herself had come along. It was terrible when he first had to go back to Melbourne after his work placement finished, but he kept texting her, telling her he loved her every single morning without fail, calling when he could. She hung out for the carnivals when she'd see him. He managed to come back once every fortnight or so for a training session and it was fun to pretend they were normal swimmer and coach. He'd stay back late those nights, and they'd go in his car to the lookout in the hills back behind the town or to one of the beaches further down the coast from Merryn Bay. They'd talk a bit, but mostly they'd kiss. A lot. He was always so patient and kind to her, telling her how pretty she was, and kissing her really slowly and checking each time that she was happy with what he was doing.

He had asked her the last night he was in Merryn Bay if she wanted to go in the back seat, where there was more room, but she had felt funny. He'd been so kind. 'That's okay, Molly. We'll only do what you want to do.'

She'd felt bad then, so she'd let him touch her a bit more than she wanted, and then she'd touched him as well. She'd felt really shy and inexperienced, but he had been so good then as well, showing her what to do, how to touch him. 'You're so beautiful, Molly. That's it, that's perfect, don't stop.' She replayed that over and over in her head as well.

He'd touched her again afterwards too, and she had felt incredible, all kind of full and open and hungry in a funny way, as if she really wanted something to eat or drink or have, in some way, but wasn't sure what it was. She'd tried to tell him that and he had given her another kiss and whispered in her ear. 'Just wait, Molly, if you thought that was good.'

It was Dean who'd suggested she go on the pill. 'I'm not putting any pressure on you, Molly. It's about being responsible. Looking out for you.'

'But wouldn't we use condoms?' She felt shy saying that, but all the classes insisted that they were the most important thing.

'For a start, if that's what you want. But condoms are only if you're not committed to the person you're sleeping with.'

'But what about AIDS? And other diseases?'

He kissed her again. 'I promise you, Molly, I don't have AIDS, or VD, or chickenpox, or even a hint of a cold. Will you do that for me? Will you go on the pill? Then when we're together, you and me, it'll be just us, skin on skin . . .'

Another long kiss. His voice whispering, 'You're so beautiful.'

'No, I'm not.'

'Yes, you are. You're like a colt.'

'A colt? A horse?'

'All long legs and silky.'

She was embarrassed about going to the doctor, but she did what her friends had done. Jenny had bragged how easy it was. It was better if you got the male doctor, she said. Tell him you are having problems with your period. Bad pains, irregular cycles, something like that. And make sure you have a cover story ready to tell your mum, in case someone tells her you were at the doctor's.

Molly told her mum she was having trouble with her ears, that she thought she might need them to be syringed on account of all the chlorinated pool water. She was worried her mother would suggest coming with her, but luckily she was busy organising the autumn brochures and was working long hours.

She made her own appointment, went confidently into the doctor and talked in detail about how bad her period pain was. After he had written the prescription for the pill, she casually asked him to check her ears, to see if they needed syringing. 'You're still swimming?' She nodded. There had been an article about her in the local paper the week before. It meant she didn't even have to lie when her mother asked her later how the visit to the doctor had gone. 'Fine, he said my ears were clear.' Once again, she'd called the question out across the office, not caring for one second about Molly's privacy.

Her mother had been the same three years before when the time came for Molly to be fitted for her first bra. Molly had nearly died with embarrassment. No one liked their private business to be broadcast like that.

'I'm going to Melbourne for the day with Molly tomorrow, Penny,' she'd called out to Molly's grandma. 'There's not a decent bra shop in this town.'

'Mum, *please*.'

'Well, there's not.'

Molly had gone out to the back of the house, very upset. Lara and Harriet were sitting there, having morning tea together.

As usual, Lara noticed something was up straightaway. 'What's up, Mollusc?'

'Mum,' she said, rolling her eyes. 'Why doesn't she take out an ad in the local paper that we're going to buy me my first bra? She shouted it to Grandma, right in front of Mr and Mrs Kingston.'

'Grandma won't tell. And Mr and Mrs Kingston are both deaf, don't worry. They wouldn't have heard.'

It helped to have two aunties. Lara and Harriet sat telling stories about their first bra-fittings. Harriet had got hers first, even though she and Lara were nearly the same age.

'I was flat-chested until I was seventeen,' Lara said matter-of-factly.

'Were you? Were you worried?'

'I don't think so.'

'You weren't,' Harriet said. 'I remember. You didn't mind one bit.'

Molly was fascinated with her aunts' relationship. She knew of course that they weren't real sisters, that Lara had come to live with the Turners when she was little. She asked them lots of times to tell her stories of things they'd done when they were kids, but usually the stories were about her uncle Austin, and all the naughty things he used to do. If Molly had had a sister, foster or real, she reckoned they would have got up to all sorts of things, tried on make-up together, put on concerts, been good friends as well as sisters, but it didn't seem like that with her two aunts. Molly secretly thought that she was closer to Lara than Harriet was.

A few nights before Lara went to England, she and Molly had sat talking for ages. For the first time, Lara talked about coming to live with the Turners. How she'd had to change schools, houses, her whole life, really. Molly had also heard about the memorial days her grandma had organised for Lara, as a way to remember her parents.

'Did it help?' Molly asked.

'Just a bit,' Lara said quietly.

'So you're not my real aunty, are you?'

'No, I'm not. Not really.'

'You feel like a real aunty.' She'd leaned over and hugged her.

Lara had hugged her back. 'You feel like a real niece.'

Molly had felt even closer to Lara since then. Which was why she really wanted to talk to her now. Of course, she was going to make her own decision, but it would be interesting to hear what Lara thought. And it wasn't as if Dean had been putting any serious pressure on her yet. He hadn't, not in any bad way at least. But she knew that if she didn't go to bed with him, he would go to someone else. 'You know I love you, Molly,' he'd said on the phone the day before, 'but I need to know you feel as strongly as me, otherwise . . .'

He hadn't had to finish his sentence. Otherwise it would be all over between them. She told him how much she loved him. Twice. 'I just need to think about it.' He understood. She'd had that beautiful I l u text from him again this morning. She'd been so relieved.

She glanced down again at the text she'd written. Would she send it to Lara? Or decide for herself? She shut her eyes and imagined Dean's face. It helped her make up her mind. She did love him and she did want to sleep with him. And, at the end of the day, it had to be her decision, not Lara's, didn't it?

She started deleting the text, letter by letter.

Kevin Hillman tapped three times on the kitchen table. 'Gloria? Gloria? Dearly beloved husband calling his suddenly deaf wife?'

Gloria turned away from the window and put down the cup of tea she'd been holding. It had gone cold without her realising. 'Sorry, Kev, were you talking to me?'

'Only for the past five minutes. That's all we need, me blind, you deaf. What's up, love? You've been distracted the past couple of days. Is it Lara or Harriet you're most worried about?'

It was Lara. But nothing about Lara that she could tell Kev about. Were promises between people still promises even after one of the parties had died? Because she was longing to talk to Kev about it. She hated being the secret keeper like this. While Penny was alive, she hadn't needed to think about it. If the subject had come up, it would have been up to Penny, not Gloria, to deal with the fallout. If there had been time, perhaps Penny would have even given her some advice on what to say. Or told her how much of the truth she had told Lara. That was the worst of it. Gloria didn't know how much Lara knew. It was like carrying something fragile, but not knowing if it was going to melt or explode in your hands.

She leaned over and touched Kevin's arm. She touched him a lot these days. That was how they communicated – physical smiles, she thought of them as. 'I'm worried about Lara. I hope she's okay.'

'She'll turn up, love. It might be her version of Harriet's breakdown. Parents dying affects different kids in different ways. Being back in England might have brought back a lot of memories of them, of both sets of parents. She might just need some time out.'

'You're probably right.'

'Are you working late tonight?'

'I am. Is that okay? I'll be back at teatime though. Did you want me to do something?'

'No, you're okay, love.'

She stood up with a sigh. 'I'd better get going. The Cuthberts are coming in this morning. Off on their annual trip.'

'Where are they going this year?'

'Spain, Portugal and Italy.'

'Again? They're getting showy since they retired.'

'We can be as showy when we retire, if you like. We can be away the whole time too. I have contacts in the travel world, I reckon I could get us a few good deals.'

'No.'

'Why not?'

'Because you're too young to retire. Because you love your job.'

'You don't believe me, do you? I'd retire at the drop of a hat.'

He was serious. 'You'd go mad with boredom at home.'

'No, you'd be here to entertain me. It's you I worry about going mad with boredom at home.'

'I'm fine.'

'Are you?'

'Course I am. The blokes from the council depot are going to drop by this afternoon.'

She could picture it. They'd shuffle around, look and act uncomfortable and then leave, glad the visit to their old blind mate was out of the way for another few weeks. It struck her again how unfair it all was. All the plans they'd had. The two of them hoping to work until retirement, and then perhaps setting off with a caravan for a few months, heading up the east coast of Australia. They'd had bigger plans than that, too. Overseas trips. Gloria had even sent away for information on a get-over-your-fear-of-flying course. They'd talked about trying to get to New Zealand first. Then maybe Europe. Kevin had a longing to eat a real Italian meal in a real Italian village. They wanted to see so much. They were lucky, they had good health, enough money.

His loss of sight had been so rapid. It was as if the diagnosis had sped things up. It went from a gradual fuzzing of his vision, to complete loss of sight in one eye two months later. He could only see the barest outlines now. Legally, he was blind. It changed things, of course it did. Kevin had been so vital, so independent. It took all her acting skills to stop herself crying when he despaired at how weak he had become, how dependent on her he was. They had talked about him maybe getting a white stick, or even a guide dog, but Kevin had resisted all of it. 'I have to get used to the idea of being blind first.'

She'd found him in tears one night. She had come into the bedroom and discovered him sitting on the side of the bed, hands over his face, sobbing quietly. He had knocked something off the table and been unable to find it, even with all the lights in the room on. His sight had been practically gone by that stage. 'I'm useless, love.'

'No, you're not. You're just going blind.' She wouldn't let him feel sorry for himself.

'I'm blind and I'm useless.'

'Never useless.'

'It's too much to ask.'

'What is?'

'For you to help me. Lead me around like some invalid.'

She'd moved to him and held him close. 'I won't be leading you anywhere. You can walk beside me or in front of me if you like, but I'm not leading you. There was nothing about that in any marriage rulebook that I read. I'll sue you for false pretences if you start making those sort of demands on me.'

'You hard-hearted witch. No sympathy for a poor old fellow like me.' He'd held her tightly. 'A poor old blind fellow like me.'

'Try as hard as you like, that won't wash with me.' She had been smiling as she said it. 'Don't think about yourself like that, Kev. Because I won't be.'

'Gloria Hillman, I —'

'Oh, Mum, Dad, stop it. That's disgusting at your age. And it's not even night-time.' It had been David, their oldest son, calling in on an impromptu visit with his youngest child.

That was nearly two years ago. Kevin had left the house hardly a dozen times since, and each time had wanted to come home early.

There in the kitchen, the morning sun shining in on them both, it seemed obvious what she had to do. The feeling was getting stronger. Time was slipping past too quickly. She kept thinking that what had happened to Penny, with Neil dying so suddenly, would happen to her. She would regret all this time spent in the travel agency, getting mad at Melissa, worrying about Austin and Harriet and Lara, being tired and no company for Kev when she got home, all out of some probably misplaced loyalty to Penny and Neil. As she picked up her bag, she told him. 'When Harriet and Lara get back, I'm going to talk to them all about retiring.'

'Gloria —'

'It's simple, Kev. I want to spend more time with you.'

'You'll get bored.'

She wasn't imagining it. There wasn't the same vehemence in his voice. She leaned over and kissed his forehead. 'I can't leave you here on your own. Any fancy lady might walk past and see you.'

'That's good, because I won't see her.' It fell flat. He seemed to know it. 'Have a good day, love.'

'You too, Kev.'

CHAPTER SIXTEEN

It took Harriet three attempts to get the microphone on the bus to work the next morning. Clive finally leaned over and, with a sigh, jiggled the cord around, gave it a thump and then handed it back.

'Should be all right now, BB.'

'Thanks.' Monkey-face, she added to herself. Clive's BB jibes were wearing very thin. She picked up her script and started reading. '*Good morning, ladies and gentlemen. Now, we met each other informally and possibly a little drunkenly last night!* (James had inserted a handwritten question here: *Possible laugh??*) *But as today is really the first full day of our formal* Willoughby *tour, I wanted to say again, on behalf of everyone at Turner Travel, what a pleasure it is to have you all travelling on this tailor-made tour with us. If you're happy, we're happy, remember! And of course, I'd like to extend another special welcome to our guest of honour, Patrick Shawcross. (Gesture at guest of honour. Possible applause.)*'

Harriet refused to do the gesture. Patrick Shawcross was less than three feet away from her. She didn't need to point him out. In any case, the group members hadn't left his side since he came down and met them in the breakfast room that morning. James had been right about the applause though. There was an enthusiastic round of clapping, a whoop from Mr Fidock, a gallant bow from Patrick Shawcross and then Clive changed into gear and edged his way out onto the main road.

Harriet was in the guide's seat at the front of the bus. Patrick Shawcross was in the seat across from her, next to Miss Talbot. She was wearing a bright blue cotton jacket this morning. It went well with her spangly runners. Harriet had given her niece Molly a similar pair for her twelfth birthday a few years ago.

Mrs Lamerton was several rows back, looking unhappy. Her seating plans had gone awry when Patrick met Miss Talbot as they came out of the hotel, and escorted her, hand on elbow, on to the bus, taking the seat beside her. Harriet had half-expected an incident, or at the very least Mrs Lamerton insisting on taking the guide's seat. At the last moment, she had moved down the bus. She was making it clear with her dark glances at Harriet that she wasn't pleased.

Harriet did her best not to catch her eye in the rear-vision mirror and sat up as straight as she could. 'If you look in charge, they will think you're in charge,' James had reminded her during his hospital briefing. 'Be first on and last off, and you'll gain a natural authority over them.' He'd made it sound as if he was talking about lion-taming rather than tour guiding. Again, though, she had to admit he was right. She'd forgotten the nice feeling of being in the front of the bus, microphone in hand, clearly the one in control.

She knew Lara had done two familiarisation trips along this route since she'd been in Bath, checking everything she had organised from Australia, timing the journeys, discovering extra places of interest, passing on all the information to James to write up. Lara would have conveyed all the information from the script quite naturally, Harriet suspected. Pointed out this landmark and that fact as if it had just occurred to her. Harriet was conscious she was reading straight from the page.

'*We'll be making our first stop of the day at the picturesque village of Boscastle, known for its beautiful medieval harbour, its charming cottages and best of all for its use as the setting for the dramatic scenes in "The Case of the Crooked Chef". In the meantime, I'd like to take this opportunity to give you a few more details about the local area. The A30 trunk road we are travelling on is the backbone of Cornwall's road network and was constructed —'*

'Out of second-rate materials if you ask me.' Even without a microphone, Clive's voice was audible throughout the bus.

'*— as part of a streamlined approach to integrated traffic control following a Government review in the mid 1990s.*'

Harriet tried to ignore a gentle snoring sound coming from the driver's seat. Clive was right. Who wanted to hear about road networks? She turned the page and tried to find a more interesting topic. She picked one at random. It was a little early, but if the group squinted they might be able to see what she was talking about in the distance.

'*We'll also be passing one of Cornwall's wind farms later today, remarkable examples of man, and woman, learning how to harness nature's own energy.*' James was really losing it now. '*Wind farms may yet be the saviour of our environment and indeed the human race.*' He'd obviously copied this down word for word from a green information pack. She quickly read down the page. No, the group didn't need to hear about the ravages of the industrial revolution and the number of species of insects that had disappeared in the past ten years. She was almost relieved when Mrs Lamerton held up her hand.

'Yes, Mrs Lamerton?' Harriet hoped it wasn't a request to visit the wind farm. She needed to stick to their schedule.

'I'd like to ask Mr Shawcross when he first decided to be an actor.'

'Thank you, Mrs Lamerton. There'll be plenty of time to ask Mr Shawcross all the questions you like once we get to our first stop. '*As you all know, harnessing wind energy* —'

Mrs Lamerton was having none of it. Her voice rose a notch in volume. 'It's just this seems like a good opportunity to hear some of his stories. Certainly, much more interesting than hearing about wind farms and motorway construction.' It may have been meant as an aside, but her words came straight to Harriet's ears.

She glanced down. James's next set of notes involved the construction methods of traditional beehives. She gave in. James would never know, after all. She put her hand over the microphone and leaned across to Patrick Shawcross. 'Mr Shawcross, would you mind starting work a little earlier today?'

He whispered back. 'No problem at all. As long as you stop calling me Mr Shawcross.'

'Thank you, Patrick.'

'You're welcome, Harriet.'

As he and Harriet swapped places and she handed him the microphone, he touched Miss Talbot gently on the shoulder. 'It's been a pleasure talking to you, Miss Talbot,' he said. She turned bright pink again.

He chose to stand in the aisle beside the guide's seat, facing them all, his hand on the back of Harriet's seat. 'Good morning, everyone. I hope you can all hear me?' They sent a chorus of yeses to him. 'Thank you very much for your question, Mrs —?'

'Lamerton,' Harriet whispered.

'Mrs Lamerton. I'm more than happy to answer it, though I have to admit I was finding that motorway history fascinating. Perhaps you'll give me some private tuition later on, Harriet?'

There was a whoop from Mr Fidock.

Mrs Lamerton ignored him. 'Thank you, Mr Shawcross. I know I am speaking on behalf of all of us when I say we have so many questions that we would like to take every opportunity we can to ask them. So if I could begin. You said in an early article in a magazine I read, the article that sparked this tour, in fact, I don't know if you heard the whole story from Lara, or indeed James or Harriet – we seem to be going through the Turners at a rate of knots' – another titter – 'but to fill you in, I am proud to say it was me who mooted the idea of the *Willoughby* tour to Turner Travel.'

'Did you? Mrs Lamerton, I owe you.'

A scoff from Clive in the driver's seat.

Mrs Lamerton was now almost simpering. 'So could you tell us, Mr Shawcross, how did you first get into acting?'

For the rest of the day Patrick – he'd insisted they all call him Patrick, not Mr Shawcross – pulled anecdotes out of thin air. He answered questions for more than an hour on the bus, on everything from his early acting roles to his favourite food. He stood with the group in front of the old mill in the harbour village of Boscastle and talked about the sixteen takes – '*Sixteen*,' Mrs Pollard had breathed – required to film the scene when Willoughby confronted the restaurant owner about the black-market produce he was selling. The director had just called the final 'cut' when it had started snowing. Not only had they been unable to do any more outside filming for two days but the entire cast and crew had been snowed in together. All the filming had been moved inside. In his opinion, it had been a better episode because of it.

'You're right,' Mrs Lamerton said, nodding enthusiastically. 'There is such an air of claustrophobia, of hidden tension, in that scene.'

'All because of the snow,' Patrick said.

'Thanks so much, Patrick,' Harriet said as she walked with him back to the bus after lunch. It was the first time alone she'd had with him all day. He looked the part again, she thought. He was wearing a dark green jumper, made from what looked like handspun wool. The colour suited him. 'They're loving your behind-the-scenes tales.'

'I'm glad.' Then he lowered his voice. 'It's just a shame they're not true.'

'They're not?'

He shook his head. 'We made *Willoughby* on a shoestring. We had the luxury of two takes, if we were lucky. And if it snowed, it was too bad, we still had to film.'

'But what about that claustrophobic scene you mentioned? With those long close-ups?'

'The cameraman had a hangover and wouldn't get up. So they locked his camera into place in one corner of the room and switched it on.'

'Really?'

He nodded.

'So nothing you've said today has been true?'

'Can you remind me again what I've said?'

They were standing together near the bus. 'You told a story about Patch the dog finding that necklace under a hedge when you were filming one day and the scriptwriters deciding to write that into the "The Case of the Smuggler's Skiff".'

'No, not true.'

'You said the actress who played Lady Garvan was in real life descended from one of Bonnie Prince Charlie's mistresses. And you hinted that your romance had spilled over into real life.'

'No. I don't know anything about her past. And she was happily married to a stockbroker in Sussex back then. They had three or four children, I think. We used them as extras now and again.'

'The story about the post van getting stalled when you were filming on the railway line? And you only just getting away in time when a train appeared?'

'No.'

'The time the whole cast got the flu, but time was so tight you had to go ahead and film anyway, and dub your non-coldy voices in afterwards?'

He shook his head again.

She couldn't stop a smile. 'It's all been lies?'

'Not so much lies as fabrications. I swear, Harriet, if I told the truth they would all be snoring in their bus seats. Most days we just turned up, said our lines then went home. It was a completely uneventful program to work on. None of us ever took it that seriously, either. I think that's why it wasn't a big success.'

'It was in Australia.'

'I apologise. God bless Australia. Though now I think of it, not everything I said today was a lie.'

'No?'

'I really did enjoy those crab claws. They were delicious, just as I said.'

He smiled at her and she got a nice warm feeling. As if they were in on this together. They were interrupted by the group returning from souvenir shopping.

There was the usual scrum over who got to sit next to Patrick on the bus. Mr Douglas somehow managed it, with a bit of nifty footwork involving his wife as a decoy. Harriet realised she was going to have to think about a seating system before they came to blows. Or more to the point, before Mrs Lamerton came to blows with the rest of the group. She was now shooting serious daggers at Mr Douglas.

The question and answer session started as soon as they were back on the road. Harriet saw Mrs Pennefeather and Mrs Hart, the two sisters, nudging each other.

'Go on, ask him.'

'No, you ask him.'

'No, you.'

Mrs Hart finally convinced Mrs Pennefeather to stand up. 'Patrick, my sister and I were just wondering something. We all read in your biography that you've been married twice already —'

'Yes, in the late eighties,' Mrs Lamerton interrupted. 'Once to the Welsh actress Caitlin Moore and then to another actress called Alicia de Vries.'

'But what about now?' Mrs Pennefeather continued. 'Are you married at the moment?' She sat down with a bump, her cheeks flushed. She got a proud rub on the arm from her sister for being so brave. She stood up again. 'If you don't mind me asking,' she added.

'I don't mind at all, Mrs Pennefeather. And no, I'm not married at the moment.'

Miss Talbot stood up so she could see over the seat in front of her. 'What are those American women doing, Patrick, letting a catch like you run free?'

'I don't know, Miss Talbot. It's scandalous, isn't it?'

'Harriet's single too,' Miss Talbot said, standing on tiptoes so she could see Harriet as well. 'Aren't you, Harriet?'

In her guide's seat, Harriet decided it was time to study the itinerary.

Miss Talbot spoke louder. 'Harriet? You are single, aren't you? You broke up with that poor Simon you were living with in Merryn Bay, didn't you?'

'Yes, Miss Talbot, I did,' Harriet said, now extremely determined to look at the itinerary.

Miss Talbot sounded pleased. 'You should ask Harriet out, Patrick. She's lovely. And I've known her all her life, so I should know.'

'She certainly is lovely. Thank you for the idea, Miss Talbot.'

Harriet definitely didn't look up then.

An hour later, they were all standing by the waterside at the small Port Isaac harbour. They had slowly made their way down the narrow steep streets from a carpark above the village, past tiny shops and pretty whitewashed cottages crammed together. Clive had offered to piggyback several of the ladies down the steepest parts. They had all declined, taking their time instead, stopping to peek inside hotels and restaurants boasting freshly caught crab and lobster.

The harbour was peaceful, the water lapping against the stone walls, seagulls squawking, the sky above them a pale blue. Patrick was telling the group about the time the director got tangled in some fishing lines and nearly went over the edge of the lobster boat they were filming in.

'Did you catch him, Patrick?' Mrs Douglas asked. 'Was it you who saved his life?'

'I'm afraid I can't take the credit for that, Mrs Douglas. It was the soundman. He threw out the boom microphone just in the nick of time and the director managed to grab hold of it.'

He caught Harriet's eye and she knew from his expression that he had made all of that up too. She shook her head, pretending to despair. As they moved to the next spot on the itinerary – a pub a hundred yards up the road, also overlooking the harbour – he fell into step beside her.

'How am I going, Harriet? Staying within the boundaries of reality?'

'By the skin of your teeth, I think.'

'It could have been worse. I was going to say a shark leapt out of the water and carried the director away.'

'I'm not sure he's the one getting carried away.'

He smiled. 'It's your fault. You're the one who invited me on the tour.' They walked on. 'Poor Simon, by the way.'

She looked at him. 'I'm sorry?'

'I said, poor Simon. You broke up with him, I believe.'

'Yes. Yes, I did.' She shot him another glance. His face was expressionless. They kept walking. She couldn't resist it. 'And poor Alicia and Caitlin.'

'Alicia and Caitlin?'

'Your wives.'

'Oh, my wives. Yes, the poor things.'

'They recovered fully from the divorces?'

'Miraculously, I believe. You'd think the marriages had never happened.'

'Patrick? Patrick? Could we have you here for a photo?'

They both turned. Mr and Mrs Douglas were standing in front of a moored blue boat, smiling eagerly. 'We think this is the actual one from that episode, don't you?'

'I think you're right,' he called over. 'Excuse me, Harriet.'

'Of course. Mind the sharks.'

He laughed and walked over to them, just as Harriet felt her mobile phone vibrate to signify a new text message. Still smiling, she took it out. The message was from Austin.

Flights organsd. Wil b with u 2moro a.m. then onto Bath. Will find L, dn't worry. U could b off hook yet!! A x

She read it twice, feeling strange. She gazed around at the group. Several of them were chatting among themselves, pointing up at the old harbour building that had been in episodes six and seven. Miss Talbot, Mrs Lamerton and Mrs Kempton were involved in a lively discussion, seated beside one another on a bench near a pile of fishing nets and lobster pots. They made a real picture, with the grey of the stone wall and the orange and green of the nets and baskets vivid beside them. Snatches of their conversation floated across. They were still arguing about Lady Garvan and her suitability for Willoughby. Clive had left the bus and was lying stretched out on a bench, his newspaper under his head, soaking up a ray of afternoon sunshine, oblivious to a large black cat doing the same thing beside him. Mr and Mrs Douglas were moving Patrick back and forth in front of the boat, trying to get the best angle. He was laughing good-naturedly.

Harriet read the text once more. She couldn't deny it. She didn't want Austin to find Lara. Not yet. The reasons why were getting more complicated each day.

Chapter Seventeen

By the time Harriet and Lara turned twelve, in some ways it was as if she had always lived with them. Three children had become four, which made games easier to play, although Harriet secretly wished she didn't have to end up partnering James all the time. Austin was always more fun.

Her parents were careful to make sure that what one of the girls got, the other did too. Two kittens. Two birds. Two goldfish. Their birthdays were both in May, yet there were always two separate parties.

Lara puzzled Harriet, though. She wasn't how she'd imagined a sister would be. She'd thought a sister would be another girl she would play with and laugh with, and be kind to and teach how to do things. It wasn't like that. Lara already seemed to know how to do most things – ride a bike, swim, do her homework. If she wanted to find things out, she asked Austin, or James, or her mum and dad, even Gloria, as often as she asked Harriet.

Sometimes it felt as though Lara was the one who had always been there, and Harriet was the one feeling her way. Lara seemed to be more confident. Harriet felt nervous about things, and often had to check with her parents or with Gloria if she had done something the right way or if she had said the right thing. Lara didn't seem to need that reassurance.

Harriet tried to put herself in Lara's shoes, the way her mother had asked her to do. To understand how hard it must have been for Lara, her own parents being killed, having to come and live with a whole new family. Harriet gave it a lot of thought. She would have felt scared, she decided. And she would have done her best to make everyone like her, and been really well-behaved and done lots of housework and not sworn and tried to be kind. In her mind, it started getting a bit confused with the Cinderella story, that she would become the unpaid slave, but it was the truth. She would have felt uncertain, that she had to behave really well so that she didn't stand out and so her new family didn't ask her to leave.

Lara didn't behave anything like that, though. She had grown-up conversations with Harriet's mother and father, talking to them in a serious way that Harriet herself had never done. Lara got on well with James too, watching cricket with him and saying quite sensible things when Harriet couldn't make head or tail of the game and found it too slow, anyway. Lara and Austin got on especially well. They did a lot of laughing.

Harriet and Lara were still sharing a bedroom. That caused more problems. Lara was extremely tidy. Harriet was the opposite. She would come back from school and throw her belongings around, while Lara would fold hers neatly. It wasn't Lara who complained, but Harriet's mother.

'It's not fair on Lara,' she said one afternoon. 'Your mess is all over the whole room, Harriet. You have to try and be tidier.'

'I try, I really do. But something happens.'

'Your clothes grow legs and run over to Lara's side of the room?'

Harriet nodded, smiling. 'It's nicer over there. It's tidier.'

Gloria came up with the solution. She'd done the same thing

with two of her sons. A line down the middle of the room. Harriet could be as messy as she liked but not on Lara's side. Lara had every right to push any of Harriet's mess over the line.

It summed up their whole relationship in a way. They got along perfectly well, as long as neither of them crossed the line. It worked well, most of the time. Then Harriet crossed it. Very publicly.

Her class was asked to write a true story from their family history as though they were an eyewitness. Her friend Emma wrote about the time her grandfather's house nearly burnt down in the 1945 bushfires. She described the smell of singed hair, the feeling of his eyeballs nearly bursting in the heat from the flames. Sitting beside her, Harriet did her best to make hers as thrilling as possible too. She started with the story of her mother and father and brothers coming out from England in the boat, as one of the 'Ten Pound Poms', and how they had lived in that hostel place for a year, but after a few paragraphs it all seemed a bit boring, especially compared to the burning trees and sirens Emma was writing about. Emma had the habit of reading aloud as she wrote, which was sometimes annoying, but often a help with school projects.

Harriet tried to think of an alternative event from her family history. She was about to settle for the time her mum had been bitten by a wasp at a family barbecue when she remembered the story of Lara's parents being killed in that car crash and how Lara came to live with them afterwards. Harriet didn't know all the details. They didn't speak about it much any more, but she knew enough to be able to write a 900-word essay. She knew Lara hadn't been there during the crash, but she decided that it would make it much more dramatic if she was. She also decided to make Lara into a baby in a car seat, rather than an eight-year-old. It didn't change it too much, after all. Lara would still come to live with them at the end.

Her story began as Lara and her parents were driving through the mountains somewhere in Ireland. Harriet wasn't sure where in Ireland the crash had happened or if there were many mountains in Ireland, but it painted a sort of scary picture, she thought. She described the noise of the engine, even the sound of the radio in the car. Their teacher had asked them to use all five senses to tell the story, so that was hearing covered, she thought. She was particularly proud of a description of the village they had driven through. There was a poster of an Irish village in the travel agency, showing lots of coloured doors and curvy lettered signs over pubs, and she'd sort of taken it from that.

Out of nowhere she had a flash of memory, overhearing a conversation between her parents about Lara's parents. About the two of them having a screaming match. Perfect. She wrote a sentence about Lara's parents shouting at each other, while little Lara slept in the back, luckily unable to hear. As she kept writing Harriet started to feel she was in the car herself. She leaned over the page, writing as quickly as she could. She imagined the squeal as the tyres hit an icy patch and Lara's dad shouted, 'It's out of control,' and Lara's mum said, 'Oh God,' turning around to look at Lara in her seat in the back. And then the car crashed through the white road barrier, skimming over rocks and gathering grass as it did so, the three of them being thrown around, the car turning once, twice, before coming to a stop in the river at the bottom of the valley. Somehow, miraculously, the seat Lara was sitting in, wedged in with extra pillows because she was so little, had been torn from its holdings and flung out of the (luckily open) window. Harriet hadn't been too sure if that was possible, but she hoped her teacher wouldn't pick her up on a detail like that. Lara's parents wouldn't have had a hope. But thank God – Harriet's hand was nearly a blur on the page by this stage – someone had driven by then and noticed the car. They'd run to a nearby phone box and called for an ambulance. It was the female ambulance driver who had found Lara, still strapped into her seat hours later, as the rescue party was about to leave the scene. 'We've got a survivor!' she shouted out into the night air, Harriet wrote. She had nearly been in tears.

Her story got the second highest mark, behind Tran Hien, the Vietnamese student whose parents had come to Australia in a terrifying trip in a flimsy boat, escaping from torture and imprisonment. Harriet was even more amazed when 'Lara's Rescue' appeared alongside 'The Boat Trip' in the annual school magazine. The teacher told her afterwards she'd wanted it to be a surprise for them both. The first she knew about it was when Lara came up to her at the end of year school assembly, looking shocked and angry. Harriet had never seen that expression on her face. It made her feel sick inside.

'Harriet, how could you do this? Why did you write it?'

She looked at the magazine in Lara's hand and blinked, in shock. Part of her was thrilled to see her name in print like that. She thought Lara would be happy for her. 'We had to write a story about something true that happened to our family.'

'But it isn't true. I wasn't in the car.'

Harriet was embarrassed. 'I know. But I didn't know how else to write it, because if I wrote it only from the point of view of your mother and father then they . . .' She stopped before she dug herself any deeper. She couldn't say because she wouldn't have been able to write about it if it was only them, because they weren't her family, only Lara was now, so Lara had to be in the car if she was to use them in the story. She'd started to explain, tried her best, but Lara interrupted her. Harriet got that frightening feeling again, that Lara was there, but a long way away, all at the same time.

'Don't ever do that again. It's my story, not your story.'

'But you're my family, aren't you. Aren't I allowed to write about you?' She was genuinely confused.

'Am I your family?'

'Aren't you?'

Lara didn't answer.

'I thought you were,' Harriet said in a small voice.

The rest of the family all read it. Mum, Dad, Austin, James. It was very dramatic, they all said. 'But Lara wasn't in the car, was she?' she heard James say. 'And she wasn't a baby at the time either, was she?'

It was talked about in the travel agency. Many of their customers had children at Harriet and Lara's school. The school magazine was read by everyone. Folding brochures one afternoon, Harriet overheard a conversation between Gloria and one of the clients.

'I didn't realise it had been so traumatic for Lara. I knew her parents had died, but I didn't realise she'd been in the crash with them.'

Gloria lowered her voice. 'No, actually, she wasn't.'

'But Harriet's story in the school magazine . . .'

'A little artistic licence.'

'But her parents did die in a car crash?'

'Yes, but Lara wasn't with them.'

Others were even blunter, and talked about it to Lara herself. 'I hadn't realised you were adopted, Lara. And under such tragic circumstances.'

Harriet felt sick. Her parents told her off, for not thinking about Lara, not thinking through the consequences of her actions. Even Gloria told her she should have thought more before she wrote it.

She'd gone to Gloria, the way she always did when her own family didn't make sense.

'I didn't mean to hurt her.'

'Are you sure?'

'Why would I?'

Gloria was serious. 'Look, I know it isn't easy sometimes for you, Harriet.'

'I've been really kind to her. I've always been kind to her.'

'Maybe she doesn't always want your kindness. Maybe sometimes she just wants to feel normal.'

It changed things between her and Lara for a while. Until Harriet went into their bedroom one night, with a carrot cake she had made herself. She knew Lara loved her cake. She had written *Sorry Lara* in icing on the top.

'I didn't mean to hurt you. I'm so sorry.'

'It's okay.'

'I didn't think.'

'It's okay, Harriet.'

Not long after that, Harriet kept coming across Lara and her parents, especially her mother, having the secret conversations again. Sometimes they were out in the garden, sitting together on the bench near the plum tree, talking quietly together. They stopped talking when Harriet came out with a basket of washing. Another time she came into the travel agency after hours to get some paper from the stationery cupboard. She surprised them, sitting close together in the waiting area. Her mother was holding Lara's hands. One afternoon she came home from a swim at the beach and walked into the living room, to see Lara sitting on the couch, crying, with her mother on one side and her father on the other.

'What's wrong? What's happened?'

Her mother's expression was obvious. 'Harriet, please, Lara needs to talk about a few things.'

In other words, Harriet, go away. It made her feel she was eight, all over again.

'Do you want to talk to me, Lara?'

'No thanks.'

'It's not because of the story, is it? I promise I won't tell anyone ever again.'

'It's okay, Harriet.'

She went back to Gloria again. 'They won't tell me what's going on. They're shutting me out.' She was going through a dramatic phase.

'There are things she wants to know about her own parents.'

'Why?'

'Because she can't remember them very well. And she wants to.'

'But she's got my parents now.'

'She still misses her own parents.'

'I suppose.' She thought about it. 'And it's not like she's adopted, is it? She can't go and find her parents. Get to know them at all, can she?'

Gloria looked at her for a long moment. 'No, Harriet, she can't.'

James started going out with Melissa the year Lara and Harriet turned sixteen. Melissa and her family had moved to Merryn Bay at the end of summer and she and James were an item within a month. As Melissa said at the first family barbecue she attended, 'I took one look at James in the main street and knew he was the one for me.'

'He didn't stand a chance,' Harriet heard Gloria say to her mother one night. She didn't think she was supposed to have heard it. But she knew what Gloria meant. Melissa frightened Harriet a bit. She was small but bossy and James seemed to almost hide behind her. He also made a big deal to Austin about the fact he had a girlfriend and Austin didn't. Harriet heard them have a horrible fight about it.

'Melissa's your girlfriend? Yes, James, that's one word for her, I suppose.'

'Meaning what?'

'Well, it's a funny thing. I often wondered what a female Rottweiler would look like in human form, and now I know. Blonde hair, tanned skin, remarkably like someone you know well, actually.'

'Fuck off, Austin,' James had said. Harriet had put her hands over her ears. She still hated it when they fought.

Austin was right in a way, but it wasn't a nice thing to say about James's girlfriend. Lara, however, didn't seem scared of Melissa at all. She talked to her, quite nicely, answered her questions and somehow didn't let her boss her around, the way Melissa was able to do to Harriet. Harriet was always surprised to find herself in the shop down the road, having been sent – ordered – by Melissa to go and buy some drinks, or a newspaper, or some chocolate. Gloria had said to her quietly one day that she should remember she was James's younger sister, not Melissa's slave.

'But she's his girlfriend. I'm being polite.'

'You don't have to let her walk all over you, Harriet. Some people like to do that to others.'

'I'll try not to let her do it any more. Anyway, they might split up soon, mightn't they?' she asked hopefully.

She'd been wrong. James and Melissa got engaged six months later, on Melissa's twenty-fifth birthday. Melissa asked Lara to be her third bridesmaid and Harriet to be one of the ushers. She'd explained to Harriet that she thought Lara's blonde hair, almost the same shade as hers, would look a bit better in the photographs. Harriet didn't think she minded, though she felt a bit strange on the day of the wedding. She'd overheard her parents saying how kind it had been of Melissa and James to ask Lara to be in the wedding party. 'It must have really made her feel one of the family.' It felt wrong to feel a bit jealous, so she did her best to hide it.

Harriet was eighteen and in her bedroom studying for her final year exams when her mum and dad came in. They both sat on the bed and formally invited her to come and work for Turner Travel.

'We'd love it if you would.' Her mother was all smiles.

'But only if you want to,' her father added. 'We want you here, but not under pressure.'

She had accepted straightaway, and not just because she wanted to make her parents happy. She'd never thought about working anywhere else. She'd always hoped that's what would happen, but she was very touched they'd asked her like that. After Austin's decision to go to music college rather than follow James and work in the agency, Harriet knew it was important to them.

It was a special moment for Harriet. Sitting in her room with her parents, hearing them say so casually that they loved the way she already helped in the travel agency, all the after-school hours she did, the way she made people feel so looked after when they called in or phoned about any of the tours.

'That's a real gift, Harriet,' her mother said. 'You make me very proud when I see you with our customers. We'd have loved you to work for us even if you weren't our daughter.'

They spoke about the sorts of things she would be doing, and asked her whether she wanted to work as a guide down the track, or stay in the office. She felt the ideas bubbling up inside her. She made suggestions there and then. What about guided tour groups to sporting events? Themed tours based around different sorts of restaurants? Historical tours, visiting towns connected with the colonial history of Australia? Her teacher at school had been brilliant the way he'd made it all come alive. Maybe he could come as a special guest speaker? Or geological tours? She'd seen a documentary and it was incredible when the history of a mountain or a bay was explained, all the things you looked at every day without ever really seeing them. Lots of people might be interested in that, mightn't they? She'd felt as though someone had thrown open a window, showing her all sorts of possibilities.

Her father had sat back and given her a beautiful smile. 'I don't think coming up with ideas is going to be a problem for you, Harriet.'

Her mother had been as happy. 'We'll have to take on extra staff to cope with all the business you're going to bring in, by the sound of things.'

'You have asked Lara to come and work with us as well, haven't you? I don't want her to feel left out.' Even as she asked, even as she genuinely hoped they had, she'd felt a stirring of her eight-year-old self. Please don't let them have asked her first.

'Not yet. We're asking her next. And we hope she'll say yes too.'

They'd asked her that same night. Harriet had been in the next room and had overheard. She'd made sure she could overhear, in fact. Lara hadn't said much. She had just gone to Mrs Turner and then to Mr Turner and held them in a very tight hug. 'I'd love to. Thank you.'

After James and Austin moved out of home, their bedroom became the Turner Travel storeroom. Harriet and Lara continued to share a bedroom, until Lara moved out of home the year they both turned twenty. She'd saved enough for a deposit on her own flat, on the first floor of one of the oldest stone buildings in the town, beyond the main street shops. They all knew, but didn't say, that there had also been a legacy from her parents.

Lara announced her plans quietly over breakfast one morning. It had come up for sale, she had been to see it, fallen in love with it.

Penny had been alarmed. 'Are you unhappy here, Lara? Oh, darling, you should have said something. We could have talked about it.'

'No, I'm not unhappy at all. It just felt like the right time.'

'You're not thinking of leaving the business, are you? Because we think the world of you, you know that, don't you?'

'No, I love working here. I'd just like to live on my own.'

They were all invited to a house-warming drinks party. It was the first time any of them had seen the flat since she'd moved in. She had kept them away, gently but firmly. 'No, not until it's perfect.'

Harriet hadn't been pleased. 'Come on, Lara. We want to see the before and after.'

'No, I'd rather you only saw the after.'

Even Mr and Mrs Turner hadn't seen it. Harriet had a feeling they were hurt by it. She'd heard her mum talking about it with Gloria one night.

'It's her first place, her first real independence,' Gloria tried to explain to Penny. Harriet had been in the staffroom, able to clearly hear their conversation, even though she wasn't sure if she should be listening. 'The first time since she came to live with you. She must have always felt like she was taking part of Harriet's bedroom. This is the first time she's really had something of her own. I think you need to respect that. Give her time.'

Whatever the flat had looked like when Lara first moved in, they didn't know. But she'd made it lovely. It was three large rooms at the front of the big stone building, which had previously been a bank. On top was a roof garden. It was one of the few two-storey buildings in the town, with a view over the pine trees lining the caravan park at the seafront. It was almost total sea view, if you ignored the car park and the kiosk, and the children's playground.

The rooms were simply but beautifully decorated. There wasn't a lot of furniture: a low sofa and two matching armchairs in soft white leather; a rectangular dining table in pale wood, with six wooden chairs, their padded seats matching the leather of the sofa. One wall was bookshelves, the books arranged neatly, art books and non-fiction on one row of shelves, hardbacks on another, paperbacks on another.

They peeked into the bedroom. It was decorated in the same pale colours, off-white walls, a cream quilt cover on the bed, a pile of soft pillows and cushions in shades of pink, light blue and pale yellow adding gentle colour. It was a very peaceful room. Even the kitchen was uncluttered, white cupboards and a stainless steel oven, with the cheery addition of a row of bright green cups and a thriving spider plant on the deep windowsill.

There were no heavy curtains over any of the large windows, just light gauze material in a soft turquoise that framed the view perfectly. A large painting hung on the main wall in the living room, an abstract seascape in different soft shades of blue and greens. It was very beautiful, the renovations thoughtfully done, the decoration stylish and feminine.

In a corner, pouring drinks, was Lara's boyfriend of six months, Tom. They had heard about Tom, but this was the first time they had seen him. Lara had met him at a travel agents' dinner in Melbourne. A pilot with one of the new airlines, he'd been one of the guest speakers.

'He's gorgeous,' Gloria said to Lara in a whisper. Not only physically, though the combination of fine Asian features inherited from his mother and height from his Australian father was striking. Later, emboldened and made giddy by too many champagnes, Harriet said to him that if she was ever destined to be in a plane crash, she hoped he was at the helm.

She realised too late what she had said. Her hand went to her mouth. Everyone looked at her, then Lara. 'Oh Lara, I'm so sorry.' No one needed to say it aloud, but they'd all been thinking of Lara's parents dying in a crash.

Lara fixed it, smoothly, gracefully. She went to Tom's side, kissed his cheek and said, 'It's fine, Harriet. Tom wouldn't crash. He's too good a pilot, aren't you?' She somehow stitched the tear in the conversation without fuss. The music was turned up, the conversation continued, the evening went on.

They'd all liked him very much, they told her at work the next week. She seemed pleased but didn't say much. Several months later she casually remarked that she wasn't seeing Tom any more. Harriet had wanted all the reasons why not, but Lara wouldn't be drawn. 'It wasn't working out between us,' she said. It was the explanation she used from then on, whenever she ended it with one of her boyfriends.

Harriet met Simon when she was twenty-six. It hadn't been an instant attraction, but she grew to like lots of things about him. How sure he was of everything. How definite he was about what he wanted to do with his life. He was nice-looking, solid, with sandy hair and an open, smiling face. Sometimes they ran out of conversation, and didn't always laugh at the same things, and she often wished he wasn't quite so quick with his lovemaking, but she reasoned with herself that she couldn't have everything. His good points easily outweighed the bad.

Austin was appalled at the news. 'A policeman? You're going out with a policeman? Oh bloody hell, Harriet. Talk about put a halt to all our gallops.'

'He's not *square*, if that's what you're getting at,' she said, stung. 'Anyway, you shouldn't be smoking drugs, if that's what you're getting at.'

'I don't smoke drugs. I inject them. Or freebase them. Sometimes I even take a bath in them.'

Lara was laughing. 'Don't mind him, Harriet, he's teasing you.'

'I know he is.' Of course she knew that. 'Don't worry, Austin, I've asked him to let you off lightly if he ever picks you up.'

'I don't know if I want to meet him. What if he starts lecturing me? Wants to teach me the right way to cross the road? "Look left, then right, no, no, Austin, not three rights and then a left. Look, if you kill yourself it's not my responsibility." '

Harriet wasn't enjoying this any more. She'd been dying to tell Austin about Simon, had saved it up for his visit home, and now he and Lara were making a joke of it. Austin had changed since he'd started touring with the orchestra, she decided. He only visited now and again, breezing in for a night here or there, sometimes midweek, sometimes on a Saturday. This visit – home for three nights – was a rarity. Harriet had pictured how it would be, Simon arriving for a barbecue, he and Austin hitting it off immediately – with a bit of teasing about Simon being a policeman of course, but then they'd find all sorts of things in common.

She made one last effort. 'Mum and Dad really like him, don't they, Lara?'

Lara nodded. 'He's very likeable.'

Harriet should have been pleased that Lara had said that. It was true. It was a statement of fact. But it felt condescending. 'Please don't talk about him like that.'

Lara frowned. 'Like what, Harriet? I meant it. He is very likeable.'

'You make him sound dull. It was like a put-down.'

Lara seemed genuinely confused. 'I didn't mean it to.' She turned to Austin. 'He is a nice man. And Harriet's right, he gets on really well with your dad too.'

That was even worse. She couldn't put her finger on it though. She could see Austin was puzzled by her reaction. On the surface everything Lara was saying was perfectly acceptable. Simon was very likeable, he did get on well with her father and, yes, he was a nice man. But it was the way she said it. Harriet rubbed her wrist, the way she had started doing when she felt under siege.

Austin came over, disarming her with a big hug, the sort of hugs he used to give her when she was small. 'Harriet, relax, would you? You're a little tense, and it's perfectly understandable. Your boyfriend is meeting your big scary internationally successful percussionist brother for the first time and you are hoping he comes up to scratch. That's your boyfriend, not your brother. But don't worry. I will sniff around him in the manner of all good dogs, and if I decide that, yes, he is good enough for my dearest baby sister, then I promise you he will see nothing but the most angelic and adorable side of my many faceted personality, okay?'

'Okay.'

'And Harriet, I'm sorry too if what I said came out wrong,' Lara said. 'I like Simon.'

There it was again. The words were perfect but Harriet couldn't stop herself from wanting to pick them up, shake them around, find out what Lara really thought about Simon. But they were both looking at her, with concern and, yes, with affection. She took a breath. Perhaps they were right. She probably was just nervous about Austin meeting Simon for the first time.

'Thanks.' She glanced at her watch. 'He'll be here in a minute.'

As she went outside she heard Lara say to Austin. 'It must be his police training, but it's amazing, he is never, ever late. You can set your watch by him.'

Harriet had never noticed it, but Lara was right. She glanced at her watch as Simon pulled up in his blue Mazda. It was exactly seven o'clock.

Their father managed the barbecue. It was nothing formal, chops, burgers, vegetarian sausages for Lara, salads, some of their mother's homemade patties, her special recipe of mincemeat, vegetables and what she said was her secret ingredient. Harriet knew it was soy sauce. Simon loved them and complimented her on them. He helped himself to several more, as well as another chop and a sausage, after offering the tray to everyone else first. They all accepted except Lara.

'You a vegetarian, Lara?'

'I am, yes.'

'Moral grounds or taste grounds?'

'Moral, I suppose.'

He bit into a chop. 'Don't think I'd last a week if I was a veggo.'

He'd announced when he arrived that he could only stay until ten o'clock as he had an early start the next day. Harriet tried not to, but as the time moved closer to ten, she noticed Austin and Lara glancing at their watches, exchanging knowing grins. She knew what they were up to. They were laughing at him.

At ten to ten she went over to where Simon was sitting talking to her father. They had discovered early in their relationship a shared passion for cricket. Simon barracked for Australia and Mr Turner supported England, despite his many years in Australia, so there was always plenty of scope for arguments and, this season in particular, even some gloating on Simon's part. The current English team was one of the weakest in memory.

'It's your batting that lets you down,' Simon was saying now, as she came up behind him and put her arms around his waist. She loved the solid feel of him. He lifted up one of her hands, squeezed it then kept talking. 'Too much focus on the opening batsmen, and the middle order are too unreliable.'

'I'd agree with you there, but the coach has to take some of the blame. They're prepared for a completely different sort of bowling style, not to mention the conditions. Harriet love, get me a beer, would you?'

'Sure Dad. Simon, you too?' She hoped he'd say yes. It would take him at least ten minutes to drink it, which would delay his departure and take those grins off Austin and Lara's faces.

He lifted up his wrist and checked the time. 'I'd better not, Harriet. I've got an early start tomorrow and I said I'd be gone by ten. I'll go and say goodnight to Penny now.' He leaned over and vigorously shook Mr Turner's hand. 'Pleasure talking to you again, Neil. And my commiserations again on your decision to back the English team.'

Neil laughed loudly. 'You young buck. We'll have the last laugh yet.'

Harriet followed Simon into the kitchen to get a beer for her dad. Mrs Turner was at the sink, rinsing out the dessert dishes.

'Thanks for a great night, Penny.'

'You're welcome, Simon. Off already? Don't tell me, early start?'

'Six o'clock.'

'Well, you don't want to be late.' She accepted his kiss on the cheek. 'See you next time. Thanks again for the flowers.'

Not her mother making digs about his timekeeping too? Harriet felt under siege from all sides. How dare they all laugh at Simon? It was all she could do to keep her temper as she walked to the car with him. He kissed her on the cheek, told her she had looked very pretty that night and that he'd enjoyed meeting Austin. 'A bit of a character, by the looks of things.'

'Yes, he is.'

She thought at first she was imagining it but then Austin's voice became louder, floating over the fence. She wasn't imagining it. He was doing a countdown to ten o'clock.

She didn't know whether Simon could hear or not. He got into his car and started the engine.

'Ten, nine, eight, seven . . .'

Simon put on his indicator.

'Six, five, four . . .'

Changed into first gear . . .

'Three, two . . .'

And drove away.

'One!' Austin poked his head over the fence. 'Ten o'clock, on the dot.'

'You're pathetic.'

In the background she saw her parents and Lara. All of them with big smiles on their faces. Austin had been playing to the gallery.

'Just helping him out, Harold. In case he lost track of the time in your fragrant company.'

'You're more than pathetic. You're pitiful.'

Austin was laughing. 'He's nice, Harriet.'

'I really like him. How dare you be so rude.'

'I wasn't rude. I talked to him. We had a long talk about sport and politics, man to man. Didn't we, Lara? You heard us.'

Harriet wouldn't look at Lara. 'I saw you laughing at him, Austin. How would you like it if you called the police in an emergency and they weren't there because they had slept in? He has to be punctual.'

Now not only Austin and Lara but her mum and dad were laughing.

'Harriet, that was the best defence of timekeeping I have ever heard,' her dad said. 'Now what about that beer, love?'

'Stuff your beer, Dad.'

When she came back from her floods of tears on the beach, it was to find her parents and Austin and Lara sitting around the back veranda. She went to her father, embarrassed but still prickly. 'I'm sorry.'

He took her hand and gave it a squeeze. 'I'm sorry too, love. I didn't mean to tease you.'

'That time of the month, Harriet?'

'Austin, stop it, would you?' The anger was still fizzing inside her. She wanted to shout at all of them – well, no, not at her parents. She wanted to shout at Austin and Lara. It was their fault. Sitting there, all cool and collected and supercilious. She liked Simon. She possibly even loved Simon. And she didn't want them to ruin it for her. It seemed important to say that. 'He means a lot to me. I didn't like that you were poking fun at him.'

Austin leaned back in his chair. 'Harriet, it's a good sign that I'm teasing him. It means he's one of the family. You'd have more reason to be worried if I was nice to him.'

Her mother patted her arm. 'He's right, Harriet. Don't be so sensitive about him.'

She wavered.

'Anyway, Harold, wouldn't it be creepier if I was really, really nice to him?' Austin stood up and made an elaborate bow. '"Really, Simon, do tell me more about your recent law-defending antics. You caught a joy-rider? My word, what an adventure. Tell me every bit of it, from the start, now. You set the alarm for six a.m. . ."'

She couldn't help herself. She started to laugh. 'You are a bastard, Austin Turner.'

Austin kept going, even as a piece of bread left over from the barbecue went whizzing past his ear. '"And tell me, Simon, how do you make those uniforms fit so snugly? Do you have any leather pants? Could I see them some time?"'

She went over and punched him on the arm. 'Bastard, bastard, bastard.'

He grabbed her. 'But lovable.'

She swiped him and went inside to help her mum make coffee.

Chapter Eighteen

Harriet looked around her hotel room. Everything was organised. She'd asked the porter for another armchair and both were now arranged in front of the TV. It made the room even more cramped, but never mind. She had also asked for a teapot and two nice cups. The two videos they'd be watching tonight were also ready to go, one of them already in the video player.

She knew all her clients were happy. Tired, full and happy. Most had gone straight up to their rooms after dinner. 'Very nice meal, thank you, Harriet,' Miss Talbot said as she walked past. Mrs Randall just gave her a big smile and said nothing.

The hotel's menu was as old-fashioned as the decor, Harriet thought, but her clients were delighted with it. Good old English comfort food, one of them called it. Soup or pâté for starters. Pork chop, grilled sole or lamb cutlets with mint sauce for mains. Ordinary vegetables like mashed potato, carrots and peas. Desserts like treacle tart, trifle or apple pie, all served with large quantities of the local clotted cream.

Even Mrs Lamerton had pronounced herself pleased. 'Thank you, Harriet,' she had said regally as she sailed past on her way to the bar for an after-dinner port. 'I do like a nice pork chop.' Harriet knew all Mrs Lamerton cared about was being seated next to Patrick Shawcross. She would have been happy eating fried ants as long as she was beside him. She had definitely made up for all the lost opportunities on the bus. No one else had got a word in with him until after dessert. The poor man would be covered in bruises too, from all the arm clasping Mrs Lamerton had been doing. If he wasn't already covered in bruises from being thrown against the seats on the bus twice that day. Clive's fault, each time.

Patrick's arrival had definitely upset him. Clive had obviously enjoyed being the alpha male or whatever position he imagined being bus driver afforded him. Now Patrick was getting all the attention and Clive wasn't happy. He had started to subtly sabotage things. The microphone had inexplicably gone off twice when Patrick was talking as they drove along the coast road earlier that day.

Clive had called out loudly, not turning around. 'Sorry about that, folks, this is an old bus. They must have given the proper bus to the *All Creatures Great and Small* tour group. That's the really popular one.'

As Patrick was standing up answering questions there had also been unexplained sudden braking when there had been no traffic or obstacles in front of the bus. Each time Patrick had been jolted up against the seat beside him. If he hadn't been hanging on to the back of Harriet's seat he'd have gone flying down the aisle.

She would have to keep an eye on Clive. But at least her clients were happy and they were her priority. Their question and answer sessions with Patrick were getting more enthusiastic each day. At lunch that afternoon he had fielded them from all sides.

'Patrick, was it just one dog playing Patch or were there several of them?' Mrs Kempton had wanted to know.

'Just the one, but he did go missing one day. After that we tried to make sure we always had a double on standby.'

Mr Fidock was leaning over the table. 'A crossbreed, wasn't he? Part sheepdog and part something else?'

Harriet had taken the opportunity to make a quick call back to Australia. She'd been about to dial the Turner Travel office when she'd changed her mind, dialing the number of James's hospital instead. She hadn't spoken to anyone at home since the night she'd rung Austin. Another of the new Turner Travel rules. Melissa had declared no news was good news. 'Let us know if something is wrong, otherwise we will assume all is going perfectly, as it should. It's what our clients expect.'

Harriet was put straight through to James. He sounded very pleased to hear from her. She ran through the tour so far. 'No problems yet, either. I think they're having a really good time.'

'It sounds like it. Well done, Harriet. I know you must have got a shock about Lara, but it sounds like you're doing a great job on your own.'

'Still no word from her?'

'Nothing. You know Austin's on his way to Bath? And to you, of course.' He didn't wait for her answer. 'Melissa thinks there might be a man involved, but I don't know about that. I think Lara will tell us in her own good time what's up. She left enough information with her flatmate so we wouldn't worry, so I'm not worrying.'

Every now and then James surprised Harriet with a dash of good sense. It was often too easy to take Austin's side and dismiss James as Melissa's lapdog. 'You think that?'

'I do. That's what Lara is like. Something's up with her, but she's obviously taken herself off to sort it out. These weren't exactly the ideal circumstances, but then it's not a perfect world. And I had full faith in you, Harriet. Sounds like you're doing beautifully. Are they laughing at my jokes in the script, by the way?'

She had just reported that yes, they were (the ones she was reading aloud, in any case) and was about to finish up when she heard a loud voice in the background. She heard James speak to the new arrival. 'It's Harriet from St Ives.'

The phone was snatched. 'Harriet, hello. Everything's all right?'

Harriet felt the tension inside. 'It's going really well, Melissa, thanks.'

'Really?'

Why did she have to sound so disappointed? 'Yes. The group are all very happy.'

'And Mr Shawcross?'

'He's happy too, I promise.'

'Is he nearby? Can I have a word with him?'

'He's busy with the clients at the moment.' Harriet realised then that she was actually handling Melissa. Old Harriet would have run and got Mr Shawcross. Old Harriet would have stammered and said, actually there's a bit of a problem with the bus driver, and I think Mrs Lamerton is upset she isn't getting to sit next to Patrick Shawcross often enough, and Mrs Kempton keeps losing things. But she was coping with it all, she realised. It was going fine. And that was all Melissa needed to know. She decided to get away while the going was good. Just in case her new confidence had a time limit. 'Can I talk to James again?'

'He's with a nurse.'

'Never mind. Would you tell him I said goodbye? And give Molly my love? I'll call if anything comes up.'

'Thanks, Harriet.' A slightly too long pause. 'And well done.'

'Thanks, Melissa.'

'And we'll let you know as soon as we track Lara down. There might still be time to get her to give you a hand.'

Several replies came to mind. Harriet pushed them all down. 'Thanks, Melissa,' she said again. 'Goodbye.'

Patrick's knock came at ten o'clock, as they'd arranged. Harriet had made sure she was changed out of the Turner Travel uniform and dressed in her own clothes, a cotton skirt that felt light and summery, her favourite red T-shirt and espadrilles. The yellow outfit was pushed right to the back of her cupboard.

'I feel like I'm cramming for exams,' he said as he came in.

'You're passing with flying colours, then,' she said with a smile. 'They'd never guess you couldn't remember the first thing about *Willoughby* twenty-four hours ago.'

'Not strictly fair, Harriet. I had blocked it out. Buried it deep in my psyche somewhere.'

'You're not unleashing too many demons, excavating it like this?'

'If I feel a psychological breakdown coming on, you'll be the first to know.'

'Can I get you a cup of tea before we start?'

'That awful tea you served me last night?' He laughed at the expression on her face. 'Harriet, it's all right. You didn't make the teabags. You take things very personally, don't you? You reacted the same way when one of the women complained about the cloudy morning. It's called nature. Weather. You can't be held responsible.'

'No. Sorry. It's just this is important to me.'

'And me too.'

'You don't have to pretend, really. Not with me.'

'I'm not pretending. I'm having a great time. If I was home, I'd be living quite a different life. Not being feted at every turn and having people howl with laughter at everything I say. Do you suppose this is what life is like for celebrities all the time?'

'Don't you know? As an actor?'

'I was never truly successful, though. I usually felt too self-conscious and, as you saw yourself, too nervous. Let's forget the tea. Will you have some wine with me instead?'

She saw then he had a bottle with him, tucked in behind the itinerary he was carrying. 'It's a good one.' He glanced at the label. 'Italian.'

'Oh, yes, thanks very much. I'd love a glass of wine.'

'Excellent. We're having a party.' He sat on the end of the bed and pulled out the cork. She looked for glasses. There were only the tooth mugs.

'I'm sorry, they're not exactly fine crystal.'

'They'll do perfectly.' He poured two mugs and handed hers across. 'You have been given the servant's quarters, haven't you? We can switch our viewing sessions to my room if you're feeling too crowded?'

'No, this is fine.' It was, too. They were more relaxed with each other tonight.

He took a sip of his wine. 'So what do we have for our viewing pleasure this evening?'

'Episode five to begin with, "The Case of the Smuggler's Skiff". It begins with a big fight between you and Lady Garvan. And then episode fifteen, "The Case of the Leaning Lighthouse".'

'Those two were even worse than the rest, if my memory serves me right. We might need to fast-forward both of them. And we're visiting where tomorrow?'

'Patrick, are you looking at the itinerary at all?'

'No, I don't need to. I'm in such good hands with you. You seem to cater to my every need and guess my every want, before it's even a half-formed notion in my head.'

'You just can't cope with my brother's writing style, can you?'

'It was your brother who wrote it?' He laughed. 'No, I'm sorry, I can't. And I'm actually using all my free time to try and remember *Willoughby* stories.'

'They're loving everything you're telling them. Even if the stories aren't strictly true.'

'They could be, you know. I might be dredging up old memories. I'm very glad they're enjoying it. They're nice people.'

'Do you mean that?' The night before he'd thought they were all mad.

'Yes, I really do.' He stretched out his long legs. 'I'm also glad it's now, not fifteen years ago. Back then I might have laughed at them for being so interested in something as flimsy as a TV program. But I had an interesting discussion with Mr Fidock today.'

Harriet had seen the pair of them talking as they walked back to the bus in Port Isaac.

'He was embarrassed at first about why he was here,' Patrick said. 'He thought he shouldn't be interested in something so silly as a long-gone TV program. But he confessed to me that it was his link with home. That he didn't want to come back and wander about looking for something in his home town that he wouldn't find, or see school friends that he no longer had anything in common with. He decided this was a safe way, a fun way, to be nostalgic. And I thought, he's right, that's what it is. This is like a public service, not an ordinary tour.' He held up his mug in a toast. 'So well done to you and all at Turner Travel, Harriet Turner.'

He took charge of the remote control. They sat silently as he fast-forwarded through the opening credits, pausing before the end, for the aerial shot of himself and the dog walking across a windswept headland. They took a sip of wine at the same time.

Harriet had watched this episode during her *Willoughby*-athon the first night she arrived. Well, fast-forward-watched it, at least. It involved a missing watch, stolen from the jewellery store in the centre of St Ives. Called to investigate it, Willoughby uncovers a chain of counterfeit jewellery smuggling. The jeweller, new to the town, is in fact a prison escapee. There is nearly a shoot-out, before Willoughby sneaks up behind and disarms the jeweller. The gun goes off and Willoughby falls to the ground. A tense moment – the ad break would have come in when it was screened on TV – before they discover the jeweller has shot himself in the foot.

Patrick pressed pause just as Lady Garvan ran towards him on screen, her face anguished. 'I remember doing that scene. They were going to have a stunt double for me. But there was a problem with the budget so I had to do it myself. The man playing the jeweller kept joking that he was going to bring in a real gun, to add realism. I remember being worried he'd done just that.'

'You were supposed to be worried, though. So it looked like good acting.'

'It wasn't. Not really. I don't think I ever got the part right. Even though it wasn't a success, I'd like to be able to look back and think I'd done my best. But never mind.'

She turned to him. 'Why are you so relaxed about it?'

'Because it was years ago. I've already had my dark nights about it.'

'I thought actors were supposed to be insecure.'

'Oh, I can be. I'm just not in the mood for it right now.'

They watched the second episode in silence. As the end credits started to roll, Harriet stood up, about to pack away the video cases, when he surprised her.

'Enough work.' He reached across and poured some more wine into her mug. 'Tell me about you, Harriet.'

'There's nothing much to tell.'

'Let me ask you some questions then. I can decide whether there's much to tell after that. I'll start with an easy one. Favourite colour?'

She smiled. 'Definitely not yellow. Purple, I think.'

'Favourite animal.'

'Hyena.'

He smiled. 'An unusual choice.'

'I thought you were doing one of those psychological tests. Where your choice of colour and favourite animal gives away your inner secrets.'

'So a hyena isn't your favourite animal? What would it have meant if it was? That you were attracted to howling men with stripes on their backs?'

'Exactly.'

'Just as well you didn't say mouse, then. I'd have been disappointed in you.'

The wine was relaxing her. 'We used to play that game all the time as teenagers. You'd give someone four things to describe and it would instantly give you an insight into all their deepest, darkest feelings.'

'That must be an Australian game. Tell me about it.'

'No, it takes a while. You must be tired.' And she wasn't sure how she'd feel hearing what his attitudes to sex, death, himself, and his ideal partner were.

'Not too tired to play an authentic Australian game. I don't have to run around in shorts or kick a ball?'

'No.'

'Well, then. Play it with me now.'

She had that feeling again that he was amused by her. She hoped it wasn't only a way of filling in time. Though of course that's what he was doing. In his normal life he wouldn't be sitting in a hotel room watching videos and playing games with a tour guide. She had that rush of curiosity again to ask him about his life, his work in America, but he was waiting for her to explain the game. 'I give you four topics and you have to tell me in four words, off the top of your head, how they make you feel.'

'Right. I'm ready when you are.'

Still a little unsure, she reached for her bag and took out pen and paper. He did seem genuinely keen to play the game. 'First of all, imagine yourself in a white room and tell me how you would feel.'

'A completely white room? White floors, white walls . . .?'

She nodded. 'White ceiling. Completely white. The first thoughts that come to mind.'

He didn't hesitate. 'Calm. Clean. Peaceful. But I'd feel a bit wary in case I left marks all over it. Perhaps I'd take my shoes off before I went in there.'

She wrote it all down. When she looked up he was watching her, with that half-smile again.

'So Professor Turner, what have I revealed about myself?'

'It's supposed to represent your attitude to death. Some people say they'd be terrified in a white room, scared, trying to get out.' She checked her notes. 'Whereas you seem to be well-adjusted about the whole idea. You'd feel calm, clean, peaceful, but worried about leaving marks. That's probably guilt.' She kept a straight face.

'Probably? Definitely. All the sins of my past coming back to haunt me. So, next question.'

She was embarrassed now. 'Patrick, really, it's just a teenage thing. You don't need to do it.'

'Seriously, Harriet. I'm intrigued now. Ask me another.'

'The next one is about your favourite colour.'

'That's an easy one. Red. The exact colour of your T-shirt, in fact.'

'You're sure about that?'

He nodded. 'It's always been my favourite colour. So now what? I give you four words to describe how I feel about the colour red?' At her nod, he shut his eyes as if to concentrate.

Sitting opposite him, Harriet studied his face. She liked the character in it, the liveliness. In *Willoughby* he had been all moody and mysterious, and his dark looks suited that. In real life he was much lighter of spirit. Carefree, somehow. He opened his eyes. She noticed the dark blue again. 'Right. I have my answer. Cheerful. Vibrant. Deep. Sexy.'

She wrote them down. It was just as she would have described him herself.

'Don't tell me, I've revealed my ideal partner is a rooster?'

She smiled. 'No, that one's about you. It's how you'd like other people to see you, or how you see yourself.'

'What did I say again?'

She had a feeling he knew exactly what he had said. 'You are cheerful, vibrant, deep and sexy.'

'How extraordinary. That's right. I am all those things. To think you Australians have been keeping this incredibly accurate psychological testing to yourself all this time. Next one?'

'This one's about water.' Which was really about sex. She felt that odd tingle again, as though she was swimming and getting out of her depth. Another reference to water, she realised. So was she thinking about sex? With Patrick? She stared at him, taking in the expectant expression on his face, the relaxed body, the long fingers holding the glass of wine. 'Again, you need to tell me —'

She jumped as a mobile phone sounded. His, not hers.

'Excuse me, Harriet.' He glanced at the number and smiled before he answered it. 'Hello there.' His voice was warm.

Harriet tried not to eavesdrop, though it was difficult enough not to in the small room. He was obviously happy to hear from the caller. She could hear the voice faintly. It sounded like a woman. She couldn't help listening. 'I'll need to check my diary,' he was saying. 'I'm not in my room just now, can I call you back? Great. Give me a few minutes. Okay, thanks.' He turned to her. 'Harriet, will you excuse me? I need to make some calls home.'

'Of course. I think we're done for tonight anyway.'

'I think so too.' This time he did kiss her. Quickly, on the forehead. 'Thank you. I'm enjoying this very much.'

'You're welcome. So am I.'

When she went to bed an hour later, she could still get the scent of his aftershave on her skin.

In her bedroom in Merryn Bay, Molly Turner was sitting looking at herself in her dressing-table mirror. She'd hardly slept all night. It was still too early to go to swimming training but there was no way she could go back to bed. There was too much to think about. The house was quiet. She imagined she could hear her own heart beating. She tried to keep her expression serious as she stared at her reflection, but a smile kept breaking through.

It was finally going to happen. She'd made her decision.

Dean had been so proud of her. 'That's fantastic, gorgeous.' She loved it when he called her gorgeous. 'See, didn't I tell you it would be easy?'

Their plans had all come together when her mother had reminded her she'd be going to Melbourne for the night later that week 'You're still okay to go and stay with Hailey?'

In that instant she'd decided. It had all fallen into place in her mind, just like that. She had calmly said, as if it were true, that she had a swimming carnival that night, didn't her mum remember? She'd told her about it the week before? She'd be staying overnight in a billet because it was so far away? So she wouldn't need to go and stay with Hailey after all. And her mum had hesitated only for a minute and then said, of course, that's right, she must have forgotten about it, how was Molly going to get there, though? And as calmly, Molly had said that Dean, her new coach, was going to come and pick them up and drive them there. That was only the tiniest of lies, saying 'them' when it would only be her, but she didn't want her mum to get too worried.

She'd rung him straightaway. He'd been taken aback at first, she could hear it in his voice, but then he sounded really pleased. He would come and get her himself. He knew which motel they'd go to, as well. 'We'll have the whole night together, gorgeous. You won't regret it, I promise you.'

She leaned forward to the mirror. Would she look different when she got back? Would it show that she had had sex? Would other people be able to tell? She folded her arms around herself. It was the right thing to do, she was sure of it. She loved Dean and he loved her, and as he said, it was time they took their relationship to the next stage.

She glanced at her mobile phone. There had been no text from Lara. She decided to take it as a sign. She had to trust her own instincts. And she did. It was what she wanted to do. She was nearly one hundred per cent sure of it.

CHAPTER NINETEEN

Austin rang Harriet mid-morning the next day to say he'd be with her within the hour. He'd flown into Plymouth airport that morning and hired a car. He'd decided he would be able to stay for an hour at the most. 'I've only got three days off, Harold. I'll have to start looking for Lara as soon as I can.'

Harriet had imagined him having lunch with them, meeting Patrick Shawcross and all the clients. Maybe even coming on the tour of Bodmin Moor that afternoon. She couldn't admit it to him, but she wanted Austin to see how well she was coping. She still hated remembering the state she'd been in when he came to her rescue in the Flinders Ranges. He had told her many times since that he had practically forgotten it, but she hadn't.

The tour group were spending the morning sightseeing around St Ives on their own, visiting galleries and tracking down extra *Willoughby* landmarks. Mrs Lamerton had loudly announced her intention to be photographed standing in front of the lighthouse seen in many of the episodes. Clive had meanly, and too loudly, remarked that she'd better be careful she didn't block out the light. They were all meeting for lunch in one of the beachfront cafes. The afternoon would be spent on the Moor, looking for moorland ponies to photograph and taking a short walk to the tor that had been the backdrop for the confrontation scene in 'The Case of the Jilted Jockey'.

Harriet had taken the opportunity of having some free time to send a postcard home to Molly and to buy some creamy toffee for Gloria and Kevin. Back in her room, she had just finished checking the itinerary for the next day when the receptionist called to tell her Austin was downstairs. She'd contemplated wearing something different from the hideous yellow outfit, but she was meeting the group at the harbour at twelve-thirty and it made more sense to be already dressed in uniform.

Austin was waiting at the foot of the stairs and slowly shook his head as she came towards him. He looked as stylish as ever, his dark hair shiny and fashionably long, his linen shirt and dark trousers hanging perfectly on his lean frame. There was also the usual spark of mischief in his eyes.

'I see that outfit hasn't got any more attractive. Melissa's on the other side of the world and you're still obeying her?'

'It's very handy. My group don't have the best eyesight.'

'They won't if they keep looking at you in that get-up.' He hugged her. 'How are you, Harold?'

'I'm great. It's brilliant to see you, Austie.'

'You too. I'm sorry I can't stay long. I want to get across to Bath as soon as I can and talk to her flatmate. I was thinking about it the whole way here. It has to be something about her parents, don't you think?'

Harriet blinked. She knew he was here to talk about Lara, but she hadn't expected it to be so immediate. She was about to answer when she heard a voice.

'Hello again, Harriet.'

Harriet turned. It was Patrick. She was very pleased to see him. She could introduce Austin to her star guest, even if they didn't get to spend any more time with him.

'Patrick, hello.' She noticed him looking at Austin and made the introduction. 'This is my brother, Austin Turner. Austin, this is Willoughby himself, Patrick Shawcross.'

They shook hands. Harriet watched as Austin turned on the charm. 'You're having a good time, I hope. My sister's not working you too hard?'

'Oh no. Your sister is a gem. She's got all of us under her thumb. Especially me, isn't that right, Harriet?'

'I don't know about that,' she said. She liked that he was laying it on so thick.

'So you're enjoying your trip down memory lane?' Austin asked.

Patrick nodded. 'Even more than I expected. I may have to make an annual thing of it. What do you say, Harriet? Could you bear me once a year?'

'Of course. I just need you to survive this one first,' she said.

There was a noise at the front door of the hotel. They looked over. Miss Talbot and three of the other women were knocking on the glass and waving. Patrick smiled and waved across. 'Will you excuse me? I'm showing Miss Talbot and some of the others the way to the art gallery. A pleasure to meet you, Austin.'

They shook hands again. 'You too,' Austin said.

'I'll see you later, Harriet.' He touched her back lightly as he spoke.

'See you, Patrick,' she said.

She took Austin for a coffee at the cafe on Porthminster Beach, down from the hotel. It was a blustery day. The sand was whipping along the beach, red and white striped canvas deckchairs flapping, bright-coloured towels gusting, children running in and out of the water, squealing and chasing spatters of foam.

Austin gazed around. 'It's a beautiful place. Incredible light.'

'Gorgeous. Everyone loves it here.'

'So what do you think? Any more ideas?'

'Well, no, not really. I'm sticking to the itinerary pretty much. That's what everyone's expecting.'

'Sorry, Harriet, I meant about Lara. I tell you, it's times like this I wish Mum and Dad were here.'

She kept her face expressionless. 'Just times like this?'

'Well, no, lots of times, of course. But we could have asked them for help now. Asked them more about Rose, and her husband. Are you like me? A bit shocked about how little we know about where Lara came from, who her parents were?'

'We knew a fair bit, didn't we? Remember the memorial days? They were all about her parents.'

'I know that. But it's the facts we don't know. A little girl came to us out of the blue, and the more I think about it, the more I realise we hardly asked a question about it or did anything special for her. We went on as if it was a normal thing, that a stranger arrived to live with us.'

'No, we didn't. Everything changed when she arrived.'

'No, it didn't. We still went to school, to the beach, helped in the office. It's just there were four of us kids, not three.'

They were interrupted by the arrival of their coffee. The wind threatened to take the foamy tops off their cappuccinos. Across from her, Austin was checking his mobile phone. 'Sorry about this, Harriet. Want to double check I've got a signal here. I was thinking about calling Lara's flatmate first, but I think I might turn up unannounced. I'm going to call into her college too, see if I can have a word with one of her lecturers or any of the others in her class. They might have noticed something.'

'Thanks for taking the time to drop by and say hello.'

He picked up her tone. 'Harriet, I'm sorry.' He leaned over and tweaked her nose. He'd been doing that since she was little and she had always hated it.

She was cross enough now to say it. 'Please don't do that. I'm not a child any more.'

'You on your cranky pills, Harold? With me, your dearest brother, here on the other side of the world with you? And you not treating me with respect and adoration? Aren't you finding your heart beating faster with the excitement of being in close proximity to me?'

She couldn't help it. She started to smile.

'That's better. You looked like you'd been drinking sour milk. Harold, I'm sorry to talk about Lara and not shower you with praise about how well you're coping on this tour. I'm not surprised, that's all. I knew you could do it. I told Lara that as well.'

'Told her what?'

'That I had complete faith in you.'

She sat up straighter. 'When did you talk to her about me?'

'The day James had his accident. She rang to see whether I thought you were up to it.'

She could feel the colour in her cheeks. 'Why did she have to check with you whether I was up to it?'

'What else could she have done? Rung you, in the middle of the night? When she knew you'd be flat out getting ready? Calm down, would you? Think about it from her point of view. She'd spent months setting up this tour and then James pulls out the day before. She was concerned and reasonably so. Don't overreact.'

'I'm not overreacting. But it's a pretty funny way of showing how much you care about something, not showing up like this.

Leaving all of us in the lurch.' She felt a hot, prickly sensation inside. She knew she was being bitchy but she couldn't seem to stop herself.

'Which brings us right back to square one. Why I'm here. To find her.'

'But what if she doesn't want to be found? What if she wants to be left alone?'

'I told you before. I'll leave her alone as soon as I know she's okay.'

'I still think if she's decided she wants some space we should give her some space.'

Austin gave her a strange look. 'Harriet, this is Lara. Lara whose parents were killed when she was eight years old. Lara who had to go and live with a whole new family. Don't you think this is out of character for her? That something's up and she might be needing some support right now? What's got into you? I thought you and Lara were close.'

The feeling again. The uncomfortable ripple of hurt and confusion. 'Things change in a family, Austin. Relationships change, people behave differently. Lara might not want you chasing after her.'

'Lara's heart would skip a beat if she saw me appear out of nowhere, just as yours did. My two little acolytes, that's how I've always seen you. My little elfin-faced Harold, and ice queen Lara. Not so much sisters as followers, I always liked to think. Such sport too, playing you off against each other, making you do my bidding. I suspect I'm part wizard, actually. What do you think, Harold?'

She stood up. 'I have to go, Austin. I'm meeting the tour group.'

'Not until lunchtime, you told me.'

'I've got work to do.'

Austin didn't move. 'Don't be like this.'

'Like what?'

'Prickly. Pretending to be tough. It doesn't suit you.'

She lost her temper. 'What am I supposed to be like then, Austin? Answer me that? Because I don't seem to be able to win in this family. I'm either too weak, falling apart, the basket-case or it's "Don't get tough, Harriet, it doesn't suit you." Which one am I?'

'You're my dear little sister Harold, that's who you are. My little anxiety bag of a sister. Come on, Harriet, sit down and calm down, would you?'

He disarmed her, as he always could. Her temper flickered and then went out. But he was wrong. She wasn't just his little sister, the anxiety bag of a child. Not any more. But he kept choosing not to see it. They fell quiet again. She made a point of slowly stirring sugar into her coffee. The mood had changed and she didn't know whether she wanted to fix it or not.

Austin broke the silence. 'I thought he was supposed to be an old man.'

She looked up. 'Who?'

'That Patrick Shawcross. He's not old at all. In fact, he's a hunk.'

'A hunk? When did you ever use a word like hunk?'

'Don't you think it suits him? He's like one of those old-fashioned matinee idols. "Hunky actor Patrick Shawcross, pictured today in St Ives",' he spoke in a bad American accent. 'If I had known my little sister was travelling around the wilds of Cornwall with a sex symbol . . .'

'Yes, a sex symbol and twelve old-aged pensioners.'

'So he hasn't tried anything on you?'

'Tried what?'

'You know. These actor-types, no morals . . .'

She knew he was trying to joke with her, but she didn't like it. 'Austin, what's got into you? You never did this big brother act when we were at home, so why now?'

He shrugged. 'Because you had Simon guarding you back then. I might be your brother but I can see these things. He's an attractive man. You're a single, good-looking woman. I know from the orchestra that you put those things together on tour and boom. I saw the two of you, getting on so well, that touch on your back . . .'

'Of course we get on well. And he's an actor. Everyone knows actors are tactile.'

'Is he married?'

'Yes, with eleven children, but he told me this morning he loves me and wants to leave them for me. Austin, listen to yourself.' She was laughing now, but she was also serious.

'Just worrying about my little sister. Protecting her, as I always have.'

She poked out her tongue at him.

' "Please don't do that," ' he mimicked her. ' "I'm not a child any more." '

She couldn't help herself. She did it again.

After waving goodbye to Austin as he drove off in his hire car, she went for a walk along the beach on her own. He had given her a nice hug, and told her he thought she was great, and the tour was obviously going well, but he'd been distracted when he said it. It was obvious he wanted to get on the road.

She walked down the beach, taking in deep breaths of the fresh air, trying to focus on the peaks of white on the water. The seagulls were loud. The weather was changing. The blue in the sky was being taken over by large dark clouds, and the wind was picking up, getting colder and gustier. The buildings and streets of St Ives were to her right, just out of her line of vision. She tried to concentrate on the fishing boats out on the water, real, solid things, not the uncomfortable thoughts pushing their way into her mind.

She'd had the dream again the night before. Reliving the phone calls that her parents were dying and she was rushing to get to them, feeling the panic in her chest that she wasn't getting closer even though she was running as fast as she could. Getting to the hospital and racing to the door, only to find it locked. To find Lara standing there behind the glass, staring at her without expression. Hearing herself call out, 'Lara, let me in.' Not being able to get her to understand, or to hear. She'd woken up then, her heart racing. It had taken her a long time to get to sleep again. If she had the dream, the bad memories always followed. Memories of the terrible conversation with Lara three months ago, the night before she left for her course in England. Like a video in her mind she couldn't erase.

She should have told Austin about it. Explained why she felt so strange about finding Lara. Told him what she had learned, from Lara herself.

One of the nurses from the hospital had set it in motion, unwittingly, at Lara's farewell party. It was the first time Harriet had seen her since the day her mother died. The young woman had put her hand on Harriet's arm and expressed her sympathies again about Mr and Mrs Turner, asking how she was getting on, in a tone of voice that gave away she knew about Harriet's breakdown.

Harriet had answered as brightly as she could. She'd told the truth. She missed her parents very badly. 'I just keep wishing I could have one last conversation with them.'

'It must have been some consolation to Lara, I suppose. Nothing takes the sadness away, but perhaps it would have helped.'

Harriet didn't understand. 'I'm sorry, I'm not sure what you mean.'

'It might have helped Lara, that she was able to speak to your mother before she died. Before she had the second stroke.'

'But Mum wasn't conscious after the first stroke. She was in a coma when she had the second one, wasn't she?'

The nurse had looked uncomfortable. 'I'm sorry. I thought you —'

'No, it's fine. Really. Will you excuse me?'

She'd gone directly to James, who was in mid-conversation with several clients. She'd pulled him to one side. 'James, did you know Mum was conscious before she died?'

'What, Harriet?' He'd looked unhappy to be interrupted.

She repeated the question.

'Harriet, why are you asking this now? What will it change?'

He didn't understand. She went to Austin, on the other side of the room, and asked him the same question.

'Harriet, don't do this to yourself.'

'I'm not doing anything. But did you know?'

'Harriet . . .'

He didn't understand either. Lara was in the far corner of the room, talking to several clients. Harriet could hear her explaining what the course in Bath was about. She knew it was rude to interrupt but she couldn't stop herself.

'Lara, can I talk to you. In private?'

They went outside to the garden. Harriet blurted it out. All the nurse had said. 'Is it true? Were you talking to Mum? Before she died?'

Harriet didn't know what she'd expected from Lara. A denial perhaps. An explanation that the nurse had got it wrong. What she hadn't expected was what Lara did.

She nodded. After only a moment's hesitation.

Harriet was shocked. 'But when? I thought she was in a coma. Why didn't any of you tell me she'd been conscious?'

'Harriet, it wasn't for long. We'd just got to the hospital and James went outside to ring Austin and Melissa and he asked me to ring you and . . .' Lara stopped there.

Harriet stared at her, trying to make sense of what she was saying. 'James asked you to ring me? To tell me Mum was in hospital? That she'd had a stroke?'

Lara nodded.

'But you didn't ring me. James rang me.' Even as she said it, a sharp memory of James's call that day seemed to echo in her mind. '*Harriet, thank God I got you.*'

Harriet saw something in Lara's expression. She knew what it was immediately. It was guilt. 'Lara, did he ask you to ring me? And you didn't?'

Lara didn't answer that time. She just kept looking at Harriet.

Harriet had to know. She had to know for sure. 'Lara? Is that true? I have to know, can't you see that? Did James ask you to ring me and you didn't?'

'Harriet . . .'

'Is that what happened?' She knew the answer from Lara's face. 'But Lara, if you had rung me, I could have got there earlier. I might have been with Mum when . . .' Back it came, the panic and the hurt and the desperation of not being with her father or her mother when they died. She could hardly look at Lara, unable to believe what she had just learned. 'I can't understand. How could you have done it?' Still no answer. 'Lara, please, you have to tell me. How could you have done it? Don't you see what you have taken from me?'

There had been no response from Lara. Nothing. That's what had stunned her. No tears, no apologies. They had just stared at each other, and then Lara had turned and gone inside.

The next day Lara had left for England. They hadn't spoken of it – spoken of anything – in the months since. Harriet hadn't known where to start. How did she begin to ask about something that she knew would hurt so badly to hear? How did she get past the fact that Lara had done something so terrible?

Should she have told Austin about it? She couldn't have, she realised. Something inside, some instinct, had stopped her. The uneasy feeling that he wasn't automatically on her side any more. Because like it or not, she knew there had always been rivalry between her and Lara over Austin. Over who spoke to him the most. Who made him laugh the most. Who he liked the most.

Austin had looked at her as if she was crazy when she dared to suggest it hadn't all been smooth sailing when Lara arrived. For once, she had heard herself voicing something close to the truth, but it had been dismissed. Austin was in his rescuer mode, and nothing was going to get in his way. He'd always been like that. Playing the older brother card, but only when it suited him.

For the hundredth time since her parents died, Harriet wished they were there, so she could ask for help and advice. She thought about what Austin had said about wanting to ask about Lara, her parents, what had happened to them.

The questions she wanted to ask them came straight into her mind. 'Did you know how much I loved you? Did you love me?

Did you love me as much as you loved Lara?' She knew what they would have said. 'Of course we did, Harriet. We had enough love for all of you.' She'd never been able to hear it enough times. And what questions would they ask her, she wondered.

Perhaps they knew all about her already. If, as she hoped, they were up in some sort of heaven somewhere, she liked to think of them keeping an occasional eye on her, or at least getting regular reports, like dossiers. She liked to imagine the two of them, sipping cocktails on some big cruise ship in the sky, a tuxedo-wearing waiter swishing up to them with a tray. 'Here's this week's report on your children, Mr and Mrs Turner.'

It had disturbed Harriet recently to discover that her memories of her parents were fading. When she tried to picture them sometimes, the edges were hazy, as though she was looking at them through frosted glass. She could remember minor details, but not the whole. The way her father walked, an upright, brisk movement. The way her mother laughed, with one hand covering her mouth, so ladylike. She could still imagine their voices, though. They'd always kept their English accents, even after so many years in Australia. Sometimes just a touch of another similar accent was enough to hear them in her head.

Harriet came to a boat pulled up on the sand. She leaned down to touch it, running her hand along the wood, the solid feel of the paint layers. *Will o' the Wisp* was written in curvy letters on its side, a bright starfish painted beside it. She traced it with her finger, counting the five points. A childhood memory came back to her. A conversation she'd had with Gloria about six months after Lara had come to live with them. Harriet had just finished her regular drawing on the travel agency blackboard. Gloria had come over to look.

'That's lovely, Harriet. But you've forgotten your starfish.'

Since doing her Christmas cards, Harriet had started putting a small starfish in a corner of all of her drawings, as a little symbol of her family. She hadn't forgotten it this time. She'd been thinking about it, picturing the five pointed arms, trying to decide what colour she would do it, when she had realised it didn't work now. 'No, I haven't. I can't do it any more.'

'Why not?' Gloria asked.

'Because there are six of us in my family now, not five.'

'You can get six-pointed starfish. Twenty-pointed starfish, even. Starfish come in all shapes and sizes.'

'I've never seen them.'

'You'll just have to search harder, then. And in the meantime, the five-pointed one can still be your family. You'll just have to look at it differently.' Gloria had drawn a five-pointed starfish on the blackboard then and there. 'See? One of you can go in the middle of the starfish – you for now, as a special treat, but you can take turns.' She'd written Harriet's initial in the centre of her drawing. 'And the other five, your mum, your dad, James, Austin and Lara, can surround you,' she'd been writing their names as she spoke, 'standing in a circle with their funny pointy heads, looking after you.'

The memory made Harriet smile and made her sad, all at once. She ran her hands along the wood of the boat again, picturing it out on the water, riding waves. As children they had built rafts and swum in the sea, but she had never spent much time sailing or boating, preferring to swim. She imagined climbing in, setting sail, going across the water for miles, until she arrived at a whole new place. Is that what Lara was trying to do, make a fresh start somewhere? Leaving the Turners, and that whole life, behind her? Reclaiming the life that would have been hers if her parents hadn't died?

Harriet suddenly had the same urge. To go somewhere, start all over again. Leave pain and sadness behind. Be happy, laugh. Out of the blue she thought of Patrick Shawcross. That lightness of spirit he had. Was it a choice he had made or was it luck that he had got through life unscathed, unshaken by grief or jealousy? She wanted to ask him. She had a hundred questions she wanted to ask him. Why he had stopped acting. What he did now. Why he was still single . . .

She thought of Austin's description of him as a hunk, a sex symbol. 'Has he tried anything on, Harriet?' What if she'd yes? What would Austin have done? Gone and punched him on the nose? Or if she had said to Austin, 'Actually, yes, we've been lovers since the first night we met. It was an instant and incredible attraction.' What would Austin have done then? He'd be shocked at her, she knew. He thought of her as a child, not an adult. No matter what she did.

As for Melissa's reaction if something were to happen between her and Patrick Shawcross . . . Harriet pictured it. The two of them, her and Patrick, spending hours of long, lazy lovemaking in her bed – no, his, it had more room, and a much better view – and finally deciding a choice had to be made. She imagined herself stretching across to the phone, dialing the international number while Patrick ran a gentle finger down her bare back, following with his lips, soft, warm kisses. 'Melissa, hello, it's Harriet. I'm ringing to let you know I've called off the tour because I'm having an affair with Patrick Shawcross and, unfortunately, the clients are getting in the way.' She would lie in his arms, still talking, while he stroked her body some more. Her voice would go husky, as Melissa shouted down the line. Finally she would simply hang up and turn to . . .

'Hello, Harriet.'

She spun around. 'Patrick!'

'Are you all right? You look quite flushed.'

She put her hands to her cheeks. Flushed? Of course she was. 'No, just windburn, I think. I'm not running late, am I?'

'No, I'm early. I saw you from the harbour steps and thought, that's either Harriet off for a walk or a yellow duck has been blown onto the beach.'

She took refuge from her embarrassment by pretending to be insulted. 'The uniform's really not that bad. Anyone would think you and Clive had never seen the colour yellow before.'

'That's right,' he said, as they started walking back to the steps together. 'He calls you Big Bird, doesn't he? Very clever. Perhaps we could hold a contest to see what names the others can come up with.' He laughed at her reaction. 'Harriet, you really do have the most expressive face. I'd call that one mutinous. Can you do heartbroken for me? Or exultant, perhaps?'

She shook her head. 'No. I specialise in worried or anxious.'

'Worried? What do you have to be worried about?'

She told the truth. 'The tour. Something going wrong. Making sure everyone is having a good time.'

He put his arm around her shoulder and hugged her against him as they walked. 'They are. I am. We all are. You're doing a great job. I meant what I said to your brother. I'd happily come back every year and do this. I'm being treated like a king. I have twelve people who seem to think I am the funniest, wittiest person they have ever met in their lives and a lovely woman minding me every step of the way.'

Her senses had sprung into life. She kept waiting for him to drop his arm, but if anything he was holding her closer against him as they walked. She was the right height to be leaning against his shoulder. She could smell his aftershave again. She tried to stay relaxed, as if walking along a windy beach with his arm around her was nothing out of the ordinary. She tried to give a normal-sounding answer. 'As long as you're enjoying it, that's the main thing.'

'I certainly am. And I know the group is, too.' They walked in silence for a while, Harriet was conscious of their closeness, the way their steps were matching. How would they look to anyone watching? Like lovers? Yes, if you ignored the fact one of them was dressed like a duck.

The weather was changing dramatically around them. There was now little blue in the sky and the wind was getting gustier. He had to raise his voice to be heard, leaning down to her height again. 'So is your brother in the travel business, too?'

She shook her head. 'He's a percussionist, touring Germany with an opera company.'

'And he came all this way to say hello to you?'

No, he'd come all this way to find Lara. But she wasn't going to go into that at the moment. She hesitated, noticing again the darker flecks in his eyes, and how good his arm felt. 'Yes, he did.'

'You're lucky to have a close family like that.'

'Yes. Yes, I am.'

They reached the steps to the beach cafe as the first spatters of rain started. Only then did he take his arm away from her.

Chapter Twenty

Austin drove along the fast lane of the motorway towards Bath, tapping his fingers on the wheel in time to the windscreen wipers. The rain had started as he left St Ives an hour before and hadn't stopped since. The sky ahead was black with clouds. He'd listened to the weather forecast. The bad weather was expected to continue for the next few days. On the seat beside him was a street directory and the scribbled directions he'd made for finding Lara's address. In the back seat was his rucksack, filled with enough clothes for three days.

The orchestra manager had been surprisingly understanding when he'd explained about Lara going missing, though only able to spare him for a short time. Austin was glad he'd been able to drop in and see Harriet, brief and all as it was. Even though she was a grown woman, he still had that urge to look after her, to make sure she was okay. He felt differently about Lara, he realised. He'd given it a lot of thought on the plane on the way over. Some of it had to be because Lara wasn't his natural sister, of course. He'd met her when she was eight, whereas Harriet had arrived as a screaming bundle. He could still hear his mother saying, 'Keep an eye out for your little sister, Austin, won't you?' Had she said the same thing about Lara? Austin couldn't remember. Lara was so different to Harriet, in any case. So much more self-sufficient.

Good fun still – he and Lara had always got on well, right from the start – but she had never needed him the way Harriet always had.

He'd liked getting another, instant sister. He knew Gloria had been all for it, too. She'd thought it would do Harriet good to have someone to play with. Not that Gloria knew he'd heard her say it. He'd overheard her talking to her husband when he had been doing some gardening for them. Nothing like open windows to keep a kid up-to-date. Back then adults seemed to be under the impression that if you couldn't see a child, then they couldn't hear you. Austin had heard more dirt by sitting still than he ever would have by asking.

Where could Lara have gone, he wondered. Was she somewhere nearby, right now, upset about something or having the time of her life, off on holiday with a new boyfriend? She hadn't given anything away last time they talked. She'd sounded fine. Normal. He was convinced of it. Would he have noticed if she had been distressed, though? Possibly not. He'd been calling in between rehearsals, with a lot of noise in the background, not really the circumstances for a heart-to-heart discussion.

He'd thought Harriet would have had more of an idea how Lara had been lately, given him some clues, but she hadn't been helpful at all that morning. She'd been odd about Lara, if anything. Women could be so weird. Best friends one minute, all moody and prickly the next. He wondered if Harriet was jealous that Lara had got to go to the tourism college. Perhaps that was it.

He tried to recall more from his last conversation with Lara. They'd had a joke about something, hadn't they? His social life again, probably. He'd always thought it funny the way she was at him to settle down, when she'd shown no inclination to do the same thing herself. He'd teased her about it often enough. 'Time's running out, Blister. Biological clocks ticking, nuclear war clocks ticking. I want to hold another niece or nephew in my arms while I still have the strength.'

'It's your fault I can't settle on any one man, Austin. You've shown me such a bad example.'

'No, I've been helpful. Showing you how not to do it. Therefore, you should want to go off and do it properly. Get yourself married, a nice little home somewhere, two and a half children. Don't ask me to babysit, though, will you? I like full children but I can't bear half-children. I never know what to say to them.'

He'd made a joke of it, as he always did. He'd had enough practice over the years, with the endless comments from Harriet, Lara, even Gloria, about his social life, asking when was he going to settle down, stop playing the field.

He wondered how they'd react if he actually answered them truthfully for once. If he told them that in fact there was nothing he wanted more than to meet a woman he wanted to settle down with. A woman he wanted to have children with. Of course that was what he wanted. He'd loved his own childhood, the fun, the freedom, living by the sea, especially. He loved the idea of giving all that to his own son or daughter. Perhaps even several of them.

He'd seen his own parents together, the respect they had for one another, the affection. The partnership and love. He wanted that as well. But it wasn't that simple, was it? Just because it was what he knew he needed didn't mean the right woman for the job was going to turn up saying, 'Here I am, Austin. Ready when you are.' A woman he enjoyed being with, enjoyed looking at, who challenged him, enjoyed the same sorts of things. Who liked him and liked being with him. It wasn't that simple. It was very difficult, in fact.

All the travelling he did didn't help, he knew that. Twice in the past five years he had been involved with women he had really started to like. Things had been going well between them – not that he'd told any of his family, in case they had started booking churches and printing wedding invitations. But both relationships had ended badly. The first woman, a teacher he'd met at one of the school workshops in Melbourne, had insisted he give up the travelling. She had started leaving newspaper advertisements around for cover bands advertising for drummers or teaching posts in suburban schools. He'd thought it was a joke and then realised she was serious. 'But I love the touring,' he'd tried to explain. 'It's not good for our relationship,' she'd said. 'I need you to be here, close by.' They had split up soon after, on the eve of a month-long tour of Asia. She had told him he would have to choose and he had realised at that moment life with her would always be too hard. He'd chosen touring.

The second woman hadn't minded his absences. She was an artist who worked part-time in a gallery in the city centre. She liked the fact he was a musician and she told him she liked the freedom his coming and going gave her. The truth was she had found someone else to fill the space whenever he was gone. Austin had discovered them together when he had arrived home from tour a day early. It had been like a scene from a film. Hurried dressing, embarrassed faces. He had been surprised how much it had hurt him. And how it had affected him afterwards. He'd become wary, he realised. Since then he had made a conscious effort to keep all relationships light, to keep any bonds flexible. He knew he was taking the easy way out but he was only thirty-eight, after all. Picasso was in his seventies when he was having children. There was no hurry, was there? Sometimes he nearly convinced himself.

He stopped at a red light and checked the map again. He decided to go off the motorway for a short while, take in the more scenic back roads. With luck the rain would clear and he'd manage to see something other than grey skies and drenched fields. He was in no hurry. Her flatmate probably worked. She might not be back until after six at the earliest. He could have stayed longer with Harriet, perhaps, but he needed to keep on the move. He needed to feel he was doing something, not just talking about doing something.

He looked out across the fields, at a village backing onto the motorway. He'd been to England several times before, twice with the orchestra, once on a quick trip to visit his birthplace. It hadn't been an emotional homecoming for him, in any way. He had hardly any memories of England. He'd left when he was six. He liked the fact being born here had given him an English passport, and he sometimes felt torn between supporting England or Australia when watching cricket or rugby, but otherwise he didn't feel any great pull either way. He had reverted to an English accent for a while in his teens, when he'd gone through his Goth and new wave stage, but that too had faded away.

He pressed the radio button to change stations. Classical music filled the car. He quickly switched to a pop station. The hire car smelt new, and felt new. Everything from the seats to the steering wheel was smooth and spotless. He liked driving. He liked any kind of travel. Just as well, considering all the time he spent on the road, in cars, buses and planes, these days.

He heard the sound of a text message arriving and swiftly checked it, taking his eyes off the road for a second. Not from Harriet, or Lara, but one of the female members of the orchestra. She'd been sending him flirty texts now for a few weeks. He liked her well enough. She was pretty, certainly. And he knew that if he wanted to take it further it would be simple, as it often seemed to be. 'Too good-looking for your own good,' Gloria had said to him once. Perhaps it was true. Perhaps that was the problem. He didn't have to try hard to attract women. But lately the heart had gone out of it for him. The term 'the thrill of the chase' came to mind. Apt, if not politically correct. The thrill had gone out of all the flirting and chasing and catching. Was it old age setting in? No, he knew it wasn't.

He had really started feeling differently about that side of his life after his parents died. He'd felt his behaviour was – he searched for the word – too frivolous. Life had become serious. Grief hurt, he'd discovered. Some friends had asked him if he thought his mother had died of a broken heart, that she had simply decided life wasn't worth living after his father died. There was no way of knowing. When it first happened, it had been too shocking to be able to analyse the reasons why. And was such a thing possible, in any case? He knew his parents had loved each other, and had had a particularly good marriage. But was it something his mother could have chosen? To die, rather than go on living without his father? He tried again to imagine feeling so strongly about a woman. Loving her on every level – physically, mentally, spiritually. Some of his girlfriends had been model-beautiful and, shallow as it sounded, that was all he had wanted from them for a while. He had other female friends who challenged him intellectually, made him defend his politics, his religious beliefs, even his sporting allegiances, but he had never been physically attracted to them. Perhaps that's what real maturity would bring, he decided. A realisation that he couldn't have everything. That he'd have to choose between beauty and brains. Sex or intellectual stimulation. Or continue along as he had been doing, picking and choosing as it suited him, ignoring the empty feeling inside himself . . .

An image of James and Melissa came to mind. No, he couldn't settle for that kind of relationship, either. Imagine wanting to live with someone like Melissa for the rest of your life. Not only the bossiness, but the noise of her. It was Molly who Austin felt most sorry for. He was very fond of his niece. James had voluntarily chosen to be with Melissa. Poor Molly hadn't been given a choice. With any luck her swimming career would take off and she could start travelling the world, participating in competitions, and get away as early as possible. If she could. He presumed she was already under pressure to stay in the family business. Melissa was making it clear she was building a family empire. He felt his temper simmer at the thought of how she had ingratiated herself into Turner Travel, starting with helping out now and again, insisting Penny and Neil take some time off. Pretending to be amazed when they offered her part-time work after she and James got engaged. She'd turned it into a full-time position within six months and had been slowly taking over ever since. He'd watched her after his parents died. It was as if she had been waiting to seize her chance. Waiting until they were all vulnerable. She had swooped in with her changes, the new uniform, the new logo, the new tours. She had no right, but no one had stood up to her. Harriet hadn't been strong enough. Lara had seemed to agree, to Austin's amazement. James, of course, had gone along with everything she suggested.

He had been joking to Harriet that he paid Gloria to spy for him, but in truth he did get regular updates from her. Just because he didn't work in the agency didn't mean he didn't want to know what was going on. Gloria had tried to be fair. 'Yes, Austin, Melissa can be a bit annoying . . .'

'It's me you're talking to, Glorious. You don't have to be reasonable. You and I are the only ones who have seen through her clever human disguise. She is the Anti-Christ. Say it after me. "Melissa is Evil. She must be destroyed."'

Gloria laughed. 'I will not say that. You say after me, "Melissa has some good ideas."'

'So why doesn't she go and start her own travel agency then? And leave us alone.'

'Because we need her. Because she is married to James, your brother. Remember him, that man with the red hair you've been picking on for the past thirty-eight years?'

'He's my brother? I thought he was some stray a visiting circus left behind.'

'One day, Austin, you will wake up and be mature and it will be a day of great celebration for all who know you.'

He was smiling at the memory as a sign for Bath appeared in front of him.

It was nearly dark by the time he found Lara's suburb. He was cursing his earlier sightseeing. He'd got stuck in a tailback when he got back on the motorway and then hit the rush-hour traffic on the outskirts of the city as well. It was now past seven o'clock. Lara was renting a room in a share house in the northern part of the city. He finally found it after getting two different sets of directions from passersby and getting lost in the busy Bath streets, distracted by the elegantly restored buildings, crowded cafes and restaurants.

He parked the car opposite Lara's house and gazed around him. Once the terrace of two-storey buildings would have been quite grand, but they were now shabby. The row of buttons beside each front door was the giveaway. Each had been divided into separate apartments. Harder to be house proud in those circumstances, he supposed, as he got out of the car.

He checked the address on the piece of paper he was carrying. Number fifty-three, flat two. He pressed the button. A buzz sounded somewhere. He waited for a voice from the intercom. Nothing. Another buzz. He was about to try again when he heard the noise of a window being opened above him.

A young woman poked her head out. 'Sorry, were you trying the door?'

He stepped back. She had short hair, dripping wet. Her shoulders were bare. He could see the top of a towel. 'Yes, hello there,' he called up. 'My name's Austin Turner. I'm Lara's stepbrother.' Brother, stepbrother, foster-brother. He'd never made the distinction, switching back and forth between the terms. 'Could I talk to you about her?'

'Oh, hi. Of course you can. Hold on, I'll be right down.' She was there at the door in a minute, her hair still wet. She was about his age, barely five foot, in cut-off jeans and an orange T-shirt. He couldn't help noticing she wasn't wearing a bra. 'I'm Nina. Sorry to keep you waiting.' She had a slight accent, not quite English, something else. 'Come in. We're on the first floor.'

He followed her up the wide staircase and onto the landing. The door opened onto a colourful living room, with a large bay window overlooking the street. The curtains were orange. There was a blue patterned rug on the floor. One corner was a riot of spider plants, rubber plants and even a palm. Someone here had a green thumb. She gestured towards a sofa covered in a bright red throw. 'Take a seat, I'll be right back.'

He looked around. He doubted Lara had had much to do with the decoration. It wasn't her style at all. He thought of her apartment in Merryn Bay, all white walls and pastel colors. This was like living in a kaleidoscope. Maybe that's why she'd disappeared. She couldn't bear to live in this mass of colour another day.

Nina came back in. Her hair was drier. He could see different colours in it now. Bright red streaks here and there among the dark brown, even some golden strands as well. She'd also put on a bra, he noticed.

'Sorry about that,' she said. 'I promise I haven't just got up and that wasn't my first shower of the day. I've been for a run.'

'It's no problem.' She had very bright eyes, he noticed. Full of life.

'So, how can I help? It's about Lara going off like that, I suppose?'

He nodded. 'Do you mind if I ask you a few questions?'

'Of course not. I'm as puzzled as you are, to tell you the truth. I thought she was in fine form. And then she announced she was going away for a few weeks, asked me not to rent out her room. It wasn't until I got all those messages on the answering machine from your sister at the airport, and then her call, that I realised something more might be up.'

'So how did she seem before she left?'

'Physically? As groomed as ever. You know Lara. She'd come out of a hurricane with her hair in place.' She smiled. 'We've had a few nights out on the tear and I don't know how she did it but she would look as bandbox fresh at the end of the night as she did at the start. I'd have mascara under my eyes, wine spilt on myself. I've never been able to wear white clothes. But she was always spotless. The brat never had hangovers, either.'

'She's never drunk much.'

'No. Imagine saying you didn't like the taste of alcohol? Chance would be a fine thing with me. But was she distressed at all, do you mean?'

Austin nodded.

She gave it some thought. 'I really don't think she was. She was focused, if you know what I mean. Pre-occupied, I suppose, but she often was, especially when one of her assignments was due. She was into her course, doing lots of extra hours. But it wasn't all slog. She said she was getting a lot out of it.'

Austin knew that already. 'So she's been living here with you since she arrived?'

Nina nodded. 'I've got an arrangement with the tourism college. I do a lot of short-term lets, students or visitors. I had a good chat with Lara the first day she came to have a look at the room. I thought at first sight she might be a bit reserved, but she's not underneath, is she? And it suited her here as well, of course, with the college down the road.'

'You're a student there too?'

'No. I'm working as a temp. I took a career break and went travelling last year. And I can't decide what to do next, so I'm doing casual work. I'm actually a scientist.' She smiled at the expression on his face. 'I know, I should be wearing a white coat. I'm a biologist, to be exact. I do lab work, research. But I got tired of being so clean all the time. And peering into microscopes. I had a permanent red mark around my eye. Terribly hard to conceal. I was going through pots of make-up.'

Austin was finding her very entertaining, but also distracting. He was here about Lara, after all. 'Would it be all right if I had a quick look in her room?'

'Of course it would. It's this way, here.'

He followed her out of the living room, past a small, equally bright kitchen and down a narrow hallway. Black and white photographs lined the walls, details of buildings, rooftops, stonework. 'They're mine,' she said. 'I'm trying to be arty. Here's Lara's room.

What we charmingly call the box room.' She opened the door and turned on the light.

It looked like Lara's type of room. A white quilt cover lay on the three-quarter size bed, heaped with pale blue and white velvet and silk cushions. Muslin hung on the window. A pile of books stood on the shelf. He glanced at them. A mixture of travel books, some fiction. A poetry book. He hadn't known Lara read poetry.

He felt uneasy, as though he was snooping. And what was he looking for anyway? A note on the pillow? *I have run away. Don't try to find me.*

'Thanks,' he said, not sure what to do next. He didn't want to start sorting through her belongings, going through her cupboards.

Nina was watching him closely. 'If you don't mind me asking, why are you all so worried about her? She's over thirty, isn't she? A grown-up? Or are you a particularly close family?'

It was hard to explain. 'It's just that it's so out of character. She's so reliable. And she was due to help out on this tour. And then she didn't turn up, or let us know there was any problem. That's not like her.'

'Tour? Oh, that TV series one? I did wonder about that, when she said she was heading away. She'd been talking about it quite a lot. And you're right, she is reliable. I think she's the only flatmate I've ever had who's always paid her rent on time.' She stepped out into the hall again. 'What about a coffee?'

'That would be great, thanks.' He followed her into the kitchen, taking a seat at the wooden table, watching as she took down cups and a silver espresso maker and prepared coffee.

'You should think about becoming a drummer,' she said.

'Sorry?'

She gestured towards his hands, tapping a rhythm on the side of the table. He hadn't realised he'd been doing it.

'Oh. Sorry about that. Actually, I am a drummer. A percussionist, at least.'

'In a band? What are you called?'

'The Southern Cross Orchestra.'

'That's catchy. Hard for some of your fans to spell though.'

'Most of the fans are over sixty, so their spelling's pretty good.'

'So you're a classical musician? Wow. I thought they were only old people too.'

'No, we're all in our thirties. It's just the formal clothes make us look grown-up.'

She smiled. 'Milk? Sugar?' As she fetched both, she looked over her shoulder. 'Can I ask you something else? Did you call yourself Lara's stepbrother?'

Austin nodded.

'I hadn't realised it was a blended family. Your father married her mother, something like that?'

'Not so much a blended family. She's my foster-sister really. Lara came to live with us after her parents were killed.'

'Killed?' She turned completely. 'Oh God, I'm sorry. She mentioned that they had both died a year ago, but she didn't say they were killed. What happened?'

'Not a year ago. More than twenty years ago. It's a bit complicated. Her real parents were killed in a car crash in Ireland. When Lara was little. That's when she came to live with us. My parents, Lara's foster-parents I suppose you'd call them, died within a few months of each other, just over a year ago.' He noticed Nina's confusion. 'She didn't tell you about it?'

'No. I mean, I don't know when it would come up in normal conversation, but when we talked about our families she said she had a sister and two brothers, and that her parents had died recently.'

'Well, that's true. She does have a sister and two brothers. Just not biological. My parents were her guardians, rather than adopted parents. So she had two sets of parents, I suppose.' He was uncomfortable talking about this so soon, but in a way that was what he was there to talk about, wasn't it? He stirred his coffee. 'So she didn't seem upset about anything lately, then? Study? Home life? Being away from home?'

'Not that she said. Nothing I can put my finger on, anyway. Look, let's go into the living room and talk, it's nicer in there.'

He picked up his cup and saucer and followed her. He'd heard that trace of accent again. A lilt, as though English was her second language. It reminded him of the waitresses in the Italian coffee shop near their rehearsal rooms in Melbourne, the daughters of immigrants, their accents a musical mixture of Australian and Italian. He should be talking about Lara, but he had to ask. 'Are you English? I'm trying to place your accent . . .'

She smiled. 'I knew I shouldn't have skipped those elocution lessons. I'm Italian. I was born there, but I've lived here since I was a teenager. My parents moved over to run a restaurant here in Bath.'

'So you went from cooking to lab work?'

'Is it any wonder I gave it up? I can't eat the results of my experiments. I think my parents had a much better idea.' She went to the bay window, pushed it up as far as it would go, then perched on the sill and lit a cigarette. It was only after she'd blown out the first plume of smoke that she asked him. 'Do you mind? I'm trying to give up, but I like it too much.'

'No, not at all. It's your house.'

'I kid myself it helps me think. I know it's not fair for a non-smoker like Lara, so I sit here, like a pigeon. Half in, half out.' She squinted. 'If I disappeared suddenly, it would be because I was having a mad love affair and my lover wanted to spirit me away.'

'You think Lara was having a love affair?'

She shook her head. 'No, I don't actually. I think there were a few guys interested in her, and she went out to see films and bands with people from her course, but no one special. Unless she'd met someone else recently that I didn't know about. And she might have. I mean, we got on well, and we'd go out together now and then, but we were both busy. Sometimes days would go by without us having a proper conversation. So she might have met someone.' She went quiet, drawing on the cigarette again, then sending another plume of smoke out through the open window. 'It would have to have been a bolt from the blue. Love at first sight, wouldn't it? I can't really picture that happening to Lara.'

'Why not?'

'Because she seems too organised. Controlled, almost. Though they say still waters run deep. That's the saying, isn't it?' She laughed. 'I used to say too many cooks spoil the bread until someone kindly pointed my error out. I thought it made perfect sense – how could a whole lot of cooks knead the bread at the same time?'

She hopped off the windowsill and started pacing the room, still with the cigarette in her hand. This time the smoke went into the room. She had a real restless energy, Austin noticed. But she was graceful with it. Like a dancer. It was very attractive.

'Have you been to her college yet? Someone there might know more.'

He shook his head. 'No, I came straight here. Via Cornwall at least. I called in on my other sister Harriet in St Ives this morning.'

'After you'd flown in from Australia? It must be a close family.'

'No, from Berlin.' He filled her in briefly on the orchestra's tour.

Again the conversation veered away from Lara, as she fired questions at him. Which cities had he been to? Which operas were they doing? She'd seen a few, but wasn't an expert. The problem with being Italian, she told him, was that people always assumed she'd spent her childhood singing *Tosca* and *Rigoletto*. In her opinion opera was an acquired taste. She frowned. 'There's not a lot for a drummer to do in opera, though, is there? Don't you just have to hit the cymbals now and again?'

'That's about it.'

'So what do you do the rest of the time? Look around the theatre a lot?'

'A fair bit.'

'That would be good fun. Because everyone in the audience would be staring at the singers, so you'd have a real chance to stare at them.'

'I do, yes.' He was about to try to bring the subject back to Lara when she stubbed out the cigarette, took a peppermint from a bowl beside her and checked her watch.

'Come on,' she said. 'We might as well go down to Lara's college now. They have classes on Wednesday and Thursday nights, so there might be someone there you can talk to. One of her classmates or one of the lecturers.'

'I can go on my own if you point me in the right direction.'

'No, I'm as puzzled as you. I want to know where she is too. Let's go.'

In her St Ives hotel room, Harriet answered the phone for the third time in five minutes. The tour group was travelling to the nearby harbour town of Padstow for a special dinner tonight and the preparations had sent most of the ladies in the group into a spin. She'd already had Miss Boyd wondering if Harriet had seen her handbag anywhere. Yes, Harriet assured her. She'd had it when they got off the bus that afternoon. 'Oh, yes, here it is. Thank you, Harriet.' Mrs Kempton had rung to ask if Harriet could loan her an umbrella as unfortunately she seemed to have lost hers. Harriet said that of course she could and she would bring it down to the foyer with her. The latest call was from Miss Talbot.

'Harriet, could you please give me some fashion advice? Would a silver halter top go better with pink trousers or a blue skirt?'

'There's a bit of a wind outside tonight, Miss Talbot. You might be happier in something warmer, perhaps?'

'Do you think?' Harriet heard a rustling of coathangers. 'That's a good idea, Harriet. I have just the thing. Thank you!'

'You're welcome.'

Harriet had barely hung up when the phone rang again. It was Mrs Kempton again. 'Harriet, I was sure I took out my favourite scarf but now I can't find it. Would you have a minute to pop down?'

'Of course. I'll be right there.'

She quickly finished her own make-up and collected her bag and wrap from the foot of the bed. En route to Mrs Kempton's room she took a quick detour and ran downstairs to check on the men. They were already changed into sports jackets and smart slacks, perfectly happy in the seaview bar with pints of beer in front of them. They didn't notice her, engrossed in the racing results on the TV. There was no sign of Patrick. He was in his room getting ready, too, she assumed. She smiled at the thought of him ringing her, too. Asking her advice about his clothes as he had that first night. 'Harriet, should I wear the white shirt or the blue shirt?' She had a memory flash of his toned brown body and had to blink it away.

As she made her way to Mrs Kempton's room she found her mind filling with more thoughts about Patrick. He had been great company again all day. He had such a nice way with the group, able to put them at ease and make them laugh. Make her laugh, particularly. Or perhaps they just had very similar senses of humour.

Clive had also finally decided he liked him. At least, he'd stopped doing the sudden braking when Patrick was standing talking to the group. She had been watching for it that afternoon, keeping a close eye on Patrick as he was answering their questions. Out of the corner of her eye she had seen Clive lean forward to the brake pedal. She'd leapt up and grasped Patrick around the waist, convinced he was about to go flying down the aisle.

Patrick had looked startled and then amused. 'Harriet, what a lovely surprise.'

She'd let go immediately. 'I'm so sorry, I thought you were going to go flying.'

'Not without special effects wires, I promise. But thank you very much anyway.'

Harriet had gone red and hurriedly sat down. Mr Fidock had given another whoop. Mrs Lamerton had just looked annoyed that she hadn't thought of doing the same thing.

On the way home from Bodmin Moor, they'd travelled to a coastal lookout near Newquay, the location for a dramatic scene in episode nine, 'The Case of the Rogues' Reunion'. They asked Patrick for memories of the punch-up on the cliff top between Willoughby and Jonas Herron, the crooked abattoir owner who featured in a number of episodes. It had been a two-part storyline, the first episode ending on a – literally – cliffhanging sequence featuring Willoughby hanging by his fingertips from the cliff edge, having been pushed over by Herron. They were enthralled as he described how he nearly fell in real life and had to be winched to safety by a crane.

Mr Douglas managed to secure the seat next to Patrick for the trip back. Harriet overheard him telling the actor about the searing heat of an Australian summer and how he'd had to have a skin cancer removed from his nose only a week before he'd left for this trip. 'It went well, I think. I'm just waiting for the autopsy results.'

'Autopsy?' Patrick said.

Mr Douglas nodded. 'I'm not that worried. I'm sure it's nothing serious.'

She and Patrick had exchanged a glance. Faces solemn, eyes laughing.

All day she'd found herself watching him, enjoying his ready humour, noticing the small courtesies, his good manners with everyone in the group. He watched out for her just as much, opening doors for her, making sure she was fine, that she was happy with how it was all going. The two of them also managed to have lots of snatched conversations, quick exchanges about the tour, or Patrick asking about previous trips she'd worked on, Harriet asking about his pre-*Willoughby* days, about America, and Boston. She'd been surprised again how relaxed he was about his acting career. He didn't seem to do much work these days, yet he didn't appear anxious about it. He was more interested in talking about books he'd read, wondering if she had read them too, or wanting to talk about changes he'd noticed in England since his last visit. The more they talked, brief as the conversations were, the more it was changing from her being the guide and him being the special guest. It wasn't just the feeling that the two of them worked very well together. Something else was happening as well. She'd become acutely aware of him. She knew if he was nearby, if he had left a room, if he had come back into a room. Not in a protective 'looking after the special guest' way. It was something different.

Harriet came up the stairs again and knocked on Mrs Kempton's door. It was opened immediately. The room was almost full. Mrs Kempton had been joined by Miss Talbot, Mrs Randall and Miss Boyd. It was like a senior citizens' sleepover. They gave her an enthusiastic welcome.

'Oh Harriet, you look beautiful,' Miss Talbot exclaimed. 'Like a sea creature.'

'Really? Not a jellyfish, I hope?'

'Oh no, like a nymph. Something glorious like that.'

Harriet had changed out of the yellow uniform into a special dress she had brought with her. She had tried it on in a boutique in Melbourne several months earlier and known immediately it was something out of the ordinary. It was made of dark green silk, and both the colour and the material seemed to catch the light in an unusual way, glistening almost. The design left her arms bare, while the scooped neckline showed off her skin and skimmed the tops of her breasts. It fitted her body, ending just below her knees. She had felt different as soon as she tried it on. Beautiful, confident, adventurous, as though she was in costume for an acting role, or an actress preparing to step onto the red carpet for a premiere. The boutique assistant had got into the spirit, bringing over pieces of expensive jewellery for Harriet to try on, making suggestions for make-up and matching glamorous hairstyles. She had also produced the perfect matching shoes. The toes were pointed, the heels high. Harriet had ignored the price and bought them immediately. She didn't regret it. She felt different when she was wearing them, too. Elegant and feminine. She carried a silk wrap with her, in a darker green than her dress. While she'd been getting ready in her room she'd tried to remember the jewellery and make-up suggestions the boutique assistant had given her. 'Go dramatic,' the woman had said. 'The dress deserves it.' She was right. The ornate earrings, smoky eyeshadow, carefully applied eyeliner and darker shade of red lipstick did suit the dress.

'I love your make-up.' Miss Boyd said, inspecting her closely. 'Have you had professional training?'

'No,' Harriet said, surprised. 'I taught myself really.'

'It's beautiful, Harriet. Could you make my eyes look like yours?'

'And do you think I would look better with a darker lipstick?' Mrs Kempton said. 'Mine's a bit too pink, don't you think?'

'Could you do us too, Harriet?' Miss Talbot asked.

Harriet checked her watch. There was plenty of time. Clive wasn't due for another twenty minutes or so. 'I'd love to,' she said. She went back to her room and fetched her make-up bag. By the time she came back, the four ladies were lined up on the bed, side by side, towels around their necks protecting their outfits.

She started with Miss Talbot. First she helped her fasten the clasp of her bright pink resin necklace, and do up the button at the back of her satin flares. Together they found a shade of lipstick and blush that matched both the necklace and the flares.

Miss Talbot lifted her face, sighing in pleasure as Harriet gently applied the make-up. 'We'll have to take a photo so I can remember this. But you have to be in it too, Harriet. I know, I'll get Patrick to take it. He'll know all about cameras and he can teach us how to pose properly too.'

Before Harriet could stop her, Miss Talbot had leaned across to the phone, rung reception and asked to be put through to Patrick Shawcross's room.

'Patrick, it's Emily. No, you don't need to call me Miss Talbot, I told you that. Would you please be able to come and take our photo? Harriet's making us beautiful and we want to treasure the moment. Oh, thank you. We're in room twenty-three, second floor.' She hung up, very pleased with herself. 'He'll be here in a minute.'

Harriet finished Miss Talbot's make-up and was just applying a soft mauve to Miss Boyd's eyelids when there was a knock at the door.

Miss Talbot answered it. 'Patrick, hello. Look, aren't I a picture?' She did a little spin. 'I feel like a girl again.'

Harriet watched her with great amusement, then glanced over her shoulder at him. 'Thanks, Patrick. We're nearly ready. I just have two more sets of eyes, three lips and a necklace to do.'

'And my belt again,' Miss Talbot said, twisting around and refastening the buckle on her silver chainlink belt. 'They don't make clothes the way they used to. Patrick, do you want to come back in a minute? When we'll be really perfect?'

'I'm happy to wait, Emily.'

There wasn't room for him to come in. He leaned against the doorway. He had changed his clothes too, Harriet noticed. He was wearing a light grey suit, beautifully cut, over a white shirt. He'd either showered or been outside for a walk. She could see drops of water in his dark curls. He was talking very seriously to Miss Talbot, who was explaining in detail how her camera worked. He glanced up at her and she had to look away. She had that unsettling feeling again. That the room was full of people, but she was conscious only of him.

Harriet added a little more blush to Miss Boyd's cheeks and a dusting of powder. She had to concentrate. Her hands seemed to be shaking slightly. She moved to Mrs Kempton, choosing a pale brown eyeshadow, and just a touch of lipgloss. Mrs Randall only needed foundation, a light grey eyeshadow and mascara. All three women were like purring cats, their faces turned up to her, as she went back and forth doing the final touches, smoothing eyeshadow here, a little bit more lipstick there, some light finishing powder on each of them.

'I'm really not an expert,' she said. 'I hope you'll like it.'

'I don't mind what I look like. It feels so nice having it put on,' Miss Boyd said. 'You've got such a gentle touch, Harriet.'

They were finally done. She stood back and watched as they took turns looking into the mirror, delighted with themselves.

Miss Boyd nearly cried. 'I love it. You've made me look years younger.'

Mrs Kempton put her hands to her cheeks. 'Oh, thank you, Harriet, I love it too.'

Mrs Randall didn't say anything, just gave Harriet a warm, happy smile.

'Photo time, everyone,' Miss Talbot declared, clapping her hands. She was getting quite giddy. 'And quickly. We may never look this good again.'

Harriet insisted on taking the first photo: Patrick with the four women. Their fingers brushed briefly as he passed her the camera. She was aware of not just him, but of herself now, too. Of how she felt when he was near her.

Miss Talbot took over then, wanting different combinations, moving them all back and forth. 'I've brought twenty films with me,' she declared. 'I don't care if I use them all up tonight. Harriet, Patrick, I want one of the two of you together.'

She moved them until they were side by side. 'Put your arm

around her, Patrick, that's it,' she called. 'Perfect. Nice and close, now.'

Harriet felt his arm touch her back, his fingers against her bare skin. A combination of hot and cold sensation shot right through her. She didn't dare look at him. She also didn't tell Miss Talbot that her thumb was over the lens. She was worried her voice would sound strange.

Miss Boyd pointed it out instead.

'Never mind,' Miss Talbot said. 'I'll take a few more. Back together again, Patrick and Harriet. Closer, that's it.'

The merest touch of his fingers on her skin felt like a caress. Harriet could barely breathe. She felt like closing her eyes in pleasure, not smiling at a camera.

There was time for one more. 'Patrick, with all of you,' Harriet said, moving away from him, needing to take back a bit of control. She arranged them all, Patrick in the centre, Miss Talbot and Miss Boyd on one side, Mrs Kempton and Mrs Randall on the other. Another brief touch, her hand on his sleeve as she moved him into place, and that sensation again, as if electricity was zipping back and forth between them. She arranged Mrs Kempton's scarf and fixed the collar of Miss Talbot's fluffy cardigan. The simple actions calmed her. She was imagining this, she told herself.

'Now we're ready,' she said, taking a step back, smiling at the looks on their faces. 'What do you think, Patrick? Aren't they gorgeous?'

'Beautiful,' he said.

He was looking at her when he said it.

Chapter Twenty-One

Austin and Nina parked the car in a side street down the road from the tourism college. It was part of a modern campus in the middle of Bath, the sleek concrete lines of the building incongruous after the tall elegant terraces and wide streets they had passed on the way. Nina had directed him in the same way she spoke, quickly, stopping and starting.

'That's the tourism section over there,' she said, pointing to a wing of a four-storey building. 'You could come back tomorrow, of course, when all the staff will probably be here. But as I said, you might see a few of her class and a couple of her lecturers tonight. Where are you staying by the way? Have you booked anywhere? Is that all your luggage?'

'I haven't booked anywhere yet. And yes, that's all.'

'A man who travels light. I used to know a quote about that too, but I forget it. Stay with me. We have a sofa bed in the living room.'

'I'll be fine in a guesthouse.'

'No, don't be mad. I insist. Lara would insist too.'

She would, too. She had already invited him to stay, when they had spoken the previous week. When she had seemed fine. No inkling of this at all. 'If you're sure.'

'I'm sure.'

He followed Nina across the open square. 'I met Lara here one night, last month,' she said. 'We were going to see a film, she came out of the classroom over this way.' She stopped a passing student and confirmed it. 'This way, Austin.' He had to walk quickly to keep up.

Half an hour later, Austin had spoken to two of Lara's classmates and her lecturer. They seemed puzzled at his concern. No, they hadn't been surprised when she wasn't in class the past couple of days. She was expected to be away on the *Willoughby* tour after all. And no, they hadn't noticed anything out of the ordinary with her behaviour before then, either.

Austin sat down at one of the desks. Nina and the lecturer, Brendan, sat opposite. He was in his late thirties, tall, lean, with glasses and tousled brown hair.

'Why do you think something is wrong?' Brendan asked.

Austin tried to explain it again. 'It's not like her. She doesn't do things like this, just disappear.'

'Maybe she felt it was time she did? I know I've wanted to make a run for it now and then.'

'Maybe.' Austin was starting to feel embarrassed. It had felt like the right thing to do when he was in Berlin, to drop everything and rush over here, like a man with a mission, the heroic rescuer. But now he was actually here, he wasn't so sure.

'You could talk to a couple more of her fellow students, if you like,' Brendan said. 'She might have mentioned something to them. They'll be back tomorrow. Or you can have a look at her computer. There might be a few clues there.'

'Clues?' Nina's eyes were bright. 'This is feeling like a detective program now. What sort of clues?'

Brendan shrugged. 'Maybe she had written a letter, or looked up some websites or something. That would give you an idea of where she might have gone.'

Austin and Nina followed Brendan over to a desk in the corner. 'The students move around a bit, but Lara generally worked on this one. I don't think any of the students keep much on the desktop, though. They save their work to disk usually. They use the computer more for research purposes, web surfing, that sort of thing.'

'We've been getting emails from her. Would this be where she sent them from?'

'Probably. Either from here, or one of the Internet cafes in town. But she'd have a password for that. You don't know it, I suppose? Or know who her server is?'

Austin shook his head. It would have felt wrong reading her emails, in any case. As it was it felt again like he was prying, looking at her computer like this. As it booted up, he saw neatly arranged folders with Lara's name on them appear on the screen. He hesitated and then clicked on one. The documents inside were also neatly labelled. Week 1, Week 2, all the way through to what must have been last week, Week 12. He clicked on one, but it was blank. That's right, the lecturer had said they saved everything on disk. So no clues there.

'She was doing well,' Brendan said. 'Some great ideas. Really dedicated, too.'

'She was looking forward to this,' Austin said. He remembered getting the call from her, when she found out she'd got the industry scholarship for the three month course. 'It's the best one in the whole world, Austie!' He hadn't heard her so happy in a long time.

Nina pulled up a chair beside the computer. 'If she packed a suitcase, she must have been going somewhere some distance away,' she said. 'So she'd had to have booked, wouldn't she? Maybe she'd have booked on the Internet?'

'Not necessarily,' Brendan said. 'She could have caught a train. Picked up a flight at the airport on stand-by. Hired a car. She could be anywhere.'

'I suppose there's no way of checking what sites she'd been looking at anyway, is there?' Nina asked.

The lecturer nodded. 'There is, actually. It's simple.' He leaned across and moved the mouse on Lara's computer. 'You go to Internet Explorer, then View, then Explorer Bar and then History. And there it is.' A long list of sites appeared on the screen.

Nina whistled. 'Everything you look at on the web gets recorded? I didn't know that.'

'Nothing ever leaves a computer,' Brendan said. 'Even if you delete it, it's still there on the hard drive somewhere.'

Austin's hopes rose. 'If she has gone somewhere, she might have been looking up info about it, mightn't she? We just need to see what travel sites she's been looking at . . .' He scanned the long list of sites Lara had accessed. There was address after address of tourism sites, airline booking sites, information for travellers. He hit his palm against his forehead in a gesture of stupidity. 'Sorry, I've just remembered where we are. A tourism college.'

The lecturer gave a wry laugh. 'Well, yes, I'd be more surprised if she hadn't been looking up travel websites. Most of the travel business is computerised these days.'

'And I couldn't know which of these Lara had looked at most recently anyway, or for how long, could I?'

'A technician might be able to tell you. There's probably a way of checking dates and times, how long they'd been looked at, but I'm sorry, I don't know how to do it.'

Nina picked up the mouse and scrolled through more of the history. 'There's some news sites, too. Telephone directories. Search engines, info on some cruise ships . . .'

The lecturer nodded. 'That was last week's project. We asked the students to put together some themed fantasy cruises.'

'That explains that one then.' She kept scrolling, reading aloud as she went. 'The Met Office, a book review site, more cruise ships, and then a whole bunch of Irish sites. One, two, three . . .' she stopped counting aloud. 'About ten of them. See, Irish newspapers. Maps. Would that have been for her course, too?' she asked the lecturer.

'Perhaps, though not necessarily. Our focus this semester was themed travel. That's why Lara applied to come here. It was in line with what she was doing at home in Australia.'

Austin moved his chair closer. 'She had a few links with Ireland herself, though. Her mother was Irish, at least she was born in Ireland, but she grew up in England. Before she and Lara's father emigrated to Australia.'

'Didn't you say her mum and dad were killed in Ireland?' Nina asked. 'Were they back there on holiday?'

'Her parents were killed there?' Brendan said. 'When? Recently?'

Austin shook his head. 'About twenty-four years ago.'

'When she was only a child? Oh, how sad.'

Nina was looking at the screen again. 'Maybe that's what's happened. She's on the other side of the world, feeling a long way from home and what family she has got, so she's gone looking for some connections. Her dad was English, did you say? Did he have family left here in England?'

Austin shook his head. He knew that much.

Nina was undeterred. 'All right, so she decides to track down some of her mother's Irish relatives. She might have found instant cousins or great uncles that she didn't know she had.' She glanced at the screen. 'Maybe she put an ad in the —' she squinted to read the name on the screen, 'the *Irish Times*, asking for information. Where was her mother from?'

'I don't know. I don't know much about her mother or her father, to tell you the truth.'

'There's no one at home you can ask?' the lecturer asked.

Austin shook his head. 'My own parents died a year ago, and it was my mother who knew Lara's mother. We have a family friend who's worked with us for years. Mum might have told her something. It's worth asking, I guess.'

Brendan turned as several students walked in. 'I'd better get back to work. I'm sorry I couldn't be more help. If I think of anything else, is there any way I can contact you?'

Austin scribbled his mobile number. Ten minutes later, he and Nina were back in the car.

Nina took Austin to her parents' restaurant in the centre of Bath. It was large, but with plenty of atmosphere: paintings of Tuscan landscapes on the wall, Italian pop songs playing in the background, and red tablecloths on each of the twenty or more tables. Most of them were full. Nina spoke briefly to her parents, her father in the kitchen and her mother looking after a large party of diners. She introduced Austin as Lara's brother, without going into detail about why he was there. He noticed Nina had inherited her mother's bright eyes and her father's big smile. They were too busy to talk long, waving Nina across to a spare table in the back section of the restaurant.

Over a pizza and a glass of red wine he filled her in on all he knew about Lara's early years.

Nina listened intently. 'I'm sorry I didn't ask her more questions when she was leaving, Austin,' she said when he'd finished. 'She seemed so matter of fact about it. Packed her suitcase. Said something about family business and off she went. And you know, with flatmates, you have to keep some distance, respect each other's privacy.'

'We might be onto something with the Irish sites. I'll know more after I've phoned Gloria tonight.'

'But just because she was looking at Irish sites doesn't mean that's where she's gone, does it?' Nina asked.

'I don't know. I'm probably jumping to conclusions . . .' He tailed off. It had seemed much more certain in the college than it was now. And Nina was right. There were lots of places Lara could have gone. And lots of reasons why.

'So is Ireland where her parents are buried? If they were killed there? Or were their bodies flown home to Australia?'

'I don't know. I don't think so.' Surely he would have remembered if Lara's parents' bodies had been flown home to Australia? Wouldn't there have been talk about it? And they would all have gone to the funerals, wouldn't they? The difficulty was there had never been much talk at home about Lara's parents, except on the memorial days his mother had instigated.

'Was Lara in the car with them when they had that crash in Ireland? Would she have memories of it? Maybe that's what's happened, it's brought back some trauma. What's it called – post traumatic stress disorder? That might be why she disappeared like that. I thought she seemed focused, but perhaps it was shock.'

Austin shook his head. 'No, she wasn't even in Ireland when it happened. Her parents were over fixing up something about a family estate, I think. Lara's grandmother had died a few weeks earlier. I don't really know all the details.' He couldn't remember why Lara hadn't gone with them. He only remembered people saying it was lucky that she hadn't, or she probably would have been killed too.

'Don't you know anything about where Lara came from? She arrived to live with you and none of you asked *anything* about it?'

He wished Nina would stop asking him such awkward questions. 'We weren't that sort of family. My mother, especially. She thought it was best not to dwell on any of it too much, in case it upset Lara. We had to be as kind as we could to her.' He could hear his mother saying it.

'So she was a charity case?'

'No. Not for a minute. We never treated her like that.' Even as he said it, he had a memory of Harriet wanting to treat Lara like that. Like one of her school 'be kind' projects. But that had passed, surely? And he and James had always thought of Lara as an extra little sister. It hadn't been a big deal at all.

'No need to be defensive, Austin. I'm sorry, I touched a raw nerve.'

He calmed. 'No, you didn't. It's a fair enough question. I suppose it must look unusual from the outside, but really, she just became part of the family.'

Nina reached over and refilled their glasses. 'Maybe that's it. She didn't want to be a part of your family any more. She wanted her own family.'

'I don't think it's that. She would have said something, to Harriet, or to me. One of us anyway.'

Nina shrugged. 'Then maybe she just wanted to go away for a while. Have some time to herself. Maybe it's as simple as that.'

Austin found himself fighting an urge to start tapping. 'Maybe it is,' he said.

Chapter Twenty-Two

The *Willoughby* group was on board the bus, en route to Padstow, a forty-mile journey from St Ives. Willoughby himself hadn't actually set foot in the town during the series, but Mrs Lamerton had seen the harbour village featured on TV and insisted a trip to a celebrity chef's restaurant be included in the itinerary.

James had suggested in his notes that Harriet lead the group in a fish-themed bus-trip singalong but Harriet had tucked that suggestion away at the back of the folder. As they came into the harbour town, Harriet glanced at his script again – *Once one of Cornwall's principal fishing ports, Padstow is now famous for its gourmet restaurants and sandy beaches* – and put it away too. There was so much chatter and laughter in the bus she wouldn't have been able to make herself heard, microphone or not. Mrs Lamerton's laugh was loudest of all. She had managed to get the seat next to Patrick again. Harriet was reminded of the bellowing sounds of a water buffalo, happily splashing in mud.

Her mobile beeped twice just as Clive pulled into the car park beside the Padstow harbour. A text message had arrived. She didn't check it immediately, first opening the door and as usual helping her group down onto the ground. They were all in high spirits. Mr Fidock practically leapt off the step. Mrs Lamerton ignored Harriet standing at the foot of the stairs, putting on a girlish voice and asking Patrick to help her.

'Of course, Mrs Lamerton.' He smiled at Harriet as he came down the step.

Mrs Lamerton alighted, taking Patrick's hand. She didn't let go once she reached the ground, holding his hand high as though they were about to do a stately dance. Patrick had no choice, unless he was going to shake her away. Harriet did her best not to smile as the pair of them went hand in hand across the car park towards the restaurant. It looked like Mrs Lamerton would be sitting next to him at dinner, too.

As she watched, he stopped and turned. 'Harriet, will we wait for you?'

Harriet could tell Mrs Lamerton wasn't pleased. 'No thanks, Patrick. You go ahead. I'll be right there.'

Once everyone was off the bus, she took out her phone and read the text message. It was from Austin. Am with Lara's flatmate. On her trail. All for 2nite. Will keep you posted. A x

She turned off the mobile and put it back in her bag. The feeling of confusion returned. Wanting to know about Lara, but not wanting to know. Wanting to stay in the cocoon of the tour, not having to think about her real life, enjoying all of this so much, the travelling, the group, Patrick . . .

'Harriet?'

It was Miss Talbot. She'd come back for her. 'Is everything all right? You look like you're miles away.'

'I'm sorry, Miss Talbot. I was just daydreaming.'

'Oh, don't be sorry. I love daydreams myself. I go to all sorts of places in my daydreams. It's good for the soul.' She lowered her voice. 'Were you daydreaming about Patrick?'

'Miss Talbot!'

'Well, I would, if I were you. Who else is there? Clive? Mr

Fidock? Mr Douglas?' She made a disgusted face. 'Perhaps that could be Turner Travel's next theme tour, Harriet? A cruise for elderly singles like myself. We could call it the Old Love Boat.'

'That's an excellent idea.' It was, too. Melissa would jump at it. 'Will we do it together? I could be your chaperone.'

Miss Talbot nodded eagerly. 'Yes please.'

Harriet took Miss Talbot's arm as they made their way to the restaurant. The group had gathered outside, already studying the menu in a glass frame on the wall. The restaurant was in a two-storey corner building, looking out onto the harbour crammed with commercial fishing boats and smaller, colourful craft. Inside the tables were wooden, the ceilings high, the atmosphere welcoming, the walls and table decorations coordinated in blue and white. There was no formal seating arrangement at their long table. They took seats as they came in. Harriet had Miss Talbot on one side and Mr Douglas on the other. At the other end of the table she saw Mrs Lamerton take a seat next to Patrick. Harriet turned away, making a point of settling Miss Talbot into her chair, helping to stow her silver handbag on the back of her chair and then reading the menu to her. She couldn't help herself, though. She looked over in Patrick's direction. He was looking at her too.

Once they finished their main courses, everyone in the tour group started moving around the table. It seemed perfectly natural for Harriet to go to Patrick's end of the table and check that everything was fine with him. It made perfect sense, too, when he very nicely asked Mrs Lamerton if she could move up a little so he could put a chair for Harriet there beside him. It was quite crammed so it also felt right for him to casually place his arm around the back of her chair as they talked. It also seemed natural that he should later visit

Harriet's end of the table to talk to the people seated near her. He stood behind her, with his arm resting against the back of her chair, close enough so her head was touching his arm. The chair beside her became free. He sat down and it also felt right that her leg was touching his, and that his arm was along the back of her chair again. Once or twice she reached for her wine glass at the same time he reached for his. Their hands touched. A glance.

'After you, Harriet.'

'No, you first.'

'Please, I insist.'

As he had a lively conversation with Mr and Mrs Douglas across the table, she couldn't stop noticing more details about him. The way he used his hands to express himself. The long fingers and square-cut nails. The silver watch on his wrist. The sprinkling of dark hair on his arms. The tanned skin on his chest, where the top button of his pale blue shirt was undone. The dark hair there, too.

She was very conscious of her body next to his. The feel of the silk material of her dress against her skin. Even the feel of her fingers against the stem of the glass. Every movement seemed charged with something. Anticipation.

They returned to the bus, everyone in great spirits. They had drunk a lot of wine. Mr Fidock insisted on taking the microphone and performing an Elvis-style version of 'I do like to be beside the seaside' as they left Padstow. Harriet expected half the group to go straight to their rooms when they returned to St Ives, but she was wrong. The hotel boasted an old-fashioned disco once a week. The receptionist had promised it was perfect for the age group. More Tom Jones than they'll be able to shake a hip replacement to, she'd laughed. All of them, Clive included, came into the function room. It had been transformed with flashing lights and clusters of armchairs, overseen by a man with an obvious toupee behind a DJ desk.

Harriet danced with Mr Fidock, Mr Douglas and even Clive. She waltzed with Miss Talbot who was feather-light on her feet. She danced with everyone except Patrick Shawcross. She knew it didn't matter whether she danced with him, or whether they talked to each other some more that night or not. It had gone beyond that. Somehow, at some stage during the night, something unspoken had been agreed between them. He hadn't said anything. Neither had she. It was the strangest sensation, as though the entire time they were talking to other people, involved in other conversations, standing at other sides of the room, they were somehow connected, as if by invisible wires. She was intensely and completely aware of him, and knew that he was aware of her. Even when she was talking to Mrs Kempton, or dancing with Mr Fidock (and having to first laughingly and then firmly ask him to keep his hands to himself) she knew if she looked up Patrick would be watching her.

It felt so good. Exciting. Exhilarating. And something deeper, sexier than that. One part of her brain was clear, telling her all the reasons why it wasn't making sense. He was thirteen years older than her. He was the special guest on their tour. Melissa would surely have something to say about fraternisation between guides and tour guests. But obstacles like that seemed a long way away, connected to the side of herself she was trying to leave behind. This new, exciting feeling belonged with the freedom she'd been sensing as her confidence had grown the past few days, as she discovered she was able to cope, make decisions, take care of a group of people. She wanted something to happen between them. It was almost a need inside her.

Just before midnight she was helping a tipsy Miss Talbot out of the disco and up to her room when she heard her name being called. She turned. It was him.

'Harriet, are you leaving?'

Miss Talbot spoke before Harriet had a chance. 'She's helping me to bed, Patrick. I've had one too many Fluffy Ducks. I'm a disgrace.'

'You're not a disgrace,' Harriet laughed, holding Miss Talbot's arm firmly. 'You're just exhausted from all that dancing.'

'Can I help?' Patrick said.

'No, thanks anyway.' She smiled at him. 'We'll be fine.'

'Could I speak to you before you go up?'

'Talk away, Harriet,' Miss Talbot said, sinking into the armchair beside them. 'I'll just sit here for a while. It will do me good. That carpet is making me dizzy.'

They moved towards the door. His voice was quiet. 'I know it's too late to look at the videos tonight —' She felt a faint shimmer of disappointment. '— but there is something I need to talk to you about. Would you be able to call to my room instead, do you think?'

'Tonight?'

'If that's all right? If it's not too late?'

'No. Of course it's not. In half an hour?'

'Good. Yes. That's good.' He smiled at her. That was all. But it felt like a promise.

Forty minutes passed before she was able to go to him. Most of the group had started going to their rooms. As Harriet was helping Miss Talbot to bed, Mrs Kempton poked her head out of her door, just down the corridor.

'Harriet, I'm sorry to bother you but I don't seem to be able to find my reading glasses. Would you be able to come and help me look?'

'Of course, Mrs Kempton. I'll just settle Miss Talbot.'

Miss Talbot took less than five minutes to settle. She tipped into the bed and was snoring gently in the time it took Harriet to take off her shoes.

Mrs Kempton was waiting at her door. 'I am a silly sausage, aren't I? I can't find them anywhere.'

The glasses were on the bedside table, in full view of the door. 'Here they are, Mrs Kempton.'

'Oh Harriet, you're an angel. While you're here, would you be able to undo the buttons at my neck for me? I'm having such trouble with them.'

Harriet undid the row of tiny buttons. Mrs Kempton favoured old-fashioned clothing and this blouse wouldn't have looked out of place in a period drama, with its high neck and puffy sleeves.

'Thank you, Harriet. And not just for this. You're looking after us so well. We were all talking about it and we all think you're lovely.'

She felt her cheeks go warm. 'Thank you, Mrs Kempton. I'm glad you're enjoying it.'

She was almost at her door when she was summoned by Mrs Lamerton from her doorway further down the same corridor, needing help with the lock on her case. That was a first. Mrs Lamerton was normally the most independent of them.

Harriet didn't have any trouble with the lock. It snapped open immediately.

'Thank you, Harriet. You must have a knack.'

'Years of practice, Mrs Lamerton. I hope you enjoyed today?'

'Yes, thank you. It's all coming together well, isn't it? All the hard work Lara and I put into it in the planning stages, I suppose.'

'I'm sure that's it. I'm really pleased you're happy.'

'Well, goodnight, Harriet. Still no chance of Lara turning up?'

'I'm afraid not, Mrs Lamerton. I understand her other commitments got very demanding. Goodnight. See you in the morning.' She was at the door when the older woman spoke again.

'So what will you do now?'

'I beg your pardon?'

'What will you do now?'

'It's after midnight. I'll probably go to bed.'

Mrs Lamerton nodded. 'Goodnight then.'

Harriet went to her room, checked her make-up, her hair, realising her hands were shaking. She took a moment to breathe slowly, to calm herself, as she stood in front of the mirror. Her eyes looked very bright. She wasn't nervous. It was anticipation. Excitement. And a feeling that this was meant to be. As if everything had been meant to happen. James's accident. This tour. Even the dinner tonight. All the tiny details coming together to this point so she would feel like this, look like this, want what she knew was going to happen with Patrick. What she wanted to happen. She stepped out into the corridor.

She didn't see Mrs Lamerton's door open or see her peer out and watch her leave.

Harriet only had to knock twice, softly, before he opened the door. He smiled. 'Harriet, come in.'

He had taken off his jacket and rolled up the sleeves of his shirt. His room looked inviting. The bed through the doorway, the table and chairs in the centre, the door to the balcony open a little way.

He had turned on all the lamps in the room and switched off the main light.

'Can I get you a drink? Some wine? A coffee? A brandy?'

'A brandy would be lovely, thank you.'

She walked out onto the small balcony and put her hands on the rail, looking out over the beach and the dark sea. The sky was thick with clouds, only a few stars visible.

She could hear him fixing the drinks. Another time she would have felt the need to talk, to make conversation. Not now. There was the sound of the waves hitting the sand, traffic noise, tyres on the wet roads behind the hotel, a car horn. Murmured voices from the cafe on the beach below them, staff tidying up, bottles being taken outside. As she stood there, it started to rain again, a faint drizzle. She felt it against her face, the water swirling into the wind. There was water everywhere she looked. Sea, rain. Water equalled sex. She stepped inside the room again as he came towards her. He wasn't carrying any drinks.

She felt nervous, but she also felt good. Sure. 'You wanted to talk to me about something.'

He nodded. 'I wanted you to know that I told the truth all day today, Harriet. All of those *Willoughby* stories actually happened.'

'Did they?' She looked up at him and smiled. 'Well done.'

'I also meant it when I said you are beautiful.'

She went still.

He came closer, gazing down at her face, her bare shoulders, the curve of her neckline. She felt it like a caress. He was serious, his look intense. 'Harriet, I think something's happening. Something with us.'

She nodded. She couldn't pretend anything else. 'I think so too.'

'I can't even get you that drink. All I want to do is kiss you.'

She caught her breath as he brushed her cheekbone with his thumb. A charge of desire went through her as she felt his hands at her waist. He kissed her, a brief, beautiful kiss.

He lifted his head and she saw his eyes had darkened. 'I've wanted to do that all day.'

He kissed her again, her lips, her neck, then her lips again. She kissed him back. It was different this time, more intense. She arched her neck at the feel of his lips, closing her eyes. There were waves of intense feeling building deep inside her. She hadn't touched a man since Simon. It was as if all the passion and longing had been saving itself for now. She could feel it with each kiss, each touch. Her body was responding instantly to every caress he gave her, on her lips, her face, her neck, lower. She could feel his body under her fingers, the heat of his lips, as they moved closer against each other, tighter, harder. She felt his hand cup her breast, felt herself swell and push against him, as her hand found his skin under his shirt, as she moulded her body against his, the kisses getting hotter and deeper —

A noise filled the room. A banging noise.

'Harriet? Harriet? Are you in there? I need your help. Now.'

Harriet pulled away. There was no mistaking the voice.

'Harriet? Are you in there?'

It was Mrs Lamerton.

It was past one o'clock before Harriet got back to her own room.

The minute before she opened the door to Mrs Lamerton had almost been funny. She had smoothed her hair, checked her clothes were in place, trying not to look as if she'd been doing what she had been doing. Patrick had done the same thing. There hadn't even been time to say anything to each other. Harriet opened the door to find Mrs Lamerton standing outside, dramatically clutching her stomach. 'Harriet, I think I have food poisoning.'

Amid loud groaning, she insisted Harriet bring a first aid kit to her room and sit with her, until she felt better. She also insisted she didn't need a doctor.

Harriet quickly went up to her room, snatching up the first aid kit, catching sight of herself in the mirror, conscious of her flushed face, her too bright eyes. When she got back to Mrs Lamerton's room, Patrick was there.

'Do you want me to do anything?' he said. 'Call anyone?'

Mrs Lamerton groaned again. 'Harriet . . .'

'I don't think so. But I'd better stay with her,' she whispered. He nodded. He didn't touch her, but it felt like he had.

When she said goodnight to Mrs Lamerton an hour later, the older woman was sitting up in bed, in a quilted bedjacket. The groaning had stopped, even though she'd refused to take any of the array of tablets Harriet had been able to produce from the first aid kit. Harriet wasn't convinced any of it had been genuine. But she couldn't have abandoned her, much as she had wanted to. And she had wanted to, very much.

'Are you sure you're feeling better, Mrs Lamerton? You'll be all right if I leave you?'

'I hope so. But if I need to ring you again, Harriet, where will you be?'

'I'm sorry?'

'Where will you be?'

It was like being back at school. 'In my room. Just ring the number and I'll come down again if you need me.'

'I didn't interrupt anything, did I? With you and Patrick Shawcross?' The tone was accusing, triumphant even.

'No, Mrs Lamerton.'

It wasn't until she was back in her own room that she wondered why Mrs Lamerton had come to Patrick's room, not hers. Had she been following her? Watching her and Patrick together? Not just tonight but the last few nights? If she had been, she would have seen Patrick come to her room every night, once with a bottle of wine, stay for an hour and then leave. Oh God. She could only imagine what the older woman had been thinking.

Outside Mrs Lamerton's door, she had stopped. Down the corridor was her own room. Upstairs was Patrick's room. She was torn, but finally she had decided not to go back there. Not yet. Not tonight. She needed to think about this.

She went into the bathroom and looked at herself in the mirror. She felt different. Patrick had looked at her tonight, kissed her tonight, caressed her, as though she was the most beautiful, desirable woman he had ever seen. It gave her a breathless feeling, like the earth was slipping away, things were out of control. It was how the panic attacks had felt, she realised. Yet this felt good. Better than good.

Wonderful.

Chapter Twenty-three

'Thanks, Molly, you've done a great job.'

Molly picked up the last box of envelopes and added them to the pile she and Gloria had been stuffing with tour brochures all morning. She had the day off school and had been in the office helping.

Gloria enjoyed her company. Molly had somehow escaped the worst of Melissa's genes, and inherited James's calm temperament. She was in fact very restful to be around. A good worker, too. A bit distracted today, though. Gloria noticed her checking her mobile phone again. She'd been doing it all morning.

'Waiting on an urgent message, Moll?'

'I still haven't heard from her.'

'From Lara?'

Molly nodded. 'Do you think she's all right, Gloria?'

'Of course she is, lovie,' Gloria said as brightly as she could. 'I'd say she just needs some time out.'

'But not from me. Not usually, anyway. She's always answered me. Especially when I told her it was urgent.'

'Is something up?'

'No, no, it's fine. Just a school thing she was helping me with.' She bit her lip. For a moment she looked like a little girl, not a fifteen-year-old.

'Can I help?'

'No.' She answered quickly. 'Thanks anyway, Gloria.'

'Well, just ask if I can.' She looked at the airplane clock. 'I'd better head out for lunch. Thanks again, Moll.' She picked up her bag and called over to the glass office. 'I'm off to lunch, Melissa.'

Melissa didn't turn around, just lifted her hand to say she'd heard.

Gloria hated the way she did that. She refused to let it bother her this time. She pulled the door shut behind her and stood there, in the shade of the veranda. She waved over at Reg from the deli, outside sweeping the footpath.

'Beautiful day,' she called over.

'Beautiful,' Reg called back. 'You're looking well, too. Everything good with Kev?'

'No worries at all.'

So she looked normal. No one was picking up anything different about her. It was only inside she was feeling sick. She had felt sick since Austin had rung and told her about Lara and the Irish websites.

He'd rung early that morning. It had been after midnight in Bath. She'd just unlocked the front door and walked into the Turner Travel office when the call came. 'Austin! What time is it there? Hold on, let me get my cup of tea. Of course, please fill me in.'

As he related the story so far, she found herself scribbling notes, out of habit when she was on the phone. *Flatmate Nina. College. Lecturer. Ireland???*

Ireland. She felt it in the pit of her stomach. The feeling of dread. 'Where are you now?'

'In Lara's flat. Nina's next door in the kitchen. She's as puzzled as we are. Said she wished she'd thought to ask Lara more questions.

She's been very helpful, actually. I think she feels like she's in the middle of a detective film.'

'Have you been to see Harriet yet?'

'This morning, briefly. She was in good form, I thought. She's got her hands full with that Willoughby, too. There's a thought. He's a detective, isn't he? We can get him onto Lara's case.' His joke fell flat. 'Maybe you were right about this having something to do with Lara's parents, Gloria. The way she said she had to go off and do some family business.' He laughed awkwardly. 'Sorry, listen to me, Austin the amateur psychologist. But Nina and I were talking about it. Maybe Lara went to Ireland without mentioning it to any of us, and it's sparked all sorts of horrible memories for her, from when her parents had that crash.'

Gloria was silent.

'Gloria? Are you there?'

'I'm here,' she said. 'Sorry, I was just thinking.'

'I realised when we were talking about it that there were all these things I didn't know about Lara's parents. Where they came from, who they were even. I don't even know where they are buried. Was it in Ireland, or in Australia?'

'They were cremated, as far as I know,' Gloria said. She knew for sure. There had been a lot of contact between the Australian police and the Irish police. The embassies had been involved as well. It was Penny again who had made the decision. She had requested the ashes be scattered somewhere in Ireland. 'I know you'll think I'm wrong, Gloria, you don't even have to say it. I'm doing it to protect Lara. It's what Rose would have wanted.' Gloria could remember her voice as clearly as if it was yesterday.

'So do you know the whole story from that time?' Austin asked.

'Not all of it,' Gloria said hesitantly.

'Has Lara asked you about any of this? I mean, she might have asked Mum and Dad about it, but we'll never know now.'

'I know they spoke about it with her a lot, around the time she turned eighteen especially.' Penny had come to Gloria, asking for advice. It had been one of the few times since that first terrible night that she and Penny had spoken about it. Lara had started asking lots of questions again about her parents and Penny hadn't known what to tell her. Didn't I tell you this would happen, Gloria had wanted to say to her. Didn't I tell you that it would all come back to bite you? They had nearly fought about it, Gloria remembered. But in the end Penny had stuck to her original story and, as far as Gloria ever found out from Penny, Lara had accepted it.

'Why wasn't Lara with her parents in Ireland that time, Gloria? Her flatmate asked me tonight and I couldn't remember.'

'I think her parents had been having problems,' she said, choosing her words with care. 'Lara had a school camp that week. Your mother told me they'd decided it was a good opportunity to go away on their own, to try and sort out a few things.'

'That's right. Mrs Robinson was always ringing Mum for help, wasn't she? For hours on end, now I think of it. So where did the crash happen in Ireland? Was it near where her mother's house was? Or somewhere else?'

'I'm not sure,' Gloria said. That wasn't true, either. She knew exactly where it had happened. Just outside a town called Clonakilty, near the city of Cork. The name had always stuck in her head. She was hating this, hating being put on the spot, having to think before she answered him. *Help me, Penny*, she implored silently. At least it was only a phone conversation. She would have found it harder to lie face to face. She tried to change the subject, to buy herself some thinking time. 'Look, Austin, you're not getting carried away with this possibility, are you? You don't think that maybe we should leave her be, wait until she decides to contact us again?'

'I can't, Gloria. Not now. It's like I said to Harriet, if we find her and she's all right, then we'll leave her alone. If she's not all right, then we'll be glad we went looking. But something's obviously wrong. She's upset about something and maybe it's got something to do with her parents and what happened in Ireland. Nina's convinced that's what it is. She's going to come and help me look for her, too.'

'Go with you? Where, to Ireland?'

'Yes. She's very fond of Lara. And she's worried now, too.'

'Have you got time to do this? What about the orchestra?'

'It'll be fine. I've still got two days off and I'll do what I can in that time. What do you reckon? It's worth a try, isn't it?'

'Yes, it is.' What else could she have said to him?

Gloria started to take her usual route home for lunch, along the beach path, but as she reached the end of the curved bay she turned right, instead of her usual left. She leaned down and took off her sandals and picked her way through the sand to the tree trunk. Bleached from the sun and the water, it had been there for as long as she could remember. She had played on it as a child. She had sat on it with Kevin when they were first dating, with their three boys over the years, and even with her grandkids. She'd sat there with Penny many times too, watching their kids swim, shriek and bodysurf for hours on summer days.

The sun was high. The water was the glowing blue she loved. There were a few people swimming, a couple under an umbrella far to her right, a mother and her two daughters trying to fly a kite. Her imagination turned the woman into Penny, and the two daughters into Harriet and Lara.

Gloria had come to this spot the night she had that awful, difficult conversation with Penny, the night they heard the news about Lara's parents. The night she'd made that promise. Gloria had regretted making it then and she regretted it now, twenty-four years later.

Gloria was in the back room of the agency, unpacking new stationery, when she heard the phone ring. She heard Penny answer it. The two of them were alone. Neil had left early to drop some tickets to one of their older customers.

Gloria finished the unpacking and was about to put on her coat to go home when Penny came in. Her face was white. Gloria's immediate thought was someone had died. Neil. Or Kevin. One of the kids. 'Penny, what is it?'

Penny told her. Gloria sat down, shocked. She was right. Someone had died. Two people. Lara's parents. Little Lara, who had stayed with the family just a few months before. Her hand went to her mouth as Penny shut the door, sat down at the table and told her the details. 'Oh God. Oh my God. That poor little girl.'

'I can't believe it, Gloria. How could something like that happen?'

Gloria shook her head, put her hand on Penny's arm. 'Did you have any inkling things were so terrible? How long was it since you spoke to Rose?'

'Just last week. Before she left. She asked me to be Lara's guardian while they were away. In case something happened. That's how the police in Ireland tracked me down. My details were in the back of her passport.'

'You think she knew? Had a feeling . . .?'

'I didn't notice anything. It was hard to tell with Rose. You know what she was like.'

Gloria knew well. She had answered the phone many times to Rose over the past few months. Rose had taken to ringing Penny during work hours, always with that edge of tears to her voice. Penny tried to be understanding about it, even while she was obviously getting impatient with the long, too regular and often increasingly drunken calls. Rose and her husband were always breaking up and getting back together. He'd moved to Queensland to live with another woman at one stage, Gloria recalled. That had sparked twice daily phone calls to Penny. Rose had nearly been hysterical, Penny had told Gloria. She would say over and over how much she loved Dennis, how she couldn't bear it if he left her again. Rose had eventually gone up there with Lara and pleaded with him to come back.

'I can't believe it, Gloria,' Penny said again. 'I just can't.'

'Who's told Lara? One of her teachers?'

'No one yet. The teachers don't know. That's why the police rang me. They want me to go and tell her.'

'Oh Penny, no! That's very hard on you.'

'It's worse than hard. It's impossible. What do I tell her?'

Gloria thought about it. 'As much as you think she can stand. Not all the details yet, but the basic facts.'

'Tell her the truth, you mean? Gloria, of course I can't. She's eight years old. What would news like that do to a child of that age? She wouldn't be able to take it in, let alone cope with it.'

'But you have to. What else can you tell her? Penny, her parents are dead. Nothing you say is going to change that. What could you say to soften it? Tell her they died in a car crash?'

'A car crash?' Penny was thoughtful. 'Do you know, I think you're right. I think that could be the best solution.'

'Penny, I didn't mean it. I was speaking hypothetically.'

'But I think you're right. What difference will it make to her if she thinks that's what happened? It won't bring her parents back if she knows the truth, will it? It might make it easier for her.'

'Stop it. You can't do this.'

'I can, Gloria. I have to. Can't you see it makes sense? I can't tell a little girl the truth. You met Lara, you saw how fragile she was. How damaging would this be for her, the rest of her life? You know how people talk. She'd never be treated normally.'

'But you can't make up a lie like that. What about her family? Uncles, aunts? Grandparents?'

'There aren't any. Rose was an only child, and Dennis's parents died before he emigrated. Her mother died a month ago, and she never knew her father. That's why Rose went over there, to finalise her mother's estate. There was no one else.'

'Penny, you can't be serious about this. You have to tell her the truth.'

'I don't. And I need you to promise that you won't tell her. I'm not going to tell Neil or the children, either. They don't need to know.'

Gloria had never seen Penny like this. 'You can't just invent a car crash.'

'I'm not inventing it.' Penny spoke in a firm voice. 'It happened. They were driving through the mountains outside Cork and bad weather came in. There are mountains outside Cork, aren't there? Perhaps I'd better just say Ireland for the time being. The road was winding. They must have lost control of the car and tipped over the cliff edge.'

Gloria could hardly believe she was having this conversation. 'You can't just make something up like that, Penny. You can't. It won't change anything, anyway. They're still dead, aren't they? How can you think this will make it easier for her to cope?'

'It'll be easier than the truth at least. Can you think of another possibility? A plane crash? A train accident? No, I think you're right. A car crash. It's ordinary enough.'

'What do you mean I'm right? No, Penny, you can't make this my idea. You need to hold off. Think about it some more.'

'There's no time. What I tell her when I pick her up from the school camp tonight is how it will be. I know it's the right decision, Gloria. I really do. I feel it in my heart.'

'But what if she comes to you when she's older and says she needs to know more about her parents? What will you tell her then?'

'That they loved her. I'll talk about what they were like, the sort of people they were. That's what she'll want to hear. What she'll need to hear.'

'I think you're making a big mistake.'

'I know I'm not. And I need you to promise me you won't tell her, Gloria. That you won't tell anyone.'

'She'll find out some other way. You can't keep something like this a secret.'

'How will she find out? It happened on the other side of the world. I told you, there isn't a big family waiting for her to join them and wanting to tell her the truth. Gloria, that's why Rose asked me to be Lara's guardian. She didn't know other people here and there wasn't other family who could take her. She always said how lucky she thought I was. And how lucky it was that we were on the same ship to Australia. That it was meant to be that we were friends. And she was right. We are lucky. We should share that luck.'

Gloria couldn't think of anything to say to that. Since she had known her, Penny had always had the belief that things were destined, meant to happen.

'I'm telling you, Gloria, because I need to, tonight at least. But I want you to promise me that you'll always keep it to yourself. You mustn't even tell Kevin.'

'I can't make a promise like that.'

'You have to. If we're to keep working together, to be friends, I need to know I can trust you. It'll be too difficult for Lara otherwise, not to mention the rest of the family. I don't know for sure, but my feeling is that Lara will be living with us from now on. It's the only possible outcome. I want her to feel welcome. And loved. And secure. I need to know that you won't do anything to endanger that.'

Gloria felt she was seeing Penny for the first time. She was like a different woman. Driven. A thought flashed into Gloria's head. From one of their conversations, during the long, quiet times in the travel agency's earliest days. Penny had confessed she'd longed to have another child, two boys and two girls, but it had never happened. 'You're glad about this, Penny, aren't you? Glad to get Lara? Your second daughter?'

Gloria saw a flicker of something in her friend's eyes, but then Penny's chin rose. 'Of course I'm not glad. How could I be glad that something so terrible happened? What I'm trying to do is make the best of it. The best for Lara and what I know Rose would have wanted to happen. Please, Gloria. I'm asking for a promise.'

Gloria hesitated, then nodded. 'I promise. I think it's wrong, but I promise.'

She'd known for twenty-four years and kept her promise. As

she watched Lara settle in to the family, go to the local schools and start working for Turner Travel, she'd reluctantly admitted to herself that Penny had been right. It had made it easier for Lara. Gloria and Penny had rarely spoken about it. One of the few times they did was at a school play, sitting in the audience, watching Harriet and Lara on stage. Lara was considered one of the Turners now. A woman went past. 'You must be so proud of your girls, Penny.'

'Oh, I am.' Penny exchanged pleasantries and then turned to Gloria and spoke in a quiet voice. 'You see? It's made her ordinary, Gloria. One of us. If people had known the truth, she would never have been able to fit in. People would always have talked about her in a terrible way.'

'It was still wrong. You were changing her history.'

'No, I was protecting a little girl.'

'You can't protect her forever. She'll find out.'

'How? You promised me you wouldn't say anything.'

'She'll go looking one day.'

'She won't, Gloria. I just know she won't. She won't need to.'

'You were wrong, Penny.' Gloria said the words aloud, staring out across the water. 'I wish you had been right, but I think you were wrong. She has gone looking.'

Her heart went out to Lara. Please, God, let her not have found out, not like this, alone on the other side of the world. There was nothing she could have done to stop her though, she realised. She had to let it happen. Let it unfold, whether she liked it or not.

She got up and wrapped her arms around herself, cold despite the sunshine. Slowly, she walked up the beach and headed for home.

Chapter Twenty-Four

Nina called out into the hallway. 'Austin, do you want more coffee?'

'More?' he called back from the bathroom. 'Have you got shares in a coffee bean plantation?'

'No, just an addictive personality. Caffeine, nicotine, and don't start me on Ovaltine.'

'Don't you have to go into work today?' Austin said, as he came into the room, freshly showered. He felt good, ready for action, optimistic, even. He'd expected to sleep badly on the sofa bed, or at least lie awake for hours. But he'd fallen asleep immediately.

'Not today. Not unless I get an emergency call that some filing needs doing somewhere.'

He and Nina fell into easy conversation again. Lara was still their main topic, but they kept veering off into side routes. What it was like living in Bath. How long he'd been a drummer. Some of the temping jobs she'd done. Whether he felt more at home in England or Australia.

She laughed easily. He found himself telling orchestra tales, spurred on by her questions.

'You can't all be well-behaved all the time, surely?' she'd asked.

He'd confessed that, no, they weren't. Musicians were terrible practical jokers. He told her about the time the cornet player discovered someone had put water into his instrument. When he picked it up and played, water sprayed out left, right and centre. Or the time the women in the first violin section turned the page on their score mid-opera to reveal some extremely explicit gay porn. The whole wind section had cracked up laughing. Only one had continued playing, to the conductor's disgust.

As she laughed, he saw again how sparkly her brown eyes were. Like a child's, he thought. He'd always noticed that with his niece Molly, how clear her eyes were. Innocent, he supposed. Untouched by life's hard knocks yet.

'So, Austin, do you have a girlfriend?'

Her sudden change of subject threw him, but he didn't show it. 'No, I don't.'

'A good-looking man like you? I'm not trying to flatter you, I'm stating a fact. I like your hair long like that, by the way. It suits you. But still no girlfriend?'

'No.'

'Surely someone fancies you or you fancy someone?'

'You sound like my sisters. They're constantly trying to marry me off.'

'You don't want to settle down?'

'I just haven't found the right girl.'

'I would have thought you'd come up with something more original than that.'

'I'm too young to settle down.'

'You're not too young. What are you? My age? Thirty-five?'

'Thirty-eight.'

'See, not too young at all. Better excuse, please.'

'Too many fish in the sea?'

'Oh, I see,' she grinned. 'You're a field player. A Don Juan.'

'A what?'

'A ladies' man. Of course you are, with those looks. And do you have much success?'

'I have my moments.'

'And is it enough?'

'What do you mean?'

'If you can play the field like that, is it enough for you mentally? Emotionally? Because you strike me as a clever man underneath all the front. Thoughtful, too. You wouldn't be here looking for Lara if you weren't a caring person.'

He was enjoying this and not enjoying it, all at once. 'You don't mince your words, do you?'

She smiled. 'I'm sorry, I actually meant it as a compliment. And yes, before you say it, I am far too nosy. I always have been, especially about people's love lives. It's the Italian in me. And I suppose I always wondered what it would be like to play the field.'

'You're good-looking yourself. You could try it. Have you got a boyfriend?'

'Alas, no, I haven't.'

They were flirting, he realised. He also realised he liked it. 'Oh, poor Nina. Do you want me to give you some tips?'

'Would you? Really? Oh yes please, great master.'

He had just started, in a mock-serious voice – 'First, identify your prey' – when the phone rang. It was Brendan, Lara's lecturer from the tourism college. He'd found something he wanted to show them.

They met him in the same classroom they'd visited the night before. He'd asked them to come as quickly as possible, before the morning classes started. He looked like an absent-minded scientist, Austin thought. His hair was even more tousled than before. His glasses kept slipping, too.

'I hope you don't think I was being nosy,' Brendan said, 'but I was mulling it over last night. I tried that Internet history search on my own computer at home, and I discovered it saves everything you've looked at, every word you've searched for on a search engine, not only the website addresses.'

They sat around Lara's computer with him. He clicked, and then moved the mouse again until the Internet Explorer page was open on the screen. 'You see, here's the history that we looked at last night, the Irish sites, the cruise ship info pages, all of that. But here's what I found on Lara's search engine this morning. I don't know, it might be helpful.'

He clicked on the search engine web address, and then clicked again. A long list appeared on the screen of every word Lara had typed into the search engine. Amidst ones they expected to see – Willoughby, Patrick Shawcross, airlines, weather bureau, airport information – was a list of more disturbing words.

Rose Dennis Robinson
Car crash
Ireland
Australian
British
Police
Two killed

There was no mistaking it. She had been looking for information about her parents.

'Did she find anything?' Austin asked.

'I don't know. I thought I'd wait until you got here before I tried searching the same words again. The history shows the terms entered, but not what results came up. It didn't feel right for me to look them up if you weren't here.'

Austin was grateful for his understanding. 'Could you try now?'

More clicks. He tried all the different combinations. Lots of random web pages came up, but nothing with any more information on Lara's parents.

'Of course, it was more than twenty years ago,' Brendan said. 'If it had been reported in any of the newspapers, and it probably was, it mightn't show up here. They wouldn't have had electronic editions back then. So if she was trying to find out more, she'd probably need to go to the offices themselves and check their archives.'

Austin sat back in the chair. It was a help, but it didn't narrow the search for her any more. 'She could be anywhere, couldn't she? Visiting every newspaper office in Ireland, asking to go through their back editions.'

'She might have phoned around first.' He pointed at the screen again. 'See, she'd done a search on all the police stations in Ireland too. They'd have the information as well.'

Nina was disappointed. 'It's like looking for a needle in a haystack, isn't it? She could be anywhere in Ireland, staying in any hotel or B&B, walking miles and miles of roads trying to find the exact spot where her parents were killed.' She sighed. 'Then again, she could be sitting in a spa, having a facial at this moment, unaware of all this fuss.'

'Not Lara. It's more than that. It has to be something to do with her parents. If we could just figure out where she was, here or in

Ireland, the next step would be easier. One island to search instead of two.'

Brendan glanced at his watch. 'I'm sorry to rush you, but I've got a class coming in a minute. You're welcome to come back if you like.'

Austin stood up, feeling flat, and pushed his chair back under the desk. 'Thanks again, Brendan. You've been really helpful.'

'Let me know if there's anything else I can do, won't you?'

'You couldn't run a check on her name on every airline leaving the UK for Ireland by any chance?' Austin said, only half-joking. 'See if we could track her down that way?'

Brendan gave a wry smile. 'No, I couldn't, sorry.'

Austin was about to turn away when Brendan spoke again, in a low voice. 'But a friend of mine could.'

In St Ives, Harriet was getting ready to go down to breakfast. She wasn't sure if she was feeling nervous or just confused. It was as if a spell had been cast over all of them the night before, she decided. The make-up and hair session with Miss Talbot and the others, the bus trip, the restaurant, the disco – the combination had acted like a potion. If Mrs Lamerton hadn't knocked on the door when she did, Harriet didn't know what would have happened. She corrected herself. Yes, she did actually. She would have kissed Patrick Shawcross for a lot longer and if those kisses had been as good as the first kiss, then she would have gone to bed with him. She would probably still be in bed with him now.

Perhaps it was as well she hadn't gone back to his room after leaving Mrs Lamerton. This morning she would see him, and it would be businesslike again and they would continue on the tour as if nothing had happened.

It was an easy day today, driving from St Ives to Land's End and then on to the Minack Theatre overlooking Porthcurno Bay. They were all dining in town together and then the rest of the evening was scheduled as free time for everyone. The group had been talking the night before about what they would do. Mr Fidock and Mr and Mrs Douglas had been investigating local pubs and had found a nautically themed one they wanted to try. Harriet was going to take the opportunity to make calls to confirm the next part of their tour. Go for a long walk. Do some reading, perhaps.

Her phone rang. It was Austin, calling from Bath.

'She's definitely gone to Ireland, Harriet. She flew there three days ago. To Cork, in the south. She left Bristol on a nine p.m. flight, the same day she was supposed to meet you. On a one-way ticket and so far she hasn't returned. Not that they've been able to tell by the bookings, anyway.'

Harriet listened as Austin explained about Lara's lecturer and his industry contacts. Lara had been cutting it fine. If their flight had been on time, they would have been arriving at nine-thirty. 'But why would she go to Cork?'

'It's got to be about her parents. Why else would she go there?'

'Has she found out where the crash was? I only remember Mum and Dad saying it was in Ireland, but I never knew where.'

'Nor did I. Maybe they knew, and maybe they told Lara years ago. Or she might have contacted the Irish police. I've checked the flights. There's one leaving Bristol for Cork later today, we might be able to catch it.'

'We?'

'Nina's as worried as we are. She's coming with me. Harriet, I'd better go. I'll ring you as soon as I have any more news.'

Harriet finished getting ready. Austin's call had brought her back to reality. That was her real life, the real world. Her family, Lara, Austin. Not what she had imagined was happening with Patrick. She had blown everything out of proportion.

On her way downstairs she stopped at the landing and looked out through the big windows onto the beach. There was only one person out there, in a billowing raincoat, walking a dog. It was still drizzling and the waves were high, but not as rough as the previous day.

The front door of the hotel opened. She knew it was him even before he appeared.

He saw her immediately. His face broke into a smile. 'Harriet.'

She walked down the final few stairs. Her legs were suddenly unsteady. 'Hello, Patrick.'

'Did you manage to sort things out for Mrs Lamerton last night?'

'I did.' She swallowed. 'Patrick, I'm sorry about —'

'I'm not.'

She fell quiet.

'Harriet, I meant it last night. I mean it this morning. Something is happening. We both feel it.' His face was serious. 'Are you sorry about last night?'

'No, I'm not. No.'

'Are you sure?'

'I'm sure.'

'Can I see you this evening? After the group dinner in town?'

'You've looked at the itinerary?'

'I have, yes.' A glint came to his eye. 'You see? If I'd known you would kiss me so beautifully, I'd have been checking it long before now.'

He hadn't even lowered his voice. The feeling came rushing

back. That warmth, the sharing, but now with something much deeper underneath it.

'Hello, Harriet. Hello, Patrick.' They both turned. It was Miss Talbot. She looked pale. 'Patrick, would you please come and peel my orange for me again this morning?'

'Of course, Miss Talbot,' he said. 'How are you this morning?'

'Not very well, I'm ashamed to confess. I think there might be alcohol in those Fluffy Ducks.'

Harriet was smiling as she followed them into the breakfast room.

They were all on the bus by ten o'clock. Harriet noticed a different mood among the group. She also knew what had caused it.

After breakfast, she had gone to her room to collect the day's tour notes when she was waylaid by Mrs Lamerton. She'd seen her in the dining room but they hadn't spoken. The older woman had been tucking heartily into kippers. It was a remarkable recovery from food poisoning.

'I need to have a word, please, Harriet. A private word.'

'Of course, Mrs Lamerton.' She stepped into her room, inviting Mrs Lamerton to come in as well.

The older woman seemed agitated. 'I've been thinking about this all night. I really don't think it's appropriate behaviour and I think Melissa would agree, if she knew. Lara, too, if she was here.'

'I'm sorry, Mrs Lamerton, I'm not sure what you mean.'

'I'm talking about you and Patrick Shawcross. You were in his room very late last night. And I've seen him go into your room late at night as well. More than once.'

So she had been spying on them. Harriet knew she had to call her bluff. 'Oh, Mrs Lamerton, have you been imagining hijinks between myself and Patrick?'

'Yes. Yes, I have. But I haven't imagined it. I've seen it.'

'Mrs Lamerton, I think I need to let you in on a secret.' Harriet stepped back, so Mrs Lamerton could see the TV and video on its stand in the corner of the room. A stack of videos was on the table beside it. The *Willoughby* titles were clearly visible. 'That's what Patrick and I have been doing.'

'Watching television?'

'Not television. Videos. *Willoughby* videos. I was brought onto this trip at very short notice, as you know, so I've been watching the videos each night. Patrick has been watching them with me, helping me to get familiar with the episodes. I knew I'd never be as familiar with them as James or Lara, let alone you and the rest of the group, but I wanted to do the best I could.' It was all nearly true. It didn't explain what she was doing in Patrick's room the previous night, but she realised then that Mrs Lamerton no longer cared about that. She was looking at the videos like a sugarholic in a sweetshop.

'You've got all the *Willoughby* episodes here with you?'

'Yes.'

'All twenty of them?'

'That's right.'

'Could I borrow them?'

'Pardon me?'

'Visiting the locations has brought back so many memories. I'd like to watch a few of the videos again myself. Tonight, if I could borrow your video player. In fact, can I take the videos now?'

'Now? But we're about to go on the bus.'

'Just so I know I have them. In case you get busy later today when we get back.'

Harriet softened. Mrs Lamerton really was the High Queen of the *Willoughby* weirdos. 'Of course you can.'

Harriet could see her in the middle seat of the bus now, taking one of the videos out of her bag and letting her neighbour, Mrs Biggins, take a look at it. Mr Fidock was leaning across the aisle. 'All twenty of them? Are you sure?'

'Yes, I've checked the titles. All twenty, right here.'

Yes, Mrs Lamerton had definitely made a full recovery from last night's food poisoning. Harriet wondered what else had happened the previous evening. Clive and Mrs Randall had been the last to get on the bus that morning, coming out of the hotel together. It might have been a trick of the light, but she was nearly sure she'd seen Clive give Mrs Randall a little pinch on the bottom before she went to sit down. He was certainly in better humour. And they had been dancing together a lot the previous night. No, Harriet had to be imagining it . . .

She took out her folder. So far she'd also done a good job of pretending nothing had changed between her and Patrick. For the sake of everyone, she'd greeted him normally when he got on the bus. She hadn't spoken to him since.

As she looked up he caught her gaze. He stopped mid-conversation with his neighbour. 'Excuse me, Mrs Douglas. Harriet?'

'Yes, Patrick?'

'I wonder would you pass me that map there beside Clive?'

'The map? Of course.' She passed it over.

A few minutes later he called her name again, thanked her for the map and asked her to put it back. A few minutes later, just as politely, he asked her to pass him the torch from the dashboard beside Clive.

'The torch?'

'I like torches.'

In the next ten minutes he asked her to pass him the St Ives street directory and then the newspaper that Clive had pushed into the seat pocket beside him. When Mrs Douglas got up to fetch something from her husband, Harriet took the opportunity to lean across to him, speaking in a low tone. 'Patrick, what are you doing?'

'Asking you to pass me things.'

'Yes, I know. I've passed you everything in the front of the bus. I'm running out of things to pass you.'

'Stop ignoring me then.'

'I'm not ignoring you.'

'Aren't you? What are you doing then?'

She started to smile. 'I'm trying to maintain a dignified and professional distance.'

'So I can't kiss you now?' That sparkle was back in his eyes again.

'No, you can't.'

'I want to.'

'You can't.'

'I'll be thinking about it.'

'I won't look at you.'

'I'll ask you to pass me more things.'

'Patrick, please.'

'I'm sorry. I'll be on my best behaviour.'

'Thank you.'

'But if you hear me say the word raven today during the question and answer session, you'll know I'm thinking about kissing you.'

'Raven?'

'Raven,' he said.

She took the microphone as usual once they got out onto the

open road and started reading. James had been surprisingly low-key in his script today. '*Welcome aboard, everyone. Just two days to go. On behalf of everyone at Turner Travel, I hope you're all enjoying yourselves and the trip is meeting your expectations in every possible way. If there is anything I can do to make it more pleasurable, you only have to ask.*' She couldn't help herself. She glanced over at Patrick. He had a big smile on his face.

She quickly looked back at her script.'*This morning we'll be visiting Land's End, England's extreme western tip and of course the scene for episode fourteen's romantic reunion between Willoughby and Lady Garvan, following her release from prison on forgery charges. We'll also be visiting the awe-inspiring Minack Theatre, the Greek-style amphitheatre set into the cliff face overlooking the spectacular Porthcurno Bay. Built in the 1930s by Rowena Cade, the theatre has seen many open air productions of operas, musicals and Shakespeare plays, but is of course also known to the* Willoughby *afficionado as the setting for the dramatic conclusion to episode twelve, "The Case of the Vanishing Vicar"*.'

She swapped seats and handed the microphone to Patrick for the usual on-the-road question and answer session. He stood next to her, his hand resting lightly on the backrest, close enough to touch.

Mrs Kempton put up her hand. 'Patrick, did you have much of a say in any of the actors who were cast in the show?'

'Not in the first series, Mrs Kempton, no. But in the second series I did. We were fortunate to hear about a talented family of actors called the Ravens. There were seven of them, all talented in different ways and, remarkably for one family, all quite different in appearance, so we used them as much as possible. There was Andrew Raven, who you might remember as the gardener in episode three. Carlos Raven, the chef in "The Case of the Crooked Chef". His sister Cassandra Raven played a waitress in that same episode. Isabella Raven, who was a maid in Lady Garvan's mansion in several episodes. Santana Raven – the family had Spanish blood, I believe – was one of the customers in the jewellery shop at the time of the siege. And of course not forgetting the twins, Delilah Raven and her sister Anastasia Raven, who played a set of twins in "The Case of the Stolen Kiss".'

Mrs Lamerton was frowning. 'I don't remember that episode. Which series was that in?'

'I do apologise, Mrs Lamerton. That was its working title. You might remember it as "The Case of the Mislaid Mail".'

'Oh yes,' Mrs Lamerton nodded. 'Now I remember it.'

'A wonderful family, the Ravens. I've been thinking about them a great deal the past few days. I'm hoping to get in contact with some of them. Tonight, possibly.' He looked at Harriet. There was laughter in his eyes, but there was that deeper, more intense look as well. He gave her the slightest of winks and then turned as another question was called. 'Yes, Mr Fidock?'

Chapter Twenty-five

In Merryn Bay, it was the end of a long day. Gloria was battling a headache. The phones had been ringing constantly. Each time she expected it to be Austin. It was making her jumpy. It didn't help that she was running the office on her own. Melissa had made a great show the afternoon before of saying she might stay an extra day in Melbourne, that it was time she did a thorough reconnoitre of the city travel agents. Gloria knew it was a lie. She had heard Melissa make the appointment in the day spa herself. This time tomorrow Melissa would be frown-free and three shades of brown darker.

'That's fine.' She'd enjoy the peace in fact. 'Are you expecting any calls? Anything I need to know?'

Melissa had been distracted, cleaning out her handbag as she often seemed to do in work hours, all the little pots of make-up lined in a row across her desk. 'Go ahead and handle them for me, would you? If anyone asks, I'm away on family business. Molly will be away too. She's got a swimming carnival in the north of the state. You'll have the place to yourself.'

Gloria had closed the office for lunch, deciding on the spur of the moment to pick up sandwiches and go home to Kevin. It was hard to leave him after the hour was up. They sat in the garden, talking, drinking tea, doing the newspaper crossword. He was better than her at the cryptic clues, but he didn't rub it in. He liked to joke that he wouldn't let a crossword come between them. When she had got back to the office at two o'clock, there had been fourteen messages waiting for her on the machine.

She went into the back room now to make a cup of tea. Just half an hour to closing time. She was counting the minutes. The phone was ringing as she came back. She had to lean over the desk to grab it in time. 'Turner Travel, Gloria speaking, can I help you?'

'Good afternoon, can I speak to Melissa Turner please?'

'I'm sorry, Melissa's not in the office at present. Can I take a message?'

'Will she be in later today?'

'I'm sorry. She's been called away on family business. Who's calling please?'

'I'm sorry, I should have introduced myself. This is Regina Lewis, calling from Matheson Travel.'

One of the largest of the national travel companies. 'I'm sure I can help you, this is Gloria Hillman speaking. Melissa's asked me to deal with any business that came in today.'

'Oh, thank you. I'm calling on behalf of Mr Alex Sakidis, our franchise and acquisitions manager. He's asked if it would be possible for him to change the date of his viewing to next Thursday, rather than Wednesday.'

'That should be fine,' Gloria said cautiously. She'd been expecting a question about one of their tours, or an exchange of information. That was common enough among travel agents, even if they were apparently in competition. 'Let me check Mrs Turner's diary.'

She opened the diary on Melissa's desk and flicked to the right date. Nothing there. Then she clicked on the computer screen to her electronic diary. Melissa was the only one who used it every day – Gloria, Harriet, James and Lara preferred the paper trail. There was something marked on that date: M.T. Matheson Travel?

'And you'd like to change that date to —?'

'The following day, if that's all right?'

'That should be fine.' Gloria put on her most casual voice. 'Could I just double-check Mr Sakidis's title?'

'Of course. He is our franchise and acquisitions manager.'

'Oh, yes.' Were they actually talking about what she thought they were talking about? 'And Mr Sakidis has the address?'

'Turner Travel, 143 Main Street, Merryn Bay?'

'That's right. And all the background information he needs?'

'Let me check.' The young woman returned after a moment. 'I'll put you through to Mr Sakidis, Mrs Hillman. It is Mrs?'

'Yes, thank you.'

A short burst of classical piano and then a smooth, deep voice. 'Mrs Hillman, Alex Sakidis speaking.'

'How are you, Mr Sakidis? Your assistant probably explained that Mrs Turner is unfortunately out of the office today, but please feel free to ask me if you need any more information.' She felt she was walking a tightrope, hoping she was saying the right things.

'We have all the figures we need, thanks, Mrs Hillman. They look very healthy. And we received the forecast material from your accountant on Monday, as agreed. I think once we see the property itself, that will help us get more of a feel for what sort of package we'd be offering. That date change isn't a problem for you, I hope? Another possible acquisition property has come up further down the peninsula, so I want to take in both.'

'No, that's fine. I hope that second property won't have any bearing on whether you will or won't buy us out?' She shut her eyes, hoping she was still on track.

'We're currently planning an exciting expansion program, so no, let me assure you, we are still extremely interested. You haven't changed your minds, I hope?'

'Oh, no. Not at all.'

'So will I be meeting you as well, Mrs Hillman, or will it just be Mrs Turner?'

'Both of us, I hope. Thanks so much for talking to me. Goodbye.'

The shop was quiet after she hung up, only the sound of passing cars filtering in from outside. She must be mistaken. They must have been at cross purposes. They hadn't been talking about selling out Turner Travel. They had been discussing some shared tours.

No, they hadn't. He had spoken of acquisitions, buy-outs, figures, future plans. She had to check. She moved to her own computer, not wanting to touch Melissa's again. On to the Internet, on to the Matheson Travel website, on to their corporate page. *Mission statement: Matheson Travel is committed to becoming a world leader in international travel package suppliers, with plans to establish shopfronts and a presence throughout Australia.* In smaller letters: *For franchise and sales opportunities please contact Alex Sakidis.* A Melbourne number followed.

She had to be sure. She rang the number. The same young woman answered. 'Oh Regina, hello, it's Gloria from Turner Travel in Merryn Bay calling back. Sorry to bother you again. We're preparing some new brochures here and I meant to check, would Mr Sakidis need a sample of more of our itineraries, to give him an idea of the sort of business he'd be buying?'

'Oh, we have all that, thanks, Mrs Hillman. Mrs Turner sent a big selection through last month. You do some great tours, don't you?'

'We sure do. That's fine, as long as you have all you need. Goodbye now.'

She hung up. A photo of Melissa in her yellow uniform was on the pinboard in front of her. Gloria stared up at it and shook her head in disbelief. 'You scheming yellow cow.'

It was pouring with rain in Bath. There had been a thunderstorm that morning. Austin and Nina had to run from the flat down to the hire car. He'd been surprised, but also glad, when Nina offered to come to Ireland with him. 'I have some time off and I've never been to Ireland. Would you mind if I came too? Between the two of us we might be able to track her down more quickly.'

They were both drenched by the time they put their bags in the boot and clambered inside. 'Not exactly ideal flying weather,' Nina said, shaking her head, sending drops of water flying around the car.

Austin glanced at her. 'You're not scared of flying, are you?'

'Not usually, no. During electrical storms, yes. That was impressive flight organisation by the way. Especially considering you're a long way from home.'

'I was reared on timetables and flight bookings, remember. Travel runs in the Turner blood.'

'But you didn't want to go into the family business?'

He pulled out into the traffic. 'I did at first. But I also wanted to play the drums and it was hard to fit the kit in the office. The others complained I made too much noise while they were on the phone.'

She didn't acknowledge the joke. 'Yours is a family company, isn't it? So there must have been some pressure to stay with them?' She caught his expression. 'My parents run a restaurant, remember. I know all there is to know about family pressure.'

'I might have thought about going into it when I got tired of touring. And if my parents were still alive. It was different when they were there. But unfortunately my older brother James made the decision to marry a woman called Melissa. A woman from the black lagoon who has been slowly taking over our family business since the day James had the misfortune to meet her.' He stopped at the traffic lights, and adjusted the wipers to a faster speed. The rain was getting heavier.

'Fantastic, Austin.'

'Fantastic?'

'I've heard of people disliking their in-laws but you take it to a whole new level. You're sure you're not secretly harbouring a passionate love for her?'

'What is it with you and my love life?' He moved forward into the traffic again.

'I like you. I think we're going to be friends. And I worry about my friends. So am I right? Do you secretly love – what's her name?'

'Melissa.'

'Melissa. Is it a case of being jealous of your brother? Of having to take yourself out of the office because it was too much for your heart and your nerves to work so closely with your brother's wife?'

'Nina, can you stop it?'

'Your nerves taut as piano wire as you brushed against each other by the photocopy machine.'

'I'm serious.'

'Eyes meeting eyes across the formica lunch table.'

'Shut up, Nina.'

Her smile disappeared. 'Don't you tell me to shut up.'

He stopped at another red light and looked over. 'I'm sorry. You hit a sore point. No, I don't secretly love Melissa. I openly loathe Melissa. And I hate what she's done to our family business.'

'But it's successful, isn't it?'

He nodded. 'Very, these days.'

'You hate that she's made it successful? I can see why you'd hate it if she ruined it, but isn't success a good thing?'

'It's complicated.'

'In what way?'

'It's the way she does things. She rides roughshod over everyone. Makes decisions without asking us. She's taken over.'

'So who works in the family business? You don't. Your parents have passed away . . .'

'My sister Harriet. My brother James. Melissa. Lara. And Gloria, an old family friend. She's been working with us for centuries. Mum and Dad left her shares in the company in their will.'

'So it's not completely a family business then? More half and half.' She counted names off on her fingers. 'In fact, the non-biological family are winning. You'll have to go back and work there so there's more of you than them.'

Nina had an annoying habit of getting right to the point. 'I don't want to. It's the last place I want to work.'

'Then you can't complain if they make decisions without you, can you?'

He opened his mouth and then shut it again. He'd liked her at the start. Now he wasn't sure at all.

He stayed quiet for the rest of the journey, telling himself he was concentrating on the road. These were difficult driving conditions, after all. She made one or two attempts to break into his silence, but he wouldn't bite. She was messing up his head, with all these opinions and nosy remarks about Melissa and the travel agency. He was regretting asking her to come with him to Ireland now. Come to think of it, had he asked her along? She'd invited herself, hadn't she?

The music from the radio filled the car. It suited him that way. He indicated as the sign for Bristol Airport came up. The rain was still beating down. They had just driven into the hire car area when she leaned over and switched off the radio.

'What's it like up there, Austin?'

He manoeuvred the car into a parking bay, not looking at her. 'Up where?'

'On your high horse.'

He stopped the car and turned to her. Enough was enough. 'Do you ever give up?'

'Nope. Are you going to sulk like this the whole way to Ireland, because it won't be much fun if you do.'

'I'm not sulking.' They were having to speak loudly over the sound of the rain hitting the roof of the car.

'Aren't you? You've just decided to have some quiet time while you're in a car with another human being? You don't like teasing much, do you? I can be respectful if that's what you'd prefer. But I thought there was more to you than a sulky boy, Austin. I thought you were more interesting than this. More fun.'

'This isn't supposed to be fun. We're trying to find Lara, remember. This is serious.'

'And life goes on while we try to find Lara. Conversation goes on, manners go on. As life has always gone on, no matter what else is happening around a person.'

She kept getting to him. It needled him again. 'Well, aren't you the philosopher. A graduate from the school of cheery optimism, I see.'

'Yes, I am. I have been ever since my husband died.'

'I beg your pardon?'

'I said, yes, I am optimistic. I have been ever since my husband died.'

He stared at her. 'Are you serious?'

'He died four years ago. We'd been married for three years. Something like that changes the way you look at life, Austin. It made me appreciate it. It's also made me impatient.'

'I'm so sorry.'

'Don't be. You didn't know.'

'What happened?' It was his turn to ask the blunt questions.

'It was an accident. A silly stupid accident. He was playing Sunday football with a gang of our friends, a social league, out in the park. And the goal net wasn't secured properly and someone knocked against it. The bars tipped over and hit him on the head. Trapped him.'

'You were there?'

She nodded. 'We got him to hospital but he never regained consciousness. He died two days later.'

He didn't know what to say. All he could do was apologise again. 'I'm so sorry, Nina. About your husband. And for sulking. You're right. I was.'

'I forgive you. You know what I mean, though, don't you? You know how it feels when someone you love dies. It makes you look at everything in a different way.'

He did know. 'But mine wasn't the same as your situation. My parents had a good life. And they died within weeks of each other. It almost felt like the right thing for them.' Not that he hadn't been devastated when they died. And he still missed them, badly. But slowly, he had recovered. He had got used to it, at least.

She put her hand on his arm. 'I'm sorry to talk about it like this, in a car park. But I wanted to explain why I am like I am. I haven't got time to hang around and wait to find things out, or to put up with people sulking. Especially when I like them so much when they're not sulking.'

Austin acknowledged the dig.

'And I'm sorry if it's hard to take sometimes. But I try to grasp life now, Austin. All and as much as I can, while I can. So please, if you get mad at me over the next few days, say you're mad, would you, and we'll try and sort it out there and then? We haven't got time to mess around.'

'I'm sorry.'

'And stop saying sorry.'

'Can I buy you a drink?'

'Now you're talking.'

They climbed out of the car, grabbed their bags from the boot and ran through the rain into the airport building.

Clive drove the bus out of the Land's End car park just as the rain started again. The group hadn't been that impressed with their time there. An amusement arcade had been built on the spot where Willoughby and Lady Garvan had run into each other's arms in episode fourteen, 'The Case of the Jilted Jockey'. Still, they all enjoyed a stroll along the coastal path, peered over the cliff at the sea churning and boiling against the rocks far below. They queued patiently to have their group photograph taken in front of the signpost showing the distances to New York, John O'Groats and the focus of all their pointing fingers – Merryn Bay – 11 897 miles away. Harriet did a headcount as they came onto the bus. So far so good, she still hadn't lost anyone. She was about to give Clive the nod to drive on when Mrs Lamerton stood up and coughed, self-importantly. Harriet's heart sank. She had seen them all whispering about something as they walked back. Please don't let her say they didn't want to go to the Minack Theatre. Harriet was longing to see it.

'Harriet, we've been talking amongst ourselves and we were wondering if that TV and video up there works.'

Harriet glanced up at the small TV built into the plastic casing behind Clive's seat. Clive had heard the question and leaned around. 'Of course it does, Mrs L. This is one of the best buses in our fleet. Not the biggest, but everything on it is in first-class working order. Including myself.'

Harriet saw Miss Talbot nudge Mrs Randall.

Mrs Lamerton reached into her bag. 'In that case, Harriet, would you mind if we watched "The Case of the Vanishing Vicar" as we make our way to the Minack Theatre? To familiarise ourselves?'

'Watch the whole episode? But it's only a few miles from here.'

'We could take the long way, couldn't we?' They'd obviously looked at the map. 'It would add to the whole experience to see it on video before we saw the real thing.'

Harriet couldn't say no.

It took Clive only a minute to get the video running. There was a cheer as the *Willoughby* theme tune started and the familiar sight of a man walking across the field appeared on screen.

'Patrick, it's you!' Mrs Kempton said happily.

'Can you turn it up, Clive?' Miss Boyd called out.

'Can we pull the curtains on the bus, Harriet?' Mr Fidock asked. 'It's a bit hard to see otherwise.'

Harriet knew from James's script that they were about to pass some of Cornwall's most beautiful coastline: coastal paths and towering cliffs, long sandy beaches and wind-ravaged trees. And they wanted to watch TV. 'Of course,' she said.

They drove into the car park of the Minack Theatre as the closing credits came up. No one had said a word for the past thirty minutes, gripped by the storyline. Clive had been driving at about five miles an hour. The volume had been turned up to maximum. Mrs Kempton grabbed Patrick's arm at several tense moments during the episode. It ended on another cliffhanger note – Willoughby looking down the barrel of a gun being held by the fugitive vicar, on the stage of the Minack Theatre. The scriptwriters had obviously specialised in cliffhanger endings. There were sighs as the credits started to roll.

'There's your name, Patrick!' Mrs Kempton said, pulling at his sleeve again.

Harriet leaned over and asked Clive to turn the video off. She reached for the microphone and started reading from James's script. '*Welcome to the Minack Theatre, everyone. As you're about to see, this outdoor theatre is truly one of the most beautiful theatre spaces in the world. Unfortunately we are here too early in the season to see any of the plays but come with me and stand among the carved stone seats, halt awhile and surely you will be able to hear the ghosts of actors past, calling out their lines, enchanting audiences old and young.*' Oh, shut up, James, Harriet thought crossly. She put down the script. 'If you'd all like to follow me, we'll begin our tour.'

Mrs Lamerton pulled back her curtain. 'But it's raining.'

'No, it's just a slight drizzle,' Harriet said.

Mrs Pollard was peering out of her window too. 'It's looks very windy. And we're on top of a cliff, aren't we? Isn't that dangerous?'

Harriet was surprised she'd noticed where they were. None of them had looked outside the bus for the past half hour. 'I promise you it's safe.'

'I think I'd feel safer in here,' Mrs Douglas said.

'Me too,' Mrs Kempton said. 'Clive, does the video work even if the bus isn't running?'

'It should do. What was happening at the end of that episode? All that shouting? I could hear it but not see it.'

'It was Reginald Camphor, the vanishing vicar. Willoughby tracked him down to the theatre, in the middle of one of the performances, and the vicar pulled out a gun. He's threatening to shoot Lady Garvan unless she tells him where she put the safe with all the diamonds.'

'Which one was Lady Garvan?'

'The aristocratic one,' Mrs Lamerton said.

'So who was the other female voice I heard?'

'That was Mrs Flanders, the elderly postmistress. Haven't you seen *Willoughby* before, Clive?' Mrs Lamerton took another cassette out of her large handbag. 'I've got the first episode here. "The Case of the Prodigal Postman". It's my favourite.' She put on a deep voice. '*There are some mornings when I wake up and see the blue of the sea and feel the freshness of the wind —*'

A chorus of voices joined in. '*And I know I'm home.*'

'Put that first episode on, Clive,' Mr Douglas called out.

'No, let's have part two of "The Case of the Vanishing Vicar",' his wife said. 'We can look at episode one on the way back to the hotel.'

'Yes, part two of the "Vanishing Vicar",' Mrs Lamerton said firmly. 'Hands up who agrees with that?'

Thirteen pairs of hands went up. Harriet was astonished. 'Does anyone want to come to the Minack Theatre?'

They all shook their heads.

'You seriously want to stay on the bus and watch videos?'

Mrs Lamerton had the grace to look a bit embarrassed. 'Would you mind, Harriet?'

Patrick stood up. 'Of course she wouldn't. Would any of you mind if Harriet and I went to look at the theatre while you were watching videos?'

Clive had already pressed play. Patch was barking in the background. Mrs Lamerton was looking at the screen as she answered. 'No. Take as long as you like.'

By the time Harriet and Patrick bought their tickets and walked down the steps to the amphitheatre, the light rain had stopped. There were three small tour groups roaming through it. Harriet stopped at the bottom of the steps. It was the most spectacular sight she'd seen on the trip.

It was a perfect amphitheatre, set into the side of a cliff, long rows of seats curving around a stone stage area. There was no backdrop, just the pure view of ocean and the coastline stretching for miles. The sky was dramatic, blue in parts, with huge billowing white and grey clouds darkening in the distance. Far below them was a curved beach, tucked into a cove. She could see a path winding down the cliffside to the sand.

Everything was in place for a theatre performance. A lighting area, a director's vantage point, even a separate higher stage for tower scenes. It was something from ancient Greece transported to modern Cornwall.

'Magnificent, isn't it?' Patrick said, beside her. He'd been watching her reaction.

'It's absolutely beautiful. Has it changed since you were here last?'

'All those centuries ago?' He smiled. 'No, except we almost have it to ourselves. It was overrun with crew and actors when we were here. It wasn't quite the same. It's better today.'

They made their way along one of the rows of seats, stopping in the centre. Celtic emblems were etched into the stone. Grass was growing on the footpaths between the seats. The sea was in front of them, blue and grey with flecks of white, reflecting the sky.

He took her hand as they sat down. It was a simple gesture but it sent a spark of desire through her.

'Talk to me, Harriet. If you won't let me kiss you in public, you have to talk to me instead. Tell me everything.'

She smiled at him. 'Where do I start?'

'With the bad news. How old are you?'

'I'm thirty-two.'

'And you're still single?'

She nodded.

'You're not pining for poor Simon?'

'No, I'm not.' She hesitated. Did she tell him all that had led to her splitting up with Simon? The anxiety attacks? The breakdown? She stayed with the simple truth. 'I broke it off with him. I realised I didn't love him enough.' She paused. 'And you, Patrick? Were you really married?'

'To poor Alicia and Caitlin, you mean?' A glimmer of a smile. 'No, Harriet, not to them. But I was married. For nine years. To an American woman. We were divorced nearly five years ago.'

'And do you have children?'

'One stepson. He lives in Boston. We see each other still. We're close. He's great.'

'And now? Are you with anyone now?' It felt important to ask all these questions.

He shook his head. 'I was seeing someone until about six months ago. But it wasn't working for either of us. It's been me and work since. Too much work, I think sometimes.'

'What do you do, Patrick? When you're not being Willoughby?'

'I haven't told you?'

She shook her head.

'No, you're right, I haven't. There always seemed to be better things to talk about. I run a casting agency. A different sort of actors' casting agency.'

'You're not an actor any more?'

'No, I haven't been for years. I was no good at it, and it was no good for me.'

'No good?'

'You saw it yourself. I had an attack of the nerves before every performance.'

She remembered the night of the cocktail party. She had thought the nerves he'd shown were just part of the process, a way of getting his adrenaline running. It had worked, too. He had been the perfect guest star that night.

'I decided it was my body telling me to give it up,' he said. 'That I wasn't good enough.'

'But you were good. I thought you were great in *Willoughby*. And you've been so good with all the group, too. They love you.'

He smiled. 'Thank you, Harriet. But it was more than being good or being bad. More than feeling nervous, too. It was a matter of choosing a different sort of life.'

'Tell me.'

'It's quite a long story.'

'I'd like to hear it. I'd love to hear it.'

'Really?' At her nod, he continued. He was still holding her hand. 'After *Willoughby* was axed, I went to America with an actor friend of mine. Two British actors planning to take over the world. I'd been offered that role in the terrible soap, the one I told you about, so I was set up immediately. I met my wife around that same time. She was a producer on the program. Then the show folded. She got another job very quickly, but I couldn't get any work for a long time. My father was a carpenter, and I'd helped him out when I was young, so I did that for a while, picking up work here and there. My friend got some acting roles, but things were fairly desperate for both of us career-wise. Then he saw an ad one day, for department store Santas. For a joke, he put both our names down. We got called in the next day and started there and then.'

'You were a Santa Claus? In one of those shop grottoes?'

He nodded, smiling. 'For one Christmas, at least. Or one holiday season, as we call it in America. The two of us, in our thirties, dressing up in full suits every day for eight hours. My friend thought it was ridiculous and gave it up after a month, but I needed the money. I wanted to be working, too. I found it fun, easy in fact, but the guy who replaced my friend didn't have a clue what to do. He asked me for tips. The manager of the chain of stores heard me passing on some actor's tricks – the simplest of things – but he asked me if I'd be interested in training some more of his Santas. I did that for the next two years, for three months of the year. Good money, great conditions. I didn't have to worry about getting nervous and I was still involved in acting, in an odd way. In a funny way.'

She could see from his expression that he still found it funny now. 'My friend said I'd taken the easy way out, that I'd given up on this quest the two of us had to break into America. That I obviously wasn't hungry enough for the good parts, that I should be more like him, suffering for my craft. My wife thought the same thing, I realised later. They were right. I didn't have that hunger. I did my Santa training and the carpentry for the rest of the year and earned enough money to keep things afloat. My friend went in the opposite direction. He took acting classes five days a week. He had his teeth done. He had an eye tuck. He worked out all the time. It became an obsession with him. All he wanted was to be a success.'

'But it didn't happen for him?'

'Oh yes, it did.' He named his friend.

Harriet's eyes opened wide. 'Him? But he's famous. Really famous.' She had seen two of his films in the past year. 'He won an Oscar, didn't he?'

'No, he was nominated, but he didn't win.'

'Were you jealous of him? Are you jealous now?'

'Never. Not for a minute.' He hesitated. 'It was my wife who was jealous. That's what she wanted for me. For us. But I couldn't hunger for something I didn't want. And I didn't want that life. I didn't want all the perfection and the pressure. I wanted to swim every day because I liked how it made me feel, not because it was good for muscle definition. And I liked acting when the roles were interesting or entertaining, or when the camaraderie was good, but I knew from my friend, from my own experience, that was rarely the case. My wife wanted me to push forward and I wanted to pull back. That's when it started to go bad between us. We separated at first and tried to work it out, but we couldn't. We got divorced a year later.'

'She didn't go on to marry your friend?'

He gave a soft laugh. 'Looking for a happy ending, Harriet? No. My friend is gay.'

'Gay? But I read about him in a magazine last month. He's seeing a French actress, isn't he?'

'No, he's not. You see, Harriet? See how seductive it is, how all pervasive it is? You, on the other side of the world, reading about a complete stranger, and all of it lies. I didn't want that kind of life. Not that there was ever any real possibility of me getting it, in any case. I kept doing what I was doing, the training, a bit of carpentry. And then I got asked to train extras for a family Christmas film that was being shot in Boston. The producer asked did I know of any more normal-looking people for some other crowd scenes he was doing. I asked around, put out the word and that's how it started. I decided to set up an agency for normal people who wanted to do some acting, not the ferocious Hollywood celebrity-style jobs or Shakespearian tragedies. Ordinary people who wanted some of the buzz, some of the fun.'

'What did you call it?'

'NPA. Eventually, anyway. My assistant thought up the name. She came to me about three years ago, wanting to be an extra. She said all her grandchildren said she looked like Whoopi Goldberg so she wanted all the roles Whoopi said no to. She gave that up when she realised it was more fun organising the extras than standing around being one all day. I'd called my business the North Pole Agency, when it was just the Santa training. She shortened it to NPA. The NP Agency. North Pole, Normal People.'

'That's very good.'

'She's full of ideas. We have two offices now. Things took off very quickly. I'm based in Boston. The other one's in California. We're small, but very busy.' He paused. 'And there it is, Harriet. My life.'

'And all true?'

'All true.' He smiled, looking almost shy. Something went straight to her heart. 'Your turn, Harriet. Tell me everything. I want to hear about your life in Australia. About your family. About everything you've ever done.'

'I've nothing to compare to that.'

'Start with the small things, then. Can you ride a bike? Have you ever surfed? What's your favourite meal? Do you speak any other languages? What book would you take to a desert island? Can you dance? Do you like horses? Can you recognise the flags of at least twenty countries?'

She was laughing.

'I'm serious, Harriet. I want to know all those things about you. At least throw me a scrap today to keep me happy.'

She thought of something. She reached into her bag and took out Gloria's list. She didn't say anything, just handed it to him.

He took the envelope and at her prompting, opened it and unfolded the piece of paper inside. He started reading it, softly. '*I have worked and supported myself for more than fifteen years. I am buying my own flat. I have travelled all around Australia. I have led hundreds of tour groups. I can touch type. I know how to cook Thai food, Italian food and Malaysian food, make jam, chutney, and tomato sauce. I have grown my own tomatoes, sweet corn, parsley, coriander and pumpkins. I once made dinner for ten people on a camp fire. I can drive a car and a tractor . . .*'

As he kept reading, she heard him laugh quietly once or twice. He came to the end and smiled at her. 'I thought you were one of the most organised people I'd ever met, but this takes the cake. You carry it around just in case someone asks you about yourself?'

'No.' Should she tell him why she had that list? She wanted to, she realised. 'I had a nervous breakdown last year. After my parents died, one after the other. A good friend of mine wrote that for me, to remind me of the things I could do before it happened.'

'Your parents died?'

'Within two months of each other.'

'Oh, Harriet. That must have been hard.'

'It was very hard.'

'Did that bracelet belong to your mother?'

She was startled. 'How did you know that?'

'You touch it whenever you seem worried about something, I've noticed in the past few days. I thought it was either a good luck charm or it meant a lot to you.'

'It means a lot to me. My father gave it to her when they first arrived in Australia, after they emigrated from England.'

'You're English?'

'My two brothers are. I was born in Australia.'

'You're close to them, by the sound of things. Has that helped?'

'In some ways.'

He took her hand again. He held it between both of his. 'Tell me about your breakdown.'

It felt easy to tell him. Straightforward. As they sat close beside one another in the open air, looking out over the cliffs and the sea, she told him what had happened, describing her parents' deaths, the anxiety attacks, the tour in the Flinders Ranges, Austin coming to get her, the three weeks in hospital afterwards. He listened, asked questions, taking it all in. When she finished, he lifted her hand and kissed her palm. He read the list again, in a different way this time. More seriously.

'What does it mean "you welcomed Lara into the family"? Is that the Lara who sent the fax to me?'

Harriet nodded. 'She came to live with us when she was eight. After her parents were killed in a car crash.'

'She's your foster-sister?'

She nodded.

'And you get on?'

She couldn't answer that. It was too complicated. She nodded instead. He read the list again, then folded it very carefully and gave it back to her.

'I'm sorry, Harriet. About your parents. About the breakdown.'

She didn't want to talk about herself any more. Not yet. Not here. 'I'm getting better. I am better, I think.'

'I think you're better than better.'

She reached up and kissed him. A quick, deep kiss. She saw his eyes darken.

'You shouldn't do that to me in public. I'm having enough trouble staying away from you as it is.'

'I'm sorry.'

'So am I. It's very hard to steal a kiss when there are twelve pairs of seventy-year-old eyes watching my every move.'

She told him about her conversation with Mrs Lamerton that morning. The mood lightened again.

He laughed. 'Then it's time we brought it out into the open. I'll make an announcement. "Ladies and gentlemen, I'm sorry to call off the tour but I've fallen in love with Harriet and we want to be on our own, so if you could all make your own way home . . ."'

'You haven't fallen in love with me. Not in four days.'

She was expecting another joke, but his face was serious. 'Haven't I? What is it then? What do I call the feeling I get when I see you? The way you laugh so easily, the way you make me laugh?

The way I feel when I watch you with the group, the way you look after them? The way you look after me? The way I feel when I kiss you? You delight me, Harriet. I've fallen in delight with you.' He paused. 'But not your yellow suit. I still don't like that.'

She laughed.

'Finish that game you were playing the other night when my assistant rang, Harriet. The question and answer one.'

'No. It's for teenagers, really. It's a silly party game.'

'Please. Finish it. There were two more questions, weren't there?'

'Yes.'

'Ask me.'

She tried to sound casual. 'The third one is about water.'

'I need to tell you how I feel when I think of water?'

She nodded.

'Let me think.' He held her hand against his lips. His breath was warm against her skin. She felt a response deep inside her again. 'I feel overwhelmed. Out of my depth. Uncertain, but also excited. Thirsty. You make me think of water, Harriet. Why would that be? Why would I think of water whenever I see you?'

She felt her heart beating. 'I'm not sure.'

'And the final question?'

'Your favourite animal.' Your ideal partner.

'My favourite animal,' he repeated. 'It's yellow, though not always, fortunately. Beautiful. It likes to travel. I think it's from the southern hemisphere.'

She pulled her hand away. 'You know this game, don't you? You knew it the whole time?'

He smiled. 'Of course. Everyone knows that game. What was it I said about water? I've forgotten.'

'You said it overwhelmed you. Made you feel out of your depth. Excited. Thirsty. And you said that I make you think of water.'

'I'm sorry, Harriet. That's not true. You don't make me think of water. You make me think of something else.' He whispered in her ear. Desire rushed through her again.

He leaned back. His tone was light, but she knew he was serious. 'What would you say if I asked you those questions, Harriet?'

'I wouldn't answer them.'

'No?'

'I'd tell you in a different way.'

'What would you tell me?'

'The truth.' She felt certain of it. 'That I've never felt like this with someone before. That you delight me too. That I think I've fallen in delight with you too.'

A group of tourists came down the steps behind them. Patrick stood up, drawing her up beside him. 'There's a path down to the beach. Do you suppose we could leave them in that bus for longer?'

Harriet checked her watch. 'There's only ten minutes of that episode left to go.'

'Then we'll have to hurry.'

The path was long and steep. They had barely reached the sand when he took her in his arms and pulled her against him. The kiss was different than the night before. This was hard, passionate, urgent. She felt it. She wanted to make love to him right there, and she knew he wanted her, too.

They had the beach to themselves. There was an outcrop of rocks to one side, almost a cave. From above they were hidden from view. The only noise was the waves crashing against the sand, the shrill cries of seagulls. They didn't speak. He took her in his arms again when they reached the rocks. The kisses deepened. Her desire was overwhelming. She was nearly in ecstasy from the touch of his fingers under her shirt, on her skin, on her breast. Her eyes were shut, his lips on her neck. The feeling was building, wave after wave.

'Harriet, I won't be able to stop soon.' His voice was heavy with desire.

'I don't want you to.'

They were moments from taking the next step, from forgetting where they were, when she heard her name being called. She stepped back from him, feeling half-drugged.

She wasn't imagining it. Someone was calling her name. More than one person. From high above them.

'Harriet? Are you down there?'

She came out onto the sand, away from the rocks and looked up. It was Clive, Mrs Lamerton and a man who looked like Mr Douglas, but could have been Mr Fidock.

She only just made out their words. 'Harriet, we need your help.'

'What is it? What's wrong?'

Mrs Lamerton's voice floated down, very clearly. 'The tape's jammed.'

Back in St Ives later that night, the hotel was quiet. Mr Fidock and Mr Douglas were in the bar. Several of the ladies were in the lounge area, playing cards. Others had gone to their rooms.

The whole group had ended up spending the evening together again, visiting an Italian restaurant on the waterfront for dinner and then moving on to the nautical pub. There had been an impromptu *Willoughby* quiz. Mr Fidock and Mr Douglas put on a five minute mini-play, stringing all their favourite pieces of dialogue together. It hadn't mattered to Harriet and Patrick that they weren't on their own. Even across the crowded room, it was as though they were linked.

They'd had a drink in the hotel bar with everyone when they returned. More talking, laughing. Around eleven he glanced at her. A question in his eyes. She nodded, the faintest of gestures. He left first, saying goodnight to each of the group. Twenty minutes later, Harriet followed. Mrs Lamerton was in deep conversation with Miss Boyd about the episode they'd watched that day. She showed no interest in doing any following that night.

Harriet went via her room. She quickly checked her appearance. No sign of the yellow outfit tonight, either. Just a simple, wraparound dress, dark red, worn with a soft cardigan. Only the opal bracelet for jewellery. Several of the women in the group had complimented her.

'You look so pretty,' Mrs Kempton said. Mrs Randall had nodded her head in agreement.

'Those colours are lovely on you,' Miss Talbot added. 'It makes those beautiful dark eyes of yours look all sparkly. Or is that a make-up trick again? Would you show me?'

It wasn't the make-up making her eyes sparkle. She felt alive again, she realised. The desire for Patrick, to be with him, touch him, talk to him, was giving her a confidence and a kind of joy she hadn't felt for a long time.

She knocked gently at his door and he answered. Barely a word was spoken before she moved into his arms and felt his lips on hers. They weren't in public. There was no one hammering on the door. They had talked about things she needed to hear. It had only been a short time, but she knew this was what she wanted to do, where she wanted to be, how she wanted to feel, who she wanted to be with. After months of indecision and fear and nervousness, it was overwhelming to feel so sure of something.

He kissed her lips, her neck, lower. He slowly undressed her, caressing her body, gazing down at her. She undressed him. They didn't speak. The kisses became more urgent and passionate. They moved into the bedroom and lay entwined, skin against skin. She could feel the strength of his body against her, his fingers stroking her and then the feel of him inside her. She wrapped her legs around his body, arching herself against him. She felt him hard and fast, the movement so perfect, so close and so beautiful. She held him tight, as tight as she could against her and inside her, waves of intense pleasure rippling through both of them, together.

She lay in his arms afterwards, his fingers caressing her back. She turned and looked at his face on the pillow beside her. His eyes were closed. She traced his features, touched the dark curls, the grey at the temples. She moved her hand onto his shoulder, his chest, placed her palm on his skin. She moved closer and kissed him. His eyes opened. She saw the blue of them again. She put her finger on his lips then leaned forward again and kissed him once more.

'Thank you.'

His lips curved into a smile. 'You're very welcome. Thank you, too.'

She closed her eyes, feeling him breathing under her cheek, the beating of his heart.

He touched the side of her face and then leaned over and kissed her lips. She kissed him back. He spoke, his mouth close against her ear. 'Harriet, how many of your company rules have we broken tonight?'

'So far?'

She felt his smile. 'Yes, so far.'

'Two at least. But I think they only count if I'm wearing yellow.'

He kissed her again. 'So if you're not wearing yellow I can do this any time I like?'

She was all sensation again. 'Yes, you can.'

'Would you do something for me?' His lips moved to her neck, then up to her ear.

She waited.

He whispered the words. 'Could you burn every piece of yellow clothing you own?'

Chapter Twenty-six

Austin and Nina had arrived at Cork Airport in the early afternoon. There was a lot of building work going on, cranes and bulldozers surrounding the small terminal. As the two of them climbed into a taxi outside, they could see half the sky was blue, but the half they were standing under was filled with heavy grey clouds, dumping sheets of rain on them. The weather was getting wild all over the UK and Ireland. It had been a turbulent flight. There had even been talk at Bristol Airport of flights being grounded until the storms passed.

'To the city centre, thanks,' Austin told the driver.

'Anywhere special?' the man asked. Austin noticed the sing-song accent, as he tried to decide. He and Nina had talked about it on the plane. Should they go straight to a police station? Or find a place to stay for the night and then start looking?

They decided to go to a hotel first. The taxi driver recommended one overlooking the river in the centre of town. He'd drop them right to it.

Nina was quiet on the journey in. Austin was glad of it, touched by her thoughtfulness. He had that feeling again, that he was rushing forward too quickly. These bold gestures were all very well, but why did he keep feeling foolish, out of his depth? He needed to stop, think it over again. What if they did find Lara in Cork? And what if she was in pieces? He had been able to handle Harriet on her Flinders Ranges tour, but would he cope with Lara in crisis?

They checked in to the hotel. It was clean, serviceable. All they needed for the reason they were here. Austin left his bag on the bed and returned to the foyer to wait for Nina. He stared out the window, at the river running through the city, the houses clustered on the hill above the city centre, out to green hills beyond. He felt a touch on his arm.

'Do you want to get a coffee first?' Nina asked. 'Before we get started?'

It was a good idea. They left the hotel, walked out along the river into the centre of the city and into a pub with a coloured stone front. Nina ordered two coffees. Austin caught himself looking at the crowds walking past the window.

'You're expecting to see her?'

He nodded, embarrassed. 'Mad, isn't it? Even if she did come here, she might have left already. She could have hired a car, driven anywhere.'

'She might have, but she might also be here still. Will we ring around to a few of the hotels and B&Bs? Ask if they've had a Lara Robinson staying? Someone might remember her.'

Austin had the weirdest feeling they were talking about her in the past tense. 'She's fine. I know she is.'

'Of course she is.'

They were both quiet, sipping their coffee. 'Austin, why didn't Lara ever change her surname to Turner?'

'Mum and Dad never officially adopted her. They were her legal guardians, but I think they thought it would be too traumatic if she had to go through the whole adoption process, talking about her parents. She called my mum and dad her guardian angels.'

'That's nice.'

'She loved them a lot.'

'Was it hard on Harriet, your other sister?'

'When Lara arrived? No, I think she thought it was great. Like getting an instant sister.'

'I'd find it hard.'

'Would you?'

'Well, if you'd been the littlest, the only girl, and suddenly you had to share the position with another girl.'

'I never thought about it like that.'

After coffee, they stopped at a shop to buy two umbrellas. The rain was coming down in sheets now, yet there was still a tantalising patch of blue on the horizon. Taunting them, Austin thought. He walked along a pedestrianised street, dodging tourists and shoppers, taking in the Irish names and lettering above the shops, pointing some out to Nina. He heard several different languages being spoken. A newspaper seller's cry kept echoing through the air. They had walked down two streets when she stopped him, putting her hand on his arm.

'Austin, we're not going to find her like this. We need to look properly. Have a plan. Let's go to the police.'

'They won't be interested. She left voluntarily. There's nothing they can do.'

'They'd have records of car crashes, though, wouldn't they? Maybe that's what Lara did, flew in here, found out from the police where her parents were killed and made her way there. So we have to copy her.'

'Follow in her footsteps?'

A glimmer of her smile. 'Like all good TV detectives. Come on.'

The main police station was easy to find, down from the city hall, away from the river. A modern building, the foyer was big and airy, an atrium filled with light and marble pillars. The policeman behind the desk was in his mid-twenties, red-cheeked, sweet-faced.

Austin introduced himself and Nina. 'We're looking for my sister. She flew to Cork four days ago and we're trying to find her.'

'You're reporting a missing person?'

'Not exactly. She left voluntarily. We don't know for sure where she is.' He explained about Lara's parents being killed in a car crash. 'We don't know where, but we think it might have been here in Cork somewhere. Would you have details of accidents going back more than twenty years?'

'We would, but you'd have to put in an application to get the files. That could take a week or more. Unless one of the people here remembered the case. I could ask if you like?'

'Would you? That would be a real help. We're short on time.'

'Can you give me more details? The names and the dates?'

'Their surname was Robinson. Rose and . . .' Austin stopped, thinking hard. 'Sorry, I can't remember her father's name. It was around the middle of March, twenty-four years ago.'

'They hit another car, or was it a single vehicle incident?'

Austin had a flash of their car hurtling off the road after hitting a patch of gravel, before realising he was thinking of the story Harriet had written for her school magazine. 'I'm sorry, I don't know.'

They waited as the young man made a phone call and repeated the details to someone. Austin had to stop himself from leaning over the counter and taking the phone himself. Nina put her hand on his arm. He relaxed.

The man hung up and shook his head. 'I'm sorry, it's not ringing bells with anyone. But that doesn't mean it didn't happen around here. Have you tried the newspaper office down the road? It would have made the news, especially the fact it was tourists. It's not far, if you want to give them a try.'

The rain had slowed to a light drizzle by the time they reached the newspaper office, a glass-fronted building, with a row of framed front pages along the outside wall. Austin pushed open the door, letting Nina go in first.

A middle-aged woman was dusting the counter as they came in. Austin explained what they were looking for.

'Oh, I'm sorry, I can't help you there,' she said. 'We only keep six months worth of back issues here. The city library has them all on microfilm and hard copy, though.'

'It's like a treasure hunt,' Nina said as they walked outside again.

Not quite, Austin thought.

The Cork City Library was on Grand Parade, two blocks away. Austin and Nina were directed upstairs to the local history section. The room was lit by fluorescent lights and lined with glass-fronted cabinets filled with old books. There were several wooden tables, chairs, and a photocopy machine. A doorway led to another room filled with racks of shelving, each shelf holding rows of black folders. The man behind the counter listened as Austin explained once more what they were looking for.

'We should be able to help you. There are two local papers, *The Examiner* and the *Southern Star*, which covers the Clonakilty and Skibbereen area, west of here. From twenty years ago, did you say? Can you be more exact with the date?'

'Middle of March, twenty-four years ago.'

The librarian was back five minutes later with a large black folder, holding the newspapers from March and April of that year. Austin and Nina followed him across the room to a table.

'Let me know if that's not the one you want. We've got decades worth you can look through.'

'Thanks,' Austin said. He and Nina pulled their chairs close to the table, turned the heavy cardboard cover and started leafing through the pages.

They found it in the sixth newspaper they opened. Austin knew it was Lara's parents as soon as he saw the headline on the top of page three. It was all there. The names. The right date. The right location.

'Oh my God,' Nina breathed.

Austin reached for her hand without thinking. He held it tightly as they both stared at the page.

Tourists found dead in family tragedy

An Australian couple was found dead in a holiday cottage outside Clonakilty yesterday in what gardai described as 'a terrible family tragedy'.

The bodies of Dennis Robinson (38) and his wife Rose (35) from Melbourne, Victoria, were discovered when the cottage owner called to the house shortly after 8.30 a.m. It is believed they may have been dead for up to two days.

Gardai said Mr Robinson had stab wounds to the chest and abdomen. The cause of his wife's death is not yet known, but foul play is not suspected.

Although still trying to establish what happened in the hours leading up to the deaths gardai have confirmed they are not seeking anyone else.

'At this stage it has the appearance of a terrible family tragedy,' a spokesman said.

The state pathologist carried out a preliminary examination at the scene yesterday morning. Later, the bodies were removed to Cork Regional Hospital where a further post-mortem examination is due to be carried out today.

The cottage owner, Mrs Flor O'Regan, who lives nearby, said she was 'completely shocked' by the discovery. She called to the house because she had not seen the couple for two days, she said.

'They booked the cottage for a week and arrived four days ago,' Mrs O'Regan added. 'They said they'd been in England before coming here.

'The woman mentioned she had Irish connections – her mother or grandmother, I think – but I don't know if she had any relatives still living in this country.

'It's hard to understand how something like this could happen. It's tragic.'

'Austin, it's a nightmare.' Nina was very shocked. 'Are you sure it's them?'

'It has to be. The same names. The right dates.' He read it again. 'It's them.'

'It's not an awful coincidence? Another couple with the same name?'

'It's them,' he repeated. He knew right then that Lara had discovered this too.

'But I don't understand it. Why would Lara have been told they'd died in a car crash?'

'I don't know.'

'And what does it mean foul play wasn't suspected? They were both found dead, weren't they? Doesn't that count as foul play?'

Austin shook his head, pointing at the page. 'He had stab wounds. The cause of her death was still to be confirmed, yet the police aren't looking for anyone else. It means . . .'

Nina stared at the newspaper. 'It means Lara's mother killed Lara's father and then she killed herself.'

Austin nodded. He read the article again. 'It doesn't say how, just that tests were being carried out. It must have been an overdose of something. Any other method would have been obvious.'

'Oh my God, Austin.' She turned away from the article. 'Do you think Lara has seen this too? That this is why she disappeared?'

'It must be.' Had she done just as they had? Come here, looked up the newspapers? Or rung the police? He had an awful image of her, innocently going into a police station or this room, wanting to know the location of her parents' car crash, doing it privately, without letting any of them know. And then discovering this, as they had. But on her own.

Nina turned to him. 'What do we do now?'

'We ring Gloria,' he said.

An hour later they were both in Austin's hotel room, sitting side by side on his bed, a copy of the newspaper article between them. Austin had started to dial Gloria's number before realising it was the middle of the night in Australia. This was urgent, but it would have to wait. He was counting down the minutes.

'Austin, shouldn't you ring the rest of your family?' Nina said. 'Your sister? Your brother?'

He knew he should, but he didn't want to. Not yet. He needed to talk to Gloria before any of them. She had been his mother's best friend. She might be able to shed even the smallest amount of light on all of this.

'I want to talk to Gloria first.' He checked the time again. Still too early. But only just. His mind was racing through all they had learned. He turned to Nina again. 'What would you do next if you were Lara, Nina? If you'd somehow found all this out?'

She thought about it. 'I'd go to the holiday cottage,' she said.

'To the house?' His horror must have shown on his face.

'You'd need to. It would be something you'd have to do. I would, anyway.'

It took just a few phone calls to find out where the house was. They started with *The Examiner* office. The reporter who had written the article had long retired. They were advised to ring the *Southern Star*, the local Clonakilty paper. The news editor at the *Southern Star* knew of the story, but hadn't been working there at the time. He suggested they ring the local gardai. The garda who answered said yes, he did know the house. Someone else had been in asking about it a few days before, in fact.

Austin went still. 'An Australian woman?'

'Yes.'

Austin took down the name of the house. It was now called Glen View. It had changed names, and owners, several times in the past twenty-four years. The garda said he thought a German couple owned it now. A local property company managed the holiday rentals.

Austin got the after-hours phone number of the property company from directory inquiries. He hesitated before dialling it. 'Lara might be gone already, mightn't she? She might have had a look at the house and driven away. She could be back in England by now. In Australia, even. Maybe it would be better if we just had a quick look ourselves and then went back to Bath, in case she —'

Nina interrupted. 'Austin, I need to say something to you. I don't think it should be me here. I think it should be you and your sister. You have to ring her. The two of you should be doing this together.'

He still didn't want to ring Harriet. Not yet. 'Let me ring this number first. See what I can find out.' He dialled the number. 'Oh, hello there.' He exaggerated his Australian accent, ignoring Nina's surprised look. 'I wonder if you can help me. My little sister's over here travelling around Ireland on holiday and I'm trying to track her down to give her a surprise. Has she been in to your office to enquire about holiday properties by any chance? Her name's Lara. Lara Robinson.'

He waited. Nina sat still beside him.

'Two days ago. Brilliant. Right. Yes please.' He grabbed a piece of paper and started scribbling down directions. 'Thanks for your help. No, it's a big surprise, so please don't tell her I'm coming if she happens to get in touch. Bye.'

The cheery tone disappeared as soon as he hung up. 'Lara's there. She's rented Glen View.'

Chapter Twenty-Seven

In Merryn Bay, Gloria was lying in bed, wide awake, waiting for the alarm clock to go off. Kevin was snoring quietly beside her. She'd had barely any sleep. She'd been too shocked and too angry to sleep. But the decision had been made. She was resigning from Turner Travel. As soon as Melissa got back from Melbourne.

She and Kevin had spent the evening talking about it. After she had hung up from Matheson Travel for the second time, she had moved into action. She had closed Turner Travel early, putting on the answering machine, pulling down the blind and locking the door. She'd practically run home and bundled Kevin into the car before he had a chance to protest.

She'd driven to another seaside town further down the coast, to their favourite restaurant. It was a small Italian trattoria, with red and white checked tablecloths, straw-covered chianti bottles, and a simple menu of pasta and pizza. They loved it. They felt comfortable and the food was always delicious. It was where they had gone over the years whenever they had something to discuss or to celebrate, either themselves or with their three boys. They hadn't been there since Kevin had gone blind.

Gloria barely let him get a word in at first, veering between disbelief and anger, going over and over her conversation with the people from Matheson Travel.

'You're sure you're not mistaken,' Kevin asked. 'Would she actually do something like that?'

'Of course she'd do it. She'd sell Molly if she was offered a good price. Can you believe it, Kev? She must have thought all her Christmases had come at once when Harriet had to leave on the *Willoughby* tour. All the Turners out of the way.'

'You don't think James knows?

'I haven't a clue. She walks all over him. Perhaps he knows and she's sworn him to secrecy. She probably broke his leg for him, so he'd be out of the way as well.'

'You a little bit angry about this, love?'

'I'm furious, Kev. Years of service and this is how she repays me. Sneaking around behind my back.'

'Is that it really?'

She stopped, and took a breath. 'No, it's not. That's not what it is. You're right. I've been well-paid. It's a job. It's not about being repaid. It's about not being told beforehand. It's the final straw.'

'For who? You or the Turner kids?'

She gave a half-smile. 'That's it, isn't it? I'm angry but on whose behalf any more? Whether James knows yet or not is immaterial. He agrees with everything Melissa does anyway. Austin doesn't care about the business and I don't know if he ever really did. I don't know for sure if this is where Harriet wants to be or should be any more. I think Lara needs to spread her wings. Going to England was part of it, I'm sure.' She shook her head. 'Listen to me, Kev. I probably know more about the Turner children than I do about our own boys.'

'That's not true.'

'No, it isn't. But it nearly is. I'm going to resign.'

'You're over-reacting.'

'No, I'm not. I'm tired, Kev. I want to stay home with you.' She leaned across and tightly gripped his hand. She could feel all the years of physical work in the rough skin, the strength in his fingers. Just thinking of the idea of him being taken away from her, as Neil had been from Penny. All the regret she would feel, that they hadn't done the things they'd been planning and talking about for years. It was going to be up to her to make those things happen, she realised. She had forced Kev into coming to this restaurant tonight because she had been so angry she wouldn't take no for an answer. Look what had happened. He'd thoroughly enjoyed himself. No one had taken any notice of them. He had spilt only one thing, and so what? There were worse things in the world than a blind man spilling a bit of soup on a tablecloth. Tonight was the start of their new life, she decided. They were going to go and do whatever they wanted, whenever they wanted. The two of them.

'You've been too quiet for too long,' he said. 'I can hear your mind ticking from here. You know that makes me nervous.'

'I'm hatching a few plans, now you mention it.'

'Let me guess. You're going to stay at home and watch me for hours every day? Not let me out of your sight?'

'That's it.'

'Be a bit boring for you, won't it?'

'Yes. So you better start learning a few tricks.'

'I've always wanted to try juggling or fire-eating.'

'Perfect,' she said, knowing he would hear the smile in her voice. 'We'll sit around to begin with. Just so we get to know each other again. But it's time we starting doing more stuff together, too. Not just around the house, either. I think we should take a few trips. Just get in the car and head off somewhere.'

'Like where?'

'I don't know. Up the coast to Queensland. Take the ferry to

Tasmania, drive around there for a couple of weeks. We could even drive over to Perth if we wanted to.'

'That all sounds pretty good.'

'You think so? Good.'

'There's just one big problem, though.'

'What's that, love?'

'I'm not sure I can do my share of the driving.'

She was suddenly laughing and crying at the same time. 'I don't mind, Kev. I don't mind one bit.'

It had been after one by the time they got home. They had lain in bed talking for another hour. Gloria checked the time now. Nearly six. She might as well get up. She switched off the alarm before it sounded. She'd get ready for work and then make Kev's tea. She wished Melissa was going to be in the office today. She was in the mood for a showdown.

She had just filled the kettle when the sound of the phone ringing made her jump. She snatched it up quickly before the noise woke Kev.

'Gloria, it's Austin. How are things?'

He'd barely given her time to say hello. How were things? Where did she start? She had found out Melissa was selling the business from under them, she had decided to resign and she'd been up all night talking about it. 'There's been a fair bit going on over here, Austin, to tell you the truth.'

He wasn't listening. 'Gloria, I'm in Cork. We've been looking at the newspapers. We've found out what happened and it's terrible. Lara's parents weren't killed in a car crash. It was a murder–suicide. Lara's mother killed her father, and then killed herself.'

Gloria couldn't answer. She'd waited twenty-four years to hear someone else say it and now the day had come she felt no relief, no sadness. She just felt numb.

'Gloria? Did you hear what I said?'

'Yes, Austin, I did.'

'Aren't you shocked?'

'No, I'm not.' She had no reason to be shocked. She realised what she felt was complete and overwhelming exhaustion.

'You're not? Why not?'

'Because I already knew.'

'You *knew*? You knew the car crash never happened?'

At last she didn't have to pretend. 'Yes, I did. I've known for twenty-four years.' She waited for the flare of temper. He didn't disappoint her.

'I can't believe this. We've been looking for her, worrying about her and you knew the whole time? Knew Cork was probably where she was going? That this was what she was going to find out? And you said *nothing*?'

'I made a promise to your mother.'

He raised his voice. 'For Christ's sake, Gloria. My mother is dead. How could you do this to Lara?'

Twenty-four years of anger welled in Gloria. How dare he talk to her like that? How dare he sound so self-righteous? She'd had enough.

'How could I do this to Lara?' Her voice was as loud as his. 'How could your mother do this to me? Do you think I wanted to be the secret keeper? The one who knew? Of course I didn't. How do you think it has been for me, Austin? It was your family, your secret. I never wanted to know, back then, or even now. I loved your parents, and I love all of you children, but I didn't want this. I never wanted it. And don't you ever, *ever* talk to me like that again.'

'I'm sorry.'

She was beyond apologies. 'You need to be more than sorry. If you stopped thinking about yourself and your own selfish charmed life for one moment, and looked out into the world occasionally, Austin Turner, then you'd have the right to talk to me like this. But you don't. So you have no right to question my relationship with your mother and you have no right to tell me what I should or shouldn't have said to you, to Lara, or to anyone. It was your mother who made the decision, Austin. She decided to change the story that night. She did it to protect Lara. She thought she was too young to hear something so terrible. That it would change the way people would treat her in Merryn Bay. And perhaps she was right, perhaps she was wrong. I don't know. All I know is I have hated knowing all these years and I still hate it.'

There was a shocked silence. 'Gloria, are you all right?'

'No, Austin. I'm not all right.'

'I'm sorry, Gloria, I'm really sorry.' A long pause. 'I'm sorry.'

There was a long silence and then Gloria spoke again. 'Tell me. What did you find out? And how?'

He told her, in a subdued voice. Gloria didn't interrupt. There was nothing she hadn't already known, nothing Penny hadn't told her that night. She knew some extra details, in fact. She knew Lara's mother had lain down next to her husband's dead body after she had taken the pills. She had been found wrapped around him, holding on to him. There was a bottle of vodka beside them. Her blood alcohol level had been at a dangerous level. The police hadn't known whether she had drunk the vodka before she killed her husband or afterwards. Gloria kept those details to herself. Austin had no need to hear them now, if ever.

'Lara must have learnt all this too, mustn't she?' Austin said. 'If we found it, she must have too.'

'I think so, yes.'

'How would she have known where to look? Had Mum told her anything?'

'I know she told her the crash happened near Cork. That would have been enough to start with. Had she been at the library, too?'

'We asked the librarian. He hadn't seen her. She might have found out some other way. The police, perhaps. Gloria, it's horrible.'

'Yes, it is.'

'What will this have done to her?'

'I don't know.' She had calmed down a little. 'I hoped at first when she went missing that it was something else. Then when you rang and said you'd found out she'd gone to Ireland, I knew she must have discovered the truth.'

'She must be so angry. So hurt. She probably thinks we knew all this time and none of us ever told her. That's even worse. It would explain so much. Why she left so suddenly. Why she left the tour. Left Harriet like that. That's why I knew it had to be something bad. She wouldn't have done that to Harriet otherwise.'

Gloria felt the exhaustion again. 'Austin, did you know that Lara and Harriet have barely spoken in the past three months?'

'They haven't? But they're so close. They grew up together. Have they had a fight?'

'Are they close? I've never really known. But yes, I think they have had a fight.' Once upon a time she would have kept her observation to herself. Now she wanted to unload every Turner secret she had. 'Something happened with your mother's death. I don't know what. Something that upset Harriet terribly.'

'She wasn't there when Mum died, I know that. Or Dad. But she came to terms with it, didn't she? And is it important right now?'

'Yes, it is. It's another fact about your family. Or is this how it will always be with you all? Hiding things, not saying anything and then suffering the consequences after?'

'Gloria, I'm sorry, but I don't know what you're talking about.'

She felt the wave of tiredness again. 'It's all right, Austin. I don't know either.'

'What do I do about Lara, Gloria? Do I go to the house? To Glen View?'

Her head was hurting. She felt like she had spent more time over the years worrying about the Turners than about her own family. She massaged her temples, trying to concentrate. 'I don't know, Austin.'

'I think I should. And I think Harriet should be there too. That feels like the right thing to do. So Lara knows we care about her.'

'Then that's what you should do.'

'But what do I say to her, Gloria?'

It was simple, at last. 'You tell her the truth, Austin. You tell her that you love her. That we all love her. And that we're sorry. For everything.'

She said goodbye then. There was nothing else to say. She had just hung up and leaned back against the chair, shutting her eyes, when she heard a noise and felt a hand on her shoulder. She turned.

It was Kevin. 'You want to tell me what that was all about, love?'

In Cork, Nina was hearing no arguments. 'Now, Austin. You ring your sister now.'

'It's a bit late. I don't know if I should.'

'Austin, ring her. You can't keep something like this to yourself any longer. Your whole family has to know.'

He tried Harriet's mobile number. It was switched to voicemail. He was about to speak when he hung up. 'I can't leave a message.

It's going to be hard enough as it is telling her news like this over the phone.'

'Then leave a message asking her to ring you back.'

'I'll try her tomorrow.'

'Why not now?'

It was complicated. He was worried news like this might tip Harriet over the edge again. But Nina was right about the whole family needing to know. He already had the other number he needed from the time he'd rung the hospital the night Lara went missing. It was early, but hospitals started early. He dialled and was put straight through this time.

'James, it's Austin. I'm sorry if I woke you up.'

'Austin? You didn't, don't worry. Have you got news on Lara?'

'I have. It's not good news, either.' Austin told him everything.

James was silent for a time. Then he spoke. 'Shit, Austin. You don't think she's gone there to kill herself too, do you?'

James had said out loud what Austin was thinking. 'I don't know. Maybe. That's why I want to get there as soon as I can.'

'You're going on your own? What about Harriet? Wouldn't it be better if you were both there?'

'Of course it would. I've tried her phone but I just got voicemail. You don't know where she'd be at the moment, do you? Is there another number for her I could try?'

'Hold on, I've got the itinerary here.' Austin heard a rustling of paper. 'They've had a free evening. Tomorrow's the last day of the tour. They're doing a quick trip to Marazion to see St Michael's Mount, then it's their farewell lunch. Mrs Lamerton's organised a *Willoughby* quiz for that, I think. And Mrs Kempton's got a Patch jumper that she's going to give Patrick Shawcross.'

Austin shut his eyes. Spare me the details, James.

James was still reading. 'After lunch they go by bus to Bath to link up with the other tour company for the *All Creatures Great and Small* and *Monarch of the Glen* tours. Harriet drops Patrick Shawcross at Bristol Airport so he can fly back to Boston and then she'll be free for a week. She could get to you in the afternoon. Could it wait till then?'

Austin ran his fingers through his hair. How the hell did he know? Was Lara at this moment getting ready to kill herself? Had she already done it? 'I don't know. How would you react if you found out something like this, James? If it had been our parents?'

James fell quiet again. 'I'd be shocked. Horrified. Angry. But Austin, I can also see why Mum would have kept it secret. Do you remember it all happened so quickly? Mum told us about Mr and Mrs Robinson being killed and then Lara was living with us the next day. I can see why Mum might have said something like that to begin with. What I can't understand is why she didn't tell Lara the truth when she was older.' He answered his own query. 'Though where would you start? When would you decide it was the right age to tell someone something like that. The poor kid.'

Not kid. Lara was thirty-two. But then so was Harriet, and Austin still thought of her as a kid. He was still puzzling over what Gloria had said about the relationship being tricky between Harriet and Lara. He didn't think it was true. They had always been best of friends, hadn't they? There must have been a few spats – he remembered Harriet storming off once or twice, but she had gone through a storming off phase for a few years. Was it because of Lara, though? He needed to talk about it. 'James, what did you think when Lara came to live with us?'

'I liked her. I've always liked her. She's my sister as far as I'm concerned. She's a brilliant tour guide too.'

'She didn't change your life?'

'Change it? In what way?'

'Affect you? Bother you?'

'No, it was just good to have another sister. It made it easier to play some of those games, with four of us instead of three. I suppose if it affected anyone, it was Harriet. She bore the brunt of it.'

'Bore the brunt?'

'Well, Harriet had been Mum and Dad's number one girl for eight years. Ours too. So I'd say it was tough for her at first when Lara came along.'

'Maybe you're right.' Nina had said that too. So had Gloria. Why hadn't he seen any of this? What had he been doing the whole time they were growing up? 'Harriet's doing really well with that *Willoughby* tour, by the way. That actor was singing her praises.'

'I'm not surprised. She just lost her confidence there for a while.'

James was making too much sense. Being too knowledgeable. Austin was feeling more and more confused. 'I'd better go. Thanks for your help.' He was surprised how helpful James had been. He felt a shimmer of guilt. Just because he didn't like James's wife didn't mean he and James couldn't get on. He was his only brother, after all. Perhaps he should have kept in touch a bit more . . .

'So you'll ring Harriet now?' James said. 'Get her to come as soon as she can? I think you should. I think it would be better for Lara if there were two of you.'

'I'll call her right now.'

'Keep me up-to-date, will you?'

'Sure.' He forced himself to ask the question. 'And Melissa's okay?'

'Fine. In Melbourne for a couple of days.'

'And Molly? All fine with her?'

'No worries at all,' James said.

In Merryn Bay, Molly was curled up on top of the bedspread, her face pressed into the pillow, trying to muffle her tears. Nobody had ever told her it would hurt this much. She wanted her mum. She wanted her dad. She wanted Lara and Harriet and all her family around her. She didn't want to be a grown-up. She wanted to be a kid again.

CHAPTER TWENTY-EIGHT

An hour later Austin still hadn't managed to get Harriet on the phone. He was getting anxious. 'Her mobile keeps ringing out. And she's not in her room, either. She can't have gone far, can she?'

'Maybe she's with one of the guests,' Nina said. 'Can you ask to be put through to another room, in case she's there?'

'I don't know the name of any of the guests. I only know the actor's name. The special guest.'

'Try his room, then. He might know where she is.'

Austin dialled the number of the St Ives hotel again. 'Could you put me through to Patrick Shawcross's room please?'

Harriet was in Patrick's bed, being kissed slowly and beautifully, her body coming alive again under Patrick's fingers. She stroked his naked body, too, loving the feel of his skin, loving —

The noise of the phone on the bedside table was like an alarm, making them both jump. They ignored it at first. It kept going. They reluctantly separated. Patrick reached out a brown arm to the receiver.

'Hello?' He listened. 'She is, yes. Just a moment.' He turned to Harriet. 'It's for you. It's your brother.'

Five minutes later, Harriet was still in Patrick's bed, naked, the sheet wrapped around her. He was half-dressed, wearing jeans, sitting at the end of the bed, watching her, his expression concerned.

She still couldn't make sense of what Austin was saying to her. Since she'd taken the phone he hadn't stopped talking about flight schedules and Nina and Ireland and police and he still hadn't told her what he'd found out about Lara. All he had said was he knew where Lara was and he wanted Harriet to fly to Cork as soon as possible and go with him to see her.

She finally managed to interrupt him. 'Austin, please, slow down for a minute. I can't come just like that. I can't abandon the tour group.'

'You won't be abandoning them. I told you. Nina's offered to come over and take your place. I've checked out all the flights. She can fly in just before you fly out tomorrow. There'll be enough time for a handover. And don't worry, Nina will be great. She's worked in her parents' restaurant for years, she's good with people. She knows the area. She'll get them to the meeting place in Bath and she can make sure Patrick Shawcross gets his flight too.'

'Austin, I'm sorry, but I still don't understand. You ring out of the blue, you won't tell me anything, you say I have to get to Cork for Lara's sake . . .'

'It's not something I want to tell you over the phone. It's awful news. Really awful news.'

Her breath caught. 'She's not —?'

'No, she's not dead. I haven't seen her yet, but she's alive.' As far as he knew. 'It's about her parents.'

The relief made Harriet impatient with him again. 'Austin, we've talked about this. That's Lara's business, not ours. If she needs to visit where the crash happened, we have to respect that, don't we? Give her some space?'

'It's not that simple. There was more to it than that.'

'What do you mean more to it? Was it drunk-driving? Was someone else killed in the crash?'

He had no choice. 'Harriet, Lara's parents didn't die in a car crash. Lara's mother killed her father, then killed herself. In a holiday cottage outside Cork. That's where Lara is. She's staying in the cottage right now.'

'No.'

'Yes.'

'No, that can't be true. You must have confused them with someone else.'

'Harriet, it's them. It's their names. The right dates. It's them. I've read the newspaper report. Spoken to the local police.'

'You're sure that's what happened? It wasn't an accident?'

'It wasn't an accident. She stabbed him and then she took an overdose.'

Harriet felt a chill. 'But how could that have been hidden from us? Surely people would have known?'

'It happened on the other side of the world. It was more than twenty years ago. There was no Internet. I don't know how, Harriet, but it happened.'

'But why would the police lie about a thing like that?'

'It wasn't the police. It was Mum.'

'Mum?'

'Mum made up the story about the car crash and the only person she told the truth to was Gloria. I don't think it was deliberate lying. Gloria said it was to protect Lara.'

'Gloria knew too? All this time? And she didn't say anything?'

'She made a promise to Mum.'

'But you don't keep a promise in these circumstances.'

'Gloria did.' He told her everything Gloria had said to him.

They were both silent for a long time afterwards. Then Harriet spoke again. 'Would Lara think we all knew already? That we've always known and kept it from her?'

'Maybe. I think so. It would explain why she disappeared so suddenly. Why she hasn't been in contact with any of us. Harriet, I'm going to go to the house tomorrow. We need to talk to her. I need you to be there too.'

'Of course I should be there. I want to be there.' She didn't hesitate. 'But Austin, I'm worried about the group being on their own. They're old people.'

'I told you, Nina can take over. She'll be able to handle anything that comes up. I'll arrange what I can from here, get all your flights sorted out. There's only a couple during the day, we haven't got a lot of choice. And I think you should read the newspaper report before you get here, as well. Let it sink in. I don't want to shock you any more than I already have. That's why I didn't want to tell you over the phone. I know you're still fragile —'

'I'm all right, Austin. I've been all right for a while. I can handle more than any of you think I can. I just can't believe it. Any of it.'

'It's true. It's horrible but it's true. I'll fax the article to you now, Harriet. And I'll see you tomorrow.'

'See you, Austin.'

She hung up, and turned, ashen-faced, to Patrick.

Nina was waiting when Austin came back to his room after faxing the article to Harriet's hotel.

He started talking as soon as he came in. 'You're still sure you don't mind taking over the tour? It should be fairly simple. You'll be handing them on to another tour leader within a couple of hours. Think of them as a flock of sheep being moved from one field to another.'

'I'll be fine. Do you need to let anyone else know it'll be me? Or can you and Harriet just change things like this?'

Austin had thought about it. It was a Turner Travel tour and he and Harriet were Turners, weren't they? They were allowed to sort it out between themselves. 'No, it's fine. I'll take responsibility for it all. As I said, it's straightforward anyway. Meet them all at the airport, take the group to the other tour company meeting point and then make sure Patrick Shawcross gets his flight home.'

She nodded. 'What's he like? Not a prima donna or anything?'

'No. He seemed nice enough. Friendly.' He got a mental image of Harriet and Patrick Shawcross together. He realised something else. Harriet had been in Patrick's room when he rang. 'Nina, could you ever have a fling with a much older man?'

'I've heard of sudden subject changes —'

'I'm sorry. My mind's all over the place. It's something I thought I saw when I was in St Ives. And something I realised now.'

'About Patrick Shawcross and one of the tour group?'

'About Patrick Shawcross and my sister.'

'Did she say something to you?'

He shook his head. 'No. It was just a feeling when I met him. The way he looked at her, or she looked at him. Something, anyway.' He knew the look well, from his own experiences with women over the years. 'And she was in his room tonight. Now.'

'How much older is he than her?'

'Harriet's thirty-two. I'd say he's in his mid-forties.'

'That's nothing. You made it sound like he was in his eighties.

You're not suffering from protective older brother syndrome, are you?'

'I am her older brother.'

'And how old did you say your sister was? Thirteen or thirty-two?'

'It's just she's been shaky lately.'

'So maybe what she needs is a nice big affair to get her back on her feet. Nothing like it to soothe the spirit, so I hear.'

'You're supposed to be on my side.'

'No, I'm not. Leave her alone, Austin. She's a grown woman.' She seemed to realise it wasn't a laughing matter. She went across and pulled Austin into a hug. 'I'm sorry, she's your sister, but that's what I think.'

He hugged her back. She felt good. 'You're probably right. I forgive you.'

She looked up at him. 'You're sure? I'd hate to leave you on bad terms.'

'I'm sure,' he said. She didn't just feel good. She felt better than good. He leaned down and kissed her.

After Austin called, Harriet quickly dressed and collected his fax from reception. She stood in the foyer and read the newspaper article three times.

She returned to Patrick's room. He'd asked her to come back. He read the fax while she sat at the table opposite and watched his face. He looked up, serious. 'It's terrible. It's a terrible thing to find out.'

'I have to go there. We need to see her, to talk to her. My brother and I.'

'Of course. Do you want to go tonight?'

She shook her head. Austin had already told her there were no flights that night. 'Tomorrow.'

He offered to take charge of the group. She explained about Nina coming over. He asked more, about Lara, about her arrival in the Turner family. The stories spilled from Harriet. She spoke about it in a way she hadn't before with anyone. The entire time the fax lay on the table between them.

She didn't stay with him that night. She couldn't. Something had shifted inside her. It was as if her confidence had gone. That happiness. It didn't seem right to feel good, to want to be in Patrick's arms, in his bed, when Lara was alone in the house where her parents had died so violently. Harriet kept getting terrible images in her head, of Lara mimicking her mother, taking pills, bringing it all in some terrible full circle.

She told Patrick she was sorry. She told him the truth, that it didn't feel right. She said goodnight and went back to her own room. She undressed, brushed her teeth, tried to read. Nothing was calming her. She tried to picture Lara's parents as they had been, not in the way the article had described them. All she had was a child's eye view, from the time they came to collect Lara, a few months before they died. She tried to picture Lara's mother, summoning only a hazy image of dark hair and nervous laughter. Her voice on the phone all the times she would ring and Harriet would answer. It was so hard to reconcile those images with thoughts of a woman stabbing her husband, then killing herself, abandoning her only child.

She couldn't sleep. She couldn't stop thinking about Lara, what this all meant for her, what it meant for their whole family. She kept trying to understand why her mother would have invented the story of the car crash. Thinking again and again of the horror that had happened to Lara's parents. And thinking, more than anything, of how Lara must be feeling right now.

The handover took place in front of Bristol Airport in the early afternoon, exactly as Austin had arranged.

Harriet had explained the situation to the group at breakfast time. She kept it simple, mentioning sudden family business, hoping they'd understand if she didn't go into detail about it and promising they would all be in safe hands with Nina. Only Mrs Lamerton had muttered about a revolving-door system of tour guides.

The final outing of the tour had been a short journey along the coast to Marazion, and a boat trip over to the small island and dramatic castle of St Michael's Mount. Harriet only half heard Patrick's talk about the *Willoughby* filming that had taken place there. He didn't seem to be telling any unusual stories. He kept it short, in fact.

On the way back to St Ives for their farewell lunch she sat in the guide's seat, looking out the front window, intensely conscious that he was sitting behind her. She knew he was concerned. She knew they needed to talk more.

There wasn't the opportunity. They returned from the bus trip with just enough time to change before they were due in the dining room. It was a lively lunch. Mrs Lamerton called out *Willoughby* quiz questions and answered most of them herself. There was some shifting of seats around the dining table to get close to Patrick for the final time, but several women in the group were already looking to the next trip, talking aloud about their favourite scenes from *All Creatures Great and Small* and *Monarch of the Glen*. Harriet made a short speech, thanking them all and presenting a bottle of whisky to Clive. The group gave her a big box of chocolates and a card they'd all signed. Mrs Kempton presented Patrick with her handknitted jumper, with the little Patch embroidered on the bottom right-hand corner. He put it on. It was at least three sizes too big. There was a lot of laughter. Harriet felt as if she was a long way away, watching it all from a distance.

Patrick had come straight to her in the breakfast room that morning. Touched her arm. 'Harriet? Are you all right? Did you sleep? Can I do anything?'

'Thank you, but no, I don't think so.'

'We need to talk. Will you have time after breakfast? Can you come to my room?'

She nodded. Twenty minutes later she was on her way to him when Mrs Kempton called out to her in the corridor. She'd lost not only her glasses but also her passport. She also had a row of small buttons on her shirt that she needed help with. It set off a domino effect in the group. Mr and Mrs Douglas broke a zip on their suitcase. The lens fell out of Miss Boyd's reading glasses. Miss Talbot lost her macintosh. Harriet had to phone Patrick to say she couldn't come yet.

There was a moment after lunch when she and Patrick were alone, but then Mr and Mrs Douglas insisted on a group photo and urged everyone outside to the hotel steps. Then she needed to make sure all their luggage was out of their rooms and on the bus. There were more last-minute hitches. Miss Talbot lost her macintosh again. Mr Fidock couldn't remember the combination of his in-room safe. Mrs Lamerton decided she wanted to take the *Willoughby* videos on the next tour with her and needed another bag to carry them in.

Now they were at Bristol Airport and they still hadn't had a chance to talk.

Nina had arrived on the early flight from Cork. She was waiting in front of the airport when they drove up in the bus. Austin had described her as small and very pretty. Harriet liked her immediately. She introduced her to Patrick, and had a strong sensation Nina knew something about them or had picked up something. The way she looked at him and then her, as if she knew. Perhaps it was obvious. Nina told Patrick she would come back as soon as she had dropped off the group in Bath to make sure he made his Boston flight. He thanked her but said there was no need for her to come back, that he was happy to look after himself.

Harriet's flight to Cork was already boarding. There was just enough time for her and Patrick to say goodbye to the tour group. They lost three minutes when Mrs Kempton announced she couldn't find her glasses anywhere. Clive eventually found them under one of the seats.

Patrick climbed on to the bus first. All the women hugged him goodbye and more than half of them kissed him, too. Mr Douglas and Mr Fidock hugged him as well. Clive just shook his hand.

Harriet said goodbye to them one by one. It wasn't even a final farewell. She'd be meeting them again in Bath in a week or so and escorting them back to Australia. Not only that, many of them lived near Merryn Bay, so she would see them again. She was still sad.

Clive started up the bus. Nina climbed on board and belted herself into the tour guide seat. She looked at home and very capable, Harriet thought as she waved goodbye.

Patrick walked her to the departures gate. The boarding sign was flashing. The flight was about to close.

He didn't touch her. 'Harriet, will you be all right?'

She nodded. She tried to sound in control. 'I'm sorry to abandon you like this. It's not our usual way of doing business.'

'I don't think much of this past week has been usual, has it? For either of us?'

'No, it hasn't.' What could she say to him? Where did she start? Thank you for being our special guest? Thank you for making me laugh. Thank you for making me feel beautiful and sexy and looked after and . . . all those things. She decided to say it as it was. 'Thank you for everything. I'm sorry it's ending like this.'

'I am too.' He touched her on the cheek and it nearly finished her. She wanted to kiss him. She wanted to talk to him and hear him talk until they ran out of words and stories. She wanted him to say, stay, don't go. She wanted him to say, I'll be here when you get back. She wanted him to say, I want to see you again, this wasn't only a dalliance for me. He didn't.

'You'd better go.' She said it first, not him.

He kissed her lightly on the lips. Then he stepped back, or perhaps it was her.

'Thank you again.' She couldn't stop thanking him. It wasn't what she wanted to say, but it was all that was coming out.

'Goodbye, Harriet.'

She walked through the gate and had to force herself not to look back.

Austin stood at the arrivals gate at Cork Airport, waiting for Harriet to emerge. His thoughts were with Nina. It was ironic. It served him right. The first woman he'd seriously been interested in for years hadn't been interested in him.

Their kiss the day before had lasted only a few seconds. He'd felt the faintest of answering pressure from her, the start of a response and then she had pulled away, her face serious for once.

'That was a very nice kiss, Austin, thank you.'

'I could give you another one if you like.'

She'd smiled and shaken her head. 'I'm sorry. It's not you. I'm just not ready.'

'I like you very much, Nina.' He did. She had touched him in a way he hadn't expected. Not just her looks, but her intelligence, her sparkiness. She made him think about things and she challenged him, too. He liked the feeling.

'And I like you very much. And I very much want to be your friend —'

'But that's all?'

She nodded. 'For now, yes, Austin, I think so.'

'For now? So we could revisit the idea in a year's time?' He tried to make light of it but he was serious. It felt important to say it. To be honest with her. 'Sooner, even? Could we keep in touch with each other?'

She smiled. 'I'd like that. Now, will we get back to work?'

She'd handled it as nicely as that. That morning before leaving for Cork she had given him a tight hug goodbye. 'I'll see you again, I know. And give Lara my love. Lots of love. Tell her the room is hers whenever she wants it. For as long as she wants it.'

'Can I ring you later? Tell you what happens?'

'Please. As soon as you can. Ring me any time you need to.'

'Nina . . .'

She waited.

'If you did decide you were ready to see someone again, would there be a list of possible candidates?'

'There might be. A small list, perhaps.'

'Could I put my name on it?'

She smiled. 'I already have, Austin.'

'At the top?'

She'd laughed then. 'I'm not telling you.' They'd shared another hug goodbye.

Harriet emerged through the gates then. She was wearing the yellow uniform. Austin stepped forward. She started talking before he even said hello.

'How would she be feeling, Aust? I keep picturing her on her own in the house. You don't think she would have —'

'No.'

'How do you know?'

'I don't know for sure. I don't want her to have done that, so that's what I'm telling myself over and over. Will we go straight there?'

She nodded.

'We've got time for you to change if you like,' he said.

His attempt at a joke. She didn't laugh but she took him up on it.

As they drove out of the airport car park fifteen minutes later, Austin looked over at her. She was now wearing black cotton trousers and a white linen shirt. She was very pale. He saw dark shadows under her eyes. 'You okay, Harold?'

She shook her head then turned to him. 'Did you know the truth, Austin?'

'How could I have known?'

'You were older. You might have heard them talking. Mum and Gloria. Mum and Dad.'

'Do you think Dad knew?'

'I suppose so.'

'Maybe he didn't. I never heard them talking about it. Not once.'

'Why wouldn't Mum have told us the truth?'

'Gloria said she wanted to protect Lara.'

There was a long pause. 'What else don't we know about them, Austin? About our family?'

'A thousand things, probably.'

They were quiet as he drove west through the winding roads towards Clonakilty. They'd gone straight from the airport grounds into countryside, past a topiary airplane perched on a roundabout outside the airport, onto a busy road beside fields lush with growth. For a time their route followed the path of a slow-moving river, edged by woods. They passed stone bridges, road signs in Irish and English, B&Bs and country pubs. The fields and the countryside looked wilder than the scenery in Devon and Cornwall. Another time Harriet would have loved looking around. She had grown up seeing posters of Ireland on the walls of the travel agency. She barely saw it now. There was too much to think about.

Austin needed to talk. He didn't like the thoughts that were filling his head when it was quiet. He glanced over at Harriet. 'So how did the rest of the tour go?'

'Good, thanks.'

'Patrick Shawcross managed to keep his hands off you?'

'No, Austin, he didn't.'

'Sorry?'

Harriet wasn't looking at him. 'No, he didn't keep his hands off me. I didn't want him to.'

'Are you joking?'

'No, I'm not.'

'So what's happening?'

'What do you mean?'

'Are you going to see him again?'

'I don't know.'

'That's it? The cad.'

She turned to him then. 'He's not a cad, Austin. He's not a hunk or a cad.'

'If he's disappeared on you, he is a cad.'

'He didn't disappear. I disappeared.'

'You have to watch out for men like that, Harriet. Ones that take advantage of —'

'Shut up, Austin.'

'I beg your pardon?'

'I mean it. I love you but shut up and mind your own business.'

'You love me but you also want me to shut up. Sounds like mixed messages to me, Harold.'

She lost her temper. 'Can you please stop joking for one minute? You've always done that. Tried to turn serious things into a laughing matter and sometimes it's wrong, Austin. Sometimes serious things have to be serious.'

'I see.' There was a pause. He started tapping the steering wheel. What had happened the past few days? Gloria going for him. Nina turning him down. James surprising him. And now Harriet attacking him as well. He had an uneasy feeling all those people couldn't be wrong. 'I suppose I could try not to joke all the time.'

'And could you please stop tapping too. Your tapping drives me crazy sometimes. It drives all of us crazy.'

'You're certainly firing on all cylinders today, Harold.'

'I'm sorry. I needed to say it.'

'That's fine. It's no problem.' He paused. 'So I won't joke and I won't tap for a little while, either.'

They were quiet for a minute, then Harriet turned to him again. 'And if you ever tweak my nose again I swear I will punch you in the face.'

Austin nodded. 'Mental note. No tweaking of Harold's nose ever again, either.'

'And stop calling me Harold.'

'Talk about the mouse that roared.'

'I mean it, Austin.'

He glanced over. 'I can see that, Harriet.'

She said nothing.

He couldn't resist it. 'Harriet the Chariot.'

She ignored him.

At Bristol Airport, Patrick Shawcross was standing at the airline desk.

The middle-aged woman in front of him ran her fingers across the keyboard. As she waited for the information to come up on the screen, she glanced at him. Did she know him from somewhere? He looked vaguely familiar. She mentally noted how blue his eyes were. Contact lens? No, he didn't look the type. If he was that vain, he would have dyed some of the grey she could see in those black curls. And he'd probably cut those black curls shorter too.

She glanced at the screen as the flight details appeared. 'Yes, sir, there are seats available on that flight. Will I go ahead and make the booking?'

'Yes, thank you.'

'You're welcome, sir.' If only all her customers were so decisive.

Chapter Twenty-Nine

It took Austin and Harriet just under an hour to reach Clonakilty. The house was outside the town. He had detailed directions from the property company. They took a road to the right before the town entrance, drove on for five miles, then took a left turn onto a long hilly lane. They were surrounded by green fields, bordered by overgrown hedges and gorse bushes, small buds of yellow flowers visible here and there. The roads were narrow. Austin had to pull over sharply twice when another car appeared. The land was lush, the trees covered in new spring growth. There were black-and-white cows in some of the fields.

The house was on its own, set back from the road. Compact, modern, painted yellow. Two half-barrels of flowers stood on either side of the front door. A carved wooden sign on the right-hand post said Glen View. A small silver car was in the driveway.

Austin pulled into the side of the road about twenty feet beyond the gate. They sat there.

'Are you ready?' he asked.

Harriet nodded. They didn't know what they would find. Lara, in floods of tears. Distraught. Or something worse.

They got out, closed their doors as quietly as possible. The gravel in the driveway sounded loud under their feet.

There was lavender among the flowers in the barrels by the front door. The scent was strong. Clean and sharp. Austin knocked once, twice, three times. Harriet stood back a little way. She realised she was holding her breath.

They could see Lara's silhouette through the glass panels. She opened the door and looked at them both. She didn't speak.

She looked immaculate. Her shoulder-length hair was tied back in a neat ponytail at the nape of her neck. She was wearing jeans and a pale blue T-shirt. Her feet were bare. Harriet remembered then, incongruously, that Lara often went barefoot. She always had painted toenails, too. She glanced down. Lara's toenails were bright red.

'Austin. Harriet.' She didn't smile, or sound surprised.

Austin spoke. 'Can we come in?'

She hesitated for only a second. 'Yes.'

They followed her into the living area. It was open plan, a bright lounge area leading onto a kitchen, large windows looking out into the green fields. A herd of cows was making its way back from milking in a long line, one after another like toy animals.

Harriet was uneasy. Lara hadn't expressed surprise to see them. She was almost too calm. Harriet wondered if she had taken tablets. Lara didn't seem to be sedated. Her eyes were clear. Harriet looked again. It wasn't calmness. Lara was icy, she realised. And angry. Very angry.

Lara turned, crossed her arms and leaned against the wall. 'You both suddenly felt like a trip to Ireland?'

Austin answered. 'We've been looking for you. We've been very worried.'

'Have you? I'm sorry about that. How did the *Willoughby* tour go, Harriet?'

She swallowed. 'Fine. It went fine.'

'That's good.'

Harriet and Austin exchanged a glance. In the kitchen behind her they could see she had been cooking. There was a chopping board, several large ripe tomatoes, and a strong smell of basil.

Austin spoke again. 'Lara, are you all right?'

'I'm fine, thank you.'

'Do you know where you are?'

'Yes, thank you, Austin. I'm in Cork. I also know I'm in the house where my mother killed my father and then killed herself, if that's what you were wondering.'

Harriet couldn't help herself. She took a step back.

Lara noticed. 'So if you've come to break some news to me, you're a bit late. I found out for myself.'

'We didn't know, Lara,' Austin said.

'No? No more lies, thanks, Austin.'

'We didn't. We didn't know until yesterday.'

Lara didn't say anything.

'He's telling the truth, Lara.' Harriet spoke then.

'Of course he is.'

Austin tried again. 'Lara, I swear. We didn't know.'

'I don't believe you. You must have known. There is no way you couldn't have known.'

'We didn't. Mum told us it was a car crash too. She came into the lounge. We were watching *Gilligan's Island* on the TV.' It seemed important to Harriet that she give all the detail.

Austin nodded. 'She said she had bad news, that your parents had been killed in a car crash in Ireland. That's all we ever knew.'

'Penny told you it was a car crash?'

Austin and Harriet nodded.

'But she knew it wasn't. I spoke to the sergeant at Clonakilty police station. The same man who rang the Australian police that night. He told them exactly what had happened. Every detail of it. He told me what he had told them. What they would have told Penny.'

'That might be true. But she didn't tell us.'

Lara's expression changed. The anger was giving way to something else. Uncertainty. She turned her gaze to Austin. 'Did Neil know the truth?'

'I don't know.'

'Harriet?'

'I'm sorry, Lara, I don't know either.'

Austin tried again. 'All we know is how hard it must have been for you to find out.'

Lara went icy again. 'Do you? How do you know that?'

'Because we've just found out too,' he said. 'Because we've had a shock too. Because you are my sister and when something bad happens to my sister, to either of my sisters, I feel it too. So I know, not as bad, I'll never know that, but I have an idea how it must feel for you.'

'And you, Harriet?'

'I'm just as shocked. It's terrible, Lara.'

'What's terrible, Harriet? The fact it happened or the fact I was lied to?'

'We were all lied to, Lara,' Austin said softly.

'But why? Why would your mother lie to me? To you as well? That's what I can't understand. I've spent the past five days trying to understand all the lies.'

'I think Gloria knows why.'

Lara turned to Austin. 'Gloria?

'She knew the truth as well. She told me yesterday. She said Mum had made her promise not to tell anyone.'

'She's known for twenty-four years?'

'She hated knowing, Lara. She didn't like being the secret keeper. She was angry about it. She thought Mum made a big mistake. Gloria said to say that to you. To say sorry. And to tell you we love you.'

Lara stayed still.

Harriet needed to help. 'Mum would have done it for good reasons, Lara. She loved you very much. So did Dad. I'm sure of that. I think she must have wanted to protect you. To make it easier for you.'

'Make what easier?'

'You joining our family. Coming to live with us. Coming to Merryn Bay.'

'Building it on lies? How would that make it easier?'

'It wasn't built on lies. It was built on love. She loved you, right from the start. I know she did.'

'How do you know?'

Harriet hesitated. 'Because I could see that she did. That they both did.'

Lara made a dismissive noise.

Harriet made herself say it. 'Because I remember feeling jealous of you.'

'Jealous of what?'

'Their love for you. The attention they gave you. And how sure you seemed of them, of yourself.' She felt a tightness around her chest. This was too big, too raw, happening too quickly. It wasn't what they were here to talk about. She could feel Austin staring at both of them, confused.

'Sure of myself?' Lara gave a short laugh. 'You have no idea, Harriet. I spent my entire childhood feeling completely terrified.'

'When you came to live with us?'

'To begin with, yes. But before then, too. When it was me and Mum and Dad.'

Austin spoke. 'Did your parents hurt you, Lara?'

'Physically? No.' Lara was quiet for a long time. 'My father used to say cruel things to my mother, and she'd get upset, throw things at him. She used to cry all the time, tell me how much she loved him, how he meant the world to her. That she couldn't live without him. She'd sleep for days or she'd start drinking, or we'd have to go in search of him. I always knew I was second best. She said she loved me. But she loved him more.'

Austin and Harriet stayed quiet. They had never heard Lara speak about her parents before. She was talking quickly, but she wasn't looking at either of them.

'I never knew what was happening. He kept leaving. I'd get taken out of school and we would pack up and try to find him. We always did and she would always beg him to come back. Plead with him or scream at him. Make me stand there and say he had to come back because of me. And sometimes he would but not straightaway. So we would live in some guesthouse until it suited him to come home with us.' She gave that laugh again. 'So was I sure of myself as a child? No, Harriet. I was never that. I was scared.'

Harriet needed to hear more. 'You weren't scared of us, though, were you? Scared of my mother and father?'

'I loved your mother and father. And that made it worse. I felt like a fraud. I felt like a fraud when I came to stay the first time and I felt like a fraud every year on those memorial days your mother wanted me to have. Because the truth was I didn't want to remember my parents. I was glad I was living with your family. I liked it much more than I had liked living with my own. I did love my mother, but I couldn't fix things for her. I knew she was unhappy but I didn't know what to do about it. When I came to stay with you that first time, and then Mum and Dad came and got me, do you remember? After a couple of days? Mum had a black eye.'

Harriet and Austin nodded.

Lara seemed deep in the memory. 'It wasn't an accident with a tree. They'd had a huge fight the week before and he had thrown something at her. A book, I think. Something that caught her eye, made it swell up. She'd thrown it straight back at him, thrown glasses and cups, a bottle of wine, anything she could get her hands on. They were always like that. I thought that's how things were for everyone and then I met your parents and they were nice to each other. And you were all nice to each other. There was no shouting or fighting. I remember thinking, stay as quiet as you can, Lara. Be as good as you can. If you stay still, don't make a fuss, you might be able to stay for longer.'

Harriet remembered. She had seen it as Lara being so self-contained. Distant.

'All I wanted to do was be as quiet and polite as I could be and then maybe I could stay with your family for a long time. All the sheets smelt so good, and you probably don't even remember this, Harriet, but you let me sleep by the window. And I knew that was your bed, and I knew I should have said no, but I loved the idea of being by the window like that, all fresh and clean, and with all the books on the windowsill. I pretended it was all mine, the bedroom, the books. I pretended that your mother was mine, and your father was mine, and that something had happened to my mum and dad, and that I had come to live with your family.' Tears were forming in Lara's eyes. 'And then three months later, I was back. Because something had happened to my mother and father. And I thought

I had made it happen. I thought I had killed them. That my wish had come true. I kept getting nightmares, that I had wished it on them, because I had admitted to myself that I didn't want to live with them any more.'

'But you didn't make it happen. It was a car cra—' Harriet stopped herself. It hadn't been a car crash.

'I thought I had. In my mind I made them have the car crash. Except now I know it wasn't that, either. My mother killed my father and then killed herself. She chose to do both those things. So now I can't take the blame, I suppose. Because they didn't want to be with me either.'

Harriet wanted to move to her, to hug her. But that wasn't how it was between her and Lara. She stayed still and kept listening. Austin was just as quiet beside her.

'I told Penny how I felt. How guilty I was. She told me again and again that they didn't die because of me. Yet all that time she must have known what had really happened.' A long pause. 'That's what I've been trying to reconcile in my head. I've been going over and over it. I can't understand why Penny said what she did, why she lied to me. All my life.'

Harriet had been trying to understand it herself. She had thought about it all night. About her mother. The way she liked everyone to be good and kind. The way she had never liked to face up to the bad things in life. She had overheard her and Gloria arguing good-naturedly about it over the years. It had been a laughing matter sometimes. But it had its serious side as well. She needed to try to explain.

She spoke softly. 'Lara, maybe Mum didn't know how to tell you, how to give you such terrible news. I don't know how it feels to be a mother. Maybe all you want to do is look after people, and protect them and love them and keep them from harm. And you keep everything bad away from them that you can. I think that's what Mum tried to do with you.'

'That's not true, Harriet. It can't be true. What about my mother? She didn't want to do any of those things for me, did she? She didn't care what happened to me. Not for a minute.'

Austin stepped closer. 'Lara, please . . .'

For a moment Harriet thought she'd made a terrible mistake saying what she'd said. But then something occurred to her. 'But she must have cared, Lara. She got in touch with my mum. She came to see us that day, when you first stayed with us. She spoke to Mum all the time, and she asked her to be your guardian when they went to Ireland. Wasn't that what she was doing? Making sure you would be all right while she was away? Caring about you? Wanting to make sure you would be looked after?'

Lara was staring at her.

Harriet was struggling, but she felt every word. 'I can't even start to think why she did it, Lara. But I believe she had thought of you. Perhaps she had us there ready as your family, just in case. She had been thinking about you.'

'But I wanted *her*, Harriet. My mother. Dad was different in a way. He came and went all the time, and he would do me drawings and we would have some fun but then he would go again. But I remember Mum. We did have some good times. She and I would go on walks or catch the tram down to the beach and pick out shells together. And she liked cooking. She would make special meals just for the two of us sometimes, with candles and cutlery and napkins, and three courses. And we would toast each other. And she would buy little chocolate mints for afterwards . . .' She stopped. 'But none of it meant anything to her, did it? She wouldn't have done this if it had.'

'She must have been so sick, Lara,' Austin said. 'I can't understand it all, but she must have been. They must have had a huge fight, maybe they'd both been drinking, she did something terrible and panicked. Maybe she couldn't see a way out. She realised what she'd done to your father and she couldn't face —'

Lara interrupted. 'I remember the night Penny told me. I was at a school camp. The teacher made me sit in a room until Penny came. No one would tell me what had happened, but I knew it had to be something to do with my parents. There was nothing else. And Penny came in, and she knelt down on the floor beside me and she said —'

Harriet held her breath.

'She said that something very sad had happened but before she told me what it was she wanted me to know that I would always be loved and looked after and I would always have a home with her. And then she told me what had happened. That there had been a crash. And that my parents —' The tears were flowing but Lara didn't blink them away.

Harriet wanted to move closer to her, but something still kept her back.

Lara kept talking. 'And I said to her, "Did I make it happen? So I could come and live with you again?" And that was so wrong. I should have been thinking of my mum and dad and been so sad about them. But I wasn't. Not until later. That's how bad I was.'

'Lara, you were eight years old,' Austin said. 'How could you have understood what it meant? It wasn't because of you. It wasn't your fault it happened.'

'That's what Penny would always say to me, when I thought I had killed them, that I'd made the car crash happen. She told me I was never to blame myself.'

'Then believe her,' Harriet said. 'Please, Lara.'

'I knew something, Harriet. I always knew there was something that Penny didn't tell me. She would tell me all these stories about my mother and father and try to make them sound all loving and happy but I knew it hadn't been like that. I could remember the fighting and the mess and the moving around. And Penny must have known I would remember that, but she always tried to paint the brightest picture of them she could. Yet I always knew that something about my parents made her uncomfortable. I thought at first that she didn't like them. But she told me she did. Then I thought about it some more, and I came up with something even better. I decided that I was your father's daughter. That he and my mother had had an affair on the ship. That I was his natural daughter.'

'Were you?' Austin asked the question.

'No.' She gave a faint smile. 'I asked him one day. I asked both of them. He said he would have been proud if I was, but I wasn't.'

Harriet had a clear memory of Lara talking to her parents in the garden, and feeling jealous. Feeling left out. She was ashamed of herself.

'You were his daughter, though,' Austin said. 'And you were Mum's daughter too. It didn't matter to them where you came from, they were just glad to have you. It's true.'

'I'll never know for sure. I can't ask them now. I can't ask Penny about any of this. I'll never know the whole story now.'

Austin noticed Harriet's eyes fill with tears, and also that she quickly brushed them away. He made a decision. 'Will you both excuse me for a minute?'

He went outside and took out his mobile phone. It was nearing twilight, the air filled with sounds of insects, birds in the hedges, the mooing cows in the distance. The light was hazy. He could see through the window into the living room. Harriet and Lara were visible. Neither of them was talking. He dialled the long-distance number. 'Gloria, I know it's very late. I'm so sorry. We're here with Lara.'

It was as if she had been waiting for his call. 'Is she all right?'

'She's fine.' That was the wrong word to describe Lara, he realised. 'No, she's not fine. She's angry, with all of us. Confused. She needs to know more.' He hesitated. 'I know you've had enough of us, and you have every right to feel that way, but please, Gloria, can you do one more thing for us as a family? Would you talk to Lara? Would you tell her anything you remember about that night? About why Mum did what she did?'

There was no hesitation from Gloria. 'Austin, I'll talk to Lara for as long as she needs. Tonight or any time she likes.'

Lara was on the phone to Gloria for nearly an hour. Harriet and Austin sat outside on a bench in the garden while she talked to her. They heard murmurs. When she came out, her eyes were red-rimmed but there were no tears. She didn't tell them what Gloria had said.

Lara didn't invite them back inside the house. The three of them went for a walk instead. Harriet wasn't sure who suggested it. They didn't go far, just to the end of the road. There was a farm, neatly painted, whitewashed buildings, a two-storey house. Harriet thought of the newpaper article, the fax folded in her bag. Was this the farm where the woman who found Lara's parents had lived?

None of them spoke much. Austin pointed out a glimpse of a lake visible between some low hills. They tried to think of the name of a bird that came flapping out of a tree beside them. Lara thought it was a rook. Harriet thought it was a jackdaw. Austin said he didn't know.

They reached the gate and the yard of the cottage again. Something stopped Harriet and Austin from going any further.

Lara spoke. 'This will sound rude, and I'm sorry, but I want you both to go now.'

Austin was surprised. 'To leave?'

Lara nodded. 'I don't want you to stay here. I need to be here on my own.'

'Lara, is that a good idea?'

The chill again. 'I'll decide that, thanks, Austin.'

'We want you to be all right. I don't like to think of you —'

'I'll be all right.'

Harriet searched Lara's face. This felt wrong. Lara shouldn't be here on her own. 'You're sure you don't want to come with us? The three of us. We could —'

'No thanks, Harriet.'

No discussion. 'Lara, what will you do?'

'I don't know.'

'Will you come back home? Back to Merryn Bay?'

'I don't know anything yet. I need to think about it. Stay here and think about it all. On my own.'

Austin said what they were both thinking. 'Lara, please promise us you won't —'

'Kill myself? No, Austin. I won't. I've got so much to live for. So many people who will miss me,' Lara said. Her tone was sarcastic.

'Lara, please —'

'I won't kill myself, Harriet.'

Austin put his hand on her arm. 'Lara, you still have us. This doesn't change anything for us.'

'It's already changed, Austin.'

'This is it? You don't want to see us again?'

'I don't know.'

Harriet needed to try again. 'Lara —'

As Lara turned to her, Harriet recognised the look in her eyes. She remembered it from when Lara came to live with them after her parents died, that faraway, scared look. It silenced her.

Austin spoke. 'We'll go if that's what you want us to do.'

'It's what I want.'

'Can we ring you?' he asked. 'Make sure you're okay?'

Lara didn't say yes or no.

They stood for a second and then Austin stepped forward and gave her the quickest of hugs. 'See you soon, blister.'

Lara didn't hug him back. 'Goodbye, bother.'

Harriet was next. It felt wrong. It felt bad to leave like this. But Lara was like a statue. She wanted them gone. She didn't want them anywhere near her. Harriet could feel the coldness coming off her in waves. 'Lara —'

'Goodbye, Harriet.'

She didn't hug Harriet back either. She stood there, still, while Harriet awkwardly put her arms around her.

There was nothing else to say. Harriet and Austin walked back to the car in silence. They didn't wave as they drove past the house again. There was no point. Lara had already gone inside.

Chapter Thirty

Austin and Harriet were on the main road back to Cork before they could talk about it. It was a beautiful spring evening. There was little traffic. Austin turned on the radio, changing the station from pop music to current affairs. He found an Irish language station and left it on there. For a while the only sound in the car was bursts of traditional music, interspersed with the rolling and rhythmic sounds of spoken Irish.

Harriet was the first to reach over and turn it down. 'Aust? Are you all right?'

'No.'

'She doesn't want us in her life any more, does she?'

'I don't think so.'

'She said goodbye. We said "see you" and she said "goodbye".'

'I know.'

'What can we do? How can we help her?'

'I don't think there's anything we can do. I think we have to wait. Let her decide what she wants to do.'

They were silent for a few minutes.

'What are you going to do now?' she asked.

'Now tonight or now the rest of my life?'

'Both.'

'I need to get back to work. We've got a performance in Cologne tomorrow night. I'll try for a flight back tonight. Go straight to the airport now. Beyond that, I don't know. What are you going to do?'

'I don't know.' She hadn't thought beyond seeing Lara. She made herself remember the itinerary. She wouldn't let herself think about Patrick. 'I need to be back in Bristol in a week to take the group back to Australia.'

'We can get a flight together. You can come with me to Germany if you want. If you don't want to be here on your own. It might be better if you're not.'

The kindness in his voice nearly undid her. She didn't know where she wanted to be. Her head was too full of Lara, of what Lara had learnt, of the expression on her face. Her mobile phone rang, the sound very loud in the small car. They both hoped for the same thing.

'Is it her?' Austin said.

Harriet looked at the number. She didn't recognise it. 'I don't think so.' She pressed Connect. 'Hello?'

'Harriet? I hope this isn't a bad time?'

'Patrick?' Harriet had been imagining him on his flight to Boston. It would have left an hour before. 'Where are you? Has your flight been delayed?'

'No, I changed my ticket. I'm in Cork.'

'In Cork?'

'Is Lara all right? Are you all right?'

'Yes. No . . . I don't know yet. Why are you in Cork?'

'I had to see you again.' A pause. 'I didn't like the way we said goodbye.'

She hesitated. 'I didn't like it either.'

'Is there anything I can do? Do you need me to come and get you?'

'No, I'm with my brother. We're on our way back to Cork.'

'Would you come and see me? When you feel you can?'

'Yes.'

He gave her the name of his hotel and the room number. She said goodbye and hung up. She wasn't shocked or surprised. She was numb.

Austin was watching her. 'Did you say Patrick? Was that Patrick Shawcross?'

Harriet nodded.

'Where was he calling from?'

'Cork.'

'But he was due to fly back to Boston today, wasn't he? Wasn't Nina looking after him?'

'He changed his flight.'

'Why would he have done that?'

Harriet hesitated. 'He wanted to see me again.'

'So he's followed you? That puts a different slant on things. Cads don't usually do any following. If he's followed you then he must —' He stopped there, sensing Harriet's mood. 'You want me to mind my own business, don't you?'

'Yes, I do.'

There was silence for a minute. 'It's hard. I want to say things.'

'You can't.'

'Can I say good luck? That I thought he seemed —'

'You only met him for a minute, Austin. You don't know what he's like.'

'No, you're right.' There was a long pause. 'Do you like him?'

'Yes, I do.'

'Very much?'

'Very much.'

'That's all right then.'

They were quiet again for a minute and then she turned to him. 'I liked Nina, by the way.'

'Did you?'

'Yes. Did you like her?'

'Mind your own business, Harold.'

'Don't call me Harold.'

'Mind your own business, Harriet.'

She smiled a little as she turned and looked out the window.

They hugged goodbye at the airport. Austin had phoned ahead. There was a flight leaving within the hour. Harriet was keeping the hire car. It was a difficult farewell.

'We have to let her come to terms with it, Harriet. If she wants that space, we have to give it to her.'

'Even if we're not sure it's the best thing?'

'Yes. This is huge for her. We have to give her what she wants. And she wants to be on her own.'

Harriet wasn't sure he was right. There wasn't time to talk about it any more. She hugged him goodbye. 'See you, Austie.'

'See you, too. Ring me. Or text me. Whenever you need to. Keep talking to me. Let me know if you hear anything from her.'

'I will. And you too. If she rings you. Keep talking to me, too.'

'Of course.' He reached over and pretended to tweak her nose. 'Only joking. See you, Harriet.'

They hugged each other goodbye again.

Harriet drove into the centre of Cork and found Patrick's hotel. She parked the car, took her bag and walked down the street. She didn't know how she felt. So sad for Lara, glad he had come, both at once.

It was a modern hotel in an old stone building, decorated with plush blue carpet, red sofas and modern art on the walls. She took the lift to the third floor, walked along the quiet, carpeted corridor and knocked at the door.

She didn't run into his arms. He didn't pick her up and sweep her off her feet. He just said her name. 'Harriet. Please, come in.'

It was a large suite with a living area, separate bedroom, a large window looking out over the city, the river shining below. The day before it had been the two of them in St Ives, in another hotel room. Now they were in a different country, looking over a river not a sea. More than that had changed.

'How is she?' Patrick asked. 'How was it?'

'I don't know yet. She's very angry with us. She's hurt. She wants us to leave her alone.'

'What do you want to do?'

'For her? Whatever she wants. Whatever she needs us to do.'

'And you? What do you want to do?'

'I don't know, Patrick. Cry. Think. Sleep.'

He opened his arms. 'Come here to me, Harriet.'

She moved towards him, feeling his warm, solid body, feeling his arms come tightly around her. She stood like that for what felt like a long time, his fingers stroking her back and her hair, hearing him murmur her name. It overwhelmed her. She pressed her face against his chest and cried and cried.

She woke. It was dark outside. She didn't know if she had slept for hours or just a short time. She was in the bedroom on her own.

Patrick had put her to bed once the tears stopped. He had pulled back the bedclothes and the crisp white sheets and helped her in. She had taken only her shoes off. Then he had lain down on the bed beside her, put his arms around her and listened as she told him all that had happened with Lara. He had asked questions. He had let her cry again. Then he held her close against him until she fell asleep.

She got out of bed. He wasn't there. There was a note on the table. He'd written the time he'd left and one sentence, in strong handwriting: *Harriet, I'll be back very soon. Patrick.* She checked the time. It was six p.m. He had just gone.

She took a shower, standing under the hot water, thinking hard. There was something she needed to do. Something she had been thinking about while she was driving here, while she was talking to Patrick. As soon as she had woken she knew it was the right thing. She also knew it was urgent. If she didn't do it now, as soon as she could, it might never be possible again.

When she came out of the bathroom, fully dressed, Patrick was back. He was sitting at the table by the window, reading. The lights of Cork were visible outside the window. There was a bottle of wine and two glasses on the table beside him. He looked over and smiled.

'Hello again.'

She walked across to him and put her arms around his neck. He drew her close against him and kissed her. It was a soft, sweet, gentle kiss. She kissed him back, feeling his body hard against hers, the cotton of his shirt, then his skin, smooth, underneath it. She wanted to be with him. She wanted to feel every part of his body again. Lose herself in him, feel safe and sure. But she couldn't. She couldn't when she knew how Lara was feeling.

She drew away. 'Patrick, I need to go back to her. Back to Lara.'

'Now?'

She nodded.

'But didn't she ask you to leave her alone?'

'She did. But I think if I obey her now, we might never see her again. She might leave our family.'

'You don't want that to happen?'

'No, I don't.'

'Do you want me to drive you? Come with you?'

'I think I need to do it on my own. I'm sorry. It means so much to me that you came here, but . . .' She hesitated. It was too soon to be able to assume anything, even though what had happened with Lara had changed things between them. Moved what was happening between them to a different stage, more quickly than might have happened otherwise. They had talked about so much, but she still felt her way through the next sentence. 'If you want to leave, I'll understand. If you need to go —'

'I don't want to go.'

'I don't know how long I'll be with her.'

'I'll wait here. If you want me to wait.'

'I want you to. I really want you to.'

'Then I will,' he said.

Chapter Thirty-One

Harriet got lost on her way back to the house. The roads were hard to find in the dark of the countryside. After taking the wrong turn and doubling back, she finally saw it ahead, the yellow house, the two barrels of flowers outside, Lara's car in the front. She felt nerves but wouldn't give in to them. She imagined her parents, Gloria, Austin, James and Molly willing her on.

Memories and thoughts of Lara kept her going, most of all. The truth had started dawning on her as she had been driving back with Austin. How little she had known about Lara. How little she had thought about how Lara must have been feeling. Not just with this devastating news, but all her life.

Something else had hit her, too. How she felt when her parents died was how Lara must have felt as an eight-year-old. Scared, alone, uncertain of the world. Yet Lara would have had none of the happy memories Harriet had to draw on to console her. Lara would have had only the terror and fear and loneliness of grief, layered over the loneliness and frightening feelings she'd had when her parents were alive.

The enormity of it shocked Harriet. It must have been so hard for Lara. She must have felt so scared as a child. And how had Harriet reacted to her arrival? Badly. She had been jealous of the attention her parents had paid her. She had been jealous of Austin getting on so well with her. Of Lara getting on with James and Melissa, too. Harriet felt sick as it all came back, how put out she had been by Lara. She was shocked at her own selfishness. And not just as a child. More recently . . .

The gravel underfoot was very loud. There was only one light on, sending a faint path out into the yard. She knocked at the door. She had to wait longer this time. At first she thought that Lara had gone out, and she wondered what to do. Then she heard a noise. Footsteps. Lara opened the door. Her eyes were red. She had been crying. She didn't say hello. Her voice was cold.

'I asked you to go.'

'I know. I came back.'

'Why?'

'Because you're my sister.'

'No, I'm not.'

'You are my sister. Something very sad has happened to you. I'm not leaving you alone until I know you're okay. Until I can tell everyone you're okay.'

'Everyone?'

'Austin. James. Your family.'

'Harriet, I don't have a family. I have no parents. I have no brothers and sisters.'

'You do. You have us.'

'No, Harriet. You're wrong. I've got nothing. I never did have anything. I always suspected it, and now I know it for sure.' She turned and went inside.

Harriet followed her. 'Lara, please, can't you see —'

Lara stopped. 'No, Harriet, can't *you* see? I have nowhere to go from here. I can't pretend things any more. I know the truth. From the police, from what Gloria told me. I can't pretend that my mother and father had sorted it all out between them. That their trip to Ireland made them realise how much they loved one another and how much they loved me. That I was the last thought on their minds when they had that terrible accident in the car.'

Harriet was shocked by how open Lara was being. 'That might have been what they were thinking. When it happened.'

'No, Harriet, it couldn't have been. I know that. Because that's what finding out what really happened to them has done. It's taken all that hope away. All the fantasy I had that my mother did love me, not as much, never as much, but perhaps nearly as much as she loved my father. But she didn't. If she had loved me she would never have done this terrible thing. She would never have killed my father and she would never have killed herself.'

'She was very sick, Lara.'

'Was she? Sick with love? Sick of me?

'Unwell. Unbalanced.'

'Just words. Different words for it. Do you see what it's taken from me, Harriet? Any life with my parents at all. I didn't get any of them. I didn't get a life with them as a child and now I am left with no happy memories, either.'

Harriet was in trouble. This was harder and darker than she knew how to deal with. 'I can't know how you feel. All I know is that it hurts me so much that my mum and dad have died, and it must be a hundred times worse for you. The way it happened. The way you found out.'

'Gloria said Penny wanted to make it easier for me. That she did it for all the right reasons. That it was a terrible thing for a child to hear. But it wouldn't have made any difference. I don't want to know it as a child or as an adult. I don't want it to have happened.'

Harriet wanted to go across and hold Lara, tell her it would be all right, somehow. That they would do all they could to make it all right for her. But there was still that distance between them. She could only listen for now.

'I don't want my mother to have killed my father, Harriet. I don't want to think that I wasn't worth living for. That he was all that mattered and that if he was gone she didn't want to live. I should have mattered to her. She should have thought of me as she lay there. I was eight. I wanted my mother and I wanted my father and she did that to me.'

'She didn't do it to you, Lara. She did it to herself. To your father.'

'But she left me behind. She left me on my own. Then and now.' Her eyes filled with tears. Harriet took a step forward, but Lara turned away.

Harriet kept trying. 'You're not on your own, Lara. You have us.'

'I don't. Not any more. It's different now, Harriet. You know yourself. Penny and Neil are gone. Who's left for me? They're the ones who made the decision to bring me into the family. You didn't have a choice.'

'It's not about having a choice. Lara, we are your family. It's true. Ask any of us. Ring Austin. Ring James. Ring Molly. You are our sister and you are Molly's aunt. You grew up with us. You're one of us. We're . . . we're part of each other. That's what a family is, isn't it?'

'I don't know.'

'It is. It must be. Because that's what we are.'

'But it's different now. It'll never be the same. After Penny and Neil died, everything changed for me. I couldn't stop thinking about my own parents again. All the things I should have asked about them. My head was filled with questions. Things I wanted to ask Penny and Neil about their lives as well.'

Harriet knew what she meant. She stayed silent.

'I couldn't tell anyone. It felt too disloyal, that we were all grieving for Penny and Neil yet I was trying to find out about my own parents. So I didn't say anything. I thought I would find out where the car crash happened. Make a visit. Leave some flowers or do something there that would make me feel close to them. Make me feel I hadn't forgotten them. I thought about it for weeks, and then the course was nearly over and I realised I had to do it now. I started making enquiries a few days before you got here. The day you were arriving I got a call back from the sergeant in the Clonakilty police station. He told me everything. And it was like . . .' She stopped for a moment.

Harriet pictured it. Imagined Lara, finding this out for herself. On her own.

'I couldn't see reason, Harriet. I thought you had all lied to me for years. I wanted nothing to do with you. I didn't care if the *Willoughby* tour was ruined. I just needed to run. I told Nina I had to go and I left. I came here. I came here where it happened, to see if I could make sense of it. If I could feel anything of them.'

'And could you?' Harriet's voice was soft.

'Nothing. I felt nothing. Just anger and sadness and . . . I just felt alone.' She was quiet for a time and then she looked at Harriet again, as if she had just realised something. 'How did you and Austin find me? How did you know I was here?'

'It was Austin. Austin and Nina, your flatmate.' She told Lara all she knew, about Austin coming over, talking to Lara's lecturer at the college, coming to Cork with Nina, going to the police, the newspaper, the library.

'Austin did all that?'

Harriet nodded.

'And you came back here, Harriet. Even after I told you to go away.'

'I had to, Lara. I wanted to.' She could only say it again. 'You're my sister.'

'Harriet, I should have rung you. From England. After the farewell party. I should have tried to explain why I did what I did.'

Harriet was caught off-guard. Lara suddenly wasn't talking about the past few days. She was talking about the day Harriet's mother had died. This was the conversation Harriet had thought about having for three months. The conversation she had dreaded. This wasn't the time. 'Lara, don't —'

'You need to know what happened. I need to tell you why.'

Harriet couldn't speak. She waited.

'It was all just chaos that day, Harriet.' Lara's voice was very quiet. 'The ambulance and nurses and doctors and moving Penny into a room and we didn't know what was happening. I was with her and then James ran in and asked me to ring you while he rang Austin and Melissa and Gloria. And I was about to, I was about to call you. But something stopped me. I needed her to myself. Just for a few minutes, before I rang you, before James came back. I sat with her, holding her hand and it was so quiet suddenly, just the two of us. I didn't say anything but inside I was willing her to get better, telling her how much I loved her, thanking her.

'And then I heard her speak. I heard her voice, Harriet. I realised she was conscious. She was talking to me.' Lara's eyes filled with tears. 'And I needed her so badly. I didn't know what she was going to say, or what I could ask her, but I needed that time with her like nothing I had needed before. And if I had gone away to ring you then I wouldn't have had that time with her. I couldn't leave her. Not even to ring you.'

Harriet had tears in her eyes now too. 'I couldn't understand how you could have done that to me. I couldn't believe it when I heard you admit it.'

'I knew it hurt you so badly, but I was hurting too, Harriet. I loved Penny and Neil so much. And it felt like Penny was my last link with my own parents. That if she died, they were gone forever. There'd be no one I could ask questions about them. No one else I knew who had known them. I panicked. I needed her to myself, even for just a minute, because I loved her, but also in case there was something else she could tell me about them.'

'Was there?'

'A little. Just a little.' She didn't say what it was. 'She talked just a bit. She said she loved us all. And I told her we loved her . . . and then just as James and the nurse came back in she had the second stroke and . . .' Lara's voice was barely audible. 'I'm sorry, Harriet. I know I can't ask you to forgive me, but I just need you to understand.'

'I do, Lara. I promise you I do.' She did. She understood now. She could imagine how Lara would have felt. The same need Harriet had felt. Wanting to be with her parents. Wanting the last minutes. Knowing this was it. But what Harriet had been through, the pain she had felt, was nothing compared to what Lara must be feeling about her own parents. Right then, right now, she would have given her mother's last week to Lara. Her father's last words. She had never imagined being able to think those thoughts. But she could. And she meant it. She took a step forward. 'Lara, how can we help you. Is there anything —'

'I don't know yet. I don't know how I feel about anything yet.'

'Will you let us help you?'

'Help me?'

'With whatever you decide to do. Whatever you need to do. If Mum and Dad were here, that's what they'd say, too. But they're not. So we have to start again. Have a different sort of family. And you are part of that. We need you.'

'You don't need me.'

'I do. We all do.'

'Why?'

'To think about. To worry about. To care about.' Harriet gestured. 'All the sister things. All the family things. Please, Lara. Let us be your family. Don't leave us.'

Lara's expression changed. She looked sad and lost. Fragile. 'I need help, Harriet. I need lots of help with this.'

'Then we'll help you, Lara. As much as we can. I promise.'

Lara started crying then. Harriet didn't hesitate. She went over and took her in her arms.

They stayed up late that night talking. Not just about their parents. Not just about their family. They spoke in a different way. Without guards. Lara talked more than she had ever talked. About what it had been like coming to live with the Turners. Of how nervous she had been of Harriet. Of not wanting to take her place or step on her toes. Of wanting to be as well behaved as she could so she wouldn't be sent away.

Harriet was overwhelmed by sadness. How must Lara have felt? Had she waited day after day for something to go wrong, to be sent away? 'They always wanted you, Lara. They did. Right from the start. I know they did. We all did.'

'It was hard on you. All of you, but you especially.'

'Lara —'

'I know it was, Harriet. Your mother knew too. She asked me to be understanding. She told me that you might find it hard, that you'd been the only girl and that I should be understanding if you got upset. Do you remember her talking to both of us about it one night? That time she came in to our room? She said she knew how hard it might be but that we both had to remember she had a very big heart, bigger than either of us could imagine and there was room for all of us in there. And you said, how come she was only a normal-sized person if she had such a big heart. And Penny said it was made out of special material that let it stretch as big as anything.'

'Did she?'

Lara was smiling. 'You don't remember? And then in science class about a month later, before you and I moved into different classes, the teacher was talking about anatomy, and she had that model of a human body and you stood up and said your mother was different from that, that her heart was made out of some stretchy type of plastic stuff, not muscle. And you refused to give in. You said you weren't sure how she did it, but all of us lived in her heart as well as out in the world. The teacher thought Penny had been teaching some strange alternative science, I'm sure of it.' She laughed softly.

Harriet felt the memory returning. Yes, her mother had come in to their bedroom and said that about her heart. And Harriet had said that in a class. She remembered Lara telling the story when they got home from school that night, and her mum and dad laughing about it. Her mum had given her that nice special smile.

'And that time with the tent-rooms, Harriet. Do you remember? Before Gloria came up with the idea to draw a line down the centre of our bedroom? Neil brought home those two tents and we slept out in the garden for a few nights. They said it was a test to see who really was the messy one. And yours was full of jigsaw puzzles and all the books and even both of our kittens within about an hour, do you remember? And then it turned out the real reason we were out in the tents was so Austin and James could paint our room for us? Remember? They'd asked us what our favourite colours were. And I said yellow and you said pink, so that's why it was half and half.'

Harriet was feeling strange. She had forgotten that too. But back came the memory now. Her parents had called it the Miss Messy of Merryn Bay competition. Harriet had won hands down. She could remember laughing about it. Her mum had even made a little paper sash.

Where had these good memories been? She could conjure up memories of being hurt when her mother went to Lara first. When her father gave Lara more attention. Dozens of times when she had been cross or hurt by things that had happened to Lara and not to her. But behind those hurts she realised were other memories that she didn't ever revisit. Of Lara shyly waking her up on her tenth birthday. Giving her a little shell-covered picture frame she had made herself, from shells found on the Merryn Bay beach. Of other birthdays. Coming out into the kitchen in the morning, still half-asleep, and Lara stopping her, saying, 'No, you're too early,' putting her hand over her eyes until she got the signal from Austin or James that the candles on her cake were lit. The whole family singing 'Happy Birthday' to her. Lara, as loudly as anyone.

Of being so sad as a twelve-year-old when her kitten was run over. Lara had come to her with a basket. 'Here, Harriet. I want you to have my kitten.'

Of Lara coming to her one afternoon after school, when Harriet was in tears because the boy she had a crush on had ignored her. 'He's not worth it, Harriet. You're much better than him. Just wait and see.'

Kindness after kindness from Lara. Had Harriet forgotten them all? Blocked them all out? She had. She had turned Lara into something she wasn't. Made her into someone who had come in and ruined her life. Lara wasn't that. Lara was someone very like her. Someone who felt as scared and frightened as she did. Someone who had lost her parents, not just once, but twice.

Lara was right. She could remember all of these things. It's just that those good memories, those funny memories, weren't the ones she kept taking out to look at again and again. She seemed to bring out the ones that made her feel sad, or scared, or lost. Or jealous.

'I do remember, Lara. Just not as easily as I remember other things.'

'You remember the sad things instead?'

Harriet nodded.

'I do, too,' Lara said. 'All the time. But I'm trying to tell myself not to.'

Harriet tried to take that in. How could Lara not think of all those sad things. Those tragic things . . . 'Is it something you can choose? Something you can decide?'

'I don't know yet.' Lara's voice was soft. 'I hope so. I have to try. I have to try to remember the good things that have happened. Try to understand the bad things, but not let them win. I've been thinking about it ever since I found out. Trying to work out what I can do. Life is all about choices, isn't it? On a physical level, what we do, where we live? Perhaps it's the same with your mind and your memory. Perhaps we can choose what we want to remember. We can choose what we think about. I hope so. I hope it's like that.'

'I'm so sorry, Lara. I should have been so much kinder to you. All the time. I should have understood. And I didn't.'

'Yes, you did. Harriet, you were allowed to be mad that I arrived to live with you. But you weren't mad all the time. Things aren't one way or the other, Harriet. You can feel lots of different things at once. That's normal. Why wouldn't it be normal?'

'Because I knew it was wrong. Because I didn't want to hurt your feelings.'

'It hurt me more when I could see you were pretending. You're allowed to have feelings, you know,' she said again.

'I have feelings. They just haven't always been the most grown-up ones.' So many memories needed sorting through. 'You've always been able to be so calm about things, Lara. How do you do that?'

'I don't know. That's just what I'm like.'

Harriet looked at her. That was it. Lara was one extreme, Harriet was the other. 'I wish I was more like you, Lara.'

'Do you?' Lara gave her a sweet smile. 'That's funny. I always wished I was more like you.'

Harriet was up first the next morning. She was filling the kettle when Lara came out of her bedroom. She was fully dressed, wearing jeans, the pale blue shirt and suede boots. She was carrying a suitcase.

Lara came straight over and gave her a hug. 'Thank you,' she said. 'For last night. For coming back.'

It felt right, natural, to hug her back, to thank her as well. Then she noticed the suitcase. 'You're leaving? Now?'

'Not yet. After breakfast.'

'You don't want to stay here any longer?'

She shook her head.

'Where will you go?'

'Back to Bath for now.'

'Do you want me to come with you? I can. Whatever you need.'

'Will it hurt you if I say no?'

'No. I want you to tell me the truth.'

'I need time, Harriet. I need to think all of this through. Let everything sink in. And I need to finish my course. And then I need to decide what to do next.'

Harriet nodded. She understood. 'Lara, will you keep in touch? Please?'

'Will you keep in touch with me?'

'I asked you first.'

'We sound like we're eight years old.'

'As a thirty-two-year-old, will you please keep in touch with me? With us all? Let us know what you decide to do? Where you'll be?'

'I will let you know, I promise, but not yet. It's too soon. When I feel ready.' Lara hesitated. 'Is that okay?'

'That's more than okay.'

They made coffee and toast. Normal day-to-day actions that changed the mood, lightened it. It allowed them to talk about different things. Ordinary things. Lara spoke about her course, about living in Bath. Then she changed the subject.

'Tell me more about the *Willoughby* tour, Harriet. Did it go well?'

Harriet had to gather her thoughts before she answered. The *Willoughby* tour felt like it had been years before. 'Yes, it did. It was good. They loved every minute of it, I think.'

'I'm sorry for leaving you in the lurch like that. Especially after you'd stepped in for James.'

'It's fine. It was probably the best thing for me.'

'Really?'

'Really.'

A shared look of understanding again. Lara smiled. 'And was Mrs Lamerton okay? Did her brooches make the trip?'

'Every one of them, I think.'

Lara's lips twitched. 'And my little Miss Talbot?'

'She loved it. She bought a new red velvet pantsuit especially.'

'Not that one from Tina's Teen Wear?'

Harriet smiled. 'The exact one.'

'And Mr Douglas?'

'I heard him say the bay reminded him of a milkpond. He also told Patrick Shawcross he's waiting on some autopsy results.'

Lara laughed out loud, properly, for the first time since Harriet had arrived. 'And what was Patrick Shawcross like? Was he difficult?'

'No. No, he wasn't. I was expecting some elderly man in a wheelchair, carrying his dentures. He wasn't like that at all.'

'No, he's hardly changed from the *Willoughby* days,' Lara said.

'You knew what he looked like?' Harriet said.

Lara nodded. 'I found quite a lot about him on the Internet a couple of weeks ago. It took a lot of tracking down but I found out he runs an actors agency in Boston now. There was a photo of him on the website. I was going to ask James to include all that in the *Willoughby* info, but it wasn't in his official biography, so I decided he didn't want it broadcast. I thought it was up to him what he told them about his life now. I had a feeling Mrs Lamerton wouldn't leave him alone if she knew how to get in contact with him.' She took a sip of her coffee. 'So you got on okay with him?'

'Yes, I did,' Harriet said. Was it too soon to talk about Patrick?

Perhaps. But Lara was her sister. And surely if you told anyone that you thought you were falling in love, you told your sister. 'Actually, better than okay.'

Lara picked up the tone. Her expression changed. A slow smile. 'Something happened between you?'

Harriet told her. Not every detail, but enough. It was the kind of conversation she had never had with Lara. She felt her way. She could see from Lara's expression that she was enjoying hearing it. Not just the story but the fact they were talking about something like this. She asked a few questions, not many, not too intrusive. Just the right amount.

'You think it might be serious between you?'

'I don't know. I hope so. I think so.' She hesitated. 'Lara, would you like to come and meet him? Before you go to the airport? I'll understand if you don't want to, but —'

'I'd love to meet him,' Lara said.

It was cosy inside the hotel bar. The chairs were made of a deep red material, soft to touch. There were lamps lit on each table, soft music playing in the background, a clink of glasses and light laughter from a small group of elderly women in the corner table.

Harriet, Patrick and Lara were at the window table, looking out over the river and Cork city. The rain had stopped. In its place was pale sunshine.

'Lara, can I get you another coffee?' Patrick asked. 'Anything else?'

She shook her head, glancing at her watch. 'Thanks, Patrick, but no. I'd better go. My flight leaves at four.' She stood up, picking up her coat and her bag.

Lara had driven back to Cork at the same time as Harriet,

following her car. For the past hour the three of them had been sitting together in the hotel bar. Harriet hadn't felt nervous. She was introducing her sister to someone she cared very much about. Lara had been reserved at first. Not shy or stand-offish, but cautious. Harriet watched her as Patrick drew her out. He asked questions about her course, about other tours she had done. He laughed at her stories. She asked him about his agency. About Boston. The three of them swapped Mrs Lamerton stories. It had been good. Gentle.

Lara smiled at Patrick now. 'Goodbye, Patrick. I'm glad the tour went so well. I'm glad we invited you.'

'I am too.' He hesitated. 'And Lara, I'm sorry, once again. For all you learned in the past few days.'

She looked at him in her serious way. 'Thank you.'

Patrick stayed in the bar. Harriet walked with Lara to the front of the hotel where her car was parked. Lara had insisted on driving to the airport on her own.

In the foyer she turned to Harriet. 'He's lovely,' she said.

'You approve?'

'Completely.'

'Are you sure you won't stay?' Harriet asked. 'For the night, or as long as you like?'

'And be the gooseberry?'

'You wouldn't be. I promise. You wouldn't be. If you need, if you want it to be the two of us, you and me, I'll explain to Patrick and —'

'Harriet, I'm teasing. No, I want to go home. Back to Bath, anyway.'

'Could we see each other next week? When I'm back to collect the group?'

Lara didn't answer for a moment. 'I don't think so. Not yet. I might go away again. I need to think about so much. I think if I saw you, if I saw the group, it would interrupt me. Do you know what I mean? I'm sorry if that sounds hurtful, I don't mean to be, I promise. I need to be away. For a while, at least.'

'But not forever.'

'Not forever.'

'Lara, would you do something for me?'

Lara waited.

Harriet took off her bracelet. Her mother's opal bracelet. 'Would you look after this until the next time we see each other?'

'Penny's bracelet?'

Harriet nodded.

'But it's so precious.'

'I know. That's why I want you to look after it.' She passed it to her.

Lara took it. She held it very carefully. 'Harriet —'

'Please, Lara.'

Lara put Penny's bracelet on her wrist. Then she hugged Harriet. Properly. For a long time.

Harriet stood on the footpath and waited as Lara got into the car, put on her seatbelt and started the engine. She was about to pull into the traffic when she stopped and wound down the window. She looked over at Harriet. 'Thank you, blister.'

Harriet smiled. 'You're welcome, blister.'

She stayed waving until Lara was out of sight.

CHAPTER THIRTY-TWO

Gloria was ready and waiting for Melissa the next day. She'd been in the office since seven-thirty. She wasn't going to pussyfoot around. If there was anything she'd learned in the past few days it was that there was a time for plain speaking.

Melissa bustled in, straight into her office, and turned on her computer. 'Morning, Gloria.'

'Good morning, Melissa.' She was right about the beautician's appointment in Melbourne. Melissa was a different colour. Gloria didn't give her a chance to get another word in. 'I spoke to Alex Sakidis yesterday, Melissa. Does the name ring a bell? Alex from Matheson Travel?'

Melissa's head shot up. 'He rang here? You spoke to him?'

'Yes. So you know who I mean?'

'He's —'

Gloria interrupted. 'Franchise and acquisitions manager. The man you were going to sell Turner Travel to. Secretly. Under all our noses. Or was James in on it too? Had you convinced him to be as sneaky, as underhand as you?'

'You've got it wrong. It's not —'

'No, I haven't got it wrong, Melissa. I spoke to him. He told me. He was coming down here to view the building. Discuss the value. Discuss a possible sale.'

'That's partly true. I did invite him down. I asked him to make me an offer. But not why you think.'

Gloria couldn't believe how calm Melissa was. How brazen could she be? 'No? It was just out of interest, was it? You were just suddenly curious how much the business might be worth? And what the largest travel company in the country might be interested in paying for it? Don't treat me like a fool, Melissa.'

'I wasn't suddenly curious. I've been curious – we've been curious, James and I – for nearly two years.'

'I beg your pardon?'

'Since before Penny and Neil died. But we didn't want to rush anyone into it, and then after they died, it was too soon. This seemed like the most businesslike way to find out.'

'Melissa, find out what? What are you talking about?'

'I'd have preferred to wait, but since you've brought it up, I owe you the truth. Please sit down.' Gloria took a seat. 'James and I want to buy you all out, Gloria. Run Turner Travel ourselves. We've been thinking about it for some time. But we wanted to be sure we were offering what the business was worth. This was the best way we could find out. It wasn't very fair to Matheson Travel, we knew that, to go on as if we really did mean to sell, but we knew it would give us the most accurate figure of what it was worth.'

'Worth to who? Who were you going to make the offer to?'

'All of you. You, Lara, Harriet, Austin.'

'Why?'

'Because it feels like time. Something has to change. All of us have started going in different directions over the past twelve months. No one seems happy. Austin has stopped coming to the meetings. I've always known he doesn't like me, in fact I don't like him either, but it was starting to impact on the business. He was stalling on decisions when we needed to move quickly. I've also not been sure this is the right place for Lara any more, either. Or Harriet, for that matter.'

Gloria could hardly believe this. Melissa had been noticing other people? Was she actually having this conversation with her? She looked around the office. Yes, it looked the same. The desks, the computers, the travel posters, the racks of brochures. Even Melissa looked the same, all blonde hair and brown skin and high energy. But she was making sense. And it sounded as though she had given all of this a great deal of thought. Gloria was still suspicious though. 'And me, Melissa? What plans did you have for me?'

'I know you've been thinking about retiring. But I didn't think you would leave until you were pushed —'

'You were going to push me?'

'No. Never. You're the backbone of this company. But I've seen it in you, Gloria. Your heart's gone out of it. And I thought – James and I thought – that perhaps a big lump sum of money might make it easier for you and Kev to make some decisions.' She gestured to the phone. 'Ring James, Gloria, if you don't believe me.'

Gloria did, still in a state of amazement. James backed up everything Melissa said. He was also more apologetic about the way Gloria had found out.

'It shouldn't have happened like that. I'm very sorry. You must have been furious.'

'That's one word for it.'

'Gloria, that absolutely wasn't our intention. It wasn't a matter of going behind everyone's backs. We just felt it was better to produce the offer as a complete package, figures and all. So we had the answers to any questions anyone might ask.'

Gloria knew it was true. James didn't lie.

'What do you think?' he asked.

She told him the truth. 'I think it's a brilliant idea.'

After she hung up from James, she felt different. The anger and shock of Melissa being so upfront passed. She relaxed. So did Melissa. She made coffee. She left the answering machine on. And she talked to Gloria in a way she had never done before. Or perhaps Gloria had never listened to her in that way before.

She wanted to organise even more theme tours, she said. The *Willoughby* tour especially had put lots of ideas in her head. People loved to travel for a reason. She was thinking of exploring food and wine tourism. Literary tourism. Historical tourism. Working with the schools and universities, putting together special offers for students. She had some new ideas for marketing, as well. Joint promotions. A new website. More regular newsletters. Gloria was impressed. She told her she was.

'Yes, they are good ideas.' Melissa was matter-of-fact about it. 'And it will be easier to put them into place if it's our company. That's if the others agree.'

'I think they will.'

'Do you? That's a good sign. You'd know.' She took a sip of coffee. 'I feel a bit underhand, I suppose, the way we've gone about getting the valuation, but I'm sure Alex Sakidis will cope. Perhaps down the track we may think about doing some joint work with Matheson Travel. His journey won't be completely wasted. Mind you, I actually think he's only coming to see your suitcase stamps.'

'The stamps? On the staffroom wall?'

'He's dying to see them. I told him all about the idea behind them. He said we should let one of the travel magazines know about it. So I did. They're thinking about doing an article on us. Great publicity.

James and I were talking yesterday about taking it one step further, if all of you agree to the buy-out. Using the stamps as our next logo and on all the stationery. Maybe even getting new uniforms made, yellow background of course, but with all the different-coloured suitcases as the pattern.'

Gloria nearly choked on her coffee. That would definitely send Harriet into a new career.

Melissa didn't notice. 'I'm going to get a photographer to take pictures of all the walls as a starting point. I actually did a count of the stamps last week.'

'You counted them? Why?'

'I was curious. Do you remember Penny saying that she and Neil would call it quits when she got to ten thousand suitcase stamps?'

Gloria nodded.

'I'm not sentimental but I wondered if we were close. If it was a good time to change hands. And there nearly is. We're about a hundred off, but there will be ten thousand by the time the buy-out goes ahead, if it does. It's a shame Penny didn't see it. But I think she and Neil would be proud. And I don't think they'd mind, do you? It'll still be Turner Travel, after all.'

Gloria didn't know if Penny and Neil would mind. It wasn't her business any more.

'I'll see what the others want to do, and you too, Gloria, of course. There's no rush. We want you to stay on as long as you like. But if we set up on our own we'll take on other staff. Non-family staff. I think it will be easier to expand that way. So much less complicated. And I want to cut back our hours a bit, too. Molly is a teenager, she's going to need us around a bit more.'

Gloria blinked. Melissa was still making sense?

'What do you think, Gloria? About all of it? I know you'll need to think about it some more, your retirement especially, but in principle?'

'I think it all sounds excellent. And I wish you well.'

'Really? Do you mean that?'

Gloria thought about it. She thought about herself and Kevin, driving off somewhere. She nodded. 'Yes, I really do.'

Ten feet away, lying in her bedroom, Molly Turner pushed the mobile phone back under her pillow. She was sure she wouldn't hear back, but even sending the text to Lara had made her feel a little bit better. I wish you were here and I could talk to you. I miss you. Molly xxx

She looked at her bedside clock. She had slept for nearly thirteen hours, after crying for what felt as long as that too. It felt like she had done nothing but cry for days. Her whole body hurt from it. She had lain, curled in a ball, on top of the bedspread, as she'd always done when she was upset as a child. It hadn't made the hurt go away, though. She was all alone and it was her own fault.

Dean hadn't turned up to collect her. She had waited and waited, ringing his mobile number, but he hadn't answered. She'd sent a text, and then another. She had been worried sick he'd had an accident. She had been about to ring the police, the hospitals, even her coach Mr Green in case he'd heard something, when her mobile phone had finally beeped. A text. She'd snatched it up.

Molly, I'm sorry. I'm not coming. It wld be wrong. D

She had rung him. The first time it had gone to voicemail. And the second. She kept ringing until he finally answered. She was in tears by then.

'But why, Dean? I thought you loved me.'

She hardly heard his explanation. He should never have kept it from her, but the truth was he had another girlfriend in Melbourne. He'd met her at university and they'd lost contact but he'd run into her again six weeks ago and it had all started between them again. He thought Molly was beautiful, the time they'd had together would always be special to him, but he'd realised, especially in the last couple of days, that it would be better if they didn't see each other any more.

His words weren't making sense. 'But you promised. That it would be so special. I was ready.'

He kept saying the same things. She was beautiful but she was so young, she'd find someone her own age in a few years, and —

She hung up on him midway through the excuses. She was angry at first. He hadn't thought she was too young in the beginning. He hadn't thought she was too young when he'd first made her fall in love with him. But then the anger went and the hurt and the tears came flooding over her. She glanced up and saw his photograph, saw him with his arm around her, and her stomach started to hurt. She knew it was childish but she reached up and tore the photo out of the frame, ripping it into little pieces and putting them in the bin. She thought it would make her feel better but it only made her feel worse. It was the only photo she had of him.

She had been crying for nearly ten minutes, curled on her bed, clutching her pillow to her, when her phone rang again. Her heart leapt when she saw the name on the display. It was him. He'd changed his mind.

'Dean?'

He spoke quickly, in that same low tone, as though someone else was in the room or nearby. 'I know you're probably upset and you've got every right to be, Molly, and I'll never be able to say sorry enough, I know. But I need you to promise me you won't tell anyone about us, Molly. It wouldn't do either of us any good if you did.'

She hung up on him once more. He didn't call back again.

She'd stayed in her room since. She'd told her mother the swimming carnival had been cancelled. She hadn't asked any more questions about it. Molly had wanted to talk about it, wanted to tell her, but she hadn't known how to start. There was no one she could talk to about it. Not even Lara any more. She felt another wave of tears start to well inside her and bit her lip to try and stop them.

She had just turned out the light and climbed under the covers again when she heard a sound from under her pillow. Her phone. She lifted it to her ear and heard a strange echoing sound as though there was a time delay, or the call was coming from a long way away.

'Hello?' she said.

'Mollusc? What's up, sweetheart?'

It was Lara.

Harriet and Patrick ignored her mobile phone when it rang the first time, early the next morning. They had woken at dawn. She felt his arms come around her again, felt his lips on her forehead, her cheek, her lips. Their skin was warm, their bodies tangled. She felt his fingers caress her, the two of them skin against skin. It was different this time. It was gentle, deep lovemaking. There wasn't the urgency. There was something richer.

They had talked so much. They had walked around Cork together, up steep hills, along the river. They had found a small restaurant, tucked into the back streets, and talked over dinner, over a bottle of wine. About Lara. And about other things. He spoke more about his life. He answered all her questions, describing Boston, his work, his house, his favourite restaurant, where he swam. Then he asked to see her list again, Gloria's list. He went through it item by item, asking her questions. Making her laugh. Making her feel good. Cared for.

She didn't know exactly what was happening between them, or what might happen beyond now. It didn't seem to matter. She knew there would be time to talk about it.

Other things in her life felt different too, she realised. When she thought about her parents, about Lara, about the future, or the past, she didn't get the jagged uneasy feeling she normally did. She felt calmer.

Her phone on the bedside table rang again. She couldn't let it ring out a second time. She reached over to it, smiling at Patrick's murmured protest. She didn't recognise the number on the display. 'Hello, Harriet speaking.'

'Harriet, it's Nina. I'm sorry to disturb you so early.'

She sat up abruptly. 'Nina? Is everything all right?'

'It's fine. Well, nearly fine. I've just had a call from the *All Creatures Great and Small* people.'

'What is it? What's wrong?'

'Would you have any idea where they might find Mrs Kempton's glasses?'

Chapter Thirty-three

Eight months later

Molly Turner smoothed down her black skirt and white shirt and looked around the Turner Travel office. It had been her idea to have the party here. She had blown up the balloons herself, and she and Harriet had moved all the desks back and decorated the staffroom so it looked all bright and cheery. About sixty people were there already and it was a bit crowded but it didn't matter. It made sense that the party was here, as her dad had said. Gloria had spent more than thirty years working in these rooms, after all.

Molly picked up the tray and started moving through the room collecting empty glasses. As she dodged her way through groups of people, she looked up and saw that the 'Good Luck in your Retirement, Gloria!' banner had started to peel off the wall. She put down the tray and went out to get some more sticky tape. She'd spent days doing that banner and she didn't want it to end up on the floor. It had already spent far too long in the cupboard as it was. She had almost been tempted to add the word 'Finally!' at the end when a confirmed date for the party was at last set. It must have been the longest run up to a retirement in history. Molly had worked it out that afternoon. It was almost eight months to the day since Gloria had said she was retiring.

Molly remembered the day clearly. It wasn't only the day she heard that her mum and dad were going to start running Turner

Travel on their own. It was also just after that awful time with Dean. Molly remembered feeling so sad, feeling so horrible and then, out of the blue, Lara had rung. Exactly when she'd needed her.

She had told Lara everything. Lara had been very, very upset. Not with Molly, but with Dean. Molly had been a bit shocked how mad she'd been, and how relieved Lara had been to hear that nothing too serious had happened between them, apart from the kissing in the car. 'What he did was very wrong, Molly, do you see that?' Lara had said. 'He was out of line, as a man and as a teacher.' She had listened to Molly saying that she had fallen in love with him, and that Dean had said he loved her, but she had stayed just as angry. 'You should have told someone, Molly. Even if I wasn't there. It felt wrong to you because it would have been wrong. If it ever happens again, anything like this, promise me you will tell someone.' Molly had promised. It had made her feel so much better. It hadn't been all her fault, after all.

Then Molly had asked Lara where she'd been the past week. They'd all been so worried, she told her. They had talked for a long time, Molly curled up on her bed, Lara in her flat in Bath. Lara had told Molly all she had found out, that horrible story about her parents. It had made Molly feel so sad and so strange. It had almost made her forget all the trouble with Dean. That hadn't seemed so important compared to what Lara had been through. She had asked Lara what she was going to do now. Lara told her that she had decided to stay on in Bath. She was going to finish the course first, maybe have a bit of time off. She was going to call James and talk about it with him in the next few days. She had other things to tell him, too. She was thinking about resigning from Turner Travel. Trying something new. Maybe even starting her own travel agency. In England, not Australia.

Molly didn't like hearing that. 'Is it because of Grandma not telling you the truth? Does it make you feel funny about being part of the family now?'

Lara had been quiet for a little while. 'It makes me think that perhaps I should try being on my own. Stay here. Be myself, Lara Robinson, not Lara, one of the Turner family, and see how that feels.'

It felt so good when Lara told her how she felt, and why. She always explained it really well. 'I'll really miss you.'

'I'll miss you too, Mollusc.'

'I wish you were here now.'

'I am there now. My voice is, anyway. You just can't see me.'

She'd needed to talk about Dean some more. Lara seemed to understand. Afterwards she'd been really kind. 'Just trust your instincts next time, Mollusc,' she'd said. 'You didn't have to ask me. You just wanted me to tell you not to do it, didn't you?'

She was right. 'But how will I know when I meet the right person, Lara?'

'I don't know. I'm not very good at relationships. I always seem to send all my boyfriends away.'

Molly had thought about it. 'That's probably because of your parents. Because you saw them fighting all the time. That would make you feel a bit nervous you were going to do the same thing.'

Lara had gone silent. 'You're probably right,' she'd said finally.

All sorts of things had changed on the surface since that day, but underneath none of it had, really. There had been a lot more talking lately. There'd even been a few family conferences about her mum and dad taking over the company and the amazing thing was she was invited in to listen. Everyone had thought it was a good idea. They would take it slowly, they decided. Everyone could stay on working there for as long or as short as they wanted. Lara hadn't come to the meetings of course, but she'd sent emails and once they'd had a conference call with the phone in the middle of the table and Lara's voice coming out of it. After she'd hung up, her dad and Austin and Harriet had all talked about Lara and her parents and they'd decided the real story was to stay within the family, that no one outside Gloria and Kevin needed to know.

Molly had felt a bit guilty admitting it to herself, and she hadn't said it out loud, but she didn't really see how knowing the truth changed anything much. As far as she could see, Lara had come to live with them because her parents had died, and that hadn't changed.

She emailed Lara all the time now. She knew that Harriet did too. Sometimes Lara copied them both in on articles she thought they'd like, or a joke or just a little story about her life in Bath. It was much better than texting. Lara had her own office in the middle of Bath. She even had a website. She'd gone into business with one of the lecturers from the tourism college she'd attended. Brendan. He sounded really nice, Molly thought. He had a nice voice, anyway. When Molly had called Lara at her new flat in the centre of Bath at Christmas time, she'd been a bit surprised when Brendan answered. She'd been expecting it to be Nina, Lara's old flatmate, if it was anyone. Molly had asked Lara in her next email if she was going out with Brendan but Lara had just written back to say he was there at the flat because she was having a Christmas party and he was her work colleague. But then a few weeks later Molly had rung again to say a quick hello and Brendan had answered again. She'd emailed Lara straightaway. Are you sure there's nothing going on with you and Brendan?

Lara had emailed her back the next day to ask her, very nicely, to mind her own business.

She'd emailed back quickly. But if he's going to be my uncle I should know.

Lara hadn't answered that one. Molly knew that was Lara's definite way of saying mind your own business.

Still, she had another new uncle to be going on with. Molly had tried to explain to her friends at school that Patrick used to be really famous but none of them had ever watched *Willoughby*. It was on at the same time as the Top 10 music videos show on another channel. Molly had watched one episode when Harriet first came back and told them all, just straight out, that something had happened between her and Patrick and she wanted them to hear it from her, not from anyone else who had been on the tour. Molly had found it hard not to laugh at the look on her mum and dad's faces.

Patrick had come to visit a few weeks after that and everyone had really liked him. She'd heard her mum talking about him to her dad. She'd been going on about how good-looking he was, until her dad had said yes, he had eyes, she didn't have to rub it in. And her mum had said, but he's not my type, you're my type. And they had actually kissed each other. Her parents! It was revolting.

Her mum was right, though. Patrick was old, sure, but he was good-looking. Molly had actually enjoyed *Willoughby* too. It was a bit old-fashioned and she thought it looked like the actors were having trouble trying not to laugh, but she thought Cornwall looked beautiful, with all the cliffs and the little harbour towns. She and Harriet had sat in the living room watching it together, a week before Patrick's first visit. Mrs Lamerton had returned the videos that day and Molly had asked if she could take a look.

'If he's going to be my new uncle, I'd better be able to recognise him, don't you think?'

Harriet had just laughed at her. They had watched from the very first episode, a dog and some cliffs, Patrick turning up in a small car, barely unpacking before he started solving crimes. Molly had paused the action so she could have a good look at him.

'Does he still look like that now?'

'No, he's old with white hair.'

'Really?'

'No, Moll, I'm joking. He still looks just like that.'

He did, too. He was pretty yummy for an old guy. And he was mad about Harriet, anyone could see that. In the past eight months he'd been out to visit Harriet twice and she had spent a month in Boston. They talked on the phone all the time in between. Molly wondered how they found so much to talk about. Whatever it was, it must be funny. She always heard Harriet laughing on the phone whenever he rang. The latest bombshell was they were getting married and Harriet was going to go and live with him in Boston full-time. Harriet had come to Molly and told her, woman to woman. She'd wanted her to know that if she had been organising a big wedding, then Molly would have been her bridesmaid, but she and Patrick had decided that they didn't want a big wedding. Molly hadn't minded at all, really. They were going to get married in Merryn Bay, on the beach. Secretly. And then when they got back from their honeymoon, they were inviting everyone over to Boston for a holiday. The whole family, Gloria and Kevin too.

Molly was really looking forward to it. Not just because Boston sounded great and Harriet had said she could spend a few days working with her in Patrick's agency if she wanted, but because she figured it was the only way she was going to be able to get to know her new uncle. Each time he had come over to Australia and Merryn Bay to see Harriet, none of them had been able to get anywhere near him. They still didn't know how word got around so quickly that he was in town.

It was happening again tonight, Molly could see. If Mrs Lamerton and Miss Talbot stood any closer to poor Patrick they'd knock him to the ground. Mrs Lamerton hadn't let go of his arm since she'd come in and spotted him across the room. Miss Talbot was trying to get a word in, but she was having trouble.

Molly always had to stop herself from laughing every time she looked at Miss Talbot. She wore the funniest clothes. Tonight she was wearing a short tartan skirt she'd bought when she was in Scotland on that *Monarch of the Glen* tour. She also had a matching vest, apparently, but it was a bit warm tonight for that. Molly had heard her dad whisper something about Miss Talbot looking like an escapee from a Bay City Rollers convention, but Molly wasn't too sure what that meant. Some band from the olden days, by the sound of things.

She checked the time. Ten to eight. Her dad had said he'd start the speeches at eight. Molly heard the door open and spun around. No, false alarm. It was only Austin and Nina. She had been out to Australia on holiday a few months before and had come down to Merryn Bay with him for a few days. This was her second visit and she was staying longer this time. Molly really liked Nina. She was like a kid in an adult's body, always ready for fun.

Molly had decided to be daring. If adults could tell teenagers what to do, then she could tell adults what to do occasionally, she'd decided. She badgered Austin to give her a driving lesson – she'd got her learner's permit three days after she'd turned sixteen – and cornered him on the subject while they were driving up and down the back roads behind the town. She casually said she thought Nina was really lovely and she thought that her and Austin made a good match. To her surprise, Austin had nodded.

'I do too, Moll. But unfortunately Nina isn't quite as perceptive as you. She's playing with my emotions. Keeping me dangling.'

'Are you in love with her?'

'I think I am, yes.'

'And she's not in love with you?'

'She nearly is. But not yet. I'm still working on her.'

'Do you want me to have a word with her? As your concerned niece? Press your case?' She'd heard the phrase on an American law program the night before and decided it was very apt here.

'No thanks, Molly.'

She'd done it anyway. The night before, when Nina arrived she had just happened to say that she thought Austin was really nice and it certainly seemed that he was very keen on her. 'I think you'd only need to say the word.'

Nina had winked. 'Thanks, Molly.'

She looked over now. Yep, Austin was definitely smitten. She could see the way he looked at Nina all the time. She saw them both talking to Gloria. Gloria was all smiles, too. Molly knew she also really liked Nina. Gloria had told Molly that. It was just as well. Molly had a feeling it was very important to Austin that Gloria liked anyone he ended up with.

Her mum went past carrying a tray of drinks. She whispered, just that bit too loudly as usual, 'Molly, would you please check if Kevin needs anything?'

Whoops. Molly had forgotten she was supposed to be keeping an eye on Kevin. She went straight over to him. He was sitting on a chair at the edge of the room talking to Mr Fidock. Molly crouched beside him. 'Sorry, Kev, I should have asked you before. Do you want me to get you another drink or anything else to eat?'

'No thanks, Molly love.' He patted the chair beside him. 'S here for a second and tell me what it all looks like.'

She sat down, a bit amazed that he had known the chair wa empty. 'It's getting really crowded. About eighty people now, I'd say but there's still more coming in. Gloria is in the corner talking to Austin and Nina. She's been talking to heaps of people all night. Sh looks really happy. She's wearing a sort of blue dress, by the way She looks very nice.' Molly liked giving Kev these reports. It made her feel like a football commentator. 'Not long now till you're off on your driving trip,' she said. 'Are you looking forward to it?'

He gave her a big smile. 'Can't wait, Miss Molly, by golly.'

Kev had become her sort of surrogate grandfather the past few months. She'd walked home with Gloria one night, helping her to carry some files back that she was going to sort through over the weekend. She'd been amazed to come in and find Kev cooking. She'd just blurted it out. 'How can you cook? You can't see anything.'

He'd explained that he still had four other senses and that he could cook simple things, as long as everything was where he could get his hands on it easily. And he said he cooked a lot with herbs because it was easy to tell from the smell how much he was using. She'd tasted the tomato casserole he was making and it was delicious. After that she hadn't been so amazed to see him doing things like gardening, even a sort of Braille jigsaw puzzle. She dropped in and out on the way back from swimming training these days, even if Gloria wasn't there. Sometimes she helped him do his cooking, or helped out in the garden, but lots of times they just talked away to each other.

Molly felt the mobile in her pocket vibrate. At last. She read the text. Am outside.

She did it as they'd discussed. She went to Harriet first and whispered. Harriet gave her a big smile then whispered something to Patrick. Molly saw Patrick smile and look pleased too. Next she went up to her dad and whispered in his ear. He looked really surprised and then gave her a big grin. 'No worries, Moll.' Then she went over to her uncle Austin. 'Are you serious?' he said. He was really happy too. He agreed to do what she asked. She saw him tell Nina. She looked surprised and then really happy as well.

Molly looked over at Harriet again and nodded, as quickly as she could so no one would see. They had hatched this up between the two of them. It had been good fun keeping it a secret from everyone. Now it was all about to be revealed.

Harriet went close to the microphone and stood there, waiting for the right moment.

Molly ran outside. There she was, leaning against her hire car just down the main street. She was smiling. Really smiling. Molly felt a big smile come over her own face.

'Hi, Mollusc.'

Molly didn't bother with hellos. She just gave Lara a great big hug. 'You're only just in time.'

'I like a dramatic ending. Are you ready for me?'

'I've been waiting for you to come home for nearly a year. Of course I'm ready.'

As Molly took her by the hand, she noticed Lara's bracelet. A really pretty one, made from opals. Molly thought it looked familiar. Then she remembered. Harriet used to have one just like it. She led Lara back towards Turner Travel. 'Wait here,' she said.

She peeked in through the door first to check it was all ready. It was. Austin and James were on either side of Gloria with their hands over her eyes. Molly gave Harriet the thumbs up. As she and

Lara came in, Harriet leaned in to the microphone and told Gloria to turn around and say hello to a special surprise guest here all the way from England.

Molly couldn't believe it. First Gloria started crying and then so did Harriet. Even her mum and dad and Austin looked like they had tears in their eyes. Molly looked up at Lara. She was crying too. What had got into everyone?

Molly didn't think it was sad. She thought it was brilliant. The whole family was together again. Now they could really have a party.